W9-CMP-869

SPECIAL EFFECTS

SPECIAL EFFECTS

The History and Technique

RICHARD RICKITT

Foreword by **RAY HARRYHAUSEN**

BILLBOARD BOOKS

An imprint of Watson-Guptill Publications/New York

First published in the United States in 2007 by Billboard Books
An imprint of Watson-Guptill Publications
A division of VNU Business Media, Inc.
770 Broadway, New York, NY 10003
www.watsonguptill.com

First published in Great Britain 2006 by Aurum Press Ltd
25 Bedford Avenue, London WC1B 3AT
www.aurumpress.co.uk

Copyright © 2007 by Richard Rickitt

All rights reserved. No part of this book may be reproduced or utilized in any form
or by any means, electronic or mechanical, including photocopying, recording or by
any information storage and retrieval system, without permission in writing from
the publishers.

The author and publishers have made every effort to contact the copyright holders
for the illustrations used in this book. The publishers should be notified of any
omission of credit.

Library of Congress Control Number: 2006924912
ISBN-13: 978-0-8230-8408-1
ISBN-10: 0-8230-8408-6

10 9 8 7 6 5 4 3 2 1 / 2011 2010 2009 2008 2007

Design by Ashley Western
Printed in China

FRONTISPIECE: *King Kong* (2005), Weta's extraordinary creation.

BELOW: Special effects have played a prominent part in many movies during
cinema's first century: *Santa Claus* (1898), *T2: 3-D – Battle across Time* (1996),
Manslaughter (1922), *When Worlds Collide* (1951), *The Living Daylights* (1987),
The Godfather (1972).

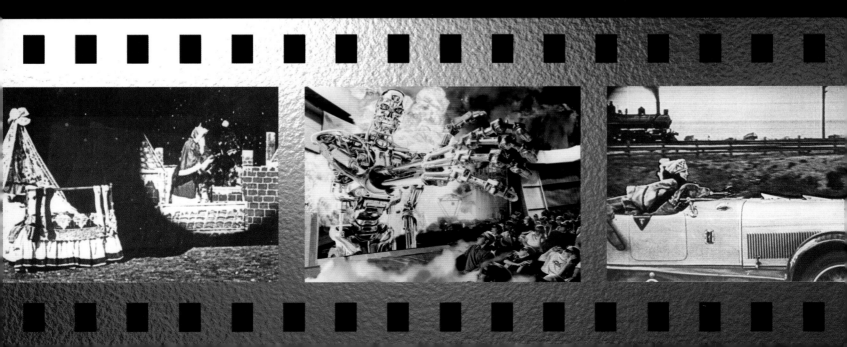

CONTENTS

FOREWORD

I am delighted to be able to contribute to this wonderful book in some way as I vividly remember how, as a youth fascinated by the mysterious world of special effects, there were no books or information of any kind available.

My childhood interest was encouraged by a visit to Grauman's Chinese Theatre on Hollywood Boulevard to see *King Kong* (1933). I was thrilled by the movie and its monsters but had no idea how those visions were achieved. Some months later I discovered a magazine article with a photograph of Fay Wray shaking hands with an 18-inch King Kong puppet. My father also had a friend who worked at the RKO studios and he patiently described the magical process of stop-motion animation.

I had until then been playing around with small home-made scenes of prehistoric creatures made in clay. But now I knew how to make them move! With a borrowed 16 mm camera I made my first tentative experiments animating a cave bear that I had made with a wooden ball and socket armature. The camera could not shoot single frames so I had to tap the start button quickly, hoping to expose only one frame at a time. When the film was developed I was mesmerized by the results. The movement was very jerky and crude, but I only saw this as a challenge and my experiments continued.

Throughout my years of trial and discovery I found very little written information about special effects and animation. This forced me to devise my own ways and means of creating and photographing smoother, more realistic animation. In spite of the many failures and pitfalls, it became my obsession – like Frankenstein, I wanted to create life where there was none. If only there had been available a book such as this to explain methods and techniques; it would have saved me many days and much frustration in my quest to film what I could see so vividly in my imagination.

Today, of course, so much information about the once mysterious process of special effects is revealed before a film is even released. In the early days I strongly felt that revealing how things were accomplished took away the entertaining quality of the final film and destroyed the magic. After all, the main purpose of any film was to tell a story and transport viewers into a world of make-believe. But now it would seem that knowing how a film is made only makes people want to watch it even more.

Over the years there have been such incredible advances in technology that it has completely transformed the making of entertainment. The complex techniques now used seem so far removed from those that I helped to pioneer. Today a book of this nature is invaluable, explaining not only to dedicated fans but also to the interested general public how the magic is – and was – achieved.

Today's 'blockbusters' suggest a demand for more 'realistic' images, but I sometimes wonder if this concept really makes entertainment more enjoyable. In the world of fantasy I feel there is a danger of bringing the amazing image down to the mundane. A debatable question. I am most grateful at least that the films on which I worked have stood the test of time.

Richard Rickitt's splendid volume is a fitting tribute to the numerous great special effects pioneers of past years whose imaginative innovations continue to inspire new generations of artists and technicians – many of whom are included within the pages that follow. It is fascinating to see how each new generation has built upon the achievements of the last. Each new film adds to the great heritage of special effects, and each one is influenced by its predecessors. Without that past there could be no future.

Ray Harryhausen

THE HISTORY OF
SPECIAL EFFECTS

PRECEDING PAGES: **In one of the most iconic images in early cinema, the understandably grumpy Man-in-the-Moon has just endured a rocket full of explorers landing in his eye. Georges Méliès's** *Le Voyage Dans La Lune (A Trip to the Moon,* **1902) was the very first science fiction film and it remains an inspiration to many lovers of movie magic to this day.**

RIGHT: **A hand-painted magic-lantern slide dating from the 1800s. Sophisticated slides incorporated mechanical elements to produce the illusion of movement, such as drifting clouds and churning waves.**

BELOW: **Edison's kinetophone improved on the earlier kinetoscope by combining moving images with a soundtrack provided by another Edison innovation, the phonograph.**

OUT OF THE SHADOWS

Cinema is now over a hundred years old. The invention of photography in the nineteenth century may have provided Victorians with a remarkable means of recording real-life images, but it wasn't long before their curiosity created the first moving pictures.

At first, the wonder of moving pictures, no matter how dull the deeds they showed, was enough to entertain and amaze. But the ordinary subjects of these early 'flickers' could not satisfy imaginative audiences, eager for the drama of the stage or the fantasy of the page. This led to the development of 'trick photography', which was used to astound viewers with visions of trips to the moon or journeys in flying cars.

As moving pictures developed, 'special effects' grew increasingly sophisticated to match changing audience expectations. What thrilled in one decade seemed quaint and creaky in the next. The animated dinosaurs of *The Lost World* (1925) would have made audiences of the 50s laugh, just as the monsters of the 50s held no terror for viewers in the 80s.

This chapter provides an overview of the development of special effects in cinema's first century. Later chapters examine specific special effects techniques in depth, showing how they have helped to make cinema the most popular and influential of all media forms.

THE PREHISTORY OF CINEMA

Cinema has many ancestors. In Europe, the period from the Renaissance to the eighteenth century saw an explosion of interest in the visual arts, architecture, painting and the theatre. The latter two were married in the ancient art of shadow puppetry, known as *ombres chinoises* ('Chinese shadows'), which came to Europe from the Far East in the late seventeenth century. Its popularity as a form of entertainment sparked a fascination for light shows of all kinds.

There were simple illuminated views, such as the Panorama, devised and patented by the Scottish artist Robert Barker in 1787. His circular paintings, which told a story, were viewed in stages, much like the narrative of a film. At about the same time the German-born British painter and stage designer Philippe de Loutherbourg developed the Eidophusikon, a sequence of paintings exhibited in a theatre, complete with lighting and sound effects to enhance the drama of the scene. Louis Daguerre, one of the fathers of photography, developed another idea with his Dioramas, which were popular in Paris in the 1820s. These were paintings made on layers of transparent gauze, hung and lit separately one in front of the other. By dimming the light on one gauze and raising it on another, primitive yet effective dissolves could be made from scene to scene.

RIGHT: Eastern shadow puppets were one of the visual forms of entertainment popular before the arrival of the cinema. This example is from Java in Indonesia.

BELOW: The zoetrope, a popular Victorian parlour toy, allowed animated sequences to be viewed through slits in a rotating drum.

A popular attraction during the Renaissance was the camera obscura (meaning 'dark room'). For centuries it had been noted that a small hole in the wall of a darkened room would permit an inverted image of the outside world to appear on the opposite wall. This process would later be adapted for the pinhole camera, but in the mid-1500s, patrons would crowd into a darkened room and thrill to the sight of moving images of the outside world that had been focused and turned the right way up with the use of lenses.

By the seventeenth century, the camera obscura's principles had been developed to produce the magic lantern. This had a light source inside the chamber, and was used to project images through a lens into a darkened room, much like a modern slide projector. Scenes were painted on glass 'sliders' (strips of glass that slid between lens and light source just like modern slides), which were manufactured on a large scale. In the nineteenth century the magic lantern reached a peak of refinement. Dissolves could be achieved using dual lanterns to project images onto the same spot. One image would slowly be replaced by another by controlling the amount of light emitted from the lanterns. Slides were manufactured with images on several layers, and by moving them by mechanical means, illusions such as beheadings and beatings could be displayed.

It was the illusion of movement that most beguiled audiences of the day, and a number of innovations were devised to satisfy this fascination. The magic of movement would not have been possible without a peculiarity of human sight. The human retina registers an image for a fraction of a second after it has gone from view. Called 'persistence of vision', this is the principle that makes a rapid sequence of slightly differing images appear continuous and is what allows us to enjoy watching film and television. The principle had been noted by the ancient Greeks and in the nineteenth century it inspired the development of a succession of 'scopes' and 'tropes' – visual toys with names derived from Greek roots.

The most famous of these was the zoetrope. A popular parlour toy from the late 1860s, the zoetrope consists of a drum with a sequence of drawings around the inside, which can be seen through equidistant slits. The drum is spun, and persistence of vision causes the slits to merge into one, while the

drawings coming into view create the impression of a moving image: a man turning a somersault again and again, for example, or a bird flapping its wings. Many other optical toys of the period worked on the same principle of revealing and obscuring images at a rate that made them appear to have motion. Developed by Emile Reynaud and patented in 1892, the Théâtre Optique used a light source to project sequential images, each of which had been painstakingly hand-painted onto a strip of translucent material. The system produced what we would now call a cartoon, but did not involve any form of photographic process.

The first fledgling photographic processes, developed at the beginning of the nineteenth century, involved light-sensitive emulsions requiring long exposure times to capture any permanent image, and so were not suitable for shots of moving images. It was not until the 1870s that emulsions sensitive enough to take a photograph in a fraction of a second became practically available, although the creation of moving pictures was still hampered by the fact that one glass photographic plate was needed for each picture.

An Englishman working in San Francisco under the name of Eadweard Muybridge (originally Edward Muggeridge) developed a system of individual stills cameras set alongside a track to record the normal movement of men, horses and other animals. His photographs, and the pioneering studies of the Frenchman Etienne Jules Marey (who invented a kind of photographic machine gun), were a major advance in the development of motion picture apparatus. They projected their pictures by slotting photographic plates into large revolving discs, in a device similar to a magic lantern called the zoöpraxiscope.

The development of a sensitized strip of celluloid film by Kodak founder George Eastman in 1888 launched a frenzy of invention. From then on, inventors in Europe and America vied with one another to patent cinematic devices, and studied others' patents with equal frenzy. Cinema as we know it was waiting to be born, but who would be the father?

WHAT THE NINETIES SAW

By the end of the 1880s, all the elements required to make moving pictures had fallen into place. In the United States, Thomas Alva Edison (1847–1931), having already recorded sound with his invention the Phonograph (1877), took up the challenge to develop an apparatus for recording moving images. In 1888 Edison, with so many other ideas to explore, entrusted his assistant, the Englishman W.K.L. Dickson (1860–1935), with the task of inventing something on his behalf.

By late 1890, Dickson had developed the Kinetograph, which could take rapid sequential images. These were then shown using loops of 35 mm film held in a Kinetoscope, a slot machine that provided a brief display of moving images to a single viewer who had to bend down as if looking through a keyhole – hence the nickname 'What-the-Butler-Saw'. Such films were 'single-shot' dramas, where there was no editing and the position of the camera remained fixed. Subjects tended to be risqué, such as women disrobing, and the devices soon began to appear on seaside piers and in special parlours on both sides of the Atlantic. It was quickly recognized that if the moving images could be projected onto a screen, a large paying audience would gather for each display.

The answer was sought in the magic lantern, and was found by two French brothers – whose surname, appropriately, means 'lamplighter' – Auguste (1862–1954) and Louis Lumière (1864–1948). The Lumières devised the Cinématographe, which was camera, film printer and projector all in one. It improved on Edison's Kinetograph by being more portable; as it did not rely on an electric motor, the film could be hand-cranked. The device used a toothed ratchet mechanism and sprocket holes to move the celluloid film, which was the 35 mm standard still used today. The cinema had come, albeit silently, into the world.

The Lumières believed their invention would be a passing craze and decided to exploit it for short-term financial gain. The brothers gave the first public exhibition of their small repertoire of short films at the Grand Café on the Boulevard des Capucines, Paris, on 28 December 1895. Early films included *A Lesson in Vaulting*, *Feeding a Baby*, *Firemen Extinguishing a Fire*, and most famously, *Train Arriving at a Station*. The latter is reputed to have alarmed audience members who thought the locomotive was about to steam out of the screen into the auditorium. The journalist G.R. Baker wrote: 'The station is apparently empty when the train is seen approaching, and gradually gets nearer and larger until the engine passes where we are apparently standing, and the train stops, the guard comes along, passengers get out and in, and all is real!'

Louis and Auguste discovered the power of their invention immediately, and engaged 200 agents to travel to almost every part of the world, exhibiting their films and shooting new ones to add to their library. The first Cinématographe display in Britain took place in London's Regent Street on 20 February 1896. The show soon transferred to Leicester Square, still the centre of film-going in London. The immense popularity of the moving films was described in the press at the time as the 'Living Picture Craze'.

The invention of moving pictures, much like the making of them, was a collective process. To single out Edison, Dickson or the Lumières as the inventor of movies is unjust to the many others who were at work on moving picture systems at that time. The efforts of men such as Louis Le Prince (1842–96), who experimented with paper rolls of film, or William Friese-Greene (1855–1921), who helped to develop a system for projecting still images at four or five frames per second, should not be forgotten.

Similarly, the creation of a cinema industry did not happen because of the business acumen of any one man or company. The Lumières captured the public imagination, but they could not hold a monopoly on the production and exhibition of films. Their invention was copied and exploited in countries where their patents did not apply. In the United States, Edison initially dominated the market, but soon had competition from people with other moving picture systems – bought or invented – such as the Vitascope of C. Francis Jenkins and Thomas Armat.

It soon became clear to all concerned that, because no particular system had a unique selling point, the only way to make a success in the business would be to produce films that told a story, rather than show the one-shot wonder of a man combing his hair or a woman dancing. Film-makers came to rely on special effects almost from the beginning in their efforts to entertain and involve the audience.

The fundamentals of film spectacle as we know it today – sound, colour, widescreen – were all being striven for within a few years of that first Lumière show. In 1900, at the Paris Exposition, the latest in cinema technology was on display. This included Cineorama, a primitive sound system relying on a separate synchronized sound disc, and hand-tinted films giving a gaudy illusion of colour.

Audience reactions to these cinematic 'effects' can perhaps be judged from these observations on 'living pictures' that appeared in a general family reference work, *The Sunlight Year-Book*, in 1898: 'This ingenious and pleasing exhibition has become very popular. The method . . . though at first incomprehensible, yet becomes fairly clear on examination . . . a French gentleman named Cordy is said to have taken a set of photographs of growing flowers at different stages of development, and flashing them thus quickly on the screen, shows you a plant growing and budding and flowering in a moment or so. This living picture, though no doubt interesting, must, however, be likely to have an unnatural effect, for in nature we do not see plants budding and flowering in a minute.'

LEFT: The Lumières' early film *Train Arriving at a Station* (1896) alarmed more nervous viewers, who thought the approaching train might actually burst through the screen.

RIGHT: In what is considered to be the world's first special effects shot, stop-action was used to create the on-screen beheading for *The Execution of Mary, Queen of Scots* (1895).

BOTTOM: This colourful poster was printed to advertise screenings of the Lumières' film *L'Arroseur Arrose (The Waterer Watered*, 1895). The short film showed a young boy enjoying the classic trick of switching off the water only to turn it back on when the gardener peers into the hose. Luckily, simply seeing moving images was enough to amuse audiences of the day.

GEORGES MÉLIÈS

The French magician Georges Méliès (1861–1938) was perhaps the most important innovator in the history of cinema. Within 10 years of discovering the wonder of film, Méliès made hundreds of short films and pioneered many of the methods that would remain at the heart of special effects production for much of the next century. Perhaps no one else has had such a profound and long-lasting influence on special effects production.

The 'father of special effects' was the youngest son of a French boot-making tycoon and was expected to follow his father and two brothers into the trade. His destiny, however, did not lie in filling the family shoes, and when his father retired the young Georges sold his share in the family business. With the considerable proceeds he purchased the Théâtre Robert-Houdin in Paris, one of the most famous magic venues in the world.

As manager, Méliès took to the sulphur and sodium life of the theatre magician with a flourish, conjuring up an array of innovative stage illusions – all of which he designed, built, painted and performed in famously comic style. Magic lantern shows were another attraction on his bill of wonders, with fantastical presentations of hand-coloured and often simply animated glass slides.

So Méliès was aware of both the science and the popularity of theatrical projection when, on 28 December 1895, he was among the first in the world to witness a performance of the Lumière brothers' Cinématographe. Realizing the potential of the new device, Méliès immediately entered into a bidding war with other Parisian impresarios, only to be told that the amazing magic box was not for sale at any price. Méliès was undeterred. Within three months he had bought a device built by Robert W. Paul of London, designed for use with Edison's Kinetoscope films. Méliès then worked with two engineers in his theatre workshop to build an enormous and unwieldy prototype camera of his own. Early warning of a growing obsession came when he took the camera with him on a seaside vacation in July 1896. The frustrations of a family holiday accompanied by a 35 kg (77 lb) camera can only be imagined. Luckily for family harmony, Méliès patented a lighter version in September 1896.

Méliès began making simple one-shot films, usually 60-second scenic views – moving versions of the magic lantern shows that had preceded them. When he was filming one such scene in the Place de

ABOVE: **Performing in his own film, Georges Méliès is amazed by the sight of his own rapidly expanding head, the fantastical result of double exposure, in** Indian Rubber Head **(1902).**

RIGHT: **A scene from Méliès's most famous film,** A Trip to the Moon **(1902). The gun, actually a painted backdrop, is about to fire a manned capsule to the moon, where fantastic adventures will unfold.**

FAR RIGHT: **Méliès, cinema's pioneering magician, spent his last years supplying toys and trinkets to the children of Paris.**

l'Opéra in Paris, a chance incident occurred that appealed to both the innovator and the showman in Méliès, and helped him to become one of the most important figures in the history of special effects.

As he turned the camera's hand-crank, the device jammed. 'It took a minute to release the film and get the camera going again,' Méliès later wrote. 'During this minute the people, buses, vehicles, had of course moved. Projecting the film, having joined the break, I suddenly saw an omnibus changed into a hearse and men into women. The trick of substitution, called the trick of stop-action, was discovered.'

In fact, stop-action photography had already been used by Edison's camera operator Alfred Clarke for the beheading sequence in *The Execution of Mary Queen of Scots* (1893). There is no doubt, however, that Méliès discovered the trick for himself, and that his application of what had been a cinematic accident would make him the world's foremost producer of 'trick films'. Méliès was soon using stop-action, double exposure, fast and slow motion, dissolves and perspective tricks in his films, which became increasingly elaborate. His love of storytelling, his zeal for illusion and his new-found photographic abilities led him to devise spectacles that would have been impossible on stage. To realize his ideas, Méliès built an impressive glass studio in the garden of his family home near Paris. The studio, perhaps the most sophisticated of its age, could claim to be the world's first special effects facility. It was elaborately equipped like a magic theatre, with trapdoors, winches, pulleys, mirrors and flying rigs, as well as workshops and scenery stores.

The convention of the age was to film the world as it was in front of the camera. Méliès created more complex films, weaving his unique spell in what he termed 'artificially arranged scenes'. Each film comprised a number of distinct scenes, filmed from a single viewpoint, as if the camera were in the front row of a theatre. The action took place within this single setting, with characters and their props entering and exiting from stage left or right.

Though Méliès produced war scenes, historical scenes, news reconstructions, operas, publicity films, dramas and comedies, his most popular and famous films were those based on fairy tales and fantasies. In *Cinderella* (1899), stop-action turns a pumpkin into a glittering coach, and Cinderella's rags into a luxuriant gown. Slow motion allowed elfin dancers to glide in the air. Some scenes were even painstakingly hand-coloured one frame at a time.

In *Indian Rubber Head* (1902) Méliès used a 'split screen' process, which involved masking off areas of the film so that they did not receive an image in the first exposure, and then adjusting the masking so that only these areas were exposed in the second take. The viewer sees Méliès in the role of a scientist, placing a duplicate of his own head on a table and beginning to inflate it using a bellows. An assistant takes over and enthusiastically pumps air into the head, which grows enormous, pulling distended faces until finally exploding. The disembodied head was added in the second exposure, and enlarged by wheeling Méliès, sitting in a specially constructed carriage, closer to the camera.

Of the 500 films that Méliès produced between 1896 and 1912, perhaps his most impressive is *A Trip to the Moon* (1902), based on the writings of Jules Verne and H.G. Wells. The 21-minute film – a sprawling epic in an age when films rarely lasted more than 2 minutes – uses every available artifice to tell the story of a group of Victorian explorers who visit the moon. The sets and props were typical of the Méliès style, simply consisting of *trompe l'œil* paintings designed and painted by Méliès himself to give the illusion of three-dimensional depth. The presentation was pure pantomime, with a dash of moonshine. Groups of leggy chorus girls help to launch the spaceship shell from its cannon. Flying through space, the ship passes stars with beaming feminine faces at their centres, while the moon's grumpy crater-face becomes even more cheesed-off when the enormous spacecraft lands in his eye. On the lunar surface, the explorers are confronted by impish aliens who disappear in a puff of smoke, and Méliès exhibits one of his most imaginative effects when the various two-dimensional moonscape elements move in relation to one another to suggest a camera perspective shift.

For more than 10 years Méliès was the most popular film-maker in the world and could justifiably lay claim to being cinema's first star. The simple storylines and visual enchantment of his films meant that they could be enjoyed around the world without subtitling, and they were frequently pirated by foreign producers. However, Méliès's visual style did not evolve, and his narratives were little more than linkage for fantastic special effects. From around 1910 audiences in Europe and the United States began to see the innovative work of the American film-maker D.W. Griffith – films with realistic locations, stories and fast-paced editing. By comparison, the films of the Parisian master magician seemed outdated. Despite conjuring up greater spectacles than ever, Méliès could not hold on to his audience.

The Théâtre Robert-Houdin was closed by the outbreak of war in 1914, and Méliès was bankrupted. He spent the last years of his life running a toy kiosk on the Gare Montparnasse. He enjoyed a minor comeback in the late 1920s, courtesy of the surrealists, who admired the dreamlike sense of adventure and the whimsical treatment of science and logic in his work – and his films continue to beguile appreciative and nostalgic audiences to this day.

OTHER INNOVATORS

The reputation of Georges Méliès as the father of special effects is undisputed, yet he was not working in a vacuum and many others were innovating at the same time. Film was still a young medium, so the simple process of solving everyday film-making problems frequently led to the discovery or invention of new techniques – making it almost impossible to pinpoint who invented what and when. Many pioneers worked in Britain, and were the founders of a tradition of innovation in the field of special effects.

Méliès bought his first projector from Robert W. Paul, a scientific instrument maker from London. Paul entered the business when he was asked to make six duplicates of an Edison Kinetoscope for two Greek showmen. Although Paul copied the machines legally – Edison having failed to patent the device – the American inventor refused to supply films to run in the machines. Not to be defeated, Paul built his own camera and projection device and went into production himself.

Like other early film-makers, Paul's first efforts were single-shot views, but he quickly realized the value of offering audiences the unusual and fantastic. In 1897 he sent a cameraman to Egypt to capture exotic travelogue scenes such as *An Arab Knife Grinder at Work*. He also produced 'trick films' in a specially built studio in north London. One of his earliest productions gives an idea of the effects that could be achieved in films of the day, using methods such as stop-action and combining elements filmed in different exposures. In the frenetically surreal *The Haunted Curiosity Shop* (1901, directed for Paul by W.R. Booth), the top half of a woman enters a shop, closely followed by her bottom half. When the elderly storekeeper attempts to embrace the woman, she suddenly changes into a mummy, and then again into a skeleton. Three pixies then arrive on the scene, dancing wildly before merging into a single pixie,

ABOVE: **G.A. Smith's** *Santa Claus* **(1898) was a charming trick film using, among other effects, the film-maker's patented process of double exposure.**

LEFT: **R.W. Paul's** *The ? Motorist* **(1906) entertained audiences with its lighthearted vision of an interstellar car journey.**

RIGHT: **Edwin S. Porter, director of** *The Great Train Robbery* **(1903) and one of early cinema's true visionaries.**

FAR RIGHT: **For** *The Great Train Robbery* **(1903), Porter filmed the live action in the telegraph office in one exposure and the train passing the window in another.**

which the old man captures in a jar. A giant head then emerges from a puff of smoke and frightens the old man away.

Of the few surviving Paul films, the confusingly titled *The ? Motorist* (1906) is the most remarkable. Equalling anything produced by Méliès in technique and ambition, the film uses every available trick to tell the story of a couple who exceed the speed limit in their car and fly off the face of the Earth into outer space. Motoring through the solar system, the model car touches down on the Sun and circumnavigates its surface before taking off for a spin around Saturn's rings. Paul did not look upon himself as a film-maker, however, and only produced films to support the sales of his company's equipment. In 1910 he abandoned film-making, sold his studio and, tragically, burned many of his films.

Another English pioneer was the photographer G.A. Smith, who built his own movie camera in 1896 and produced a number of trick films. In 1897 he took out an English patent on the process of double exposure, and used the method to create the ghost in *The Corsican Brothers* (1909). Smith later joined forces with Charles Urban, a business manager whom Edison had originally sent to England in an attempt to prevent the piracy of his machines and films. Their company produced several notable films, including *Airship Destroyer* (1919, directed by W.R. Booth), in which London is attacked by a fleet of mysterious airships. A large and minutely detailed model of London was bombed and destroyed before the film's hero was able to defeat the zeppelins with radio-controlled missiles.

Among other notable film-makers in Britain was Cecil Hepworth, whose trick films included the evocatively titled *Explosion of a Motor Car* (1900), *How It Feels to Be Run Over* (1900) and *Alice in Wonderland* (1903).

After the dramatic early coup of the beheading in Alfred Clarke's *The Execution of Mary Queen of Scots* (1893), American film-makers remained surprisingly slow to use tricks in their fiction films. There was innovation, however; where Europeans favoured spectacular films in which tricks were the stars, American producers preferred a more subtle approach. A popular form of entertainment was the news film – a short film that claimed to portray real events as they had happened. In fact, many such 'events' were faked for the cameras.

In 1898, artists Albert E. Smith and J. Stuart Blackton, who together formed the Vitagraph Company, filmed *The Battle of Santiago Bay*. The bay was created by laying one of Blackton's paintings face-down and filling the canvas-covered frame with water to produce a small pond. The warring ships were cut-out photographs, pinned to floating wooden bases and pulled along on strings. Explosions were created using gunpowder attached to the back of the photographs. The drifting smoke of battle was produced by Mrs Blackton and an office boy, who stood off-camera and blew cigar smoke into the scene. The result was remarkably convincing. Vitagraph's next reconstruction was of *The Windsor Hotel Fire* (1899), in which small dolls fell from burning cardboard buildings, and water squirted from toy guns suggested the gallant efforts of the fire department.

Vitagraph was not alone in its techniques; other early studios, such as Biograph, Lubin, Selig and Edison, regularly counterfeited current events. Several companies produced films that showed both the real aftermath of the 1906 San Francisco earthquake and reconstructions of the disaster itself. Biograph produced a particularly spectacular model of the city, which was filmed as it burned and fell apart. It may seem extraordinary today that the viewers of such scenes rarely questioned their authenticity, but this was a time when moving pictures themselves seemed a miracle to most and few paused to consider that what they saw might be in any way fake.

The most significant American pioneer of this time was Edwin S. Porter. Joining Edison as a projectionist in 1900, he quickly assumed the rank of director. Porter produced several important films in which he challenged the conventions of editing, but his major contribution to the history of special effects came with *The Great Train Robbery* in 1903. This early 'Western' used shifting camera viewpoints and naturalistic settings, and startled audiences with one of the first known close-up shots. But the film's most significant breakthrough probably passed audiences by at the time – literally.

While the robbery takes place in the railroad telegraph office, a train can be seen steaming past the window. Later, in a mail car, a real moving landscape is seen going past an open doorway. To create these moving backgrounds, Porter adopted the matting techniques that Méliès had used to make himself appear twice in the same shot in *Indian Rubber Head*. In another scene, Porter tinted three frames red to simulate the firing of a gun – a dramatic device that would be used again by Alfred Hitchcock in *Spellbound* (1945).

Porter is remembered for having advanced the use of special effects to increase the naturalism of scenes and to further the drama. Whereas Méliès, Paul and other early film-makers had used trick photography for its own sake, Porter exploited special effects as unobtrusive tools to help tell a story.

THE 1910s

By 1910 film-making and exhibition was becoming a major business, and was beginning to assume the structure that would characterize the industry for much of the century. What was once a cottage industry gave way to film factories – nickelodeons (the first movie theatres) became goldmines.

Many small production companies emerged during this period, including Rex, run by Edwin Porter, who had left Edison in 1909. A considerable number of these companies disappeared almost before they arrived, while a few would survive and go on to dominate world film production for more than three-quarters of a century. Porter's company was among the early casualties. Moving out of production into technical research and manufacture, he was wiped out in the 1929 stock market crash.

As the industry found its feet, artistic pioneers continued to develop the art of film-making. Foremost among these was David Wark Griffith (1875–1948). Griffith joined Biograph in 1907 and quickly began to revolutionize film grammar through his command of editing, camera placing and movement, shot composition and lighting. Not an effects pioneer like Méliès, D.W. Griffith did however standardize a number of photographic effects for storytelling.

He used shot transitions, such as the fade-in and fade-out, to indicate the lapse of time between scenes. Such effects were achieved during photography by opening and closing the camera aperture diaphragm to control the amount of light reaching the film. If a fade was required after photography, the camera negative was lowered slowly into bleach until the start point of the fade was reached. The negative was then slowly withdrawn, producing a linear fading of the image on the negative.

Around 1913, Griffith also began to make frequent use of the iris-in and iris-out for dramatic effect. There is some dispute as to whether the device was pioneered by Griffith or by fellow director Thomas Ince (1882–1924), though it

was undoubtedly Griffith who developed the art of the technique. The iris was a simple device that fitted in front of the lens and could be opened and closed to progressively reveal or conceal areas of the frame. Griffith used the device to draw the eye to the centre of the drama or to reveal previously hidden elements of a scene. In *The Birth of a Nation* (1915), a mother and her children are shown huddling in the upper left-hand corner of an otherwise black screen. The object of their concern is revealed as the iris opens to show the Northern armies marching through the family's devastated town.

By 1914 the movie industry was well established in southern California, where the fine weather and extreme distance from New York's Motion Picture Patents Company (which prosecuted anyone caught using its film equipment without authorization) made for ideal working conditions. Though Europe had developed its own thriving film industry, the outbreak of

1910s PROFILE **MACK SENNETT**

Buying their tickets, the majority of early movie-goers expected to be entertained. Weepies were fine, but weeping with laughter was better. Visual comedy was loved the world over, and no one developed the art of screen slapstick more than Mack Sennett (1880–1960) – the 'King of Comedy'.

In 1912, after a stint as actor, gagman and comedy director at Biograph, Canadian-born Sennett persuaded two ex-bookmakers to lay money on his sure-fire idea for movies about a blundering troupe of policemen. He called his studio Keystone, and its comical, car-chasing Kops were to arrest audiences for much of the next decade.

Keystone was a laughter factory where two-reel comedies were churned out like custard pies from a bakery. At the peak of production, several films a day emerged from the strictly run studio. Teams of writers, performers and prop builders manufactured gags that formed the cornerstone of all Keystone comedy: the fall from dignity.

Keystone performers underwent all manner of punishing pratfalls to make gags work. Helping them

raise their laughs were a stable of effects men, perhaps the most skilled of their time. Any day might find them making rubber bricks, rigging telegraph poles to collapse on cue or building fake houses for cars to smash through. Central to the Kop films was the patrol wagon. Designed by Del Lord, the vehicle's heavy chassis and specially designed brakes allowed it, loaded with lunatic lawmen, to perform some astonishing stunts.

Sennett was notoriously tightfisted, refusing to pay his performers their worth – names such as Charlie Chaplin, Harold Lloyd, Fatty Arbuckle, Gloria Swanson and even the director Frank Capra passed through the studio on their way up the ladder. The studio flourished in the 1910s, but by the 20s its comedy was seriously challenged by the likes of Hal Roach Studios, whose stars included Harold Lloyd, Harry Langdon and Laurel and Hardy. Though Sennett had made a fortune from investing in oil and real estate, he was bankrupted in 1933 when the Wall Street Crash left him with debts of over $5 million.

war effectively ended all commercial production. With its European competition crippled by war, Hollywood was set to dominate the hearts, minds and screens of the world.

Typical Hollywood film units consisted of a small all-purpose (and all-male) crew. At the head was the director, and under him the cameraman. Any good cameraman was capable of producing a number of 'live' tricks during the hand-cranked filming process. Among them were the basic fading and iris effects. Cameramen could produce dissolves, by which one image merges seamlessly into another. The effect was achieved by reducing the camera's aperture at the end of a sequence to produce a fade to black, rewinding the film, starting a second exposure and opening the aperture as the new scene was shot. By varying the speed at which they cranked the camera, cameramen could also produce fast or slow motion. The average cranking speed for cameras and projectors at this time was 16 frames per second. Undercranking the camera would speed up the action in the film when it was projected, and became a favourite trick of helter-skelter slapstick comedies.

Methods that required running the film through the camera twice, such as split screens and double exposures, became much more practical after the introduction of the new Bell and Howell type 2709 camera in 1912. This new all-metal camera was unique in the way it moved film and held it steady in front of the aperture on fixed register pins during exposure. The ability to produce steady images, combined with an accurate frame counter, made the Bell and Howell ideal for producing in-camera special effects, which required the exact placing of images on film.

The creation of any unusual effect was generally the responsibility of whoever came up with a workable on-the-spot solution to a problem. However, some people gradually began to specialize in particular techniques and gained a reputation for those skills. One such individual was Norman O. Dawn, Hollywood's first effects man (245>).

Dawn pioneered the glass shot, whereby scenery could be altered or extended on film by the use of highly detailed paintings. The technique was typically used to add additional height to studio sets that were only built one or two storeys high – the upper levels were added by painting them on a sheet of glass positioned in front of the camera. He later developed the in-camera matte shot, a technique that enabled filmed scenery to be combined with paintings.

The decade also saw the emergence and exploitation of the film 'star'. At first, film actors were happy to appear anonymously; film work was often seen as a sign of failure on the stage. But audiences gradually grew attached to their favourite performers, and came to know them by their nicknames – Mary Pickford was known to millions simply as 'Little Mary' and 'The Girl with the Curls'. Producers and exhibitors quickly grasped the potential drawing power of these audience favourites, and the 'star' was born. By the end of the decade, performers such as Pickford, Douglas Fairbanks and Charlie Chaplin were among the most famous and best loved people in the world, commanding huge followings and staggering salaries.

In 1916 cameraman Frank Williams devised a method of filming actors in front of a black background so that a new background filmed at another time and place could be added later. The results were crude but it was the first example of travelling matte photography (57>), a technique that would become a mainstay of special effects production.

Among the decade's other developments was the introduction of the feature film format. Exhibitors had nursed the belief that audiences could only concentrate for the length of one reel, normally around 12 minutes. When D.W. Griffith found himself unable to tell the story of *Enoch and Arden* (1911) in less than two reels, exhibitors insisted on releasing it in two halves. Films several reels in length emerged from Europe at the beginning of the decade, and in 1912 the French four-reeler *Queen Elizabeth*, featuring the distinguished classical actress Sarah Bernhardt, was an international hit. In the United States, producer and future Paramount boss Adolph Zukor took the lead when he began making feature-length productions of 'Famous Players in Famous Plays'. By the end of the decade, the feature film – usually around 90 minutes in length – was on every cinema bill.

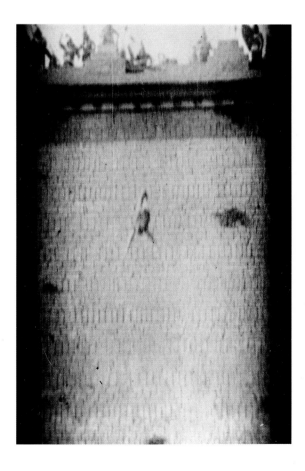

ABOVE LEFT: **Many film companies settled in southern California in the 1910s. Universal Studios was built among the orange groves of the San Fernando Valley, where film-makers enjoyed fresh air and clear skies.**

RIGHT: **D.W. Griffith masked the sides of the frame to emphasize the length of a fall from the walls of Babylon in this scene from his epic** *Intolerance* **(1916).**

FAR RIGHT: **Griffith and his cameraman Billy Bitzer (*left*) pioneered new standards of motion-picture photography and editing that would be used for decades.**

THE 1920s

American film-making flourished in the 20s. Film-makers began to branch out beyond the artistic and technical boundaries established by the pioneers of the previous decade, and came to rely increasingly on special effects to tell their stories. The Hollywood studio system was up to speed, and film-making was an efficient, rationalized and highly profitable business.

Under the fledgling movie moguls, specific departments were created to deal with each aspect of movie production, from scripts and costumes to props and editing. There is uncertainty over which studio established the first department dedicated to the creation of special effects – some claim that it was Fox, while others are sure that it was MGM. Either way, the term 'special effects' received its first screen credit in the 1926 Fox picture *What Price Glory?* It referred in this case to both the film's physical and mechanical effects.

New techniques were developed to help film-makers present the lavish or historical settings their films demanded. The first travelling matte processes, allowing actors filmed in the studio to be placed within settings from a different time and place, were crude but enabled a degree of realism (57>). These processes were helped by the development of much-improved camera and lighting equipment, and faster, finer film stocks (53>).

Since the earliest days of the industry, film-makers had built small models of any object or location that was too big, expensive or impractical to be filmed in any other way. In the 20s, as production budgets soared in line with film-makers' ambitions, studios became increasingly dependent on the use of money-saving models. As a result, effects technicians became highly skilled in the building and shooting of accurately scaled-down landscapes, buildings and vehicles, and in the combination of such footage with live-action full-scale photography for films such as *The Crowd* (1928) and *Just Imagine* (1930).

German films were a major influence on American film-makers of the 20s. Douglas Fairbanks (1883–1939) was particularly impressed by what he saw emerging from the studios of Europe. *The Thief of Bagdad* (1924) used opulent sets and the best effects Hollywood could buy. Fairbanks admitted that they were designed to compete with the German films of the time. Some of the scenes were effective, such as the flying carpet sequences (when the wires didn't show), but *Thief* mainly served to demonstrate that

ABOVE: **The sluggish science fiction musical *Just Imagine* (1930) was enlivened by shots of a magnificent model city inspired by Fritz Lang's *Metropolis* (1926).**

LEFT: **Douglas Fairbanks rides a flying carpet suspended on wires above hundreds of extras populating the enormous sets built for *The Thief of Bagdad* (1924).**

RIGHT: **Adventurer Bessie Love cowers beneath one of Willis O'Brien's animated dinosaurs in the classic effects film *The Lost World* (1925).**

while American technicians could build enormous sets, they still had a lot of ground to cover in the field of special effects.

Epics on the scale of *The Thief of Bagdad* were popular, often demanding sets of biblical proportions. *Ben Hur* (1925) required the creation of a full-scale Circus Maximus and a fleet of seven huge Roman galleys on location in Italy. But a number of incidents – including the burning of the galleys (in which some extras are reputed to have drowned when the galleys accidentally caught fire) – combined with bad weather and Italian labour disputes, brought the production back to California. The film was completed in rebuilt sets with significant use of miniatures.

Films created using animation grew in sophistication and popularity. In 1923 Walt Disney (1901–66) began production of his *Alice* comedies, in which a live-action Alice was combined with two-dimensional cartoon figures. The combination of live action and animation went further in *The Lost World* (1925). This ambitious version of Sir Arthur Conan Doyle's novel used startling stop-motion animated dinosaurs created by pioneering animator Willis O'Brien (1886–1962, 182>).

The greatest technical development of the period came towards the end of the decade. The coming of sound was no surprise – sound systems of varying effectiveness had been around for much of the decade. By the time Al Jolson broke into song on film on 6 October 1927, many audiences had experienced Fox Movietone newsreels that used the sound-on-film methods pioneered by Lee De Forest (1874–1961). But Warner Brothers' release of *The Jazz Singer* (1927) – in a last-ditch effort to stave off bankruptcy – fired the public imagination and signalled that the 'talkie' was here to stay.

GERMAN SPECIAL EFFECTS

In the 20s Hollywood was undisputed as the world's leading film factory, but the special effects of German film-makers, combining their technical flair with a traditional love of fairy tales, were far superior.

The German actor and director Paul Wegener (1874–1948), considered by many as the 'father of the horror film', was a great advocate of special effects. In a 1916 speech, which was more prophetic than probably even he imagined, he envisaged the development of a 'synthetic cinema' in which totally artificial scenes would be created by the abilities of the camera. Wegener made significant use of special effects, notably in his religious meditation *Living Buddhas* (1923). For one dramatic sequence, a sophisticated matte technique was used to create the impression of a Buddha in the sky directing a ship lost at sea to safety.

UFA, Germany's largest studio, made the country's most spectacular productions, with Fritz Lang (1890–1976) as their star director. Lang's two-part epic *Die Niebelungen* (1924) was filmed entirely on enormous studio sets and featured an awesome 18 m (60 ft) mechanical dragon – a far cry from the awkward reptile of Douglas Fairbanks's *The Thief of Bagdad*, made in the same year. The production also exploited the Shuftan process (114>), which used mirrors to combine full-sized sets with miniatures – a technique for which German cinema would become famous.

Lang's effects masterpiece was *Metropolis* (1926), a visionary science fiction fable that made stunning use of model animation, matte painting, early rear projection and full-scale mechanical effects. Although a financial failure, *Metropolis* had a huge impact on contemporary American film-makers, and it continues to be one of the most influential films ever made. Futuristic artistry and technical excellence have secured its place in popular culture.

Ironically, by 1930 many of Germany's leading directors and technicians had left for Hollywood. Lang was one of the last to take flight, lingering in Germany to produce *Frau im Mond* (*The Woman in the Moon*, 1929). Though the film was science fiction, Lang strove to make it as accurate as possible, hiring Professor Hermann Oberth (who later designed the Nazis' terrifying V-1 rocket bomb) and Willy Ley (later a designer of rockets for the USA) to work as consultants. The resulting scenes of rocket construction were so revealing that prints of the film, and model rockets used during filming, were later confiscated by the Gestapo.

Film-makers of the 20s often
sought economical ways to bring
large-scale settings to the screen.
For this scene (*above*) in *Dorothy
Vernon of Haddon Hall* (1924), only
the lower portion of the castle was
constructed as a full-size set. A
miniature of the upper parts (*left*)
was positioned much nearer to the
camera so that the two halves
appeared as one when seen through
the lens.

THE 1930s

Despite the success of *The Jazz Singer* (1927), the new phenomenon of the 'talkie' was largely ignored in most Hollywood studios. For Warner Brothers, however, the gamble had paid off. Audiences couldn't get enough of the talkies. Using their Vitaphone sound-on-disc process, the studio hastily added snippets of music and dialogue to the silent films already in production, and began planning all-talking future projects. Fox also added sound to their films, using their rival technique Movietone – a sound-on-film process that would later become the industry standard. The rest of Hollywood remained silent, resisting sound as no more than a fad.

But the public appetite for talkies was not to be starved, and by the mid-30s, the big studios were producing all their major films in sound. Others, notably the Chaplin Studio, remained to be convinced, and it was another 10 years before Charlie Chaplin was first heard in *The Great Dictator* (1940).

The coming of sound brought massive changes to an industry that was still settling into departmentalized production routines. New studio departments were tasked with sound recording, mixing and dubbing, as well as the scoring and performance of musical soundtracks. Stages needed to be soundproofed and movie theatres equipped for sound.

By the late 20s, silent films had achieved extraordinary finesse. Directors knew how to position and move their cameras to heighten dramatic impact, and when to use intertitles – written cards displayed between and during scenes – to represent dialogue and express plot points. The arrival of sound hijacked everything. Early sound recording was a delicate and demanding process, and the needs of the soundmen began to dictate every aspect of shooting. Cameras were noisy and drowned out dialogue, so they were housed in soundproof sheds, with cameraman and lens peering through a glass window. Action had to be performed before this fixed camera, becoming almost as confined and stagy as it was in Georges Méliès's day.

Early microphones were weak, and actors often suffered the indignity of delivering emotional dialogue into a microphone disguised as a telephone or a vase of flowers. Many early stars didn't progress that far, finding that their voices were unsuitable for the talkies, or that their voices didn't fit their images. They were replaced by a constellation of newcomers, often from the stage, whose richer diction had the approval of the sound department.

From about 1933, sound recording restricted filming on location, and for the next 20 years the great Hollywood outdoors would be filmed almost entirely within studio walls. The coming of sound is often held solely responsible for this wholesale move into the studios. In truth, the move probably had as much to do with increasing control by studio bosses who, after location nightmares such as those on *Ben Hur* (1925), preferred to keep wayward productions and problematic directors well within view.

For special effects departments, sound brought some new challenges. With films being made exclusively on the studio lot, effects technicians had to find ways to bring exotic and even everyday locations to the set. One result was the first practical form of rear projection, a process enabling background scenery to be projected onto a screen behind actors while filming in the studio (82>). Over the next 20 years the technique would be perfected for use in almost every Hollywood production – providing backdrops for ocean-going romances, stagecoach chases, and journeys in trains, cars and planes.

Although rear projection often replaced the need for travelling mattes (57>), effects technicians continued to perfect travelling matte photography. The development of advanced optical printers, which enabled the various elements necessary for travelling matte shots to be combined on film with greater control, meant improved image quality. The optical printer also found favour in the production of many 30s musicals whose spectacular dance sequences needed flamboyant scene transitions, such as the star-wipe (70>) and the now iconic spinning newspaper effect used to proclaim headline news.

By the middle of the decade, special effects had advanced so much that a single department under the umbrella title of 'special effects' was not enough, and each studio's effects department found itself with a number of subdivisions. At MGM, for example, the special effects department was responsible for rear projection, miniatures, and physical and mechanical effects, while the optical department dealt with matte paintings and optical printing (54>).

Special effects became an integral aspect of movie-making during the decade, perhaps as much for their ability to save time and money as their

1930s PROFILE JAMES WHALE

The English director James Whale (1896–1957) came to Hollywood at the end of the 1920s to make the film of *Journey's End* (1930), a play tracking the horrors of war. An enigmatic man, his best films smiled darkly at terrors of the imagination. Under contract at Universal, Whale then took the director's chair for *Frankenstein* (1931), the success of which would both bless and damn his career.

Frankenstein's laboratory sequences and spectacular lightning effects were created by Kenneth Strickfaden, whose 'Electrical Properties' boosted the fading current of many horror movies of the 1930s. Modelwork by John P. Fulton (69>) was used for the laboratory and the blazing mill at the end of the film. These techniques, combined with Jack Pierce's iconic monster design (272>) and expressionistic lighting, produced a science fantasy unlike anything Universal had made before.

Whale made three more horror films for Universal. *Bride of Frankenstein* (1935) embellished the achievements of its forerunner with technically superior effects, supervised again by Fulton. The two men also worked together on *The Invisible Man* (1933), in which Fulton used the Williams process (58>) to ensure that when Claude Rains shed his bandages, he revealed nothing. *The Old Dark House* (1932) employed modelwork to create a devastating landslide.

Whale directed two more films of note: *Show Boat* (1936), a musical that convincingly re-created a Mississippi riverboat entirely with models; and *The Man in the Iron Mask* (1939), where double exposure techniques allowed Louis Hayward to speak to himself – his other lines were spoken to him by a stand-in (the young Peter Cushing), who was later edited from the composite image.

Whale became increasingly frustrated by the limits of the horror genre. Like Frankenstein, he had unlocked the mysteries of creation, but all the studio gods expected him to create was horror.

FAR LEFT: **A young Alfred Hitchcock listens to actress Anny Ondra during the filming of *Blackmail* (1929). The camera stands in a soundproof chamber so that the noise from its motor does not interfere with the sound recording.**

LEFT: **Disaster movie *The Rains Came* (1939) won an early Academy Award for its special effects. A variety of techniques, including the split-screen combination of live action and miniatures, was used to depict the devastation caused by earthquakes and floods.**

power to create the fantastic or the seemingly impossible. As a result there was good investment in technology, and leeway for innovation. In 1932 Carl Laemmle (1867–1939) ordered the construction of Universal's first dedicated special effects stage, inaugurated with the filming of the miniature aeroplanes for *Air Mail* (1932) under the supervision of John Fulton (69>), and soon used for the production of classics such as *The Invisible Man* (1934) and *The Bride of Frankenstein* (1935). Special effects men began to earn considerable respect within the studios, although they rarely received any notice from the outside world, studio bosses believing audiences would feel cheated if they discovered the secrets of on-screen deception.

The studios of Hollywood began to develop distinct personalities in the 1930s. A film's studio pedigree was often clearly recognizable without reading its titles. The type of pictures a studio produced depended largely on its roster of contract stars. The Warners house style, for instance, was built around a string of crime dramas and gangster movies featuring James Cagney, earnest biopics starring Paul Muni, Errol Flynn swashbucklers, and a series of 'women's pictures' starring Bette Davis. Each studio established output patterns related to its stars, market position and resources.

The kind of film a studio produced affected the resources dedicated to its special effects department. Universal maintained a substantial department to provide optical, physical and make-up effects for its famous stream of horror movies, begun with Tod Browning's *Dracula* in 1931 and established by James Whale's *Frankenstein* later the same year. The series, eventually comprising some 24 films, centred on the characters of Dracula, Frankenstein's Monster, the Invisible Man, the Mummy and the Wolf Man, later combining two or more of these characters. At RKO, a particularly good optical department provided prominent effects for their series of Astaire and Rogers musicals, and contributed astonishing effects to the landmark smash hit *King Kong* (1933). Despite the success of *Kong* and some of Universal's horror movies, special effects films did not flourish in their own right in this decade. Effects people spent most of their time perfecting the type of unglamorous methods that allowed Hollywood's stars to drive convincingly in front of rear-projected traffic.

The craze for talkies had shielded the major studios from the world's financial crisis in the 30s, and at the end of the decade Hollywood remained in good financial shape – unchallenged as the supplier of the world's most popular form of entertainment. The end of the 30s also witnessed one of the greatest periods in Hollywood production history, with the release of classics including *The Wizard of Oz*, *Mr Smith Goes to Washington*, *Stagecoach*, *Goodbye, Mr Chips*, *Wuthering Heights* and *Gone with the Wind* (all 1939).

Special effects were now so important to movie production that they even received the ultimate recognition: their very own category at the Oscars. The first Academy Award for Achievement in Special Effects went to *The Rains Came* (1939), featuring a flood of biblical proportions masterminded by Fox's effects maestro, Fred Sersen (1890–1962).

THE 1940s

The 40s began auspiciously with the production of Orson Welles's *Citizen Kane* (1941). The film, now ranked as one of the greatest ever made, was a tour de force of matte paintings, miniatures, animation, and ingenious optical printing techniques. Perhaps it is a tribute to their invisibility that the film was not even nominated in the recently created special effects category of that year's Academy Awards.

Most of Hollywood's leading effects people now had well over a decade's experience in studio production behind them and were masters of the various techniques available to them. Rear projection, optical printing, matte painting, and to a lesser degree, travelling matte photography, played a key role in the majority of studio productions, and were considered a vital part of the production process.

The rise of colour photography, however, brought significant changes to the industry – although it did not cause a revolution on the scale that the arrival of sound had provoked in the previous decade. Colour film processes had been around since the early days of film, but few systems had been either practical or particularly pleasing to the eye. The first popular system, introduced in the late 20s, was Technicolor's two-strip process (56>). But with very slow film speeds requiring blinding amounts of light – often resulting in false colours on a grainy image – the two-strip technique did not enjoy widespread use. The early 30s saw the introduction of a three-strip Technicolor process (56>), whose colour reproduction was superb. Three-strip Technicolor was first used commercially for Disney's cartoon short *Flowers and Trees* (1932), and RKO's *Becky Sharp* became the first live-action feature to use the process in 1935.

Filming with early three-strip Technicolor still required three to four times as much light as black-and-white photography, so it was largely impractical for interiors. In a break from the studio-bound regime of the 30s, a number of prestigious productions were shot on location in three-strip Technicolor, a move also facilitated by improved sound technology. The first film shot entirely outdoors was Henry Hathaway's *The Trail of the Lonesome Pine* (1936). However, the introduction in 1939 of much faster film stock – requiring far less light – made three-strip Technicolor a viable option for studio production in the 40s.

For effects technicians, colour was a challenge. Rear projection in colour was at first a vivid but unattainable dream. The background images projected onto a screen behind actors in the studio were not bright enough to be filmed in colour. However, faster film stocks and a powerful new projection system devised at Paramount helped to overcome this problem in the early 40s.

Travelling matte techniques (57>) also needed modification to accommodate colour. The first successful new method was pioneered in the UK and used in the 1940 version of *The Thief of Bagdad* (61>).

The effects technique most affected by the arrival of colour was matte painting (244>). In black and white the painter and subsequent photographer had to worry about matching the greyscale tones of painting and live action. In Technicolor, every colour and shade of the painting had to match exactly those of the original footage *after* both had been combined under different lighting conditions *and* after the original exposure had been stored undeveloped for some time. The first major display of Technicolor matte painting was *Gone with the Wind* (1939) – an often sumptuous blend of painting and live action born out of months of patient experimentation.

Despite the success of Technicolor, it was both an intensive and expensive system, generally reserved for prestige productions. The majority of films in the 40s continued to be shot in black and white.

The involvement of Europe and the United States in World War II meant that a large proportion of Hollywood's 40s output was devoted to boosting the morale of those in the armed services and their families back home. The number of films made by Hollywood studios fell from an average of 50 pictures a year per studio to a wartime average of 30. But with fewer films being made, more resources were available for the on-screen version of a world at war.

The re-creation of battlefields, destroyer-prowled oceans and fighter-filled skies fell to the effects technicians. Full-scale armaments were out of the question, so war films relied heavily on models and miniature photography – often on an epic scale. The demand for realistic sea battles led to advances in marine model-making and shooting in studio tanks – huge outdoor pools in which naval confrontations were staged. The tank at MGM was 92 m (300 ft) square, but the 15 m (50 ft) vessels that it often contained – such as those for *Thirty Seconds over Tokyo* (1944) – were so cramped that the water had to be pumped past the ships to give the impression that they were steaming forwards at speed. Filming water to scale will always be a problem, though the experience gained in the 1940s brought the art as close to perfection as it would ever be.

Aerial combat was re-created using squadrons of miniature aircraft, held aloft and manoeuvred by complex systems of wires. One of the most remarkable uses of the technique saw two dozen model aircraft take off in convincingly precise formation for *Mrs Miniver* (1942). War films also meant the frequent use of explosives, and Hollywood powdermen were kept busy supplying carefully devised miniature explosions for the destruction of models, in addition to convincing (but safe) mortars and bullet hits for full-scale live-action combat sequences.

Wartime box office takings soared in the US and the UK, more than compensating for the loss of important revenues from much of war-torn Europe and Asia. But after the end of hostilities box office revenues began to slump, partly because of the growth of suburban housing developments away from city cinemas, and increasingly because of the arrival of a mighty challenge to the dominance of the big screen: television.

LEFT: The filming of *Trail of the Lonesome Pine* (1936) was dominated by the presence of the enormous early Technicolor camera.

BELOW LEFT: The use of early blue-screen travelling mattes enabled child star Sabu to sit in the hand of a giant djinn for *The Thief of Bagdad* (1940).

RIGHT: Like many films of the period, *Ships with Wings* (1942) relied on model ships, planes and miniature pyrotechnics for its portrayal of a world at war.

1940s PROFILE **ALFRED HITCHCOCK**

Alfred Hitchcock (1899–1980) is celebrated as the undisputed master of the thriller genre, but is less often credited as an important special effects director. He entered the film industry as a title card illustrator in 1919, but soon graduated, via scenario writing, to directing – making his first feature, *The Pleasure Garden*, in 1925.

Hitchcock directed Britain's first acknowledged sound film, *Blackmail* (1929). Not content with merely capturing sound, he also employed some adventurous special effects. Using the Shuftan process (114>) – which he had noted during a visit to Germany's UFA studios – he combined models and live action for a large-scale finale that the film's modest budget could not otherwise have provided.

Hitchcock's technical virtuosity continued to grow in the 1930s, with films such as *The 39 Steps* (1935) and *The Lady Vanishes* (1938) demonstrating the director's ability to combine witty scripts and characters with deft camerawork and subtle special effects. Quickly latching

onto the potential of the new process of rear projection (82>), Hitchcock devised some of the most imaginative uses ever of the technique for films such as *Foreign Correspondent* (1940; 83>).

Hitchcock moved to Hollywood in 1940. With *Rebecca* (1940), his first American production, he started to explore the increased potential for special effects that higher budgets allowed, making particular use of miniatures and rear projection. Later experiments included *Lifeboat* (1944), a film set entirely within the confines of a drifting boat, and *Rope* (1948), a film cleverly filmed to appear as one continuous shot. Later films were increasingly reliant on effects, most notably *The Birds* (1963) which used a number of techniques to create both the flocks of birds and the destruction wrought by them. Hitchcock's position as the most creative and influential director of the period was unchallenged. His bold and imaginative use of special effects could not be matched.

THE 1950s

In America, television took hold quickly. Many families moved out of the city to the mushrooming post-war suburbs, and TV provided a cheap and accessible form of entertainment in their new homes.

The massive rise of television ownership terrified Hollywood. With free viewing in their living rooms, families didn't need to visit city centre theatres for their entertainment. For the first time in its history, Hollywood's position as the foremost provider of the nation's entertainment was seriously challenged; average weekly attendances plummeted from around 90 million in 1948 to 51 million in 1952.

But Hollywood's troubles did not end there. In the 30s the trading practices of the big studios became the subject of a US Federal anti-trust investigation. In 1948 the Supreme Court ruled that ownership of both the means of film production (the studio) and the means of distribution (the theatre) was monopolistic. The studios were forced to separate their production and exhibition activities by selling off their theatre chains. The newly independent theatres could show films made by any producer – be it major Hollywood studio or small independent production company. Hollywood had lost the previously guaranteed outlet for its films – good or bad.

Hollywood reasoned that it could win back audiences with innovation and technology. It began with the quality of the image. The small screen provided a fuzzy, black-and-white picture of variable quality. The big screen could dazzle, with enhanced images – huge, sharp and colourful.

The availability of good, economical colour systems, such as Eastman Kodak's single-strip Eastmancolor process, effectively ended Technicolor's market monopoly in the early 50s. In their attempt to outshine television, the studios splashed colour into the majority of their films. Later, it became evident that colour made little difference to the commercial success of most films and after the initial boost, the proportion of films made in colour declined to around 50 per cent from the middle of the decade. Ironically, the number of colour films did not increase significantly again until the mid-1960s, when the TV networks switched to colour broadcasting, and films made in colour became worth more when sold for broadcast.

Efforts were also made to improve the size and quality of the image. In 1952 Cinerama was introduced: a widescreen projection method, using three synchronized projectors to produce an exceptionally wide image with multi-track stereo sound. Spectacular though it was, Cinerama nevertheless caused more problems than it solved, since it required theatres, already desperate to cut costs, to invest in additional screens, projectors and projection staff.

CinemaScope was a more successful widescreen process, which used an anamorphic lens that squeezed wide 'letterbox' images onto film during photography and unsqueezed them during

RIGHT: Effects-filled science fiction fantasies such as George Pal's production *When Worlds Collide* (1951) did much to tempt younger audiences back to the cinema.

BELOW: The widescreen epics of the 50s strove to re-create history in spectacular fashion. This scene from *Ben Hur* (1959) combined live-action photography with a matte painting by Matthew Yuricich to depict a legion's triumphal return to Rome.

1950s PROFILE **GEORGE PAL**

Though many film-makers ventured into the realms of science fiction during the 1950s, few of them produced so consistent and successful a body of work as George Pal (1908–80).

Pal was born in Hungary, the son of famous stage-acting parents. Though he had planned to be an architect, a clerical error at his Budapest college led Pal to enrol in art classes, sparking a love for animation. Pal's first job was as an animator at Budapest's Hunnia Studios but his knowledge of architecture soon led to a job as a set designer for Germany's renowned UFA Studios in Berlin, where within two months he became head of the animation department. The rise of Hitler prompted Pal to move to Paris, where he established a successful animation business, until the spectre of Nazi invasion forced him to move to Holland and then again to the US.

In the US, Pal secured a contract with Paramount to produce a series of animated puppet films called 'Pal's Puppetoons', employing the young Ray Harryhausen as an animator (188>) and winning a special Oscar for the

techniques that he developed. Following the success of his Puppetoons, Pal secured finance for his first feature film, *Destination Moon* (1950). Pal gave his first film the high production values that would come to distinguish all of his features – even hiring the German rocket scientist Hermann Oberth to ensure the film would be scientifically accurate. As producer – and in later films director – Pal's use of special effects was typically restrained; he recognized when it was best to allow character and dialogue to tell a story, and when to rely on special effects and action.

Pal's later productions contained less science and more fantasy, but his commitment to detail, high production values and judicious use of superb special effects ensured that his films, such as *When Worlds Collide* (1951), *The War of the Worlds* (1953), *The Conquest of Space* (1955), *tom thumb* (1958), *The Lost Continent* (1960) and *The Time Machine* (1960), were among the most popular, critically acclaimed and best remembered of the period.

fiction genre, considering it the fodder of cheap serials and B movies produced by the Poverty Row studios. But the popularity of sci-fi literature and movie serials among young people – now the front row of film audiences – made it appear a safe bet for greater investment.

Destination Moon (1950) was the first major sci-fi film of the decade. Produced by George Pal, who was to create several of the decade's most significant science fiction films, *Destination Moon* was a critical and commercial success, sparking a meteor shower of similar movies. The fears of the 50s – atomic annihilation and Communist invasion – were echoed vividly in tales of aliens visiting Earth intent on domination and destruction.

From the middle of the decade, a rash of movies offered variations on a range of sci-fi themes, and all kinds of monsters were seen to be populating the planet. These included beasts forgotten by time (*The Creature from the Black Lagoon*, 1954), angry monsters stirred from the deep by atomic explosions (*The Beast from 20,000 Fathoms*, 1953), creatures mutated by atomic experiments (*Them!*, 1954), people whose bodies or even souls had been invaded by aliens (*Invasion of the Body Snatchers*, 1956) and people harmed by modern science (*The Fly*, 1958).

All of this meant plenty of work for Hollywood's special effects departments. Model-makers were kept busy fashioning spacecraft, often in the now classic flying saucer design – though there were notable exceptions, such as the sleek manta-like ships of perhaps the decade's most memorable science fiction film, *The War of the Worlds* (1953). Many sci-fi movies of the 50s were produced on tiny budgets by independent producers, such as the cinematically challenged director Edward D. Wood (1924–78), whose weird, wired and wobbly efforts have become classics in their own right.

Aliens and monsters of the 50s were generally men in rubber suits, with little subtlety of movement or performance. Perhaps the most famous, that which emerged from the infamous Black Lagoon, was a wholly typical creation, requiring stuntman Ricou Browning to flail around in a rubber suit that was half monkey and half lizard in design. A number of notable mechanical creatures did appear, however, including a crude but effective giant ant in *Them!* and the popular Robby the Robot in *Forbidden Planet* (1956). Perhaps most spectacular was the giant squid in Disney's *20,000 Leagues under the Sea* (1954). The mechanical beast, built by Bob Mattey, was originally scheduled to appear in a tranquil sunset scene but its clumsy pneumatic and cable-controlled performance eventually had to be obscured in a tempest whipped up by studio technicians. The genuinely thrilling results won the studio an Oscar for Best Special Effects.

There were some important effects innovations during the decade. In Britain, the J. Arthur Rank Organisation pioneered a superior new travelling matte system using sodium vapour lighting (64>), later adopted and refined by Disney. There were also mechanical inventions, such as an early motion-control system (146>) called a 'repeater', developed at Paramount. This recorded camera motion so that shots of separate elements, such as models and live action, could be taken with identical camera movements, enabling them to be combined effectively.

The decade also saw the rise of the only effects artist ever to become a household name. Gaining attention with the stop-motion ape in *Mighty Joe Young* (1949), Ray Harryhausen (1920–; 188>) continued to produce spectacular animated creatures for a series of 'monster on the rampage' films, including *It Came from Beneath the Sea* (1955) and *Twenty Million Miles to Earth* (1957). Harryhausen ended the decade with the first of a series of spectacular mythical fantasies: *The 7th Voyage of Sinbad* (1959). To produce the Arabian Nights adventure, Harryhausen used perspective tricks, split screens, over- and undersized props, mattes and stop-motion animation of unparalleled complexity.

Hollywood ended the 50s in a beleaguered and somewhat bewildered state, unsure of how to prevent its dominance slipping further from its grasp. The good times were a fast-fading memory as Tinseltown dug in to prepare for whatever the 60s might bring.

projection. The only investment required by theatres was the new lenses, which could be fitted to existing projectors. Fox pioneered the process and unveiled it spectacularly with *The Robe* in 1953. Within a year, every major studio – except for Paramount (which used its own VistaVision process) and RKO (which used SuperScope) – had adopted CinemaScope. By 1957, 85 per cent of the movie theatres in the US were equipped to show films in 'Scope'.

The other major attraction of the 50s was pure gimmickry – *Bwana Devil* (1952) promised audiences 'A lion in your lap!' Persuading itself that 3-D films might be the industry's saviour, Hollywood forced its new perspective on all kinds of film, from musicals (*Kiss Me Kate*, 1953) to thrillers (*Dial M for Murder*, 1954), and from horror films (*House of Wax*, 1953) to Westerns (*Hondo*, 1953). Audiences disliked wearing the special glasses that the process required and within 18 months of its much-touted launch, the 3-D craze had sunk almost without trace.

Studios tinkered with more than image quality. As families sat at home watching Lucille Ball and Jackie Gleason on television, movie audience demographics changed. The movie theatre was now the darkened haunt of teenagers and young couples, glad to slip away from their parents. Drive-in theatres sprang up in response to the post-war boom in car sales and the rise of suburbanization. By 1956 the United States had over 4,000 of these out-of-town sites, and at their height, more people sat in cars to watch a movie than in the traditional theatres. Despite their popularity, the drive-ins did little to stop the overall decline in film-going.

Pulp science fiction novels and comics had become hugely popular since the 40s, but the Hollywood majors had hardly explored the science

THE 1960s

Hollywood entered the 60s with trepidation. Film audiences around the world had dwindled by millions, and once-profitable theatres were closing by the thousand. Still struggling to win back audiences from television, studios continued to produce a broad range of mainstream genre films. With the persistent conviction that size was the one attribute they could offer that television could not, the studios embarked on the production of a number of spectacular historical epics, where scale was everything. Films such as *Spartacus* (1960), *Exodus* (1960), *El Cid* (1961), *Mutiny on the Bounty* (1963) and *The Greatest Story Ever Told* (1965) hyped their casts of thousands and enormous sets.

The most excessive example was Twentieth Century Fox's production of *Cleopatra* (1963), which reputedly spent $6,500 on a crown of real gold and employed 10,000 extras in period costume. Cleopatra's capital, Alexandria, was rebuilt as an 8-hectare (20-acre) set of huge palaces and temples; the 5-hectare (12-acre) reconstruction of Rome's forum was bigger than the original; and Cleopatra's barge was a full-scale floating vessel built at the cost of $250,000. The finished film cost an unprecedented $44 million (around $300 million in today's money), and its epic failure at the box office almost bankrupted Fox.

However, Fox got rich again with its version of Rodgers and Hammerstein's *The Sound of Music* (1965), which became the most successful film in history and helped to underwrite the continuing policy of lavish adaptation of successful stage musicals, plays and classic stories. Fox also profited from *Fantastic Voyage* (1966), a tremendously entertaining science fiction adventure, which reconstructed

ABOVE: *Fantastic Voyage* (1966) captured the public's imagination with its action set inside the human body.

RIGHT: One of cinema's most popular science fiction series began with *The Planet of the Apes* (1968). The superb ape make-up was created by John Chambers, who later won a special Academy Award for his work.

LEFT: **Rear-projected cars chase secret agent 007 (Sean Connery) in** *Dr No* **(1962), the first of James Bond's big-screen adventures.**

BELOW RIGHT: *2001: A Space Odyssey* **(1968) established a new benchmark in special effects photography. Its meticulously rendered space scenes remain an inspiration to this day.**

the organs of the human body as enormous sets in which wire-suspended actors floated around. Other sci-fi successes of the decade included *Planet of the Apes* (1968) – an impressive film, pointing towards the maturity of science fiction cinema. The superbly expressive ape make-up allowed for subtle and believable performances that no 50s creature could have achieved.

Continuing the theme of excess, movies in general became increasingly fast-paced, action-packed and violent. The beginning of the decade saw audiences shocked by the graphic horror of *Psycho* (1960). The 1962 release of the first James Bond film, *Dr No*, delighted large audiences with a new style of flamboyant macho action. Soon the limits of on-screen violence were being extended, as audiences responded positively to faster chases, fiercer fights and bigger explosions in films such as *A Fistful of Dollars* (1964) and *Bonnie and Clyde* (1967). The 'bigger is better' ethos continued with war films such as *The Great Escape* (1963), whose makers crashed real planes instead of models. *The Hellfighters* (1968), an oil-fire drama, capitalized on audiences' love of explosions by setting the entire film against a backdrop of blazing oil rigs. Even comedy had to be of epic proportions – *It's a Mad Mad Mad Mad World* (1963) combined an all-star cast with over three hours of increasingly frenetic slapstick comedy, chases and explosions.

The 60s hunger for the spectacular had little use for the traditional skills of Hollywood's special effects departments. Where biblical cities might once have been rendered by the matte artist or the model-maker, 60s epics had to have reality. Planes crashing into trees were full-scale aircraft flown by living pilots, and real racing cars were fired from pneumatic cannons to create spectacular crashes (*Grand Prix*, 1966). The predominance of such extravagant physical effects (306>) and the increasing reliance on location shooting – diminishing the need for rear projection (82>) or travelling matte effects (57>) – reduced many special effects departments to workshops for producing mundane optical effects and titles.

Hollywood had started to streamline operations in the late 1940s. The severe financial difficulties faced in the 60s, combined with the new policy of distributing more independent films (by the early 60s two-thirds of films distributed by the major studios were independently produced), increased the drive to downsize facilities and reduce overheads. In the climate of the 60s, the effects departments became a costly overhead that studios no longer wanted to bear.

By the end of the decade, only Disney maintained a full-time effects department to service its range of fantasy-based family entertainment films, such as *The Nutty Professor* (1963) and *Mary Poppins* (1964). Elsewhere, a generation of artists left their departments. Some discovered a life outside the studios and set up their own small companies to service independent productions. Many, reaching the end of their working lives, chose to retire for good. The accumulated skills of more than a quarter of a century were discarded in order to save a few dollars, and like silent stars faded by the blare of the talkies, special effects were reduced to bit parts.

But in 1968 a film of unprecedented visual impact, drawing on the most astonishing special effects yet seen, was released to critical bewilderment and impressive box office business. Stanley Kubrick's *2001: A Space Odyssey*, with its balletic space stations soaring to the music of Strauss, challenged everyone's concept of space travel, and made the real moon landing of the following year something of an anticlimax. For Kubrick, realism was the key, and his quest to make the film the most visually arresting portrayal of man in space led to an obsession with the quality of his special effects. The production of *2001* was also responsible for the only major effects technology developments of the decade. Rear projection was not effective enough for Kubrick's vision, and so the relatively untried process of front projection (84>), which offered the potential of much bigger, brighter and clearer background images behind actors, was developed and used for the first time in a feature film. A new process of mechanically repeatable camera control, the forerunner of modern motion control (146>), was also developed for the photography of the film's enormous model spacecraft. Most visually striking of the film's innovations was the now legendary 'Stargate' sequence, produced using an inventive animation method dubbed 'slit scan' (178>).

Audiences had never seen anything like it, and it seemed as if the success of *2001* might make the studios regret the closure of their effects departments.

1960s PROFILE **ROGER CORMAN**

When the studios were at their most vulnerable, one director found a way to make a profit, quickly becoming one of the most prolific and commercially successful film-makers in Hollywood history.

Roger Corman (1926–) entered the industry as a messenger boy at Twentieth Century Fox before finding work as a story analyst and scriptwriter. Frustrated by studio interference during the shooting of his first script, *Highway Dragnet* (1954), Corman decided to form his own company to shoot his next script, *The Monster from the Ocean Floor* (1954).

By the time he directed his own first feature, *Apache Woman* (1955), the Corman formula was in place. His productions were invariably characterized by offbeat plots and quirky characters. They were made at lightning speed (sometimes in under a week) on minuscule budgets, with largely untried performers and young crews.

Although Corman's science fiction films and creature features cried out for lavish special effects, budgets dictated otherwise. Effects were generally limited to the simplest physical or mechanical methods – avoiding the use of costly post-production processes. Occasionally budgets stretched to elaborate monsters, such as the 4.5 m (15 ft) radioactive crustacean that sidled into *The Attack of the Crab Monsters* (1957) to snap up $1,200 of the film's $70,000 budget. More often, budgetary constraints meant that alien invaders would be no more than actors wearing special contact lenses, as in *Not of this Earth* (1957).

The 50s fare of monsters and aliens gave way to slightly more sophisticated horror in the following decade. Corman's Edgar Allan Poe adaptations had time and money 'lavished' on them – they could be in production for as long as three weeks. Despite their almost crippling constraints, however, some have become classics of film horror.

Corman has made over 200 films to date, and has prospered in one of the toughest industries in the world. Despite the sometimes laughable quality of his films, Corman has earned great respect in Hollywood – not only for his ability to produce profitable movies on shoestring budgets, but also for the start he has given to many ambitious youngsters, including Martin Scorsese, Francis Ford Coppola, Peter Bogdanovitch, Joe Dante, Jonathan Demme, Penelope Spheris, Robert De Niro and Jack Nicholson.

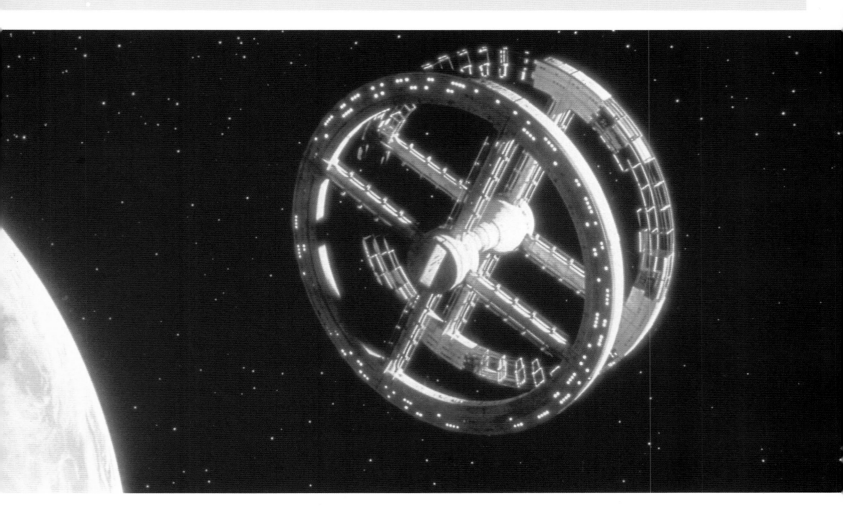

THE 1970s

The success of *2001: A Space Odyssey* (1968) was heaven-sent. At 141 minutes long it had no big stars, an ambiguous narrative, and no one could say for sure whether or not it had a happy ending. In Hollywood, where the popularity of one film normally has studios scrambling to cash in on any perceived trend, *2001* was something of a mystery. Executives didn't quite know what had drawn audiences to the film – although the popular rumour that it was best enjoyed while stoned was suspected of having some influence. Stanley Kubrick's film was a freak success, made by a brilliant, obsessive director, who went over schedule by a year and doubled his original budget.

2001's special effects were undoubtedly stunning, but they were created by a disparate group of talents in a studio in England, halfway across the world from Hollywood. How these skills could be profitably re-employed was unclear. The studios needed to identify a much more predictable, and repeatable, formula before they could take advantage of any 'trend'. Although there were some effects-laden science fiction films in the wake of *2001* – such as *Journey to the Far Side of the Sun* (1969) – it would be a decade before the influence of Kubrick's masterpiece would truly be felt.

After the poor performance of its costly late-60s musicals and historical epics, Hollywood had entered the 70s in its most perilous financial condition ever. Tinseltown had been run by movie people for half a century, but the financial vulnerability of the studios in the late 60s had led to a series of takeovers and mergers. Much of Hollywood now lay in the hands of business conglomerates for whom movie-making was a sideline.

The new Hollywood management rang the changes in film marketing. For decades studios had used a pattern of releasing films gradually. Starting its run in big city theatres and gradually moving out into smaller regional venues, a feature film might have gone on release for over a year. In the early 70s the studios began to use television and the national press as launch pads. Rather than going the rounds, a film now opened in hundreds of theatres simultaneously to capitalize on a nationwide campaign built around a single release date.

While they couldn't define – and therefore exploit – the success of *2001*, the executives interpreted the popularity of *Airport* (1970) as proof that audiences would pay to see disaster on a major scale. The studios embarked on a series of star-stuffed disaster epics, in which people were threatened variously by doomed ocean liners (*The Poseidon Adventure*, 1972), flaming skyscrapers (*The Towering Inferno*, 1974), seismic catastrophes (*Earthquake*, 1974) and even an ill-fated airship (*The Hindenburg*, 1975). These films brought some good opportunities for Hollywood's underemployed special effects artists, and many found temporary work producing and shooting miniatures, matte paintings and pyrotechnics.

Massive national promotion leading to a blanket release made these films early beneficiaries of the new marketing strategies. Although the disaster cycle was largely successful, studios realized that traditional genres with their built-in audience bias (Westerns aimed at the male audience, melodramas for women, science fiction for teenagers and so on) would require adaptation. With the rapidly increasing cost of production and national promotion, it was imperative that films should appeal to broad cross-sections of the modern audience. To help meet this need, the studios turned to a new generation of film-makers.

Later dubbed the 'movie brats', the young directors of the early 1970s were mostly film school graduates with a deep love of classic Hollywood cinema. These directors, including Francis Ford Coppola (1939–), George Lucas (1944–) and Steven Spielberg (1947–), felt indebted to the traditions of Hollywood but were keen to make the type of big-budget, broad-appeal genre films that the new-style studio marketing sought. Beginning with Coppola's hit *The Godfather* (1972), the young directors started to produce movies of unprecedented mass appeal. Lucas's first success, *American Graffiti* (1973), was made on a small budget, but its surprising enormous success was only the starter. The main course was Spielberg's *Jaws* (1975). The young director caused a sensation with the first film to make over $100 million for a studio. The film was the prototype for an important new marketing strategy that would later become known as the 'event movie'.

Jaws used mechanical special effects to produce an occasionally

1970s PROFILE **IRWIN ALLEN**

Irwin Allen (1916–91) entered film production in the early 1950s, after a career that had included stints as a magazine editor, Hollywood columnist, literary agent (clients included P.G. Wodehouse) and radio producer. After producing some modest features such as the comedy *Double Dynamite* (1951), starring Frank Sinatra and Groucho Marx, and several award-winning documentaries including the Academy Award-winning *The Sea Around Us* (1953), Allen made the 1956 documentary *Animal World*, which included 12 minutes of dinosaur footage animated by Ray Harryhausen (188>).

In 1960 *The Lost World* marked the beginning of a long and profitable relationship between Allen and Twentieth Century Fox. The film was a colourful but flimsy interpretation of Sir Arthur Conan Doyle's novel of the same name that forfeited the delights of Harryhausen-style animation in favour of live lizards with stuck-on appendages to portray its dinosaurs. Despite its many failings, the film offered the right mix of action, adventure and romance to make it a major financial success.

Allen then produced several effects-heavy adventure films such as *Voyage to the Bottom of the Sea* (1961), but concentrated on producing fantasy and sci-fi television, including a TV series of *Voyage to the Bottom of the Sea* (1964–8), *Lost in Space* (1966–8) and *Land of the Giants* (1968–70). Ever resourceful, Allen liked to recycle his feature-film footage – especially the dinosaur material from *The Lost World*, which regularly reappeared in his various TV productions.

Perhaps the films for which Allen is most remembered are his disaster epics *The Poseidon Adventure* (1972) and *The Towering Inferno* (1974), and to a lesser extent *The Swarm* (1978) and *The Day the World Ended* (1980), all of which helped to earn him the title 'Master of Disaster'. These movies were object lessons in how stars, large-scale action and impressive special effects, such as models of burning skyscrapers and sinking ships, could be mixed into a box office winner despite the lack of a first-rate script or interesting characters – an irresistibly profitable equation that has guided some producers ever since.

TOP LEFT: **The temperamental mechanical shark built for Steven Spielberg's** *Jaws* **(1975) worked long enough to keep summer audiences sitting in movie theatres and out of the sea. It was the first film to make $100 million at the box office.**

TOP RIGHT: **Spielberg's second big hit,** *Close Encounters of the Third Kind* **(1977), featured some of the most magical and awe-inspiring visual effects photography ever created.**

ABOVE: **Turning tragedy into entertainment,** *The Hindenburg* **(1975) was one of a series of 70s disaster epics that used special effects to replicate scenes of destruction.**

convincing performance from an oversized rubber shark, but the film itself did not advance the art of special effects. Indeed, the difficulties of filming with the temperamental mechanical beasts caused the movie to sail beyond its original schedule and budget, and served as a warning to anyone considering a similar enterprise.

But it was the subsequent offerings of these young directors that would have a significant role to play in the revival of movie special effects.

George Lucas's *Star Wars* (1977) was like no other science fiction film that had gone before. In fact, Lucas played down the film's science fiction heritage with the now legendary opening titles – 'A long time ago in a galaxy far, far away. . .' – which promoted the film as fantasy and legend rather than science and futurism. The film relied heavily on spectacular special effects to portray its unique blend of mythology and science fiction. Lucas had been inspired by the quality of the effects in *2001*, but the graceful waltz of elegant space stations was not his style – nor did he have the time and money that such work would take. With no studio effects department to call on for help, Lucas decided to build his own. He assembled a team of talented young artists and technicians, many of whom had cut their teeth in the world of TV commercials, where creative demands and budgets often allowed more innovation than modern features did.

For space battles, Lucas wanted to re-create the speed and excitement of the airborne dogfights of World War II movies. Existing effects technology did not permit the production of this type of material, which involved filming many fast-moving spaceships and then filming background elements with the same, complicated camera movements, to enable them to be combined seamlessly. As a result, Lucas's team of technicians built a new computer-linked camera control system, to record and repeat the exact movements of a camera – the first of its kind. Many traditional effects were also employed with renewed vigour; optical effects, matte paintings, models, make-up, effects animation and pyrotechnics all helped to produce the vividly alien worlds that Lucas had imagined.

Steven Spielberg's *Close Encounters of the Third Kind* (1977) was equally reliant on breathtaking special effects. Again, this film was not science fiction in the traditional sense, and although clearly influenced by science fiction of the 50s, Spielberg shunned the shock tactics of earlier alien-invasion movies to create a powerful fusion of science, myth and religious iconography. To help him create his vision, Spielberg assembled a team of effects talent, including some of the crew from *2001*. Making extraordinary use of convincing Earthscape models, miniature spacecraft, matte paintings, animation, optical effects, mechanical creature effects and clever camera tricks, Spielberg and his collaborators produced one of the most visually stunning spectacles ever to illuminate the screen.

Star Wars and *Close Encounters* were phenomenal box office successes, earning their creators sizeable fortunes and giving them unparalleled power in Hollywood. The studios hadn't known how to react to *2001*, but they had now seen the light and there seemed no doubt about what audiences wanted to see. Large-scale action films with show-stopping special effects were the order of the day. The closing years of the 70s saw vintage special effects equipment dusted off, effects artists coaxed out of retirement and new talent given its opportunity with the production of extravagant, effects-intensive movies, such as *Superman* (1978), *Star Trek: The Motion Picture* (1979), *The Black Hole* (1979) and *Alien* (1979). While the studios continued to release smaller movies of all types, the emphasis was on finding the next blockbuster, and studio executives developed an almost fanatical faith in the money-spinning properties of spectacular special effects.

THE 1980s

Jaws (1975), *Close Encounters of the Third Kind* (1977), *Star Wars* (1977) and the films that rode on the back of their phenomenal success brought new hope to Hollywood.

The studios were making money again. In executive minds, there was no doubt about the type of films they should be making: the quest was on for the next $100 million blockbuster.

Movie theatre admissions were on the rise. In 1985 the anti-trust legislation of the 40s (<28) was reversed and some of the studios began to invest in theatre chains once more. Smart new multiplex theatres were springing up everywhere, funded by studio cash.

Home video became available in the mid-70s, and within 10 years, half the homes in the United States owned a VCR. The studios initially feared the effect of video on movie-going, but it soon became evident that video 'sell-through' and rentals could provide important additional income. By 1986 the US revenues from video cassette sales matched those from movie theatres. What's more, video actually renewed public interest in the movies and helped to revive film-going culture.

Studios also began to discover the worth of their libraries of vintage films, as increasing demand on video and the rise in cable and satellite broadcasting brought new markets for the movies of yesteryear. In the 30s a film was considered a 'spent' product within two years of its release, but by the mid-80s the post-theatrical life of a movie promised to be long and profitable – especially for a blockbuster.

The production of 'blockbuster-style' films was expensive. Hollywood now planned about 100 major releases annually, compared with 350 in the 40s, but these films had much bigger budgets. The films of the 80s became increasingly glossy, action-packed and violent, youth-oriented and special effects-intensive.

As the decade began, the immediate future for science fiction and fantasy seemed assured. George Lucas had promised at least another two *Star Wars* films, and sequels of *Star Trek* and *Superman* seemed almost perpetual. Enthusiastic audiences for futuristic and fantastic films led to the production of movies such as *Flash Gordon* (1980), *Blade Runner* (1982) and the record-breaking *E.T. the Extra-Terrestrial* (1982).

An affluent and influential youth market also displayed an appetite for comedy. Steven Spielberg's expensive belly-flop *1941* (1979) had been a huge disappointment, and led for a while to less ambitious fare such as *Airplane!* (1980) and *Trading Places* (1983). Though not exactly brain food, they were mouth-wateringly successful. Producers went on to perfect another recipe for profit – comedy, action and spectacle, mixed in a pot of money – in films such as *Ghostbusters* (1984) and *Back to the Future* (1985).

The action genre was pumped up in the 80s with the musclebound, high-density efforts of Stallone and Schwarzenegger. In-your-face heroics and comedy were combined in films like *Lethal Weapon* (1987) and *Die Hard* (1988). Romantic, swashbuckling action resurfaced in the triumphantly popular *Indiana Jones* trilogy (1981, 1984, 1989) and its various imitators.

For their big earners, the studios became increasingly reliant on 'event movies' – high-profile films with major stars that were released at key dates (Christmas, Easter and summer holidays) to a fanfare of publicity. These films were not cheap to produce. In 1972 production costs for the average movie were $2 million. By 1980 the average cost had reached $10 million, and by the end of the decade it would be $23 million. The intense pressure for films to perform led to enormous publicity campaigns that could send costs spiralling. *Alien* (1979) cost $10 million to produce and an estimated $15 million to promote.

The huge cost of films was partly due to the growing demands of big-name stars and directors, whose fees could equal a film's other production expenses. The price of movies was kept down, marginally, through a reliance on independent production. By the 80s the major studios had largely given up making films, preferring instead to commission movies from smaller production companies. In a typical arrangement, Spielberg's Amblin Entertainment – the most successful 'independent' company of the 80s – was provided with a lavish home at Universal Studios in return for offering its productions to Universal first for financing and distribution. This method of production cost the studios less, but it also meant receiving a smaller portion of eventual profits.

The reliance on sophisticated special effects was another factor in the escalating price tag of major movies. Special effects were no longer just a way

LEFT: **Ridley Scott's atmospheric science fiction classic *Blade Runner* (1982) was among the stream of effects-packed movies to emerge in the wake of *Star Wars* (1977).**

RIGHT: **Steven Spielberg's *E.T. the Extra-Terrestrial* (1982) combined cutting-edge visual effects and special effects make-up with a heart-warming story to create box office magic.**

of producing difficult or impossible shots – they were becoming the star of the show, and audiences wanted to see more. *Star Wars* had been the first film to promote itself partly on the quality of its special effects. As the film took off, articles were written and documentaries made about how the special effects were achieved. For the first time, the movie-going public became familiar with the concept of matte paintings and blue screens. Rather than destroying the magic, as the old moguls had predicted, people actually wanted to know about the technology behind what they saw. A knowledge of how special effects were produced appeared to fuel public interest in a film, and helped die-hard fans to get inside their favourite movie.

In the wake of *Star Wars*, independent companies were established to service the increased demand for film and television special effects. George Lucas's own outfit, Industrial Light and Magic (ILM), was temporarily disbanded after *Star Wars*, but reassembled permanently for its sequel, *The Empire Strikes Back* (1980). During the 80s ILM grew into the most successful special effects house in the world, serving the films of Lucas and Spielberg as well as many other landmark productions. The effects business became a well-established, if not especially stable, sector of the film industry. When films went into production, special effects houses would break down scripts to assess their potential effects content and bid for the work on a competitive basis. Of the many small companies established, most were short-lived, though others would prosper and grow into the next decade, forming a core of dominant industry leaders.

The sheer bulk of special effects-dependent movies led to an unparalleled period of research and development. The early blockbusters had made significant use of effects, but for the most part these involved skilful variations on traditional methods. The major breakthrough in effects technology had been the use of simple computers to control the movement of cameras filming models. The real revolution came when the computers began to generate visuals.

In 1982 Disney produced *Tron*, a film based largely within a computer. Several minutes of footage were computer-generated, and Disney used this as a major promotional tool. The failure of *Tron* at the box office might have short-circuited the immediate interest in computer-generated imagery (CGI), but research continued. Several important CGI sequences were created in the following years, such as ILM's 'Genesis sequence' in *Star Trek II: The Wrath of Khan* (1982) and the space battle elements of *The Last Starfighter* (1984). But it wouldn't be until the 90s that the dazzling potential of computers would become fully apparent.

Hollywood had undergone a remarkable revival; 1989 was the most successful year in Hollywood history, with the American public spending $5.03 billion at the box office. The film business was an integral part of the global leisure industry, and hit movies spawned enormous sales of merchandise: computer games, toys, books, clothing and music. Many of the studios – now really clearing banks for celluloid commodities – were owned by multinational conglomerates, including soft drinks manufacturers and Japanese electronics firms. The 80s may not be remembered as a golden age for quality, but it was a time of plenty for the money men, and paid for a remarkable renaissance in the art and technology of special effects.

1980s PROFILE **GEORGE LUCAS AND STEVEN SPIELBERG**

Studying film at the University of Southern California, George Lucas (1944–; *left*) made a 20-minute dystopic vision of the future, which – with the backing of his friend Francis Ford Coppola (1939–) – he later developed into a feature film. *THX 1138* (1971) was a stark, intelligent science fiction film that gained cult status and earned Lucas the mantle of an 'intellectual' film-maker. He next surprised everyone with *American Graffiti* (1973), a semi-autobiographical film crystallizing teenage life on one night in 1962. Made for a pittance, it took a fortune at the box office, becoming one of the most profitable films of the decade. The success of Lucas's next project, *Star Wars* (1977), is legendary, and – together with Spielberg's *Close Encounters of the Third Kind* (1977) – resurrected the big-budget sci-fi/fantasy movie and ushered in the age of special effects on a grand scale.

To furnish the effects for *Star Wars* (1977), Lucas created his own facility, Industrial Light and Magic (ILM) – a company that would become an industry byword for innovation and quality. ILM has since contributed many of the most memorable special effects to modern films, and earned dozens of Academy Awards for its extraordinary work. Lucas himself, with his Lucasfilm organization, has played a key role in the development of digital visual effects and other digital cinema innovations.

Making *Star Wars* (1977) was such an ordeal for Lucas that for the next 20 years he gave up the director's chair for the role of creative producer, becoming the architect of massive commercial success with the *Star Wars* sequels (1980, 1983) and the *Indiana Jones* trilogy (1981, 1984, 1989). Indiana Jones was revived in the popular *Young Indiana Jones Chronicles* TV series (1991), which pioneered the use of digital visual effects in television production.

Despite immense commercial successes, there have been occasional disappointments for Lucas, including *Willow* (1988), *Tucker: The Man and His Dream* (1988) and *Howard the Duck* (1986).

After two decades, Lucas finally returned to the director's chair to bring the long-awaited *Star Wars* prequels to the screen. *Star Wars*: Episode I *The Phantom Menace* (1999), Episode II *Attack of the Clones* (2002) and Episode III *Revenge of the Sith* (2005) received a mixed reception from fans and critics but were smash hits at the box office. The three films were a showcase for the dazzling potential of digital visual effects, using techniques largely pioneered by and promoted by Lucas and his organization.

Unlike Lucas, Steven Spielberg (1946–; *right*) had no formal film training, learning his craft and polishing a natural talent with a series of childhood home movies. His college film *Amblin'* (1969) won critical praise and, more importantly, a contract to direct at Universal. After a number of television assignments, including episodes of *Night Gallery* (1969, 1971) and *Columbo* (1971), the apprentice moved up the ladder to TV movies. The popularity of *Duel* (1971), in which a lone driver is pursued relentlessly by a mysterious, menacing truck, earned Spielberg the opportunity to direct his first theatrical film, *The Sugarland Express* (1974). Though it was not a commercial success, by the time it was released, he was already directing *Jaws* (1975).

The worldwide popularity of *Jaws* (1975), and then *Close Encounters* (1977), was not matched by Spielberg's rip-roaring misfire *1941* (1979), though what the film lacked in dramatic subtlety it compensated for in some exquisite miniature work. However, the first collaboration between Spielberg and Lucas, *Raiders of the Lost Ark* (1981), was a barnstorming success that demonstrated the value of fantasy and dazzling special effects in the creation of earthbound historical adventures.

The 80s were a golden time for Spielberg. In addition to his own directorial projects, he mined an endless seam of popular movies produced by his company Amblin Entertainment. *Gremlins* (1984), *The Goonies* (1985), *Back to the Future* (1985), *Innerspace* (1987) and *Who Framed Roger Rabbit* (1988) were just some of the hits that emerged. All were heavily reliant on ILM's visual treats.

Spielberg continued to helm popular blockbusters throughout the 90s and 2000s and also garnered critical acclaim with a series of more personal movies including *Schindler's List* (1993) and *Saving Private Ryan* (1998). With partners David Geffen and Jeffrey Katzenberg, Spielberg even formed his own studio, DreamWorks SKG, to produce and distribute movies, music and computer games. The live-action part of the business was sold to Paramount in 2006, but DreamWorks Animation, parent to the successful *Shrek* movies (2001, 2004) continues to operate under Spielberg's influence.

More than any others, George Lucas and Steven Spielberg were responsible for the commercial rejuvenation of cinema in the 80s. They made movies that aimed unashamedly to please their audiences and their emphasis on visual spectacle and ground breaking special effects demanded technical achievements that would benefit the entire industry.

THE 1990s

By the centenary of its birth in 1995, the American film industry had developed into an efficient money-making machine and the country's most profitable export. The cost of making movies continued to mushroom, and by the middle of the decade, the average studio film cost $50 million to produce, and the big seasonal blockbusters considerably more. By their very nature, blockbusters must surpass whatever has gone before if they are to attract a large audience; the concepts must be more outrageous and the special effects more stunning. In an attempt to limit the risks involved in investing so much money in a single movie, studios came to rely heavily on sequels in the 90s. In a notoriously volatile business, the sequel's potential for success seemed marginally more predictable.

The 90s also witnessed the resurgence of the feature-length animated movie. After years in the doldrums, Disney followed its smash hit *The Little Mermaid* (1989) with *Beauty and the Beast* (1992), which was an even greater box office success and became the first animated feature to be nominated for a Best Picture Academy Award. Other major studios, including Twentieth Century Fox, Warner Brothers and the newly created DreamWorks SKG, developed their own feature animation programmes, banking on a share of Disney's box office magic.

The profits from animated features can be enormous, even though the majority of tickets sold are for low-priced children's seats. Box office success is just one part of the equation, however, and Disney – more than any other studio – became supremely accomplished at extending the commercial value of its films by licensing its animated characters for use in every imaginable consumer product, from toys and books to clothing, computer games and fast food tie-ins.

In 1996 the launch of the DVD format resulted in the fastest consumer adoption of any new technology in history. Within five years, 40 million US households owned a DVD player and were spending an annual $20 billion buying movies to watch at home – more than twice what was spent at the box office. In addition to the actual film, DVDs offered a host of extra features, spawning a new industry to produce behind-the-scenes footage and 'making-of' documentaries for both new and classic movies. Chapters showing how a film's special effects were created became a particular favourite, helping to reinforce the role of visual effects 'hype' in the marketing of a major movie.

In the realm of visual effects production, the 90s saw a monumental breakthrough in digital imaging. Although generating original imagery with a computer had become faster and easier by this time, such images still had to be manipulated and incorporated into film footage using traditional optical techniques. However, the development of fast and reliable scanning and recording technology (92>) at the beginning of the decade allowed film images to be converted to the digital medium, manipulated within a computer and recorded back onto film for exhibition. The ability to get film in and out of the digital realm with no loss of quality opened the floodgates for Hollywood's digital revolution.

1990s PROFILE **JAMES CAMERON**

James Cameron (1954–) began his film career working for Roger Corman (<33) as art director, miniature set builder and rear-screen photography supervisor for *Battle Beyond the Stars* (1980).

Cameron made his directorial debut in 1981 with *Piranha II: The Flying Killers*, which he co-wrote. The film barely betrayed the talent of its director, but did signal Cameron's interest in science fiction and special effects, which resulted three years later in *The Terminator* (1984), an exciting and inventive sci-fi thriller that was the first of several collaborations with action star Arnold Schwarzenegger.

Aliens (1986) saw Cameron using striking visuals and Oscar-winning special effects to create a landmark in science fiction action films. *The Abyss* (1989) was a critical and commercial disappointment, but featured some ground-breaking computer-generated effects that helped to assure the future of digital imagery in film-making and won Industrial Light and Magic an Oscar for its work on the film.

Terminator 2: Judgment Day (1991) relied on the computer-generated wonders of ILM to provide one of its key characters – a shape-shifting android that could assume any form or texture that it wished. The stories that Cameron wanted to tell had become so reliant on cutting-edge special effects technology that after making *T2* he became a partner in a new visual effects facility, Digital Domain.

True Lies (1994) saw the director's first foray into real-world action adventure, and the use of digital effects to create naturalistic environments and events – perhaps a rehearsal for his epic *Titanic* (1997), which became the first film to pass the $1 billion figure at the box office. With *Titanic*, Cameron showed that digital effects could be equally effective at conjuring historical eras as they were at creating futuristic ones.

Perhaps more than any other film-maker of the 1990s, James Cameron had the imagination and ambition to harness the potential of both traditional and cutting-edge special effects techniques. He has since pioneered the use of 3-D video technology to produce several IMAX documentary films and is planning to make his future feature films in stereoscopic video.

ABOVE LEFT: **Audiences were amazed by ILM's incredible computer-generated character effects in James Cameron's *Terminator 2: Judgment Day* (1991), a landmark in digital visual effects production.**

BELOW LEFT: **The massively popular *Jurassic Park* (1993) awed audiences with its magnificently realistic computer-generated dinosaurs. More than a decade later, its pioneering creature effects still hold up well.**

James Cameron's *Terminator 2: Judgment Day* (1991) offered stunning, digitally created characters that performed feats impossible to achieve in the physical world. Audiences were amazed. Steven Spielberg's *Jurassic Park* (1993), which used computers to produce amazingly lifelike images of extinct dinosaurs, took digital imaging to a new level of sophistication and became the highest-grossing film in history at that time.

The special effects industry was taken by storm. *Jurassic Park* confirmed that digital effects were the way of the future. Almost overnight, machinery and skills that had been in use for over half a century became outmoded. Special effects facilities scrambled to recruit people who had never touched a frame of film in their life, but who could operate computers and write code. Producers were impressed by the new technology, and scripts whose impossible scenarios had made their productions unfeasible in the past were dusted off and put into production.

Toy Story (1995) became the first entirely computer-generated feature film. Its stunning images, appealing characters and compelling storyline ensured that it was a huge hit. Several wholly computer-generated films followed, including Disney/Pixar's *A Bug's Life* (1998) and DreamWorks' *Antz* (1998).

As the decade progressed, digital technology, once the preserve of big-budget movies, quickly became affordable and available to even the most modest productions. Crowds could be replicated, removing the need for hundreds of extras in expensive costumes. Physical effects were made practical and safe because safety wires used to protect actors during filming could easily be digitally removed. Futuristic or historical locations could be conjured up with the minimal use of sets and locations. Directors could make grass greener and skies bluer at the touch of a button. The most glaring on-set errors could be corrected during post-production, to the extent that effects artists commonly complained that careless filming methods were causing unnecessary digital work at a later stage of production.

At the end of the century, George Lucas released *Star Wars*: Episode I *The Phantom Menace* (1999), the long-awaited addition to the *Star Wars* saga, which had sparked a big bang in special effects 20 years before. Taking advantage of the progress in digital effects technologies that had developed largely as a result of his own earlier successes, Lucas produced a landmark movie in which otherworldly locations and fully interactive characters were created almost entirely within the computer. Lucas even experimented with digital video as a means of capturing images, challenging the supremacy of film as the movie-making medium for the first time since its invention.

For the first time in the 100-year history of the cinema, film-makers were able to put literally anything that they could imagine onto the screen. It remained to be seen whether such power would truly benefit the art of cinematic storytelling.

Westchester Public Library
Chesterton, IN

THE 2000s

Hollywood entered the new century in a position reminiscent of that enjoyed by film-making pioneers exactly 100 years earlier. The extraordinary technological advances made in previous years meant that they had at their disposal powerful new image-making technologies that had been almost inconceivable just a few years earlier. The world waited to discover what wonders would be conjured to delight them.

The start of the decade saw several big-budget, effects-laden successes that spawned sequels and imitators that would dominate our screens for the following five years. Landmarks among these were a trilogy of trilogies in the form of the *Star Wars*, *Matrix* and *Lord of the Rings* films. Each movie pioneered new effects techniques and worked hard to amaze us with increasingly elaborate imagery. A remarkable series of movies that would span the decade also began in 2001 with the first adaptation of J.K. Rowling's *Harry Potter* books. These epic films with superb visual effects have been produced at a rate of one a year and have been phenomenally popular, taking almost $1 billion per film at the box office.

The ability to create any image desired, particularly scenes of mass destruction, prompted a clutch of movies based on the adventures of comic-book superheroes. Spider-Man, the Hulk, the Fantastic Four, Hellboy and the X-Men, among others, made the leap from page to screen with varying degrees of critical and commercial success.

The popularity of *Gladiator* (2000) seemed to show that 'sword and sandal' epics, largely abandoned since the 60s, could again blow the dust off the history books to create cinematic gold. Digital technology was used to conjure vast armies and spectacular historical vistas in films such as *Troy* (2004), *Alexander* (2004) and *Kingdom of Heaven* (2005). But unlike their computer-generated armies, these films performed less than impressively in the battle of the turnstiles.

One reliable source of success remained the computer-generated feature film. Following its early triumphs with the *Toy Story* films (1995, 1999) and *A Bug's Life* (1998), Pixar again showed how solid storytelling, colourful characters and plenty of well-timed comedy could be mixed with breathtaking digital animation to create sure-fire hits with *Monsters, Inc.* (2001), *Finding Nemo* (2003) and *The Incredibles* (2004). Meanwhile, DreamWorks had a monster success with two films starring a lovable green ogre (*Shrek*, 2001 and *Shrek 2*, 2004) and again with a zoo full of pliable animals in *Madagascar* (2005). The almost unbroken record of success for these films has encouraged many other companies to establish their own CGI animation divisions. Twentieth Century Fox, Disney, Sony Pictures Imageworks and Lucasfilm, among others, have invested heavily in the format.

Budgets in the first half of the decade continued to rocket. Due largely to their reliance on extravagant visual effects and big-name stars, the so-called 'tent-pole' movies, genetically engineered to prop up cinema-going in the important holiday seasons, cost an average of $120 million. The biggest productions could make the studios dig even deeper into their pockets; *Terminator 3: Rise of*

ABOVE: **Increasingly sophisticated digital effects made it possible to successfully simulate natural phenomena including rain, snow and storms in movies such as** *The Day After Tomorrow* **(2004).**

RIGHT: **Digital technology allowed film-makers to paint on the largest possible canvasses.** *Gladiator* **(2000) was the first of a series of historical dramas that re-created the past on a scale that the makers of 60s epics could only dream of.**

BELOW: **By the beginning of the new century, digital effects had made anything possible in the movies, including the aerial antics of superheroes such as Spider-Man. Smash-hit sequel** *Spider-Man 2* **(2004) featured exhilarating scenes of computer-generated characters fighting in digital city environments.**

2000s PROFILE **ROBERT ZEMECKIS**

Chicago-born Robert Zemeckis (1952–) was a keen film-maker when still at high school. While studying film at USC his student movie *A Field of Honor* brought him to the attention of Steven Spielberg (<39). Spielberg helped Zemeckis and his writing partner Bob Gale get a studio deal for one of their screenplays, a project which later became Spielberg's World War II comedy *1941* (1979).

Zemeckis made his feature-directing debut in 1978 with *I Wanna Hold Your Hand*, followed by *Used Cars* (1980), both written with Gale and made in association with Spielberg. Zemeckis hit the big time with his next film, *Romancing the Stone* (1984), a large-scale action-adventure starring Michael Douglas and Kathleen Turner.

After trying to sell their next idea to a number of unimpressed executives, Zemeckis and Gale found themselves working with Spielberg again to produce their ingenious sci-fi action-comedy *Back to the Future* (1985). The film was a massive hit, spawning two elaborate sequels and allowing Zemeckis to employ increasingly sophisticated visual effects to tell his stories.

Back to the Future saw Zemeckis's first collaboration with visual effects supervisor Ken Ralston (299>), who would become a vital contributor to all his future films.

Who Framed Roger Rabbit (1988) was a technically ambitious combination of live action and cartoon animation that dazzled audiences worldwide. *Death Becomes Her* (1992) saw Zemeckis relying again on cutting-edge effects to tell his story. This time the fledgling technology of digital image manipulation was used to conjure the film's comically gruesome events. Zemeckis next made *Forrest Gump* (1994), a box office smash that starred Tom Hanks and some technically astonishing, often subtle effects work. Zemeckis won an Oscar for his direction.

With films such as *Contact* (1997), *What Lies Beneath* (2000), *Castaway* (2001) and *The Polar Express* (2004), Zemeckis has continued to create strong, story-driven entertainment that uses pioneering visual effects both to dazzle the audience and underpin the narrative. He is indisputably one of the great special effects directors.

the Machines (2003) smashed its way through a budget of $170 million and *Superman Returns* (2006) swooped in with an estimated bill of $250 million. The cost of hyping these films to the point where the movie-going public feels obliged to see them can add as much as half again to the overall bill.

The time taken to get movies off the storyboard and onto the screen began to diminish during this period. While projects might still spend several years languishing in development, once a film has been green-lit and vast sums are committed, it is expected to start earning its keep as soon as possible. Steven Spielberg, never one to linger over the making of his films, produced *War of the Worlds* (2005) in a dizzying 10 months from the first day of pre-production to delivery of the final cut.

The desire for films to make their money back quickly has been reflected in the shrinking time between a movie's theatrical premiere and its release on DVD and home video. *Star Wars*: Episode III *Revenge of the Sith* (2005), for example, was released in cinemas in mid-May and was on supermarket shelves by early November the same year. Rapid release for home viewing helps to beat piracy and quickly recoups production costs. It also allows films to piggyback their original marketing hype while it remains fresh in people's minds. At a time when box office revenues are faltering, studios now make most of their money from home entertainment. The theatrical run of a film therefore often serves as a marketing exercise to support its future retail release.

The need for movies to be completed quickly has changed the way that visual effects are created for a film. In previous decades the job of providing effects for a movie was typically awarded to a single vendor – with possibly one or two others supplying additional specialized services. Today's tight schedules mean that it is only possible for the largest of facilities to create all of the effects for a major film. Visual effects are now tendered out on a shot-by-shot basis to studios known for their expertise in particular areas. *Harry Potter and the Goblet of Fire* (2005), for example, employed no fewer than 10 companies to create its visual effects.

This system has helped create a tiered structure of effects houses. At the top are the biggest studios such as ILM, Digital Domain, Rhythm and Hues, and Sony Pictures Imageworks. These facilities employ hundreds of artists, possess vast computing networks, and have the resources to research and develop new technology. Such companies tend to be awarded the most difficult and expensive effects shots, often involving character animation or complex environmental scenes. Next are the medium-sized companies, typically employing 50–100 artists. These may do some original research and development but mostly use off-the-shelf technology to help them provide sophisticated work for major films or perhaps provide all of the shots for smaller productions. Finally there are the 'boutique'

ABOVE: **Entirely digital films continued to wow audiences of all ages.** *Shrek 2* **(2004) combined entertaining stories and loveable characters with new animation techniques to create one of the most popular CGI films to date.**

2000s PROFILE **PETER JACKSON**

Growing up in New Zealand, Peter Jackson (1961–) made miniature war epics and James Bond spoofs with his parents' 8 mm camera. With what would become trademark resourcefulness, the budding auteur built his own equipment, made models, animated puppets and created gory make-up effects.

Jackson spent four years of weekends creating his first feature *Bad Taste* (1987), which was critically acclaimed and became a cult hit among horror fans.

Meet the Feebles (1989) was a gory, vile, and often hilarious puppet movie that strengthened Jackson's reputation and resulted in offers from Hollywood. But Jackson was determined to make films his own way and in his own country. Though shockingly violent and grisly, *Braindead* (1991) was well crafted on many levels, using superb miniature effects to recreate 1950s Wellington. *Heavenly Creatures* (1994) was the true story of two teenagers whose obsessive relationship drove them to murder. Slick and compelling, it was Jackson's most mainstream movie to date. The film's special effects requirements led Jackson to establish Weta, his own effects facility.

When Jackson and partner Fran Walsh were approached by Robert Zemeckis (<43) to write an

episode for his *Tales from the Crypt* TV show, Zemeckis liked the resulting script so much that he asked Jackson to direct a feature-length version. *The Frighteners* (1995) was disappointing commercially but did showcase Jackson's growing mastery of visual effects and complex action.

The world was astonished by the size, scope and visual splendour of Jackson's next offering. With *The Lord of the Rings: The Fellowship of the Ring* (2001) Jackson achieved what many had thought impossible: a version of Tolkien's classic that satisfied both fans and a general audience. Spectacular and innovative effects helped make this and its two sequels among the most commercially successful films ever. The films earned Jackson and his collaborators a clutch of Oscars and established Weta as one of the world's leading effects facilities.

In 2005 Jackson released *King Kong*, the fulfilment of a long-term dream to remake his boyhood favourite. Praised by critics, though less commercially successful than predicted, the movie was nevertheless an outstanding effects achievement with superb miniature and digital environments and a breathtakingly emotive central performance from an all-CGI Kong.

ABOVE: **Almost three decades after the original *Star Wars*, George Lucas's *Revenge of the Sith* (2005) displayed digital visual effects of extraordinary sophistication that would have been unimaginable to a previous generation. This battle scene was made massively complicated by setting it just above the surface of a planet, so that atmospheric effects such as smoke, fire and water were required to obey the laws of gravity.**

companies. These tend to employ perhaps only a dozen artists using a few modest computer workstations. These companies might be hired to produce one or two stand-alone shots for a big feature film – perhaps a digital matte painting, for example. They may also do the more mundane and less visible effects work such as relatively simple wire-removal shots.

The astonishing developments in digital visual effects technology mean that top-quality work can now be produced by any talented person with the money to buy the necessary off-the-shelf software and hardware. For less than $10,000 a 'desktop studio' can be used to create imagery that the biggest companies would have struggled to deliver less than a decade ago. It is now possible to rent an office, lease workstations, recruit artists and be ready to create feature-film effects within a few months. Some companies have even been established solely to provide the effects for a single film, such as World of Tomorrow, which was set up to produce over 1,000 shots for the modestly budgeted *Sky Captain and the World of Tomorrow* (2004). However, the biggest studio productions can still spend huge sums on effects, particularly if any significant research and development is required. As much as 40 per cent of the $200 million spent on *Spider-Man 2* (2004) was lavished on its Oscar-winning effects work. Studios consider this investment a worthwhile risk, however. Nineteen of the top 20 box office earners have been effects-reliant productions.

Visual effects remain a significant part of the marketing for any major movie. Effects vendors are typically obliged to finish their most spectacular shots early enough for them to be used in advance trailers and, increasingly, internet sneak previews. They will also find themselves demonstrating their techniques as part of the movie's DVD bonus features.

It is now no longer a case of whether any visual effect is possible but of how quickly and economically it can be done. Today much effort is put into developing systems and production 'pipelines' that allow spectacular work to be achieved more efficiently. Like many other industries, outsourcing to foreign companies is becoming more common. Countries such as Korea and India have rapidly developing visual effects sectors and are likely to become major competitors to the traditional vendors in the US and Europe.

Whether or not digital technology has enhanced the *art* of film-making is open to question. But there can be no doubt that, with access to such powerful tools, directors now have the means, more quickly and perhaps economically than ever before, to produce the film that they have conceived in their mind's eye. Given a computer and some powerful software, it can only be imagined what wonders Georges Méliès might have produced.

ACADEMY AWARDS

On one night every year, over a billion people around the world tune in to watch the Oscars, the most glamorous and anticipated event in the Hollywood calendar.

For weeks beforehand, the world's media will speculate about which performer, director or movie deserves to walk away with the treasured trophy. Less often discussed in this flurry of excitement, however, are the more technical nominations such as cinematography, sound editing and visual effects. Yet the list of past winners in these categories provides a fascinating insight into the development of film-making skills and technology through the decades.

The Academy of Motion Picture Arts and Sciences (AMPAS) was established in 1927 and held the first of its award ceremonies on 16 May 1929 at the Hollywood Roosevelt Hotel. Guests paid $5 per ticket to attend a banquet followed by a ten-minute inaugural awards ceremony. However, that first ceremony had little of the drama and suspense that we associate with today's Academy Awards. With the results made public several weeks earlier, the evening was simply a formal occasion to present trophies to the winners. Their prize, the iconic golden statuette later nicknamed 'Oscar', was designed by MGM art director Cedric Gibbons, who would eventually win 11 of the awards during his career.

The first awards contained just 12 categories, compared with today's 25. Given the limited number of prizes in that first year, it is perhaps surprising to find the inclusion of an award for 'Engineering Effects'. The winner was the Academy founding member Roy J. Pomeroy (1892–1947), who had created a range of fires, crashes and explosions for the World War I flying epic *Wings* (1927).

However, it wasn't until the 11th ceremony in 1938 that the Academy again recognized the importance of special effects by giving a 'special award' to *Spawn of the North* (1937). This was for 'Outstanding Achievement in Creating Special Photographic and Sound Effects'. From then on an 'Achievement in Special Effects' category was included in each year's nominations, covering both photographic and sound effects with one award. In 1964 photographic and sound effects were separated into two distinct categories.

In addition to the regular competitive categories, the Academy also bestows occasional discretionary awards for particularly outstanding achievements. These have included an Academy Honorary Award to Walt Disney in 1938 for *Snow White and the Seven Dwarfs* (1937), which was considered a 'significant screen innovation'. Charmingly, the animator was presented with one normal-sized Oscar and seven small ones.

The Academy also honours several classes of Scientific and Technical Awards to those who have created and developed innovative new film-making technology. These are chosen by a technical committee and awardees have included Dennis Muren (see panel) and Stuart Ziff for their creation of the Go-Motion animation system for *Dragonslayer* (1981), for example.

In 1995 AMPAS created a Visual Effects branch to select the films to be nominated for each year's Visual Effects Oscar. The chairman of the branch since its formation has been Richard Edlund, himself the recipient of multiple Academy Awards (79>).

'The Visual Effects branch is currently comprised of about 250 distinguished effects professionals who represent the many various disciplines of our craft,' states Edlund. 'Prospective branch members, except in exceptional circumstances, must have worked in a key creative position for at least eight years before being eligible to become members of the Academy.'

Edlund explains the process of selecting the films that are nominated for each year's Visual Effects Oscar: 'Every year a Steering Committee of forty members will be charged with the selection of seven movies which contain the most outstanding visual effects.' The selection process proceeds as follows. 'We begin by reading off the titles of the movies that have qualified for Academy consideration – usually about 250 films. We then select those which are considered to have significant special effects work in them, usually resulting in a list of perhaps forty movies. We then discuss these in more detail, our objective being to narrow the field down to a short list of less than twenty contenders. We then vote,' continues Edlund. 'Each Committee member is asked to complete a ballot on which they list what they consider the ten best visual effects efforts in order of merit. The accountants of Price Waterhouse Coopers then tabulate those votes and the seven top films are officially announced the next day.'

Letters are then mailed to the producers of the seven productions, inviting them to formally submit their movie for consideration in the form of written material and a demonstration reel of visual effects, not to exceed 15 minutes.

'These producers are asked to select up to four individuals who most contributed to the visual effects on each film,' Edlund continues. 'These are

PROFILE **DENNIS MUREN**

Fascinated with the creation of moving images from an early age, Dennis Muren (1946–) began making films with an 8 mm cine camera at the age of 10. Before long Muren was experimenting with techniques such as stop-motion and rear projection.

Muren studied business at California State University but invested his spare time in the production of an ambitious science fiction film, *The Equinox*. The picture was later bought by a distributor who replaced almost everything except the impressive effects before releasing it in 1970.

Realizing that special effects were his talent, Muren spent several years shooting TV commercials before finding work at Industrial Light and Magic as second cameraman on *Star Wars* (1977), specializing in stop-motion and miniature photography. After working with Douglas Trumbull (1942–) to film the mothership sequences for *Close Encounters of the Third Kind* (1977) and a stint on TV's *Battlestar Galactica*, Muren returned to ILM as director of effects photography for *The Empire Strikes Back* (1980).

Muren is currently senior visual effects supervisor at ILM, having overseen the creation of groundbreaking work for many important special effects films. In 1989 he took a one-year sabbatical to learn about computers and digital technology. Since then he has supervised some of the most important digital visual effects films including *The Phantom Menace* (1999), *Hulk* (2003) and *War of the Worlds* (2005).

Muren has won more Oscars than any other living individual, with Awards for his work on *The Empire Strikes Back* (1980), *E.T. the Extra-Terrestrial* (1982), *Return of the Jedi* (1983), *Indiana Jones and the Temple of Doom* (1984), *Innerspace* (1987), *The Abyss* (1989), *Terminator 2: Judgment Day* (1991) and *Jurassic Park* (1993). He was also awarded a technical Oscar for his contribution to the development of Go-Motion for *Dragonslayer* (1981). In 1999 he became the first effects artist to be honoured with a star on Hollywood's Walk of Fame.

ABOVE LEFT: **William A. Wellman's *Wings* (1927) was the first film to win an Oscar for its special effects. At the first-ever Academy Awards ceremony, the film was presented with a statue for the 'Engineering Effects' used to re-create the aerial battles of World War I.**

BELOW: **At the 78th Academy Awards ceremony in March 2006, Joe Letteri, Brian Van't Hul, Christian Rivers and Richard Taylor proudly display their Oscars, received for Achievement in Visual Effects for *King Kong* (2005).**

the people who will actually receive an Oscar should their film win. This in itself is always a tough decision since in the digital age hundreds of people will often contribute to the effects in a film.'

'Finally, we have what we call the "bakeoff", the night when the entire branch comes together to view the reels and to then nominate the three films that will be in competition on Oscar night.'

The bakeoff takes place in the Academy's Samuel Goldwyn Theatre in Beverly Hills. The 250 members of the Visual Effects branch and their guests gather to view submissions from the teams behind the seven selected movies. A line forms early for those anxious to get a good seat as this widely anticipated event is also open to all members of the visual effects community – on a first come, first served basis.

The programme begins with the first visual effects supervisor, who gives a five-minute presentation followed by up to fifteen minutes of clips from the finished film. Finally, the team of four come onstage and are allowed up to three minutes to answer any questions. 'Twenty-three minutes doesn't seem like much time to persuade people that you deserve a nomination,' admits Edlund. 'But we do have to pack seven presentations into one meeting. It's a great evening all round, and a rare chance for so many people from the effects industry to meet and catch up.'

Asked about what makes the effects in one film more deserving than those in another, Edlund can only speculate: 'We don't have any written criteria by which we must judge the effects in each film – I don't know if that would ever be possible. How could you compare a sea battle from *Master and Commander* with the animation of Gollum, for example? These are two completely different challenges that have been successfully met in very different ways.'

At the end of the bakeoff, the members of the Visual Effects branch will vote to determine which three films will be nominated for the year's Academy Award: the three finalists will then be listed on the final ballots which will be cast by the 6,000 Academy members who vote in each of the major categories.

On Oscar night a small band of special effects professionals will attend one of the most spectacular ceremonies to be held anywhere in the world. Technicians and artists who rarely get away from their cameras or computers find themselves sharing the red carpet with some of the most famous names on the planet.

It is recognized that an Oscar win can transform the career of an actor and massively improve a film's box office performance. But what does winning an Academy Award for Visual Effects mean for those involved? 'I'm not sure if winning an Oscar for Visual Effects would make a great deal of difference at the box office,' muses Edlund, 'though just printing how many Academy Awards a film has won on the posters helps enormously. But winning an Oscar for Visual Effects can really help to establish an artist's name and boost their career. In the end, to receive a nomination or an Oscar is the ultimate reward, because you know that your own peers – those who are in the trenches with you and who really understand what you have achieved – have judged you. That's what makes that golden statue such a treasured goal in our industry.'

See appendix for a full list of Visual Effects Academy Award winners.

2

OPTICAL EFFECTS

OPTICAL ILLUSIONS

Moving pictures had barely been invented when enterprising film-makers began to experiment with the unique properties of motion picture photography to conjure up new and sometimes fantastic images. At the heart of most cinematic experiments was the selective combination, on a single piece of film, of several images filmed at different times and places. The earliest method of combining images in this way was the simple double exposure, in which one part of the image was filmed in one take and the rest captured in a second.

Film-makers had various reasons for wishing to transform reality. The motivation was partly practical – an image of actors filmed in the studio combined with one of the pyramids alleviated the need for a time-consuming trip to Egypt. Cost factors also played their part; if models or even paintings could be filmed and combined with live action then the cost of building large and expensive sets could be avoided. And there were artistic reasons, too – the illusion of fantastic and otherwise impossible events could be achieved through the manipulation of several realistic elements.

Early methods of image combination were crude, but, as the century progressed, film-makers began to develop more sophisticated techniques that took advantage of the optical and photochemical principles of film itself. The potential of light, lenses, filters and film was harnessed to enable new forms of photographic alchemy. This chapter explores the basic principles of motion picture photography before examining in depth the image-manipulation processes that have been used over the last hundred years, from the crudest early optical tricks to today's breathtaking digital technologies.

PRECEDING PAGES: **A triple-head rear projector in use at London's Pinewood Studios.**

ABOVE: **The Panavision Millennium, one of the most sophisticated 35 mm movie cameras in the world.**

THE CAMERA – LENS – FILM

THE CAMERA

Despite its complex engineering and precision mechanisms, the movie camera is, in principle, a relatively simple device. The camera holds a detachable magazine (fig. 1 (a)) that contains two lightproof chambers. During photography, unexposed film leaves the first chamber, travels through the camera for exposure and is fed into the second chamber, where it is stored until being removed for processing.

Film travels through the camera at a continuous rate – in the case of normal sound photography, at 24 frames per second. As the film approaches the gate where it will be exposed to light (b), a claw mechanism (c) engages the film's sprocket holes. The claws hold each frame motionless in the gate for exposure before pulling the next frame into place.

Film is exposed to light that has been gathered and focused by a lens (d), which is attached to the front of the camera. An adjustable diaphragm, or aperture (e), can be opened or closed to admit varying amounts of light through to the gate. The camera's shutter (f) is a continually revolving disc with gaps in it that can be made larger or smaller. The width of the gaps determines the length of time that the film is exposed to light coming through the aperture. While the film is held in the gate, the revolving shutter opens to let light onto the film. As the shutter closes, the film is moved on. While the next unexposed frame is being moved into the gate, the closed shutter's mirrored surface reflects light into the camera's viewfinder (g), enabling the camera operator to see the image being photographed. Images sent to the viewfinder can also be diverted to a video camera, allowing scenes to be recorded on tape. This allows directors to view a scene on a monitor during filming or to immediately review it without waiting for the film to be developed, a process known as 'video-assist'.

All movie cameras employ mechanical methods to ensure that each frame of film is correctly positioned, or 'registered', in the gate during exposure. Without such a device, images exposed on the film would move slightly from frame to frame, causing 'image weave' when projected onto a screen. While a small degree of image weave is acceptable when watching a film, it cannot be tolerated in any shot that is to become part of a visual effects sequence. Visual effects procedures require the precise placing of images on film so that multiple elements can be combined effectively to achieve the desired result. To register film in the gate, cameras used in visual effects production feature a system of 'pilot pins' that slot into the sprocket holes of each frame of film and hold the film absolutely steady during exposure. Cameras with this feature are known as process cameras.

Once developed, film is displayed on a screen using a projector – essentially a camera in reverse. Rather than outside light entering the device through the lens, light is generated within the machine and channelled out through the lens. The light first passes through the film, where it picks up an image, and is then focused by the lens on a distant screen. Like cameras, projectors also have a rotating shutter. Although pictures recorded at 24 frames per second are sufficient to establish the illusion of smooth movement, they have a noticeable 'flickering' effect when projected. It is a feature of human vision that the faster the flickers occur, the less we perceive them. To present apparently flicker-free pictures, the shutter closes momentarily during the projection of each frame of film, so we actually see each frame twice and are presented with 48 images a second.

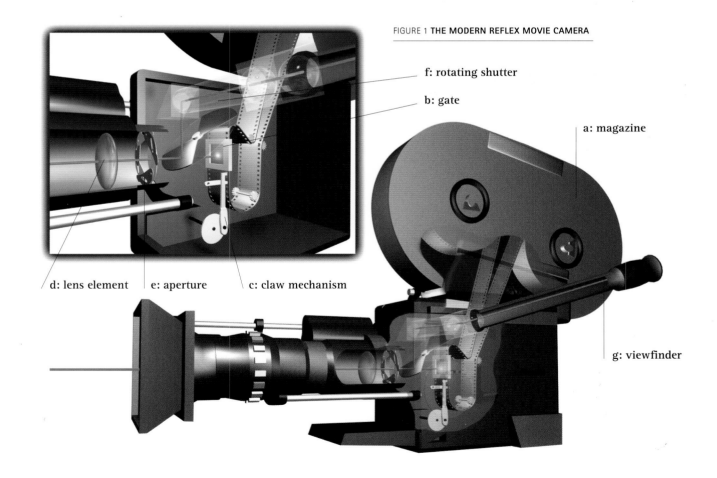

FIGURE 1 **THE MODERN REFLEX MOVIE CAMERA**

f: rotating shutter

b: gate

a: magazine

d: lens element   e: aperture   c: claw mechanism

g: viewfinder

THE LENS

The most important component of any camera is its lens. The purpose of the lens is to collect all the light waves emanating from a single point on the subject matter and to make them converge at a single point on the film. Different-coloured light waves do not focus at the same point if channelled through a single lens element, however, so several lens elements with different properties are combined to ensure that the image is focused correctly on the film. These glass elements are arranged in a lens barrel, which, when turned, moves the elements towards or away from the film, allowing the image to be focused correctly. The lens barrel also contains an adjustable diaphragm, or aperture, that can be opened and closed to control the amount of light reaching the film. Lenses are generally classified according to their focal length – that is, the distance between the optical centre of the lens, where all incoming light converges, and the film plane (fig. 2). A wide-angle lens (a) with a focal length of 28 mm has its optical centre very near to the film plane and is able to photograph objects from a very wide area around the camera, making it ideal for photography in confined spaces. A long, or telephoto, lens (b) with a focal length of 125 mm, for example, has its optical centre further from the film plane. It has a narrow field of view and will make objects that are in fact a great distance away from the camera appear much closer, making the telephoto lens suitable for filming distant wildlife, for example. In 35 mm photography, a lens with a focal length of 50 mm is considered 'normal', since the field of view in pictures filmed with such a lens most approximates what can be seen by the human eye.

Focal length also affects the ability of a lens to keep subjects in focus. With a wide-angle lens, objects both close to and far from the camera remain in focus. With a long lens, only objects a small distance apart from each other will remain in focus. The distance within which objects remain sharply in focus is known as depth of field, a phenomenon that is also influenced by the amount of light in a scene, the aperture of the diaphragm and the sensitivity of the film being used (115>).

The focal length of a lens also affects the depth perception of a shot. Where two objects are placed at varying distances from the camera, for instance, a wide-angle lens will exaggerate the space between them, while a long lens will make them appear to be closer to one another.

Though most lenses used in motion picture photography are of a fixed focal length (known as 'prime' lenses), zoom lenses can also be used. The zoom lens has a variable focal length that can be altered during photography to make subjects that are a fixed distance from the camera appear to move nearer or further away. The distance between subject and camera does not have to change during a zoom, so it is not necessary to refocus the lens during the movement, which would be the case were camera and subject to change their relative positions.

The Trombone Shot

Alfred Hitchcock (<27) made startling use of the optical principles of lenses during the making of his psychological thriller *Vertigo* (1958). The director wanted to create a visual impression of the feeling of vertigo experienced by a character while looking down the stairwell of a high bell tower.

The shot was designed and photographed by second-unit cameraman Irmin Roberts. Knowing that depth perception changes with the focal length of a lens, Roberts set up a track with a camera and zoom lens at one end, and a large model stairwell laid on its side at the other end. Looking towards the distant stairwell, the camera's lens was zoomed in so that the model appeared close, filling the whole frame. During filming, the camera was moved rapidly along the track towards the model while the lens was simultaneously zoomed out. Although the camera got nearer to the model, zooming out meant that the stairwell appeared to stay exactly the same size (fig. 3).

The resulting footage showed a stairwell that remained the same size in the frame whilst the drop from the top to bottom of the stairs appeared to

FIGURE 2 **LENS ANGLES**

a: wide-angle lens   b: 'long' or telephoto lens

FIGURE 3 **THE TROMBONE SHOT**

Altering the focal length of the lens while the camera moves towards an object results in the object remaining the same relative size in the frame while its background appears to change.

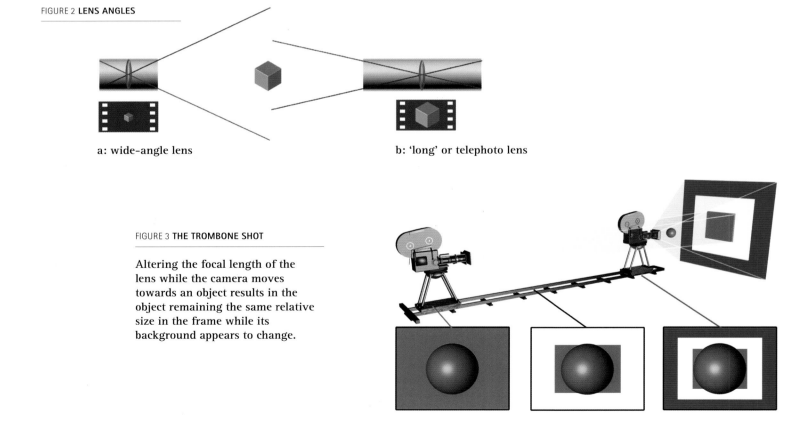

RIGHT: **James Stewart confronts his fear of heights in this scene from** *Vertigo* **(1958). Hitchcock used an innovative filming technique to indicate how Stewart's character felt when suffering from vertigo.**

increase considerably – the floor pulling away from the viewer as if to exaggerate the distance. The shot is astonishingly effective in simulating the fear felt by a vertigo sufferer. The technique, subsequently dubbed the trombone shot, Hitchcock zoom, contra-zoom or Vertigo effect, has since been used to create a sense of unease in a number of other films, notably *Jaws* (1975), *Goodfellas* (1990), and *The Fellowship of the Ring* (2001), as well as in many horror films, TV shows and commercials.

THE FILM

Film is the medium traditionally used to capture, store, manipulate and deliver motion picture images. It is a flexible strip of transparent cellulose acetate that is coated with a light-sensitive emulsion in which tiny crystals of silver halide are suspended in gelatin. Black-and-white film consists of one layer of light-sensitive emulsion; colour film consists of three layers, each one sensitive to a different colour – red, green or blue. When exposed to light, the silver halide crystals undergo a chemical change which makes them turn dark when the film is later processed in a laboratory. Crystals not affected by light are washed away during processing to leave clear areas on the film. The result is a 'negative' image of the original scene.

In the case of black-and-white film, the negative is purely tonal – that is, a mixture of dark and clear areas, with light from a bright area of the subject affecting more silver halide crystals than light from a dark area. Colour negatives, on the other hand, record both tone and colour – red light affects the silver halide crystals in the red-sensitive layer of the film, green light affects the green-sensitive layer and blue light the blue-sensitive layer. During processing, a coloured dye forms where the silver halide crystals have been affected in each layer of the film, and the crystals are then bleached away. The dyes that form in each layer of the negative are in that layer's 'complementary' colour (56>) – that is, cyan dye forms in the red-sensitive layer, magenta dye in the green-sensitive layer and yellow dye in the blue-sensitive layer. When negatives are copied onto film or paper to produce a 'positive' image, the dark areas on a black-and-white negative become light again, and light areas dark, and the dyes in the colour negative are reversed to their original colours.

The speed of film – that is, how much light it needs to record an image – is determined by the size of the silver halide crystals held in the emulsion. Slow films have small silver crystals, needing a large quantity of light to produce an image. The small crystals, however, produce a high-quality, fine-grained image. Fast films, on the other hand, can produce a picture in low light conditions, but the large silver crystals needed result in a much grainier image.

DUPLICATION AND FORMATS

DUPLICATION

At the heart of all optical special effects was the ability to copy images from one film to another. During the copying process, images could be manipulated in various ways – for example, to extract selected elements from the frame or to prepare them for combination with other images at a later stage. Although optical effects have now been entirely replaced with digital alternatives, film images must still be copied in order to produce the thousands of finished prints that are screened in movie theatres across the world (fig. 4).

Until the widespread adoption of optical printers (70>) in the late 20s, the copying of images from one film to another was done entirely through a process known as 'contact printing' (fig. 5). To transfer an image, two films are sandwiched together, emulsion to emulsion, and light shone through them, thus copying the image from film to film. Continuous contact printing, in which two films are moved without pause through the printer, is still used today to produce 'rushes' (the previous day's footage watched each morning by the director and key crew) and to copy large numbers of prints at low cost for general release.

From the 20s onwards, the copying of images was increasingly carried out using the process known as optical printing, which entailed projecting the image from one film to another through a lens. This allowed changes to be made to the image during copying, for example by using a filter to change colours (72>). Before the introduction of slow-speed, fine-grained duplication stock in the 50s, each subsequent copy of a film brought a noticeable deterioration in picture quality – rather like making a photocopy of a photocopy. Even using today's sophisticated film stocks, copying images from film to film inevitably causes some increase in grain and contrast levels.

FILM FORMATS

The shape and quality of the image we see on a cinema screen is largely affected by two factors: the size of the film on which it is shot and presented, and the aspect ratio at which it is presented (fig. 6).

FIGURE 5 **CONTACT PRINTING**

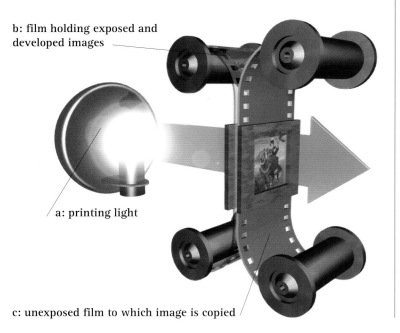

b: film holding exposed and developed images

a: printing light

c: unexposed film to which image is copied

FIGURE 4 **FILM GENERATIONS**

When films are copied from negatives or positives, they are named according to their place in the production chain. Each copy is known as a generation, and each generation can be given a number of names.

1. ORIGINAL CAMERA NEGATIVE. The film that is held in the camera during photography and subsequently developed into a negative. This may now be scanned to produce a digital negative, which will be used in all subsequent post-production work. Also called the master negative.

2. MASTER POSITIVE. First-generation copy of the original negative. Such copies were traditionally used in the production of special effects where a positive image of the highest quality was required – for rear projection, for example. Also called the interpositive.

3. INTERNEGATIVE. Made from copying the master negative onto reversal film to produce another negative, or by copying the master positive onto negative film. Many additional positives can be struck from this film – edited release prints, for example. Also called an interdupe or colour reversal intermediate. Today, a final negative used for creating release prints might be recorded to film after going through an entirely digital post-production process.

4. RELEASE PRINT. Thousands of release prints may be made of a film to be sent to cinemas around the world.

The standard width of film used in professional cinematography and projection is 35 mm. The aspect ratio of a standard 35 mm image is 1.33:1, which means that it is 1.33 units wide for every one unit that it is high. This ratio was standardized by the Academy of Motion Picture Arts and Sciences in 1932 and is known as the 'Academy ratio'. Most feature films were shown in this ratio until the 1950s, when it was also adopted as the standard for television screens.

It was the massive success of television that prompted experimentation with different screen formats for the movie theatre. If television used the ratio 1.33:1, it was reasoned that film theatres might win back audiences by producing images that appeared to be much bigger. This was initially achieved simply by masking off the top and bottom of the 35 mm frame to produce a wider-looking 'letterbox' image. This method is still commonly used today, and (in the UK and the US) films shot in 1.33:1 ratio have a mask applied during projection to produce a widescreen image of 1.85:1 (the standard European widescreen is 1.66:1).

To produce much wider images from 35 mm film, the use of anamorphic lenses became popular in the 1950s. Anamorphic lenses squeeze an image horizontally, so that a very wide image can be fitted onto narrow 35 mm film. When projected, another lens returns the image to its normal proportions. The anamorphic process (meaning 'to form anew' in Greek) was pioneered by Henri Chrétien (1879–1956) for use in tank sights during World War I, but the process was not widely adopted for feature film use until Fox patented the process under the name CinemaScope in 1952. CinemaScope produced an incredibly wide image with a ratio of 2.35:1, and was first used in the filming of *The Robe* (1953). Today, the anamorphic process is often called 'Panavision' – after the company that produces the most widely used anamorphic lenses.

While most studios embraced anamorphic techniques, Paramount adopted a different approach. It developed the VistaVision system, which was first used for *White Christmas* (1954). VistaVision ran 35 mm film horizontally through the camera rather than vertically, like other systems. This produced a negative with the standard 1.33:1 aspect ratio, but one that was more than twice the normal size, resulting in very high-quality images. Few theatres installed the special projectors needed to show VistaVision, however, so most productions filmed in the format were optically reduced to standard 35 mm, but still benefited enormously from the high definition of the original negative.

The 1950s also saw a rise in the use of large-format film techniques, mostly using 65 mm negative film, which was then printed onto 70 mm release prints, allowing an extra 5 mm for the soundtrack. Only large theatres in major cities adopted 70 mm systems, and most 70 mm productions were reduced to 35 mm for screening in conventional theatres. Today, most 70 mm presentations are actually 35 mm films that have been blown up to 70 mm, though occasionally, prestigious films such as Kenneth Branagh's *Hamlet* (1997) are still filmed in 65 mm.

Large film formats are now generally only used for the production of special effects shots, since the several processes that images traditionally go through before completion degrade the image substantially. This was especially so in the case of traditional optical techniques, which required the duplication of an image many times, each copy resulting in a loss of quality. Initial large-format image quality is so high that images for effects sequences can be shot, copied and manipulated several times, and the results copied onto a 35 mm release print without looking any worse than the standard 35 mm photography. Even in the digital age, where images are scanned in and out of a computer with no loss of quality, special effects photography still often uses larger formats where budgets permit, because they allow post-production processes such as cropping or image reframing to be carried out.

VistaVision is a popular format for effects photography. The process had fallen into disuse until it was rediscovered during the production of *Star Wars* (1977) to film large-sized plates for optical effects work. VistaVision has the further advantage that it uses standard 35 mm film stock, so it can be processed and handled in the normal way, unlike 65 mm film, which can only be handled by a few laboratories.

FIGURE 6 **FILM FORMATS**

Academy ratio 1.33:1 (35 mm unmasked)

widescreen ratio 1.85:1 (35 mm unmasked)

anamorphic, 2.35:1, squeezed and unsqueezed

65 mm negative

70 mm print

VistaVision, also known as '8' perf

OPTICAL EFFECTS **55**

THE PRINCIPLES OF COLOUR

A number of optical visual effects processes relied on the selective use of colour for their results. A basic understanding of colour, light and film is therefore helpful in understanding such processes.

Light forms part of a wide range of energies that together make up the electromagnetic spectrum. This spectrum includes gamma rays, X-rays, ultraviolet radiation, infrared radiation, radio waves, microwaves and visible light. Light forms only a tiny portion of the spectrum's wavelengths and is the only radiation energy visible to the human eye.

Natural white light is a mixture of these visible wavelengths. When a beam of white light is shone through a prism, the various wavelengths that combine to make white light are bent, or refracted, by varying amounts. The separated wavelengths emerge from the prism and can be seen as an array of colours if a white card is placed in their path. The colours always appear in the same order: violet, blue, green, yellow, orange and red. A similar process occurs when sunlight passes through mist and forms a rainbow. Photographically, there are two ways to create all the colours that are visible to the human eye. One method, known as the additive process, involves mixing a number of coloured lights together to produce other colours, including white. The other, the subtractive process, entails removing various colours from white light to produce other colours (fig. 7).

In the additive process, the primary colours from which all others are produced are red, green and blue. Each of these consists of about a third of all the wavelengths in the visible spectrum. Recombining all three will create white light. They can also be combined in various quantities to create other colours. Early colour film techniques used the additive process to produce colour pictures. Two separate copies of the same image were filmed using black-and-white film, one through a red filter, the other through a green filter. A red filter (simply a piece of red-coloured glass) only lets red light through to the film and absorbs all other colours, while a green filter only transmits green light. The result was two almost identical black-and-white images, one of which contained a black-and-white record of the red content of the scene, the other a record of the green content. These two images were projected onto a screen, each through the corresponding red or green filter to restore colour to the image. The addition of the red and the green content of the scene created a relatively satisfactory image (albeit without any true blue) – hence the name 'additive' process.

Though the additive process was used in early colour photography, the subtractive process provides far more satisfactory colour reproduction and is the basis for all modern colour film systems. In this process, the three colours used – cyan (which absorbs red), magenta (which absorbs green) and yellow (which absorbs blue) – are the 'complementary' colours of the red, green and blue used in the additive process. A cyan filter will let blue and green light pass but absorb red light, and so on. Some early subtractive processes involved the use of two colours, but the three-strip Technicolor process introduced in 1932 was the first truly effective subtractive colour film system; it used filters and a prism to split white light entering the camera into its red, green and blue components. Each of these constituents was directed to one of three black-and-white films held in the camera, resulting in black-and-white records of each colour. These were developed and used to create three more pieces of film, each containing an image in relief of the colour content in the scene. Each image was covered with the dyes of the complementary colours necessary to block the transmission of anything other than the primary colour involved. Thus, for example, the relief of the red image was treated with magenta and yellow dyes so that only red would be transmitted if light was shone through it. When the three dyed images were printed together on a single piece of film, the result was an image in cyan, magenta and yellow which when projected would show the final image with realistic colours.

Modern colour films work in much the same way as the Technicolor process, but the three separate strips of film are replaced by a single piece of film coated with three layers of light-sensitive emulsion, each designed to record either the blue, green or red content of a scene (fig. 8). Some optical special effects processes printed the colour negative through red, green and blue filters onto black-and-white film, to produce black-and-white colour separations – three separate strips, of the red, green or blue content of the scene, which could be selectively recombined and filtered to produce various optical effects (61>).

FIGURE 7 **ADDITIVE AND SUBTRACTIVE COLOUR**

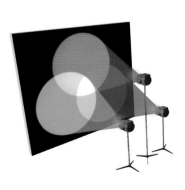 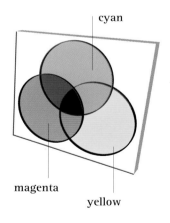

a: Additive process
Red, green and blue light
combine to create white.

b: Subtractive process
Cyan, magenta and yellow
will progressively block light
from a white source.

FIGURE 8 **MODERN COLOUR FILM**

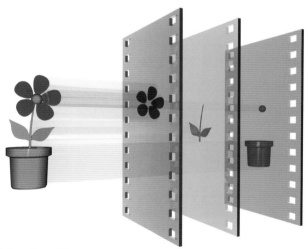

Single-strip colour film
consists of three layers, each
of which captures the red,
green or blue content of an
image.

FIGURE 9 **THE NEED FOR TRAVELLING MATTES**

Without mattes, the combination of
two film elements leads to the
ghosting of images.

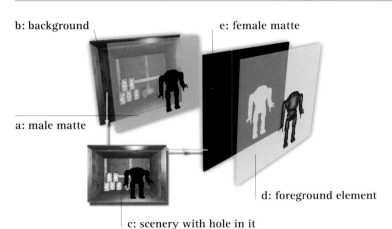

b: background

e: female matte

FIGURE 10 **THE PRINCIPLES OF TRAVELLING MATTES**

a: male matte

d: foreground element

c: scenery with hole in it

f: final composite

TRAVELLING MATTES

Since the earliest days of motion picture history, film-makers have sought ways to convincingly combine, on a single strip of film, images that have been filmed at differing times or locations. Méliès and Porter, among other early film-makers, used a simple technique of blocking, or 'matting' out, parts of the frame during initial photography in order to preserve an area of unexposed film on which other elements could later be photographed. Such simple 'split-screen' processes, performed on the original piece of film, could be effective if the additional action was to remain in a fixed area of the frame without interacting directly with the rest of the picture – in order to replace the view out of a window, for example. More attractive to film-makers, however, was a method that would allow an actor, or other element, to move in front of a separately filmed background with absolute freedom. Such a system would allow characters filmed in a studio to appear to inhabit places that were located on the other side of the world, or that only existed as small models or paintings created by the special effects department. Producing the two elements to be combined is a simple process. The desired background can be photographed on location or on a special effects stage on one piece of film, and the foreground element – usually an actor performing against a blank studio backdrop – on another piece of film.

Combining the two pieces of film is where difficulties begin to arise. If the separately shot film of an actor, who is to appear in the foreground, is simply placed or printed on top of the film of the desired background, a composite will be produced in which the actor may indeed appear to be at that location. But due to the transparent nature of celluloid film, the background element will be visible through the actor, making the performer appear ghostlike (fig. 9).

The only way to combine the two elements convincingly is to produce a background image that contains an unexposed hole exactly the same size and shape as the moving actor. The photograph of the actor can then be slotted into this hole to produce the desired result. To produce such a combination of images, several additional elements must be created. First is a 'male' matte, which is a black silhouette of the foreground performer on a clear background (fig. 10 (a)). This silhouette is placed over the desired background image (b), and the two are printed together to produce a piece of as yet undeveloped film that has been exposed to the background except in the areas covered by the matte (c). This piece of film must then have the image of the foreground performer (d) copied into the area left unexposed by the male matte. This involves the use of a 'female' matte, an exact opposite of the male matte and entirely black, except for a clear area the size and shape of the foreground actor (e). The female matte is placed over the undeveloped film that has already been exposed to the background, the black areas covering the already exposed background areas to prevent them from receiving more light during exposure and leaving uncovered only the as-yet-unexposed area of the film. The image of the foreground actor is then copied into the area of the film not concealed by the female matte. When this piece of film is developed, the result is a combination of the desired foreground and background elements known as a 'composite' (f). Since the male and female mattes must change in shape, position and size for every subsequent frame of film in order to accommodate the actor travelling about the frame, techniques in which they are used are known as 'travelling mattes'.

All travelling matte techniques rely on the same fundamental principle of creating a background element with an empty hole in which a foreground element containing nothing but the moving object is to be placed.

Optical travelling mattes, created by taking advantage of the properties of light and film, have been central to special effects creation since the early 1900s. Today, travelling mattes of extraordinary sophistication are created within the computer, but for almost a century special effects artists struggled with an array of complicated and often temperamental equipment and techniques to achieve their visual wonders.

The following pages describe the principles and processes of creating optical travelling mattes, a range of techniques now made entirely redundant by digital technology.

OPTICAL EFFECTS **57**

THE WILLIAMS PROCESS

Invented in 1916 and patented in 1918 by one-time Keystone Kops cameraman Frank Williams, the Williams process (also called the black-backing travelling matte process) was the first practical and widely used travelling matte technique. The foreground element, be it actor, monster or model, was photographed in front of an evenly lit plain black (or sometimes white) backdrop (fig. 11 (a)). The background element with which this foreground action was to be combined was usually filmed in advance (b), so that directors and performers could refer to it in order to choreograph movement.

Once a shot of the foreground element against its black backdrop had been filmed (c), this was copied a number of times using high-contrast film, which turns variations of tone into either black or white. This produced a clear background with the black silhouette of the foreground element (d). The film containing no image other than a black silhouette was then sandwiched, or 'bi-packed', with the film containing the desired background element, and contact-printed onto a new piece of film, thus producing an image of the correctly exposed background with an unexposed area at its centre.

This piece of film, still undeveloped, was then bi-packed with the developed strip of film containing the correctly exposed image of the foreground element with an opaque background. These two elements were run through the printer and re-exposed to light, thus printing the foreground element into its prepared hole (e). The developed piece of film combined foreground and background elements relatively satisfactorily – although it was not uncommon to see a telltale black outline (known as a 'minus' or 'matte line').

The Williams process was used in a number of films in the 1920s, becoming especially popular after it helped Rudolph Valentino to rescue Gloria Swanson from a perilous mountain-top situation in Famous Players Lasky's *Beyond the Rocks* (1922). It was also used to great effect in *The Lost World* (1925) and *Ben Hur* (1925).

Perhaps the most creative use of the technique was for James Whale's *The Invisible Man* (1933), for which John P. Fulton (69>), head of Universal's special effects department, produced some extraordinary 'invisible' moments. Scenes in which the film's star is totally imperceptible were relatively simple to produce – his presence was indicated by using fine wires to manipulate scenery and objects as he apparently interacted with them. The problematic scenes were those in which the invisible man is seen to fill his otherwise empty clothes. To create the image of an empty set of apparel wandering about, Fulton and his team prepared a studio draped entirely with black velvet – a fabric often used in the film industry because it is the most light-absorbent of materials and reflects no highlights. The team then dressed a performer in the clothes worn by the invisible man, having first covered all areas of his body from head to toe in black velvet, including his head, where he had a suffocating headpiece, with no holes for eyes or mouth. Air was

FIGURE 11 **THE WILLIAMS PROCESS**

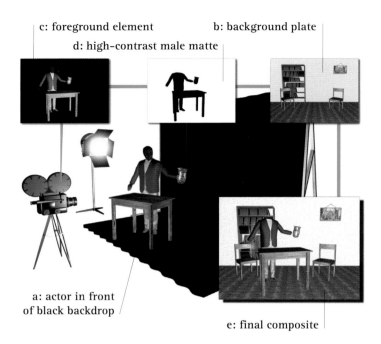

c: foreground element   b: background plate

d: high-contrast male matte

a: actor in front of black backdrop

e: final composite

supplied to the actor through tubes fed up his trouser leg, further impeding his movement. Fulton and the actor rehearsed each shot for hours in order to find ways in which the character could move naturally without allowing a black-gloved hand to pass in front of any clothed area; any black areas would become see-through after going through the Williams process.

Producing these scenes was painfully slow. The actor could not see where he was going and could barely hear the directions bellowed by Fulton, who stood just yards away with a megaphone. If a shot was completed in 20 takes, Fulton considered it a triumph. But the finished result *was* a triumph. The foreground element of the actor in the suit was copied onto high-contrast film, enabling the removal of his black-velvet-covered head, hands and neck. This allowed the foreground element of the mobile set of clothes to be combined with the desired location element. The technique was so successful that a number of sequels to the film were produced in which Fulton used increasingly elaborate 'invisible' effects. Even after the development of more satisfactory travelling matte techniques, the Williams process continued to be used in a number of 'invisibility' films, including *Topper* (1937) and its various sequels.

LEFT: The Williams process was used to combine foreground car with background train in Cecil B. DeMille's *Manslaughter* (1922). A black matte line can be seen around the edge of actress Leatrice Joy's scarf.

RIGHT: Claude Rains despairs in one of his more visible moments from *The Invisible Man* (1933).

FIGURE 12 **THE DUNNING-POMEROY SELF-MATTING PROCESS**

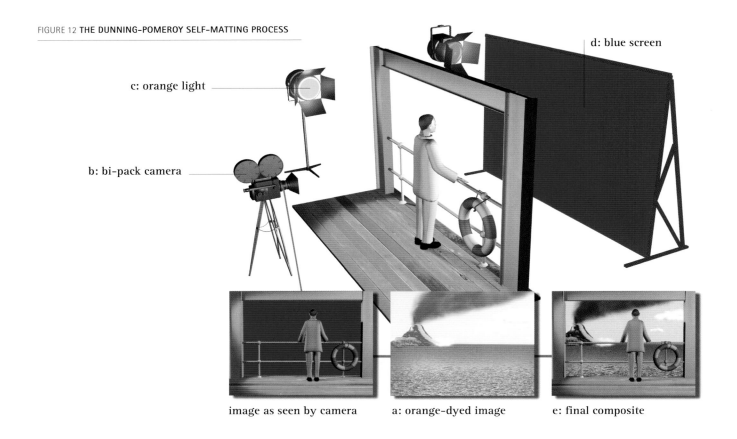

d: blue screen

c: orange light

b: bi-pack camera

image as seen by camera   a: orange-dyed image   e: final composite

THE DUNNING-POMEROY SELF-MATTING PROCESS

The colour-matting method that first became widely used in Hollywood was the process pioneered by C. Dodge Dunning and later refined by Roy J. Pomeroy, winner of the first-ever special effects Oscar (<46). The Dunning-Pomeroy process allowed actors to be filmed in the studio while their image was combined simultaneously with a previously filmed background plate without any additional photographic processes. The production of the necessary mattes and their combination to produce a final black-and-white composite image was achieved entirely in-camera during studio photography.

The background scene was filmed and developed in the normal way, and then printed to produce a positive black-and-white image. This strip of film was then bleached in the silver areas (the exposed part of the image) and then submersed in a dye that turned the bleached areas a deep orange. The result was not a black-and-white image but an orange-and-white image (fig. 12 (a)). The orange-and-white positive was bi-packed with ordinary unexposed black-and-white negative film in a camera capable of running two films together (b). When exposed, light would therefore pass through the orange-and-white film before reaching the unexposed negative film behind it.

In the studio, the foreground was set up and its various elements – actors and props – were illuminated by orange light (c). Behind these bright orange foreground elements was placed a flat screen, which was evenly illuminated with blue light (d). During photography, light from the orange foreground elements entered the camera and travelled equally through both the orange and the clear portions of the orange-dyed positive film – thus forming a normally exposed negative image of the foreground elements on the undeveloped film behind. However, the light from the blue screen that surrounded the foreground elements hit the orange-dyed film and was absorbed where it hit orange areas, and transmitted where it hit the clear areas – thus copying a negative image of the desired background onto the

undeveloped film behind. When developed and printed, the black-and-white film produced a composite of the desired foreground and background elements (e); by blocking the blue light, the performer served as a 'living' travelling matte.

Ingenious though the theory was, the Dunning-Pomeroy process was unfortunately a lot less practical than it sounds. The density of the orange-dyed background plate and the balance of the orange-and-blue-lit studio elements were all critical, and any imbalance led to incorrect exposure or 'ghosting' of the foreground elements. The preparation and dyeing of the orange component was a tortuous process, and once the film was bi-packed in the camera, there was no way of judging whether an actor's performance married with the action of the background element until the footage was developed. Despite its drawbacks, the Dunning-Pomeroy process was the only truly practical and effective method of combining separately filmed foreground and background elements in its day. The technique was widely employed in Hollywood from the late 20s and early 30s, and can be seen in use in films such as *Trader Horn* (1931) and *Tarzan the Ape-Man* (1932). Though the development of effective rear projection soon made the process obsolete (82>), it remains of interest because it was the first technique to use the properties of coloured light to produce a matte – a method that would become integral to all future travelling matte developments.

BLUE-SCREEN COLOUR SEPARATION PROCESS

In the early 30s, rear projection (82>) replaced the Dunning-Pomeroy process as the dominant means of combining separately filmed images. The introduction of colour photography in the 40s and 50s created technical difficulties that rear projection could not immediately overcome, however, and a new method of combining foreground and background elements was sought. The Dunning-Pomeroy process had used the properties of coloured light to produce travelling mattes, but its use of orange and blue light, which remained unnoticed in black-and-white photography, made it unsuitable for

FIGURE 13 **BLUE-SCREEN COLOUR SEPARATION PROCESS**

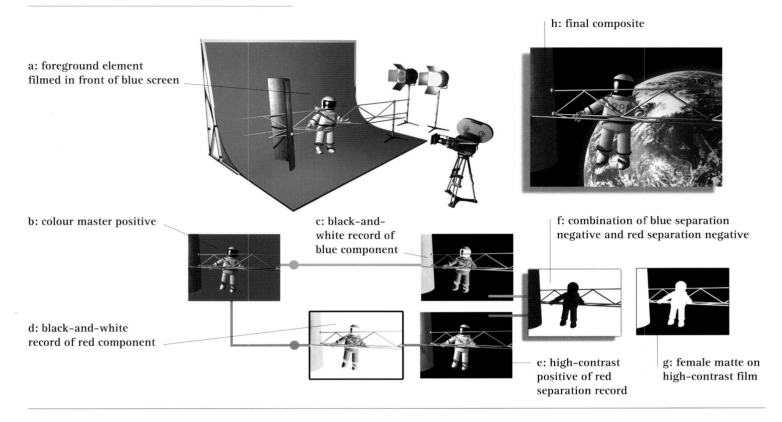

a: foreground element filmed in front of blue screen

h: final composite

b: colour master positive

c: black-and-white record of blue component

d: black-and-white record of red component

e: high-contrast positive of red separation record

f: combination of blue separation negative and red separation negative

g: female matte on high-contrast film

use in colour. A new process, using similar principles but capable of rendering the colours of the final image realistically, was therefore sought.

In the late 30s, the Technicolor laboratory in London experimented with methods of creating travelling mattes using the three colour separations produced in the three-strip Technicolor process. They discovered that by filming foreground elements in front of a blue background screen, the blue and red colour separations of the scene could be used to generate high-contrast male and female mattes. The first feature film to employ this process was Alexander Korda's production of *The Thief of Bagdad* (1940), which used it to produce scenes with a flying horse and a giant genie. In the 50s, the Technicolor three-strip blue-screen process was developed and improved for use with single-strip colour film stocks such as Eastmancolor. Known as the blue-screen colour separation process, the new method was the basis for modern blue-screen techniques.

As in all travelling matte photography, the process required two basic elements: a background plate and a foreground element that could be used to produce a male and female matte. The foreground element was filmed in front of a bright blue background screen (fig. 13 (a)). Great care was taken that the screen, which was effectively a large blue reflector, did not cast blue light onto the foreground subject. Such blue 'spill' could make the production of clean mattes extremely difficult to achieve. To help separate the foreground element from the blue screen behind it, a weak yellow filter was sometimes added to the foreground lighting in order to prevent the emission of any blue light. The foreground element, with its blue background, was then filmed on colour film stock and developed into a negative in the usual way.

The developed camera negative was then printed to produce a colour master positive (b). This was in turn printed onto black-and-white film through a blue filter to produce a colour separation negative that was a black-and-white record of the blue component of the scene. In this negative, the background screen area was now black (c).

Another copy of the master positive was then made on black-and-white film. This time a red filter was used. This produced a separation negative of the red component of the scene (d). In this negative, the background area was clear. This was then printed onto high-contrast black-and-white stock to produce a positive image in which the background screen area was black (e).

As a result of these processes, the blue separation negative and the red separation positive both had black backgrounds. The two pieces of film were then printed onto the same strip of high-contrast black-and-white film stock. The black backgrounds on both separation strips prevented any light from reaching the background area on the new strip of film, while the combination of negative and positive images of the foreground element ensured that the whole of the foreground area was exposed to light. The resulting negative (f) was clear in the background area and solid black in the foreground area – this was the male matte (also known as the hold-out matte). A positive copy of this produced the female matte, which was clear in the foreground area and solid black in the background area (g). These elements were then combined with the master positive of the foreground and the master positive of the desired background element in an optical printer to produce the final composite image of foreground and background objects (h).

While the blue-screen colour separation technique was an effective method of producing travelling matte shots in colour, it did have its pitfalls. Any transparent foreground element through which the blue screen was visible – for instance, a glass of water – became invisible in the final image. Semi-transparent objects – for example, smoke, fine hair or soft-edged items such as out-of-focus or fast-moving objects – often inherited a hazy blue fringe.

Interesting examples of this blue-fringing effect can be seen in the rapid scenes of *The African Queen* (1951) and the closing of the Red Sea in *The Ten Commandments* (1956). In both cases, the edges of water spray have a dramatic blue or green halo. Despite its limitations, however, the technique was at the time the only way to successfully combine large-scale foreground and background elements in colour.

ABOVE: The blue-screen colour separation process was used to create many composite shots for the science fiction extravaganzas of the 50s. For this shot, actor Lewis Martin was filmed in front of a blue screen in order to composite him with footage of model alien spacecraft for *The War of the Worlds* (1953). The performer's fine hair has caused some blue-fringe problems on the left-hand side of his head.

ABOVE: The sodium vapour process was used to combine live action with animated characters and backgrounds in a number of 60s family movies, as in this scene from *Mary Poppins* (1964).

FIGURE 14 **SODIUM VAPOUR PROCESS**

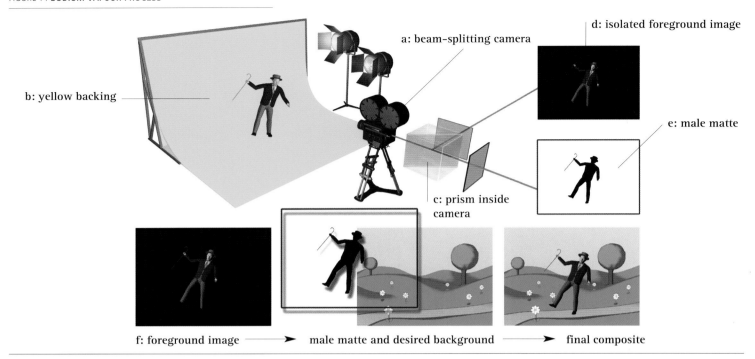

a: beam-splitting camera

d: isolated foreground image

b: yellow backing

e: male matte

c: prism inside camera

f: foreground image ⟶ male matte and desired background ⟶ final composite

SODIUM VAPOUR PROCESS

In the mid-50s an alternative method of colour travelling matte photography was devised in France and developed for practical use by the Rank Organisation in England. The sodium vapour process resembled the Dunning-Pomeroy method in being a 'dual-film' system that produced the travelling matte while the action was being photographed. While the older method combined background and foreground elements in-camera, the sodium vapour technique involved the in-camera production of a live-action foreground negative and a separate travelling matte element on two different pieces of film that could be combined with a separately filmed background image at a later stage.

The process required the use of a camera that could hold two separate films which could be exposed to the same image simultaneously. The system developed in England employed specially built cameras, whereas in America, obsolete three-strip Technicolor cameras were modified to take two rather than three strips of film (fig. 14 (a)). The films loaded into the camera were a standard colour stock (to record the foreground image) and a black-and-white stock (to record the travelling matte image). As in other processes, the foreground action was staged in front of a coloured backdrop. In this case, the backing was a brilliant yellow, further illuminated with yellow light from sodium vapour lamps (b), similar to those used to light roads at night. Normal lights used for the foreground action were equipped with a filter coated with didymium (a mixture of elements that absorbs yellow light) to subtract monochromatic yellow from the foreground lighting.

During filming, light entered the camera through the lens and hit a beam-splitting prism (c). This prism divided the light, sending identical images of the scene towards the two separate films contained in the camera. Light heading for the colour-negative stock was passed through a didymium filter, which blocked the yellow light from the background, resulting in an image which when developed showed the foreground action surrounded by black (d). The light directed towards the black-and-white film passed through a filter that transmitted only the yellow light of the background, thus producing a black area around a clear foreground (a female matte). This could be copied to produce a male matte (e). The developed elements were then combined (f) to produce exceptionally fine results.

As well as producing accurate mattes, the process allowed for the

photography of transparent objects; an actor could now enjoy a drink during photography, and in the final composite image the matted-in background would be visible through the glass and liquid. The sodium vapour process was first used by Rank during its production of *Plain Sailing* (1958) and was then adopted by the Walt Disney Studio, which developed the system under the guidance of its head of research and development, Ub Iwerks (1901–71). The technique was used to enliven many Disney productions in the 60s and 70s, an early and spectacular example being the combination of the live-action antics of Julie Andrews and Dick Van Dyke with animated cartoon elements in *Mary Poppins* (1964). Alfred Hitchcock also used the method to produce many of his travelling mattes for *The Birds* (1963).

The sodium vapour process was the most successful of a number of similar methods that were developed at around the same time. Alternative systems differed in their use of background light; rather than using sodium vapour light, some employed either infrared or ultraviolet light to produce mattes. These systems required additional processing after initial photography and so were less accurate, practical and popular.

BLUE-SCREEN COLOUR DIFFERENCE PROCESS

Dual-film travelling matte techniques such as the sodium vapour process produced high-quality travelling mattes that were far more versatile and effective than those produced using the blue-screen colour separation process. However, dual-film methods required the use of specialist cameras that were unwieldy, expensive to hire and which could not be used with the anamorphic CinemaScope lenses that were popular from the mid-50s onwards.

A system of producing travelling mattes was sought that combined the quality of the dual-film sodium vapour technique with the convenience of the blue-screen colour separation process, which derived its mattes from a single negative shot in a standard production camera.

A number of methods were devised in response to this need, most of which worked on principles similar to that of a system first developed and patented by Petro Vlahos of the Motion Picture Research Council. His system, which he called the blue-screen colour difference process, became the basis for the most widely used method of producing travelling mattes from the mid-60s until the advent of digital alternatives in the late 80s.

In its photography and subsequent optical processes, the blue-screen colour difference system resembled the original colour separation process. However, the newer method differed from its older cousin in several important ways, one of which was a reduction in the number of duplication generations needed to produce the final composite of background and foreground action. The system was a complicated one, but its basic principles were as follows (fig. 15).

The live-action element of a scene was filmed in front of a carefully illuminated blue screen. While early blue screens could be a wall or any other surface that had been painted blue and illuminated with blue light, the colour difference process required such pure blue that new screens had to be developed for the purpose. Such screens were typically made from a translucent blue material and lit from behind with banks of flicker-free fluorescent tubes (a).

After processing, the negative of the foreground action was copied onto high-contrast black-and-white film stock through a blue filter, whose colour exactly matched that of the blue screen (b). The filter absorbed the blue light from the scene but allowed red and green to pass through, resulting in a black-and-white separation record in which the blue-screen area was transparent (c). However, in most cases the foreground element was likely to contain some traces of blue – perhaps in an actor's costume or make-up. These traces of blue would appear partially transparent in the separation

ABOVE: **The crew of the** *Enterprise* **perform in front of a blue-screen window in which a space scene will later be composited for** *Star Trek: The Motion Picture* **(1979).**

FIGURE 15 **BLUE-SCREEN COLOUR DIFFERENCE PROCESS**

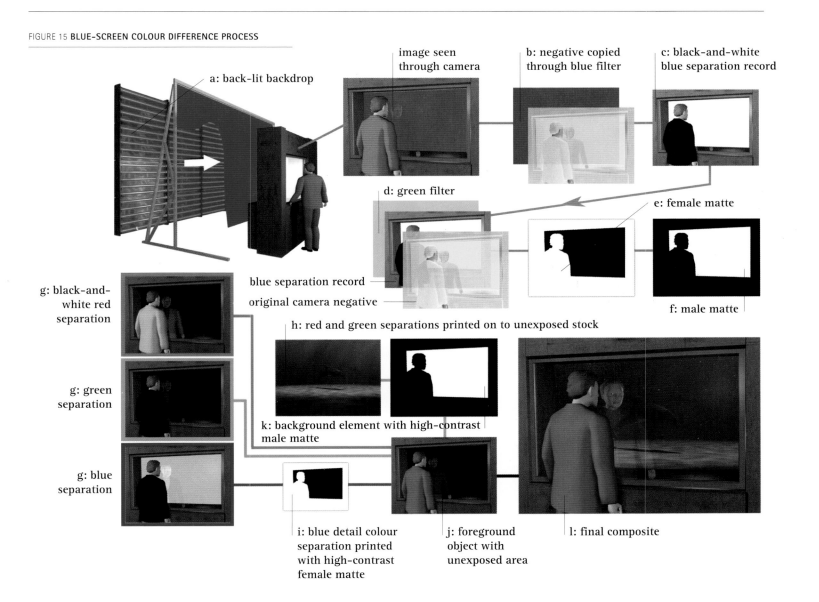

a: back-lit backdrop

image seen through camera

b: negative copied through blue filter

c: black-and-white blue separation record

d: green filter

e: female matte

blue separation record

original camera negative

f: male matte

g: black-and-white red separation

g: green separation

g: blue separation

h: red and green separations printed on to unexposed stock

k: background element with high-contrast male matte

i: blue detail colour separation printed with high-contrast female matte

j: foreground object with unexposed area

l: final composite

record. To remedy this, the black-and-white separation record was bi-packed with the original negative and printed again onto high-contrast stock, this time through a specially balanced green filter (d). This produced a high-contrast female matte that was transparent in the foreground area and black in the blue-screen area (e). A negative was taken from this to produce a high-contrast male matte, in which the blue-screen area was clear and the foreground was black (f).

Once the mattes had been produced, red, green and blue colour separations were made from the original camera negative onto normal-contrast black-and-white film (g). These contained all of the essential colour information from the scene. The red and green colour separations were then printed onto a single piece of unexposed colour film stock through their corresponding colour filters, to produce an image in which the background area remained clear, while the foreground details were recorded (h). Next, the blue colour separation was printed onto the colour film stock, through both its corresponding colour filter and the high-contrast female matte. The transparent area of the female matte ensured that the blue details in the foreground image were exposed, while the black area of the matte stopped the background blue-screen image from transferring to the colour film stock (i). The result of combining the colour separations in this way was a foreground object surrounded by an unexposed area of film (j). This film was then combined with the high-contrast male matte in order to record the desired background element. The male matte prevented any unwanted light from reaching the already exposed foreground elements, but allowed light to fall onto the unexposed areas of the undeveloped film – that is, the background area (k). The required background was printed into the previously unexposed area of the film, thereby completing the illusion that the foreground and background elements were filmed simultaneously (l).

The advantage of using this system was that, because each separation was taken directly from the original negative, fine details such as hair or grass were not lost through 'image spread', which occurs whenever film images are repeatedly duplicated. Since reflections from semi-transparent objects were also represented in each colour separation, their detail was present in the final composite. This made the process suitable for filming transparent objects such as windows and water, which would become invisible or suffer from blue-fringing if the colour separation process were used.

'The colour difference process was a major development in the production of travelling mattes,' explained the British effects supervisor Roy Field (1932–2002). 'We had been trying all sorts of systems with varying degrees of success for years, but the colour difference process was the basis of a system that really enabled us to produce travelling mattes of pretty much anything we wanted.'

Field put his abilities to the test during the production of *Superman* (1978), which required the hero in a blue costume to appear in many blue-screen shots. 'On *Superman* I was slightly perturbed to find that the main character's costume was going to be blue – which isn't ideal when you're planning blue-screen shots,' laughs Field. 'I tried to persuade the producers to change the colour – but it had to be blue. I then spent six months testing all sorts of different blues and turquoises to find which we could use in conjunction with a blue screen. Eventually I found an extremely narrow band of blue that could be filmed in front of a blue screen and which could be utilized to produce mattes using a variation of the colour difference method. After persuading DC Comics to allow us to use this particular shade of blue – which was different to that used in the comics – we had to find a way to get costume material made to this exact colour. Eventually we found a company in France that could get it just right.' Though Field won an Oscar for his work on the film, he was never entirely happy with all of it. 'There's one shot in particular that we never got right,' he says. 'It's where Superman is flying around the dam – his costume is far too green-looking. Unfortunately, we had a tough schedule, but with a little bit more time we could have got that one right.'

The blue-screen colour difference process enabled Superman (Christopher Reeve) to soar over Metropolis despite his inconveniently blue clothing.

FIGURE 16 **THE ROTOSCOPE**

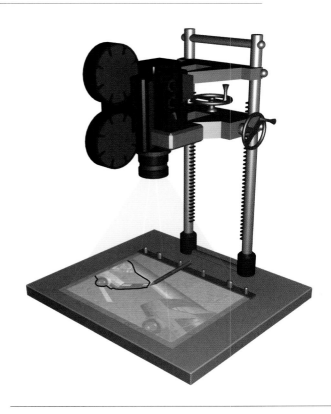

HAND-DRAWN MATTES

For those occasions when filming with specialized cameras or backdrops was impossible or impractical, travelling mattes and split screens could still be produced without resorting to complicated photochemical techniques. In such cases, effects artists drew their mattes by hand.

The equipment used to draw mattes is based on that invented and patented by the animator Max Fleischer (1889–1972) in 1917. Fleischer developed the process known as rotoscoping as an aid to drawing cartoon animation (174>), but a variation of the technique has been used for many aspects of effects production. The rotoscope (fig. 16) – also often called the 'down-shooter' or 'rostrum camera' – was simply a large, sturdy frame onto which a downward-pointing camera was mounted. The camera was adapted to operate as both a camera and, with the addition of a lamp, a projector.

To produce a travelling split screen, various aspects of the same shot were filmed in different takes (fig. 17). If, for example, a shot of an actor running across the road, narrowly avoiding a traffic accident was required, the actor might be filmed safely crossing the road in one take (a), and the accident in the next (b). The two takes would then be combined. To achieve the desired result, one of the films was loaded into the camera–projector. In this example, it might be the film of colliding vehicles. The first frame of film in the sequence was projected downwards and focused on the animation table, on which specially punched paper was held in precise registration by a peg-bar.

The first 'split' was then traced on the paper in pencil. The split formed the dividing line where the separate takes would be joined together – the image on one side of the line coming from one take, the action on the other side of the line from the other. Splits were usually drawn around well-defined lines that already existed within the image – in our example it is where the front of the vehicle enters the frame (c). When the outline of the first split had been drawn, the film in the camera projector was advanced by one frame and the next split drawn on a new piece of paper. This continued through the sequence to produce a series of pencil drawings that represented a moving outline progressing across the screen.

The pencil lines were then carefully inked in and the area on one side of the line painted black – the part of the screen to be occupied by the oncoming vehicle, in our example. The projector – still locked in exactly the same position – was then converted back into a camera and loaded with high-contrast black-and-white film which was used to photograph the painted artwork one frame at a time in the correct order. This produced a strip of film on which the blacked-out areas formed a travelling matte. This film was then copied to produce a counter-matte element (d), in which the film on the opposite side of the line was black – in our example, the area where the actor will be seen running.

In an optical printer, the footage of the crashing car would be printed along with its female matte to produce a strip of film that is exposed only in the area occupied by the car (e). This film, still undeveloped, would then be rewound and exposed to the footage of the running actor, using the counter-matte to protect the area of the frame already exposed to the footage of the car. The actor would now appear to be running across the road, avoiding the colliding vehicles by just inches (f).

Rotoscoping could also be used to enhance the impression that the various elements matted into a shot are not simply placed on top of the scene, but are actually *within* it. In *Return of the Jedi* (1983), animated walking vehicles were matted into real forest scenes. By creating hand-drawn split screens, the vehicles were 'sandwiched' between live-action elements and appeared to walk in between trees and bushes as if actually interacting with the environment. To achieve the effect, the live-action forest environment was rotoscoped to produce mattes that split the image into its 'foreground' and 'background' planes (fig. 18). Travelling mattes of the animated vehicle were then produced using blue-screen techniques. To assemble the final composite, the background forest area was first printed onto unexposed film using the male mattes from the foreground forest area and the vehicle to prevent exposure in these areas. The vehicle was then printed into the new composite by using mattes to cover the already exposed background as well as the areas reserved for the foreground. Finally the foreground was added by covering the already exposed background and vehicle areas with their mattes to prevent additional exposure.

FIGURE 17 **ROTOSCOPING**

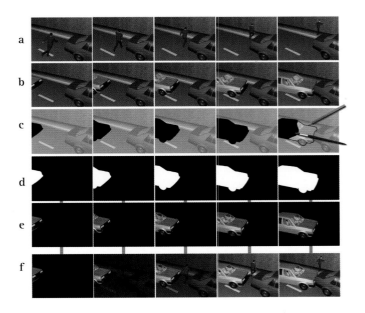

The best aspects of two similar shots, (a) and (b), can be combined using hand-drawn mattes – (c), (d) and (e) – to create a new shot (f).

FIGURE 18 **ROTOSCOPING WITH MATTES**

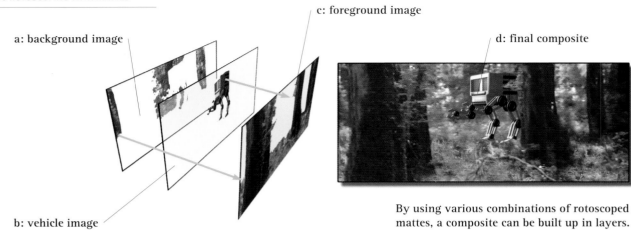

a: background image

c: foreground image

d: final composite

b: vehicle image

By using various combinations of rotoscoped mattes, a composite can be built up in layers.

It was also possible to achieve intricate travelling mattes using a rotoscope. Objects that needed to be placed into a scene, but which had not been filmed in front of a blue screen, could be traced frame by frame, inked in, and the resulting mattes and counter-mattes used to place them into their new background. Drawing such mattes was an intricate and time-consuming process. For Alfred Hitchcock's *The Birds* (1963), a shot required that hundreds of seagulls be seen descending towards a town from a bird's-eye point of view. The nature and scale of the shot meant that filming birds in front of a blue screen was impossible. Instead, the gulls were filmed from a clifftop as they swooped towards the shore where food had been placed. The resulting footage was then rotoscoped – every gull painstakingly hand-traced to produce a matte that would separate it from its background, and allow it to be placed into an aerial view of the town – which was itself a combination of a matte painting by Albert Whitlock (249>) and live-action footage shot looking down from a hill at Universal Studios (fig. 19). Rotoscoping the 500 frames in this one shot took two artists three months to complete.

The rotoscope was also useful for removing any unwanted items from a shot or for cleaning up images before compositing. When models or puppets are filmed in front of blue screens, they are usually attached to various rods and wires. These are sometimes painted blue to enable them to be 'automatically' removed during the generation of optical, now digital, blue-screen mattes. If this is not possible, the shots are rotoscoped instead. Although now done digitally, this was once a manual task, the rods being

individually hand-traced to produce a separate matte for each frame of film. Furthermore, since large blue screens can be difficult to light, performers, puppets or miniatures are often placed in front of a screen that is just large enough to isolate their edges – foreground objects need only have a small area of blue around them to produce a matte using blue-screen methods. However, if a small blue screen is used, the clutter of studio surroundings (lights, camera tracks, technicians and so on) will also be photographed. To clean up the shot, the rotoscope was once used to create 'garbage mattes' (also called 'junk mattes') that obscured all the unwanted elements at the edges of the shot.

Garbage mattes were sometimes hand-painted for each frame, but, since they did not have to follow the edge detail of an object accurately, they were more commonly generated by arranging and photographing sheets of black paper that covered up all of the detail outside the blue-screen area. If the camera or object moved during the shot, the paper was reconfigured every few frames to keep the unwanted areas covered. Optically created garbage mattes sometimes show up around flying superheroes or spacecraft when older films are watched on television (fig. 20). They are usually invisible in the cinema because film records a huge range of subtleties. Television, however, is a relatively coarse medium and is unable to reproduce as many variations of colour and contrast, especially when an image has been brightened for home viewing, with the result that optical garbage mattes do not always blend in with their surroundings.

FIGURE 19 **HAND-DRAWN MATTES IN** *THE BIRDS*

a: original gull footage

b: hand-drawn mattes

c: mattes and backdrop combined

d: final composite

PROFILE **JOHN P. FULTON**

John P. Fulton (1902–65), son of Fitch Fulton, who painted scenic backdrops for movies such as *Gone with the Wind* (1939), became hooked on film-making when, as a teenager, he watched D.W. Griffith (<18) directing. In the mid-1920s, Fulton secured a job as an assistant cameraman, later graduating to cinematographer. After shooting *Hell's Harbour* (1929) and *Eyes of the World* (1930) for the director Henry King, Fulton took a job in Frank Williams's optical laboratory, where he learned the art of 'trick' photography.

In 1930 Fulton became the head of Universal's special effects department, where he oversaw effects for all of the studio's films including its classic horror movies such as *Frankenstein* (1931) and *The Mummy* (1932) and its Sherlock Holmes films such as *The Scarlet Claw* (1944).

In 1945 Samuel Goldwyn hired Fulton from Universal to produce the effects for the Danny Kaye film *Wonder Man* (1945). Kaye was so impressed with the effects that enabled him to appear twice in the same shot

that he called Fulton 'the real star of the film'. Equally impressed was Goldwyn, who offered Fulton a contract with the promise of directing. Fulton never got his chance to direct a feature, although he did direct second-unit footage on several films, including *The Secret Life of Walter Mitty* (1947), again with Danny Kaye.

Fulton became the head of special effects at Paramount in 1953 following the death of Gordon Jennings (147>). Fulton's greatest achievement at Paramount was the effects for *The Ten Commandments* (1956), including the famous parting of the Red Sea sequence. He also created effects for a number of Hitchcock films including the dizzying 'trombone shots' in *Vertigo* (<52; 1958).

In a career that embraced hundreds of classic films, Fulton supervised some of the most important special effects work in Hollywood history, winning Oscars for his contributions to *Wonder Man*, *The Bridges at Toko-Ri* (1954) and *The Ten Commandments*. He died in London in 1966 while working on *Battle of Britain* (1969).

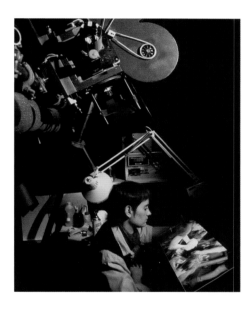

ABOVE: A special effects artist studies a frame of film using the rotoscope at Boss Film Studios.

FIGURE 20 **GARBAGE MATTES** [RIGHT]

Garbage mattes are used to remove unwanted details from travelling matte shots. They are sometimes visible as low-contrast areas around composited elements when older films are shown on TV.

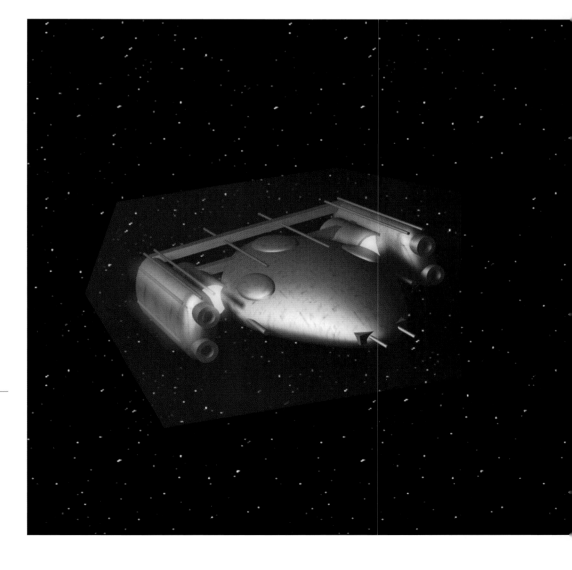

OPTICAL PRINTING

When all the elements of a visual effects shot have been produced – models, animation, live action, travelling mattes – the separate pieces must be reassembled to form a single, completed image for inclusion in the final version of the film. The process of fitting all the pieces together is known as compositing. Until the arrival and rapid dominance of digital techniques in the 1990s, almost all compositing was done using a machine called an optical printer. For decades optical printers were at the very heart of visual effects production and were the most important and treasured pieces of equipment in any effects studio.

The early copying of moving images was done by contact printing – the film to be copied was sandwiched in contact with unexposed film, and light shone through the two pieces to produce a copy. However, some early film-makers wished to do more than simply copy their images – they wanted to alter them in the process. Around the turn of the century, the British film pioneer Cecil Hepworth devised a system by which he pointed the lens of a projector into that of a camera and, by projecting and photographing one frame at a time, could rephotograph an image. Hepworth used his technique of 'projection printing' to produce *The Frustrated Elopement* (1902), in which the forward-moving action occasionally reversed, mid-scene, to make characters and action move backwards. This was achieved simply by changing the direction that the film moved through the projector during rephotography.

The copying of moving images in this way was generally avoided until the mid-20s, since rephotographing early film stocks led to a significant deterioration in image quality. The emergence of a film stock specifically designed for duplication in 1926, followed by greater improvements in the early 1930s, meant that the potential of optical printing could be explored by the fledgling special effects departments of the studios.

Early optical printers were hand-built to cater to the individual needs of the department in question, and were designed to incorporate whatever equipment was available to them. Such printers typically consisted of a process projector (called the printer head), which faced an adapted production camera (fig. 21). Both camera and projector featured fixed-pin registration, so that the film was held absolutely steady during the copying process. The camera and projector were mounted on a heavy base, typically a cast-iron lathe bed, to prevent any form of vibration during operation.

SCENE TRANSITIONS

The ability to copy images efficiently and effectively meant that optical tricks, which were previously achieved in-camera, could be left until post-production. While the skilled camera operator had once been responsible for the 'live' production of fades and dissolves during original photography, the optical printer could now be used to produce these effects with more control at a later stage, with no danger of spoiling the original negative.

To produce a fade-out, the master positive of a scene was loaded into the printer head, and rephotographed one frame at a time by the camera. The fade-out was produced by incrementally closing the camera's shutter in order to reduce the amount of light that reached the copied film. To create a dissolve from one shot to another, the editor studied the film and marked the points at which a dissolve should start and end. The first scene was loaded into the printer head, and the camera's shutter gradually closed during rephotography to produce a conventional fade-out. The second shot was then loaded into the printer head, the film in the camera back-wound and a second exposure made. This time the camera's shutter was gradually opened over the same period that it was previously closed. The second image therefore faded in as the first faded out, the two appearing to dissolve into one another.

As well as basic dissolves and fades, a plethora of elaborate scene transitions could be achieved. A simple wipe from one shot to another was produced by fitting the camera with a set of 'blades' that were moved mechanically. During the copying of the first shot, the blade was moved horizontally, vertically or diagonally across the frame, progressively obscuring the image and leaving a portion of the frame unexposed. The camera film was then back-wound and the second shot run through the printer while the wipe blade repeated its movements in reverse – thus printing the second shot onto the unexposed portion of film. The result was a transition in which one shot was replaced by a second as it wiped across the screen. By sliding the projector head sideways at the same rate as a wipe blade, the wipe could be turned into a 'push-off' – one image pushing the other off the screen.

A major pioneer of transition effects was Linwood G. Dunn (72>), head of the RKO optical department. Dunn first experimented with scene transitions in the short film *This Is Harris* (1933), and achieved such good results that he added several to the studio's next musical feature film, *Melody Cruise* (1933). The enthusiastic reaction to his optical transitions persuaded Dunn to add even more elaborate ones to the studio's next

FIGURE 21 **A SINGLE-HEAD OPTICAL PRINTER**

Simple, single-head optical printers would be used for basic copying tasks and for adding basic fades and wipes.

RIGHT: The optical printer was used to produce many fanciful scene transitions in films of the 30s, including this star-wipe from *Flying Down to Rio* (1933).

PROFILE **LINWOOD DUNN**

Linwood G. Dunn (1904–98) began his career in the movie business as an assistant cameraman for Pathé in 1925. After moving from New York to Hollywood Dunn worked at a number of studios until, in 1929, he was offered two days' work in the photographic effects department of the newly established RKO Radio Pictures.

Dunn stayed at RKO for the next 28 years, producing effects for hundreds of films and eventually becoming head of the studio's photographic effects department. He was known as the first master of the optical printer.

Optical printers had been custom-made machines until Dunn was asked to design a device to be mass-produced for US military film units during World War II. After the war, the printer, which Dunn had designed with his associate Cecil Love, was marketed as the Acme-Dunn Optical Printer – the first commercially produced off-the-shelf printer. Dunn and Love won a Technical Academy Award for their design in 1944.

During his career at RKO, Dunn created pioneering composite shots for many classic films including *King*

Kong (1933), *Flying Down to Rio* (1933), *The Last Days of Pompeii* (1935), *Bringing up Baby* (1938), *The Hunchback of Notre Dame* (1939) and *Citizen Kane* (1941).

When RKO ceased production in 1957, Dunn leased the studio's redundant effects facilities for use by his own independent company, Film Effects of Hollywood, which he founded in 1946. The company continued to produce sophisticated visual effects for films such as *West Side Story* (1961), *It's a Mad Mad Mad Mad World* (1963), *My Fair Lady* (1964), *Airport* (1970), and television productions including the original series of *Star Trek* (1966–9). Dunn received an Academy Award for his contributions to *Mighty Joe Young* (1949), a Special Academy Award for lifetime achievement in 1979, and another in 1981 for having designed the Acme-Dunn Optical Printer.

Dunn sold his company in 1985 but continued to work in the field through his involvement in many industry societies and committees. His technical skills moved with the times, and he was busy working on a digital projection system at the time of his death in 1998.

production, *Flying Down to Rio* (1933), the first pairing of Ginger Rogers and Fred Astaire. Dunn merged shots with kaleidoscopic starbursts, rotating swirls, circular 'clock' wipes and zig-zag 'saw' wipes. David Lean's naval drama *In Which We Serve* (1942) employed more subtle techniques. Watery dissolves between shipwreck scenes were created by moving a piece of rippled glass between camera and projector during printing. Similar methods were used to achieve the wavering transitions to flashback scenes and dream sequences for decades to come.

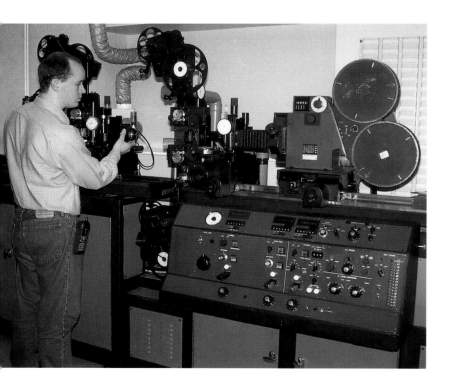

OPTICAL TRICKS

The optical printer, at first used for simple copying jobs and scene transitions, soon became a major tool for the creative manipulation of film footage. If a chase sequence needed a little more impact, every third or fourth frame could be skipped during printing in order to speed up the appearance of the action. A scene that seemed a little too fast, on the other hand, could have some frames double-printed to slow the action down. By projecting and copying a single frame, a freeze-frame could be produced – a technique employed with dramatic effect by L.B. Abbott for the final shot of *Butch Cassidy and the Sundance Kid* (1969). By moving the camera closer to the projector, the original image could be reframed – perhaps to crop out an unwanted object such as a microphone, or to turn a long shot into a close-up. A shot originally filmed without any camera movement could be brought to life by adding a small pan or zoom during the copying process. Tilting the camera from side to side during printing added the sway of the seas to elements shot in land-locked studios. To help solve a difficult cutting problem, editors might request that a shot be 'flopped' to produce a mirror image. Adding filters to the camera could turn scenes filmed by day into night, make a clear day foggy, or add a glowing sunset to an overcast sky. Simple cut-out masks could produce 'through the keyhole' shots or views through binoculars and periscopes.

Similar processes could be used to salvage footage that might otherwise have been unusable. During the editing of *Flaming Gold* (1933), it was noticed that a passing truck had an objectionable phrase written on its side. The footage was sent to the optical department, where a glass slide was placed in front of the camera and the offending words blotted out with a fine grease pencil. The glass was moved, frame by frame, to follow the truck as it passed through the shot and the words in question were blurred unnoticeably.

By masking different areas of the camera negative, several exposures could be made on a single frame of film to produce complex multiple-image shots. To produce a shot containing four different images, for example, a matte device was slotted in front of the camera to obscure three-quarters of the frame. One image was then projected onto the unmasked area of film. The camera film was then back-wound and a new mask inserted, this time revealing a different quarter of the frame of film. The next image was then printed onto that area and so on, until each quarter of the frame had been exposed to a different image. This method was cleverly used in *Grand Prix* (1966), in which multiple images informed the viewer of different events that were taking place simultaneously during the course of a motor race.

Sophisticated moving split-screen shots could be achieved entirely within the printer using a variation of the moving-blade system employed to produce wipe transitions. Shots that required the interaction of two elements that could not be filmed together for reasons of practicality or safety could instead be filmed in two takes and then selectively printed together to produce a convincing composite. For some scenes in *Wonder Man* (1945), Danny Kaye was required to play identical twins. Under the supervision of John P. Fulton, each shot was filmed twice (once for each twin), and in each the actor's movements were carefully planned to correspond to those of his twin. During filming, the camera remained locked in one position, and care was taken that the actor did not enter or cross the part of the shot that his twin would later occupy. In the optical department, the images from one of the films were projected into the camera. As the first twin moved around the frame, a split-screen matte was moved with him to ensure that only the area occupied by the actor during that frame was exposed to the camera film. The camera film was then back-wound and the second film printed onto it, using a moving counter-matte to expose footage of the second brother onto the areas of unexposed film. Ensuring that the two moving mattes complemented each other frame by frame was an exacting business, but the results allowed two Danny Kayes to perform together convincingly, walking from side to side of the frame, in a way that fixed-position, in-camera split screens never could.

Even films that required no special effects traditionally relied on optical printing for the addition of titles and credits. Wording was produced as black-and-white artwork and photographed onto high-contrast black-and-white film. The resulting negative and positive were used as a matte and counter-matte to superimpose the wording onto live-action footage. By using an optical printer with two printer heads, this could be achieved in one simple operation (fig. 22, 76>) and, by adding filters to the process, title sequences could be produced in colour.

BELOW LEFT: **This optical printer at Pinewood Studios was specially built for the production of *Superman* (1978). It remained in use to create titles and optical effects until 2002.**

BELOW: **This multiple-image shot was assembled in an optical printer using a system of mattes and counter-mattes for the film *Grand Prix* (1966).**

CITIZEN KANE

Orson Welles (1915–85) had an auspicious early career. His 1938 radio adaptation of H.G. Wells's book *The War of the Worlds* sent shockwaves across the United States, causing panic on the streets when people believed it was genuine news coverage of an alien invasion. An impressed RKO offered the 23-year-old Welles a movie contract. The terms: carte blanche. The result: what many consider to be the greatest film of all time.

Welles arrived in Hollywood in 1939, admitting that he knew nothing about film production. An RKO researcher was asked to tutor Welles in basic film terms and techniques, patiently explaining the difference between a close-up and a long shot. Welles then watched John Ford's *Stagecoach* (1939) every night for a month before he felt ready to make his own film.

Vital in creating the astounding look of *Citizen Kane* (1941) was its cinematographer Gregg Toland (1904–48). Toland had asked to photograph Welles's first film as he realized the young director's great vision and scant experience meant his creativity would know no bounds. As Welles himself later admitted, 'I thought that you could do anything with a camera that the eye could do, or the imagination – I didn't know that there were things you couldn't do, so anything I came up with I tried to photograph.' The combination of Toland's skill and Welles's vision resulted in cinematic perfection.

Also responsible for much of the film's imagery was Linwood Dunn (<72) of RKO's photographic effects department. The master of the optical printer carefully explained the potential of the device to the young director – a kindness he would come to regret. 'Telling Orson about the optical printer was the kiss of death,' Dunn later recalled. 'He used it like a paint brush, which was fine – except that he asked me to do things that I'd never done before. However, he had enough power at the studio to OK the time and money it would take – I learned a lot from it.'

Dunn's optical printer was used to combine elements in many pre-planned shots – for example, extending the production's modest sets into seemingly huge spaces. During post-production, however, Welles began to feel that many scenes lacked the impact that he sought and Dunn was asked to improve many additional shots. Typical of these was the scene in the Thatcher Memorial Library, which started with a camera pull-out from a chiselled inscription on a huge statue plinth to reveal a secretary sitting behind a desk (*below*). Only the plinth had been built and filmed, but Welles decided he would like to see the entire non-existent statue. 'I had a statue made – about two feet high,' explained Dunn, '. . . and I made a straight shot of it, and on the optical printer I made a motorised pan-down from it. Then I made a pan from the scene with the girl and I matched [the two] with a travelling split-screen.' The finished shot looks just as if a monumental statue had indeed presided over the filming.

The entire film is littered with effects work, from the stop-motion-animated construction vehicles of the opening sequence to the shots of the Kane mansion, newspaper offices and political rallies created by matte painters Chesley Bonestell, Fitch Fulton and Mario Larrinaga. The greatest effects, however, were those achieved by Dunn and his optical printer. Dunn later estimated that over 50 per cent of *Citizen Kane* was optically improved or altered, and that only he and editor Robert Wise (1914–2005) might ever be able to identify all the changes made.

Citizen Kane is hailed by many as one of the greatest films ever made. Its narrative structure, performances, editing and cinematography have earned volumes of praise. It also demonstrates the most impressive and fascinating display of special effects of its time – assembled by a precocious young film-maker who didn't know enough about Hollywood convention to know when he was breaking with it.

OPTICAL COMPOSITING

While optical printers were used to create many visual tricks, perhaps their most important function was to combine the multiple elements of travelling matte shots in order to create a final composite image. Digital techniques allowing extremely refined composites have now replaced optical techniques throughout the world but the optical processes once used to produce effects remain fascinating and informative.

Optical compositing involved copying the master positive of the background plate, along with the male 'hold-out' matte of the foreground element. These two elements were threaded into the printer head and projected into the camera. The result was a copy of the background scene with an unexposed area that was the shape and size of the foreground element. The film in the camera was then back-wound to the starting position and then exposed to the foreground plate, along with the female 'hold-out' matte. The female matte obscured the already exposed background, allowing the foreground element to fit into the unexposed area of the film. Providing all the elements had been correctly prepared, aligned and exposed, the developed result would be a satisfactory composite of separately filmed background and foreground elements.

Though the principle of compositing travelling matte shots is a simple one, in practice the task was a laborious and exacting art that required the work of highly skilled operators to achieve successful results. Elements that were incorrectly exposed or misaligned by mere thousandths of an inch would result in matte-lines – thin black outlines around the matted elements that made them look as if they had been stuck on top of their environment.

One of the complicating factors of optical printing was the number of elements sometimes required to produce a composite image. Travelling matte composites produced using the blue-screen colour difference process could comprise three individual colour separations (each of these black-and-white images needing to be printed with the correct amount of blue, red or green light), male and female mattes, and the background plate. Six separate pieces of film, therefore, had to be carefully combined to produce the seventh, final, image. When a composite shot included more than a single travelling matte element – such as a space battle involving many spacecraft – dozens or even hundreds of individual film elements may have had to be printed onto the final composite.

The number and complexity of elements that sometimes needed to be combined meant that, in addition to the technical expertise required to operate the printer, first-class administration skills were necessary. During the production of *Star Wars* (1977), Bert Terreri was hired to keep track of all of the optical elements being used. 'When I came on board the film, 50 per cent of the special effects photography was already done', recalls Terreri, now a visual effects supervisor at Rhythm and Hues animation studio. 'They had created thousands of bits of film and no one knew where they all were. I spent six months tracking down all those different pieces of celluloid, logging and preparing them so that the optical printer could put them together.'

As well as identifying and labelling the various elements, an optical administrator oversaw the preparation of those elements and the printing instructions that had to be given to the printer operator – a task called optical line-up. 'The line-up people would plan the actual compositing process', explains Terreri. 'They would look at all the shots to be combined and line them up so that they knew what went with what, and which order it should be assembled in. They would check that all the mattes matched and that no elements overlapped. All the bits of film would then be cleaned and given to the printer operators with a line-up sheet that plotted exactly how every piece of film was to be combined, what type of filters were to be used and so on. A single shot could involve hundreds of bits of film – it was a logistical nightmare and the tiniest mistake could ruin hundreds of hours of work.'

For a composited shot to be successful, its separate elements, all filmed at different times and places, must appear to fit together as a unified whole. One of the keys to the success of such a shot is the relative movement of its individual elements. For example, if an element such as a miniature castle is composited into a background plate of a real landscape, the slightest movement of the castle element will make it appear to slide against its environment, shattering the illusion.

Elements to be composited are therefore usually filmed with a 'locked-off' camera to prevent any movement or with a motion-control camera (146>) to replicate identical camera moves when filming each separate element. However, compositors are sometimes presented with two pieces of film containing images whose movements bear no relation to one another and which must be locked together to produce a convincing composite. In such cases, the exact movements of one image must be 'tracked', so that the other element can be moved frame by frame to match it during compositing. When compositing elements digitally this is an automated task, but in the days of optical printing such shots were a major task.

Fantasy II Film Effects is a much respected Hollywood effects facility that has dealt with some particularly tricky optical tracking shots. 'One of the hardest tracking shots we did was for *Bram Stoker's Dracula* [1992]', says Fantasy II owner Gene Warren. 'There was a sequence in which a coach carrying Keanu Reeves approached Dracula's castle and Keanu had to look from the coach window to see some big blue flames in the distance. Unfortunately, the camera used to film this shot was mounted on the coach itself, so the image was bouncing all over the place. We somehow had to composite a nice steady shot of some blue flames into a shot that was moving about quite dramatically.'

Warren began by studying the film of the background to find an element that could be used as a tracking marker. 'The shot was taken at night and was very dark, but I found a little white pebble in the distance that just caught the light. That was the point that I used to judge the movement of the shot.' Warren then measured the position of the pebble every five frames throughout the 55-frame shot to identify the gross movements of the camera. Those movements were translated into north, south, east and west coordinates, and the flame element was moved accordingly every five frames during the first optical printing test. Test composites were printed onto black-and-white film, which could be developed quickly and studied on a moviola (editing machine). 'I carefully studied each test, and for every frame I noted whether the flames should go a little more to the north, south, east

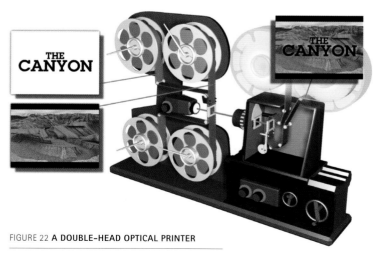

FIGURE 22 **A DOUBLE-HEAD OPTICAL PRINTER**

The double-head printer could be used to combine two images in each pass, making it ideal for creating titles. In the example shown, the black-and-white title card acts as its own matte.

or west in relation to that pebble. I repeated this task over and over, each time refining the movements a little more. Eventually you need to see the film projected on a big screen, because looking at the film on a small moviola you might not spot a very small movement, but on a big screen the flame might still look as if it is moving three feet from left to right.' Warren eventually did 35 black-and-white test shots before the flame elements looked as if they were actually sitting in the background plate. The shot was then composited in colour, and over two weeks of work resulted in two seconds of convincingly blended images.

Once tests had been carried out to ensure that the elements being optically printed actually fitted together, the final look of the composite had to be refined. This involved making sure that the colour of the various composited elements matched perfectly. Again, Gene Warren has had plenty

of experience in making very different elements match. 'We optically composited the shots in the opening battle sequence of *Terminator 2* [1991]', says Warren. 'These shots were combinations of miniature landscapes with model tanks and flying machines and full-scale, live-action shots of real people fighting. Both the full-scale and miniature elements had fires, explosions and laser bursts going off. Our task was to match the elements so that as a big fireball went off in one element, the quality of light in another element of the shot changed in response – as if the fire were casting its light onto that part of the scene.'

Since every element being optically combined usually existed as three black-and-white colour separations, each one could have different amounts of coloured light added to it during printing, thus changing the characteristics of the final image. 'Every frame of those shots had to be

ABOVE LEFT: *The Thief of Bagdad* (1940) was the first film to use an optical printer to combine travelling-matte elements produced using the Technicolor blue-screen process.

ABOVE RIGHT: This optical printer remained in regular use at Gene Warren's Fantasy II Film Effects until 2002, when digital alternatives rendered it obsolete.

RIGHT: An optical line-up sheet. This was used to plot the way in which every element of a composite shot was combined in an optical printer.

VistaVision film, would throw their images into a beam-splitting prism that combined them and redirected them into the camera. By using the Quad, a simple travelling matte shot could be produced in one pass, while complicated shots that contained several hundred elements, like those from the asteroid chase in *Empire*, could be achieved in a fraction of the time that it would take on a traditional printer.'

Edlund's Quad printer was the first to use specially built telecentric lenses, which helped to create highly accurate matte shots. 'When normal lenses emit light, it travels outwards in a cone shape', explains Edlund. 'When you change the focus of something, it not only blurs, it also changes in size. But telecentric lenses emit totally parallel bundles of light, which meant we could alter the focus of the matte, but it would not change size, as would normally be the case. The bottom line was that we could have a hold-out matte in the rear projector of the printer and the colour separation element in the front projector. We could then change the focus of the matte slightly to blur its edges and make it fit the element better. This allowed us to produce some extremely subtle travelling matte shots.'

Edlund started his own effects facility, Boss Films, in 1983, where he continued to design and build state-of-the-art optical printers. By the mid-80s, computers had begun to affect all areas of film production, and they were incorporated into new optical printers to allow precise and repeatable control of focusing, camera and projector movement, and exposure levels. 'At Boss we built two of the finest optical printers ever constructed', states Edlund. 'The ZAP [zoom aerial printer] and the Super Printer were utterly reliable 70 mm printers. We could control the accuracy of matte-fits to within a thousandth of an inch. But the photochemical process of optical printing is ultimately flawed. We spent hundreds of thousands of dollars building precision equipment and controlled every stage of the process as much as we could. But optical processes are affected by variables such as temperature, the quality of the chemical bath being used by the lab to develop film that day, voltage changes, weakening lamps, fading filters, and on and on and on. There are just so many variables that even with the best equipment in the world, a good optical composite relied partly on science and skill, and a little bit on good luck.'

Though he had been responsible for some of the finest optical equipment ever built, when optical compositing began to be replaced by digital alternatives in the early 1990s Edlund was relieved. 'I have no love lost

fiddled with to make the light in the live action match the model, or the model match the live action', says Warren. 'Sometimes we changed the focus on elements slightly, or cut out little filters to affect the light reaching one small area of the film. Sometimes the colour of an element had to be tweaked so minutely that even the most subtle filter was too much and we'd have to print a shot at half exposure with the filter in, back-wind the film and re-expose it with no filter. The amount of work that goes into making shots like that is immense, and when the director sees it and asks for one corner to be just a little bit greener, you have to go back and do it all again!'

Optical printers traditionally consisted of one or sometimes two projectors, but to cope with the increasing demands of modern special effects shots, optical departments began to build machines with additional projectors. Optical printers with three and even four heads were ultimately built (fig. 23).

For Industrial Light and Magic's work on *The Empire Strikes Back* (1980), effects supervisor Richard Edlund (see panel) designed an Academy Award-winning four-headed optical printer that became known as the 'Quad'. 'The Quad was a great time-saver when we were compositing on *Empire*', recalls Edlund. 'The Quad had two projectors mounted at a right angle to another two projectors. The projectors, which could handle both standard 35 mm and

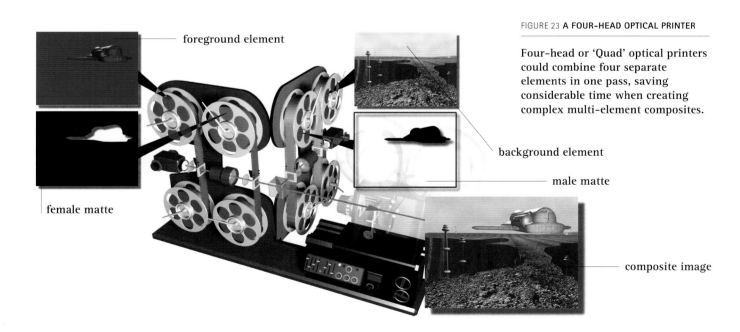

foreground element

female matte

FIGURE 23 **A FOUR-HEAD OPTICAL PRINTER**

Four-head or 'Quad' optical printers could combine four separate elements in one pass, saving considerable time when creating complex multi-element composites.

background element

male matte

composite image

PROFILE **RICHARD EDLUND**

Fascinated by photography from an early age, Richard Edlund (1940–) was trained in high-speed photography and camera maintenance while serving in the US Navy. Edlund then studied at the USC School of Cinema, before learning about special effects production while working at the Joe Westheimer special effects studio in Hollywood.

In 1975 he joined Industrial Light and Magic, the fledgling team that George Lucas had assembled to produce the effects for *Star Wars* (1977). Edlund helped to design the pioneering motion-control system (146>) used to film the fast-paced space battles, a technique that later became a cornerstone of effects production. He also developed the use of blue-screen travelling matte photography and resurrected the VistaVision film format – both of which would become key technologies in the effects revolution that followed the film's success.

While at ILM, Edlund supervised groundbreaking effects for a number of smash-hit films which have now become special effects classics. Among his most memorable achievements were the thrilling asteroid chase in *The Empire Strikes Back* (1980), the supernatural finale of *Raiders of the Lost Ark* (1981),

and the extraordinary imploding house at the climax of *Poltergeist* (1982).

In 1983 Edlund formed his own effects facility, Boss Films, where he continued to oversee the development of sophisticated equipment and effects techniques for films such as *2010* (1984), *Die Hard* (1988) and *Cliffhanger* (1993).

Though Boss Films worked on the cutting edge of technology – contributing early digital effects to *Ghost* (1990) and *Batman Returns* (1992) – Edlund felt unable to continue making the massive investments required to sustain a major independent effects company in the digital age. In 1997 he closed Boss and has worked as an independent effects supervisor since then.

Since 1996 Edlund has been the chairman of the Academy Visual Effects branch. He has himself received Oscars for his contributions to *Star Wars*, *The Empire Strikes Back*, *Raiders of the Lost Ark* and *Return of the Jedi* (1983), and three Scientific and Technical Oscars for the development of the Quad optical printer, the Empire Motion Picture Camera (motion control) system and the 65 mm Zoom Optical Printer.

for the optical printer, he claims. 'In terms of optical printing and photochemical technology, we got about as far as we could go. I had started to realize that we still had all the same limitations that we did back on *Star Wars*. The improvements that we could make to the process were so subtle that, frankly, they just didn't matter.'

Today, the rhythmic click of optical printers has been replaced by the hum of computers in every effects facility around the world. 'We finally stopped using our optical printer in 2002,' says Gene Warren with some

sadness. 'Right up to the end we could still create stunning composites with our old machines. But eventually we just couldn't compete with kids who'd spent a few thousand dollars on a workstation and some software. Anyone can now throw a few layers together at the touch of a few buttons, but there's no doubt that knowing how to really make a shot work – whether digitally or optically – is an art. But the time-honoured technique of coaxing a great shot out of those big old machines is now redundant and that traditional skill will soon be lost for ever.'

FAR LEFT ABOVE: **Despite its state-of-the-art technology, Boss Film's Super Printer was still constrained by the limitations of the optical photochemical process.**

LEFT: **This shot from *Return of the Jedi* (1983) was optically composited by ILM using over 100 separate elements.**

ABOVE: Gene Warren optically composited this combination of miniature background and full-size foreground elements with animated laser beams for *Terminator 2: Judgment Day* (1991). The explosions were created by pyrotechnician Joe Viskocil.

REAR PROJECTION

The shift to studio production with the coming of sound in the late 20s brought the need to simulate realistic outdoor scenes within the confines of the studio. Early methods of travelling matte photography were never wholly successful, failing to produce the quality or quantity of shots necessary to replace location shooting. The solution came with the development of rear projection. This system used a projector positioned behind a translucent screen in order to display previously shot footage of outdoor scenery. Actors were then filmed performing in front of this screen to produce a combination of performer and background scenery.

Rear projection was not a new idea. Special effects pioneer Norman O. Dawn (245>) had experimented with rear projection (sometimes known as 'back projection') for *The Drifter* (1913). Dawn projected photographic stills onto a small frosted glass screen to produce the background for two close-up shots. Finding the results discouraging, however, he abandoned the process to devote time to the more successful development of other effects techniques.

Dawn had experimented with the projection of still images. However, what studio-bound film-makers really needed was the ability to project and photograph moving images behind their actors.

Though the concept is a simple one, the projection and subsequent rephotography of moving images relied on several crucial technical factors. Film cameras and projectors let in or throw out images when their continuously opening and closing shutters are open. Therefore, to photograph a projected moving image, the shutter of a camera has to be synchronized with that of a projector so that the two open and close simultaneously. If the camera shutter is open at the instant the projector shutter is closed, no background image will be photographed. Furthermore, in order to be thrown onto a large screen and photographed clearly, a projected image has to be very bright, demanding the use of a projector of unusually high power. The effective photography of such an image also depends on the utilization of highly sensitive film stocks.

Some success was achieved in the early 1920s when a system was devised for the production of *Sahara* (1923). The shutters of projector and camera were synchronized mechanically by connecting them with a 24 m (80 ft) drive shaft between a specially woven silk projection screen. The system worked, but it was impractical. A similar method was used to create

the images seen on futuristic television in *Metropolis* (1926); in this case, the images were projected onto a ground-glass television screen by projectors concealed at the back of the set.

By happy coincidence, the sound technology that imprisoned film-makers in the studios, making rear projection so desirable, also enabled the effective electronic synchronization of cameras and projectors. Simultaneously, big-screen projection developments meant the creation of particularly powerful projectors, and much faster film stocks were produced. With these developments, rear projection evolved into a highly practical production method just when it was needed most. From the early 1930s it was used to combine foreground studio action with pre-filmed background scenery in every type of production. The method became so routine that rear-projection shots came to be known nondescriptly as 'process shots'. In 1930, Paramount used 146 process shots. By 1932, the figure had risen to over 600.

A method so essential to effective, economical production attracted investment and quickly became highly sophisticated. The first screens used for rear projection were small, fragile, frosted-glass sheets. These were difficult to illuminate evenly and were so small that they could not be used to provide a background to anything more than a close-up of an actor. As the process gained popularity, other screen materials were developed, the standard becoming a form of translucent celluloid pioneered by Sidney Saunders and first used during the production of *King Kong* (1933; 184>). Early celluloid screens could be up to 3.5 m (12 ft) in width, but as directors' rear-projection needs expanded, so did the screens. By the 1940s, screens 14.5 m (48 ft) wide were being used.

Throwing images onto such large screens was a trial for any projector. Projectors used for process shots were not merely high-performance versions of regular cinema apparatus, which allows a degree of 'image weave' – images twitching up and down or from side to side – during projection. Rear-projected images had to be held solidly in register with absolute accuracy, since with fixed scenery objects in the foreground, the smallest imperfections in projection would cause supposedly immovable mountains or cityscapes to appear to wander across the screen, shattering the illusion of reality. To avoid this, process projectors used pilot-pin registration: each frame of film was lifted onto fixed pins and held tight before being projected. Large screens were sometimes serviced by several projectors, each of which threw a segment of the background image onto a portion of the screen – the joins being concealed by judiciously placed

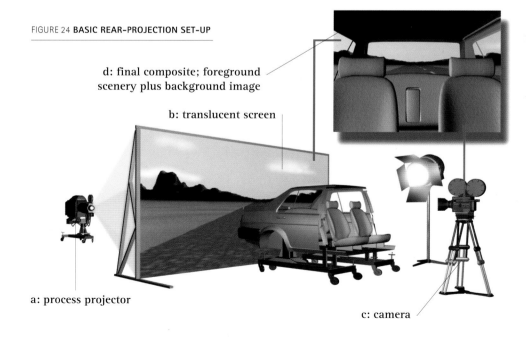

FIGURE 24 **BASIC REAR-PROJECTION SET-UP**

d: final composite; foreground scenery plus background image

b: translucent screen

a: process projector

c: camera

TOP LEFT: **Pre-filmed dinosaur footage was projected behind a studio mock-up of a submarine for** *The Land that Time Forgot* **(1975).**

TOP RIGHT: **Elvis on the beach in** *Fun in Acapulco* **(1963). The sand in the studio foreground does not quite match that in the rear-projected background.**

ABOVE LEFT & RIGHT: **To film large rear-projected backgrounds in colour, a triple-head projector was used to throw three identical overlaid images onto the screen. This system was used at London's Pinewood Studios in the 50s.**

foreground trees or lamp-posts. Large single images could be thrown onto a screen by powerful projectors placed over 45 m (150 ft) behind it. Such projectors used water-cooling devices to prevent the intense heat of their massive lamps from melting the celluloid film.

As with all composite photography, producing a good union of images depended greatly on the ability of a director of photography to reproduce the qualities of the pre-filmed background plate in the foreground action. The focal length of the lens used to film the background had to be replicated on the studio camera. The lighting conditions in the background plate also had to be matched exactly – the human eye can spot the smallest of lighting inconsistencies. Matching studio conditions with those of the background was a complex task. When the background images were rephotographed, their qualities would alter somewhat. Rephotographed images tend to gain contrast, so footage used for rear projection was printed at a lower contrast than normal. Done properly, rear projection could produce an almost seamless blend of foreground and background images. Done badly, it is obvious to even the least sophisticated movie-goer; we have all seen unconvincing driving scenes in which the retreating background scenery appears to bear no relation to the motions of the foreground car.

Some of the most successful applications of the technique were those that used it as an integral part of the storytelling process. Alfred Hitchcock

was a keen exponent of the method and employed it to great effect in many of his films. A particularly ingenious application can be found in Hitchcock's thriller *Foreign Correspondent* (1940). A passenger aircraft hit by gunfire from a German ship dives, out of control, towards the ocean. As it hits the surface, thousands of gallons of sea water smash through the windscreen, flooding the cockpit. To achieve the effect, the studio cockpit set was prepared with white paper windows. During photography, from the inside of the cockpit, footage filmed from an aircraft as it dived towards the ocean was rear-projected onto the paper windscreen, thereby giving the impression that the mock-up plane was plummeting from the sky. As the plane appeared to hit the water, thousands of gallons of water were released from tipper tanks outside the plane. Bursting through the paper windows and replacing the projected images, it engulfed the hapless crew in an instant. The passengers scrambled out of the sinking plane into the water, in a brilliantly staged sequence that involved rear-projected ocean waves and studio water effects.

The arrival of colour photography presented special effects experts with many problems, not least how to adapt rear-projection processes for colour. Early colour film required much more light than black-and-white photography, and even the most powerful rear-screen projectors were incapable of producing bright enough images for rephotography. The problem was solved by the special effects department of Paramount Studios, headed by Farciot Edouart (1897–1980), which devised a system using three powerful projectors. Each projector was loaded with an identical film. By a system of mirrors, their images were overlaid on the screen, providing an image three times as intense. The triple-head system, as it became known, worked particularly well, since rear projection had always produced a slightly grainy background image. With three images focused on one screen, the minute differences between each projected image helped to soften the picture.

Rear projection became less popular after the 50s as travelling matte photography grew more sophisticated and modern equipment allowed for more location shooting. However, the technique continued to be used sparingly for a surprisingly long time – usually providing barely noticeable moving backgrounds during travel scenes, such as the aircraft interior shots for *Air America* (1990). Though still sometimes used in TV production, the process has now been superseded by digital blue-screen techniques.

FRONT PROJECTION

As the name suggests, the technique of front projection involved the projection of background scenery from in front of the action rather than from behind it, as was the case with rear projection. Experiments with the process were made as early as the 30s but it was not until the 50s that interest in the method resulted in the development of a number of practical systems. An American science fiction writer, William Jenkins (nom de plume Murray Leinster; 1896–1975), designed and patented a system in 1952. In 1962 two French inventors, Henri Alekan and Raymond Gérard, patented a similar system, which was taken up by the Rank Organisation in England. This system was then improved by Phillip V. Palmquist, Dr Herbert Meyer and Charles Staffell, who jointly received a Scientific Academy Award for their work in 1968.

The emergence of practical front-projection systems was made possible through the invention in the late 1940s of a reflective road sign material called Scotchlite. Made by the 3M Company, Scotchlite is made of millions of glass beads, each less than 0.25 mm (1/100th in) in diameter. When light hits these beads, it is almost entirely reflected back to its source, a process called retroreflection.

Front projection worked by mounting camera (fig. 25 (a)) and projector (b) at precisely 90° to each other. Placed at 45° between them was a two-way beam-splitting mirror, which reflected 50 per cent of the light that hit it, and allowed the remaining light to pass directly through (c). During photography, the projector threw the background image onto the mirror. Half the light from this image went through the mirror and was wasted. The remaining half was reflected off the mirror toward the acting area. This projected image hit the actors and foreground objects as well as the reflective Scotchlite screen behind them (d). Light hitting actors and foreground objects was refracted in many directions, and, combined with the overpowering effect of foreground lighting, effectively became invisible. Light that hit the reflective background, however, was directed straight back to the source from which it came, with minimal loss of intensity. This reflected light was able to travel back through the half-silvered mirror from which it was previously reflected and then passed directly into the lens of the camera. It was then recorded as an image behind, and surrounding, the foreground objects (e). To a viewer standing to one side of the camera, the shadows of actors or foreground objects on the background screen would be obvious. From the camera viewpoint, however, all foreground objects would cover their own shadows, resulting in a perfectly combined image.

Front projection had a number of distinct advantages over rear projection. Because Scotchlite is so reflective, the projected image did not need to be as strong as that required for rear projection, enabling the use of much smaller projectors. Front projection could be used in a relatively small studio space, since both camera and projector were mounted on the same side of the screen; rear projection, on the other hand, required as much space behind the screen as in front. The life of the cinematographer was also made easier when using front projection. With rear projection great care had to be taken to ensure that the lighting of the foreground elements did not fall onto the backing screen – any such 'spill' would wash out the projected image in those areas. Such problems were minimal with front projection, because any spill would be directed back to its source rather than into the camera.

The first time front projection was used for a major feature film was in *2001: A Space Odyssey* (1968). Though many appreciated that the stunning space scenes were created using superior special effects, few probably gave a second thought to the early sequence of prehistoric apes fighting in the desert.

FIGURE 25 **FRONT PROJECTION**

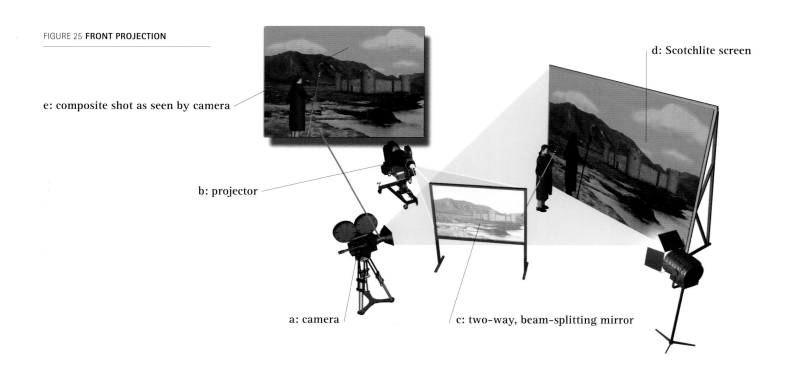

e: composite shot as seen by camera

d: Scotchlite screen

b: projector

a: camera

c: two-way, beam-splitting mirror

Kubrick didn't travel to Africa to film the so-called 'dawn of man' sequence, although it certainly appears to take place in an expansive natural environment. For this, and several other sequences in the film, Kubrick used front projection. After this outstanding debut, the process was signed up for a number of large-scale features, notably *Battle of Britain* (1969), *On Her Majesty's Secret Service* (1969), *Silent Running* (1971) and *Young Winston* (1972).

Ingenious use of front projection was made during the filming of *Tora! Tora! Tora!* (1970). The American effects veteran L.B. Abbott had planned to employ it for a shot in which American aircraft attack a surfaced Japanese submarine. Footage of the attacking aircraft was to be filmed elsewhere, while Abbott and his crew built a full-sized mock-up of the submarine with a Scotchlite screen behind it. But when the aircraft footage arrived, it was unsuitable. Abbott decided to achieve the scene by using a blue-screen shot instead – adding the aircraft footage at a later date. Finding that a big enough blue screen was not available, Abbott and his team thought again. They realized that they could convert their front-projection screen into an instant blue screen, by a kind of secondary special effect. Abbott filled a small glass container with blue water. This was placed in the projector of the front-projection set-up and used to create a front-projected blue screen. Amazingly, the improvised blue screen had significant advantages over a traditional blue screen. Normally, the water and wet submarine decks in such a scene would have reflected the blue of the screen and caused blue-spill problems during the compositing process. But in this case, because most of the front-projected blue light was reflected directly back into the camera by the Scotchlite screen, there was not a gleam left to reflect off the water. The principles of Abbott's experiment were later developed into a system called 'The Blue Max', which was successfully used to achieve large-scale composite photography in films such as *2010* (1984).

Scotchlite has been used in a number of films for purposes other than front projection. Much of the Krypton set in *Superman* (1978) was covered in the material to lend it a glowing, ethereal look. The radiant white costumes of the actors in these scenes were also made from Scotchlite. The material has also been adopted by model-makers, who have employed it to produce glaring spacecraft lights or vehicle headlamps where the use of miniature electric lighting within the model itself would be impractical or uneconomical.

ABOVE: **Superman (Christopher Reeve) speeds to avert another disaster in this Zoptic shot from *Superman* (1978).**

ZOPTICS

Superman (1978) was also the first film to use an imaginative variation of front projection. The plausibility of the film depended on convincing audiences that Superman was actually flying – like a bird or a plane. Among other means used to get actor Christopher Reeve off the ground was a method patented in 1978 by the optical expert Zoran Perisic, dubbed 'Zoptics' (fig. 26).

It was initially thought that scenes where Superman was required to fly towards or away from the camera could be achieved by suspending Reeve from wires and physically propelling him over considerable distances. Not only would this have been uncomfortable and dangerous for the actor, however, it was also about as feasible as location filming on the planet Krypton. A large and complex flying rig would have been needed, built over a long distance, with massive lighting set-ups to light the actor through the

FIGURE 26 **ZOPTICS**

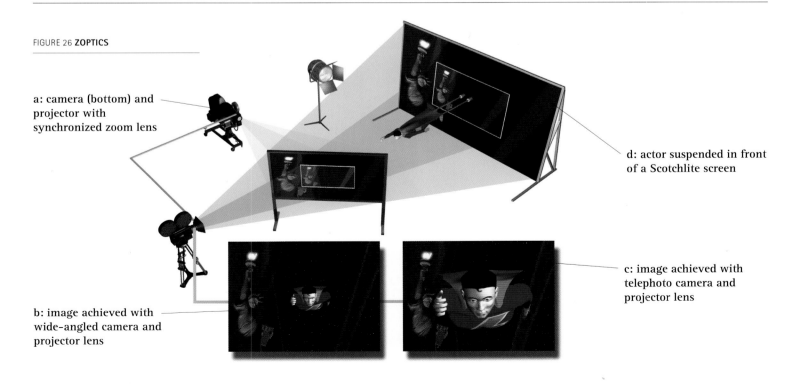

a: camera (bottom) and projector with synchronized zoom lens

d: actor suspended in front of a Scotchlite screen

b: image achieved with wide-angled camera and projector lens

c: image achieved with telephoto camera and projector lens

flight – and a superhero of a camera operator to keep focus on the hurtling man of steel. The Zoptic system allowed Superman's long flights to be achieved in a small studio without any of these problems. To achieve the effect, both the camera and projector of a front-projection set-up were fitted with matching zoom lenses (a). The lenses were both set at the same focal length and electronically linked to zoom in and out in unison. This meant that if the projector lens was used at a short focal length – throwing a large image onto the screen – the camera lens would also be at a wide angle in order to photograph the whole picture (b). If the projector lens was altered – so that the image on the screen grew smaller – the camera lens would also change, zooming in to keep the projected image exactly the same apparent size when photographed (c).

With the size of the projected image growing and shrinking on the screen, and the camera lens changing to keep the photographed image the same size, any object placed in a fixed position between camera and screen would appear to be moving, rather than the other way around (d). In this case, Superman was suspended in front of the screen, and as the projected image behind him shrank and the camera's zoom lens followed it, he appeared to fly towards the camera.

INTROVISION

A variation on front projection has been used to place actors within pre-filmed backgrounds. In a complex process perfected by the Introvision Corporation in the 80s, a 2-D projected background could be divided into a number of apparent 'layers', with performers seeming to act 'within' these layers – thus transforming a 2-D image into a convincing 3-D view.

Like all front-projection processes, Introvision (fig. 27) used a camera (a)

and a projector (b) set at 90° to one another with a half-silvered beam-splitting mirror placed at 45° between them (c). This mirror reflected half of the light from the projector onto a Scotchlite backdrop (d), which reflected the light back into the camera. The other half of the light from the projector passed directly through the half-silvered mirror. In other front-projection processes, this light was 'wasted' and was simply absorbed by a piece of black velvet. Introvision, however, made use of this light by replacing the black velvet with another Scotchlite screen (e), in order to reflect the second portion of the image back to the camera. The camera therefore received two identical images, both of which had come from the same source, but had taken different routes back to the camera.

The technique used a system of carefully placed male and female mattes (f) such that the images to be returned to the camera from the Scotchlite screens were split into the background (g) and foreground (h) parts of the original projected image. In the final composite (i) the foreground was in effect superimposed on the background so that an actor placed in front of a background (j) could be made to appear as if they are moving about between the background and foreground elements, creating a 3-D effect.

The Introvision process was first employed extensively in *Outland* (1981) to combine actors with models of the mining colony of Con-Am 27. It was also used in *Under Siege* (1992), *Army of Darkness* (1993) and in *Stand by Me* (1986), where it placed a group of children on a bridge as a speeding train approached them. The same process thrust Harrison Ford into a shot of a train smashing into an overturned bus in *The Fugitive* (1993). This composite shot would normally have needed complex post-production, but Introvision enabled Ford to defy death 'live' in the studio.

FIGURE 27 **INTROVISION**

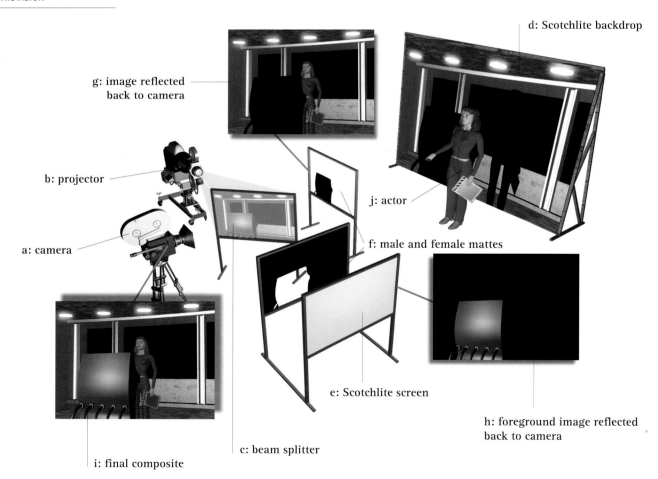

g: image reflected back to camera

d: Scotchlite backdrop

b: projector

j: actor

a: camera

f: male and female mattes

e: Scotchlite screen

h: foreground image reflected back to camera

c: beam splitter

i: final composite

LEFT: Introvision was used to insert Harrison Ford into a shot of a spectacular train crash for *The Fugitive* (1993). The train-crash footage was filmed using a miniature train (*far left*).

BELOW: Jaws (Richard Kiel) pursues James Bond down a South American river in *Moonraker* (1979). The performers and the boat were filmed in Pinewood Studios, while the pre-filmed river footage was added using front projection.

2001: A SPACE ODYSSEY

Based on a short story by Arthur C. Clarke, *2001: A Space Odyssey* (1968) has stood the test of time, remaining one of the most admired and influential visual effects films ever created.

Director Stanley Kubrick (1928–99) recognized that the minimalist dialogue and esoteric drama of his film might confuse audiences, and that the power of its visuals would have to redeem the lack of a conventional narrative. To Kubrick, the popcorn fantasy of Hollywood's earlier space-travel films was anathema – he was determined that his film would be scientifically accurate and the closest encounter that audiences might ever experience. To help achieve this vision, the director assembled an effects team that was a unique combination of old-time experience and gifted young talent. For over two years the team occupied London's Elstree Studios, painstakingly creating the most astonishing special effects that had ever reached the screen.

In the 'dawn of man' sequence, mankind's apelike ancestors inhabit an arid and rocky landscape. The apes, played by performers in costumes, used a revolutionary new type of facial mask designed by Stuart Freeborn (283>) who, many thought, deserved an Oscar for his work (ironically, it went instead to John Chambers for *Planet of the Apes*). To provide the prehistoric landscape Kubrick turned to the veteran British effects supervisor Tom Howard, Oscar winner for effects on *The Thief of Bagdad* (1940) and *Blithe Spirit* (1945).

Howard persuaded Kubrick to attempt the relatively untried process of front projection, and built an apparatus to project 20 x 25 cm (8 x 10 in) transparencies of African landscapes onto an enormous 12 x 27 m (40 x 90 ft) Scotchlite screen. Production designer Ernie Archer constructed a rocky landscape set on a revolving platform, which allowed it to be filmed from various angles against the fixed background screen. The composite images are extraordinarily convincing; their fakery can only be spotted in a leopard's eyes which, acting like Scotchlite, glow eerily as they reflect projected light back into the camera.

To produce the space sequences, an early motion-control system was built to move the camera past the enormous spaceship models. Dismissing blue-screen and other travelling matte processes, Kubrick insisted that as much compositing work as possible be done in-camera. Producing shots of the model spacecraft with live action seen inside their cockpit windows involved filming each model twice. A first pass of the camera filmed the model with its windows blacked out; a second pass then filmed the spacecraft draped in black velvet with only the windows showing. Fitted with miniature Scotchlite screens, these windows had pre-filmed cockpit footage projected into them.

To place the ships in a star-filled space environment, thousands of hand-drawn mattes were traced and inked by teams of students before being printed together with photographed star artwork and then combined with the first-generation spaceship footage to produce composites of the highest quality.

Perhaps the film's most startlingly original effect was the climactic psychedelic light show known as the 'Stargate' sequence. Kubrick didn't know exactly what he wanted to see, asking only that the camera appear to 'go through something'. The task fell to the youngest member of the effects team, Douglas Trumbull. Trumbull devised a system that he called 'slit scan' (178>), and spent nine months photographing backlit artwork one frame at a time to produce a streaking rush of colour and light the like of which had never been seen before.

Initially released to a mixture of hostility and frank bewilderment, *2001* was not a huge commercial success but it did acquire a considerable cult following. In the following 30 years there have been many outstanding special effects achievements – often directly influenced by the innovations of *2001*. Yet it is testimony to the vision of its makers that when viewed today, the film remains visually convincing. In the words of the film's own publicity, *2001: A Space Odyssey* remains 'the ultimate trip'.

ELECTRONIC ADVANCES

Optically combining separately filmed elements – either by a system of travelling mattes or by front or rear projection – was a time-consuming and ultimately inexact process. Even using highly skilled operators and the most sophisticated equipment, merging images in this way always involved some degree of image degradation and placed limitations on creative possibilities.

In the mid-70s, new developments in computer processing power and digital technology ushered in a new era, since it became possible to combine and manipulate the relatively low-resolution video images used in television production in ways that were previously impossible. In 1973 the UK company Quantel developed a practical system for converting analogue TV signals into digital ones, thereby enabling them to be altered in the digital realm. Audiences around the world saw TV coverage of the 1976 Montreal Olympic Games transformed by early digital processes, which enabled the use of small on-screen inserts showing events from multiple camera angles simultaneously – a dramatic new experience.

In 1978 Quantel introduced the first machines that could alter digital television images to produce an array of visual effects. Having watched flat television images for 30 years, audiences began to see their TV pictures turned like the pages of a book, or rolled up like a newspaper. In the 80s, Quantel continued to create revolutionary tools for manipulating television images and effectively created the market for television graphics. The introduction of their 'Harry' system in 1986 allowed the live multi-layering of video images and the creation of a host of other spectacular visual effects.

Digital technology is an immensely powerful tool for film and television production because it offers complete control over image quality. Film is an analogue medium: it records and stores a representation of the images to which it is exposed through a process of transcription. As light hits the film emulsion, a likeness in one medium is transferred, or transcribed, into another medium. In other words, the physical qualities of the photosensitive emulsion on a piece of film are directly altered by the qualities of the light that hits it. Similarly, when an image is recorded onto analogue videotape, light (measured in lux) enters the camera and is transcribed into an electrical signal (measured in volts), which is recorded by physically altering the magnetic field on the tape. In all analogue systems, transcribing one quality into another quality with a direct physical relationship means that some attributes of the original subject are lost, and degradation of both master and copy is inevitable when further copies are made.

BELOW: **An example of the spectacular 'page turn' effect achieved with a Quantel Mirage system in the 80s.**

RIGHT: **A shot from the television coverage of the 1976 Montreal Olympics. Multiple picture-within-picture effects were achieved courtesy of Quantel's digital technology.**

BELOW RIGHT: **An operator uses a graphics tablet and pen to manipulate and composite television-quality images using Quantel's pioneering Paint Box system.**

Digital systems, on the other hand, deal purely in abstract numbers. When an image or sound is recorded digitally, its qualities are measured and converted into a series of binary numbers. Binary numbers have only two states: 1 and 0. These can represent on and off, high and low, or black and white, for example, and are the basis of the mathematics used in digital systems and computing. In digital image recording, light is converted into an abstract string of numbers that have no intrinsic physical relationship to the original image. The resulting digital file, simply a huge string of zeros and ones, can be manipulated by a computer according to mathematical formulae, or algorithms, in order to change, filter and refine the information contained in the file. The information can then be copied or transferred repeatedly without any loss of quality because a computer cannot misinterpret a zero or a one and accidentally convert, warp or dilute it.

With the startling progress of digital television technology in the early 80s, those involved in film production began to seek ways to apply digital techniques to the world of celluloid-based imagery. If a way could be found to process film in much the same way that TV images were being manipulated, then processes such as optical printing and rear projection, with their associated problems and constraints, would be a thing of the past.

Two major problems faced those who wished to use digital technology for the manipulation of filmed images. Motion picture images are of a significantly higher resolution than television images, and an immense amount of processing power and memory is therefore needed to store and manipulate them. Computers in the early 80s were neither powerful nor cost-effective enough to process and store more than a few frames of film-resolution images. Even if the massive amounts of data involved could be handled, no one had yet devised an economical and efficient way of converting analogue film images into digital information and, after alteration, converting the finished work back into film for distribution and exhibition. A practical means of getting film images in and out of the digital realm would be the key to unlocking the potential of the computer in the production of film special effects.

THE DIGITAL GATEWAY

Finding an effective way of getting filmed images in and out of the digital realm became the prime goal of a number of people in the mid-80s. Among them was Dr Mike Boudry, co-founder of The Computer Film Company (CFC – now called Framestore CFC). 'In 1984 we realized that there was the potential for using the computer to combine the sort of image manipulation that was emerging in TV production with the tasks that had traditionally been done optically on film', says Boudry. 'We thought that this could radically change the type of effects that could be achieved for feature films'.

However, Boudry and his colleagues quickly discovered that their goal was still beyond the power of the computers of the day. 'We did a few early calculations and realized that the type of computer needed to achieve what we were looking for would have to be much faster than anything available in 1984', he explains. 'However, computers were evolving so fast that we thought it would only be a matter of time before machines that were affordable and fast enough would become available, so we continued to develop the system that we had in mind'.

'Our goal was to start with filmed images, get them into a computer, manipulate them and then put them back onto film with no loss of quality', explains Boudry. 'We looked around for anything on the market that could do anything vaguely like what we wanted', he remembers. 'We found a fairly primitive camera that was designed to scan and digitize printed documents. It turned out to be completely useless for our purposes, but we butchered it, found out how it worked, and reused its useful components in our own film scanner'. Boudry and his team built one of the first practical film scanners. Their machine, completed in mid-1987, was the computer-age equivalent of the optical printer. Instead of copying images from one film to another, their device converted analogue film images into digital files. 'Our scanner was loaded with the film to be digitized', explains Boudry. 'A very bright light source then illuminated the whole frame of film, which was focused through a lens onto a CCD [charge-coupled device] array. The CCD converted light from the film into electrical signals that were then converted into digital information. The scanner produced digital information at a rate of two megabytes per second – which doesn't sound like much now, but back in 1987 that was pretty awesome'.

The next task was to create a method of recording the digital images held in the computer back onto film. 'We didn't have time to build a proper recorder by the time we started doing commercial work', admits Boudry, 'so we got a really high-resolution Sony monitor and stuck it at one end of a cupboard and put a film camera at the other end. We basically filmed the finished images directly off the screen – and the results were surprisingly good. We used to talk in awestruck tones about our "recorder" whenever we met our clients, but we never let them anywhere near it in case they noticed it was effectively just a camera and a monitor in a cupboard!'

Within a year, the CFC team had built a much more professional device, replacing the monitor with a high-resolution cathode-ray tube which presented digital images to a camera with specially designed lenses. 'By the time we had our scanner and recorder ready, we had developed the hardware and software to manipulate the images', says Boudry. 'We did our first feature film work for a movie called *The Fruit Machine* [1988]'. The low-budget British film featured a character obsessed by dolphins, who in one scene imagines himself actually turning into a dolphin. 'We had footage of the character diving into the water and got some footage of a dolphin in roughly the same position', remembers Boudry. 'After scanning the two pieces of film into the computer, we used our new software to change the man into the dolphin by producing a sort of mix of the two elements. It wasn't a "morph" [109>] – we called it an "artistic transition". It's quite embarrassing to look at now, but at the time it knocked everybody's socks off'. Boudry is careful to point out that their dolphin shot certainly was not the first digital work to go into a feature film. 'By that time Disney had used digital effects in *Tron* [1982], and ILM had done the digital effects for *Young Sherlock Holmes* [1985]. But those films had used digital elements that were produced within the computer and then output to film, before being composited in the old-fashioned optical way. As far as I'm aware, our dolphin shot was the first full-frame digital composite to go into a feature film'.

The experience of Boudry and his colleagues was not unique. In the late 80s a number of companies wishing to work in digital effects independently developed their own scanning and recording equipment. In 1995 the Academy of Motion Picture Arts and Sciences awarded technical Oscars to Mike Boudry and a number of other individuals and companies who had been simultaneously instrumental in the development of the technology. Today, scanning and recording equipment is commercially produced by a number of manufacturers and can be purchased by any company that can afford the huge sums that such systems cost.

Modern film scanners work on the same principles as the original machine built by Mike Boudry and his team. Several types are commercially available, but the Northlight scanners operated by the visual effects company Cinesite Europe are of typical design. 'Scanning is a very expensive operation', says Mitch Mitchell, head of imaging at Cinesite. 'When the first edit of a film has been completed, we get instructions from the editor about which footage will be needed for some sort of digital manipulation. We scan only the footage that is needed – with a "handle" of a few frames either side'.

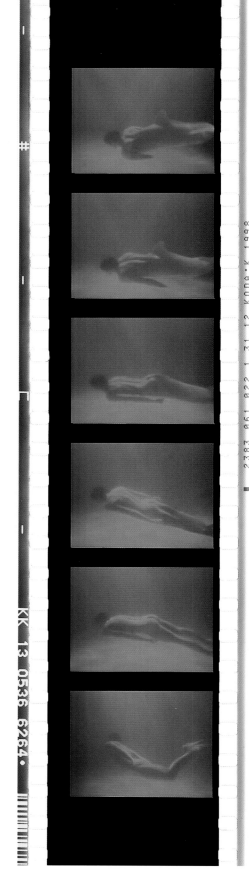

ABOVE: **Early digital film effects were used to turn a human swimmer into a dolphin in this groundbreaking sequence from** *The Fruit Machine* **(1988).**

FIGURE 28 **FILM SCANNER**

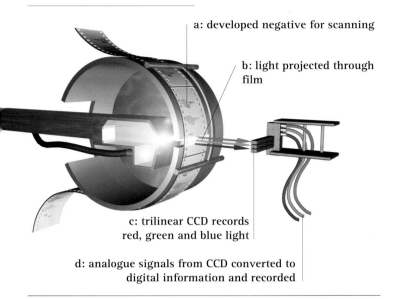

a: developed negative for scanning

b: light projected through film

c: trilinear CCD records red, green and blue light

d: analogue signals from CCD converted to digital information and recorded

Once selected, the length of original camera negative is loaded onto the scanner, an impressive device that stands inside a room kept at a positive atmospheric pressure so that dust is not sucked in when its doors are opened. Once the machine has been loaded with the negative, it is operated from a computer in a separate control room.

The film to be scanned is passed through an assembly (fig. 28) in which high-intensity light is shone through the negative so that it can be photographed by a trilinear charge-coupled device (CCD). CCDs contain thousands of minute sensors called 'photosites', each of which measures the quality of the light hitting it. A trilinear CCD has three layers, each of which is sensitive only to red, green or blue light. When each photosite has measured the light to which it is exposed it creates an analogue electrical signal which is then converted into digital information that can be recorded on tape or on a computer hard disk.

During scanning, the analogue medium of film grain is converted into its digital equivalent: pixels. Pixels (derived from the term 'picture elements') are the basic building blocks of a digital image.

When examined closely it can be seen that a digital image is simply a mosaic comprising millions of tiny coloured squares – pixels. The pixels are so small that when seen from a distance they 'merge' to form a complete picture. The more pixels used to define an image, the higher the resolution and the better the picture quality (fig. 29).

'At Cinesite we scan our 35 mm film images, at a resolution of 4K,' says Mitchell. 'That means that during scanning our CCD array divides an image into a grid that is about 4,000 pixels [4K] horizontally, to be precise it is 4,096 pixels wide and 3,112 pixels high. This produces an image that is made up of over 13 million pixels. A 4K image is about 50 megabytes of information – which is far more than we need for most purposes,' explains Mitchell. 'So once we've captured the 4,000 horizontal pixels, we normally subsample them by taking a reading of each pixel and its neighbours to produce a sort of "average". The computer then calculates a new image that is 2K. With 2,048 pixels horizontally it's half the resolution of a 4K image and at 12 megabytes is about one-quarter the digital file size. This allows our computers to work with the images much more quickly. The proprietary downsampling process we use at Cinesite is known as super2k and it produces much sharper images than a straight 2K scan.'

As well as choosing the number of pixels used to build a picture, the number of colours used to describe each pixel is also optional. Film is such an effective medium for capturing images that it actually records far more colour information than the eye can perceive. For example, our eyes can detect the difference between two very similar dark colours much better than the difference between two very light colours. Because of this, most scanning systems do not capture all of the information held within an original negative. Instead, they save on memory and processing power by selectively filtering out some of the colour information that our eye will not perceive. This process, called 'compression', is used in one form or another by most equipment used to acquire, store or manipulate digital images.

Each pixel is composed of three component colours: red, green and blue. By varying the quantity of these colours in each pixel, every colour in the visible spectrum can be reproduced – just like mixing paints on a palette (fig. 30, 94>). The number of different shades of red, green and blue available for adding to the mix is dependent on the number of 'bits' (binary digits) of information used for each component element. This is known as 'bit-depth' (94>) or 'colour-depth.'

'There are differing opinions about how much colour detail it is necessary to capture from an original image,' explains Kevin Wheatley, Senior Technology and Network Systems Architect at Cinesite. 'The bit-depth [fig. 30] that different effects facilities work at depends very much on the type of work that needs to be done and the system being used. Video effects facilities creating work for television often work at eight bits, but film is processed in at least ten bits. This means that our images have a palette of over 1.7 billion possible colours. For some purposes images are captured at as much as sixteen bits, and that gives us a palette of over 280 trillion different colours – but it's very impractical.'

FIGURE 29 **PIXELS**

A digital image is made up of thousands of tiny coloured squares, or pixels, which become increasingly apparent when the image is magnified.

Once an image has been scanned, it is saved as a digital file on digital tape or disk. The digital file for each image consists of two elements. A header contains all the information that the computer needs to read the image, such as its bit-depth and resolution plus important data such as the original film key codes – barcoded numbers that run along the side of modern 35 mm film to identify each frame. This is followed by the bulk of the information about the individual pixels and their characteristics. This data can be downloaded into a computer system and used anywhere in a digital environment to achieve the necessary image manipulation. Once the images have been altered and approved, they are recorded back onto film.

There are two methods of recording digital images onto film. Cinesite uses ArriSpeed laser recorders, which 'paint' the image onto film with a laser. 'Our images are normally subsampled down to 2K during scanning,' says Mitchell, 'but before putting them back to film, the same process is applied in reverse to produce images that are 4K resolution once again. These are then fed to the recorder to produce a new negative on extremely fine-grained film stock. A release print derived from this negative is virtually indistinguishable from a print optically copied from the original camera negative.'

Laser recorders (fig. 31) contain three different-coloured lasers: red, green and blue. As the digital file is read, each of the three lasers emits the quantity of coloured laser light needed to produce the colour in each pixel to be recorded on film. The three separate laser beams are then mixed to produce a single beam that is precisely the correct colour for each pixel. This laser is directed onto a spinning mirror, which focuses the light onto a piece of unexposed negative film. The moving mirror draws a single line of the image onto the film, then the frame of film is moved up one pixel and the next line is drawn. An ArriSpeed laser recorder takes approximately four seconds to emit, mix and record the 13 million pixels in a 4K image.

The alternative to the laser recorder is the cathode-ray tube (CRT) recorder (fig. 32). The CRT recorder is essentially a high-quality film camera (a) focused on a high-resolution black-and-white cathode-ray tube (b). Each digital image is displayed on the CRT screen three times – once for each of its three colour components (c). The camera has a set of three coloured filters that mechanically swing in front of the lens during the recording of each image (d). Each frame of film takes approximately 20 seconds to record (e).

Once the images have been recorded onto film it is developed to produce a negative which can be edited into the final version of the movie.

FIGURE 31 **LASER FILM RECORDER**

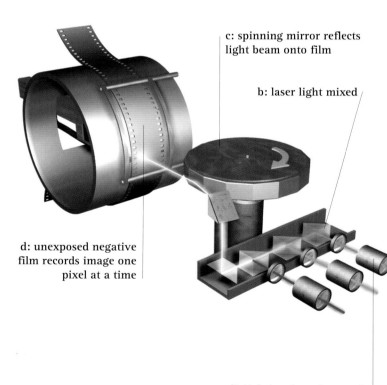

c: spinning mirror reflects light beam onto film

b: laser light mixed

d: unexposed negative film records image one pixel at a time

a: digital signal produces red, green and blue laser light

FIGURE 30 **BIT–DEPTH**

 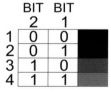 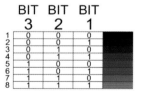

One mathematical bit can define only two gradations of colour (on and off); two bits can define four, three bits eight, four bits sixteen, and so on. Feature-film work is normally achieved with either eight or ten bits per channel. Using eight bits per channel, for example, produces a 24-bit image (eight bits for each of the red, green and blue channels). Eight bits per channel means that each of the three colour components can have 256 possible gradations, and the three combined can produce a pixel with almost 17 million potential colour variations. As well as the red, green and blue channels, each pixel normally contains a fourth channel, known as the alpha channel. This is used to control the tranparency of pixels and to produce mattes for digital compositing.

ABOVE: Negative film to be converted into digital files is threaded into the Northlight scanner at Cinesite Europe.

ABOVE RIGHT: Finished scenes are transferred back onto negative film using this Arri laser recorder at Cinesite.

FIGURE 32 **CRT FILM RECORDER**

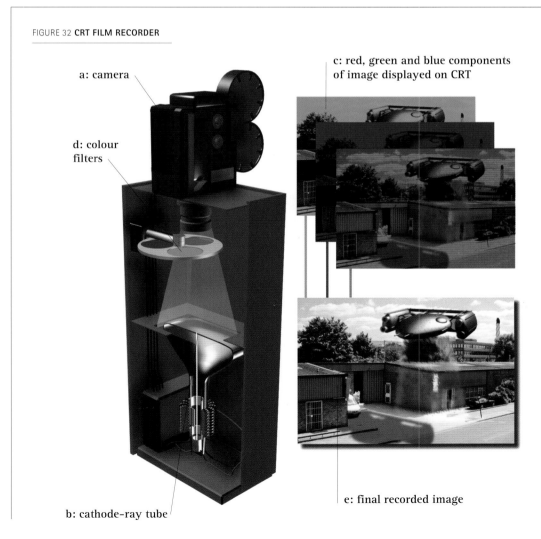

a: camera

d: colour filters

c: red, green and blue components of image displayed on CRT

b: cathode-ray tube

e: final recorded image

FIGURE 33 **VIDEO INTERLACING**

Video images are made up of interlacing 'odd' and 'even' fields. These are scanned onto cathode-ray TV screens one line at a time. The two sets of scan lines merge to form a complete image.

DIGITAL CINEMATOGRAPHY

The scanning and recording of filmed images is an expensive and time-consuming part of the visual effects post-production process. While most movies are still originated on 35 mm film, high-definition (HD) digital video has now become a viable method of capturing, processing and recording high-quality motion picture images. Footage filmed in this way starts life as digital information and so does not need to be scanned before it is ready for use in a digital post-production environment.

Video has traditionally been a hugely inferior medium: its resolution, colour information, exposure range and depth of field falling far below the abilities of film. Recent technical advancements have now addressed many of these deficiencies. However, the greatest difference between ordinary video cameras and those now used to shoot feature films is the way in which the picture signal is recorded. Unlike film, which photographs and displays 24 'whole' images per second, video divides each image into hundreds of horizontal 'scan' lines. These lines are numbered and then recorded as two separate sets of information or 'fields'. One field contains all the even-numbered lines and the other field contains the odd-numbered lines (fig. 33).

The Sony HDW-F900 was the first camera widely used for digital motion picture photography.

When video images are displayed on a television screen all the even-numbered lines are first written on the screen from left to right, top to bottom. Next, the odd-numbered lines are written to fill in all the gaps. The process of recording and displaying alternating video fields in this way is called 'interlacing'. In the US, where TVs show 30 frames per second, 60 separate interlaced fields are therefore displayed every second. In Europe, TVs show 25 frames, or 50 fields, every second.

Video's use of interlaced fields is in stark contrast to the comparatively simple way that motion picture equipment captures and then displays 24 photographic images every second. When feature films are transferred to video each frame of film must therefore be split up into fields and interlaced. Furthermore, the 24 frames that make up every second of a feature film must also be converted into the 30 frames that are required for every second of television (25 in Europe). To do this, film is run through a Telecine machine, which scans each frame and converts it into two interlaced fields. Some of these fields are then recorded twice, repeating some picture information in order to create 30 new video frames out of every 24 original film frames (fig. 34).

The high-definition digital cameras used when shooting feature films are known as '24P' cameras. This means that they can record 24 complete 'progressive' frames per second: the horizontal lines in each frame are recorded progressively, one after the other to produce one complete image, rather than splitting them up into two separately recorded interlaced fields. This footage is therefore directly comparable to that created with a motion picture camera and can easily be recorded onto celluloid for exhibition in a theatre.

The first video camera widely used in movie production was the Sony HDW-F900. This camera was developed for feature film use by Sony in conjunction with the lens manufacturer Panavision and the production company Lucasfilm, who planned to shoot some of *Star Wars*: Episode I *The Phantom Menace* (1999) and all of Episode II *Attack of the Clones* (2002) digitally.

Digital cameras record images by channelling light through a lens onto a CCD (<92). In the case of the Sony HDW-F900 and its successors, three CCDs each measure either the red, blue or green content of the scene. Each of these CCDs has an array of 1,920 horizontal photosites and 1,080 vertical photosites. This results in a 2K image that is made up of over 2 million pixels, similar in resolution to the film prints used to display feature films in movie theatres. In addition, specially designed Panavision lenses and advanced image-processing algorithms mean that the latest cameras are capable of producing uncompressed 10-bit colour images of a quality comparable to film.

Most digital cameras process their images during filming, regulating white balance and correcting gamma (a measure of contrast) in order to produce a pleasing image before it is recorded on tape. The Grass Valley Viper FilmStream camera, however, sends all of the image information that it

FIGURE 34 **FILM TO VIDEO CONVERSION**

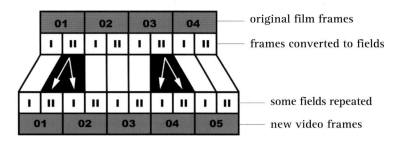

original film frames

frames converted to fields

some fields repeated

new video frames

When film is converted to video, some fields are repeated in order to stretch the 24 frames used in each second of film to the 30 frames per second required by video. Here, four frames of film are converted to five frames of video.

collects directly to a hard disk recorder without any form of compression or image signal processing. The resulting images, which look somewhat flat and have a green tinge, contain far more information than those produced by camcorders recording to tape, and this data can be processed and manipulated with great flexibility during post-production. At 8 megabytes per frame this camera produces almost a gigabyte (1 billion bytes) of information every five seconds while filming, requiring a fibre-optic cable to carry the data stream from the camera to a hard disk recorder.

Opinions vary as to whether digital cinematography will become the dominant form of origination for motion pictures. A number of high-profile feature films, including *Sky Captain and the World of Tomorrow* (2004), *Star Wars*: Episode III *Revenge of the Sith* (2005) and *Superman Returns* (2006), have already been shot digitally and many more are being planned. Many

directors and cinematographers think that video will never rival the aesthetic qualities of film, while others believe that it already has that ability. A number of directors including George Lucas and James Cameron have declared that they will never shoot on film again, whereas others, including Steven Spielberg, have said they will continue to use film until it is no longer available. Whatever people feel about digital cinematography, however, there can be no doubt that the medium does offer a number of distinct production advantages over the use of film.

The principal advantage is that of cost. A 50-minute digital videotape costs around $80 (and can be reused). The same amount of 35 mm film would cost approximately $4,000 to purchase, process and print. *Star Wars* producer Rick McCallum has estimated that $1.8 million was saved by shooting the 220 hours of footage for *Attack of the Clones* on video rather than film. If a camera is linked to a hard disk recorder then no tape need be used at all during acquisition.

Digital cinematography also has a number of practical benefits. Because HD tapes are 50 minutes in length they need to be changed less frequently during a day's filming. Film cameras, on the other hand, can only shoot for about 10 minutes before the reel of film needs to be replaced and the camera mechanisms checked for dirt or hairs. This difference can save several hours a day when shooting digitally. It can also help elicit better performances from actors whose concentration is not continually broken while the film is changed.

In the past, directors had to wait until the following day's 'rushes' to see if the previous day's work was successful or if retakes would be necessary. But when shooting digitally, directors and cinematographers can immediately review shots on large high-definition monitors in order to evaluate lighting, camera moves or performances. It is also possible for pre-produced visual effects or pre-viz material (230>) to be quickly and temporarily combined with live action for on-set test viewings. Because digital footage does not have to be developed and processed, scenes shot in the morning can already be cut into the working edit of a film by lunchtime.

Perhaps the greatest advantage of digital cinematography is the fact that images are recorded as high-definition digital files. These files can then be copied and manipulated during the post-production process without the need for expensive and time-consuming film scanning and without any loss of quality.

RIGHT: **George Lucas (***seated, centre***) and his crew view the filming of scenes for** *Star Wars*: Episode III *Revenge of the Sith* **(2005) on high-definition monitors, allowing them to study each shot in minute detail during and immediately after recording.**

-PRODUCTION

rs have become increasingly reliant on digital post-
litionally, movies were edited in a manual fashion.
?ces of positive film, shot by shot, and stuck them
.g ... or tape.

ıaking advantage of technology developed for television production,
film-makers now use computers to edit their productions. Movies shot on
film will have their negative celluloid footage developed in the traditional
way and then selected takes will be scanned to videotape at low resolution
and then stored on the hard drive of a computer. The movie is then edited
digitally, with the editor and director watching the film take shape on a
monitor as they assemble and rearrange their shots in a timeline. When
editing is finished, negative cutters will cut and splice the actual celluloid
negatives to create a final version of the film. This negative can then be used
to produce hundreds of prints for distribution to theatres.

This system, well established since the late 80s, is now seeing major
changes itself. The falling cost of film scanning, combined with faster
computers, larger hard drives and sophisticated software, means that the
celluloid footage of an entire movie can now be scanned, edited and
manipulated digitally and then recorded back onto negative film. The
technique of finishing films entirely within the computer is known as the
digital intermediate (DI) process. Though expensive, DI is rapidly becoming
the favoured way to complete big-budget movies, especially those
containing many visual effects.

A feature film using the digital intermediate process first has its celluloid
footage developed in the traditional way. The editor then uses low-resolution
scans of this footage to edit the film on a digital editing system. This edit is called
the 'offline edit'. Scenes that need visual effects added to them will usually be
completed first so that effects artists can begin work on the chosen shots.

When the entire film has been edited and the director is happy with the
result, the edit computer will generate an edit decision list (EDL). This is a
precise record of how and where each shot has been used down to the exact
frame. It also contains information about any dissolves, fades or other forms
of image manipulation used by the editor.

The EDL is then sent to the company charged with creating the digital
intermediate of the film. They will then use it to select and scan the correct
portions of original celluloid negative to produce high-resolution digital files.

Original Red Layer | Original Green Layer | Original Blue Layer

Red Filter | Green Filter | Blue Filter

Technicolor Red Layer | Technicolor Green Layer | Technicolor Blue Layer

ABOVE: **For Martin Scorsese's** *The Aviator* **(2004), scenes shot using modern film stock were digitally graded, filtering each of the red, green and blue components to re-create the rich, saturated look of three-strip Technicolor.**

LEFT: **During the digital intermediate process, highly skilled colourists use software such as Discreet's Lustre to grade each shot in a movie. The colourist can alter the mood of a scene by changing the colour, brightness and contrast of the whole image or specially selected parts of it.**

FAR LEFT: **In a grading suite at Pacific Title, a movie's cinematographer and director can sit comfortably while discussing a scene's visual quality with the nearby colourist.**

LEFT: **The digital intermediate process requires massive amounts of hard disk storage and processing power. This is the machine room at E-Film in Hollywood, where ranks of Silicone Graphics Onyx systems are housed in an air-conditioned environment.**

This is an expensive process so only the exact shots listed in the EDL will be scanned. Usually a 'handle' of a few frames on either side of a shot will also be scanned to allow small editorial changes to be made. If the movie was shot digitally no scanning will be necessary and it is simply a matter of transferring digital files from one system to another.

Most films go through the digital intermediate process at a resolution of 2K (each frame is 2,048 pixels wide and 1,556 pixels high, <93). However, negatives are often scanned at 4K (4,096 x 3,112 pixels) before being downsampled back to 2K using a process that results in a better-quality image than if the film had been scanned at 2K originally. A 2K scan of a 35 mm frame of film results in about 12 megabytes of information, so just storing the 173,000 frames that comprise a two-hour movie requires 2 trillion bytes, or terabytes (TB) of disk space. In addition, any visual effects shots may comprise a number of separate layers, dissolves will need additional lengths of footage so that they can be merged into one another, and several versions of some scenes may be created before the director is happy. As a general rule, movies going through DI at 2K will require 10 TB of storage and a 4K movie will require a massive 50 TB of storage.

After it has been scanned the digital footage will be 'dust busted' to remove any tiny specks of dust or small scratches that may have been on the original negatives. Using the EDL for reference, a high-resolution digital version of the film will then be assembled within the computer. This version of the film is the 'online edit' and it will be exactly the same as that produced by the film's editor but will be of an extremely high quality. Any completed visual effects shots will also be added at this stage and shots can be re-edited if the director is still not entirely happy with the film.

With a high-resolution digital version of the film completed, final adjustments can be made to the picture quality. Traditionally, a movie's cinematographer will attend 'grading' or 'timing' sessions at a film laboratory. Working with a highly skilled colourist, the cinematographer specifies how much red, green or blue light should be added to each shot in order to produce the image they want to see in the final version of the movie. This is done to ensure that there are no noticeable changes of colour between shots that may have been filmed at different times and in different conditions. Grading is also used for artistic reasons – adding more blue to a sad scene to emphasize a character's mood, for example. A film's look can also be affected by complex photochemical procedures during processing, such as 'bleach bypassing' or 'skip bleaching', which can increase contrast or suppress certain colours. Colourists working in both the photochemical and digital realms are vital to the final look of a movie. They are among the most highly paid of film technicians and many directors and cinematographers have a favourite colourist who is the only person to whom they will trust their film.

Digital grading now offers cinematographers unparalleled creative freedom to polish their images. In addition to directly altering the colour content of a scene, cinematographers can also address the contrast, saturation, sharpness and other attributes of an image, making it easy, for example, to make a shot filmed in the afternoon look like early morning. Furthermore, while changes to a scene once had to be applied in broad strokes – an entire shot having to be tinted one colour, for example – digital grading now allows small areas of the frame to be selectively altered. If a movie was shot in the spring but is meant to be set later in the year, the green leaves on a tree could be turned golden, for example. Small areas can be isolated and altered even if they are moving around the frame – the eyes of an actor walking through a shot could be tracked and changed from brown to blue. The apparent exposure of shots can also be altered, perhaps by adding or subtracting light in chosen areas of the frame to draw the viewer's eye to an important piece of action.

Perhaps the most interesting function of digital grading is the ability to create an overall stylistic 'look' or 'mood' for a film. Cinematographers may once have spent weeks or months testing different film stocks, filters and lighting techniques to produce a distinctive visual style that served the narrative of the movie. While most cinematographers still strive to achieve as much as they can in-camera, digital grading allows them to quickly produce effects that would previously have been very time-consuming or impossible. For the digital grading of his period biopic *The Aviator* (2004), director Martin Scorsese wanted to emulate the look of the films that were made during the period in which the movie was set. Working with Technicolor Creative Services in Hollywood, visual effects supervisor Rob Legato therefore devised a series of digital filters that could make the film look as if it was shot with either early two-strip Technicolor or the three-strip Technicolor process that took over in the mid-30s (<56).

DI is particularly popular for the production of major visual effects movies as it facilitates the streamlined management of large numbers of digital image files that may arrive from multiple visual effects vendors, often at a very late stage in the schedule. Visual effects shots can then be graded to ensure that they blend seamlessly with the rest of the film.

When a movie has been fully approved by director, cinematographer and production executives it is recorded to film to create a master negative that will be used to produce hundreds of prints for distribution to movie theatres around the world.

The digital master, the digital file that contains the entire movie, can then be used to create home video, DVD, broadcast and foreign versions of the film, all of which would normally need expensive and time-consuming remastering. It can also be used for projection in a digital cinema (358>) or to produce high-resolution IMAX prints (358>).

At present DI is an expensive process, adding an estimated $300,000 to the cost of creating a major motion picture. However, as more films use the process and more facilities begin to offer the service this cost will undoubtedly fall considerably. In the near future it is likely that DI will become the standard for all commercial movie production.

DIGITAL COMPOSITING

Optical printers, grand machines that once sat proudly at the heart of every effects facility looking like something imagined by Jules Verne, have now been replaced by computer software and hardware with names like 'Flame', 'Combustion', 'Shake' and 'Toxik'.

Although the tools have changed, the principle of digital compositing is exactly the same as its old-fashioned optical equivalent. Live-action images shot at different times and places still need to be invisibly combined with additional elements such as models, matte paintings and computer-generated animation and effects. Elements to be composited must still be photographed in a manner that best allows them to be isolated and recombined using a system of mattes and counter-mattes. In the optical era, producing mattes was a skilled job in which photochemical processes were painstakingly cajoled and tweaked to produce an acceptable result. In the digital world, producing mattes is a more automated process in which operators rely on the powerful, pre-programmed mathematical algorithms that lie at the heart of their image-processing systems. However, the process still needs to be overseen by highly skilled artists and it can be a time-consuming and frustrating activity.

When all of the elements have finally been composited satisfactorily, a finished shot will be recorded onto celluloid for editing into the final cut of the film, or it will be sent as a high-resolution digital file to be added to the movie at its digital intermediate stage (<98).

DIGITAL MATTES
The first stage of compositing is to gather together all of the elements that need to be combined to produce the final shot. These elements will then be used to generate the mattes and counter-mattes that will later allow them to be layered on top of one another.

Many of the elements to be composited into a scene are now likely to be computer-generated. Images of digital characters, scenery, models or environmental elements like smoke, water and fire will have been created by animators and rendered out in several layers (236>). In these cases the necessary mattes will come 'for free' and the compositor need do no further work to prepare them for use.

Any elements which started life in the real world and which have been photographed on film or video, however, will need to be scanned into the computer before having mattes created for them. The process of producing mattes digitally is called 'keying', though operators refer to the process as 'pulling a matte'. As with the production of optical mattes, there are a number of ways to pull a matte from a digital image, depending on the content of the image and the way in which it has been filmed.

Actors, puppets and models are still filmed in front of blue or green screens in order to produce an image that can easily be divided into foreground and background elements. This technique is known as colour matting or chroma-keying (chrominance is a measure of the hue and saturation of colour in an electronic image). In fact, black, red or any other colour that contrasts with the foreground element can be used as the backdrop for a digital colour matting shot, but green or blue are favoured for several reasons. Green backdrops require less light than other colours to be illuminated sufficiently, so the cost of hiring and operating lighting equipment may be reduced marginally. Green is also popular for productions filmed on video. Video cameras are most sensitive in their green channel and so anything green is usually recorded with finer detail, which can make pulling a good matte easier. Blue is generally the most popular colour when actors are to appear in a shot, since its extraction during the matting process does not greatly affect the appearance of a performer's skin.

ABOVE: While blue was once the only colour used as a background when filming travelling-matte shots, digital techniques mean that any colour can now be used. Here a red screen is being used to film the blue-and-white model plane used by Boss Films for *Air Force One* (1997).

BELOW: Digital composites can now hide any trace of manipulation – even when travelling-matte shots contain traditionally difficult elements such as glass or hair – as in this shot composited by Framestore CFC for *The Saint* (1997).

FAR RIGHT: Entire movies can now be filmed in blue-screen studios with minimal props. Virtual environments can be added later, as in this scene from *Sky Captain and the World of Tomorrow* (2004).

Blue or green screens can be created by painting any suitably flat surface with paint that is commercially mixed to the required shade, or made from lengths of pre-dyed fabric that is stretched over a frame. The two sequels in the *Matrix* trilogy were so reliant on green-screen filming that they used an incredible 8 square kilometres (3 square miles) of this expensive material.

To produce a matte from an image with a coloured backdrop, the operator simply identifies the colour to be removed from the image and the computer software automatically produces a matte. If the foreground element contains an area of colour that is in the background – a performer wearing a blue tie filmed in front of a blue screen, for example – the software can be instructed to ignore that particular area of the foreground image. Unlike in optical processes, the precise shade of the backing colour is not critical when setting up and filming a shot for digital manipulation. By sampling a few pixels of background colour, the computer can be calibrated to remove only those exact shades. It is therefore quite possible – though not by any means ideal – to photograph a blue object against a blue background, as long as the two blues are measurably and consistently different.

Performers can now be isolated from a coloured background and placed within new environments so convincingly that many scenes in effects-intensive movies are shot in entirely green or blue surroundings. Every scene for *Sky Captain and the World of Tomorrow* (2004) was shot in a studio decked in green or blue, with just a few small pieces of detailed scenery with which performers could interact. With no expensive sets to build or time-consuming locations to visit, this can be an extremely efficient way of creating a film. The live action for *Sky Captain* was filmed in just six weeks.

As well as background colour, a number of other image characteristics can be used to produce a matte when keying. One of the most commonly used alternatives is luma key – a method that derives its mattes from luminance, a measure of the brightness of a colour. Luminance might be employed to produce a matte of an explosion, for example. An explosion can contain a wide range of colours, making it difficult to use colour as a method of pulling a matte. However, an explosion is so bright that luminance can be used to separate it from its background – increasing or decreasing the measure of luminance used to isolate the element until a satisfactory key is achieved.

There are, in fact, a variety of ways to measure the visual information in a scene, and often a number of different keying techniques are combined to produce the perfect matte for each shot.

For example, a performer shot on location may be filmed with a portable blue screen behind them. However, such screens are normally small and parts of the performer – for example, the top of their head – may extend beyond the edge of the blue screen as they move around during the shot. In this case colour matting could be used to pull a matte around the areas of the body that are in front of the blue screen, while luminance matting might be used to pull a matte around the head area which has areas of bright sky behind it.

Often it is not possible to rely on the convenience of placing a large coloured screen behind the subject that you are filming, and the background luminance may not contrast sufficiently with the foreground to make luma-keying possible. In such cases, a technique called 'difference matting' may be used. Difference matting requires two versions of a scene to be shot – one containing the element that needs to be isolated, and one without it. The two shots are then compared by software which can automatically detect the differences between the two images and produce a matte based on the changes. This technique might be employed to turn a shot of a busy city centre into a deserted one – as people and vehicles move about the scene, the computer detects the changes in each frame and builds up a shot that contains only those elements that remain the same from frame to frame, such as immovable buildings and roads.

LEFT: Digital software allows travelling mattes to be created using a variety of techniques in each shot. For a scene such as this from *Master and Commander: The Far Side of the World* (2003), a range of methods including manual rotoscoping were used to separate the land-locked replica ship from its studio background. The ship was then placed within a stormy sea environment.

RIGHT: In a typical digital composite, elements to be combined might include miniatures, digital animation and live-action plate photography. To ensure that separately filmed objects appear to interact with each other, it is often necessary to use a number of atmospheric elements to simulate contact. Here, various elements are being simulated by dropping blue objects into soil. When the blue is removed from the image, the remaining bursts of soil will be composited over shots of computer-generated spacecraft hitting a live-action background.

ROTOSCOPING

When 'automatic' methods of producing a matte are inappropriate or ineffective, mattes can be produced using the digital equivalent of the traditional technique of rotoscoping. The image from which a matte is to be pulled is displayed on a computer monitor and an operator using a graphics tablet and digital pen manually draws around the objects that are to be isolated from the scene. By significantly enlarging the image on the screen, pixel-accurate matte lines can be drawn. This task can be semi-automated by hand-drawing the matte lines only every few frames and instructing the software to calculate the matte for the frames in between. Automation usually only works for simple shapes that move in a relatively linear fashion, however, so, more often than not, every matte in a sequence has to be hand-drawn and its edges carefully blurred to deal with any motion in the subject. Such techniques may be used when a complex live-action background plate is to have new elements placed within it and it can take many days to create the mattes for one short scene. For *King Kong* (2005) the computer-generated ape as well as dinosaurs and live-action performers needed to be placed into model jungle environments. Rotoscope artists at Weta Digital spent many months selecting or manually tracing the outline of every single leaf and blade of grass in the foreground of each frame. The result was a series of split screens that allowed Kong and his co-stars to be layered into each scene.

COMPOSITING THE IMAGE

Once mattes for each of the elements in a shot have been prepared, the scene can be composited. Starting with a blank 'canvas' on the computer monitor, the operator first introduces the background plate – typically a scenic environment. The rest of the elements are then layered one by one to build up a new image.

Traditionally, the average optical composite might have contained perhaps half a dozen elements plus their various mattes. Digital composites, however, can contain many hundreds of elements. This is

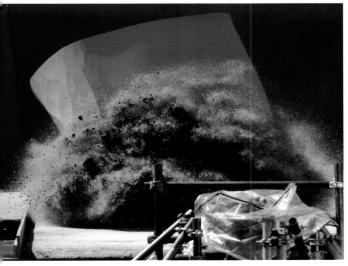

due in part to the complex requirements of many modern visual effects shots, but it can also be a result of the flexibility that is typically built into any elements that are computer-generated. Any single element that has been created in the computer is typically rendered out (236>) to a large number of layers or 'passes'. Each of these passes contains a different visual aspect of the same image. By adjusting the qualities of each of these passes during compositing, the final appearance of the element can be controlled with great precision.

As a basic example, a shot of a computer-generated spaceship might be supplied to the compositor in the following separate passes: The first pass might show the ship with its basic unlit colour detail. This is called a colour, or diffuse, pass. Another pass will show how the ship is illuminated by the lights set up in the computer by the animator (237>). This lighting pass may in fact be several separate passes – each showing how the ship is illuminated by the individual lights that surround it. This allows the compositor to adjust the lighting on the ship so that it best represents the ship's relationship with the various light sources contained in the final shot. Another pass will contain specular highlights. These are bright areas of overexposure that, in this example, might occur where the chrome machinery of the spaceship is very shiny. A further pass might show only the interior of the ship as seen through its windows. Another will hold the actual glass of the windows so that their final transparency can be determined by the compositor. Any landing lights or engine emissions will be contained in other passes. Each of the above elements will also have a corresponding black-and-white matte for compositing purposes.

As well as the passes that describe what the ship looks like, the animator may also supply a 'Z-depth map', also known as an 'ID pass'. This is a 2-D image that contains information about three-dimensional aspects of the element. Rendered out as a separate pass, this image can either use greyscale (ranging from white through the greys to black) or hue (various colours) to identify how far away parts of the image are from the camera, or perhaps the distance from the top to the bottom of an object. In our example the areas of the spaceship that are furthest from the camera might be white and this will gradually darken until the areas of ship nearest the camera are black. Z-depth maps allow objects to be integrated into environments much more realistically. For example, rather than simply having a layer of smoke placed over the top of the spaceship, the ship can be made to look as if it is flying *through* the smoke. This is done by using Z-depth information to make the smoke appear thicker over areas of the ship that are further from the camera. Using such 2-D information about the 3-D aspects of an element, it is also possible, to a certain degree, to relight objects during the compositing process. For example, this might allow the compositor to change the highlights and shadows on our spaceship should it be decided to include a previously unplanned explosion in the shot.

With perhaps 20 or 30 elements in a shot and with each element itself consisting of several passes, digital composites can quickly become extremely complicated. Compositors can find themselves individually addressing hundreds of layers in an attempt to make the shot look convincing. Though compositing is a highly technical occupation, the true skill of a compositor is in identifying which single element, of perhaps several hundred, needs minutely adjusting in order to make a shot work. For this reason many compositors are trained photographers or artists.

In optical printing, an operator only ever discovered if a composite was successful when the final film was developed and returned from the processing laboratory. The smallest mistake meant performing the entire compositing process again. Fortunately, digital compositing is a non-linear process and a shot can be progressively built upon and improved. If an element needs to be added, changed or removed, the layer in question can be accessed at any stage of the process. As with computer word processing, if the operator wants to try something different, one version of a shot can be saved while a new version is tried.

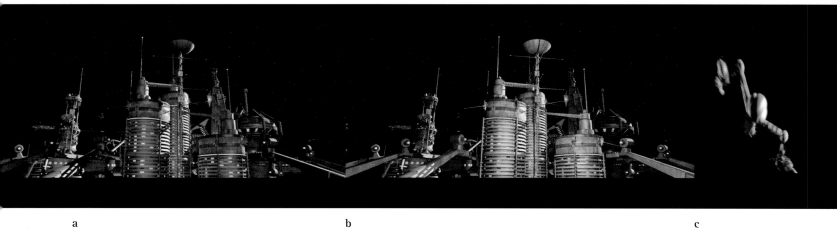

a   b   c

   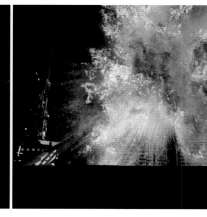

h   i   j   k

Twenty-five separate elements including a computer-generated (CG) city background, motion-control model freighter and miniature pyrotechnic explosions were combined by London's Magic Camera Company (now Cinesite Europe) to create this shot from *Lost in Space* (1998).

Elements used included:

a: CG city
b: CG city with bright-coloured light for use when ship explodes
c: CG fighters
d: female matte for fighters
e: explosion highlight from engine of freighter
f: green-screen motion-control beauty pass of freighter
g: freighter female matte
h: background explosion
i: foreground explosion
j: CG explosion debris
k: CG city and background explosion combined
l: background elements and freighter combined
m: background elements combined with freighter and engine explosion highlight
n: background, freighter and foreground explosion combined
o: final composite including CG fighters and debris

n

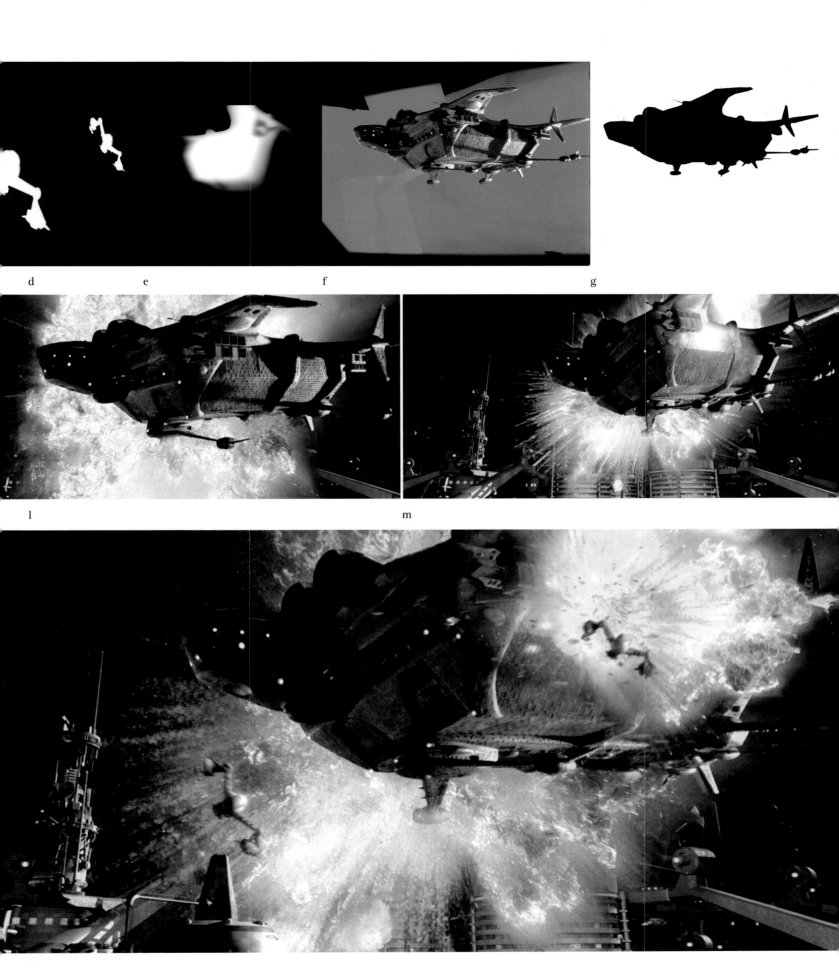

d   e   f   g

l   m

o

DIGITAL IMAGE MANIPULATION

Since digital images are really no more than an abstract collection of numbers, they can be subjected to almost limitless manipulation through the use of specially written image-processing software. By selectively applying mathematical algorithms to their digital architecture, images can be twisted, warped, stretched, flipped, squeezed, enlarged, shrunk, sharpened, blurred, coloured or dissolved. They can then be repeatedly copied, layered and combined without any loss of resolution or quality.

The platforms used for this work range from relatively inexpensive software that runs on a desktop PC to purpose-built stand-alone systems that can cost hundreds of thousands of dollars. All systems feature an array of built-in digital image manipulation software. Many effects facilities also write their own unique solutions in order to address the specific requirements of the projects on which they work. In the increasingly cut-throat visual effects industry, where competing companies often use the same commercially available image-processing systems, this proprietary software can become a jealously guarded asset in a company's arsenal of services. The only consistent requirements for this work are the massive amounts of processing power and disk space that are essential when dealing with multiple film-resolution images.

During the compositing process, images can be manipulated in a number of ways to ensure that the different elements of each shot integrate seamlessly. Various 2-D processes are explained here; 3-D processes are discussed in subsequent chapters.

COLOUR AND CONTRAST

When compositing an image, the operator begins by making sure that the colour of each of the separate elements in the shot is uniform. The type of film stock, lighting, lens and exposure level used when shooting live elements can affect their colour value – some elements may look slightly blue, while others look red by comparison, for example. Computer-generated elements will also have their own various colour values. The operator decides on a desired tone for the whole scene and then calibrates the colour of each element so they all look as if they were filmed at the same time. At this stage the aim is to ensure that all of the elements within a composite match so that the finished shot looks convincingly integrated. Once the finished composite has been edited into the final version of the film it will be graded to give it the same look and feel as the rest of the movie (<99).

The colour of an object can be controlled by measuring and manipulating its chrominance values. Chrominance is a measure of the hue and saturation of a colour, and it can be used to isolate an object or even a single pixel of an exact shade or within a range of shades. Once selected, chrominance values can be altered to create new colours. This is useful for making grey skies blue or turning parched grass green again. When shooting location scenes for *Jerry Maguire* (1996), the film crew were unable to find a car that matched the one used in the rest of the film. A vehicle that was the same model but a different colour was used during filming and changed from red to the correct shade of silver by selecting and altering its chrominance during the post-production process.

It is particularly important that the contrast levels of different elements in a shot match, since the human eye is very good at detecting uneven contrast, particularly in areas of darkness. Contrast is checked by comparing the darkest areas in each element, typically the shadows. If one element has dense black shadows and another has grey ones, the contrast of the two must be equalized.

SHADOWS

An element such as a performer or a computer-generated model that is composited into a new background will look much more natural if it casts a shadow onto its new environment. Shadows act like a kind of sticky-tape that can help to bind two artificially combined elements together – they are a visual cue used by the human eye to assess the spatial relationship between objects. Even if the lighting in a scene would not naturally cause a composited object to cast a shadow were it actually in that environment, compositors will still often add a subtle shadow which helps the human eye to link the two objects together.

The processes used for the production of digital mattes are so refined that any shadow cast onto a blue screen by an actor or a model can be extracted and added to the final composite. Elements often come without shadows, however, in which case they must be created artificially. A common method of achieving this during compositing is to copy the male matte of the foreground element and reposition it so that it joins an actor's feet or hangs beneath a model. By distorting or stretching the shape of this shadow matte, it can be made to correspond to the direction of the lighting in the scene. When blurred and made semi-transparent, this shaded element can be made to follow the foreground object around to produce a convincing shadow.

FOCUS

Elements in the extreme foreground or background of a multi-layered shot may represent objects that are supposed to be great distances apart. In a normal live-action scene, objects in the middle distance would

ABOVE: **For a location shot in** *Jerry Maguire* **(1996), a car of the correct colour could not be found. Instead, a car that was the same model but a different colour was used. During post-production, the red car was changed to silver, the overall image was given more colour and the featureless sky was replaced.**

RIGHT: **Most of the images on the monitors in this scene from** *Snake Eyes* **(1998) were added to the shot during post-production. The crosses on the screens were used to track the movement of the camera. The same movement was then applied to the TV images being added to the scene so that they would 'stick' to the screens.**

FIGURE 35 **LENS DISTORTION**

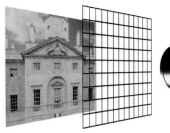 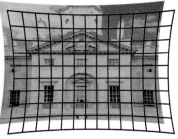 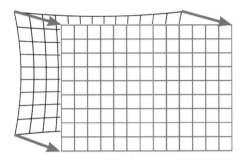

Scene and grid are filmed with the same lens.

The resulting images are warped by the lens.

By calculating, mathematically, by how much the grid has been distorted, the image itself can be corrected.

typically be in sharp focus, while those very near to or far from the camera are likely to be out of focus. To produce a realistic sense of depth in a composited image, the focus of different elements should vary subtly. Since the eventual spatial relationship between the elements in a composite may not be known during photography, each element is filmed in perfect focus. Once the elements have been layered within the computer, each one is then defocused according to its supposed distance from the camera. The focus on any moving element can then be animated to change as it moves towards or away from the camera.

Defocusing an element involves digitally blurring the image. While this gives a convincing impression of image depth, it also has the effect of blurring the 'grain' in any elements that have been shot on film. Grain is a randomly moving pattern of minute coloured dots caused by the millions of tiny silver halide crystals in the emulsion of the original piece of film, and is one of the almost imperceptible qualities that make film look different from video. To add grain back into a blurred element, an area of constant colour from the original camera negative is sampled and used to create a grain 'filter'. This artificial grain is applied to any grain-free or blurred elements in the composite shot. Since computers generate images composed of grain-free pixels, any computer-generated elements in a shot will also have film grain applied to them. Much time is spent adding or removing grain from the elements in composited shots – a process known as 'grain management'.

LENS DISTORTION

Though the images that we see on a cinema screen look 'normal' to us, closer inspection reveals that supposedly straight lines are often curved – especially as they reach the edges of the screen. This effect – called barrel distortion when the sides of an image bulge outwards or pincushioning when the sides are pinched in towards the centre – is a characteristic of almost all photographic lenses. Every camera lens is unique in the way that it distorts the images that it photographs, so visual effects supervisors try to ensure that elements to be composited together are filmed using the same lens. However, since models, miniatures and live-action elements are often filmed simultaneously in different parts of the world, this is rarely possible or practical. Furthermore, any computer-generated elements included in a scene will be distortion-free because they have never been 'filmed' through a real lens.

Compositing elements with varying degrees of distortion can lead to an unconvincing final image. To remedy this problem, the distortion created by a lens can be removed and then reapplied to images during compositing. First, each of the lenses employed to film the various elements of a shot is used to photograph the same grid of squares. The different images of this grid are then scanned and used to determine the amount by which each lens distorts its image. Distortion information can also be obtained by scanning elements of a lens with a laser. Most lenses rented out for movie production now come with unique distortion data.

Before compositing, images are undistorted using the curvature information for the lens with which they were filmed. The resulting optically perfect images are then combined with one another to produce a non-distorted composite. Although distortion is an 'imperfection', without it images tend to look a little false – it is another visual cue used by our eyes when scanning an image for traces of fakery. The distortion information from one of the lenses – normally that used to film the live-action element of a scene – is therefore reapplied to the entire composite image to produce a uniformly distorted picture that will match the rest of the film (fig. 35).

TRACKING

To composite multiple elements that have been filmed with a moving camera, or which are themselves moving within a shot, a process called 'tracking' is employed. Tracking is used to map the relative motion of objects within a scene so that any element added to that shot during compositing can be matched or 'locked' to that movement.

Tracking within optical compositing was not impossible, but it could be extremely time-consuming (<76). In the digital world, however, the efficiency and accuracy of tracking is hugely improved, allowing far more complex combinations to be achieved.

The background plate that is to have other 2-D images composited into it is studied for a number of discrete reference points – usually corners of architecture, distinct landscape details or intentionally placed luminous 'tracking markers'. These points, just a few pixels in size, are registered by special tracking software. By automatically recording the movement of these groups of pixels as the shot progresses, their relative motion within the scene can be used to form a 'map' of their movement or of the changing position of the camera used to film them. A single tracking point is sufficient to keep track of the subject's vertical and horizontal movement, and two points are enough to measure its rotation and spatial arrangement. More points can be used to gather in-depth detail of a complicated camera move so that computer-generated three-dimensional elements can be added using a process called 'match moving' (235>).

Once the tracking information for a shot has been obtained, the exact motion can be applied to any element that is to be added into the shot in order to tie the two elements together. This method might be used in scenes of spaceship interiors or mission controls, where the camera needs to roam freely while a number of television screens and computer monitors display images. Filming televisions so that their screen images are both visible and synchronized with the main action of a scene is extremely complicated. Instead, such scenes are filmed with blank television screens. As the camera roves around the room, the corners of each television monitor are tracked and the appropriate images are later composited onto each screen. The technique is also frequently used to track new skies into dull panoramas, or cover commercial signage in city centre scenes.

Tracking is among the least visible of all effects techniques since its result is simply a set of 'invisible' motion data. However, its ability to allow the subsequent layering of multiple moving objects makes the process a fundamental cornerstone in the creation of modern visual effects.

DIGITAL PAINT

A range of versatile image manipulation tools allows effects artists to 'touch up' their images in a multitude of ways. These include a variety of painting, cloning and erasing tools which together come under the title of 'digital paint'. This work is usually invisible in the final scene but it is essential to the production of many modern films.

Removing unwanted objects from a scene is relatively easy in the digital domain. If it is known that an object will need to be removed from a shot, two versions will usually be filmed – one plate with the object, and one clean plate without it. By layering one image on top of another within the computer, the objects that need to be removed can simply be 'erased' from the top layer to reveal the clean layer below. This makes the rods, stands and wires used to hold up models or suspend stunt performers extremely easy to remove. If a clean plate is not supplied, wires and rods can be removed in a number of other ways. Moving objects can be removed by tracking their movement as they cross the frame, and then placing clean background information – extracted from the preceding frame in which the object was in

another position – into the relevant areas.

Stationary objects can be removed by cloning areas of colour or detail from surrounding areas and 'painting' over the object to be removed. Using a cross-hair marker, the operator identifies the area of the scene which will be copied and then uses an on-screen brush tool controlled by their mouse or graphics pen to paint detail from one part of the image over another. This is extremely useful when making historical films – removing modern electricity pylons by painting over them with detail cloned from nearby trees, for example, or perhaps covering graffiti on a brick wall with detail from the clean bricks that surround it. Smudge and blur tools can subtly remove brand names from clothing or shopfronts.

Digital paint is also useful for removing evidence of the film-making process – removing the reflected camera crew from a window, for example, or hiding the microphone that momentarily creeps into the top of a shot. Digital paint was invaluable during the production of the three recent *Star Wars* films. Many scenes were filmed in completely blue or green studios. However, one key character, the robot C-3PO, is made entirely of highly polished metal. Many hours were spent painting out the blue or green that was reflected in the fussy droid's shiny metalwork.

CROWD REPLICATION

Film-makers who wish to film a crowd scene without overextending their budget (extras have to be hired, transported, fed and costumed) can use a computer to turn a modest collection of extras into an epic cast of thousands. To produce a throng from a small gathering, a shot can be filmed a number of times. In each take, the crowd moves to a different part of the screen, and in order to escape recognition, individuals may swap costumes. During filming, a portable blue screen may be placed behind the crowd to enable a matte of its edges to be pulled. More commonly, a difference matte will be extracted by comparing the shot with the extras to one without them. Each take can then be combined, allowing groups of people to be layered on top of one another to form a dense crowd. If the camera needs to pan or track past the crowds, a motion-control rig (146>) can be used to ensure that the camera movement is exactly the same in each take.

WARPING

Digital images can be distorted in countless ways by using software filters that stretch, displace or combine pixels. This is useful for a number of compositing tasks. To help tie a model spacecraft to a landscape into which it is being composited, for example, the background plate can be reversed, distorted and tracked onto the spacecraft windscreen to create convincing reflections. Similarly, any water contained in the real scenery can have a warped reflected image of a spacecraft tracked onto its surface as the model passes overhead. If a fire is to be composited into the foreground of a scene, the image on the background plate can be distorted to look as if it is being seen through the heat of the flames. A matte of the fire elements will be used to isolate the area of the background plate that is behind the flames. This part

ABOVE: **Industrial Light and Magic morphed the image of actress Iman into that of William Shatner to create this sequence in** Star Trek VI: The Undiscovered Country **(1991).**

LEFT: **This scene from** The Alamo **(2004) was filmed using a limited number of costumed extras. By filming the extras in several positions, Matte World Digital was able to combine several takes in order to swell the ranks. The image was further enhanced by replacing the sky with a more dramatic cloudscape.**

of the background plate is then slightly enlarged, blurred and warped, before being placed back into the composite image, to simulate heat distortion.

MORPHING

Morphing is one of the few modern special effects techniques to have become a household word. The technique's striking ability to metamorphose one image into another was first brought to public attention when it was used by Industrial Light and Magic for the film *Willow* (1988). George Lucas's mythical story required a character to change seamlessly into a number of different animals in a single shot. To achieve the groundbreaking effect, a selection of real creatures and performing model animals were filmed normally in similar positions; the models were built to mechanically perform the more extreme alterations that were needed. The animal images were scanned, and software specially written by Doug Smyth was used to distort each image into the next and create an extraordinary blend (Smyth, along with Tom Brigham of MIT, received a technical Oscar for the development of morphing techniques in 1992).

Morphing is a mathematical process, in which the computer calculates the changes that need to be made to turn one image into another. To achieve this, the original images in a sequence are analysed by the operator to find areas of shared similarity – in the case of a human head, eyes will be matched with eyes, ears with ears and so on. A series of curves is created to surround the boundaries of each of these key areas on the first image in the sequence (fig. 36 (a)).

These boundary curves are then transferred to the second image, where they are manually distorted to conform to the characteristics of the new object (b). Having been instructed which areas of one image are to be merged with the corresponding areas of another, the computer software calculates the necessary changes in colour and shape that will turn one image into the other over a set number of frames (c).

The sensation caused in the entertainment business by the use of morphing in *Willow* proved that computer graphics had become a powerful tool in the production and manipulation of images. Morphing one character into another became an overused trick in films, television commercials and music videos in the early 1990s, but has since become a powerful and subtle tool in the creation and compositing of visual effects.

Morphs are frequently used to change a shot of a movie star into one of a stunt performer just before a dangerous stunt is performed, or indeed change a computer-generated stunt performer into the film's star just in time for their close-up. A model spacecraft composited into a sequence can come to land and be morphed seamlessly into a full-sized prop spacecraft that has been built on the live-action set. In Kenneth Branagh's *Much Ado About Nothing* (1993), some scenes appear to have been filmed in extremely long takes, as the camera swoops impossibly over hedges and trees to follow characters moving around the garden of a Tuscan villa. The aim was to produce the effect of the camera following the characters' every step, so a number of separately filmed shots were subtly morphed into one another, creating the illusion of continual camera movement.

FIGURE 36 **MORPHING**

a

b

a: The first subject has key boundary lines identified and colour-coded.

b: The second subject has corresponding boundary curves selected.

c: The first image is converted into the second over a specified number of frames.

c

IMAGE INTERPOLATION

The ability of computers to analyse and interpret images means that they are now capable of creating completely artificial images that are indistinguishable from the real thing. If a frame is missing from the middle of a sequence of images, for example, specialized image interpolation software can study the frames on either side to create a replacement. This is achieved by studying small groups of pixels over a period of several frames. The computer detects the tendencies of those pixels and calculates their likely 'in-between' positions in order to synthesize a brand new frame.

This technique has been used to restore classic films where frames have been irretrievably damaged or lost. However, the ability to artificially create new frames also means that the speed of any on-screen action can now be altered during post-production.

Slow-motion shots traditionally need to be filmed with expensive high-speed cameras that can film at more than the normal 24 frames per second (133>). But image interpolation techniques mean that ordinary footage can be slowed down to any desired speed by the creation of additional new frames. In fact, movement can be both slowed down and sped up at almost any rate desired, adding a fascinating new dimension to action sequences.

Perhaps the most striking use of image interpolation techniques has been for the creation of 'time slice' or 'bullet time' sequences. Although this startling effect had been developed beforehand, it first came to prominence in *The Matrix* (1999) where in a number of shots the camera roams freely around a scene in which the action appears to have paused at one moment in time.

The technique requires an array of individual still cameras to be positioned around the subject (fig. 37). Each of these cameras is programmed to take a single photograph simultaneously. The resulting still photographs are then edited together to form a succession of images which, when viewed at the normal speed of 24 frames per second, produces a sequence in which it appears that a single movie camera is moving around a subject whose movements have been frozen. If the shutters of the still cameras are released with a fractional time delay, rather than remaining frozen, the subject will appear to move in extreme slow motion.

To achieve scenes like these for *The Matrix*, visual effects supervisor Jon Gaeta first pre-visualized (230>) each shot in the computer. This resulted in a computer model that described exactly where to place each still camera, and at what intervals the photographs should be taken. An array of 120 stills cameras was then arranged in a pattern around the performers, using laser positioning to ensure that they were accurately placed and aimed. The cameras were concealed behind a circular green screen so that the resulting images of the actor could later be isolated and composited into new computer-generated backgrounds.

As actors performed, each camera took its single photograph – sometimes with as much as one second of real time lapsing between photography of the first and last picture in the sequence. When the 120 frames were projected at 24 frames per second, the result was a sequence that stretched one second of action into a five-second moving camera shot. Using frame interpolation these images were then used to create additional synthetic in-between frames of action, turning a five-second sequence into a ten-second one. When completed, the 'bullet time' footage of the actor was composited into computer-generated 3-D backgrounds. Information from the original computer pre-visualization of the sequence was used to create the same virtual camera (233>) movement on the 3-D backgrounds so that they matched the bullet time foreground material exactly.

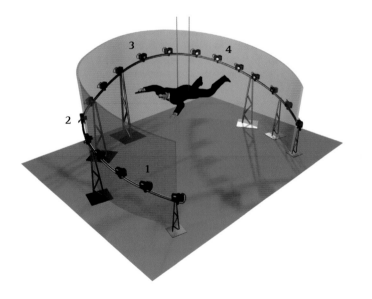

FIGURE 37 **BULLET TIME**

Using an array of still cameras, action is simultaneously photographed from multiple angles. The result is a sequence of images showing the same moment in time as seen from many different perspectives. The images are then interpolated to create the final sequence in which the camera appears to move around action that has been frozen in time.

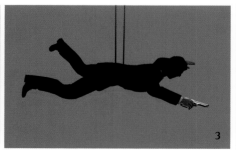
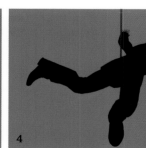

ABOVE: Neo (Keanu Reeves) and Agent Smith (Hugo Weaving) tackle each other mid-air in this exhilarating 'bullet time' shot from *The Matrix* (1999).

RIGHT: Dozens of still cameras are arranged in a circular array to photograph a bullet-time sequence for *The Matrix*. The white cube in the middle of the array is part of the laser positioning device used to ensure that each camera is in exactly the right place. The cameras will later be concealed by a green-screen wall so that they can be easily removed from the shot.

3

MODELS

INTRODUCTION

Whether for buildings, vehicles or landscapes, film-makers have long relied on the use of models to provide the props and backdrops for their productions.

Some models are built because the object or location that they represent simply does not exist in the real world; others are created because the genuine version is either too expensive, difficult or far-flung to use.

Models are generally much smaller than the object or location that they are built to represent; spaceships, ocean liners, futuristic cities and vast mountain ranges can all be constructed at a fraction of their real or supposed size. Many models are built solely to be destroyed – it being far cheaper, safer and easier to stage earthquakes, floods, fires and explosions at scaled-down proportions.

In the earliest films, models were of the simplest variety; toy cars pulled on string were passed off as the real thing, and cardboard cut-out boats floating on small ponds used to represent naval exploits. Such models were usually shown in self-contained shots that were intercut with the main action of the film. However, as techniques developed in tandem with audience expectations, models became increasingly realistic and their combination with live-action footage more convincingly interactive. Today, models can be built, lit and 'filmed' entirely within the computer, though there remains much demand for miniatures that can be lit, filmed and destroyed in the old-fashioned way. The history and techniques of model creation and photography constitute one of the most fascinating areas of special effects production.

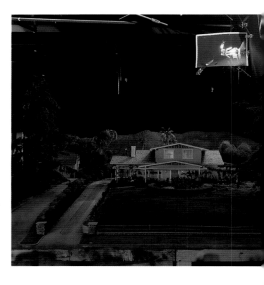

THE SHUFTAN PROCESS

Mirrors have always played a part in magic tricks and visual illusions. A technique known as 'Pepper's Ghost' was used in eighteenth-century stage productions, and even in early films, to induce the appearance of transparent phantoms. The process involved placing a disguised semi-transparent mirror at a 45° angle to the audience or camera. With careful lighting, the viewer could look directly through the mirror without noticing the glass itself. When the lights were raised on a performer standing off-stage, their image appeared as a ghostly, semi-transparent reflection in the mirror.

The extensive use of mirrors for movie special effects was pioneered by the German director of photography Eugene Shuftan (born Eugen Schüfftan; 1893–1977). Shuftan is said to have invented a method of using mirrors to combine models and full-scale sets in 1923, though there is evidence that other film-makers were using similar techniques even earlier than this. However, it was undoubtedly Shuftan who perfected and popularized the technique in European film-making from the mid-20s.

The Shuftan process uses mirrors to create the in-camera combination of miniature sets, paintings or rear-projected images with full-scale partial sets and performers. A large mirror (fig. 1 (a)) is placed at

FIGURE 1 **THE SHUFTAN PROCESS**

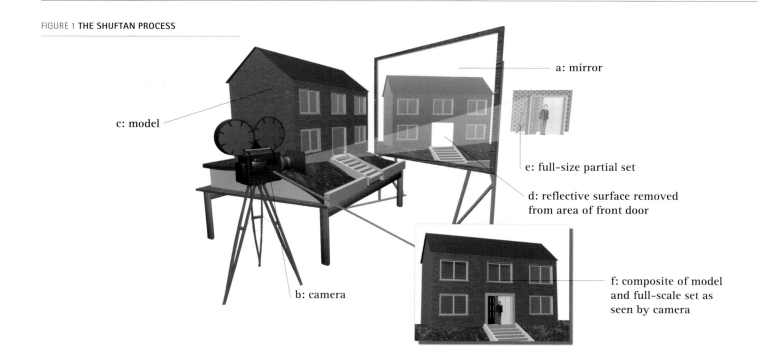

a: mirror

c: model

e: full-size partial set

d: reflective surface removed from area of front door

b: camera

f: composite of model and full-scale set as seen by camera

a 45° angle to the camera (b). A model or painting is then placed at a 90° angle to the camera (c), so that its reflection in the mirror can be seen through the camera. The areas of the reflected image that are to be replaced by full-scale scenery are marked on the surface of the mirror. These areas are then scraped clear of the silver backing that makes a mirror reflective (d). The result is a reflected image of the model or painting that contains a hole through which the area immediately behind the mirror is visible. The full-scale partial set (e) is then aligned with this area so that the camera sees a combination of the reflected image and the full-scale scenery in which actors can perform (f).

Shuftan used this technique to produce a number of shots in *Metropolis* (1926). The method was also used during the climax of Alfred Hitchcock's *Blackmail* (1929) to place characters inside the British Museum, and in *Things to Come* (1936) to locate crowds of people within the modelled environments of H.G. Wells's futuristic city Everytown.

Though an old technique, the Shuftan process has been used occasionally in modern films. Special effects supervisors Robert and Dennis Skotak (131>) are famous for using traditional techniques to produce stunning images. 'For *Aliens* [1986], we needed a shot of two characters entering a bar in the boom town, but we had no time or money to build a whole set', explains Robert Skotak. 'We built a full-size door area that actors could interact with and a matching miniature of the building and surrounding areas. The two parts were combined during filming using a mirror. To help merge the two halves convincingly, we blew clouds of dust across both the miniature and the full-size set, and strung hanging cables across the miniature that matched cables across the full-scale set. As the cables moved in the breeze, it was very difficult to detect any join between the miniature and the full-scale set. Even in the digital age, these techniques still work perfectly, and you can get your shot done in one take without any additional processes.'

SCALE, SPEED AND DEPTH OF FIELD

When used well, miniatures can be combined with full-sized live action without an audience suspecting that there is anything 'special' about what it sees. However, while most of us will never spot a good model shot, an unsuccessful one will look fake even to the most uncritical eye. To make a miniature shot indistinguishable from the real thing, much depends on the quality of the models themselves. However, the most important element in ensuring the success of a miniature is the way in which it is filmed. 'You can have the best models in the world, but if you don't photograph them correctly, you can throw away months of a model-maker's hard work in a single morning's shoot', says Nigel Stone, whose miniature photography has appeared in films including *Lost in Space* (1998), *Entrapment* (1999) and the Harry Potter movies. 'It's easy to ruin good models with bad photography', claims Stone, 'but good photography can often save the day if the models themselves are not quite as detailed as they could be.'

One of the first considerations when photographing a miniature is depth of field – the distance over which objects within a scene are in focus. Normal motion picture photography usually has a relatively deep depth of field – objects that are in the extreme background or foreground tend to look slightly out of focus or 'soft', but the majority of the action in the middle distance is perfectly sharp.

To help models look full-size, it is necessary to reproduce a similar depth of field in miniature photography to that normally achieved in full-scale photography. 'To photograph models so that they look like full-sized objects, the camera must often get very close to them', explains Stone. 'If we filmed a full-sized car with a camera 3 m [10 ft] away from it, we would probably get a shot in which the car and most of the background is in focus. To reproduce this look with a model car that is built at 1:10 scale, our camera would have to be nine-tenths nearer the car – only about 30 cm [1 ft] away. Then our problem is making sure that we have enough depth of field to ensure that the car is in perfect focus as well as the rest of the miniature set behind it.' Ensuring that both car and miniature background are perfectly focused can prove difficult, since most lenses, when focused on objects extremely close to the camera, will make anything in the background look out of focus – in other words, the shot will have a very shallow depth of field.

Depth of field can be controlled in a number of ways. Wide-angle lenses with a short focal length (<52) usually produce images that have greater depth of field than lenses with a long focal length. This is convenient for model photography since when cameras have to be close to models, wide-angle lenses are generally used to replicate the look that would be produced by a longer lens on a full-scale set. Depth of field is also affected by the size of the lens aperture. Opening or closing the aperture not only alters the

PRECEDING PAGES: **To film this shot from** *Batman Returns* **(1992), an actress is suspended above a miniature of Gotham City Plaza. In reality, the plaza is just a few metres beneath the actress. Dozens of tiny model people were jostled on wires from beneath the set to make them look alive.**

ABOVE LEFT: **In the movies, even the most mundane shots can involve some sleight of hand. This model of suburbia was featured in** *Poltergeist 2* **(1986). When properly lit, the miniature house and landscape are indistinguishable from the real thing.**

RIGHT: **In** *Darby O'Gill and the Little People* **(1959), deep-focus photography made the actors in the distance look tiny compared to those much nearer to the camera.**

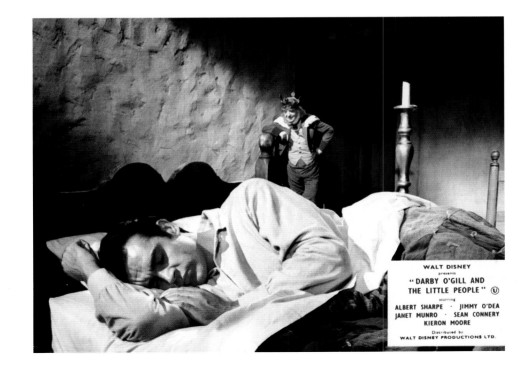

WALT DISNEY
presents
" DARBY O'GILL AND
THE LITTLE PEOPLE " Ⓤ
starring
ALBERT SHARPE · JIMMY O'DEA
JANET MUNRO · SEAN CONNERY
KIERON MOORE
Distributed by
WALT DISNEY PRODUCTIONS LTD.

amount of light that reaches the film, it also affects the depth of field. A small aperture allows a small amount of light into the lens but results in a deep depth of field (deep focus). A large aperture lets in a lot of light, but results in a shallow depth of field. To produce correctly exposed deep-focus miniature shots with a small aperture, a model can be lit with extremely bright lights or filmed using a fast film stock, which needs less light to record images than slow stock.

'When shooting miniatures you're constantly juggling the amount of light you use with the speed of the film, the focal length of the lens and the aperture you're shooting at,' says Stone. 'It becomes quite a complicated equation, but it can make all the difference to the success of a shot. On top of all these factors you also have to consider the camera speed at which you shoot the models. Ordinary films are shot at 24 frames per second [fps]. If you film a moving full-sized car at 24 frames it will look normal, but if you film a model car at 24 frames it will look like a toy car. That's because of the difference between the scale of its size and the scale of its weight.' A full-sized car might be 3 m [10 ft] in length and weigh around 1,360 kg [3,000 lb]. A model built at 1:10 scale will therefore be 30 cm [1 ft] in length, but its weight is likely to be disproportionately small. As a result, models tend to look unconvincingly lightweight when filmed at the usual 24 frames per second – a real car will sway steadily as it turns a corner, while a miniature car will wobble and jolt in response to every small bump in the road, just like a toy. To lend miniatures the sense of weight that they lack, they are filmed at higher than usual frame rates (see formula, right). When the film is projected at normal speed, the small, irregular movements that reveal a model's true weight are slowed down and smoothed out to give a sense of mass.

To calculate the frame rate at which a model should be filmed, cinematographers use an equation that takes into account the comparative scale of the full-sized object and its model. However, this formula is just a starting point when deciding the speed at which to film a miniature. 'Although working out camera speeds mathematically is helpful to a degree,' says Stone, 'there are lots of other factors to consider, such as the lens you're using, what the model is doing, how it's going to be used in the film and so on. You usually end up guessing the best speed based on a mixture of science and gut feeling. When we shot the *Jupiter 2* spaceship crash for *Lost in Space* [1998], we had five cameras shooting the 3.7 m [12 ft] model at between 72 and 250 frames per second. This gave us a selection of shots each of which looked the appropriate speed and could be edited together to look quite convincing.'

Another factor that needs to be considered when trying to make a model look real is depth perception. When we look into the distance, even on a clear day, far-away objects appear to be pale and diffuse. This is because the atmosphere that we are looking through contains traffic fumes, pollen, humidity and distortion from heat waves. 'When you build a 1:10 scale model, you also need to create a 1:10 scale atmosphere to make distances appear correct,' explains Nigel Stone. 'We therefore have to make the atmosphere that we film in ten times denser.' Miniatures that require an artificial atmosphere are filmed in a sealed and smoke-proof studio, which is filled to the correct density with a fine smoke during filming (310>). 'Models shrouded in smoke look a little odd during filming,' says Stone, 'but when the film comes back, if you've got the exposure and lighting correct, small model landscapes can look absolutely huge – you don't notice the smoke at all.'

CALCULATING CAMERA SPEED

The following mathematical formula can be used to calculate the correct camera speed when filming miniatures.

D = dimensions of full-scale object (in feet)

d = dimensions of model object (in feet)

fps = correct speed for filming (frames per second)

$$\sqrt{\frac{30}{3}} \times 24 = 76 \text{ fps}$$

For example, to film a scene in which a full-scale truck measuring 30 ft in length (D = 30) is represented by a model truck that is 3 ft in length (d = 3), the equation would result in a filming speed of 76 fps.

Therefore a 1:10 scale miniature needs to be filmed at 76 fps. When the finished film is projected at the standard rate of 24 fps, an event that lasted just one second during filming will be extended to a little over three seconds.

LEFT: **This beautifully constructed miniature of 40s Hollywood Boulevard appeared in Steven Spielberg's *1941* (1979). The street scene included thousands of miniature lights, moving vehicles, miniature shop-window displays and even tiny Coca-Cola bottles littering the gutter.**

BELOW LEFT & RIGHT: **From off camera, the miniature component of the arena for *Ben Hur* (1925) is clearly visible. When viewed from the correct angle, however, the combination of enormous full-scale set and miniature is seamless.**

FIGURE 2 **FOREGROUND MINIATURES**

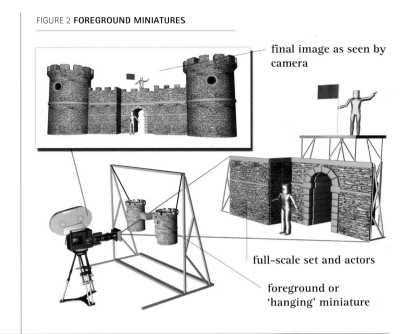

final image as seen by camera

full-scale set and actors

foreground or 'hanging' miniature

FORCED PERSPECTIVE AND FOREGROUND MINIATURES

Film-makers often need to show apparently huge environments, but do not have the time, money or space to build them full-scale. The obvious answer is to construct miniature environments, but sometimes these can also prove too large or expensive to be practical. One solution is to construct sets and miniatures that artificially exaggerate the effect of perspective.

When we look at any scene, objects that are further away will always appear much smaller than similarly sized objects that are very near. By artificially shrinking the size of objects, so they get smaller much sooner than would normally be the case, set-builders and model-makers can create the illusion of great distances in a relatively small space. This trick, called 'forced perspective', has long been used to make stage sets built within the confines of the theatre look much larger than would otherwise be possible. The technique works equally well for film, with sets and models rapidly shrinking as they recede from the camera. In such cases progressively smaller performers and props can be used to reinforce the illusion of distance. This

technique was used when constructing exterior sets for *Charlie and the Chocolate Factory* (2005), enabling apparently long city streets to fit into the relatively confined backlot of Pinewood Studios.

Another solution is to construct only those parts of the full-size set that performers will interact with. Using a carefully crafted miniature that is placed much nearer to the camera, this scenery can be extended during live-action photography, avoiding any post-production compositing work. Such models, called 'foreground miniatures', are carefully designed so that their lines of perspective match those of the full-scale set precisely, allowing the two elements to merge seamlessly when the miniature is correctly positioned and viewed through the camera (fig. 2).

Foreground miniatures are usually hung in the top of a frame to complete the lower half of a partially built full-scale set, and so are sometimes called 'hanging miniatures'. The method was frequently used in the 30s and 40s to provide open-topped studio sets with a ceiling, thus obscuring the overhead paraphernalia of lights and microphones. Designing and building a three-dimensional model to match a full-scale set is a complicated and time-consuming task, but it has distinct advantages over the similar alternative method of using a two-dimensional painting (244>).

film didn't exist on location,' explains Richardson. 'There was just a fairly unimpressive bridge about the same length as the one you see on screen, but only about 6 m [20 ft] high. So we built a model bridge over a miniature ravine with a cellophane river at the bottom. The miniature bridge, which was about 6 m [20 ft] long and 1.2 m [4 ft] high, was placed about 6 m [20 ft] in front of the camera with the real bridge about 300 m [1,000 ft] behind it. With everything positioned correctly, real horse riders and tanks moving across the full-scale bridge in the background looked just as if they were actually using the miniature.' Richardson loves to use traditional methods when filming. 'Despite all the amazing things you can do with a computer,' he says, 'simple in-camera tricks like these have always worked – and will always work – and they can be cheaper, faster and are certainly a lot more fun to create.'

Ingenious in-camera scale effects were also used to create a range of different-sized characters in some shots for *The Lord of the Rings: The Fellowship of the Ring* (2001) and its sequels. Simple shots combining the diminutive Frodo Baggins and the towering Gandalf, such as an early shot of the two sitting next to one another in a wagon, were achieved by having Frodo much further from the camera than Gandalf, making one look much larger than the other. While Gandalf sat on a normally sized section of wagon, the piece on which Frodo sat, which was further from the camera, had to be made to a larger scale – making the two distant parts look like a single piece. This classic illusion has been used many times over the years, most famously in *Darby O'Gill and the Little People* (1959) in which a 'large' Sean Connery, placed near to the camera, interacted with 'little' actors placed much further away. To achieve the seamless combination of both foreground and background objects in such shots, it is essential that the photographer achieves a good depth of field, making both near and far objects appear equally in focus.

Using modern technology, *The Fellowship of the Ring* also brought an ingenious twist to the traditional method of achieving forced-perspective shots. While such shots can normally only be filmed with subtle camera movements by using a nodal tripod (see below), director Peter Jackson wanted his forced-perspective shots to have the same dynamic camera moves used for the rest of the film's photography. For shots where Frodo and Gandalf drink tea at a kitchen table, two sections of table were built: one smaller foreground piece and one larger background piece. The sections of table, each dressed with differently scaled props, were lined up with Gandalf sitting at the foreground table, near the camera, and Frodo standing next to the

Lighting conditions will produce matching shadows and highlights on both 3-D model and full-scale set, and a model can be built to include moving parts, making it ideal when action is required in the faked part of the scene.

Foreground miniatures with moving parts were made by Arnold Gillespie and Cedric Gibbons for *Ben-Hur* (1925). The massive full-scale Circus Maximus set was built only a few storeys high. Once the camera angle for establishing shots was decided, Gillespie and Gibbons made the top half of the arena in miniature. The minutely detailed model was then hung in front of the camera so that it matched the distant set perfectly, giving the impression of a stadium built on a vast scale. The model included thousands of tiny wooden figures that could be jiggled to produce the effect of a restless crowd.

Certain precautions must be taken when using foreground miniatures. During filming, actors and moving objects must not be so high that they are cut off by the model. Similarly, atmospheric elements such as dust, fog and rain must be avoided – any such elements on the full-scale set would also disappear behind the model. Foreground models also have the disadvantage that they can only be viewed from a limited number of angles. Any change in camera position and perspective may mean that the model and the full-scale set no longer match. Even a tiny movement during filming will cause the top half of a construction to appear to slide against the bottom half, shattering the illusion of unity.

Though it is usually essential that neither camera or model is moved during filming, some camera movement is possible using a specially designed tripod. Normal tripods tilt or swing a camera about its own centre, causing a significant change in the perspective of the lens. For limited panning and tilting on foreground miniatures, however, a special 'nodal' tripod can be used (fig. 3). Nodal tripods place the pivot point of a pan or tilt at the nodal point of the lens instead of at the centre of the camera. The nodal point is the optical centre of the lens, where all light travelling through the lens converges. By swinging the camera and lens about this point when filming foreground miniatures, the view of the subject can be changed but the perspective remains the same, keeping foreground and background elements locked together.

Effects supervisor John Richardson has cleverly used foreground miniatures in many James Bond films, including *The Living Daylights* (1987). During a sequence set in Afghanistan, Bond's allies are chased by Russian tanks across a bridge over a deep gorge. 'The spectacular bridge seen in the

FIGURE 3 **NODAL TRIPODS**

A normal tripod tilts a camera around its own central axis.

A nodal tripod tilts the camera around the nodal point of its lens.

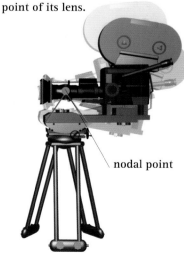

nodal point

LEFT: **A foreground miniature was used for the bridge and everything below it in this shot from** *The Living Daylights* **(1987). The hill, castle, aircraft and explosion are all full scale. The top of the real bridge, across which horses and vehicles travelled during filming, is just visible in the background.**

BELOW: **To fit a long street onto a short studio backlot, this set for** *Charlie and the Chocolate Factory* **(2005) was built using forced perspective. The second car is slightly smaller than the first, and the houses and telegraph poles quickly shrink as they progress up the hill. The last few houses and the factory are a painted backdrop.**

background table. The view from the camera made both sections of table merge, with Gandalf looking much bigger than Frodo. However, Jackson wanted his camera to dolly past the end of the table. This would normally shatter the illusion – the moving camera causing the foreground table to move disproportionately in relation to the background table and therefore revealing the join. To enable the camera to move, a motion-control rig (146>) was built to drive not only the movement of the camera but also that of the foreground piece of table. As the camera tracked past the scene, the foreground table automatically slid in a reciprocal fashion. Because the foreground table maintained its relative position in relation to both the camera and the background table, both sections of table appeared to remain 'joined'. The result was a moving-camera forced-perspective shot that created the perfect illusion of small and large characters inhabiting the same space.

CITYSCAPES

Since Fritz Lang's *Metropolis* (1926; 124>), models have been used to create the futuristic cityscapes of our dreams and nightmares. More often, however, film-makers rely on architectural models to replicate the ordinary world. 'These days we are more often asked to build models that represent not mythical or alien cities, but the modern cities and building styles that audiences know very well. The terrific thing about making these models today is that digital techniques now allow them to be populated with real traffic and crowds of people, which are the perfect finishing touch,' says Matthew Gratzner, a partner at New Deal Studios, whose architectural model work has appeared in films including *Godzilla* (1998), *Terminator 3* (2003) and *The Chronicles of Riddick* (2004).

According to Gratzner, replicating modern buildings in miniature is a greater challenge than constructing the cities of alien civilizations or of our own future. 'Modelling contemporary architecture is so hard because everybody is an expert on what these places look like,' believes Gratzner. 'We all have a little mechanism in our brain that screams "Fake!" when we see something that isn't totally convincing. Often the audience doesn't know why a shot looks fake – it just senses that there's something not quite right about it. Building realistic models of everyday environments is therefore about the hardest thing that can be done, and it takes the skill and knowledge of the best artists and technicians.'

For Gratzner, planning the way in which models will be filmed is the first step to take in the creation of successful miniatures. 'We like to approach the filming of models like ordinary first-unit production,' he explains. 'With models it is possible to do incredibly fancy shots with the camera flying around on a crane, but that rarely has any storytelling purpose – it's just showing off. The audience will instantly realize that there's some sort of trickery going on and it's the effect that becomes the focus of attention and not the story. So we always try to restrain model photography to the normal type of shots that a live-action unit, with all its physical constraints, might produce.'

TOP: **A model of New York City's famous Flatiron Building is positioned for shooting in** *Godzilla* **(1998). To save modelling time, the façade was built from repeatable sections cast in plaster.**

ABOVE: **Before digital techniques made it easy to composite people into miniatures, adding human life was always a challenge. For long shots in** *Batman Returns* **(1992), minute models of people were moved with wires from below the set.**

RIGHT: **This miniature building from** *The X-Files* **(1998) was constructed pre-destroyed (***near right***). Each room was filled with miniature office furniture and even accurately scaled-down sheets of paper. The blue cut-out trees allowed debris from the collapsing miniature building to appear as if it was travelling around real trees in the final composite (***centre right***). In the final shot (***far right***), the collapsing miniature built by New Deal Studios has been composited into footage of a real landscape. The older building and parkland to the right of the frame are a matte painting.**

Once it is known what is required of a model, plans are drawn up for its construction. If the model is of a city or a building that already exists, hundreds of photographs and measurements are taken to help the model-makers reproduce every detail. 'Once we know the design of a building, we begin to break it down into easily constructed sections. We do this for several reasons,' explains Gratzner. 'Firstly, the models may be filmed many miles from where we manufacture them, so they often have to be made in sections and then transported to the studio for assembly. At the studio, each section of building is affixed to a custom-built steel frame designed to make the model structurally sound. Secondly, we always study a building for any repeated patterns. Once we've identified parts of a building that are the same – usually brickwork or sections of façade – we can model them, then create a mould and cast as many copies as are needed to make up the whole building. When you only have eight weeks to produce an entire block of buildings, finding techniques like this becomes really important.'

Wood, metal, foam and plastic can all be shaped and sculpted to produce the repeatable parts of a building. Most materials, other than metal, can be cut using a computer-controlled laser or router to create the precise design required. Once completed, the cut-out design is covered with liquid rubber, which sets to form a mould that can be peeled off. The completed mould can then be filled with the type of material needed to produce an exact copy of the required design.

'We fill the moulds with different types of plaster, fibreglass, resin or foam, according to what is required of the final buildings,' explains Gratzner. 'Fibreglass and resins will produce a lightweight and strong shell that is suitable for many types of building. However, increasingly the models we make have to be destroyed during filming so we use materials that, when exploded, will produce many tiny chunks that are the correct scale for a building of that particular size.' To produce a building that will blow up realistically, its façade is moulded from specially mixed plaster. 'Destructive plaster is made with baking soda, sawdust and any other materials that will make it light and crumbly when set,' explains Gratzner. 'This mixture ensures the models will blow up perfectly, but they can become so fragile they are a real pain to work with.'

Models to be destroyed also have to have some sort of interior that will be revealed during the explosion. 'We often build one layer of rooms around the inside of a building and fill them with miniature furniture, fittings and carpets,' explains Gratzner. 'Then, at the edge of the floors and ceilings, we fit twisted miniature I-beams, joists, air-conditioning ducts and so on, as if the front of the building had been blown off and all this stuff has been left exposed. Once this pre-destroyed interior has been arranged and filled with dust and debris, we carefully place the façade of the building over the front and prepare it for destruction with compressed air or miniature pyrotechnics [130>].'

Sections of building that are to be destroyed are frequently reproduced numerous times. These sections are filmed being destroyed from one angle and then rapidly replaced while cameras are set up to film the destruction from another position. 'For *The Aviator* [2004] we produced a quarter-scale Beverly Hills house that a model aircraft would smash into. The undercarriage of the plane needed to gouge out a long section of roof tiles as it flew over. Most of the roof was solid but in that section the tiles were made of brittle plaster that exploded as the wheel dragged through them. Between takes we simply replaced the tiles with new ones.'

Once built, the exterior of the building is painted. 'Painting is one of the most vital parts of model construction,' stresses Gratzner. 'It makes a building the correct colour, but also gives it authenticity and character. Woods, metals and other materials may have been reproduced in plaster, so they need to be painted to look like the correct material. Then, once all the colours are right, we begin the vital process of ageing and weathering.'

Nothing in the real world is perfectly clean. From the moment an object comes off the production line, it becomes dirty, greasy and imperfect. For Gratzner, these imperfections are vital in persuading the audience that what appears on the screen is the real thing. 'In the real world most objects are pretty dirty,' says Gratzner. 'Absolutely everything is affected by environmental elements such as rain, wind, dirt, smog, smoke or the sun – and we paint all of that into our models. Whenever I look at buildings I see the way that rainwater has stained the brickwork, or how the corners of the windows have been missed by the window cleaner. Most people may never notice this kind of detail, but if it's not in a model, that little voice in their head will shout "Fake!"'

Gratzner's obsession with the limitations of the real world is observed throughout the model-making process. 'Straight lines are another thing that rarely occur in real life,' he claims. 'We all think that skyscrapers are about the most regular, perfectly angular buildings that it's possible to find, but if you stand at the foot of one of those buildings and look up at them, you'll see that the lines that should go vertically upwards actually wobble all over the place. We try to replicate that in our models. What's more,' Gratzner adds, 'if you stand at the right angle to the light, you'll notice that what you would assume are perfectly flat sheets of glass are actually rippled. Each sheet of glass used on these buildings is so huge that it bulges under its own weight, so we try to reproduce that by using sheet acetate that has similar kinds of ripples in it.'

The scale to which miniature cityscapes are built depends on a number of factors. 'There are mathematical ways of working out what scale buildings should best be built in,' says Gratzner, 'but the biggest factor in deciding a scale is practicality. If you're building a vast city, you could build the whole environment with every building at the same very small scale, which might make good photography difficult,' explains Gratzner. 'Or, you could build the whole city from very large models and then hire the world's biggest stage to house it all. Alternatively, you could work out which angles you were going to shoot from and build the models in that area a good size and have them get gradually smaller from then on.'

'In a forced-perspective shot we diminish the scale of buildings the further they get from the camera,' explains Gratzner. 'We might have 1:8 scale buildings in the foreground with every little detail perfect, then a couple of blocks further down we might go to 1:10 scale and the buildings will have a little less detail. The buildings will carry on getting smaller, and with each step down in scale, we will take a step down with the detail. Nothing makes a model look less convincing than too much detail on distant objects,' Gratzner believes. 'If you look into the distance in a real city, you can see buildings but you can't make out actual details, just suggestions of detail. Colours also get less defined the further away objects are. We might build a city with exquisite models in the foreground and end up arranging grey and lavender-coloured shoe boxes in the distance. For the most distant buildings, we can just use black-and-white photos of the foreground buildings stuck on mounting board and cut out to produce 2-D silhouettes.'

ABOVE LEFT: For *The Aviator* (2004), New Deal Studios built miniature aircraft and filmed them crashing into the roofs of buildings.

FAR LEFT: For close-up shots of destruction, only parts of the aircraft and buildings were made to collide.

ABOVE: New Deal Studios prepare a miniature roof for destruction. Plaster tiles were cast in repeatable sections so that the set could be quickly re-dressed between takes.

LEFT: The miniature aircraft was attached to a track so that it would collide with exactly the right part of the roof. The arm holding up the aircraft was later digitally removed from the shot.

METROPOLIS

Despite the struggling economy of mid-20s Germany, the country's giant film studio UFA (Universum Film Aktiengesellschaft) embarked on a series of lavish productions directed by the expressionist film-maker Fritz Lang. After the success of *Dr Mabuse* (1922), a brooding thriller in which an arch-criminal leads a gang of murderers in a series of crimes, and *Die Niebelungen* (1924), the tale of the legendary German hero Siegfried, Lang took a trip to the United States to learn about American production techniques. While sailing into New York harbour, Lang gazed at the Manhattan skyline and conceived the vision for his next film, *Metropolis* (1926).

Metropolis was the first great science fiction feature, a futuristic tour de force that established many of the themes and motifs that we expect in the science fiction movies of today. The film contrasts the ruling classes, frolicking in the luxury of their utopian skyscrapers, with the underclasses who toil below ground to keep the massive engines of industry in production. The story of *Metropolis*, with its simplistic themes and sentimental romance, today seems rather weak, but its dynamic images of a great city whose citizens are divided by their status remain powerful.

It is the image of the great city of Metropolis itself – towering, gleaming and optimistic – that remains most striking and influential. The city, designed by Erich Kettlehut, was a model with beautifully detailed skyscrapers up to 3 m (9 ft) high. Endless streams of animated traffic travelled along over 1,000 m (3,000 ft) of model roadway, while biplanes glided on invisible wires through the man-made canyons. The city was more fiction than science, however, and Lang, a trained architect, must have known that the updraught around such huge buildings would make it impossible for light aircraft to fly around them. The film's depiction of television and video phones (achieved through rear projection) was more prophetic, however.

Part of the underground city, the machine room and the Cathedral Square were built full-size and populated by some 30,000 extras. Even UFA's enormous stages could not contain the full scope of the city, however, and many sets were built in false perspective – buildings and props shrinking in size to create a false sense of distance. Watertight walls were built around these sets so that thousands of gallons of water could be released from dump tanks while filming flood sequences. Many scenes of city life were conjured with matte paintings or the clever use of mirrors to place actors 'within' models, a system invented by the film's cinematographer Eugene Shuftan (<114).

The film's other major contribution to the science fiction movie genre was Maria the robot, the first-ever screen cyborg. Built in the film by mad scientist Rotwang, Maria was in reality created by the film's sculptor, Walter Schultze-Mittendorf. Using a plaster cast from the body of actress Brigitte Helm, who played both the human Maria and the robot created in her likeness, Schultze-Mittendorf sculpted the beautiful art deco curves of the character's outer shell using hard-setting wood filler. The shell was divided into pieces that the actress could wear like a suit of armour. Each piece was sanded to a smooth finish, sprayed with metallic paint and polished until gleaming. Helm was extremely uncomfortable while wearing this costume, the sharp edges digging into her skin with every movement. A similar fate was suffered by actor Anthony Daniels half a century later when, wearing a suit remarkably similar in both design and construction, he played the robot C-3PO in *Star Wars* (1977).

After 18 months in production and a cost of over a million marks, *Metropolis* was a financial disaster and almost bankrupted UFA. It was, nevertheless, the greatest effects achievement of its age. Several years later the American musical *Just Imagine* (1930) featured a direct (though largely inferior) copy of the city of Metropolis, and its design has influenced the cityscapes of films such as *Blade Runner* (1982), the *Star Wars* series and *The Fifth Element* (1997) – among many others.

NATURAL ENVIRONMENTS

Rebuilding the cities we see every day is demanding, but reproducing natural landscapes can be equally challenging. 'Copying Mother Nature is a skill that can only come from lots of careful observation, a fair amount of research and often plenty of experimentation,' says Richard Taylor (1965–), the infectiously enthusiastic head of New Zealand's Weta Workshop, where exquisite miniature landscapes have been crafted for films including the *Lord of the Rings* trilogy (2001, 2002, 2003), *The Legend of Zorro* (2005) and *King Kong* (2005).

Referring to much of the work produced by Weta's talented staff as 'miniature' would be misleading, however. This is intricacy on an industrial scale. 'For our miniature work on Peter Jackson's *Lord of the Rings* movies we affectionately called the models "bigatures",' says Taylor. 'Many of our models for those films were bigger than the average house.'

Weta chooses to create such enormous miniatures for several reasons. 'Quite simply, the bigger a model is, the more detail we can build into it, the easier it is to photograph well and the better it will look on film,' says Taylor. 'Our biggest models so far have been for *Lord of the Rings*. These represented huge environments and often required very delicate detail to reflect the wonderful concept designs of Alan Lee and John Howe. The models had to be big because the camera often needed to move in from wide shots to close-ups showing digital and live-action characters performing within the environments.'

RIGHT: **One of the hundreds of reconstructed miniature trees built by Weta Workshop for** *King Kong* **(2005). Thousands of artificial leaves adorn the branches, while carefully crafted rubber vines hang below.**

BELOW: **In this dam-bursting scene from** *Earthquake* **(1974), the scale of the model is given away by the unconvincing appearance of the water and the oversized grass and bushes.**

Weta's models for *Lord of the Rings* were created at a range of scales, with an 8 m (26 ft) high model of the city of Minas Tirith built at 1:72 scale, a 1:35 scale, 20 m (65 ft) diameter model of Isengard, a 1:14 scale cave of Khazad-dûm that was 20 m (65 ft) long and 14 m (45 ft) wide, and a 1:6 scale dam that stood 8 m (26 ft) high and was ultimately destroyed with 35,000 gallons of water. Most of the environments built for *King Kong* were re-created at 1:10 scale while those that needed to be seen in close-up were produced at as much as 1:3 scale.

For both *Lord of the Rings* and *King Kong*, Weta needed to create many rocky environments such as cliff faces and mountainsides. 'Referring to conceptual art, a modeller, under the watchful eye of senior miniature builder John Baster, first builds a polystyrene and Plasticine-covered maquette – a small version of the model so we can see what the final version might look like,' explains Taylor. Again, describing Weta's maquettes as 'small' is something of a misstatement. Where most maquettes will fit in the palm of your hand, Weta's are typically the size of a double bed. 'We dress our maquettes with vegetation or model buildings, anything to make them resemble their final appearance. Then Peter will come and have a look. Luckily we're pretty attuned to what he likes now, but any alterations can be made there and then – he may even dig in and sculpt changes himself – he's a very skilled artist in his own right.'

With the maquette approved, Weta must upscale it to create a larger model for filming. Using a giant bandsaw each maquette is cut into many thin slices. These cross-section profiles are each traced onto sheets of plastic with grids printed on them. These are then used as a reference to hand-draw a much larger copy of the profile onto huge sheets of polystyrene – Weta's staff carefully copying the outline by eye from each small square into each big square. Each profile is then cut out using a hot wire to slice through the polystyrene.

Modern production techniques have introduced changes to the way that the cross-sections for some models are produced, as Taylor explains: 'Films with lots of action now rely heavily on computer-generated pre-viz sequences [230>]. These are 3-D animated scenes used to plan a movie before filming starts and they can include quite sophisticated CG environment models. When Peter particularly liked what had been created in *Kong*'s pre-viz sequences we would reproduce that as exactly as possible in miniature. The most important area of the model is what we call the "red carpet". This is anywhere that the computer-generated pre-viz characters touch their environment – mostly the areas they walk on. If we reproduce the CG pre-viz models exactly then animators basing their final character

animation on that pre-viz will be able to place their digital characters into our miniature environments much more efficiently.'

To create models based on *King Kong*'s pre-viz sequences, Weta utilized the actual digital models that were used to produce the pre-viz animation. These digital models were sliced up in the computer and then used to drive a 'Shopbot' computer-controlled routing machine that carved faithful polystyrene cross-sections at a large scale.

Whichever way they are produced, the finished polystyrene cross-sections are finally arranged next to each other like the bleached ribcage of some long-dead monster. In the case of the canyon created for the brontosaurus stampede in *King Kong*, this 'miniature' structure was 30 m (97 ft) long, 8 m (26 ft) wide and 7 m (23 ft) high.

With their basic skeleton complete, the models are ready to be transformed into intricately detailed environments. 'We use a lot of real rock in our models, or at least copies of real rock,' says Taylor. 'There's a certain type of rock around here in Wellington, called greywacke. It's a wonderful shattered, rotten rock with a very busy surface and it's useful because it essentially has no scale. You can put your hand on it and it looks like a normal piece of small rock, or you can composite a little inch-high climber on the same piece and it will look like they're scaling the side of a mountain.'

To transfer rock from the real world into their miniatures, Weta technicians select interesting formations and cover them in silicone (279>), working it into the cracks to make sure every detail is captured. The delicate silicone is then sprayed with urethane, a type of expanding foam which hardens to form a rigid casing. When the silicone has set, the moulds are taken back to the workshop where copies are made before production begins. 'We always make copies of the master mould because the urethane foam used to produce our model rocks degrades the silicone mould. We can only use a mould about 30 times before we have to replace it,' explains Taylor.

Hundreds of chunks of rock are cast and then painted with the right colour and texture. 'For *Kong* we spent a long time studying the rock on various South Pacific islands. At first it just looks black but seen up close it's actually a complex mixture of different oxides that combine to create a kind of mouldy black effect. Just painting the rocks black didn't produce this look so our artists built up layers of different-coloured paint, using a roller to push the wet paint around, taking it off the high spots to reveal the various shades below.'

Once painted the urethane rocks are used to 'skin' the polystyrene cross-sections. Each piece of rock is carefully selected for its shape, size and texture before being pinned to the cross-sections with wooden shish-kebab sticks. 'This is one of the most important stages because it is what will be seen on camera,' says Taylor. 'We're not just randomly sticking these rocks on so they look nice, we're art-directing the rock surface. We have to reproduce naturalistic strata details and fault lines at the same time as creating a highly evocative, dramatic environment. Our model-makers spent a lot of time studying photographs of the rock formations of the Indonesian islands to get this right.' Finally, urethane filler is sprayed into any gaps between the rock pieces and then sculpted and painted to match the surrounding detail.

Once the groundwork of a model has been laid, attention turns to dressing it with plants and trees. Miniature trees are traditionally produced by sculpting trunk and branches in clay, making moulds, and using the moulds to produce foam rubber castings. After being painted, plastic or paper leaves are painstakingly hand-glued to every branch and twig. For *King Kong*, however, Weta drew directly on nature to create their trees. 'Peter wanted all the foliage on Skull Island to look as if it had been affected by the island's savage environment. He envisaged the trees to be twisted and eerie. He also wanted them to be constantly moving in the wind that blew in from the sea,' says Taylor. 'By good fortune there is a mountain a few hours from our workshop in Wellington. The wind that hits this mountain comes directly from the South Pole – it's strong and cold. As a result the trees that grow there are twisted and gnarled and dwarfed. A local farmer was clearing his land of these trees and he couldn't believe his luck when we offered to buy the lot!'

LEFT: A miniature environment created for *King Kong* (2005). Intricately painted styrofoam rock structures have been carefully dressed with real lichens, mosses, vines and miniature trees. It will resemble a verdant jungle when expertly lit and photographed.

FAR RIGHT: A photo cut-out ship sits behind model buildings and photo cut-out railway carriages in this shot from *Titanic* (1997).

BELOW RIGHT: For *Tank Girl* (1995), Robert and Dennis Skotak created a devastated city in miniature. Despite looking like carefully modelled buildings, much of the architectural detail was created by glueing photographs of real buildings to the sides of the models.

Taylor's team transported the trees to their workshop, where they were oven-dried for two days so that their leaves, which were of a normal size, could be carefully picked off the wizened branches. The trees were then cut into pieces that could be reassembled to create new trees of the necessary character and size, ranging from 1 to 3 m (3 to 10 ft) in height.

'Because the trees had to move in the wind we reconstructed them with different diameters of springy wire inside their joints. The lower branches were connected with wire about as thick as your thumb while for the topmost twigs the wire was thinner than pencil lead. The result was trees with joints that got increasingly flexible as they got towards the top and which swayed to scale. Where the branches joined we had to leave a gap so that they could actually bend back and forth. We filled that gap with coconut fibre then covered the join with a skin of flexible latex or tissue paper. Over that we sculpted putty to look like the surrounding branch.'

The completed tree structures were painted with fine bark detail to impart a greater sense of scale. The naked structures then needed to be rejuvenated with a covering of leaves. 'Because these weren't meant to be any recognizable form of tree, we designed a range of new leaf patterns. Two of our staff then spent three weeks visiting every artificial plant factory that they could find in China until they discovered one that could make leaves to our specifications. Using our designs they injection-moulded hundreds of thousands of beautiful, delicate leaf sprays that had just the right colour and translucency. In the end we used two tons of them!'

Weta model technicians gave some of the leaves additional coats of paint and flocking to create a range of shades and textures. Thousands of tiny leaf sprays were then patiently glued to the 350 subtly flexible trees that were created for the production. When blown by giant fans and filmed at 48 frames per second, the resulting forests stirred with a primeval realism.

For *Kong*, Weta's obsessive attention to detail even extended to perfecting the perfect miniature vine. 'Skull Island needed a lot of vines. We could have used small-sized real vines, but scaled down they wouldn't have hung in the right way,' states Taylor. 'Real vines hang in a perfect parabolic curve and we thought it was important to get that right.' To create their vines Weta sprayed dyed brown liquid latex onto sheets of glass. When set, the thin latex sheets were rolled up, incorporating leaves

and moss as well as lead shot that would stretch the latex to produce perfectly scaled curves when strung between trees.

The final stage of creating each model was to dress it for camera. This meant moving the sometimes massive miniatures from the workshop to the shooting stage, where a team of model technicians under the guidance of Paul van Ommen turned the newly painted polystyrene structures into atmospheric jungles. After placing Weta's pre-sprung trees and latex vines, a range of artificial and real plants were carefully arranged to re-create the random beauty of nature. These included over 20,000 stunted ferns that were collected from the same mountain that had provided the dwarfed trees. These were nurtured in a specially built greenhouse using zero-nutrient soil to prevent any sudden growth spurts due to their comfortable new environment.

The dressing of environmental models has its own array of clever tricks. Grass can be reproduced in miniature using a range of materials including dyed goat hair and green desiccated coconut. Moss and lichens are gathered from the wild and glue-gunned into place before being scorched with a blowtorch to make them look more to scale. The contents of a certain type of fruit tea bag can make the perfect leaf litter for miniature forest floors. Even sand can look the wrong scale in a miniature and might be replaced with talcum powder or micro-balloons – minute glass beads used as an industrial filler.

The attention to minute detail that produces a perfect miniature environment can become something of an obsession, even a way of life, as Taylor admits: 'You do tend to journey through life looking at the world in a certain way,' he says. 'Everything you come across might have some sort of model-making potential. It also means you take much more notice of everything that's around you – that interesting seed pod on the ground while you're waiting for a bus, or the way the leather on a car dashboard cracks. All that stuff creeps into the work that will eventually be up on the screen. Ultimately that's what helps us achieve our goal of producing miniature environments that are indistinguishable from the real thing. We create a lot of make-up effects for fantasy creatures here at Weta and I always say that's a bit like taking an English exam – your success is open to the eye of the interpreter. But making miniature environments is more like a maths exam. If you don't get the equation right, it's just plain wrong!'

PHOTO CUT-OUTS

2-D images have been used to simulate 3-D reality in movies ever since Georges Méliès (<14) painted *trompe l'œil* spacecraft and settings for films like *A Trip to the Moon* (1902). The method of using 2-D photo cut-outs to create apparently 3-D sets has proved a useful and labour-saving one ever since.

Robert and Dennis Skotak have used photo cut-outs to great effect in productions such as *Aliens* (1986) and even the digital effects extravaganza *Titanic* (1997). For *Titanic*, the Skotaks were asked to produce a view of the doomed liner as seen from the window of a dockside pub. 'We took several photographs of the 13.5 m [44 ft] model that was being used to film many of the effects sequences, and glued them together to produce one huge 5 m [17 ft] photo of the ship', explains Robert Skotak. 'That giant photo had to be touched up a bit since the model used for filming was in several sections and a bit worse for wear by the time we photographed it. The main body of the photo cut-out ship looked quite convincing, but the rounded funnels looked a bit fake from the oblique angle that we were filming from, so we cut them out separately and angled them so that they looked more convincingly 3-D from the position of the camera. Then we dressed the photo with real model masts and rigging to give a better sense of depth.' The surrounding dockside area was also partly re-created using photo cut-outs. 'We built detailed miniature warehouses and needed to put some railway carriages in front of them', says Skotak. 'We purchased some large model trains, but these were very expensive – even for the budget of *Titanic* – so we photographed the models, then scanned them into the computer where we retouched the pictures to produce a number of variables such as wagons with open doors and windows and so on. We then printed out these

photos and mounted them on cards which we added to the model to produce a much more impressive-looking railway yard.'

To finish the shot, the Skotaks resorted to digital technology. 'We now find that the computer is a really useful tool for helping us to achieve the last 10 per cent of an image that used to take us a disproportionate amount of time to get right during actual filming', comments Skotak. 'Now we can spend more time making sure that we get the lighting right on the model and it doesn't matter too much if any bits of equipment stray into a shot because they can be removed digitally later on. In the *Titanic* dockside shot we digitally tweaked the ship's tonal values to make it look more realistic, and we added a plume of steam coming out of one of the funnels.' The photo cut-out shot was finally digitally composited into the live-action pub sequence in which Leonardo DiCaprio's character wins tickets for his trip on the *Titanic*.

MINIATURE PYROTECHNICS

For many people, high-octane action is what going to the cinema is all about. Big explosions are one of the most important ingredients in any modern action-adventure movie but, ironically, the biggest explosions to engulf our screens are usually created in miniature. Miniature pyrotechnics are used in film-making for many of the same reasons that models are used – blowing up real buildings and vehicles would be time-consuming, expensive and, above all, dangerous.

'Every kid wants to blow things up!' exclaims Academy Award winner Joseph Viskocil, one of the world's leading miniature pyrotechnicians. 'For me, the inspiration was the Saturday morning serials with effects by the Lydeckers [145>], and the Gerry Anderson puppet shows like *Thunderbirds*. As a kid I didn't know these things were done in miniature; I thought they were out there blowing up a new warehouse every week. When I discovered it was all models, I decided that was what I wanted to do.'

Viskocil's work on a project begins by discussing what type of explosion is required with the film's director and visual effects supervisor. 'What the explosion must do, and what it must look like, will affect a number of factors,' explains the pyrotechnician. 'It can influence the way a model is built, the way it is filmed, and what type of explosives and chemicals I will use for the job.'

Once plans for a shot have been confirmed, Viskocil works with the film's model-makers to make sure that the miniature to be destroyed is built to the correct specifications. 'A model for destruction is quite different to one that is used for normal shooting,' he explains. 'Most models are built to look good and perform, but destruction models must look good and blow up convincingly – it's a very different thing.' While most models are built to survive the rigours of filming, destruction models must be designed to come apart in all the right places when detonated. The way that a model comes apart is largely dependent on the materials used for its construction. 'The material a model is made of is very important,' states Viskocil. 'Plastics may be no good because they may just melt; on the other hand, metals might not break apart so well. When it comes to buildings, plaster is the best material; it blows up in nice chunks that can be controlled by the consistency of the plaster that is used. It can look totally convincing.'

Once a model is built, Viskocil takes it apart again. 'Models that explode have to be told *how* to explode,' states Viskocil. 'If you just rig a model with explosives, there's no telling what it might do, so we weaken them first.' Simply obliterating a model can be visually uninteresting, so by scoring and pre-weakening it, the model's destruction can be engineered so that particular parts break away or remain intact.

Viskocil also considers the way in which an explosion should be filmed. 'The speed we choose to film at will depend on the size of the model and what it will be doing,' he says. 'Most model explosions are done at about 96 or 120 frames per second, which will normally make an explosion look pretty good. Generally speaking, the smaller the model, the faster we will film it.' Camera position must also be considered. Most explosions are filmed with two cameras, though more are used for shots that can only be filmed in one take. 'You have to make sure you've got all the angles covered,' explains Viskocil. 'It's not so important with things like aeroplanes, because the modellers usually make a number of copies, but with a big building like the White House that I destroyed for *Independence Day* [1996], you're talking about blowing up models that cost tens of thousands of dollars each – sometimes hundreds of thousands. You don't want to have to ask them to go build you another if you get it wrong!'

ABOVE: **Joe Viskocil's Death Star explosion for** *Star Wars* **(1977). The camera is on the floor, looking up at the explosion.**

BELOW LEFT: **Joe Viskocil (***extreme right***) prepares a miniature version of the White House for destruction in** *Independence Day* **(1996).**

BELOW: **The attack on the White House as it appeared in the final film.**

PROFILE DENNIS AND ROBERT SKOTAK

Growing up in Detroit, Dennis Skotak (1943–; *above*) and his brother Robert (1948–; *below*) were influenced at an early age by a Saturday matinee screening of George Pal's (<28) classic *Destination Moon* (1950). The boys became obsessed by space travel and science fiction movies. In order to relive their favourite movies, the two would take photographs of scenes featuring homemade model spaceships. Taking photographs soon developed into making movies. In 1958 the pair made an ambitious 30-minute adaptation of H.G. Wells's novel *The Time Machine*. The effects-laden mini-epic was the first 8 mm film shot in Cinemascope and won the creators awards in a Kodak competition for young film-makers.

Dedicated to pursuing a career in movies, the Skotaks moved to Los Angeles in 1976 and found work producing imaginative zero-budget effects for Roger Corman's (<33) company New World Pictures, where they befriended James Cameron (<41). The Skotaks became known for their ability to create dazzling in-camera visual effects for films like *Battle Beyond the Stars* (1980) and *Escape from New York* (1981). For James Cameron's *Aliens* (1986), they made extensive use of foreground miniatures, mirrors, photo cut-outs and a host of other extraordinary effects on a limited budget. It was the start of a working relationship that would include most of the director's future output.

Though the Skotaks have gained great respect within the industry for producing amazing effects with minimum resources, the two brothers have also embraced the digital medium. They now enjoy creating a clever hybrid of sophisticated in-camera techniques and modern digital technologies. The best of both disciplines have been combined for the benefit of films such as *House on Haunted Hill* (1999) and *X-Men 2* (2003).

The Skotaks have won Academy Awards for their work on *Aliens* (1986), *The Abyss* (1989) and *Terminator 2: Judgment Day* (1991).

As the shoot approaches, Viskocil prepares the explosives themselves. 'The first thing I will consider is safety. The work I do could easily kill, and no one should try anything like this without an awful lot of experience and technical know-how', explains Viskocil. 'After considering the safety aspects of a shot, I will work out what the explosion needs to look like and which explosives will achieve that look. There are basically two types of explosion that I use', he explains. 'One is largely cosmetic; it produces lots of fire, sparks and smoke. The other type of explosion is purely destructive and is used to rip things apart physically.'

Gasoline is the basic ingredient used to produce billowing clouds of fire. By adding various chemicals to the gasoline, explosions can be made to appear orange, red, blue or green. 'For the TIE fighter explosions in *Star Wars* [1977], I produced green explosions using gasoline and powdered zinc', remembers Viskocil. 'George Lucas had specifically asked for green because he said it represented all the money that was being blown on the film!'

Surprisingly small quantities of gas are needed to blow up miniatures effectively. Blowing up the 2 m (7 ft) model gas tanker in *The Terminator* (1984) involved just 7 litres (1½ gallons) of gas to create the apparently huge ball of fire seen in the film. Additional ingredients can be mixed with the gas to produce other effects. Adding titanium powder results in a shower of silver-blue sparks; gold sparks

BELOW LEFT: **Joe Viskocil prepares a model gas tanker for destruction in a climactic sequence from *The Terminator* (1984).**

BELOW: **The final explosion as seen in the film.**

are produced using iron filings. 'I produced a really nice sparky explosion when we were shooting some test explosions for *Star Wars*', recalls Viskocil. 'When we watched the results the next day, someone saw this explosion and said, "That's the one we'll use for the Death Star!" I'd never even heard of the Death Star by this point so I didn't know what they meant, but that explosion was the one that they used at the end of the film.'

Gasoline explosions are frequently achieved using a mortar – a metal tube that is planted at the point where the explosion has to appear. 'A mortar is used to shape an explosion', explains Viskocil. 'Ultimately all fire will always go upwards, but using a mortar you can force an explosion in the direction you want it to go.' A detonator is placed at the bottom of the mortar, and on top of this goes a polythene bag containing the gas and other chemicals. Debris – usually bits of material left over from the modelling process – is the last thing placed in the mortar, so that it will be projected outwards to produce chunks of wreckage that are silhouetted by the ball of fire behind them.

For gas explosions in the zero gravity of space, pyrotechnics are filmed in a high-ceilinged building. The camera is placed on the floor pointing up at the explosive device that hangs from the ceiling. After detonation the cloud of combusting gas and sparks propelled down towards the camera seems as if it is travelling outwards in the vacuum of space, while the unwanted smoke rises to the ceiling, concealed by the explosion in the foreground.

Underwater explosions are an unusual challenge that Viskocil is occasionally asked to meet. For *XXX* (2002) he created the impressive underwater explosion of the 2.5 m (8 ft) long model of the submersible hydrofoil *Ahab*. 'The main thing to remember when you're underwater is that you're not going to get the smoke and fire that normally makes explosions look impressive', reveals Viskocil. 'To make the destruction of *Ahab* look good I detonated black-powder bombs which forced the craft apart and created lots of high-pressure bubble clouds. To make the explosion look really destructive I used dozens of old-fashioned camera flashbulbs. These aren't manufactured any more and supplies are dwindling, I have to import mine from Ireland. The bulbs are waterproofed and placed against the back of the object being destroyed so that they won't be seen directly when firing. When the bulbs went off they backlit the pieces of model and the bubbles caused by the explosion, making it look much more powerful.'

To physically destroy objects, an explosive rope called Primacord, also known as Det-Cord, is used. Primacord can be wrapped around, or threaded through, objects, and when detonated by an electrical charge, explodes at a speed of 6,700 m (22,000 ft) per second. 'It's a strange substance', remarks Viskocil. 'You can carry it around in rolls like normal rope and even throw it into a fire and it won't explode, but if you hit it with a hammer, you can say goodbye to your hand.'

Detonating explosives is a job that requires considerable planning. 'Normally we may have a dozen or more explosions in one shot', Viskocil explains. 'Usually we film at around 120 frames per second, and the average explosive shot may need to be on screen for two, maybe four seconds. At 120 frames, a four-second shot will actually take about three-quarters of a second to film, so we may have dozens of explosions going off in less than a second – it gets pretty complicated.' The exact order in which a sequence of explosions should be detonated is calculated carefully, taking into account the varying speeds at which different charges will explode and the position of each camera. If an explosion near the camera were to go off before those in the distance, the foreground explosion would obscure the background action. Once a shot has been planned and wired, a test is conducted using flashbulbs in place of explosives. The sequence of flashbulbs is filmed at the correct camera speed and the result studied to make sure that each 'explosion' is in the right place at the right time.

Once tests have been approved, the shot can be filmed. All of the wiring and mortars are already in place, so setting up the shot is a matter of installing the pre-prepared charges. Each charge is linked to an electronic firing box that can detonate the explosives at intervals of anything from one hour to one-thousandth of a second. 'We do a lot of checks and rehearsals before setting off an explosion', says Viskocil. 'Everyone has to know the exact running order. We deal with potentially lethal events, so if, at any point during a shot, I have the slightest doubt about anything, the whole thing will be shut down – even if there are tens of thousands of dollars at risk. Safety is number one on the set – there's no two ways about it.'

When asked about his favourite shot in his 30-year career, Viskocil is quick to respond. 'I received an Oscar for *Independence Day*, and I loved supervising the effects for *Team America* [2004], but the work I like best is from *True Lies* [1994]', he admits. 'There's a shot where a truck is travelling across a bridge and the bridge is blown up by missiles. It was filmed down in the Florida Keys using a model bridge in shallow water. Everything about that sequence worked so well that most people are convinced that it's a real bridge being destroyed. When I look at shots like that one, I realize what a great job I have – people actually pay me to blow stuff up. What schoolkid wouldn't want a job like that?'

HIGH-SPEED PHOTOGRAPHY

To film models and explosions at higher than normal frame rates, special high-speed cameras are used. Cameras designed by the Photo-Sonics Corporation, originally manufactured for filming NASA rocket launches, will run at 360 frames per second (fps).

The high-precision instruments use a vacuum pump to suck each frame of film into place behind the lens and hold it securely during exposure. The cameras have to be operated by specialist engineers who lubricate the moving parts between each shot.

An even faster Photo-Sonics camera can film at an incredible 3,250 fps, making a one-second event last over 135 seconds when projected at the normal speed of 24 fps. At this speed it is impossible to hold each frame of film still for exposure, so a rotating prism is used to bend the light from the lens and 'project' it onto each frame of film as it passes (fig. 4).

High-speed cameras take a few seconds to attain the right speed and so could waste hundreds of feet of film before anything useful is filmed. To avoid this the camera is brought up to speed before the film is released through the camera, travelling at a rate of over 5 m (16½ ft) per second. Such high speeds are normally reserved for filming small but intense explosions, which look massive and slow-moving when projected at normal speed.

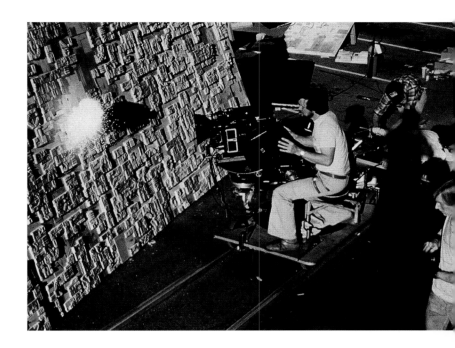

ABOVE FAR LEFT: **Joe Viskocil (wearing cap) prepares to detonate a miniature bridge built in the shallow waters of the Florida Keys for** *True Lies* **(1994).**

ABOVE LEFT: **The exploding bridge as seen in the final film. Detonations were triggered by the model truck as it travelled along the freeway. Computer-generated missile trails were added during post-production.**

ABOVE RIGHT: **Richard Edlund uses a high-speed camera to film a miniature explosion on the surface of the Death Star for** *Star Wars* **(1977). The camera is being moved along a dolly track to simulate the point of view of a passing spacecraft.**

FIGURE 4 **ROTATING PRISM CAMERA**

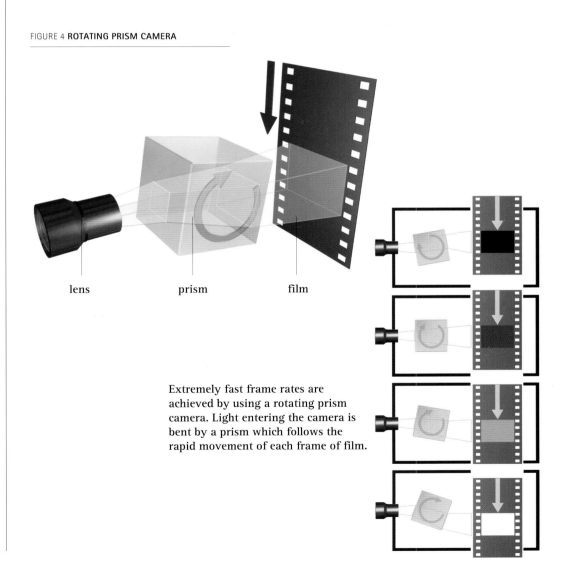

lens   prism   film

Extremely fast frame rates are achieved by using a rotating prism camera. Light entering the camera is bent by a prism which follows the rapid movement of each frame of film.

LEFT: Technicians stage an indoor battle for *Jack Ahoy* (1934) in the Gaumont-British studio in Islington, London. The camera is placed at water level to make the ships look larger, and a studiohand is ready to use a wedge-shaped paddle to produce waves.

BELOW: The destruction of a beautifully detailed 7.5 m (25 ft) ship in the pirate adventure *Cutthroat Island* (1995).

RIGHT: Filming a shot for *Interview with the Vampire* (1994) in Pinewood's huge water tank, among the biggest in the world.

FAR RIGHT: The problems of making water look to scale are apparent in this model shot from *The Poseidon Adventure* (1972).

BATTLESHIPS AND SEASCAPES

The maritime history of the movies is a long one. As early as 1898, J. Stuart Blackton and Albert E. Smith of the Vitagraph Company were sailing cardboard cut-out ships on improvised ponds to re-create the *Battle of Santiago Bay* (1898). Their later depiction of the Battle of Manila is said to have been so convincing that even naval officers present at the real conflict mistook the film for documentary footage.

Sea-going dramas have always been popular, and by the 40s, special effects departments were well equipped to provide miniature pirate galleons or battle cruisers whenever called for. Techniques were greatly refined during World War II. With limited access to naval resources and the coast during wartime, special effects artists relied on the studio 'tank' – a large pond with a painted backdrop – to provide the setting for sea battles and any other scenes that involved water. Today, model ships are still used as much as ever in films like *Pirates of the Caribbean* (2003), *Master and Commander* (2003), and *Peter Pan* (2003).

Effects supervisor Martin Gutteridge, based at London's Pinewood Studios, has overseen miniature maritime sequences for films including *Cutthroat Island* (1995) and *Interview with the Vampire* (1994). 'Miniature ships are still the most effective way of achieving any sort of action at sea,' says Gutteridge. 'Real ships are cumbersome, they take a long time to manoeuvre, they rely on the right sort of weather conditions, and they need a large crew to operate. It's also quite hard to find anyone who will let you blow up their boat and sink it!'

The greatest problem when filming miniature ships has always been the difficulty in making water look to scale – while it is possible to make small boats, it is quite impossible to make 'small water'. Whatever is done to it, water always remains the same scale. 'There are few things you can do about water,' says Gutteridge, sighing. 'It is physically impossible to scale down. There are a few tricks that we use to make things a little better, but on the whole you need to design model shots so that water appears for the shortest time possible.'

One of the most important areas of water in a model shot is that immediately in front of the camera. When filming miniature ships, the camera is kept as close as possible to the water level, and is sometimes even partially submerged so that its lens remains just above the surface. This low angle helps to make model ships look larger and also ensures that the sky detail painted on the tank's backdrop is seen as a reflection in the water. Such a low angle does, however, mean that the water may be just inches in front of the lens and a very large depth of field must be used to keep both foreground water and distant ship in acceptable focus. Out-of-focus foreground water is an instant giveaway to the presence of model shots and can be seen in many wartime films shot without the advantage of modern fast film stocks.

Much of the art of filming miniature sea battles lies in the way that water is persuaded to perform for the camera. 'We spend as much time on the performance of the water as we do on almost everything else,' says Gutteridge. Small waves are produced by placing huge fans around the edge of the tank to blow winds across the water and create the desired wave pattern. Some people add a little detergent to the water to encourage slightly foamy wave tips, though just a few drops too much can turn an ocean into a bubble bath. By positioning wedge-shaped paddles that move up and down at the edge of the tank, larger waves and rougher sea conditions can be created.

Storms and tidal waves are produced using 'tipper-tanks', which can release thousands of gallons of water into the tank to crash into boats and simulate treacherous seas. Successful wave patterns can often only be sustained for a few seconds before they reach the opposite wall of the tank and rebound to cause new and unrealistic counter-ripples. Wave patterns are therefore set up and tested before shooting commences. Once ships and cameras are in position, the desired pattern is created just moments before the action begins.

The camera speed used to film model ships is influenced more by the need to create realistic water conditions than by the scale of the models. Small waves can be made to look larger by filming at faster frame rates. This has the effect of slowing down their movement when the film is projected at the normal speed. However, rather than looking larger, waves can look thick and oily if they are filmed too fast. 'Depending on the scale of model

that we use, we tend to film most of our water sequences at somewhere between 75 and 125 frames per second,' says Gutteridge. 'This will usually give quite acceptable-scaled water. One way to get water to look totally convincing, though, is to film at night – the dark is very good at hiding scale problems in a water shot.'

To help with problems of scale in water shots, all models are built as large as possible. 'When working out at what scale to build a ship, we tend to do it in reverse,' explains Gutteridge. 'We like working with ships that are around 7.5 m [25 ft] in length. A ship that size is relatively easy to move, it's not a bad size in terms of water scale, and we can physically climb on board to make adjustments during filming. We can also comfortably float a small fleet of ships of that size on the Pinewood tank at the same time. Therefore we tend to look at the measurements of the full-size ship and derive a scale to produce a ship that is about the size we need.'

Model ships are built from a variety of materials, depending on the type of vessel being replicated. Modern naval vessels are often constructed using a fibreglass hull with wood and metal fittings. Traditional galleons, on the other hand, are crafted entirely from wood. 'Old-fashioned ships are our favourite to re-create,' says Gutteridge. 'We construct our models just like a real ship, using traditional methods to produce a scaled-down hull onto which we attach miniature planks of wood. We find that ships that are constructed in the correct way will move in all the right ways when floating in the water.'

After the hull is complete, it is given decking and every external detail, from capstan to crow's nest, is carved in wood, painted and placed on board. Masts as high as 4.6 m (15 ft) are fitted with historically accurate, hand-tied rigging and hung with lightweight sails designed to undulate like heavy canvas when filmed at high speed. Several sets of rigging are normally made for each boat, since they tend to be the first part of a ship to suffer from battle damage.

The finished masterpieces, often weighing over a ton, are lifted into the tank by crane, ready for filming. 'Moving ships around in a tank is quite a complicated business and we use a number of different methods,' explains Gutteridge. 'We can actually sail a boat by using huge fans to fill the sails and blow it along. But it's hard to get a ship to sail exactly where you want it to go and the fans can cause problems with the wave pattern. We can also build motors into the ships and sail them by radio control. More commonly, however, we use a system of underwater cables to push and pull the boats.'

Each vessel is built with a series of rings along the bottom of its keel. The rings are threaded onto an underwater guide cable that is arranged along the path that the ship needs to follow. A second underwater cable is then run through an on-shore winch and attached to the bow and stern of the boat. When this cable is moved backwards or forwards the boat moves along the guide cable at the desired speed and in the correct direction. 'With

six or eight ships being operated at once, which isn't uncommon in sea battles, there can be a real maze of wires under the water and it can become quite complex,' says Gutteridge.

The staging of sea battles is something of a military operation in itself. 'The thing about models is that we spend months building them only for editors to spend their time trying to show them as little as possible,' explains Gutteridge. 'That's because even the best models shouldn't be on screen for too long, otherwise the audience has the chance to scrutinize the image and see that it is actually just a miniature – especially where water is involved.' As a result, Gutteridge and his team often spend their time producing shots that will be on screen for perhaps four seconds or less. 'A lot can happen in four seconds,' says Gutteridge. 'Our problem, however, is that in a typical miniature ship sequence we will be filming at about 100 frames per second – four times normal speed. That means that in reality we have to perform a four-second shot in just one second. In one second we may have to manoeuvre six ships, fire a dozen cannon and blow up a mast. We have to plan things like explosions to hundredths of a second,' he explains. 'We can make a small explosion filmed at high speed look totally convincing, but when you're dealing with explosions in or around water, they will only look real during the explosion itself. Water and debris looks fine while it's on the way up, but as soon as it comes back down and hits the water, the patterns and ripples that it produces are totally unconvincing. So we always plan explosions to happen at the end of a shot so that the editor can cut away before things start to look wrong.'

Filming at four times normal speed means that ships need to be manoeuvred around the tank at a surprisingly fast rate of knots. However, these speeds are rarely enough to simulate the look of a real ship ploughing through the oceans. 'To give the impression that our small ships are actually cutting through the waves, we have to cheat a little,' admits Gutteridge. 'A normal ship travelling at speed will have waves and spray around its bow. We can't achieve that at the speeds our models move, so we fit the front of each ship with a pipe that pumps a stream of water up in front of the bow to give the impression that the ship is slicing through the waves. A similar device may be used to create a ship's wake.'

A watery grave is the fate of many model ships, and sinking them is another complex operation. Most studio tanks are just 1–1.2 m (3–4 ft) in depth but include a much deeper 'sinking hole' at their centre. This central well will allow 6 m (20 ft) ships to up-end and go down. 'To sink ships, we sometimes divide their hulls into a number of ballast tanks. These are fitted with remote-controlled valves and can be filled with air or water to control the way in which a ship lists,' says Gutteridge. 'For dramatic sinkings, however, we attach ships to a submerged hydraulic rig that will twist the vessel in any direction we want as it goes down below the surface.'

MODERN MARITIME MARVELS

Although creating the convincing illusion of ships at sea has traditionally been one of the hardest of all special effects challenges, the latest digital production methods can now be harnessed to produce incredible results. *Master and Commander: The Far Side of the World* (2003) used an ingenious combination of both old and new techniques to produce a stunning portrayal of historic naval vessels at war.

Much of the live action was filmed aboard full-scale replica ships built in a huge studio tank in Mexico. Perfect in every detail, the star vessel of the film, the 60-ton *Surprise*, was mounted on a massive hydraulic gimbal. At the flick of a switch the underwater gimbal could mechanically rock the ship, emulating anything from a gentle swell to a full-scale storm. But for long shots of ships at battle or riding storm-tossed seas, a combination of full-size and miniature ships, real ocean footage and CG elements was carefully assembled.

Miniatures of the two ships featured in the film were built by Weta Workshop in New Zealand. Workshop supervisor John Baster was in charge of building the maritime masterpieces, which took three months to complete. 'The ships' bodies were made of timber on a steel framework. They had to be extremely strong as they were going to be treated really roughly,' recalls Baster. With their basic structure complete, the ships were then dressed with minute replicas of every prop found on their full-scale sisters. 'We built small guns, shrunken swords, miniature oil lamps, even tiny chicken coops,' says Baster. Among the trickiest details to achieve were the sails and rigging. Sailcloth specially woven in Hong Kong was sprayed with layers of lacquer to make it undulate heavily with the right sense of scale before being dressed with over 10 km (6 miles) of painstakingly knotted rope.

Water being the hardest thing to film to scale, it was decided that the finished models, each about 9 m (30 ft) long and 7.5 m (25 ft) high, would be filmed on dry land and the water added later. 'We shot the ships in front of a blue screen in the studio,' explains Baster. 'We originally considered programming a computer to mechanically move the models as if they were being tossed in the sea, but in the end we got a more natural look by having long handles attached to the ships and swaying them by hand. It made them feel more alive.' However, computers were used to control the firing of the ships' cannon. 'We rigged the portholes so that they would open one after another,' explains Baster. 'As soon as a porthole was open its cannon would emerge and then recoil as if having fired. This action was computer-controlled so that it could happen in rapid succession. We then filmed the action with a high-speed camera, resulting in slowed-down action that gave everything a sense of scale. During filming, lights were flashed onto the area around each porthole to look as if it was the light from a firing cannon. The actual fire and smoke coming from each muzzle was added digitally during post-production.'

Real water was only used to create shots in which the *Surprise* had to be hit by massive waves. During filming, tipper tanks dumped up to 3 tons of water onto the ship at once, swamping the decks and smashing much of the intricate modelwork, which had to be repaired between takes.

ABOVE: **Every deck-top detail was re-created with extraordinary precision, from ship's wheel to tiny fire buckets painted with the royal crest.**

BELOW LEFT: **Staff at Weta Workshop construct the hull of the *Surprise* by creating timber cross-sections onto which scaled-down wooden planking will be attached.**

BELOW: **Filmed in front of a blue screen using high-speed cameras, the model of the *Surprise* was moved by hand to simulate the rocking of the sea while hundreds of gallons of water were dumped onto its decks.**

RIGHT ABOVE & BELOW: **Weta crew members apply the finishing touches, including scaled-down rigging and accurately tied nautical knots.**

With the models filmed, the resulting footage was sent to Asylum, a visual effects facility in Los Angeles. 'Weta did a fantastic job creating totally convincing miniature ships,' explains Asylum boss Nathan McGuinness. 'However, it was the digital addition of traditionally difficult to film environmental elements such as smoke, fire and water that really helped to make shots of the model ships indistinguishable from the real thing.'

Asylum originally planned to create digital seas for the model ships to sail in, but as the nature of the film became more apparent they developed a different approach. 'Although CG water is very good now, everything in this film had a very rough, organic look, and we decided to try and use real water,' explains McGuinness. 'So we sent a cameraman on a voyage around Cape Horn and he came back with hours of footage of real waves.' Artists at Asylum then spent weeks studying the ocean footage. 'We would look at each shot and say we like this wave here – and the tip of this one, and so on. In the computer we then rotoscoped [174>] each of the waves we liked so that we had it as a separate layer. We could then composite these layers one on top of another – building up a new seascape that would look dramatic and match the footage of the model ships.'

As well as placing both model and full-size ships into digitally manipulated seas, Asylum added many additional elements to enhance the sense of scale and realism. CG bow spray and wakes were created to help the ships 'sit' in the water. CG sailors were added to climb the miniature rigging. Live-action elements such as smoke and flame were filmed and added to the model guns with real water splashes being used when cannon balls needed to hit the water. Fog, rain, clouds and other environmental elements were also layered into each shot. Asylum even produced totally CG model ships for use in some of the longer shots. The models were perfect replicas based on Lidar scans of actual ships (160>) and had rigging and sails programmed to move like the real thing.

'At any point in the finished movie you could be watching a model ship in a CG sea or a CG ship in a real sea or even the cannon of a CG ship firing real fire and smoke at a model ship in a real sea,' says McGuinness. 'That's the beauty of modern visual effects, we can merge the best of old and new techniques, crafting every shot to ensure that we create a sense of complete realism. There are over 400 visual effects shots in *Master and Commander* and since it isn't what you might call a special effects movie, I hope not a single viewer even considered that what they were watching was not totally real.'

a

b

c

d

e

f

g

h

i

To create dramatically authentic 19th-century sea battles for *Master and Commander: The Far Side of the World* (2003), visual effects studio Asylum often composited dozens of separate elements generated using a variety of different techniques.

a: This shot was first planned using computer-generated pre-visualization techniques.

b: Exquisitely detailed miniature ships were built by Weta Workshop. The ships were filmed at high speed to make the sails undulate with the appropriate sense of scale.

c: A large pan of shallow water placed next to the miniature ship was used to film accurate reflections.

d: Live-action footage filmed at sea provided an ocean background with natural-looking waves.

e: Live-action splashes were filmed at high speed to simulate cannon balls falling into the water.

f: Miniature pyrotechnics were filmed at high speed to simulate cannon fire.

g: Live-action smoke was filmed against a black background to produce a foggy atmosphere.

h: A second, more distant ship was created using computer animation.

i: The movement of the miniature ship was tracked so that computer-generated sailors could be added to the decks and rigging.

j

j: Captain Jack Aubrey's frigate
Surprise engages the French
privateer *Acheron* in this final
composite, made up of multiple

CLOUD TANKS

For *The Beginning or the End* (1947), director Arnold Gillespie (see panel) was asked to re-create the explosion of an atom bomb. Gillespie's first problem was discovering what such an event looked like, since the only existing footage of real atomic explosions was classified at the time. To create the mushroom cloud eventually seen in the film, Gillespie remembered the way in which he had seen fake blood form billowing clouds in water when filming Tarzan movies years earlier. The effects man built a large glass tank, and after experimenting with various dyes, filmed an underwater mushroom cloud. When superimposed over background footage, it created an impression of an explosion so convincing that the shot was used in air force training films for years afterwards.

Similar methods have been used to provide brooding cloud formations in films such as *Close Encounters of the Third Kind* (1977) and *Ghostbusters* (1984). To create the effect of clouds billowing towards the camera, a large glass tank is half-filled with a heavy saline solution. A layer of plastic sheeting is then floated on top of the saline liquid and fresh water gently poured over it. After the water settles, the plastic sheeting is carefully removed, causing as little disturbance as possible. Salt and fresh water have different densities, and this causes an invisible barrier called an inversion layer to form where the two liquids meet.

Various liquids can be employed to create the clouds themselves, though the most commonly used is a mixture of thinned grey emulsion paint. The paint is injected into the tank and, since it is heavier than fresh water, it sinks until it reaches the dense salt water. It then starts to spread out, creating the effect of rolling clouds. The process is normally backlit and filmed at high speed through the glass sides of the tank. When projected at the normal rate of 24 frames per second the resulting clouds look vast and heavy.

To create the effect of lightning within the cloud formations, waterproofed photography flashguns can be suspended in the water and fired when engulfed by the paint mixture. For the threatening clouds that cloak approaching spaceships in *Independence Day* (1996), a horse-shoe arrangement of coloured lights was pushed through the water while attached nozzles squirted paint, to create clouds that moved in front of the travelling rig.

To produce a convincing World War II bombing raid in *Memphis Belle* (1990), effects supervisor Richard Conway produced the aerial view of bombs hitting the ground by covering the bottom of a large water tank with an aerial photograph. The targets on the picture had valves placed beneath them and as the camera passed overhead, puffs of paint were squirted out of the valves to give the realistic impression of bombs hitting their targets.

Even though particle systems can now be used to create very convincing digital clouds and smoke (310>), cloud tanks are still a practical and economical solution and were used to produce smoke elements for *King Kong* (2005), for example.

Any material that is required to fly, float in the air or blow with the wind can be suspended in water for photography. In *Poltergeist* (1982), the hair-raising phantom that threatens the mother was actually a puppet filmed in a tank of water. Underwater, the ghoul's long hairs floated eerily around its body. For *The Good Earth* (1937), Arnold Gillespie filmed a tank of water to which an assistant added handfuls of coffee grounds. The image of thousands of drifting particles was superimposed over footage of rice fields, to create a convincing plague of locusts. While Americans had used coffee to portray a plague of locusts, English effects supervisor Cliff Richardson preferred to use tea leaves to create his swarm of mosquitoes for *The African Queen* (1951).

ABOVE: **A cloud tank being used by Gary Platek and Gary Waller at ILM to film a tornado effect for** *Poltergeist* **(1982).**

RIGHT: **Dark clouds roll ominously across the sky in this scene from** *Independence Day* **(1996). The clouds are actually grey paint injected into water, while the lightning was created using camera flashbulbs.**

FAR RIGHT: **The** *Super Star Destroyer* **from** *The Empire Strikes Back* **(1980) was one of hundreds of exquisite models built by ILM for the** *Star Wars* **series. Thousands of tiny holes were hand-drilled in the model to create the numerous lights.**

PROFILE **ARNOLD GILLESPIE**

Contributing to over 600 films spanning 50 years, Arnold 'Buddy' Gillespie (1899–1978) was perhaps the longest-serving special effects creator in Hollywood history.

Beginning as an art director at MGM in 1924, Gillespie worked under Cedric Gibbons, designer of the famous Oscar statuette. In the days before heavy unionization, Gillespie's early career included work in diverse roles on hundreds of films. He spent nine months in Italy filming *Ben-Hur* (1925) and was dressed as a soldier on a Roman galley during the infamous sinking in which extras are reputed to have drowned. With Gibbons, Gillespie built the hanging miniature that was used to add additional storeys to the film's Circus Maximus set (<117–18). Gillespie's career was so lengthy that he had the rare opportunity to work on the originals and remakes of both *Ben-Hur* (1925 and 1959) and *Mutiny on the Bounty* (1935 and 1962).

In 1936 Gillespie became the head of MGM's special effects department where he oversaw the effects for hundreds of films including classics such as *The Wizard of Oz* (1939), *Forbidden Planet* (1956) and *North by Northwest* (1959). Gillespie is best known for his work in MGM's enormous water tank. During World War II Gillespie spent much of his time up to his waist in water overseeing the filming of sea battles using increasingly sophisticated model ships, including the 16 m (54 ft) hydraulically operated aircraft carrier built for *Thirty Seconds Over Tokyo* (1944). Gillespie didn't always resort to such dramatic solutions, however; for *Mrs. Miniver* (1942) he re-created the flotilla of Dunkirk rescue ships from hundreds of cardboard cut-outs pulled through the water on strings. The result was surprisingly effective.

Gillespie won Academy Awards for his work in *Thirty Seconds Over Tokyo*, *Green Dolphin Street* (1947), *Plymouth Adventure* (1952) and *Ben-Hur* (1959).

AIRCRAFT AND SPACESHIPS

Aeroplanes and spacecraft have traditionally been among the most called-for model effects in film-making. Model aircraft need to be particularly strong, since they often undergo considerable stress during filming. They must be able to withstand the heat of intense studio lights, occasional collisions with camera equipment, rough handling by technicians and even falls from great heights when support cables fail.

The strength of such craft comes from within. Model builders usually construct aircraft from a honeycombed framework of wooden or aluminium cross-sections. This skeleton must be light enough to allow the model to be handled easily, but strong enough to support the whole model when it is suspended on a pylon at a single point. Aircraft are normally built with a number of mounting points, so that a support pylon can be hidden behind the body of the model regardless of the angle from which it is being filmed. Models are usually clad with an exterior of lightweight plastic or fibreglass panels. These can be removed easily to allow access to interior mechanisms, and quickly replaced after the filming of explosions or collisions. Model-makers often save time and money by decorating the exterior of their creations with ready-made items. A favourite resource is commercial model kits, whose moulded plastic components can provide instant detail for a film miniature. For *Silent Running* (1972), parts scavenged from over 650 German tank kits were used to embellish the exterior of the 8 m (26 ft) model spaceship *Valley Forge*.

TOP: **An effects technician prepares a Martian spacecraft for** *The War of the Worlds* **(1953). Wires were used both to suspend the craft and to supply power for their various functions.**

ABOVE: **Joe Viskocil prepares to fly a model aircraft using the Lydecker technique on the set of** *Independence Day* **(1996).**

LEFT: **The Skotaks and their crew prepare to film the complex drop ship scenes for** *Aliens* **(1986).**

LEFT: Matthew Gratzner watches New Deal Studios crew members as they attach a 6 m (20 ft) wide wing to a model of Howard Hughes's Hercules, built for *The Aviator* (2004).

BELOW: The finished Hercules was filmed in front of a green screen using natural lighting which would reflect realistically from the silver paintwork. The aircraft was attached to a motion-control rig, allowing it to tilt and bank as if flying.

BOTTOM: This model of Howard Hughes's XF-11 was built by Aero Telemetry Corporation using military drone engines.

FAR RIGHT: This model aircraft was built and filmed for the forest-fire scenes in *Always* (1989). The model was suspended from a complex travelling rig which allowed it to tilt and bank during flight. The suspension wires were made to vibrate so that they would not be visible when photographed.

Model aircraft and spaceships often have a number of mechanical features, such as hinged wing-flaps, spinning propeller blades or intricate puppet pilots whose heads can be turned during flight. The models must also accommodate the motors and gears that control their movement and the batteries that power them. The mechanisms themselves may be operated by radio control or via a bundle of electric cables that trail behind the model during filming.

Planes, and especially spacecraft, often need some form of internal lighting. This can be provided by drilling tiny holes in the body of the model to allow a bright interior light source to shine through. For *The Empire Strikes Back* (1980), the 1.8 m (6 ft) model of Darth Vader's Star Destroyer was drilled with over 250,000 tiny holes that twinkled with light from interior neon tubes. Occasionally, a bundle of fibre-optic cables is placed inside a model and the luminous end of each cable laboriously threaded into each porthole. The 3.7 m (12 ft) mothership model for *Independence Day* (1996) was illuminated by over 10,000 individually fitted fibre-optic cables – 45 km (28 miles) worth in all. This cargo of lights and motors can become extremely hot during the long hours that it usually takes to photograph each shot, so some models are fitted with extractor fans to prevent a meltdown of plastic components.

Once model aircraft have been constructed, they are ready to take to the skies. The simplest and perhaps easiest approach is to hang them on wires – a method favoured since the earliest days of movie-making and perfected by the legendary effects artists Howard and Theodore Lydecker (see panel). Wire techniques have been used more recently by modern effects legends Robert and Dennis Skotak. 'We built quite a sophisticated flying rig to move some of the spacecraft for *Aliens* [1986],' remembers Robert Skotak. 'One of the most complex shots that we achieved was where a drop ship had to land at the deserted colony of Acheron,' he states. 'The ship had to arc across the shot and then land in exactly the right spot on the miniature colony set. The doors of the craft then had to open up so that a remote-controlled personnel carrier could drive out. The 1:12 scale fibreglass spacecraft, approximately 1.8 m [6 ft] in length and weighing some 27 kg [60 lb], was suspended from four wires, one at each corner. The wires went up to a T-shaped support rig that was itself attached to a 3.5 m [12 ft] boom arm mounted on a platform that ran on rails. Two or three

PROFILE **THE LYDECKERS**

The Lydecker brothers, Theodore (1908–90; *above*) and Howard (1911–69; *below*), worked for Republic Pictures, a 'poverty row' studio that churned out B-movies and adventure serials featuring heroes such as Captain Marvel, the Rocket Man and Commando Cody. As joint heads of the studio effects department, it was the Lydeckers who oversaw the filming of the underwater cities, flying superheroes and rocket ships that kept thousands of children on the edge of their Saturday matinée seats throughout the 40s and 50s.

Republic's meagre budgets meant that the brothers had to create their effects on a shoestring – almost literally. As well as creating a host of spectacular miniature crashes and explosions, they perfected a new method of flying model aircraft and even full-scale papier mâché superhero models. Their technique involved fitting aircraft or model people with two thin, parallel copper tubes. In the case of a human dummy the tubes – one placed on each side of the body – entered the figure's shoulders, travelled the length of the body and exited at the heels. Piano wire – rather than shoestring – was threaded through the tubing, with talcum powder for lubrication. One end of each piano wire was firmly secured, while the other was attached to handles that were operated by the Lydeckers or an assistant. Keeping the wires taut, the operator could twist them to make the flying model bank and turn. By slackening the wires or pulling them tight, the model could be encouraged to take off or land. A fixed central cable was added to pull the model forward or back. The 'Lydecker technique' was so effective that it is still used to this day.

In 1959 Republic Pictures went out of business and the brothers sought work elsewhere. Howard found employment at Universal providing effects for features such as *Sink the Bismarck!* (1960) and *Doctor Dolittle* (1967) as well as the TV series *Lost in Space* (1965–8). After an unhappy stint at Disney, Theodore also joined Universal where, among other projects, he created the mechanical birds for Hitchcock's *The Birds* (1963).

people pushed the platform to give the ship forward and backward movement,' explains Skotak. 'Another person sat on the platform and operated a steering wheel mechanism that was attached to the wires to control the roll of the model. Another person controlled the pitch of the model, and another its rise. A further person operated the swing of the boom arm. All of these people had to coordinate their actions perfectly so that the ship would fly on the desired flight path, pass within a few inches of the camera – which also had to follow the action – then land at the correct place. The director, Jim Cameron, had asked that the craft have a hard landing, but the model's landing gear was quite delicate, so we found a way to give the model a rough-looking touchdown without putting too much weight on its legs. Once the ship had landed, a door opened and the radio-controlled personnel carrier had to drive out without hitting the door or getting snagged on any of the rocks on the set. We were filming at 60 frames per second, so the whole sequence of events had to be done at two and a half times the speed that it appears on screen. To make things worse, the shot was filmed in rain and we had a fan blowing to break up the falling water to make it look more to scale. Getting all the variables right was almost impossible. Every time one part of it worked, something else went wrong. We eventually got the shot but it took about 50 takes.'

When flying by wire, some thought must be given to hiding the method of suspension. 'Today we can remove wires digitally without any difficulty,' says Skotak, 'but even without computer assistance, there are all sorts of tricks that we can use to try to disguise wires. A little Vaseline smeared on a lens filter in the area above a ship can help to soften the image and conceal wires. A little extra smoke in that area of the image will do the same thing. Or, if a craft is flying in a linear sort of fashion, the sky above the ship could be painted on a sheet of glass and placed near to the camera and in front of the wires. It also helps if there is rain in the scene – a little backlit rain will hide wires very well.'

Another method used to hide wires is to vibrate them by attaching small motors. Wires that shake at a high frequency become blurred and unnoticeable. Providing the model is relatively heavy and the motor relatively small, the shaking wires will not affect the flight performance of the model itself. This technique was used by ILM when filming scenes of aircraft flying over forest fires for Steven Spielberg's *Always* (1989).

Most aircraft are filmed within the confines of the studio but occasionally model aircraft are actually allowed to take to the skies. For *The Aviator* (2004) several very large miniatures were reconstructed as radio-controlled flying models. A quarter-scale version of Howard Hughes's futuristic XF-11 was constructed by Aero Telemetry Corporation using technology and engines normally used to build military drones. The 340 kg (750 lb) aircraft, with a wingspan of 8 m (26 ft), flew at speeds of up to 277 km (172 miles per hour) and was filmed from a helicopter. Other flying models for the film, built in conjunction with New Deal Studios, included a half-scale prop-driven H1, and a 1:16 scale miniature of Hughes's legendary HK-1 Hercules, or *Spruce Goose*. The model *Spruce Goose*, with a wingspan of 6 m (20 ft) and weighing 159 kg (350 lb), was filmed taking off from the water at the same Long Beach location used by Hughes to test-fly his own aircraft 60 years earlier.

MOTION CONTROL

Since the success of *Star Wars* (1977), the method employed to film model spaceships and aircraft in flight has centred on the use of travelling matte techniques. In such cases, static models are suspended in front of a blue screen (<64) and held aloft on some form of arm or pylon. Rather than the models moving past the camera, it is the camera that moves past the models – which are themselves often manipulated to produce additional movements such as banking and rolling. The resulting blue-screen shots are used to place the models into environments such as skies and star fields. The technology utilized to move cameras around models in this way is known as 'motion control'.

The successful combination of separately filmed elements has traditionally depended on ensuring that there is no movement in any of the cameras used to film the various components. If a model castle was filmed in one shot, and a full-scale castle set in another, the two images could only be combined successfully if there was absolutely no camera movement in either shot. The slightest movement of one element in a composite causes it to 'slide' against its neighbouring image, shattering the illusion of a unified whole. Film-makers traditionally avoided this problem by using a static camera to shoot all of the elements that were to be combined in the final sequence, although this proved visually limiting.

The only way to have camera movement in a composite shot is to use a camera that can precisely repeat the same movements while filming each of the shots that are to be combined. This is the basic principle of motion control – using mechanical or electronic means to program or record the movement of a camera and reproduce that movement wherever and whenever different elements of a composite shot are filmed.

Though motion-control photography has only become a practical solution in the past two decades, the idea is not a new one. As early as 1914, one of Thomas Edison's (<12) camera operators, James Brautigam, built a mechanical system that allowed a camera to repeat its movements over and over again. For *The Flying Duchess* (1916), Brautigam wanted to double-expose a shot so that an actor introduced during the second exposure would appear as a transparent, ghostly figure. The basic approach was not unusual, but Brautigam realized that creating a double exposure while moving the camera would be a unique and logic-defying special effect. Brautigam's camera was mounted on a 21 m (70 ft) track and moved manually using a block-and-tackle winch rig. By carefully marking the winch drum and the winch cable with distance indicators, and with some careful timing, Brautigam was able to manually match a second camera movement to the first. The system was hardly efficient or precise, but it worked. The effort and technology involved in mechanically repeating camera movements, however, meant that it was rarely attempted over the next 20 years, and it was not until the 40s that any practical systems of motion-controlled photography were developed.

In the mid-40s an MGM sound engineer called O.L. Dupy developed a machine known as the Dupy duplicator. Dupy's system was incredibly sophisticated for its time. The camera's pan and tilt motions were recorded directly onto a phonographic record, which repeated the camera's movements when played back in subsequent takes. The system was first used to combine live action with a matte painting for the 'Fifth Avenue' shot in *Easter Parade* (1948) and later used with great success during the filming of *An American in Paris* (1951) to combine stock footage of Paris and scenes filmed on the MGM backlot with a matte painting of the French capital. At about the same time, Gordon Jennings (see panel) was working on a similar motion repeater at Paramount. Jennings's device recorded camera motion on a strip of film, but the motion itself was plotted mathematically before any sets or miniatures were built. Jennings studied construction blueprints and calculated the necessary camera moves by using stand-ins on an empty stage. Once the motion track was recorded, the camera ran automatically while filming each shot of live action, matte painting or miniature. The system was most spectacularly used to combine live-action and model elements in the temple destruction scene of Cecil B. DeMille's *Samson and Delilah* (1949). Dupy and Jennings were awarded technical Academy Awards for their systems in 1951. Though sophisticated, the rather cumbersome and unreliable machinery that they designed did not enjoy widespread use.

The work of the experimental film-maker John Whitney is perhaps the next link in the development of motion control. In 1957 Whitney acquired an army-surplus mechanical analogue computer – previously used as part of an anti-aircraft gun system – and rebuilt it to control the movements of a camera and lights so that he could film streaks of coloured light for an abstract film called *Catalog 61* (1961). His goal was to give visual representation to the pattern, colour and dynamics of a piece of music. Whitney did not employ the technology that he pioneered to produce special effects as we know them, but the method was adopted for the production of the streak-photography graphics that became widely used in television advertising and films. The technique was further developed for the production of the Stargate sequence in *2001: A Space Odyssey* (1968), whereupon it was dubbed 'slit scan' (178>).

The method of repeating camera movement for the Stargate sequence of *2001* was also used for the photography of the film's giant spaceship models. The 16.5 m (54 ft) model spacecraft *Discovery* was too large to hang on wires or be physically moved past the camera. It was decided, therefore, that the camera should move past the model. Next to the huge model spacecraft, which was anchored on steel supports, a 45 m (150 ft) camera track was constructed on which a camera platform was moved back and forth by worm gearing (178>). The camera was moved incrementally past the model, and in each new position, the shutter opened to expose the next frame. The fact that the movement of the camera could be repeated meant that additional identical 'passes' could be made to film the different elements of the same shot.

PROFILE **GORDON JENNINGS**

Gordon Jennings entered the film industry as an assistant cameraman in 1919, and quickly established a reputation for innovation by inventing the first moving titles – he painted credits on glass and slid them over painted backdrops.

In 1933 Jennings became head of special effects at Paramount where, over the next 20 years, he oversaw the effects for hundreds of classic movies. For *Cleopatra* (1934), Jennings stretched a meagre budget by using mirrors and double exposure to turn just two model galleys into a fleet of 30. For *When Worlds Collide* (1951), he oversaw the construction of a huge miniature of eight blocks of New York before destroying it with a massive tidal wave. The film's miniature rocket sequences are some of the most memorable of the time.

Jennings is perhaps best remembered for his work on George Pal's special effects tour de force *The War of*

the Worlds (1953). The film's pulsating manta ray-like spacecraft were 1 m (3 ft) flexible rubber models that were inflated by concealed air pumps. Internal coloured light bulbs glowed eerily through the plastic bodies. The Martian craft's famous death rays were created by melting welding wire with a blowtorch to create a stream of sparks. The craft are now science fiction icons.

Soon after the completion of *The War of the Worlds* Jennings died, and his department was taken over by John Fulton (<69). Jennings, whom Cecil B. DeMille called 'the best special effects man I have ever been privileged to work with', won Oscars for his contributions to *Spawn of the North* (1938), *I Wanted Wings* (1941), *When Worlds Collide* and *The War of the Worlds*. He also received technical Oscars for the design of a nodal-head tripod in 1944 (<118), and a motion-control device in 1951 (<146).

Douglas Trumbull, part of the team responsible for the effects on *2001*, continued to develop the technology of motion control after the film's release, producing the visual effects for *The Andromeda Strain* (1971), which employed a new electronic system that recorded camera movements using an ordinary stereo tape recorder. The recording was then used to control stepper motors that moved the camera in a repeatable fashion. Trumbull later developed this system, dubbed the 'ice box', for use in the production of *Close Encounters of the Third Kind* (1977).

However, it was the release of *Star Wars* (1977) that brought the potential of motion control to the world's attention. Using the latest in microchip technology, Industrial Light and Magic, headed by John Dykstra

(148>), built the first computer-controlled motion-control rig, which was capable of memorizing and repeating sophisticated camera movements with absolute precision (150>). Motion control became an essential part of production for the many special-effects-driven movies that appeared in response to the success of *Star Wars*, and many companies devised their own motion-control systems based on the one built at ILM.

Today, motion-control rigs (fig. 5) can be purchased from a number of companies that manufacture the equipment using the latest motor and computer technology. One of the world's leading manufacturers is Mark Roberts Motion Control. 'We make three types of motion-control rig,' explains the company's founder, Mark Roberts. 'Our Cyclops rig is a large rig

---

ABOVE FAR LEFT: **Early motion-control photography was used for this composite of full-scale live action and miniature temple set in** *Samson and Delilah* **(1949).**

ABOVE LEFT: **The huge model of the spacecraft** *Discovery* **in** *2001: A Space Odyssey* **(1968) remained motionless in the studio. Filming with a motion-controlled camera gave the impression that the craft was gliding through space.**

A motion-control camera is linked to a computer and can repeat pre-programmed movements precisely. The camera is mounted on a multi-axis arm which travels along a track. When the camera moves past it, this stationary model spacecraft appears to be in motion.

FIGURE 5 **MOTION–CONTROL PHOTOGRAPHY**

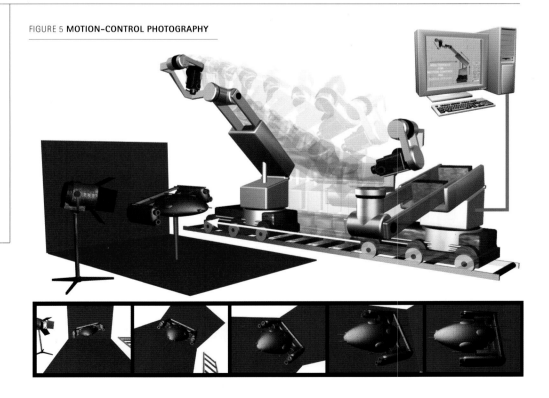

for studio-based shooting, our smaller and more popular rigs are called Milo and Juno. These grew out of the need to make motion control much more of a first-unit filming device. Early motion control like that used during the filming of *Star Wars* was a cumbersome, studio-based technology that was highly specialized and incredibly time-consuming to program and shoot with. Our smaller rigs respond to modern production needs in which motion control is used for a lot more than just a few select effects shots. These rigs can be taken anywhere in a few flight cases and be set up and operational in 45 minutes.'

The Milo, which is most popular for studio-based visual effects shots, offers 13 axes of movement and, as well as physically moving the camera, can control its focus, zoom, aperture and other mechanisms. The device sits on a 1 m (3 ft) wide length of track, along which it can travel at 2 m (7 ft) per second. The system is controlled by a powerful software program called 'Flair'. To program a camera movement, the operator instructs the software how many frames there will be in a sequence. The operator then uses a hand-held remote-control device to move the camera to its starting position. The axis and other camera information for this point are logged by the computer. The operator then moves the camera to a second position, changing the camera's angle and focus as necessary, and instructs the software to log all of the key information once again. Depending on the complexity of the move, the operator may log from two to ten key-frame positions (205>). The software then calculates an arc based on the key frames to determine the exact position of the motion-control rig and camera for all the frames in the sequence between the key frames. Once a move has been programmed, the motion-control unit can repeat the movement in real time – or at one frame at a time – to within thousandths of an inch wherever and whenever asked. The software contains a number of automatic functions that help the operator to achieve perfect results. If the device is being used to film a shot in which one item is to remain central in the frame, the operator can measure the distance from that object to the lens in the first and last position of the sequence. The computer software will then automatically track the target object in all its camera movement calculations to ensure that the item remains in the same part of the frame throughout a complicated camera move.

Increasingly, motion-control rigs act as the link between the real-world environment of the film studio and the digital world of the computer. A typical special effects shot today might contain live-action footage, miniatures and computer-generated animation. The shot may first be pre-visualized (230>) in the computer using digital models of the sets, models, performers and motion-control rig. Once the shot has been decided, the movement data from the digital motion-control rig can be exported to the real motion-control rig, which then repeats the movement when shooting the live-action element of the shot. The same camera movement is then used to film any miniatures that are to appear in the shot. However, because models are smaller than the live-action elements, the movements of the camera must be scaled down accordingly. Scaling movements was once a mathematical problem for operators, but today the comparative scale of a model is simply entered into the motion-control software, which automatically calculates the camera move required. A model may be filmed a number of times using identical camera movements but with different lighting conditions in each pass. A 'beauty pass' films the model in its most perfectly lit state; a 'shadow pass' captures the shadow elements of a model; and a 'matte pass' records the blue or green screen under optimal lighting conditions. Additional passes may be employed to capture any lights that are part of the model's construction – these are normally too weak to be visible under normal exposure conditions. Each pass is captured on a separate piece of film and is later selectively combined during compositing. Finally, the movement data may be applied to the virtual camera that is used to 'film' any additional elements that are generated within the computer (233>).

In today's increasingly international production environment, motion-control filming might take place in one part of the world while the movement data is emailed to multiple facilities in other continents for the generation of additional elements with identical camera moves.

Some shots that once relied on motion control, however, no longer need to use the process. Sophisticated 'match-moving' techniques (235>) now mean that even complicated hand-held camera moves shot on location can have their movement data extracted after filming, without the need for any form of motion control. This data can then be used to film computer-generated elements, such as animated creatures, so that they will fit perfectly into the finished shot. Despite this, motion control is still used to create reliable, predictable camera moves for many visual effects shots. *Revenge of the Sith* (2005), for example, used motion control to film multiple elements for over 500 shots that contained a combination of actors, models and computer-generated elements.

PROFILE **JOHN DYKSTRA**

Interested in mechanics and photography from an early age, John Dykstra (1947–) studied industrial design at Long Beach State College, California. After leaving college he combined his interests when he worked with Douglas Trumbull on the special effects for *The Andromeda Strain* (1971) and *Silent Running* (1972; <233).

Next Dykstra worked for Berkeley's Institute of Urban Development, building small-scale city models and filming them using an early form of motion control.

In 1975 Dykstra was appointed special effects supervisor on *Star Wars* (1977). Of the film's many achievements, Dykstra is most associated with the revolutionary motion-control system dubbed the 'Dykstraflex' in his honour. Dykstra won an Oscar for his work on *Star Wars* as well as a Scientific and Technical Oscar for the creation of the Industrial Light and Magic facility.

Dykstra was then chosen to create the special effects for the high-budget TV series *Battlestar Galactica* (1978–80). As a result Dykstra and a group of colleagues established Apogee, a facility that became a leader in special effects innovation through its work on films including *Star Trek: The Motion Picture* (1979) and *Firefox* (1982).

Apogee closed its doors in 1993, but Dykstra has continued to supervise the production of cutting-edge effects for films such as *Batman Forever* (1995) and *Batman & Robin* (1997). Since 1998 Dykstra has worked with Sony Pictures Imageworks, supervising the effects for *Stuart Little* (1999), *Spider-Man* (2002) and *Spider-Man 2* (2004), for which he won an Academy Award.

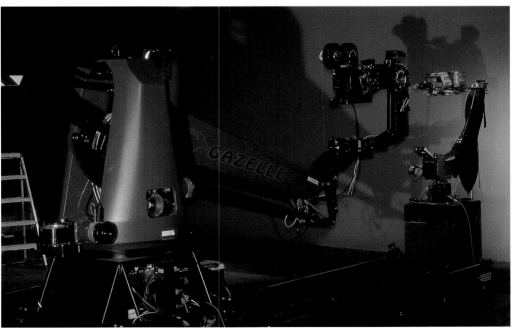

ABOVE: A Cyclops motion-control rig being prepared to film Ian Holm in *The Borrowers* (1997).

LEFT: To create a scene for *Lost in Space* (1998), a motion-controlled camera rig is being used to film a motion-controlled model spaceship.

STAR WARS

'A long time ago in a galaxy far, far away...' When these legendary words first crawled onto our screens three decades ago, science fiction movies, special effects and film technology had changed forever.

Everyone knew that the effects in *Star Wars* (1977) were truly special, but few were aware of just why those thrilling space battles seemed so realistic, or why the *Imperial Star Destroyer* looked so awesome as it thundered overhead. The enthralling realism of these scenes was due to the development of a new computer-controlled method of moving the camera.

Richard Edlund (<79) was a member of the pioneering team which, under the banner of 'Industrial Light and Magic', would make special effects history. 'Our work on the battle sequences began when George Lucas showed us a reel of black-and-white film footage of World War II aerial dogfights,' remembers Edlund. 'That was when we realized this was going to be no kid's sci-fi movie with spaceships floating around on wires. We realized we would need to film our spaceship models with an electronically controlled camera capable of motion in a number of axes, and which could be programmed to perform and repeat moves whenever we required them.'

Edlund was part of a team headed by John Dykstra (<148), who spearheaded the design and construction of the microchip-controlled motion-control system dubbed 'Dykstraflex'. 'Each category of camera movement would be stored as an individual channel in a microchip,' explains Edlund. 'I always thought it pretty ironic that we were using technology developed for NASA's space programme to make our own space movie! The chip could store twelve channels of movement, which we programmed individually by adjusting a potentiometer to control the motors operating the various parts of the system. I would begin by programming the required forward movement of the camera. Then I would do the pan movement, then the tilt and so on, slowly building up the overall movement. We didn't have any form of video feedback, so while the camera was moving I would be up and down a ladder twisting my neck to look through the viewfinder to see what the shot looked like.'

'Once we had programmed a move, we could repeat it whenever we wanted,' says Edlund. 'This meant we could use the same move several times to film models situated in different parts of the picture. I could then develop black-and-white tests of these shots and lay them on top of one another to make sure none of the ships would cross over any of the others when they were composited.'

The Dykstraflex was essential in producing the film's fast-paced space battles because, once programmed, the intricate camera moves could be performed one frame at a time while the shutter was open. Moving the camera past stationary models while exposing the film meant the resulting images were blurred as if genuine fast-moving objects had been filmed. This motion blur was essential in making the space battles unique for their time.

In addition to modern motion-control methods, a plethora of traditional techniques were employed with renewed vigour and style. Many of the film's incredible locations were created using matte paintings (254>). These included distant views of the Mos Eisley space port, the vast hangars and looming chasms of the Death Star interior, and the climactic shots of the rebel's ceremonial temple. For shots showing a row of rebel X-wing spacecraft docked in a hangar, a full-scale craft was placed in the foreground and giant cut-out versions were arranged in the distance.

The film's exotic characters were created in a number of ways. The robots C-3PO and R2-D2 were costumes containing actors, as was Chewbacca, a giant 'walking carpet' with an expressively articulated face engineered by Stuart Freeborn. Other supporting aliens were rendered by fledgling make-up artist Rick Baker (292>). A quirky game of chess in which the pieces were holographic miniature monsters was stop-motion animated by Phil Tippett (194>). Animation was used to create the glowing blades of the Jedi light sabres and the laser fire of weapons. Early computer animation also provided cockpit readouts and the rebel's briefing film (155>).

The combination of exhilarating space battles, vivid characters and environments as well as rich sound effects helped *Star Wars* smash box office records around the world, allowing George Lucas to make five more *Star Wars* films and establish a business empire which would be the leading force in special effects production for the next 30 years.

LEFT: Despite massive advances in digital model-making techniques, miniatures remain a cost-effective and efficient method of creating highly realistic environments. This beautifully constructed 1.5 m (5 ft) tall and 6 m (20 ft) long miniature hangar was built by New Deal Studios for *The Aviator* (2004).

BELOW RIGHT: Miniatures can now be made more realistic with the digital addition of details such as people and atmospheric elements. In this final shot the miniature hangar has been brought to life by adding digital construction workers, smoke from the model crane and showers of welding sparks.

THE FUTURE OF MINIATURES

For almost a century the only practical way to film many objects and locations was to build miniatures and models. But the development of photorealistic computer-generated imagery now means anything that can be built in miniature can also be built in the computer. When CG methods rapidly took hold in the mid-90s many predicted the swift demise of traditional effects techniques. However, miniatures are still widely used for a number of reasons, though whether that will remain the case is still a subject for debate.

Some believe that the dominance of computer-generated effects has led to the increased use of certain types of miniature. 'Once, large environment shots were almost exclusively created using 2-D matte paintings', comments Richard Taylor of Weta Workshop. 'But now computer technology has made audiences expect to see much more than static establishing shots of big environments. As a result we get to build complex miniature environments that the camera can swoop down and get close to. Digital visual effects also mean that live-action characters can be placed much more effectively within these environments, and CG elements like rain or snow can be used to give added realism. In the future it may become much easier to create large environments in the computer but at the moment it's hard to emulate the atmosphere and genuine sense of place that comes from actually using thousands of real leaves, or the surfaces of real rocks. Building these environments for real also means they can be beautifully lit without hours of complex rendering.'

Dennis Muren (<47) agrees that there is still a place for traditional miniatures, even when similar effects can be achieved in the computer. 'There's a shot in *War of the Worlds* [2005] where a huge road bridge is ripped apart in the background and then a street of houses is destroyed in the foreground. The bridge was CG while the houses were miniatures. We could have done the road bridge as a miniature but it would never have been so convincing and we couldn't have made it perform as dramatically. On the other hand the buildings could have been CG but instead we used traditional miniatures that were reasonably fast to build and film and looked totally convincing when destroyed. I suppose one day we might completely replace miniature work with CG, but all the time the old techniques look great and

are cost-effective, I say let's use them. I also believe that mixing a range of techniques, combining CG with traditional miniatures, brings much more texture and depth to a shot.'

One category of miniatures greatly affected by the coming of CG is that of aircraft and spaceships. 'Sadly that's something that CG does really well', admits Matthew Gratzner of New Deal Studios. 'You used to have to build these beautiful model aircraft and then they were meticulously photographed with motion control. Now it's a lot easier to build a CG model and have it flying any way you want. And if you don't like the way it flies you can just re-animate it rather than going back to the motion-control stage. We were really lucky to build model aircraft for *The Aviator* [2004], there won't be many more shows like that. But there are many things that models and CG can do equally well and many things that are still best done in miniature. I'm not sure there will ever be a time when CG is always quicker, cheaper and more effective than miniatures.'

ILM visual effects supervisor John Knoll has witnessed first-hand the rapid move from miniatures to CG. It's a trend that he believes will only continue: 'As time goes by we'll definitely do fewer miniatures. *The Phantom Menace* [1999] was one of the biggest model shows ever, but a few years later for *Revenge of the Sith* [2005] we did far more with CG. One of the main reasons was that we can now light models in the computer so much better. It used to be that you couldn't easily re-create the naturalistic lighting you get in miniatures, especially interiors. But now we can use radiosity [238>] and get our CG environments and models looking as good as the real thing. When we choose whether to do something as a miniature or as CG the deciding factor is more about time and money than how it looks – we know we can make CG look as good as the real thing.'

But Lorne Peterson of the ILM model shop is not sure that the rush to create everything digitally will render his skills redundant. 'Often we'll be filming or making something and someone from the digital department will wander past and say "Hey, *that's* what I wanted to do when I got into visual effects!" I think a lot of people relish the idea of making and filming real things. Maybe when a new generation of visual effects supervisors are in charge – people who have never seen anything done outside a computer, they'll realize that doing some things the old way can be just as effective – and an awful lot more fun!'

PROFILE **STEVE GAWLEY AND LORNE PETERSON**

ILM model supervisor Steve Gawley (*above*) and model project supervisor Lorne Peterson (*below*) both joined ILM in 1975 as part of the original 15-person visual effects crew for *Star Wars* (1977). Three decades later, they both still work at ILM and between them have been responsible for some of the most memorable miniature work ever created for film.

Steve Gawley studied industrial design at California State University and within a year of graduating was hired to make models for *Star Wars*. As well as building models such as the iconic *Star Destroyer* spaceship, Gawley also lent his pick-up truck to the production. With a camera fixed to the back he drove it at high speed to film point-of-view shots of the exploding Death Star surface. He also appeared briefly in the film as a technician who shields his face as a huge laser beam is fired from the Death Star.

After studying art at California State University Lorne Peterson started his own industrial design company, creating items including furniture and drinking fountains. In 1975 he was hired to make models of the Death Star for *Star Wars*, also contributing to the famous X-wing and Imperial TIE fighter models. He was also filmed on the top of a Guatemalan pyramid for a brief shot as a rebel look-out. He has since built models for all six *Star Wars* movies and received an Oscar for his work on *Indiana Jones and the Temple of Doom* (1984).

The list of projects to which Gawley and Peterson have contributed their beautifully detailed miniatures reads like a roll call of the most significant and successful visual effects movies of the past 30 years, including *Raiders of the Lost Ark* (1981), *Poltergeist* (1982), *E.T.* (1982), *Back to the Future* (1985), *Jurassic Park* (1993), *Men in Black* (1997), *Hulk* (2003) and *War of the Worlds* (2005). Sadly, ILM closed down its model shop in 2006.

COMPUTER GRAPHICS

Star Wars (1977) may have been among the first films to use a computer to control its camera, but computers had already started to replace the camera altogether for the creation of wholly synthetic 3-D images.

Synthetic electronic imagery became a goal in the 50s when scientists at the Massachusetts Institute of Technology (MIT) produced the first numerically controlled industrial production tools – drills and milling machines that could be programmed to perform simple and repetitive tasks during the manufacturing process. The technique became known as CAM (computer-aided manufacture), and once it had become a viable technology, the MIT scientists began to engineer a complementary technology that could be used as part of the design process, a technique that became known as CAD (computer-aided design).

The system created at MIT as a result was called Sketchpad, and its foremost architect was the computer scientist Dr Ivan Sutherland. Sutherland used the Sketchpad system to create the first computer-generated 3-D objects. Until then, early computers had been used to produce basic 2-D pictures, but these images had been described to the computer as flat scenes that could only be viewed from one angle – much like a drawing on a sheet of paper. Sutherland's breakthrough technique was to describe not the picture that he wanted to see but the object. By programming the coordinates of an object, and describing the way in which each aspect of its shape related to the others, Sutherland created objects that could be viewed from any angle. In 1964 Sutherland used the Sketchpad tool to create a short film called *Sketchpad*. Though crude, the film was perhaps the first 3-D computer animation, and was the launch pad for the incredible CGI (computer-generated image) systems that are used today to create stunningly sophisticated 3-D models and animation.

3-D graphics systems rely on the description of coordinates in terms of their depth, width and height. This method is known as the Cartesian coordinate system, after the French mathematician René Descartes (1596–1650), who created a system by which points, lines, planes and shapes could be described with algebraic equations. Using Cartesian coordinates, a 2-D shape is described using two perpendicular axes called the Y axis (vertical, or height) and the X axis (horizontal, or width). Each axis includes positive and negative numbers, as measured from an arbitrary starting point or 'origin'. The position of any single point, or 'vertex', in 2-D space can therefore be defined by a pair of numbers, which are the point's 'XY coordinates' (fig. 6).

3-D objects can be created using points that are located within a three-axis system of coordinates (fig. 7). The third axis, the Z axis, is perpendicular to both the X and Y axes and gives depth to an object. Using this system, the size and shape of theoretical objects, be they a cube or a sphere – or even a dinosaur – can be modelled within the computer.

ABOVE: **Pioneering computer scientist Dr Ivan Sutherland inspects the memory of an enormous early computer at MIT.**

RIGHT: **In 1977 *Star Wars* used one of the first examples of 3-D computer graphics in film. Vector graphics were used to show wire-frame views of the Death Star surface. The images were created by Larry Cuba at the University of Illinois.**

FIGURE 6

FIGURE 7

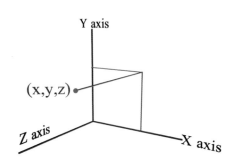

Y axis

(x,y)

X axis

Y axis

(x,y,z)

Z axis

X axis

THE CARTESIAN COORDINATE SYSTEM

Cartesian coordinates are used to describe the position of a point in two-dimensional space using X and Y coordinates (fig. 6). A point in three-dimensional space requires a third, Z axis (fig. 7).

Early graphics systems, such as that used by Sutherland, were extremely basic, and images could only be built up by instructing the computer to place one dot of light at a specific coordinate at any one time. By the mid-60s, however, hardware and software had advanced, and designers were able to use graphics 'pens' to draw shapes that immediately appeared on the computer screen. Even so, computer technology was so expensive, and so electronically and mathematically complex, that it could only be supported by the largest universities and corporations. The software and hardware for these imaging systems could not be purchased anywhere, so those wishing to work with computer graphics had to build their own systems and write original software from scratch.

The first truly practical use of computer graphics was in the aerospace industry, where the technology was not only used for computer-aided design purposes, but was also developed for the first flight simulators. It was this flight simulation hardware and software that fuelled the computer graphics revolution in the entertainment industry. The world's foremost manufacturer of flight simulation graphics hardware was a company called Evans and Sutherland. Its co-founder was Ivan Sutherland.

Early 3-D computer images were drawn using a method called 'vector graphics'. Vector graphics is a simple way of describing objects in terms of single points connected by straight lines, and generally results in see-through computer-generated shapes known as 'wire-frame' models. It is possible to create solid-looking objects with vector graphics by filling spaces with many single lines, but the method cannot produce subtle shading, highlights or textures. The alternative to vector graphics is 'raster graphics'. The raster process is capable of creating graphics by individually addressing the qualities of each pixel on the screen. The process can therefore produce images that contain large areas of solid-looking colour with many subtleties of light and shade. Raster graphics require large amounts of computing power and only became practical in the early 70s when the availability of frame buffers (a form of memory) made it possible to store the information about each of the thousands of pixels in a picture.

The only system that can synthesize realistic-looking objects, raster graphics was used for the production of television commercials by American companies such as Robert Abel and Associates as early as 1973.

At about this time, high-resolution computer graphics also began to make occasional appearances in feature films. In 1973, Gary Demos and John Whitney Jr (son of the computer art pioneer John Whitney; <146) were nominated for an Academy Award for the robot vision sequences that they produced for *Westworld* (1973). The images showed the heavily pixelated point of view of a robot played by Yul Brynner. Demos and Whitney, who worked for a company called Triple-I, were then asked to produce a computer-generated simulation of Peter Fonda's head for the film's sequel, *Futureworld* (1976). The resulting sequence was one of the first fully computer-generated elements for a feature film. Throughout the 70s, the film industry remained sceptical about the potential of the computer for generating images. Brief vector-graphics sequences were used for the Death Star trench graphic in *Star Wars* (1977), the computerized black hole graphic in *The Black Hole* (1979) and the cockpit computer graphics of outside terrain in *Alien* (1979). In each of these films, computer graphics was actually used to create representations of basic computer graphics – few people were interested in its potential for simulating photorealistic objects. One notable exception was Steven Spielberg, who approached Demos and Whitney about the possibility of producing computer-generated glowing cubes to fly around people during the climactic scenes of *Close Encounters of the Third Kind* (1977). However, the concept was ultimately dropped from the production.

Frustrated by the continuing lack of industry interest in computer graphics, Demos and Whitney decided to demonstrate the potential of the computer by preparing a test shot for *The Empire Strikes Back* (1980), which George Lucas was then preparing for production. Using a model of an X-wing fighter craft provided by Lucasfilm, Demos and Whitney built a photorealistic computer model using raster graphics and produced a test scene in which five of the craft flew in space. Lucas was impressed enough to begin negotiations with Triple-I, but the cost and practicality of such simulations proved prohibitive. However, after this demonstration of the potential of the computer, Lucas established his own computer graphics division, Pixar. While computer-generated imagery was not used for the *Star Wars* sequel, the opportunity would come instead with the production of Disney's *Tron* (1982; 162>).

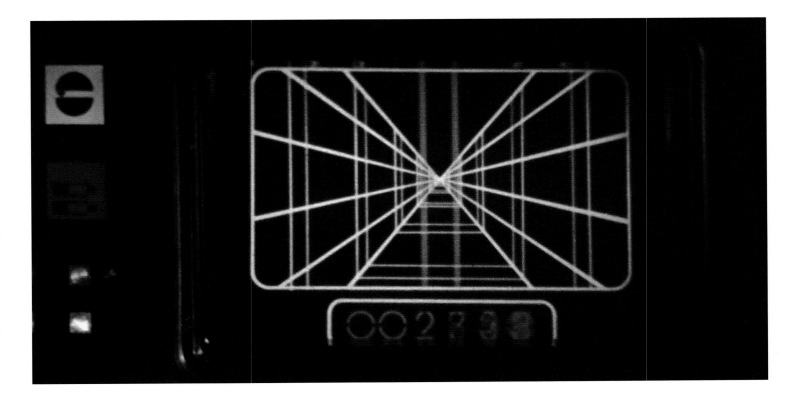

DIGITAL MODELLING

Today, computer-generated imagery can be created by anyone who can afford the relatively low cost of the off-the-shelf software and hardware used to produce such work. Most visual effects companies use the same inexpensive, commercially available software packages with names such as Maya, Houdini, Lightwave and 3D Studio Max. Many rely solely on the built-in features included in such software, while larger companies employ their own programmers to write the additional modelling, animation and rendering solutions needed for each production.

Modern modelling software is designed to be intuitive and simple to use. Most computer modellers need no specialized knowledge of computing or software code. The most important skill that a computer modeller must possess is the ability to study a shape or form and find the most appropriate way to turn it into a model within the computer. For every designer, whatever software they use, the basic principles of producing digital 3-D models are the same.

During production, modelling is generally divided into two broad categories. 'Hard surface' modelling refers to the creation of geometric, 'solid' objects such as cars, buildings or aircraft. These may eventually have animated movements such as opening doors or spinning wheels, or may possibly need to explode or deform. 'Organic' modelling refers to the normally more complex creation of models that represent living beings. These will need to have lifelike features such as faces, muscle and skin and will be animated to appear as if walking, flying or talking. The rest of this chapter largely addresses the creation of hard surface models; organic modelling will be covered in the next chapter.

The basic unit of any computer model is the 'vertex', a single point whose position in 3-D space is defined using the Cartesian coordinate system. On its own, one vertex is not very useful – just a small point in space – but by adding a second vertex, a connecting line can be drawn between the two. The distance and direction of one vertex relative to another is called a 'vector', and the line that joins them is called a 'segment' or 'edge'. Segments are also fairly useless on their own, but by adding a third vertex, a triangle – called a 'polygon' – can be formed (fig. 8). Polygons are the essential building blocks of any computer model – they are like the single patches that are sewn together to create a patchwork quilt. When clustered together to form an object, a group of interconnected polygons is called a 'mesh'. The mesh for a model of a basic cube, for example, could be made from eight vertices (one for each corner) connected by 12 segments (one for each edge), and six or 12 polygons (each of the six sides is made up of either one square or two triangular polygons). During the modelling process designers can view the

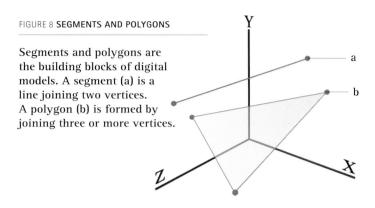

FIGURE 8 **SEGMENTS AND POLYGONS**

Segments and polygons are the building blocks of digital models. A segment (a) is a line joining two vertices. A polygon (b) is formed by joining three or more vertices.

object they are making either as a wire mesh showing all of its vertices and polygons, or as a simple shaded object with solid sides.

When modelling, a computer screen is normally divided into a number of windows, known as orthographic projections, in which different views of the modelling environment can be seen. Normally there are windows that show the model from the top, front and one side, with an additional 'camera' or 'perspective' viewport in which the designer can move around the model while working on it. Starting with this empty canvas, the designer begins by studying the object that is to be built in the digital environment.

'We get all sorts of reference material from the production company of the films that we work on,' says Gary Coulter, a digital modelling supervisor at Fuzzygoat, who has worked on films such as *Tomb Raider* (2001), *K-19: The Widowmaker* (2003) and *Sahara* (2005). 'Sometimes we get photographs of sets or props that have been made for the film. Sometimes we actually get real models that have already been built and filmed by the miniatures unit. Other times we may get blueprints or concept designs from a production designer, or we may go through books and magazines to find pictures of the things that we need to make.'

Designers carefully study the object that they have to re-create in order to break it down into a number of discrete parts that can be modelled as separate pieces. 'When we look at an item to be modelled, we will mentally disassemble it into its constituent parts,' explains Coulter. 'We look for small

FIGURE 9

Pulling a vertex away from a 3-D object produces a spike.

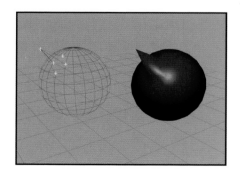

FIGURE 10 **SUBDIVISIONAL MODELLING**

A basic model made using very few polygons can have its surfaces multiplied and refined using a process called 'subdivisional modelling'. By applying this technique, a crudely modelled hand automatically becomes more organic-looking.

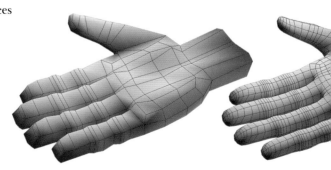

chunks of detail that can be individually re-created. Once those parts are made, they will be recombined to produce the final model. If we were going to build a wooden chair, for example, we would break it down into legs, seat, arms and back. Within those chunks we will look for what we call primitive shapes – spheres, cubes and so on. These are our basic building blocks, and it's surprising how many complex items can be made by starting off with these simple shapes. We also look for any symmetry in an object,' says Coulter. 'As soon as we've spotted any symmetry or repetition, our job is halved because we only need to make one portion of that object and clone it to make duplicates, or instruct the computer to make a mirror image of that portion.'

All modern modelling packages come with a range of ready-made 'primitives' – shapes such as spheres, cubes, cones and cylinders. These objects can be summoned onto the screen at the touch of a button. The designer can define the exact number of vertices, segments and polygons that the primitives contain, depending on the amount of detail needed in a model or the way in which the object is later to be manipulated.

'Once we have a wire-mesh primitive, there are all kinds of ways that it can be tweaked into the shape that we want,' says Coulter. 'It's a bit like having a ball of clay and being able to mould it to shape – the more polygons a mesh has, the more we can refine its detail. The usual method is to start with a fairly simple shape and then iteratively add detail, gradually refining the original simple form into a more complex one.'

Primitives can be modified or 'deformed' to resemble the various parts of the model that they are to represent – a cube can be stretched to produce a rectangle, squeezed to make a tile or have one end tapered to form a wedge shape, for example. A polygon's wire mesh can also be selectively 'edited' to amend its shape. For instance, by selecting a single vertex and pulling or 'extruding' it away from the surface of the object, a spike can be produced (fig. 9). Whole groups of vertices can also be selected and pushed around with a range of modelling tools to produce the shape required.

Starting with basic low-poly primitive shapes, it is possible to 'sculpt' very sophisticated, organic models. To produce a human hand, for example, a modeller could start by creating a very basic hand shape using a number of oblongs and cubes. The computer can then be instructed to subdivide the existing polygons in this model. This technique, called 'subdivisional modelling', adds more polygons to the mesh and then automatically 'smoothes over' any angular joints or edges (fig. 10). By repeating the process the faces of a model will become increasingly smooth. In the case of a hand, subdivision quickly makes the initial boxlike model look more human, turning cubes into simple fingers. Once the correct overall shape has been produced, the high number of smaller polygons makes it possible to manually sculpt the model. In the case of the hand this would mean manually selecting vertices and moving them to create features such as knuckles and

fingernails. Whenever increased detail is needed, small areas can again be selected, subdivided and further refined.

'Sometimes an object is just too complicated to be made from a primitive. In these cases, there are a number of other methods we can use,' says Coulter. 'If something is an odd shape, we may study it to see if it has a cross-section – a constant shape that runs right through it. Once we identify such a shape, we re-create its cross-section by arranging and connecting vertices to form that shape in 2-D. Sometimes we scan a plan or a blueprint into the computer and use that as a template to get the shape we want. Once we have the right outline, it can be "extruded" – that is, pulled outwards to form a 3-D object of any length [fig. 11]. It's a bit like pushing children's modelling clay through a hole to produce one long sausage of the same shape.'

A number of different shapes can be arranged in a line and linked to create a single object whose cross-section alters from one end to the other. This process, called 'lofting' (fig. 12, 158>), requires each of the shapes along the path to contain the same number of vertices, so that each vertex in one shape can be linked to a corresponding vertex in its adjoining shape.

Any circular object can be created through a process called 'lathing' (fig. 13, 158>). To produce a model of an ornate table leg, for example, a profile of one half of the vertical leg is made. This template is then rotated around its vertical axis to create a perfectly circular object that has the same profile all the way around. The shape can be swept through different axes to create a number of different objects if required.

Once objects have been made, it is possible to punch holes through them using a process called constructive solid geometry (CSG). A model that is the shape of the desired hole is created, then 'intersected' with the main object at the place and depth that the hole is to occur. In an operation called a 'Boolean' (fig. 14, 158>), the first object is subtracted from the second, leaving a hole in its place. CSG operations can also be used to merge, split, carve and join objects in various ways.

'Once we have created our basic model parts, we start to put them all together,' explains Coulter. 'It's a bit like making a hobbyist's modelling kit where you have to assemble all the little pieces first, and make sure that they're all going to fit before you actually glue them together. Sometimes the bits don't fit very well, but it doesn't matter too much because, unlike a plastic modelling kit, our objects can be stretched, shrunk, rotated and endlessly altered until they do.'

Since the models created in a computer are not actually solid, they can be assembled by simply pushing one object through another. If one model part needs to be affixed to the side of another object, it can simply be dragged to the object and placed against the object's side. If part of it protrudes too far, it can be pushed a little further into the main object. Once

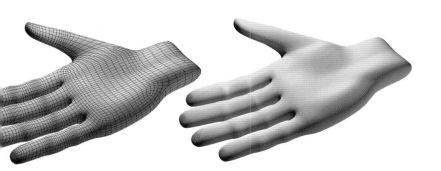

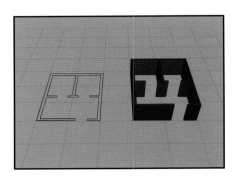

FIGURE 11

Extruding a 2-D shape along a path creates a 3-D model.

FIGURE 12

Two or more differently shaped 2-D shapes can be connected along a path to create a 3-D shape with a changing cross-section. This process is called 'lofting'.

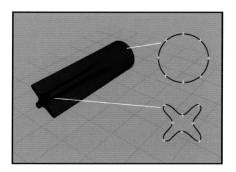

FIGURE 13

Creating a 3-D model by rotating a 2-D shape around a central axis is known as 'lathing'.

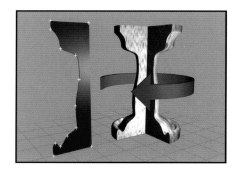

FIGURE 14

In a Boolean operation, model (a) is intersected with model (b) and subtracted to form model (c).

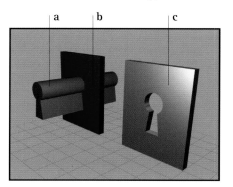

the position is satisfactory, the two parts are attached (parented or grouped) to each other so that wherever the main object goes, the smaller part follows. Should the two elements need readjusting at any time, they can be separated (unparented or ungrouped) and addressed individually. If the union is completely satisfactory, however, the two parts can be merged to form a single, inseparable object.

The final process in making a polygonal model is to 'clean' it. 'We sometimes use more vertices or segments than we really need when making a model,' explains Coulter. 'The more vertices and segments a model has, the more polygons there are in its surface. While more polygons means a more refined surface, it also means that the computer will take a lot more time to process the model during the lighting, animation and rendering stages.' One of the biggest costs in digital effects production is machine time – the time that it takes for computers to prepare images so that they are ready to be transferred onto film. This is a process called 'rendering', whereby the computer uses all the information it has been given about models, lighting and the camera to produce a film-quality 2-D image (236>). The more polygons a model contains, the more calculations a computer has to make during rendering. Rendering time can be reduced by many hours per shot by removing a model's redundant polygons.

'It's surprising how much detail can be removed from a model before it starts to look bad,' says Coulter. 'A lot of apparent detail will be added at the texturing stage so we need to know what the model's final surfaces will look like (164>). Much also depends on how big a model will be on the screen in the final shot. If a model will be very close to the camera, it should have more detail; if it will be further away, we will use a lot less. If the model starts near the camera and moves away during the shot, we may change the model to a less detailed "proxy" model as it moves into the distance – there's no point having an incredibly detailed model in a shot if it only looks like a distant moving shape.'

To reduce the number of polygons in a model, the designer studies the surfaces to decide which vertices and polygons can be removed without adversely affecting the quality of the model. During modelling, many individual parts may have been constructed and joined together. Part of one object's detail will be hidden 'within' the other object where they intersect. Any polygons hidden inside a model will not be visible when rendered and can therefore be removed. Large flat surfaces also need very few polygons to be represented successfully.

SPLINE-BASED MODELLING

Polygonal modelling is the most popular method of creating digital models, but there are other ways of producing objects within the computer. Spline-based modelling can be used to create models with complex, smooth surfaces that would normally require many polygons. A spline is a path or shape that is created by linking a number of vertices or control points. This path can be straight or curved.

The most common spline-based modelling system is known as 'NURBS' (non-uniform rational Bézier splines). The system is based on the use of NURBS 'patches'. A NURBS patch is a 2-D shape whose surface is formed using a number of splines. By changing the position of control points along the path of a spline, the surface of a NURBS patch can be distorted to create the desired shape (fig. 15). It is perhaps easiest to envisage a NURBS patch as a square of flexible rubber that is pinned to a surface at its corners. By attaching a number of strings to this rubber, its surface can be pulled and stretched into different shapes. Using just a few control points, a single NURBS patch can produce a complex shape that would otherwise require a mesh of hundreds or thousands of polygons. Because of its low number of shape-defining vertices, the modelling, animation and rendering of a NURBS model requires less processing power than a similarly shaped polygonal model would. To produce a complete model, many individual NURBS patches can be 'stitched' together like a patchwork quilt.

In a polygonal model one vertex can be moved in order to reshape one particular aspect of its form. In a NURBS model, however, changing one aspect of one spline will reshape the whole of the patch. For this reason small areas of NURBS patch can be converted to a polygonal mesh which can allow precise local refinement.

FIGURE 15 **SPLINE-BASED MODELLING**

Control points positioned on or around a NURBS patch can be assigned differing amounts of influence in order to manipulate its shape.

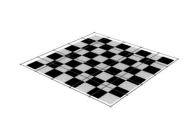

Cinesite Europe built this model Tiger helicopter as part of their work for the James Bond film *The World Is Not Enough* (1999).

a: This screen grab shows a typical modelling environment in which 3-D models are built. In this wire-frame version of the model, each component is shown in a different colour for easy identification.
b: The wire-frame model can be given simply shaded surfaces for preview purposes.
c: During modelling, the object can be studied from a number of separate 'orthographic' views.
d: Individual components can be viewed and manipulated in close-up.
e: This colour map is applied to the model to give it its exterior markings and highlights. Other maps will include a transparency map to make the glass windows see-through.
f: Fully rendered views of the final helicopter model.

a

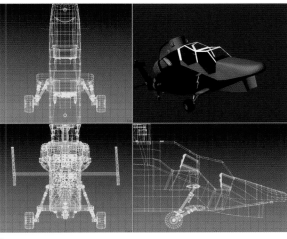

b

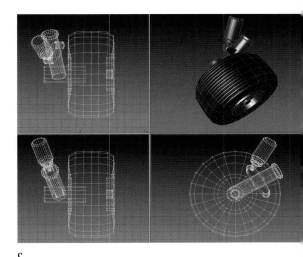

c

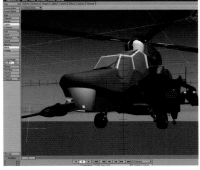

d

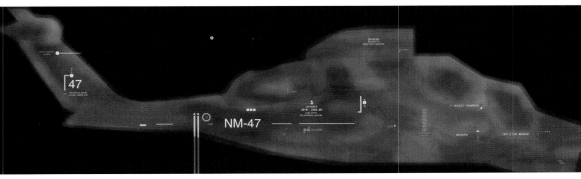

e

f

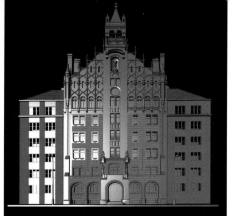

FAR LEFT: **To produce digital models of an existing apartment building, scanning specialists Gentle Giant Studios used helicopter-mounted Lidar equipment to scan the building and the surrounding area.**

LEFT: **The Lidar information was 'cleaned up' to produce this accurate model, ready for texturing.**

LIDAR SCANNING AND IMAGE-BASED MODELLING

LIDAR SCANNING

Complex organic forms such as plants and creatures are difficult to create using conventional modelling methods and so are often 'scanned' using a laser to read their surface properties and convert them into a digital model. These techniques are commonly used when creating models of digital characters (195>) but a variation can also be used to produce accurate digital models of large-scale objects such as vehicles, buildings, and even entire landscapes. In such cases a scanning technique called 'Lidar' (Laser Imaging Detection and Ranging) is used.

Lidar scanners are employed for a wide range of industrial, military and research purposes, from monitoring volcanoes for threatening bulges, to creating models of cities to aid urban planning. They work by firing a laser at the area to be scanned and measuring the quality of the reflected beam in order to build up a digital model. To create models of large areas of landscape a scanner can be suspended beneath a moving helicopter.

For visual effects production, Lidar scanners can be used to accurately survey locations or sets used during filming. The resulting digital models are extremely dense, containing millions of polygons, and so are reduced in resolution before being used. The scans can be used directly, mapping textures onto surfaces to create realistic environments, or indirectly, as a framework on top of which a new, more functional model can be built.

To create a digital city for *The Day After Tomorrow* (2004) scanning specialists Lidar VFX spent 3 months scanning 15 blocks of Manhattan using a laser with a range of 5 km (3 miles). The resulting 1.5 terabytes of data was used to construct a massive model of the city that was accurate to within a centimetre. Over 50,000 images of the city's buildings were photographed and used to create textures that were mapped onto the Lidar model. The result was a photorealistic Manhattan model that was used by several visual effects companies to create scenes of freezing snowstorms and massive tidal waves.

IMAGE-BASED MODELLING

There is not always the time or budget to use complex laser scanning equipment to capture scenery or objects when filming in a studio or on location. In such cases it is still possible to create accurate digital models by extracting the information from a number of ordinary photographs. This process is called image-based modelling, or photogrammetry.

All that is needed are two or more photographs of an object, a building for example, each taken from a different angle. The resulting photographs are then scanned into a computer and used to construct a model using specialist software.

To create a model, the first photograph has a number of 'locator' points or lines manually positioned at key features, for example at the corners of walls or along the tops of roofs. The second photograph then has locator points placed in exactly the same positions on the building, as seen from this different angle. Using triangulation the software is able to compare the relative position of each locator point when seen from different angles. It then extrapolates the differing angles from which the images were photographed and reconstructs an accurate model of the object in 3-D space. This model will not include the object's fine surface detail, but will be exact in its overall shape and proportions. Ordinary modelling techniques can then be used to build delicate 3-D details such as architectural features that match those of the actual location.

When a basic model has been constructed the computer can be asked to project the original photographs back onto its surfaces. Each photograph is projected onto the model using the camera position from which it was originally photographed (as extrapolated by the computer). Once textures are projected onto the model it can be filmed by a virtual camera (233>) that can move around the model and view it from any angle. Techniques such as these were used to create many of the environments for *The Matrix* (1999) and its sequels.

RIGHT: **To create a mountainous landscape for** *Stealth* **(2005), Digital Domain used its own procedural modelling system to generate the environment automatically. The digital model was built up one element at a time, as follows:**

a: The basic valley model, based on topographical satellite survey data.
b: An analysis of the model paints the steepest areas of cliff white. This will be used to determine the way the rock and soil is later modelled. A small plateau on which a fort will sit is created and added manually.
c: Procedural textures add basic rock and soil detail.
d: The automatic scattering of grass and small plants is based on the position and angle of slopes.
e: Strata are added to the sides of mountains procedurally.
f: The angle and shape of cliffs are automatically analysed and altered to represent the effects of erosion.
g: Rock surfaces are procedurally cracked and crumbled to produce additional detail.
h: Trees are hand-placed around the valley, a 3-D fort model is added to the plateau and mist is generated in the lower part of the valley.
i: The final composite, complete with CG aircraft and jet-engine trails.

a

b

c

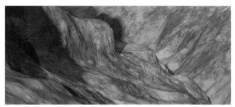

d

e

f

g

h

PROCEDURAL MODELLING

Many aspects of digital image production can be automated in order to save time, effort and money. Any task that contains some form of repetition or pattern, be it the building of models, the generation of textures (165>) or the animation of objects or images (219>), can be reduced to a set of rules or 'nodes' that can be described as a mathematical formula or algorithm. By selectively adjusting various parameters, these algorithms can be used to automatically generate work that would be difficult or time-consuming to create manually. These automatic functions are called 'procedural' tasks.

Most computer-generated models are composed of many highly different components and so each piece must be individually crafted by a digital modeller. However, models that contain large amounts of similar or repetitive information can be created procedurally. As a simple example, the model of a chequerboard could be built by manually arranging alternate black and white cubes next to one another. Though hardly a taxing modelling job, this could be reduced to a set of rules that state: 'wherever there is a black cube, create white cubes either side, and vice versa'. By changing the parameters slightly the modeller could ask the computer to produce two black cubes for every white, or more white cubes than black ones, and so on.

Procedural rules are now being used to generate incredibly complex models. For the production of *Stealth* (2005), Digital Domain needed to create vast areas of landscape for the movie's supersonic aircraft to fly over. Rather than painstakingly modelling the equivalent of thousands of square miles of varied terrain, the models were created procedurally. 'We used a proprietary program called EnGen that draws on data from the US Geographical Survey and other topographical data,' states the film's visual effects supervisor Joel Hynek. 'What we had was a digital elevation map of the entire planet. We just had to say which part of the world we wanted to fly over and that topographical data was used to create a polygonal model with mountains, valleys and rivers. The model was generated at different resolutions in different areas, automatically building in more polygons wherever we were going to get closer with the camera.' Generating the geometry of the terrain was only the first part of the process; it then had to be dressed to look like a real landscape, as Hynek explains: 'We had thousands of rules or "nodes" to control the procedural generation of everything seen on the surface of the landscape. The computer would look at a mountain and say at what altitude there should start to be snow on the ground. Based on how steep the sides were it would calculate how much and what type of vegetation would grow there, or where there should be piles of rocks due to landslides. According to where we were in the world, the computer would apply the right kind of rock patterning and soil colour. We could even say that we wanted a road going from one place to another, and the computer would build one with a route calculated according to the topology, even shaving areas out of steep slopes so the road could climb up the side.'

When procedural models had been generated by the computer, Digital Domain artists could alter them manually, adding additional geographical features where necessary, painting areas with additional textures and placing trees or rivers to produce a more art-directed landscape. 'We finished those models off manually,' states Hynek. 'But we could never have created such huge and varied vistas without sophisticated procedural modelling techniques.'

i

TRON

Tron (1982) was the first major motion picture to include fully realized sequences of computer-generated animation. The film was the brainchild of the animator Steven Lisberger, who believed the fledgling technology of computer graphics could be combined with more traditional forms of animation to tell a story set mainly within the body of an arcade video game. Lisberger initially tried to finance the film independently, but when the resources involved in creating such an ambitious film became apparent the Disney organization was persuaded to finance the production.

To produce the characters who inhabit the computer world, actors were dressed in costumes that were covered with black-and-white computer circuitry designs. Each frame of this live action was then transferred to large black-and-white transparencies, which were placed on a backlit animation stand and rephotographed through coloured filters. With coloured light shining through the white areas of their costumes, the resulting characters appeared to glow as if lit from within.

While optical processes were used to create all of the film's computerized characters, real computers were used to generate much of the world that they inhabited. From the tiny selection of American companies then capable of producing film-resolution computer images, Disney chose four outside groups to produce the computer graphics for *Tron*. At this time off-the-shelf graphics hardware and software packages were not available, so most computer graphics companies differed greatly from each other in the techniques and technology they used and the type of images they could produce. Each of the four companies was therefore given work that most suited its own capabilities.

Robert Abel and Associates used vector graphics (<155) to produce the film's title sequence as well as a scene in which the main character, Flynn (Jeff Bridges), first enters the world of the computer. Digital Effects Inc. produced a character called The Bit, and a short sequence of graphics at the beginning of the film. Triple-I and MAGI contributed 16 minutes of raster imagery (<155), including the memorable light-cycle sequence.

To produce the 3-D models needed for its portion of the film, MAGI first built a series of primitives (uniform geometric shapes; <157). The light-cycle models that the company produced were made entirely by intersecting these primitives to build up the body of the object – rather like building a model using children's toy bricks.

Triple-I, however, used a more sophisticated method to build the models for its share of the animation. After preparing detailed blueprints of the objects to be modelled, Triple-I mounted the plans on a digital encoding table – the early equivalent of today's graphics tablets – and recorded the position of each vertex (<156) by using an early mouse device with a cross-hair viewfinder. With this encoded information the computer was able to construct the models in three dimensions.

The system used by MAGI was favoured for the production of mechanical objects like the police Recognizer robots, while Triple-I worked on the more organic images such as the 'solar sailer' and the 'sea of simulation'.

As the first movie to make extensive and widely publicized use of digital graphics, much of the industry treated *Tron* as a test for the viability of computer-generated imagery in feature films. Although its revolutionary computer animation was stunning for the time, the film's failure at the box office was proof to many that the future of CGI was limited. The fact that computers had been used to re-create the world within a computer did nothing to alter people's opinion that computer graphics could only ever represent artificially stylized objects and locations.

TEXTURE MAPPING

Once the geometry of a computer model has been completed, attention turns to its outer appearance. Basic computer models are grey and dull – in fact, they look remarkably similar to an assembled plastic model kit. Like modelling kits, computer models must be finished with a coat of 'paint' and additional exterior details. It is this part of the process that truly defines a model's visual characteristics and brings it to life. By applying different colours, textures and surface properties to its exterior, the same basic sphere can be made to look like anything from a golf ball to an apparently vast planet with sparkling seas and swirling cloud formations.

Surface materials are applied to models in a process called 'texture mapping' during which texture maps containing information about how a surface should look are placed or 'mapped' onto a model. Texture mapping is actually a somewhat misleading term since although part of the process can involve physically altering the surface geometry of a model – making it more bumpy, for example – most of the time what is added to a model is not 'texture' but simply 'flat' colour detail.

To receive texture maps, the surfaces of a model first have to be 'unwrapped' to create one of a series of flat canvases called 'UV maps'. In the same way that X, Y and Z coordinates are used to refer to positions in 3-D space (<154), U and V are used to refer to points on the surface of a 2-D image. Each point on a UV map is a coordinate that relates directly to a point on the surface of the model.

The flat UV maps are used as a template on which colours or patterns can be painted to produce a texture map. When painting has been completed a texture map is 'wrapped' back onto the surface of the model in the same way that it was originally unwrapped. Wrapping may be a useful analogy to use when describing texture mapping, but this term is also somewhat misleading. Texture maps that are applied to a digital model are not physically wrapped around an object at all. The texture map is distorted by the computer according to the UV mapping coordinates, then 'projected' onto the surface of the digital model, much like the image from a slide being projected onto a wall from a distance. There are several basic methods of wrapping and unwrapping maps and these can be used for the majority of models.

The simplest form of mapping is 'planar mapping' (fig. 16). Planar mapping is similar to the process of applying wallpaper to a flat wall. Like wallpapering, if a pattern needs to be repeated – such as brickwork on a wall, for example – one small piece of texture can be repeated or 'tiled' along the wall's length and height. As with wallpapering, planar mapping only works well if the model's surface is relatively flat and featureless.

'Cylindrical mapping' is used for surfaces that have a little more curve to them – like wrapping a label around the body of a bottle (fig. 17).

'Spherical mapping' is similar to cylindrical mapping in that a linear measurement, such as image width, is converted into a circumference measurement. However, while cylindrical mapping takes only the curve of the object's circumference into account (as a cylinder's sides are straight over its entire height), spherical mapping takes into account both the curve of an object's circumference and the curve of its height – a sphere's 'sides' are curved over its height (fig. 18).

Most UV maps are generated automatically by the software used to create the digital model itself. The software looks at the shape of the model and searches for distinct joins and edges where a surface can be separated, unwrapped, and then rejoined after painting without a highly visible seam. This process is simple for uniform objects such as cubes and cylinders, but is much more complicated for irregularly shaped models. For particularly difficult forms digital artists may need to manually choose where they want the various joins to appear (fig. 19). Very complicated models, such as the body of a character, will normally have their textures applied using a different process called 'projection mapping' (203>).

Once the flat UV maps of a model's surfaces have been obtained they need to be turned into texture maps that will determine the model's outer appearance. At their simplest, textures are a combination of two main elements. The first is a basic colour or 'diffuse' map. This is simply an image of what the surface will look like and contains only colour information. To turn a model cuboid into a realistic brick, either a painting or a photograph of the surface texture of a brick needs to be mapped onto each of its sides, for example. The second element to a texture is an instruction that describes exactly how light interacts with that surface. This instruction is a mathematical algorithm called a 'shader', and it will be used during the final image-creating process of rendering (236>). The shader applied to the brick

FIGURE 16 **PLANAR MAPPING**

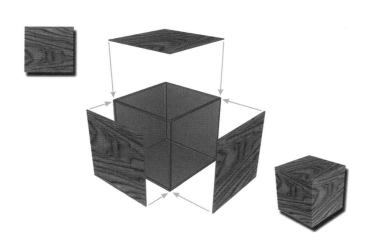

FIGURE 17 **CYLINDRICAL MAPPING**

FIGURE 18 **SPHERICAL MAPPING**

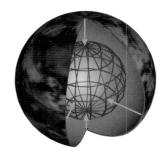

could make it look like it is made of matt plastic, shiny metal, or just crumbly old brick. Shaders are covered in greater detail overleaf.

Colour maps are produced in a number of ways. Very basic maps are created using the 'material editor' that comes with every modelling software package. The designer can choose from a range of ready-made 'stock' materials that most programs contain. These are usually basic surface materials such as brick, wood, concrete, stone, fabric, and so on. Some of these textures do not actually need to use UV mapping coordinates to position them on the surface of a model. These textures, called 'procedural textures' (or 'texture shaders'), are created using a mathematical algorithm that refers to the geometry of the object to generate its exterior appearance. This technique might be used to produce a marble vase, for example. The computer will use a mathematical description of what marble looks like and apply that to the surface of the model to produce a pattern that works well in that situation. The designer can adjust various parameters such as colour or size of pattern to influence the final appearance of the marble.

Most textures used for high-quality feature film modelling will be created specifically for each model. These colour images, also known as 'bitmaps', will either be painted by hand using a digital paint package such as Photoshop or produced from photographs of real surfaces. Most designers build up a personal photographic collection of interesting textures such as stone, brick, wood, water, grass, fabric, animal fur, mud, clouds – anything that might conceivably be used as the basis for a model's texture. These need to be photographed in flat lighting conditions so that the surface of an object does not have shadows and highlights 'built in'. Combining photographs and original artwork, often in many editable layers, designers will gradually build up the texture map for a model, frequently placing it onto the model to see how it works and where more detail is needed.

As well as colour maps, a variety of additional maps can be created to affect the appearance of the surface of a model in other ways. These maps are normally hand-painted greyscale maps – that is, images whose patterns range from black through grey to white. In these maps how light or dark an area is will affect the degree to which the surface of a model is affected by the properties that the map represents. Maps such as these can be used to influence details such as shininess or wetness, for example. In such cases the greyscale map is used to inform a shader (167>) where to apply those particular properties to the surface of a model during rendering.

To bring more detail to the surface of a model, a special texture map called a 'bump map' may be used (fig. 20, 166>). Although a bump map is 'flat', when it is added to a model, the computer renders areas of the greyscale map that are white to look as if they are raised from the surface, and areas that are black to look as if they are sunk below the surface. The actual surface of the model remains physically unaffected, but the bump map is used by the shader to change the way that light reflects from areas of the model's surface to produce an impression of texture. A bump map may be used to save modelling time when building a complex model like a ship, for example. The hull of the ship may be modelled as a perfectly smooth object. A separate bump map containing the detail of the thousands of rivets on the hull can

FIGURE 19 **UV MAPPING**

Specialist software such as UVLayout can be used to determine the best place to divide up the surfaces of complicated models in order to produce a series of flattened UV maps. In this case the division lines, in red, can be seen on the model of the kangaroo, resulting in a set of five UV maps ready for painting.

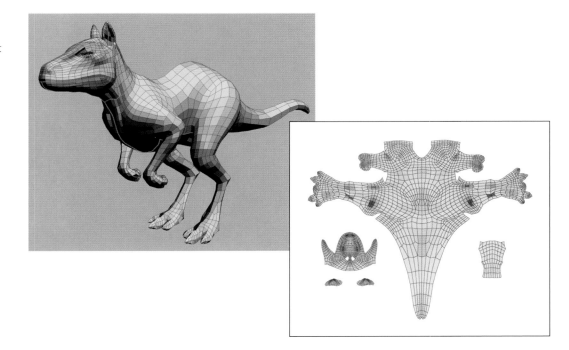

FIGURE 20 **BUMP AND DISPLACEMENT MAPS**

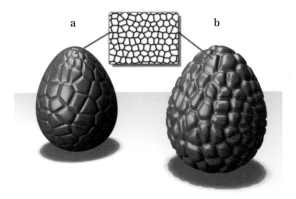

A greyscale map can be used either as a bump map (a) to make a smooth surface appear to have 3-D detail, or as a displacement map (b) to alter the actual geometry of a surface.

FIGURE 21 **OPACITY MAPS**

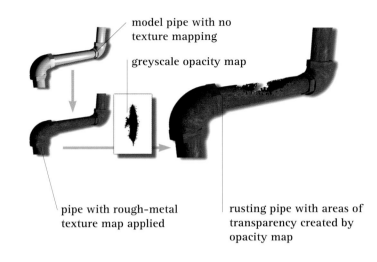

model pipe with no texture mapping

greyscale opacity map

pipe with rough-metal texture map applied

rusting pipe with areas of transparency created by opacity map

then be manually created or made from photographs of a real ship. When applied to the hull model, the bump map will give the impression of a much more complex and believable form without the modeller having to make and apply each rivet.

In addition to bump maps, modellers can use 'displacement maps' (fig. 20). Displacement maps are similar to bump maps in that they use light and dark areas to represent areas of surface detail that are raised or sunk. However, during rendering a displacement map physically alters the geometry of a model, pulling areas of highlight outwards and pushing areas of shade inwards, to create a more complex and realistic model.

Another variety of greyscale map, called an 'opacity map', can control the solidity or transparency of a surface (fig. 21). These maps are useful for placing holes in complicated models, allowing the artist first to build a perfect model and attach various texture maps to it before making alterations. As with any texture map, opacity maps can be animated so that an object appears to turn transparent – bullet holes appearing in the side of a computer-generated car, for example. Opacity maps were used by ILM

during the making of *The Mummy* (1999). The computer-generated mummy, Imhotep, was first built with many layers of skin, flesh, muscle and bone. Opacity maps were then applied to create the holes and fissures that revealed the mummy's underlying flesh and bone. These maps themselves could be animated to show areas becoming increasingly transparent as a shot progressed.

To create reflections on digital objects, a 'reflection map' can be used. If a digital car with shiny paintwork and chrome is to be composited into live-action footage, reflections from the live-action surroundings can be added to the digital car. After assigning shiny, reflective surfaces to the computer model car, a cube or dome can be placed around it. Moving footage of the location in question is then mapped onto the cube or dome, which is itself made invisible to the virtual camera so that only the moving images that it holds are reflected in the paintwork of the car. The finished image will be a digital car with real location reflections, so that when the car is composited into the live action, it will look as if it was filmed within the real environment.

FIGURE 22 **DIFFUSE LIGHT**

Diffuse light is reflected evenly in all directions according to the relationship between the object and the surrounding light sources.

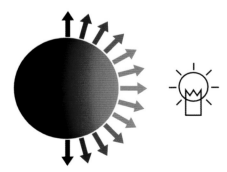

FIGURE 23 **SPECULAR LIGHT**

Specular highlights are bright spots on the surface of an object. Their intensity is affected by the angle between the light source and the camera.

SURFACE SHADERS

During the process of texture mapping, digital models have 'flat' colour images of textures and materials placed onto their surfaces. Although these might be enough to tell us that a surface is supposed to be made of brick or wood, they will not be sufficient to impart the range of more subtle visual information that we expect to receive from objects in the world around us.

For example, in our home we may have two pieces of oak furniture. Yet although in both cases the colour and grain of the wood is identical, the surface of each piece of furniture may still look very different. This could be because one piece has been varnished while the other has not. Or perhaps one has been sanded until its surfaces are smooth while the other is still relatively rough. Were we to make digital models of this furniture each piece could be given exactly the same oak texture map. But to make the wood look rough or smooth, shiny or matt, we need to define the way that light interacts with the surface. This is the job of what are called 'surface shaders'.

A surface shader is a mathematical formula that describes how light is redirected by the surface of an object. This formula is used by the computer to create a finished image during the rendering process (236>). It does this by calculating the quality and quantity of light that hits each polygon on the surface of a model. Each polygon already has its own colour, as defined by its texture map, and so the computer combines the colour of the incoming light with the colour of the texture map to produce a new colour for that polygon. The surface shader then instructs the computer how that coloured light will be reflected away from the surface of the polygon according to the angle of its surface (known as its 'surface normal'). Depending on what angle the model is viewed from, the viewer will see thousands of polygons of differing colour and brightness that combine to tell us what surface qualities an object has.

There are three main types of light interaction whose effects are calculated and combined by a surface shader in order to create the final appearance of an object.

Ambient light is a constant low level of light that is added to the surface of a model no matter what other lighting is placed in a scene. Ambient light keeps any unlit, shadow areas from turning pitch black, which would be unrealistic.

Diffuse light can come from any light-producing source within a scene. When this light hits an object it is scattered according to the position of the light and the angle to which each polygon on the surface of the object is oriented. The more a polygon is angled away from the light, the darker its surface becomes (fig. 22).

Specular light is light that is reflected from the surface of a polygon in a particular direction. This means that specular light is view-dependent – its intensity depends on the angle between the incoming light and the position from which the object is viewed. Specular calculations produce bright, focused highlights on the surface of an object, making it look shiny (fig. 23).

Surface shaders combine differing amounts of ambient, diffuse and specular lighting to simulate the look of different types of material. For example, a sphere with a low level of diffuse light and very strong specular highlights will look like a shiny snooker ball. The same sphere with little specular highlights and lots of diffuse light will look like a soft rubber ball (fig. 24).

A number of pre-designed surface shader models can be used as the basis of most surface types. These are normally named after the person who wrote them and have names such as Blinn (written by James Blinn), Phong (written by Phong Bui-Tong), Gouraud (written by Henri Gouraud) and Lambert (written by Johann Heinrich Lambert). These shader models and others like them can be used to reproduce the surface qualities of the majority of everyday objects. More unusual objects or materials will need specific shader models written for them. Most visual effects facilities have a shader writer whose job it is to edit existing shader models or write new ones in order to create exactly the look required for each object's surface. More complicated shaders can be written to describe the specific look of translucent materials such as glass or water, the unique way that hair and brushed metals stretch reflections perpendicular to their length to produce bands of highlight (called anisotropic shading), or the very complex way that light is absorbed and reflected by human skin (called subsurface scattering, 204>).

In addition to surface shaders several other types of shader will ultimately be used in every computer-generated scene. 'Light shaders' are descriptions of the quality and quantity of illumination emitted by any lights in a scene. 'Volume shaders' calculate what happens to light as it passes through a volume that represents fog or smoke. 'Transformation shaders' recalculate the angle of each polygon's surface (its 'surface normal') in order to artificially create the appearance of a bumpy surface (bump mapping, <165), and 'displacement shaders' actually prompt the physical alteration of a model's surface during rendering (displacement mapping, <166).

Shaders are one of the most abstract and complicated areas of computer graphics production and are fully understood by only a select few working in the industry. Shader writers have a rare combination of skills, being able to study the subtle natural interplay of real-world objects and light sources to produce mathematical descriptions of those interactions. Their complex work ultimately allows computers to turn numbers into light.

FIGURE 24 **SURFACE SHADERS**

A surface shader will combine differing amounts of ambient light (a), diffuse light (b), and specular light (c) to give an object the desired appearance (d). The object can be further refined with other types of map including bump maps or opacity maps.

a + b + c = d

4

ANIMATION

INTRODUCTION

The principle at the heart of moving pictures is the ability to project still images at the speed of 24 frames per second, thus creating the illusion of continuous movement. Animation takes advantage of the fact that the filming of such images need not be continuous, and that each frame in a sequence can be photographed individually with any amount of time between exposures. By manipulating objects incrementally from frame to frame during this time, animators are able to give inanimate objects the appearance of movement and life when the film is ultimately projected at the normal speed.

There are two broad categories of animation. 2-D animation mainly involves the photography of flat artwork such as drawings or paintings to produce what we might call a cartoon. Such methods are used to produce short films featuring popular characters such as The Simpsons or, in their most complex form, animated feature films such as *Pinocchio* (1940) or *Beauty and the Beast* (1991). Less well known is the practice of animating 2-D artwork to create visual effects for live-action films. Elements such as sparks, lightning and laser bolts can all be drawn by hand and photographed one frame at a time before being added to live-action images. These traditionally painstaking and laborious processes have been greatly affected by the emergence of the computer, but the principle of animating 2-D images remains essentially unchanged.

3-D animation processes, on the other hand, involve manipulating the physical position of dimensional objects such as puppets and environments from frame to frame. Such techniques are best known for creating the performance of fantastic creatures for films such as *King Kong* (1933) or *The 7th Voyage of Sinbad* (1958). 3-D animation has also been greatly affected by the digital revolution and many stunningly realistic images, from dinosaurs to spaceships and even clouds of dust, are now created and animated entirely within the computer.

Animation, in all its varied forms, is perhaps the most important and widely used of all special effects techniques and has enabled the production of some of the most memorable and breathtaking moments in the history of the movies.

2-D ANIMATION

It was a decade after the emergence of moving pictures that 2-D animation, the ancestor of the modern cartoon, became a recognizable mode of production. In 1906 J. Stuart Blackton (1875–1941) produced a film called *Humorous Phases of Funny Faces*, in which an artist's hand sketched faces in white chalk on a black background. Once drawn, the caricatures assumed a life of their own and performed exaggerated facial expressions. The film was made by a process of exposing a frame or two of the drawn face, then redrawing the face in its new position and exposing it for another frame or two.

In 1908 the French caricaturist and comic-strip artist Émile Cohl (1857–1938) made *Fantasmagorie*, a two-minute film of hand-drawn, moving stick figures. Between 1908 and 1910, Cohl contributed animation to over 75 films for the Gaumont company, and invented many of the tools that became standards of the trade, including the vertically mounted camera animation stand and charts for plotting character and camera movement. Cohl's surreal animations, in which fantastic drawings metamorphosed into one another with no apparent logic, were highly successful, and in 1912 Cohl moved to the United States to produce a series of animations based on a newspaper comic strip called *The Newlyweds and Their Baby*.

A number of American newspaper cartoonists were encouraged by the success of Cohl's films and began to make animated adaptations of their own work. Among them was Winsor McCay (1871–1934), who drew the popular *Little Nemo* comic strip for the *New York Herald*. In 1911 McCay drew and filmed 4,000 images to produce a short film called *Little Nemo*. Before the animation itself, McCay appeared on screen to demonstrate the way in which thousands of individual drawings were photographed to create the impression of movement. McCay actually painted directly onto the black-and-white celluloid images, to produce the first colour animated film.

After a year's work, McCay then produced *Gertie the Dinosaur* (1914) – not, as is often claimed, the world's first cartoon, but certainly the first to feature a character with a personality. Gertie appeared to move with a feeling of ponderous weight, was shy but liked to show off, and could even shed tears. The film was presented by McCay himself, who would stand to one side of the screen giving instructions to which Gertie appeared to respond. To create the film, McCay drew every detail of every frame on thousands of sheets of paper. The paper was semi-transparent, enabling McCay to trace the previous image and make the slight differences that would produce movement when the pictures were filmed and shown in rapid succession.

In 1914 the cartoonist and producer John Bray (1879–1978) pioneered a method of painting the background scenery of a shot on a clear cellulose acetate sheet, leaving the area where the moving characters were to appear unpainted. The acetate sheet was then placed on top of the characters – still

drawn individually on paper – and filmed. The system made production much quicker since only the moving characters and not the static background scenery had to be redrawn for each shot. Bray's system was improved later in the same year by Earl Hurd (1880–1940), who more logically reversed the process, using a single elaborate background painting over which cellulose sheets or 'cels' containing changing images of the characters were laid. The method of producing characters on see-through cels has formed the basis of 2-D animation ever since.

Realizing the potential of animated cartoons, the Edison company financed what is thought to be the first cartoon production company, Barré Studio, under the supervision of Raoul Barré (1874–1932) and William Nolan (1894–1954), who together devised several techniques that became industry standards. Around 1914, Nolan and Barré added a row of pegs to drawing boards and animation stands, on which cels and backgrounds with perforations could be laid to ensure perfect registration during drawing and photography. They also introduced an assembly-line production regime in which separate teams of people drew animation, painted it, photographed it and so on. Even the process of drawing animation itself was streamlined, with lead animators sketching characters' most extreme poses, while lower-paid artists drew the actions in between – a process that became known as 'tweening'.

By the 20s, the animated cartoon was an established part of every movie theatre programme, and animated characters such as Koko the Clown and the incredibly popular Felix the Cat were as widely recognized as their live-action co-stars. In 1923 a young and ambitious animator moved to Hollywood from Kansas City, where he had been producing humorous animated advertisements called 'Laugh-O-Grams' for a local theatre chain. Within five years he was producing the most popular and sophisticated cartoons in the world, and his name soon became synonymous with animation.

Walter Elias Disney (1901–66) and his partner Ub Iwerks (1901–71) produced, among other projects, a series of *Alice* comedies (1923–7), technically advanced cartoons that combined a live-action character called Alice with a cartoon world and cartoon characters. Disney and Iwerks made over 50 *Alice* films before creating a new character called Oswald the Lucky Rabbit in 1927. The cartoons starring Oswald were a success, so much so that their distributor, Charles Mintz, poached most of Disney's staff and set up his own studio to produce the films without Disney's input. Disney vowed that he would never again make films for anyone else. Looking for a new character to revive his fortunes, Disney shortened Oswald's ears, gave him a long tail and turned him into a mouse called Mickey.

Disney produced two Mickey Mouse cartoons in 1928, but, unable to find a national distributor, decided to make a third with sound. *Steamboat Willie* (1928) was not the first sound cartoon; Oswald the Lucky Rabbit had already been set to music, as had the work of Max and Dave Fleischer (174>) and the Terrytoon cartoons made by Paul Terry (1887–1971). However, *Steamboat Willie* was the first cartoon to use synchronized music and sound effects, including a whistling mouse and cats that miaowed when their tails were pulled. Audiences and critics loved the seven-minute cartoon and demanded more. Disney never looked back. In 1932 Disney won an Oscar for *Flowers and Trees*, the first cartoon made in three-strip Technicolor (<56), and went on to collect every Academy Award for animation over the next 11 years.

While other American animators were happy to produce cartoons that portrayed a slapstick, almost surreal version of the world, Disney developed a unique form of stylized realism combined with a close attention to narrative and characterization. By the mid-30s, Disney felt that the art of animation had developed sufficiently to support the production of a feature-length animated film. In 1934, against the advice of almost everybody, Disney began production of *Snow White and the Seven Dwarfs* (1937).

PRECEDING PAGES: **The mighty *King Kong* (1933), one of cinema's first great animated characters, and still one of the best loved.**

ABOVE LEFT: **Simple hand-drawn stick figures were animated in Émile Cohl's early cartoon *Fantasmagorie* (1908).**

LEFT: **Gertie the Dinosaur was one of cinema's first cartoon stars. Winsor McCay drew every frame by hand, even creating a cartoon version of himself to interact with the characterful dinosaur.**

RIGHT: **Enjoying the new medium of sound, Mickey Mouse uses a cow's teeth as a xylophone in Walt Disney's pioneering cartoon *Steamboat Willie* (1928).**

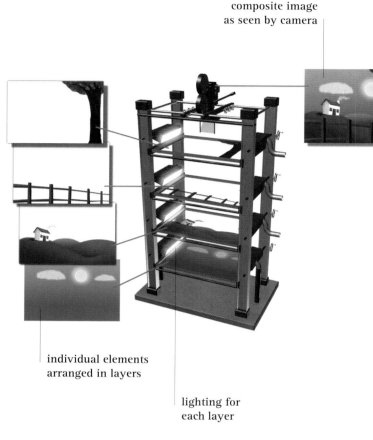

FIGURE 1 **THE MULTIPLANE CAMERA**

composite image
as seen by camera

individual elements
arranged in layers

lighting for
each layer

Disney knew that the limitations of normal 2-D cartoon animation would constrain the aesthetics of the feature-length film that he had in mind. Disney's main concern was to find a way of making his cartoons look less flat and two-dimensional. In the real world, a camera that pans over any scene will make objects in the distance appear to move very slowly, while those in the foreground appear to move much more quickly. This phenomenon is a vital cue to the depth of a scene and is known as 'parallax shift'. Since the painted cels used in ordinary animation are placed directly on top of one another with no distance between them, there is no shift in parallax when the camera moves over them. Furthermore, real scenes of objects that are some distance apart are affected by depth of field (<115), which makes foreground and background elements appear more or less in focus. Sandwiched acetate cels have no distance between them, so every layer remains in constant focus.

To overcome the lack of depth in ordinary animation, the Disney technical department built the first multiplane camera (fig. 1) – an award-winning and revolutionary piece of animation equipment. The camera was a towering device in which several animation cels were layered vertically with some distance between them. The camera, which looked down onto the stack of cels, was then sharply focused on a single layer so that the elements in front and behind were in soft focus. The cels could also be moved horizontally so that particular elements, such as the branches of overhanging trees, could be moved out of the way to give the impression that the camera was moving through a scene. Lengthy tracking shots were achieved by moving long sheets

of painted acetate or glass past the stationary camera. The cels in the foreground were moved much faster than those in the background to give a convincing sense of depth. Each layer of animation was individually illuminated to enable the creation of interesting lighting effects.

Using the multiplane camera was a complicated process. The movements of each of the separate layers of animation were painstakingly calculated and plotted before photography began. Complex sequences involving the movement of multiple layers, sometimes with dozens of characters, could involve using a team of animation photographers to service the requirements of each layer of imagery. After days of work, the success of a shot would only be confirmed when the developed film was returned from the laboratory.

Before being used for *Snow White*, the multiplane camera was given a trial run for the short film *The Old Mill* (1937), for which it created richly atmospheric images with a sense of depth that had never been seen in 2-D animation before. The incredibly realistic feeling of depth in *Snow White* was partly responsible for the film's massive commercial success when it was released in February 1938. Walt Disney had proved to his critics that the public would pay to see feature-length animated films, and his studio embarked on the production of an ambitious and profitable series of animated features, many of which have become classics that are enjoyed to this day. Though Disney's storytelling became increasingly sophisticated, the place of the multiplane camera at the heart of the animation production process remained unchanged until the arrival of computer-aided techniques in the 80s.

SPECIAL EFFECTS ANIMATION

Although creating the illusion of life with a few strokes of a pencil could be considered a special effect in itself, traditional 2-D animators distinguish between character animation and special effects animation. Anything that moves that isn't a character is usually animated by the effects department. This can include rain, snow, water, falling leaves, fire, smoke, shadows – anything that brings the scene to life.

As with so many aspects of animation, Walt Disney was an early innovator in the field of special effects. Character animators were traditionally responsible for drawing their own special effects, and as a result, such elements often remained crude and ineffective compared to the advances that were made in stylistic character animation. Disney was aware that his first feature film, *Snow White and the Seven Dwarfs* (1937), would rely just as much on the credibility of its environment as it would on its characters. To create the world he envisaged, Disney established the first special effects animation department and staffed it with artists whose talents lay in the portrayal of the natural world. These animators spent months studying the way in which different types of rain fell, how rivers flowed and flames danced. With nothing to animate but special effects, the skills of the effects department staff developed so greatly that, as *Snow White* neared completion, the effects animation created at the beginning of production had to be redesigned to match the sophistication of the later work.

One of the major innovations made by the Disney effects department was a new method of creating complex shadows. Traditionally, characters looked rather flat because there were no shadows on their bodies. The shadows that characters cast on the ground and the objects around them, which are so important in tying a character to its environment, were usually limited to amorphous dark patches that randomly followed the characters around. For *Snow White*, the Disney effects artists completed the character animation and painting, then placed another cel on top of each character on which they drew the outline of a shadow area. The shadow area was then painted solid black. During photography, the shadow cel was laid on top of the character cel and the two were photographed for around 70 per cent of the time required for a good exposure. The shadow element was then removed and the character painting was photographed on its own for the remaining 30 per cent of exposure time. The result was an image that contained a character with a transparent shadow area – the character detail could actually be seen beneath the shadow. By varying the proportion of exposure time given to the shadow element, shadows could be made darker or lighter depending on the mood and lighting of the scene.

'Shadows continue to be a large part of an effects animator's job', says Jon Brook, an animation effects supervisor who has worked on modern animated features such as *Who Framed Roger Rabbit* (1988) and *An American Tail: Fievel Goes West* (1991). 'You might think that creating a shadow down the side of a character is simply a case of drawing an area of darkness over the body, but in fact, shadow style varies greatly from scene to scene and film to film, depending on the overall production design. Shadows can be hard-edged and bold, or soft-edged and subtle so that they wrap themselves gently around the body. Shadows also have to be animated according to the content of the scene; as a character moves past a light source, the direction and quality of a shadow will change. If there's a fire in the scene, a shadow will shudder and move in response to the mood of the fire.'

Perhaps the greatest challenge for an effects animator is water. Water is transparent, elastic, constantly moving, sometimes heavy, sometimes light and frothy. Re-creating water with a few hand-drawn pencil lines is an extraordinary skill. A wave is not simply a crest that can be drawn with a single line – a wave has shadows, currents and smaller waves that grow and die within it as it moves. 'A simple little splash has so much thought put into it', says Brook. 'It has to grow and die in probably less than a second, yet in that 24 frames we must draw a series of droplets that separate out and rise up to a crest before falling back down convincingly, all within the specific style of the production. We don't simply draw a standard splash when one is needed; we spend a great deal of time designing the feeling of the splashes in any production so that they fit in with the overall art direction – they might be hard, spiky splashes or delicate, soft ones.'

An effects animator is often called upon to draw objects as they move and change position. A classic example is leaves blowing in the wind. Each leaf must change its shape, colour and shadow as it is twisted and carried by the breeze. Some of the most extraordinary examples of this artistic skill can be seen in Disney's *Fantasia* (1940). For the Nutcracker Suite sequence, animator Cy Young created a beautiful moment when a delicate white blossom drifts down to land on the surface of a pond before being reborn as a graceful ballerina swirling up into the sky. This moment is one of hundreds of sublime animated effects in the film and, despite being over half a century old, *Fantasia* remains perhaps the finest example of the art that has ever been produced.

FAR LEFT: **Invented in 1937, Disney's multiplane camera brought a new sense of depth and realism to 2-D cartoon animation. The vast monolith took a large crew to operate and required each scene to be plotted in minute detail – but the results were spectacular.**

RIGHT: **Examples of irregular movement, particularly natural phenomena such as splashing water, are painstakingly designed and drawn by special effects animators. These production designs were created by animation effects supervisor Jon Brooks.**

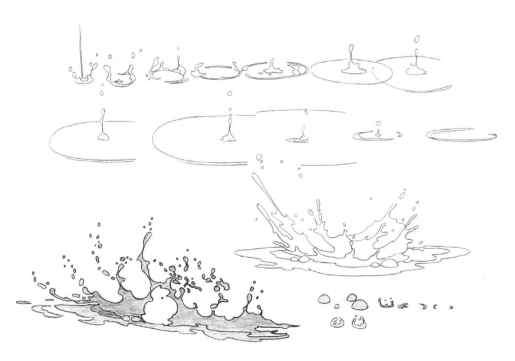

ROTOSCOPING

The use of effects animation is not confined to films featuring cartoon characters. Many live-action feature films make extensive use of hand-drawn 2-D animated special effects.

In 1917 the animator Max Fleischer (1883–1972) patented the rotoscope, a device that projected pre-filmed footage of a performing actor onto a sheet of glass. The movements of the actor were then traced onto sheets of paper one frame at a time, and these were used as templates to draw cartoon characters that, when animated, had incredibly lifelike movements. Fleischer and his brother Dave (1894–1979) used the rotoscope to produce their popular *Koko the Clown* cartoons of the 20s and the *Betty Boop* and *Popeye* cartoons of the 30s. The rotoscope did not revolutionize the production of cartoons in the way that Fleischer had hoped, though it has been used to produce character motion for a number of films including Ralph Bakshi's animated version of *The Lord of the Rings* (1978). Most character animators, however, have preferred to use a stylized hand-drawn form of human movement.

Though rarely used in the production of animated cartoons, rotoscoping has found other important uses in the field of film special effects. By projecting pre-filmed images onto a flat surface, they can be traced to produce hand-drawn travelling mattes (<67). The process can also be used to hand-draw a variety of 2-D animated elements, such as lightning, lasers, gun blasts and shadows.

Steve Begg is one of Britain's leading special effects artists and is recognized for his skill in hand-drawing animated special effects elements. 'One of the most commonly required animation effects is lightning and electrical charges', says Begg. 'To produce such effects optically, we first load a registration print [the developed print of the sequence that needs an animation effect added to it] into the rotoscope projector. Each frame of the sequence is then projected down onto a piece of paper. Using the projected image for reference, we hand-draw a rough version of the actual animation itself, or trace reference points from the scene that we can use as a guide for our animation later.' The artist then sketches the animation in pencil before going over it with black ink or paint.

'There are a number of ways of getting lightning to look real', says Begg. 'Some people like to draw the tip of the bolt of lightning as it emerges from a cloud and then extend it down towards the ground over three or four frames. For natural lightning, I think it looks best if it snaps down to the ground instantly. If it's some sort of fantasy film and you want the lightning to appear to have a life of its own, you can draw it so that it twists

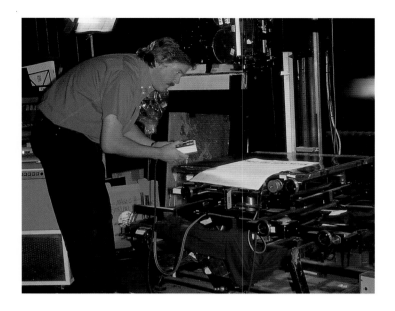

FAR LEFT: **The mighty dragon Vermithrax is struck by hand-drawn lightning effects created by ILM for** *Dragonslayer* **(1981).**

LEFT: **Effects supervisor Steve Begg photographs flat artwork using the rotoscope at The Magic Camera Company.**

BELOW: **Actors fought with wooden sticks during the making of** *The Empire Strikes Back* **(1980). The glowing light sabres were later hand-drawn and painted before being added to the footage during compositing.**

and curls in an organic-looking way before recoiling back into itself. It's important to try to give it that life.'

Once the animation of lightning or lasers has been drawn and painted, it is photographed. Each sheet of animation is laid back on the rotoscope stand and photographed sequentially onto high-contrast black-and-white film. When developed, the result is a series of black negatives with white (transparent) animation on them; in other words, the black-painted lightning becomes a clear area on the negative. This film is then loaded into an optical printer (<70) and combined with the film of the original scene. 'We will often print animation in several passes', explains Begg. 'Drawn animation is usually quite sharp-edged. This is fine for sharp electrical sparks and lighting, but lasers and other effects often look better if they have a soft glow. To achieve this, we first print the animation in what we call a "core pass". This gives a bright, sharp centre to the effect. Then we rewind the animation and print it a second time using a diffusion filter that blurs the image. This produces a soft glow around an intense centre. By placing a coloured filter in front of the animation during printing, the lightning or laser bolts can be made any colour that you want.'

As well as creating areas of light, effects animation can be used to create areas of darkness. When real aircraft fly over a real landscape, they cast shadows beneath them as they travel. When model aircraft are composited into real or model landscapes, the two elements have no physical relationship and no corresponding shadows. By using the rotoscope to plot the path of a flying object, shadows can be drawn by hand that trace the shape of the aircraft on the contours of the ground below. By adding the shadow of one object onto another, the separate elements of a scene are effectively 'tied' together, as if filmed at the same time. Fine examples of this method can be seen in *The Empire Strikes Back* (1980). When the *Millennium Falcon* is pursued across the surface of an asteroid by Imperial TIE fighters, the spaceship's shadow can be seen rippling over the rocky surface below.

Rotoscoped effects animation can also be used to create more down-to-earth effects. 'Over the years there has been one simple effect that we have been asked to do probably more than any other', explains Gene Warren, head of Fantasy II Film Effects. 'Lots of films contain shooting, and getting a gun to look as if it's firing can be a hit-or-miss thing. Firstly, the person using the gun has to remember to pull the trigger – in all the excitement of an action scene, they sometimes forget to do this. Secondly, even if the gun does go off, the flash of the gun lasts for just a fraction of a second and it is quite possible for it to occur between frames when the shutter of the camera is closed. We often end up having to rotoscope the muzzle blast on guns into a scene; we've done this hundreds of times over the years.'

'We do muzzle blasts just like normal rotoscoped animation', explains Warren. 'The shot is projected down onto paper and the position of the necessary flash is traced and then shaded in pencil. Pencil shading is great because it gives you a random, grainy look that is perfect for muzzle blast and it only takes about five minutes to draw. The drawing is then photographed and printed into the shot in the optical printer. The last little touch is to place a filter in front of the image during optical printing and put a dab of petroleum jelly onto the filter. With a fine brush, we just draw the grease out along the path of the bullet – this gives an almost imperceptible blur as if a bullet really is coming out of the gun. One of the biggest jobs we did this for was *Point Break* [1991]. We did nearly all the gun blasts in the bank robbery scenes. A few of those muzzle blasts are real and lots of them are fake, but it's totally impossible to tell which is which – I'd have to go and check our records to find out which ones we did because even I can't see the difference!'

Today rotoscoping and effects animation is achieved digitally with artwork being either hand-drawn and scanned into the computer or painted directly in the computer using specialist digital paint software (<108).

WHO FRAMED ROGER RABBIT

Film-makers have always been fascinated by the potential of combining live-action performers with animated characters. Max Fleischer's (<174) *Out of the Inkwell* series of cartoons (1919–28) featured animated characters that left their artificial environment for a jaunt in the live-action world. Walt Disney (<171) reversed the conceit in his *Alice* comedies (1923–7), in which a live-action actor was placed within an animated environment populated by cartoon co-stars. Later feature films such as *Anchors Aweigh* (1945) and *Pete's Dragon* (1977) combined human and cartoon characters, but the blend was never particularly subtle.

When director Robert Zemeckis (<43) and executive producer Steven Spielberg (<39) decided to make *Who Framed Roger Rabbit* (1988) they knew that modern audiences would only watch the film if human characters and 'Toons' coexisted with a level of realistic interaction that had never been achieved before. After two years in production, the film that was finally released blurred the lines between animation and live action until they were almost unrecognizable. Audiences were thrilled by a world that included such inconceivable marvels as a cartoon car with a human passenger being chased by a real car driven by a gang of cartoon weasels.

The first stage of production involved filming the live-action scenes into which animation would eventually be inserted. Because the film had to go through numerous optical processes before completion, the entire movie was shot in the large VistaVision format (<55), which helped to retain good picture quality. It was the first film shot entirely in the format since the 50s.

Star Bob Hoskins endured months of reacting to non-existent characters. To help Hoskins, voice artist Charles Fleischer dressed in a Roger Rabbit costume and read Roger's lines from off-camera. Hoskins was also surrounded by dozens of technicians operating a host of remote-controlled props that had been cleverly created by physical effects supervisor George Gibbs (330>) to indicate the presence of an unseen co-star. Coats bulged with the contortions of an invisible rabbit, chair seats depressed and puffed out dust as imaginary characters sat down on them, and guns floated around in the hands of a transparent pack of weasels – Zemeckis referred to the proceedings as 'the most elaborate invisible man film ever made'.

Once live-action photography was completed, the film was edited into a semblance of its ultimate form. Scenes awaiting Toon performers were then enlarged into a series of photographs. These blow-ups were used as a guide by the 375 animators working under the supervision of master animator Richard Williams at his London studio. Williams produced rough pencil-line performances and combined them with the live-action backgrounds for the director's approval. Animation was particularly taxing because Zemeckis had filmed many scenes with a moving camera. To create cartoon characters that fitted into these scenes animators had to draw Toons whose perspective altered as if filmed by the same camera.

Once approved, animation was redrawn, inked and painted. To help bring a sense of 3-D life to the 2-D characters, a new method of producing shadows was devised. Since the 30s shadows had been painted in black and double-exposed into a shot (<173), which gave all the shadows the same grey, sometimes muddy tone. To help the Toons blend more realistically with their surroundings, all shadow detail was painted in coloured tones; Jessica Rabbit's red dress was fringed with dark burgundy shadows and scarlet highlights, for example. Additional layers of animated effects – sparkling sequins in the case of Jessica's dress – were also created. Extensive rotoscoping (<174) was used to produce hand-drawn travelling mattes (<67) so that Toons, humans and real-life props could be composited together as if actually interacting.

The 82,000 frames of hand-drawn animation were then optically composited at Industrial Light and Magic to produce over 1,000 shots – equivalent, according to visual effects supervisor Ken Ralston (299>), to creating the effects for all three *Star Wars* films. Upon its release, *Who Framed Roger Rabbit* was a huge hit, earning millions at the box office and an Academy Award for its innovative and painstakingly produced special effects.

SLIT SCAN

For the tunnel of light known as the 'Stargate sequence' in *2001: A Space Odyssey* (1968), director Stanley Kubrick simply told his effects crew that the camera should appear to 'go through something'. Several options were considered, but it was a proposal from Douglas Trumbull that caught Kubrick's imagination.

Experiments in abstract streak photography had been carried out as early as the 40s by brothers James and John Whitney. In the 50s John Whitney (<146) acquired an army-surplus analogue computer and rebuilt it to photograph patterns of light for an abstract film called *Catalog 61* (1961).

In the system developed by Trumbull with Con Pederson, Bob Abel and Colin Cantwell, an animation camera (fig. 2 (a)) was placed on a 4.6 m (15 ft) track, on which it could be moved slowly and smoothly backwards and forwards using worm gearing (b). Two large sheets of glass were placed at the far end of the track, each sheet about 1.5 m (5 ft) high and 3 m (10 ft) wide. These sheets could be moved vertically and horizontally. The sheet of glass farthest from the camera held transparent, backlit artwork (c). The sheet of glass nearest the camera was masked in black material, apart from a small slit (d), from which the system derived its name. This slit allowed only a small area of the backlit artwork to be visible to the camera at any one time.

To produce the streaking effect seen in the film, the camera began with its lens close to the slit so that the artwork behind it reached the edges of the frame. The shutter on the camera was then opened to expose a single frame of film to the image. Still exposing the same frame of film, the camera was moved away from the slit until it reached the end of the track. As the camera moved backwards, gears ensured that its lens kept the shrinking artwork in focus. At the same time, the artwork itself was moved horizontally or vertically across the slit to provide distortion. When the camera reached the point farthest from the artwork, the shutter was closed after having exposed, on one frame of film, a distorted streak of coloured light as it travelled away from the camera towards the middle of the screen (e). The process can be compared to taking photographs of roads at night, where long exposures register passing vehicles simply as the blurred streaks of headlights.

Next, the film was rewound and the process repeated with the blur of light travelling from the opposite side of the frame towards the centre. The process was carefully programmed so that for each subsequent frame filmed, the movements of the camera and the artwork were repeated with minute, sequential differences. The result was the effect of travelling through the light tunnel.

No hard-and-fast rules were followed when producing the sequence. Each filming session was set up with different variations of artwork, movement and exposure, and after many hours of laborious work, the result might be, according to Kubrick, 'like carpet going by' or one of the most dazzling, kaleidoscopic light shows ever to have been captured on film. After slit scan's spectacular debut in *2001*, it was used to create streaking title effects for films such as *Superman* (1978) and the wormhole sequence in *Star Trek* (1979).

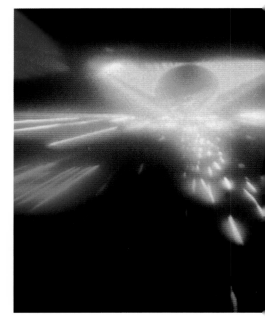

ABOVE: **The ultimate trip, courtesy of Stanley Kubrick's *2001: A Space Odyssey* (1968). The psychedelic light show of the Stargate sequence was created using slit-scan photography.**

RIGHT: **The use of tens of thousands of digitally animated 3-D characters gave a sense of massive scale to the Exodus sequence in DreamWorks Animation's *The Prince of Egypt* (1998).**

FIGURE 2 **SLIT SCAN**

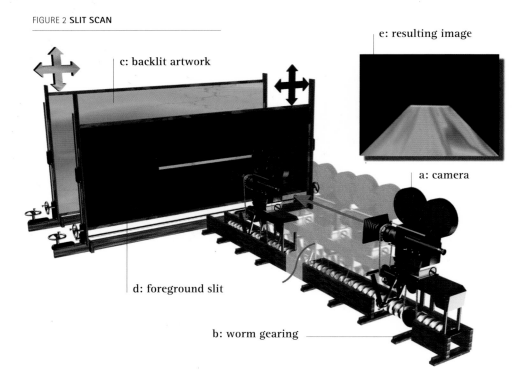

c: backlit artwork

e: resulting image

a: camera

d: foreground slit

b: worm gearing

2-D COMPUTER ANIMATION

Everything about traditional hand-drawn animation is laborious and painstakingly slow, so when computers began to affect other areas of movie production, animation studios wasted no time in finding ways to streamline their own production methods.

In 1986 Disney, in association with Pixar, began to develop CAPS (computer animation production system). CAPS was designed to perform many of the tasks of the traditional animator within the computer. First, the black-and-white artwork was drawn by hand in the traditional manner before being scanned into a computer. Each drawing was then coloured on screen using a digital paint system. The rows of artists who had once worked amid pots of freshly mixed paint were replaced by a few computer monitors. While one artist could hand-paint perhaps 20 cels a day, a single computer operator could now complete around 200. As well as painting images, CAPS could also be used to generate certain special effects and to assemble multi-layer scenes without the use of a multiplane camera (<172). The first feature film entirely painted and assembled using CAPS was *The Rescuers Down Under* (1990).

2-D animators also wanted to take advantage of the computer's ability to create 3-D images. While traditional animators could draw scenes that replicated a complicated camera move, the process was highly skilled, time-consuming, and not always successful. In the computer, however, objects created in 3-D could have any movement or change in camera angle applied to them at the touch of a few buttons.

In the 80s several systems were developed to turn 3-D computer-generated objects into 2-D animation. These systems allowed relatively simple geometric shapes to be modelled, animated and 'filmed' in the computer. The resulting sequences could be printed on paper as a series of 2-D frames in which objects had black lines around their edges. These frames could then be individually painted and combined with traditional backgrounds and character animation. This technique was first used for some scenes in Disney's ill-received *The Black Cauldron* (1985). It was used more effectively for the climactic scenes of *The Great Mouse Detective* (1986) when it produced dynamic shots of Big Ben's ticking clock mechanisms.

Computers are now an essential part of the production process of 2-D animated feature films. At the forefront of modern animated feature production is DreamWorks Animation, whose ambitious first movie *The Prince of Egypt* (1998) was a landmark in feature animation. '*The Prince of Egypt* was an epic story told on an epic scale,' comments 3-D layout artist Harald Kraut. 'We felt that traditional 2-D multiplane camera work – or at least today's computerized equivalent – wasn't up to the scope of the story. We didn't want all of the wonderful Egyptian architecture to look like pieces of flat artwork sliding past each other; we wanted to create a real sense of environment.' To help create this environment, DreamWorks developed a new animation system called 'Exposure'.

The Exposure system is based on the principles of normal 3-D animation production, in which a 3-D environment that has been built, textured and lit in the computer has a virtual camera (233>) placed within it. The camera is then animated to move around and 'film' objects from any angle. Using Exposure,

DreamWorks artists construct digital 3-D buildings and objects in the usual way, but rather than applying computer-generated textures (<164), the exterior of the objects is left flat and without details. 'We position the virtual camera to look at each object from an angle that shows the largest amount of surface area on that model', explains Kraut. 'We then print the shot out on a sheet of paper, which traditional background artists use as a template to paint the detail of the object. All of the exterior detail and definition on the object is added at the painting stage – all the cracks, weathering, water stains and so on. We didn't want to use computer-generated lighting – which often looks too perfect – so all of the shadow and light information was added as 2-D detail in these paintings. When finished, they were scanned into the computer and then projected onto the model from the position that they were originally filmed from. Two or more projectors may have been used for each object to cover the detail of all of its sides.

'What we ended up with was the computer equivalent of the sound stage', says Kraut. 'To build a street within the computer, we would position two rows of buildings, place another object underneath for the road, position a background painting in the distance and place a large dome with a sky painting mapped on it over the whole thing. The buildings with their projected surfaces looked like 2-D pictures, but we could animate our virtual camera to move past them, look around and do all the normal things that a live-action camera could. We wrote lots of software that would do things like blur the edges of the objects, so that they looked more than ever like 2-D paintings rather than hard-edged 3-D objects. For the first time ever, animation directors could actually create dynamic cinematography just like a live-action director, but their images looked like a camera was moving through a painting. If they didn't like a camera angle, the directors could just move the camera.'

Though the main characters in *The Prince of Egypt* were hand-drawn and animated in the traditional way, much of the film's additional cast of thousands was generated by computer. 'Descriptions of the Exodus in the Bible actually mention 600,000 Hebrews. We didn't have quite as many as that, but we still had scenes with many thousands of people that could never have been achieved using traditional techniques', says crowd animator Wendy Elwell.

'The first big crowd scenes are right at the beginning of the film, when we see hundreds of male slaves building a new temple complex', explains Elwell. 'For these scenes we built a single 3-D digital character that matched the drawn characters. He was then reshaped to create a total of twenty different characters. These were then dressed with different hair, beards and clothing so that each person in the crowd looked more unique. We then animated walk cycles – sequences of movement that can be repeated as required – so that characters could walk for as long as was needed in any scene. Four separate cycles were used to give more variety of movement. The characters were then placed into scenes as 3-D objects, but they were rendered [236>] with flat colours and black outlines to make them look like hand-drawn 2-D characters. They were originally intended only to be in the background, but as the directors got used to using them, they put them nearer and nearer to the camera until their detail didn't hold up any longer. When the 3-D digital characters got too near the camera, they were automatically swapped with 2-D hand-drawn ones – though I defy anyone to spot where they change.'

Despite automated methods making their production more efficient than ever, the future for 2-D animated films currently seems somewhat uncertain. Disappointing box office returns for productions such as DreamWorks' *Spirit: Stallion of the Cimarron* (2002) and Disney's *Home on the Range* (2004) have been massively eclipsed by the popularity of 3-D animated films such as *Shrek* (2001) and *Madagascar* (2005). As a result, the major studios are now investing heavily in 3-D rather than 2-D production. Among the more successful 2-D productions of recent years have been the films of the Japanese animation director Hayao Miyazaki. His stylish and often stirring films, such as *Howl's Moving Castle* (2004) and the Oscar-winning *Spirited Away* (2001), have established a considerable following with Western audiences who might not normally consider watching a 'cartoon'.

3-D ANIMATION

The principle behind the animation of models is broadly the same as that which brings life to flat artwork, the only change being that it is three-dimensional objects rather than two-dimensional pictures that are moved fractionally and photographed frame by frame to produce the illusion of movement.

Dimensional animation was explored long before the advent of moving pictures. The popular zoetrope (<11) was not confined to giving displays of animated artwork. Rather than pictures, some zoetropes contained a series of carved models in varying poses – a spin of the wheel might send a wooden bird on a graceful flight around the tin drum, or make a small dog leap through a hoop. When photographic moving pictures arrived on the scene, the technology was quickly seized upon to breathe life into otherwise inanimate objects.

The fantasies of Georges Méliès (<14) were built around the ability to stop the camera, make alterations to the scene and commence filming again. Méliès used the 'arrêt' method (literally meaning the 'stop' method) to create many cinematic wonders. Producing the impression of motion by stopping the camera, moving an object or model and then starting the camera again has since become widely used and is known as 'stop-motion' animation.

As early as 1898, Méliès produced a short commercial in which wooden alphabet blocks danced around the screen and arranged themselves into the spelling of an advertiser's name. A year before, Albert E. Smith, a founding partner of the Vitagraph company, had enlisted the services of his daughter's wooden toys and, with partner J. Stuart Blackton, produced a short stop-motion film entitled *Humpty Dumpty Circus* (1897) in which the toys moved about the screen with a life of their own.

Perhaps due to the availability of ready-made objects for manipulation, the technique of stop-motion animation seems to have been considered especially suitable for the production of children's films. Biograph produced the animated *Dolls in Dreamland* (1907), featuring a troupe of dancing dolls and a sprightly teddy bear. The ever-inventive director Edwin S. Porter (<17) spent a week of 12-hour days creating the imaginative march of six teddy bears for his rather less imaginatively entitled film *The Teddy Bears* (1907).

There were also a number of early uses of stop-motion for films aimed at a more adult audience. The English producer Arthur Melbourne-Cooper animated a collection of matchsticks in a Boer War propaganda film called *Matches Appeal* (1899). Edwin S. Porter produced *The Dream of a Rarebit Fiend* (1906), in which nightmares induced by a late-night snack of cheese haunt a sleeper who envisages the contents of his bedroom dancing around him before the bed itself takes flight into the night skies.

As the live-action feature film and its narrative forms developed, stop-motion was used for short, usually humorous films and was rarely considered for anything more adventurous. However, in around 1914 a young man obsessed by the magic of bringing life to inanimate objects began to produce short animated films that would develop into the most spectacular and influential film fantasies ever seen. The early story of stop-motion in feature films is the story of Willis O'Brien.

LEFT: While 2-D animation faces an uncertain future in mainstream cinema, the beautifully rendered films of Japanese animator Hayao Miyazaki, such as *Howl's Moving Castle* (2004), have won a dedicated following and many awards.

BELOW: English producer Arthur Melbourne Cooper animated a collection of ready-made toys in a surprisingly realistic model town for his children's film *A Dream of Toyland* (1908).

PROFILE **WILLIS O'BRIEN**

Born in Oakland, California, the young Willis O'Brien (1886–1962) worked as a marble cutter, cowboy, prize fighter, and cartoonist for the San Francisco *Daily News* before being hired to create sculptures for the 1913 San Francisco World's Fair. While preparing some small clay figures for an exhibit on boxing, O'Brien carried out an experiment that would change both his life and the course of cinematic history.

Using a borrowed newsreel camera, O'Brien moved the clay pugilists a fraction at a time before exposing each frame of film. When the film was developed, O'Brien saw a jerky, spasmodic boxing match in miniature. The images were not perfect, but O'Brien had created life where there had been none, and he was gripped.

For his second experiment with what he came to call 'animation in depth', O'Brien produced a one-minute film featuring a caveman and a dinosaur. He spent the next two months filming in the basement of a San Francisco theatre to produce *The Dinosaur and the Missing Link* (1915), a five-minute comedy starring an apeman, cavemen and various prehistoric creatures, crudely fashioned from wooden skeletons with soft clay bodies. The film was so good that it was bought by the Edison film company for distribution, and O'Brien moved to the East coast with plans to produce more films under the banner of Mannikin Films Inc.

O'Brien's company produced a number of animated shorts for Edison between 1915 and 1918, with titles such as *Prehistoric Poultry* (1917) and *Curious Pets of Our Ancestors* (1917). Most important was a film called *Nippy's Nightmare*, in which O'Brien intercut his increasingly sophisticated dinosaur animation with separate shots of live actors in matching environments. This was perhaps the first time that a real person had co-starred with stop-motion animated creatures.

Hungry for better subjects and bigger films, O'Brien embarked on the production of a feature film, *The Ghost of Slumber Mountain* (1918), of which only 15 minutes survive. The animator worked with the American Museum of Natural History to produce dinosaurs that were thought to be scientifically accurate in appearance and behaviour. The film's poster declared: 'These giant monsters of the past are seen to breathe, to live again, to move and battle as they did at the dawn of life!' O'Brien even appeared in the film as an old hermit called Mad Dick. The picture was a great success and earned the attention of the film producer Watterson R. Rothacker, founder of the Industrial Motion Picture Company, which encouraged the development of special effects techniques.

Rothacker owned the rights to Sir Arthur Conan Doyle's novel *The Lost World* (published 1912) and on the strength of his previous efforts, O'Brien was hired to bring Conan Doyle's dinosaurs to life. Conscious that his dinosaur puppets – pliable clay bodies sculpted over wooden jointed skeletons – would not be sophisticated enough for *The Lost World*, O'Brien hired a young sculptor called Marcel Delgado, whom he had met at art classes.

Using the classic dinosaur paintings of Charles Knight for reference, Delgado spent two years coaxing 50 exquisitely detailed prehistoric beasts back from extinction. Each 45 cm (18 in) creature was given an anatomically correct steel armature, complete with articulated spine and tiny ball-and-socket joints for every moving limb and digit. Once complete, the skeletons were painstakingly built up with cotton wadding and pieces of sponge to represent bulging muscle and flesh. Some models were fitted with air bladders that could be inflated and deflated during animation to mimic the animal's laboured breathing. The skeletons were supplemented with wire inserts where extra movement might be required, such as in the lips, eyebrows and cheekbones. Each body was then given an outer skin of liquid latex. Warts, scales and other surface textures were cast in latex and individually stuck onto the dinosaurs before being painted.

While Delgado laboured over the models, O'Brien oversaw the construction of the environments that they would inhabit. The Lost World itself was a miniature landscape, 60 x 90 m (200 x 300 ft), built at First National's Hollywood studios. The tabletop world had mountains, lakes and scaled-down tropical foliage with leaves made from sheet metal so that they would not grow, wilt or move in any way during the lengthy animation process.

By June 1922 O'Brien had completed a reel of animated dinosaur footage and it was shown to Conan Doyle, who was visiting the US on a lecture tour at the time. The author was delighted with the footage and could not resist a joke at the expense of his friend Harry Houdini. Houdini, who was highly sceptical about Doyle's belief in spiritualism, invited the author to the annual meeting of the Society of American Magicians in New York. At the meeting, Doyle screened O'Brien's dinosaur footage without explaining its origin. The audience was amazed and, incredibly, took what it saw to be genuine. The front page of the following morning's *New York Times* announced that prehistoric beasts had been discovered with the headline 'Dinosaurs Cavort in Film for Doyle'. Doyle immediately issued a statement revealing the true source of the footage. It was great publicity for the film and, above all, confirmed that O'Brien was producing extraordinary work.

With the effectiveness of his animation confirmed, O'Brien continued work on the film. He wanted to show something that had never been seen before: real people sharing the same space as animated creatures. This was achieved by building sections of full-scale set (usually trees or boulders) that matched the miniature set. The dinosaurs were then animated with a small area of the camera lens masked out (usually a lower corner), so that a portion of the frame was left unexposed. When the animation was complete, the film was rewound and a counter-matte placed over the lens so that only the unexposed area of the film was left uncovered. The film was then passed through the camera a second time to expose the performers in the full-scale set, apparently reacting to the prehistoric beasts in the rest of the frame. This static split-screen process was used throughout the film to combine not only actors and dinosaurs, but also dinosaurs and real locations. In the scene in which a

tyrannosaurus fights a triceratops, the matted-in Los Angeles river flows past in the foreground, helping to lend a sense of scale.

Not content with putting people into miniature scenes, O'Brien decided to place an animated brontosaurus into full-scale live-action scenes. Two thousand extras were filmed reacting to an invisible dinosaur in a London street set. The model creature was then animated in front of a plain white backdrop using a camera perspective matching that used for the live-action footage. Using the Williams process (<58) to create a travelling matte, the dinosaur was combined with the live-action plate. The result was convincing enough for contemporary audiences, though the heavy matte lines around the dinosaur seem obvious now. A full-scale tail and foot were also built for actors to interact with in these scenes.

The Lost World was a huge success when released in 1925; audiences flocked to see the two-hour, ten-reel film with its realistic scenes of dinosaur life. O'Brien's

animation was a triumph, not only as a technical achievement but for the subtlety with which his creatures performed. O'Brien gave his creatures personality and filled their performances with detailed character nuances, in the way they move, flail their tails or prepare to pounce. Tragically the film only survives in fragmentary form, much of the footage having been lost or destroyed since its release. An effort to restore the film has had some success, and a number of missing sequences have been rediscovered, restored and reintroduced for modern audiences to enjoy.

Despite the success of *The Lost World*, O'Brien did not work again immediately – the film industry had found a new gimmick in sound, and studios were more interested in hearing the voices of Broadway stars than seeing stampedes of dinosaurs. However, in 1930 O'Brien persuaded RKO to let him begin work on a film called 'Creation', which he believed would be the greatest dinosaur film of all (184>).

During the depression of the early 1930s, RKO hired Paramount producer David O. Selznick (1902–65) to help the company stave off bankruptcy. Selznick's assistant in this task was Merian C. Cooper (1893–1973), who, with Ernest Shoedsack (1893–1979), had made a series of successful adventure films including *The Four Feathers* (1929). One of the first decisions made by Selznick and Cooper was to cancel Willis O'Brien's Creation project, which had already cost the studio $100,000 and showed no signs of nearing completion.

However, Cooper believed that O'Brien might be the only person who could bring life to a story that had been gestating in his mind for some time. After O'Brien produced some successful test footage, the project was green-lit under the working title of 'Production 601', later becoming known as 'The Beast' and then 'The Eighth Wonder'. Eventually, the film was revealed to the world as *King Kong* (1933).

For *The Lost World* (1925), O'Brien had built a large set that could be photographed from all angles. For Kong he created another exotic world for the film's star to inhabit. Before starting work on the film O'Brien had discovered the engravings of the French artist Gustave Doré, whose illustrations of forest scenes with shadowy fringes and scattered pools of hazy sunlight had a prehistoric feeling of impenetrable depth. O'Brien decided to re-create this look by building a number of small sets, each designed to look like a Doré engraving come to life.

The miniature jungle sets were filled with gnarled trees made from modelling clay and palm fronds fashioned from sheet metal. Each tabletop set was arranged in a number of planes, one behind the other. Each plane was separated by a sheet of glass on which Doré-style scenery had been painted by production artists Mario Larrinaga and Bryon Crabbe. Once properly aligned and lit, each forest scene gave the impression of great depth. O'Brien's multiplane model system was the stop-motion precursor of the system used to bring depth to the flat animation of Disney a few years later (<172)

Marcel Delgado was called upon to create the marvellous model creatures. The mighty Kong was portrayed by six 46 cm (18 in) puppets made using the same build-up technique that had given the creatures of *The Lost World* their convincing muscle and flesh. For Kong, Delgado even stretched rubber tendons between joints to give the ape a realistic

FIGURE 3 **MINIATURE REAR PROJECTION**

sheets of painted glass

rear projector

miniature projection screen

animation puppet

THIS PAGE: **One of cinema's most iconic images: Kong battles for his life atop New York's Empire State Building.**

BELOW LEFT: **Kong battles with one of Marcel Delgado's beautifully modelled dinosaurs. The influence of Gustave Doré is clear in the multi-layered jungle backdrop.**

LEFT: **A performer cowers before a mighty monster. In fact, the performer and the tree are placed in front of a large rear-projection screen, and the dinosaur is an animated model just a few inches high.**

BELOW RIGHT: **Kong battles a pterosaur while clutching a puppet of the screaming Ann Darrow (Fay Wray). Such scenes used ingenious combinations of live action, stop-motion and rear projection to create their groundbreaking images.**

sinewy appearance. Covering the ape's complex body was a patchwork of trimmed black rabbit fur. The steel armatures in Kong and his prehistoric co-stars were built with keyholes in the base of their feet. This allowed them to be secured firmly to the floor between takes using 'tie-down' pins screwed up through a grid of holes on the floor of the tabletop set.

Again, O'Brien needed to mix real-life actors with his animated wonders, but he wanted to avoid the process of double-exposed split-screen mattes that he had used in *The Lost World*, which was slow and carried with it the risk of ruining the original footage. The process of rear projection was being perfected in the early 30s and RKO was an early leader in the field, pioneering the use of a new type of background screen invented by paint department head Sydney Saunders. The first scenes to use the new Saunders screen were those of Fay Wray perched in a treetop while pre-animated footage of Kong fighting a tyrannosaurus is seen in the background. The new process took some time to perfect due to the difficulties in preventing foreground lighting spilling onto the background screen – one shot of Wray in the tree was achieved only after an exhausting 22-hour session.

Cooper asked O'Brien if the process could be reversed in order to place rear-projected actors into the miniature tabletop scenery. After much experimentation, O'Brien and his team perfected a method of miniature rear projection (fig. 3, <184). The model jungle settings in which actors needed to appear were built with small areas where images could be rear-projected onto miniature screens made from stretched surgical rubber. Before each shot was filmed, many tests were made in order to match the lighting of the miniature set with the exposure of the rear-projected images. During animation, the model creatures were manipulated fractionally, the rear-projected image was advanced by one frame, and a single frame of the composite image photographed before the process was repeated.

One of the first scenes to use the miniature rear-projection process was that in which Bruce Cabot (John Driscoll) hides from Kong in a cave. A miniature cliff was built with a small cave in its wall, and a rear-projection screen was set just inside the cave. Footage of the actor performing in a large-scale cave set was projected onto the screen one frame at a time, while the model of Kong was animated rampaging on the cliff above. This shot was later cut together with a close-up of the performer interacting with a giant arm that reached into the cave.

The animation of King Kong took 55 weeks to complete. Its key actors were called back to the studio every few weeks to film scenes in which they had to react to recently completed animation, or provide the performances needed for the next batch of miniature rear-projection shots. Some animation sessions turned into marathon events; the animation team quickly learned that shots begun one day and completed the next often took on awkward changes of pace or style mid-scene; once started, the animation of a shot therefore continued until it was finished.

There were other unexpected hitches in the animation process. On one occasion an animator was halfway through a shot when he noticed that a pair of pliers left on the set was just visible in the bottom of the frame. Not wishing to start the sequence afresh, the animator slowly animated the out-of-focus grey shape out of the shot, hoping it would look like a passing jungle creature. In another scene a primrose planted as part of the jungle foliage chose the day of filming to come into bloom. No one noticed the flower's cautious emergence during animation, but when the finished shot was viewed, the scene's prehistoric star was upstaged by the energetic emergence of a giant flower, wasting hours of work.

While the team of animators achieved much of the animation of Kong in long shot, O'Brien animated particularly emotional scenes and close-ups himself. As a result, Kong remains one of the most emotive creatures to have been created for the screen. Even Kong's often criticized bristling fur coat – caused by disturbance of the stiff rabbit fur during animation – seems to add to the great ape's personality.

King Kong was a sensational hit on its release in 1933 and again when re-released in 1952. The public flocked to see the film, thrilled both by the story and the wonders of a lifelike giant ape. Kong was undoubtedly the most extraordinary technical achievement of its time and a catalogue of the most modern special effects techniques, including animation, rear projection, miniature rear-projection travelling mattes and matte paintings, as well as clever optical work by Linwood Dunn (<72).

It is testimony to the remarkable and emotive personality of O'Brien's Kong that a number of remakes and imitations of this landmark film have been attempted. Despite the technical brilliance and extraordinary realism of Kong's most recent reincarnation (2005), however, his original performance retains a power and innocence that thrills to this day.

PROFILE **RAY HARRYHAUSEN**

In 1933 the 13-year-old Ray Harryhausen (1920–) watched the newly released *King Kong* at Grauman's Chinese Theater on Hollywood Boulevard. 'This ape was so huge, and there were so many awesome dinosaurs as well,' he remembers with glee. 'I've never been the same since I walked out of that theatre!'

The young Harryhausen became obsessed with *Kong* and with discovering the magic behind its creation. 'There had been other ape films before *King Kong*, where the gorillas were played by men in suits. I knew for sure that *Kong* was different, but I didn't know how. It took me over a year to figure out the glories of animation, and eventually I found a magazine that had an article that explained all about the stop-frame method.'

On discovering the technique, Harryhausen began to experiment with animation on his family's porch and later in a small studio built by his father in the garage. One day Harryhausen plucked up the courage to phone his hero, Willis O'Brien. 'O'Bie [O'Brien's nickname] kindly invited me over to MGM where he was preparing to shoot *War Eagles* – a film that never got made because of the war. I went to the studio and took along some of the dinosaurs I'd been making. He looked at my stegosaurus, which had won second prize in a competition at the local museum, and he said: "Its legs look like sausages. You need to learn about anatomy and how muscles work." So then I began to study anatomy, life drawing, sculpture and photography.'

Harryhausen's animation skills quickly developed, and in 1940 he gained employment as an animator on George Pal's Puppetoon series (191>). After spending the war as an assistant cameraman and animator in Frank Capra's special-services film unit, Harryhausen began to

make his own series of animated fairy tales. Then, in 1947, having kept in touch with his mentor, Harryhausen accepted a job as O'Brien's assistant animator on *Mighty Joe Young* (1949).

'Working with O'Bie was a dream come true,' recalls Harryhausen. 'I helped during the whole pre-production phase, and when we got the go-ahead from the studio, RKO, I began work on the animation. I eventually did about 80 per cent of the character animation on *Joe Young*. O'Bie spent much of his time supervising all the other elements.'

The production of *Mighty Joe Young* used many of the techniques developed for *King Kong*. One small but significant advance was the use of rubberized fur for the gorilla puppets. Kong had been covered with rabbit fur, but the finer hair on unborn calf hide offered a better sense of scale for the smaller, 30 cm (12 in) Joe puppet. In a process invented by the taxidermist George Lofgren, the fur was embedded in paraffin, leaving only the skin exposed. The skin was then removed with acid and replaced with liquid latex. The finished fur, with its roots in latex, sprang back into place when touched during animation. Kong's bristling fur, which had annoyed some yet endeared him to many more, was not a feature of Joe's character.

After the release of *Mighty Joe Young*, Harryhausen was asked to be chief animator on the low-budget monster movie *The Beast from 20,000 Fathoms* (1953). '*Beast* had a ridiculously tiny budget [$150,000] considering its subject matter,' remembers Harryhausen. 'Doing things the O'Bie way was out of the question. He used big painted sheets of glass in several planes that gave a wonderful atmosphere but which were expensive

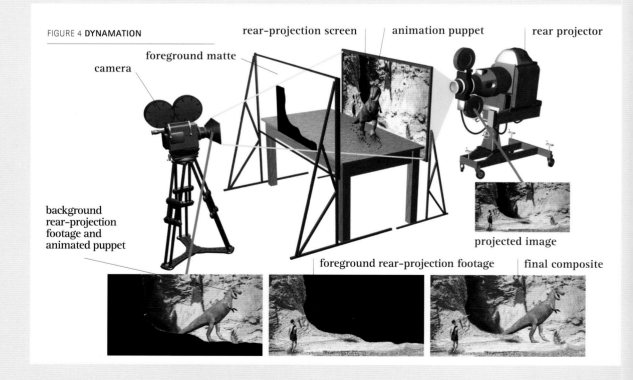

FIGURE 4 **DYNAMATION**

camera

foreground matte

rear-projection screen

animation puppet

rear projector

background rear-projection footage and animated puppet

projected image

foreground rear-projection footage

final composite

RIGHT: *The Beast from 20,000 Fathoms* (1953) was Harryhausen's first major film as chief animator. For scenes such as this, he devised a method of sandwiching stop-motion characters into live action using a split-screen rear-projection process that would become the basis for all of his later work.

BELOW: This sequence of images shows how Harryhausen combined rear-projected live action (a) with animation (b) to produce convincing composites (c). The final image (d) is a rare glimpse inside Harryhausen's studio during the filming of *The Valley of Gwangi* (1969). The model balloon and cage containing the dinosaur puppet are placed in front of a rear-projection screen. The wooden leg to the right of the image is part of the frame on which the animator placed mattes to conceal parts of the image during filming.

a

b

c

d

and restricted the camera to a single view. Also, the glass could crack in the heat of the lights. For *Beast* I devised a way of combining live-action actors with animated creatures and miniature backgrounds. It was the basis of the system that I used for the rest of my working life.'

The system that Harryhausen devised, which became known as 'Dynamation' for publicity purposes, was in many ways the opposite of that favoured by O'Brien. Rather than placing rear-projected actors into a miniature environment, Harryhausen used rear projection to place his animated characters into real environments containing real people. During live-action photography, performers reacted to the invisible creatures, sometimes looking at a cardboard head on a long stick as a guide. Harryhausen then studied the developed footage to ascertain what movements the animated creature should make in relation to the actors and their environment.

In his studio, Harryhausen then prepared an animation table (fig. 4) with a floor contoured to match the one that the creature was to traverse in the live action. A static split-screen matte that matched this contour was fitted to the bolted-down animation camera and used to mask out the bottom half of the frame, containing the animation table and other paraphernalia. The image exposed to the camera showed the puppet down to foot level, with the top portion of the rear-projected live-action background plate behind it.

Animation then proceeded as usual. Surface gauges (positional metal rods on stands) were placed at important points around the puppet's body to help mark the last position of its nose, tail, feet, and so on. The puppet's new pose was then created in relation to the action in the rear-projected frame of film and to the old positions marked by the gauges. When the new position was satisfactory, the

gauges were removed, the animation lights switched on and a frame exposed. The surface gauges were then brought back in, the rear-projected footage was advanced one frame and the next pose was created.

When the whole sequence had been animated, the puppet and animation table were removed from in front of the rear-projection screen. The camera negative and rear-projection footage were rewound to the start frame, and a counter-matte was applied to the camera to mask out the top section of the frame that had already been exposed. The camera negative was then exposed to the lower section of the background plate, so the two halves were married along the matte line. The final developed negative was a seamless composite of live-action footage and animated creature.

Harryhausen also made changes to the type of puppet he used for animation. 'Delgado's build-up method was terrific,' says Harryhausen, 'but it was time-consuming, and if a breakdown occurred during filming, the whole puppet might have to be stripped down and rebuilt.' Instead, Harryhausen sculpted his creatures in clay. These clay shapes were covered in plaster to create a mould. The creature's ball-and-socket armature was placed inside the mould, which was then filled with liquid foam rubber. When baked, the rubber set. The rubber creature was then painted and dressed with eyes, clothing, hair and props. If a mishap occurred during filming, the puppet could be stripped off and an identical rubber model quickly made. Harryhausen did not rely on this method to produce all of his creatures, however. For *Mysterious Island* (1961), a giant crustacean was made by fitting an armature inside a real crab shell. Another notable shortcut was to give the giant octopus from *It Came from Beneath the Sea* (1955)

ABOVE: *Jason and the Argonauts* (1963) is perhaps Ray Harryhausen's best-remembered film. This sequence, in which the Argonauts battle with animated skeletons, is certainly one of his most extraordinary achievements.

just six arms instead of eight. 'No one could have counted all those writhing arms, and it saved a lot of animating!' chuckles Harryhausen.

After a series of 'monster on the rampage' films in the 1950s, Harryhausen turned to the subject matter for which he became best-known. 'I had animated monsters destroying LA, Washington, San Francisco and New York – and there's a limit to the number of times you can do that sort of thing,' he explains. 'Charles Schneer [Harryhausen's long-term producer] and I decided that we wanted to move on.'

The 7th Voyage of Sinbad (1958) became the first in a series of films based on the *Arabian Nights* tales and Greek myths. Harryhausen considers this work to be his best, partly because stop-motion was so suited to the subject matter. 'I feel mythological stories are best served by stop-motion because the process produces a sort of dreamlike quality. It's true that the animation is not very realistic, but we never tried to mimic reality. We played on the melodramatic aspects of film, and Greek mythology is very melodramatic.'

Harryhausen's work in these mythological films was technically and artistically stunning, with the animator paying more attention than ever to the subtleties of characterization in his creations. 'I always tried to give my characters little habits that made them seem more believable,' he explains. 'It doesn't take much, just small habits such as taking a quick look at the ground before they step forward. I would also consider a creature's physique when planning their movement. In *The Golden Voyage of Sinbad* [1974], Kali moves in an unwieldy way because she is so top-heavy, and Talos in *Jason and the Argonauts* [1963] was actually criticized by one journalist for being jerkily animated – but he was designed to move that way because he's a giant metal statue with rusting joints!'

In the early 1960s, Harryhausen and Schneer moved their operations to England, which was closer to the

European locations that they often used and allowed them access to the sodium vapour travelling matte process (<64), which only Disney was licensed to use in the United States. During this period Harryhausen developed many new techniques for combining live action and animation more realistically. 'I tried all sorts of methods to make the two separately filmed elements look as if they were filmed together,' he says. One of the animator's cleverest deceptions involved using objects that appeared to cross the boundaries between live action and animation.

Typically, a live-action character might throw a spear through the air and it would appear to stick in the side of an animated creature. Such shots were achieved by animating the creature in front of rear-projected live action in the usual manner. As the rear-projected actor threw the spear, the weapon would, of course, disappear *behind* the model creature rather than stick into it. As the rear-projected live-action spear began to disappear behind the model, Harryhausen hung a miniature spear inside the miniature set so that, from the camera's viewpoint, the model spear covered the image of the rear-projected spear. As the live-action spear disappeared behind the creature, Harryhausen animated its miniature replacement so that it impaled the rubber model, producing the illusion that both live-action and animated elements were sharing the same space.

A different method was used to create the illusion that live-action characters with swords were interacting with animated creatures. Harryhausen mounted a sheet of glass in front of the puppet so that as a character thrust a sword at the creature, the tip (which in reality disappeared behind the model) could be painted onto the foreground glass frame by frame.

One of Harryhausen's most memorable and technically exacting achievements is the famous skeleton fight in *Jason and the Argonauts*. 'For that sequence I had to plan the movements in every single frame meticulously in order to animate seven skeletons simultaneously. Each skeleton had five appendages, so this meant I had to animate 35 separate movements for each frame, and each movement had to synchronize perfectly with the movements of the three live-action men.' It is hardly surprising that Harryhausen averaged just 13 frames a day during the four-and-a-half months that the short sequence took to complete.

Such dedication could be physically and mentally punishing, especially as Harryhausen was personally responsible for every frame of animation in all of his works, with the exception of his last film, *Clash of the Titans* (1981), when Jim Danforth and Steve Archer helped with some scenes. Extraordinarily, the master magician never received an Oscar for any of his films. In 1992, however, he received a special Academy Award in recognition of his lifetime's work. He also has a star on Hollywood Boulevard's Walk of Fame.

To this day, the methods used to create some of Harryhausen's best shots remain a secret. 'I never give everything away,' he muses. 'When a magician gives away all of his secrets, no one is interested any more!' Whether the technique behind his art remains a secret or not, the films of Ray Harryhausen continue to beguile.

REPLACEMENT ANIMATION

Most stop-motion animation is produced using a method called displacement animation, in which flexible models are moved fractionally between exposures. An alternative method involves substituting the entire model, or parts of it, between exposures. This rarely used technique is called replacement animation.

George Pal is often credited with pioneering the replacement method of stop-motion animation. Pal used replacement legs for his Puppetoon stars to produce their walking cycles. Whenever characters were required to walk, rather than reposition a flexible puppet between exposures, the entire bottom half of the puppet was replaced with one of a sequential set of carved wooden legs. Each set of around thirteen pairs of legs formed a walk cycle that was unique to the puppet in question. In 1943 Pal received a Scientific Academy Award for his development of the Puppetoon animation system.

One of the most groundbreaking modern uses of the replacement technique was for the stop-motion animated feature *Tim Burton's The Nightmare Before Christmas* (1993), directed by Henry Selick. The film used traditional ball-and-socket displacement armatures for the bodies of its main characters, which necessitated some 230 puppets in all. However, because the characters were required to talk, sing and express emotions beyond the range normally expected of stop-motion puppets, each of the major characters had a supply of replacement heads. A dialogue animator was employed to draw every conceivable combination of mouth and facial expression. The resulting 400 designs were then sculpted in modelling clay, moulded in rubber and cast in polyurethane plastic resin. Each head was then airbrushed to give it the correct colouring. One key character, Jack Skellington, required around 800 heads, allowing the expression of every possible emotion.

The finished heads were then photographed, digitized and stored in a computer databank. Each scene was then studied and the dialogue of every character broken down into frame-by-frame increments detailing the necessary phonemes and facial expressions. Using the computer database the various facial expressions were then assembled in the correct order to produce a video test of what the finished animation should look like. When approved, the computer performance was output on a breakdown sheet, telling the animators which heads to use in which order. During photography, animators first manipulated the ball-and-socket puppet body in the usual way before fixing on the necessary replacement head for each shot.

ABOVE: **George Pal sits among some of the many replacement animation figures used for his Puppetoon series in the 40s.**

BELOW: **Computer-aided replacement animation was used to give life to the quirky characters in** *Tim Burton's The Nightmare Before Christmas* **(1993).**

MOTION BLUR

Successful stop-motion animation can breathe the illusion of life into inanimate objects, but the method has a serious flaw that can prevent even the greatest animators from producing completely lifelike images.

When a real moving object is filmed at the standard rate of 24 frames per second, the shutter of the movie camera is actually open *during* the movement of the object. Since the object being filmed is in motion while its image is being exposed onto photographic film, the result is a photograph that contains a degree of 'motion blur' – a visible blurring that follows the most extreme movements of the object. Motion blur helps to impart the illusion of smooth, realistic movement when the still images are later projected onto a screen at rapid speed.

However, stop-motion animation creates the illusion of movement by projecting images of *still* objects in rapid succession. An animated object is moved *before* it is photographed, so its movements have no motion blur. The object's incremental yet distinct movements appear to jump from one position to the next during projection instead of flowing like real live-action photography. This jerky movement, which is called 'strobing', is most pronounced in fast-moving animated objects that change position substantially from frame to frame. It is also particularly noticeable when animated objects that have no motion blur are combined with live-action actors that do have motion blur.

Many people believe that it is the very absence of motion blur that gives stop-motion animation its unique, almost magical quality. Without motion blur, the mythical monsters animated by Ray Harryhausen certainly have an ethereal presence that makes them particularly effective in the fantasy films in which they appear. However, for many productions absolute realism is the goal, and without motion blur, stop-motion animation can never be mistaken for live action.

The animator Jim Danforth used a time-consuming method to create artificial motion blur when animating a number of dinosaur sequences for *When Dinosaurs Ruled the Earth* (1970). The method involves exposing each frame of stop-motion animation three times. The puppet is moved into position and photographed at one third of the exposure normally needed to capture a good image. After moving the subject again, the animator exposes a second image onto the same frame of film, again at one third of the correct exposure. After repeating this operation a third time, the result is a single correctly exposed frame of film in which the animated object appears in three positions. The fast-moving parts of the subject – such as its legs – look partially transparent, because in these areas the three exposures record images of background scenery either before or after the object was moved in front of it. Though effective, this method requires the artist to animate three poses per frame of film, each pose covering one-third of the movement normally needed for one frame of animation. Rather than 24 separate movements per second of finished film, the process requires 72 moves, making it extremely time-consuming and impractical.

Another method of creating an artificial area of blur around an object is to smear petroleum jelly onto a sheet of glass placed between the camera and the object being animated. This process is also fairly time-consuming, because the grease regularly has to be cleaned from the glass and reapplied to match the motion of the object. Though not true motion blur, the unfocused edge around objects that this method produces can be quite convincing. The technique was used by Peter Kleinow to bring life to the Terminator robot in his animated sequences for *The Terminator* (1984).

ABOVE: **The charm and humour of Nick Park's characters Wallace and Gromit have helped to ensure a place for stop-motion in modern cinema.**

LEFT: **This still from Ray Harryhausen's *Sinbad and the Eye of the Tiger* (1977) shows one of the flaws inherent in traditional stop-motion animation. While the live-action characters are blurred due to their movement, the leaping sabre-toothed cat remains completely sharp.**

RIGHT: **Phil Tippett admires the complex Go-Motion device built by ILM for the production of *Dragonslayer* (1981).**

TOP RIGHT: **While still requiring the consummate skill of highly talented animators, modern stop-motion films rely on digital technology to help create their imagery. After animation, this shot from Tim Burton's *Corpse Bride* (2005) was finished off by London's Moving Picture Company. Support rods were digitally removed from the main characters, background scenery was added, an otherwise difficult to animate veil was created digitally, and CG birds were made to flutter overhead.**

Motion blur can also be produced in stop-motion animation by physically moving a puppet during exposure. This method was used by Phil Tippett (194>) while animating the ED-209 robot for *RoboCop* (1987). After moving the robot puppet to each new position, a single frame was filmed in the usual manner. However, while the camera shutter was open and the film exposed, the model was physically 'wobbled' very slightly. Moving the model during exposure added a small amount of motion blur to the image, resulting in a very convincing animation.

Before Phil Tippett worked on *RoboCop*, he had already been part of an experiment that had culminated in some of the most effective model animation ever produced. During the making of *Star Wars* (1977), Industrial Light and Magic had pioneered the use of computer-operated motion-control cameras (<150) to film spaceship models one frame at a time while the camera moved past them. Since the camera moved while its shutter was open, the result was fast-moving spacecraft with realistic motion blur.

For *The Empire Strikes Back* (1980), the ILM team tried to apply this technology to the stop-motion animation of the woolly ice-creatures called 'tauntauns'. The tauntaun puppets were fixed to a motion-control mechanism that could move them backwards and forwards and up and down. The finer actions of the running tauntaun, such as its head and leg movements, were animated by Tippett in the usual fashion, but during photography, a motion-control mechanism moved the model vertically and horizontally while the shutter of the camera was open. The result was a form of motion blur that helped to eliminate some of the problems of traditional stop-motion.

Soon after working on *The Empire Strikes Back*, the ILM animation team were able to further develop their techniques for the production *Dragonslayer* (1981). The motion-control technique that had been used to animate *Empire*'s puppet tauntauns was developed into a system that could control specific joints on the film's flying dragon. This system involved computer-controlled gears and motors that moved six rods. These rods were attached to key joints on the puppet dragon. The other ends of the rods were attached to a motion-control unit that could travel backwards and forwards on a 2.4 m (8 ft) track. The whole contraption was connected to a computer that could record and play back 19 channels of movement.

To produce the animated dragon sequences, the puppet dragon was animated in the normal fashion. Rather than photographing the dragon when the animator was happy with its pose, the exact position of the rods during each frame was recorded by the computer. Once the whole sequence

was programmed to the satisfaction of the animator, it was played back, the dragon mechanically repeating the movements given to it earlier. During playback, the dragon puppet's performance was filmed, its movements actually occurring *while* the shutter of the camera was open. The result was a dragon that moved with an astonishing fluidity and realism, thanks to the presence of real motion blur. This computer-age refinement of stop-motion was named 'Go-Motion'.

Though incredibly effective, Go-Motion is a time-consuming and expensive method and has only been used occasionally, perhaps most memorably to create the flying bicycles in Steven Spielberg's *E.T. the Extra-Terrestrial* (1982).

Today, computer-generated animation has largely superseded stop-motion animation as a method of creating naturalistic characters for the movies. However, modern audiences still enjoy the quirky immediacy of movies created entirely using stop-motion, though their painstakingly slow production means such films are few and far between. Aardman has had great success with its beautifully crafted crowd-pleasers *Chicken Run* (2000) and *The Curse of the Were-Rabbit* (2005), while Tim Burton built on the achievements of *The Nightmare Before Christmas* with his elegantly macabre *Corpse Bride* (2005). Though such films are still created using predominantly traditional techniques, their makers also now call on the latest technology to bring their visions to the screen.

Replacing the large film cameras normally used for stop-motion, *Corpse Bride* was shot using ordinary digital SLR stills cameras. London's Moving Picture Company (MPC) then used extensive digital paint techniques to erase the rods and wires used to support puppets as well as the complex motion-control rigs that moved the cameras during animation. They also added computer-generated elements that were carefully designed to look as if they had been traditionally hand-animated. These included the bride's flowing silk veil which would have been extremely difficult to animate with stop-motion. Environmental elements such as smoke, fog and water which are hard to create effectively using traditional methods were also produced digitally.

While modern stop-motion films still depend on the skills of talented animators, digital techniques now make production quicker and easier, helping to create the more sophisticated action and imagery that is expected by modern audiences.

PROFILE **PHIL TIPPETT**

After seeing *The 7th Voyage of Sinbad* (1958), Phil Tippett (1951–) became obsessed with animation. At the age of 13 he bought an 8 mm cine camera with money earned from mowing lawns and began to teach himself the art of stop-motion animation.

While still studying art at the University of California, Tippett gained experience animating a number of popular commercial characters such as the Pillsbury Doughboy and the Jolly Green Giant. Tippett's big break came when he joined the production team of *Star Wars* (1977), where he worked on alien designs and animated the holographic chess game between Chewbacca and R2-D2.

Tippett became a regular contributor to ILM projects and was part of the team that animated the AT-AT snow walkers for *The Empire Strikes Back* (1980). He also animated the film's renowned tauntaun sequences and developed a new method of producing stop-motion animation with motion blur. Tippett helped to refine the process, named Go-Motion, with

breathtaking effect for *Dragonslayer* (1981). By 1982 Tippett was head of ILM's creature shop, where he designed and built characters for *Return of the Jedi* (1983), winning an Oscar for his efforts.

In 1983 the animator established his own company, Tippett Studio, to provide sophisticated stop-motion animation for movies such as *RoboCop* (1987) and *Honey, I Shrunk the Kids* (1989). Tippett's work with ILM on *Jurassic Park* (1993), which led the animator to enter the fledgling world of computer animation, earned him a second Oscar.

Despite running a large studio, Tippett has still managed to closely oversee work that combines digital technology with the performance skills of the traditional stop-motion animator. His studio has produced some stunning examples of CG character animation for films including *Starship Troopers* (1997), *Hollow Man* (2000), *Evolution* (2001), *Hellboy* (2004) and *Charlotte's Web* (2006). Tippett also directed the feature film *Starship Troopers 2* (2004).

3-D CHARACTER ANIMATION

3-D animation for feature films is now almost exclusively created with the computer. Like conventional stop-motion animation, 3-D computer animation requires the construction of models (albeit digital ones) that can be manipulated to produce moving images. 'Hard-surface' objects, such as spaceships and cities, are usually created using a selection of geometric objects that are combined and altered using a variety of modelling processes as described in the previous chapter (<156). CG models of 'organic' objects, such as human beings and creatures, however, require the creation of highly detailed forms that bear little resemblance to geometric building blocks like cubes and spheres.

There are several stages to creating a CG character model. Each stage can be achieved in a number of ways depending on the complexity of the character, how it will be required to perform, and the equipment and software used by the effects company producing the work. What follows is a broad overview of how CG characters are created and animated.

CHARACTER MODELLING
No matter how a CG character is to be produced, it will always start life as a series of drawings and paintings produced by a film's art department or concept artist. Paper designs approved by the movie's director will usually be turned into a series of small clay sculptures called 'maquettes' which allow a character to be studied from all angles before any further development.

When the final design of a character has been agreed, a much larger, fully detailed version will be made. Final character models are usually sculpted in a material such as Sculpey, a polymer modelling clay that is baked solid to create a permanent reference model. This final model is normally made in a neutral 'T' pose with the limbs fully extended to allow access to every area of the body. Complicated characters are sometimes sculpted in several separate pieces – such as body, head, and limbs – and these are only stitched together to form a complete character once all the parts are finally in the computer. A character's face will usually contain much more subtle detail than the rest of its body and so facial sculptures are often produced at a larger scale. To save time only half of a face or torso can be sculpted. When that half is in the computer a mirror-image copy can be made before being stitched back to the original to produce a whole, symmetrical character.

Once final character models are sculpted they need to be digitized – converted into digital models that can be further refined and animated in the computer. There are two common methods of turning a physical sculpture into a digital model: touch probes and laser scanners. It is also possible to extract 3-D information from photographs of sculptures using photogrammetric techniques (<160).

Touch probes were the first widely used method of converting sculptures into digital models. When using this method the topology of the digital model is first planned by hand-drawing a grid on the surface of the sculpture. The grid divides the surface of the model into various sizes of square.

BELOW: **Here a touch probe is being used to digitize a sheep sculpture to create a digital model for *Babe 2: Pig in the City* (1998).**

BELOW RIGHT: **During a cyberscan (*left*), a laser beam scans the object or person to be digitized. The resulting 'cloud' of points can be greatly reduced without losing key detail (*centre*). The final model (*right*), once surfaced, has the scanned colour information mapped back onto it to produce a digital head.**

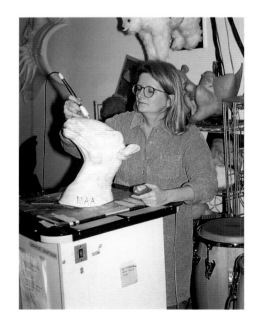

Sparsely detailed areas that won't move very much, such as the back of someone's head, are covered by large squares, while delicate areas that will be extensively animated, like a face, are covered by many smaller squares.

The sculpture to be digitized is placed on a surface that emits a magnetic field. Connected to this surface is a digitizing probe – similar to a pen. The position of the probe's nib can be measured wherever it is placed within the magnetic field. Holding the probe, the modeller systematically works their way over the surface of the model, touching and recording every intersection on its surface grid. The result is a digital 'cloud' of points. These points are vertices [<154], and when they are connected together they form a mesh of polygons – a digital copy of the clay sculpture.

After digitizing, a mesh model needs to be 'cleaned'. This involves addressing the mesh to make sure there are enough polygons to produce the detail in areas where it is needed, but not so many that the model is too complicated to be used efficiently. Attention is also paid to complex areas, such as where ears join with a head or a tail meets a body, to make sure there are no complicated folds or intersecting polygons. At this stage a polygonal model might be converted into a NURBS model (<158) or it may have areas that require lots of subtle detail to be turned into subdivisional patches for further refinement (<157).

Touch-probe scanning has now largely been replaced by laser scanning. This method, also known as 'cyberscanning', uses a laser to optically measure the surface of an object and convert it into digital information. 'Laser scans are very good for capturing any object with very fine features, especially human faces', explains Sean Varney, head of metrology at London's Framestore CFC (metrology being the science of measurement). 'The touch-probe process is completely impractical for capturing human features', continues Varney. 'Most actors wouldn't be very happy about having a grid drawn on their face before being poked with a digitizing probe for an hour. They would also have to sit impossibly still within the magnetic field during the whole process. A laser scan, on the other hand, takes about twenty seconds'.

Scanners used for small objects, such as models and sculptures, have a fixed scanning head that shines its laser onto a small turntable. The object being scanned then rotates so that every part can be read by the laser. There are also hand-held scanners that resemble the devices used to read the bar codes on larger items at supermarket checkouts. These devices are swept over one small section of surface at a time. The information gathered in separate passes is then recognized by the computer and automatically 'stitched' together to form a complete model. Scanners used to digitize human faces and bodies are usually much larger and are mounted on a rotary arm that swings the laser head itself in a complete circle around the subject.

'We can scan sculptures, props, animatronic characters, an entire human body, or even a live horse if you want', says Varney. 'But most of the time it is just the face of an actor that is needed. In this case the subject to be scanned sits on the scanner platform with their head directly at the centre of the scanner's circular path. Before a scan, we give any hair on the head or face a dusting of cornflour. Hair can cause problems because it can work like thousands of prisms that refract the laser light in all directions. By giving hair a sprinkling of flour, more of the laser light is reflected back into the scanner to produce an accurate model. During scanning the scanner swings around the subject, shining a vertical beam of harmless laser light onto the face. The laser light is reflected back into two CCDs [charge-coupled devices (<93)] that convert the light into digital information. The scan records the physical contours of the face but also its colour information'.

As with the touch probe method, the result of a laser scan is a cloud of vertices that are linked to create a polygonal mesh. 'The scan collects a vast amount of information about the subject', says Varney. 'In fact, the technique produces far more data than is needed for most purposes, so we edit the data according to how the model is going to be used. Automatic decimation software studies all the vertices and works out how to produce a highly detailed model with fewer vertices, then we finish it off by manually removing vertices or adding them back in where they are needed. A human head for use in a feature film usually starts life as a mesh of around one million polygons that can be edited down to about 10,000 polygons and still look very good. This produces a model with fewer polygons where they aren't needed, and more around areas that need to be flexible when animated – such as the corners of the mouth and eyes. Once the polygonal model has been finalized, the colour information that is also collected during the scan can be mapped back onto the model to create a convincing replica of a human head'.

According to Varney, laser scanning is becoming an increasingly popular safety tool for large-budget special effects productions. 'These days movies are altered so much during post-production that it pays to have a scan of all of the lead actors. If an important new shot is needed after filming has finished, it's possible to graft the scan of an actor's head onto the body of a double. Increasingly therefore, we are asked to scan the whole cast of a film', says Varney. 'When we scanned the cast for *The Phantom Menace* [1999], we took our equipment to the studio and the performers had their scans done whenever they had a spare half-hour in their schedule. For bigger productions we also routinely scan props and even whole film sets so that alterations can be made long after filming'.

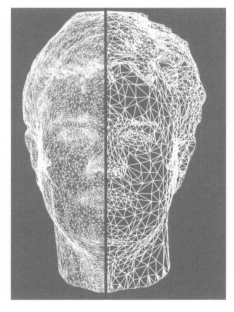

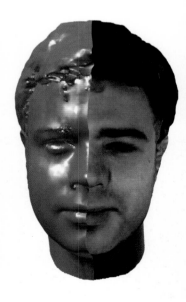

DIGITAL SCULPTING

Complicated organic forms have traditionally been difficult to create digitally, making it necessary to scan detailed clay sculptures in order to produce digital character models. However, a revolutionary software program called Z-Brush now means that intricate models can be sculpted directly within the computer without the need to make and scan sculptures in clay.

'Z-Brush has totally changed the way we make and animate digital characters,' claims computer graphics supervisor Vince Cirelli of Luma Pictures, who used Z-Brush to create characters and environments for *Underworld: Evolution* (2006). 'Z-Brush is exactly like having a lump of digital clay that can be sculpted on the computer monitor. A few years ago only computer experts could make sophisticated digital models, but now we can hire traditional artisans to sculpt directly in the computer.'

To produce a character using Z-Brush the artist begins by assembling a series of simple spheres and tubes to produce the rough, overall form of a character. This is exactly like throwing together lumps of real clay to make a basic sculpture – with a lump for the head, one for each leg and each foot, and so on. With the rough shape assembled, the computer then moulds it into a well-ordered polygonal mesh, quickly turning a crude collection of primitive shapes into something that already resembles a completed character.

The artist then starts to add more refined detail to the polygonal mesh, perhaps bulges for muscles or depressions for the ribcage. This is achieved using a series of paintbrushes that work like traditional sculpting tools, adding or removing clay where needed. To create a ribcage, the artist can simply paint onto the model with the appropriate size and strength of brush and an indentation is sculpted out of the surface. This happens in real time, as if clay was actually being carved out of a physical model. According to Vince Cirelli, very delicate detail can even be sculpted automatically, saving huge amounts of production time: 'In the past, if a sculptor wanted to create a lizard they would painstakingly scratch each scale into the clay with a toothpick,' he says. 'Now they can take a photograph of a real lizard and use a clone brush to copy the scales in the photograph, producing actual sculpted scales on the surface of the model.'

As the model progresses the artist creates increasingly fine detail, moving from bold anatomical shapes through to delicate features such as wrinkles and skin pores. Each time the sculptor wants to add more subtle detail they can create a new resolution level, each new level quadrupling the number of polygons used to describe the surface of the model. If at any time more significant alterations are needed, the artist can go back to any of the previous levels of detail – even as far back as the original collection of spheres – and make that change. That alteration is then automatically updated in all existing levels of detail.

When sculpting is complete the result is an extremely refined polygonal model with an incredible level of detail. Such complex models would be slow and impractical to animate, so the final model is used to produce a black-and-white displacement map (<166), which is a 2-D record of all the delicate surface information.

'When we've made displacement maps we can take our final polygonal mesh and strip away almost all of the detail. A mesh with over a million polygons can be reduced to a mere 50,000,' explains Cirelli. 'We then use that low-polygon model for animation purposes. When we've finished animation the displacement maps are used to add back all the complex surface information during rendering, producing an incredibly detailed final image.'

Even the amount of detail created by a displacement map can be varied. 'For *Underworld: Evolution* we created an extremely complex castle model using Z-Brush,' says Cirelli. 'The displacement maps created the physical geometry of every single brick and tile during rendering. However, much of the time that extreme level of detail was not needed and would take an unnecessary amount of time to process. Therefore, we linked the level of surface displacement to the proximity of the camera to the building. If the camera was a long way off the walls remained relatively flat, but as the camera moved nearer the bricks literally "grew" outwards from the walls and became far more detailed.'

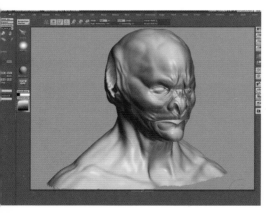
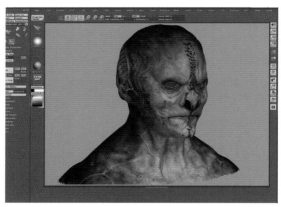
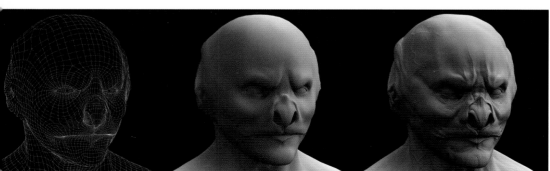

LEFT: **Z-Brush was used by Luma Pictures to sculpt digital character models for *Underworld: Evolution* (2006). The character is sculpted with fine surface detail (*top left*). This detail is saved as a displacement map. Very subtle colour information can be painted onto the digital model (*top right*). Even a highly complex model can be reduced to a low-polygon mesh (*bottom left*). When surfaced, the basic mesh shows little detail (*bottom centre*). When displacement maps from the original sculpt are applied, the surface of the character becomes minutely detailed (*bottom right*).**

TOP RIGHT: **The final CG version of the vampire Marcus, as seen in *Underworld: Evolution*.**

PROFILE **JOHN LASSETER**

Like many contemporary American animators, John Lasseter (1957–) was a graduate of the Disney Character Animation programme, run by the California Institute of the Arts in the 1970s.

While working on Disney features like *The Fox and the Hound* (1981), Lasseter saw the early computer animation being created for *Tron* (1982), and became fascinated by the potential of the computer. Lasseter then produced his own experimental film based on Maurice Sendak's book *Where the Wild Things Are*, showing how traditional hand-drawn animation could be combined with computerized camera movements and environments.

In 1984 Lasseter left Disney to join the computer graphics division of Lucasfilm, where he worked on a number of 3-D computer animation projects including the short film *The Adventures of André and Wally B.* (1984). He also animated the CG stained-glass knight for *Young Sherlock Holmes* (1985).

In 1986 Lucasfilm sold its graphics division to Steve Jobs and Pixar Animation Studios was born (198>).

At Pixar, Lasseter created a number of groundbreaking shorts including *Luxo Jr.* (1986) and *Tin Toy* (1988), which became the first CG film to win an Oscar.

Lasseter became widely praised for his extraordinary skill in creating strong characters from expressionless objects. In *Luxo Jr.*, for example, he created a touching father-and-son relationship between a pair of animated desk lamps in the space of just 90 seconds.

In 1991 Pixar signed a three-picture deal with Disney. The result was *Toy Story* (1995): co-written and directed by Lasseter, it was the world's first computer-generated feature film. It was a huge commercial and critical success and Lasseter received a Special Achievement Oscar. Lasseter has continued to oversee the creation of Pixar's innovative films and has directed *A Bug's Life* (1998), *Toy Story 2* (1999) and *Cars* (2006).

With Disney's acquisition of Pixar in 2006, John Lasseter was named chief creative officer, charged with overseeing all of Disney and Pixar's animated output and even contributing to the design of new attractions at Disney theme parks.

TOY STORY

Released in November 1995, *Toy Story* was the world's first completely computer-animated feature film, with over 70 minutes of 3-D digital animation.

Toy Story was created by Pixar, a company that began life as the digital research division of Lucasfilm. Under the leadership of Dr Edwin Catmull since 1979, Pixar created software used by ILM to provide effects for films such as *The Abyss* (1989) and *Jurassic Park* (1993). However, finding themselves more interested in producing original animation rather than technology for others to use, the Pixar division decided to split from Lucasfilm and in 1986 was bought out by Steve Jobs, co-founder of Apple Computers, for $10 million.

After producing a number of groundbreaking short films, Pixar's aim became the creation of a full-length feature film. Working towards this goal, Pixar developed three core software systems: 'Marionette', a program for modelling, animating and lighting; 'Ringmaster', a program for scheduling and coordinating animation during production; and 'RenderMan', a sophisticated rendering program for producing vibrant, photorealistic images (237>).

In 1989 Pixar signed a three-picture deal with Disney and they began to plan their first feature. For their debut, Pixar decided to play to their strengths. Although their software was not yet capable of portraying convincing human characters, in his short films director John Lasseter (<197) had managed to elicit extraordinarily emotive performances from objects such as desk lamps and, in particular, toys.

The final script was storyboarded and assembled into an 'animatic' – a rough shot-by-shot version of the film with temporary dialogue laid over it. As production progressed, these elements were gradually replaced by low-resolution test animations, actual voice-overs and final rendered shots, slowly building up the finished film.

After the various characters, sets and props had been designed on paper, they were either built directly in the computer or were digitized from traditional clay sculptures. The computer models were then given varying numbers of control points that could be animated to produce performances. A complex character such as Woody had as many as 100 facial controls. To make life easier for the animators, some of these controls were clustered into basic movements and expressions – to create a smile the animator simply turned up the 'smile' control, for example. Performers such as Tom Hanks were videotaped during the recording of voice-overs and their movements and expressions were used by animators as a guide when creating the performance of their digital alter egos.

One of the complaints about early computer animation was that it looked 'plastic'. *Toy Story* proved that stylized yet natural-looking environments and characters could be produced and sustained. Every element of a scene was carefully painted to produce a detailed 'caricature' of real life. Even skirting boards were scuffed and carpets stained. It took 1,000 megabytes to store the movie's 400 models and 3,500 textures and the final rendering process took 500,000 machine hours – that is, 57 machine years.

Toy Story was a massive worldwide hit. Although much publicity was gained from its status as the world's first computer-generated film, reviewers and audiences alike appreciated the film for its exciting story and delightful characters. Pixar has since continued to create increasingly sophisticated and successful productions including *Finding Nemo* (2003), *The Incredibles* (2004) and *Cars* (2006). In January 2006 Disney acquired Pixar in a deal worth $7.4 billion.

CHARACTER RIGGING

When the digital model of a character has been constructed, the result is a mesh of polygons or NURBS patches (<158) that form the character's outer shape. To make this empty skin suitable for animation, it must be filled with the digital equivalent of flesh and bones and then instructed how to move. This is a process called 'rigging'.

'At this studio the rigging department is called the Puppet Department,' explains Tippett Studio puppeteer Eric Jeffery, who has rigged characters for movies including *The Adventures of Sharkboy and Lavagirl in 3-D* (2005) and *Shaggy Dog* (2006). 'The term is a hangover from the stop-motion days when our puppets were painstakingly engineered with ball-and-socket joints and rubber muscles. Today we're essentially doing the same thing, but with digital models instead of physical ones.'

'Before we start rigging a character we read the script, study storyboards and talk to the animators about how they plan to use the model,' says Jeffery. 'We need to know exactly what a character will be required to do. We also look at a lot of reference material and photographs of real animals. This helps us get a sense of a creature's anatomy and how the bones and muscles should work together to make the character move.'

When a new mesh is received from the modelling department, riggers first create a very simple skeleton that will allow the character to be tested by the animators. 'It takes us about a week to build the initial skeleton and get the character moving,' explains Jeffery. 'Then we give that low-resolution version to the animators, who produce a few sequences of the character walking, running and moving in extreme poses. This enables us to see if the mesh is functioning satisfactorily, whether it's capable of moving in the right way, or whether it needs any changes to the design. When we've made any alterations and are sure everyone is happy with the model we then pass that low-res rig back to the animators and they use it to begin producing animation. While they do that we start work to produce a fully rigged version.'

The full rigging of a character begins with the building of a refined skeletal structure. With the character positioned in a neutral pose (the classic 'T' stance in the case of bipeds), joints are placed inside the mesh and arranged exactly like those in a real skeleton. These joints can be programmed to rotate, twist, scale (change in length, height, or width) and 'translate' (move in any direction to a new position). 'Unless we're working on particularly flexible characters such as those we made for *Son of the Mask* (2005), we constrain each joint so that it can only perform in the way that it would in nature,' says Jeffery. 'That way the animators can be sure it will behave accurately when they create a performance. However, we always give the animators the ability to switch off these constraints – nature often has to be tweaked just a little to make a shot work.'

With the joints in place, riggers consider what type of skeletal structure to build. 'We have two approaches to building skeletons, depending on the type of character we're working on,' says Jeffery. 'If it's a principal character, or one on which we will be seeing a lot of bare flesh, such as our Abe Sapien character for *Hellboy* [2004], we tend to construct an anatomically accurate skeleton made up of

RIGHT: **To create the incredibly lifelike aquatic character Abe Sapien for** *Hellboy* **(2004), Tippett Studio built up layers of anatomically accurate muscle which would be seen stretching and bulging beneath the character's skin.** *Top:* **The original background plate showing an empty tank of water into which the character would be placed.** *Centre:* **CG set-up showing muscled version of Abe.** *Bottom:* **Final composite, complete with watery atmosphere in front of CG character.**

BELOW: **This digital model of a horse was built by Tippett Studio. The first image shows the basic underlying skeleton and joints. Subsequent images show the anatomically accurate layers of bone, ligament and muscle that were layered over the top. The final low-resolution horse is what the animator sees when manipulating the character on their computer screen.**

realistically shaped bone geometry. This will give us somewhere to fix muscles and will help to produce realistic movement on the surface of the character. However, if the character will only be seen in a few shots, or is perhaps covered in clothes or fur, such as our Templeton the rat for *Charlotte's Web* [2006], we won't bother with any bones and will connect the mesh directly to the joints.'

With joints and any bones in place, riggers next define the way they can move in relation to one another. A skeleton's joints are programmed to act in a hierarchical fashion, each joint forming part of a chain that is linked in a one-way relationship. A hierarchy begins with a parent object. Branching from that parent can be any number of child objects. Each of these 'children' can also act as 'parents' to further child objects, and so on. For example, the pelvis would be parent to the leg bones which would be parents to the feet which, in turn, are parents to the toes. When a parent object is moved during animation, it influences each of its child objects, but moving a child object does not necessarily affect the movement of its parent. Hierarchies are useful in many modelling and animation situations but are particularly appropriate when creating characters, since the skeletons of most creatures work in a hierarchical fashion. When a human being moves an upper arm, for example, the forearm, wrist, hand and fingers will all move in response.

'Skeletons end up consisting of a number of parent–child groupings,' elaborates Jeffery. 'These hierarchies branch backwards from the outer extremities to an overall parent object, which is usually located at the creature's centre of balance – typically somewhere a little above the pelvis in a bipedal character. The animators can move this central point around depending on the performance that is needed. For example, if a character is going to hang from its hands during one scene, their centre of balance will be much higher on the body; probably somewhere near the neck. The whole hierarchy will therefore be rearranged to link back to a parental point at the top of the spine, around which most of the character's motion will then swing.'

A hierarchical system in which the movement of parent objects affects the movement of child objects is called forward kinematics (FK). However, a more sophisticated hierarchical system called 'inverse kinematics' (IK) can be used to make many of the most complex movements of a model work 'automatically' during animation. Inverse kinematics uses a hierarchy that is engineered to work backwards – that is, the movement of a child object can affect the movement of its parents as an automatic function during animation. 'Inverse kinematics is a really great way of animating complicated movements such as walking,' says Jeffery. 'If you use forward kinematics to animate a walk cycle you have to individually move the upper leg, then the lower leg and then the foot, making sure at the end of the pose that the leg is bent in the correct walking position and that the foot is touching the ground appropriately. But if you then decide to change the leg position even slightly the foot will move in response and will need to be repositioned again. But with IK the animator can grab the feet and move them around and the parent legs will automatically follow, bending in the right way.'

Inverse kinematics is a useful tool that can save animators a great deal of time and frustration. However, some animators try to avoid such automation because they believe it can make character actions appear artificial and predetermined. 'We usually place both IK and FK skeletons inside our characters,' comments Jeffery. 'That way the animator can switch between the two to get the best motion for every movement a character makes.'

Once the skeleton of a character has been built, it is used as the framework for more internal construction. When Marcel Delgado built stop-motion puppets for Willis O'Brien (<182), he padded their metal skeletons with wads of cotton to represent the flesh and muscle beneath the skin. Digital character models are usually constructed in a similar way.

'Once the anatomical bones are set up we start to add the padding that goes on top,' says Jeffery. 'All the major muscles are replicated as meshes that have the appropriate elasticity and which will maintain their volume when they stretch or contract. The ends of the muscles are then attached to the bones in the correct places so that they flex, bulge and slide realistically when the joints move. We have to build the muscles up slowly, making sure that each new muscle works correctly and doesn't adversely affect those already in place.

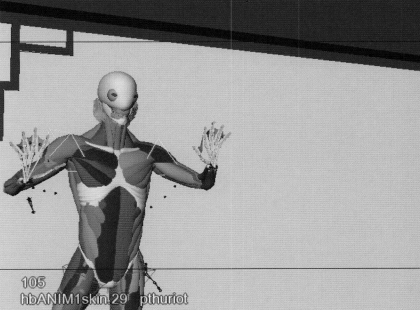

Sometimes a muscle can get confused and pop inside out, flip back-to-front, or just break – messing up everything that is linked to it. Just like a real body it can be a pretty carefully balanced system.'

The complex construction of anatomically correct muscles is not always necessary for the creation of convincing characters. Those creatures whose skin surface will not be seen in detail are not normally given bones or muscles; instead, riggers use a technique called 'skin cluster weighting'. With this system the outer mesh of the character responds directly to the movement of the joints below. Several layers of greyscale maps are attached to the surface of the mesh, indicating the degree to which each area of skin is influenced by the underlying joints. When animated, the surface of the mesh will therefore move primarily in response to the motion of the nearest joint. It will also react, though to a lesser degree, to the combined movement of the other joints in the wider area. This system can sometimes produce unrealistic body forms, however. For example, a bending elbow joint can cause the surrounding mesh to lose its volume, resulting in an arm bend that looks more like a kink in a garden hose. In order to ensure that anatomically correct body shapes are maintained during a character's movement, the computer can detect what forms a mesh is tending towards and automatically place pre-sculpted 'blend shapes' (213>) in that area. The mesh will then blend in and out of these shapes over a period of several frames to produce the correct overall body form.

For models that do have a full system of anatomically modelled bones and muscles, the final additions to the body interior are areas of loose 'flesh' or 'fat' that are programmed to automatically jiggle with varying degrees of flexibility in response to the movement around them.

Finally, the outer mesh or skin of the model must be instructed how to move over the underlying biomechanics. 'The skin of all living creatures varies greatly on different parts of the body,' says Jeffery. 'With humans, for example, it can range from the very taut skin which is fitted quite closely over a kneecap to the taut yet loosely connected skin of the upper back which allows the shoulder blades to move freely beneath. Then there are flabby or loose areas of skin like those on the average person's

stomach. All these qualities need to be replicated in our more complex digital characters.'

The performance of the skin is driven by the motion of the underlying fat and muscle which is itself driven by the motion of the joints. 'We have to tell the skin exactly how to move in reaction to those various inner motions,' says Jeffery. 'Again, we paint a number of greyscale maps which instruct each area of skin how to operate. These maps can affect how thick the skin is and therefore the degree to which it might wrinkle during movement. They can also determine how stretchy the skin is when movement causes it to be pulled over a bulging muscle. They can even identify the points at which the skin is actually attached to the body and the degree to which it can move away from those points. This can be imagined as lots of bits of elastic tying the skin to the body at various points. The bits of elastic can be attached to different parts of the body and some pieces can be longer or tighter than others, thus affecting how the skin moves around during a character's motion.'

The final visual look of the skin, its colour and texture, is the result of hand-painted texture maps created in the studio's paint department (203>).

Once a character has been fitted out with bones, muscles and skin, riggers make the final preparations before animation. Their aim is to make the control of a character as simple and intuitive as possible for the animators. 'Each character will eventually have dozens of controls that the animators can use to produce a performance,' says Jeffery. 'The most fundamental are the handles used to push, pull, and place the limbs during animation. We build large boxes around the major body parts such as hands and feet so that they can be quickly grabbed and dragged around the screen just as if the animators were using a traditional puppet.'

Riggers also set up a range of automated actions that will help create a convincing character. 'The idea is that many subtle movements will occur as an automatic response to the broader performance created by the animators,' says Jeffery. 'For example, we will program the muscles in the legs and thighs to jiggle when the animator makes a character stamp its foot down to the ground. We will also create a breathing cycle in which the character's chest rises and expands, the shoulders move back and the stomach pulls in. This will be layered into the performance without the animator having to think about it. However, we do give animators the option of altering various parameters in order to change the speed of the breathing or make it heavier, should the action require it.' Control of all of a character's functions can be accessed through a series of on-screen pick-lists which sit alongside the puppet. These menus start off with the broader, most frequently needed groups of controls and are then subdivided down into increasingly subtle aspects that the artists may only occasionally want to manipulate during animation.

When the fully rigged character is complete it is ready to have the motion being produced by the animators applied to it. 'The full-size rigs are very large and complicated models that are impractical for use during animation,' says Jeffery. 'The animators use the much lower-resolution version that we made for them earlier in the process so that they can move it around on their monitor in real time and animate really quickly. This version often shows the character as little more than a few connected pieces of primitive geometry – boxes for bodies and spheres for heads – but it's enough for them to see how their motion is working. When they have finished animating or want to see how a performance is looking, their low-res puppet is temporarily attached to the high-res version. The low-res puppet then drives the motion of the high-res puppet and we can see how things are working.'

Once a character is handed over to the animators the job of the rigger is still not finished. 'We will continue working on a character right throughout production,' says Jeffery. 'The animators will always ask us to add new functions or features. Then the character might malfunction and we'll have to trace things back to the point where they went wrong – there's always quite a bit of maintenance to be done. Sometimes the director may even decide they want to change the look of the character altogether and we will have to rig a new mesh and merge the animation that has already been created with that new model. By the end of a show we may have been working on a character for over a year. We get to know them pretty well.'

CHARACTER PAINTING

One of the final tasks in the creation of a computer character is the painting of texture maps (<164) to add both colour and detail to the modelled exterior. Several methods can be used to create character texture maps, depending on the needs of the character and the techniques preferred by the visual effects studio.

A character's skin might be 'unwrapped' to produce UV maps – 2-D images that look as if the skin has been peeled off in sections and laid flat (<164). These flat maps are then digitally painted before being wrapped back onto the character. The main flaw of this system is that some warping or stretching of the 2-D texture is inevitable when it is wrapped back onto the 3-D model. Furthermore, painting a representation of 3-D detail onto a 2-D image is hardly an intuitive way for artists to work.

More commonly, characters are painted using a technique called 'projection painting'. This process allows artists to see painted detail appearing directly on the surface of the model as they work. To paint a character in this way, the artist first views the model from one fixed angle on the monitor – the side profile of a face, for example. They then start to paint over this view using digital brushes and paint. The artist is not actually painting onto the 3-D surface of the model, rather the digital paint is being applied to a sheet of virtual 'glass' that is placed just in front of the model. This sheet of glass works somewhat like a slide in a projector – throwing the painted image onto the surface of the model. When the artist is satisfied with how the colour and texture look from this angle, the model will be turned around so that another view is presented – the front of the face, for example. As the model is rotated, the first painted texture map moves with it, still being projected onto the side profile for which it was designed.

The front view of the face will not yet have had any paint applied to it. However, some areas will display detail that is spilling over from that being projected onto the side profile. This is just like some of the image from a projected slide missing the edge of the screen and falling, distorted and out of focus, onto objects in the background. In the case of a model head, some of the colour painted along the edge of the nose in the side profile will probably now be streaking along the cheek. The artist paints the front view of the face on a new sheet of glass, covering up any of the distorted detail that has spilled over from the side-profile projection. This process continues around the model, using a new piece of glass for every angle painted, each time covering any spillage from the previous projection. A human head would typically be painted in eight equal sections. The result is eight 'stacked' layers of glass which can be collapsed down into a single layer – the top layers permanently covering any of the spilled and distorted paint from the lower layers. This single final image looks distorted and stretched, but once projected back onto the model it creates a perfect surface that can be viewed from any angle.

Projection mapping can also be used when creating a digital version of an actor for use in shots where a computer-generated character is used to perform stunts, or a real stunt performer has their head replaced by that of the star. In such cases the star will be photographed from numerous angles and projection painting used to make each projected photograph blend seamlessly with the next on the surface of a cyberscanned (<195) model head.

As with other texturing processes (<164), colour is just one of the attributes that need to be created for the exterior surface of a character. Artists will also paint black-and-white bump and displacement maps (<165) as well as maps able to affect the skin's opacity, specularity, reflectivity or iridescence. These will all be used in conjunction with shaders (<167) to produce the final look of the skin.

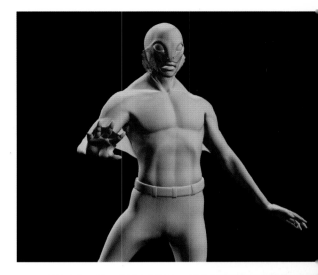

TOP: **The finished, untextured model of Abe Sapien in** *Hellboy* **(2004), showing the sculptural detail.**

ABOVE: **The final version of Abe Sapien composited into a watery environment. Various painted texture maps have been applied to the model to create the appearance of his skin.**

LEFT: **Two texture maps used to add colour and detail to Abe's body. These two were painted for his chest; many more were created to cover every part of his body.**

FAR LEFT: **While animatronic creatures were used for many shots on** *Hellboy*, **Tippett Studio created CG versions when they were required to leap or jump, such as this shot of the multi-tentacled character Sammael.**

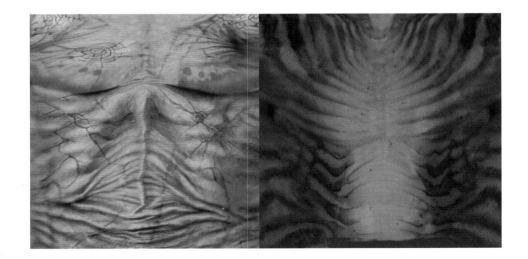

Created by Weta Digital, Gollum was one of the first digital characters for which subsurface scattering was used to produce incredibly subtle and lifelike skin.

DIGITAL SKIN

One of the greatest barriers to creating convincing computer-generated characters has been the ability to synthesize natural-looking skin. In 1993 ILM created photorealistic digital dinosaurs for *Jurassic Park*. These creatures had thick, leathery skin that was perfectly suited to the computer's ability to render solid materials from which light would bounce directly. But eight years later the beautifully modelled computer-generated humans of *Final Fantasy: The Spirits Within* (2001) remained unconvincing because light was still bouncing off their skin, making it look solid and waxy.

To solve this problem a new form of shader model has been developed that accounts for the fact that organic materials such as skin contain large amounts of water, through which light easily passes. The new technique, called 'subsurface scattering', is a mathematical description of how light that penetrates the surface of skin is absorbed or scattered by layers of subcutaneous flesh and blood before re-emerging at varying angles and with different colours (fig. 5). The result has been subtle and naturalistic computer-generated skin for characters such as ILM's Dobby the House-Elf in *Harry Potter and the Chamber of Secrets* (2002) and the green star of PDI DreamWorks' *Shrek 2* (2004). One of the first examples to make it to the screen was Gollum, the extraordinarily convincing character created by Weta Digital for *The Lord of the Rings: The Two Towers* (2002).

'When I took on Gollum I knew that creating a believable 3-D animated performance was no longer a major issue and that the key to believability was going to come down to the quality of his skin', states Joe Letteri, who won Oscars for his work as visual effects supervisor on both *The Lord of the Rings: The Two Towers* and *The Return of the King* (2003). As he began working on Gollum, Letteri discovered the new research into subsurface scattering and thought it might provide the solution he was looking for. 'People were starting to experiment with subsurface scattering', recalls Letteri. 'However, in order for it to work they were actually modelling everything under a character's skin for the light to interact with, including capillaries, blood vessels and fatty tissues. This seemed a tremendous amount of work for details that would never actually be seen on the screen. Then one day I saw a silicone model of Sean Bean's head that had been made by Weta Workshop. It looked so real – as if the actor's head had just been chopped off. The skin looked like it had great depth and that all those natural details were actually lying below the surface'. Letteri learned that the head was made of solid silicone that was dyed a base flesh colour. On top of the silicone a number of thin layers of colour pigment had been hand-painted to build up the impression of depth.

'I realized this might be a practical method of creating realistic skin for Gollum', recalls Letteri. 'The method we devised as a result involved developing a base digital flesh material that was equivalent to the silicone used for the model head. Then we layered a number of detailed colour and texture maps on top to form the skin. In this way light would first pass through Gollum's skin layers picking up colour detail, then enter the flesh layer where the photons of light were absorbed or scattered before exiting back through the skin layers to pick up more detail'.

The result was the most believable photorealistic digital character yet seen on film. 'Subsurface scattering really did add something to our creative toolkit', remarks Letteri. 'We could put Gollum in bright sunlit scenes next to Sam and Frodo and his skin would just soak up the sunlight, making him look just like his human co-stars. It's a breakthrough that adds a vital level of realism. We can now push light into skin and get real softness and richness. We used it for all our CG characters in *Return of the King* and *King Kong* [2005]'.

FIGURE 5 **SUBSURFACE SCATTERING**

Normal rendering techniques (a) calculate the way that light bounces off the surface of objects. Subsurface scattering (b) simulates the way that light penetrates translucent materials, being absorbed and refracted before exiting with different qualities.
Subsurface scattering is capable of producing incredibly realistic-looking CG skin.

a   b

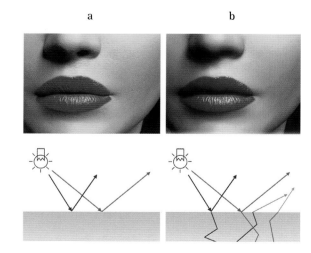

FIGURE 6 **KEY-FRAME ANIMATION**

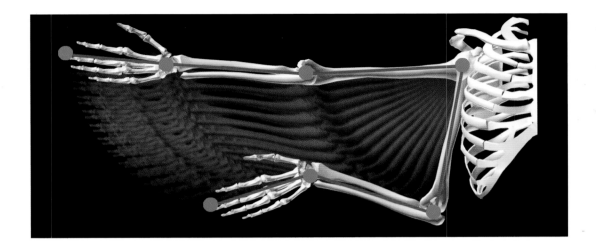

As the result of setting just two key frames at either end of a large movement, the computer automatically calculates each position in between. To produce this lifting arm motion, for example, the computer animator need only move the model twice. A traditonal stop-motion animator might move their model six times to produce the same effect.

ANIMATING DIGITAL CHARACTERS

A single second of film comprises 24 individual frames. A stop-motion animator must therefore painstakingly position and photograph a puppet 24 times in order to produce just one second of movement. At best, traditional animators might work 'on twos', which means that they expose two frames of film at once, thereby cutting their workload in half. But if the animators make a mistake, they may have to discard hours of work and start again.

Computer animators have several distinct advantages over traditional stop-motion animators. Since computers can mathematically interpolate movement, animators can create a minimum number of character positions per second and rely on the computer to intelligently calculate the rest for them. Furthermore, a computer animator can refine work endlessly, gradually building up a performance and only finishing a piece of animation when it has been approved by the client.

The computer animator's primary tool is the 'key frame'. Each key frame is the point in time at which an animator manually changes one aspect of the object or character that they are bringing to life. Creating animation in this way is called 'key-framing' and it is the technique used to produce most computer animation.

An animator first informs the computer how many frames there will be in a shot. This creates a timeline with each frame in the sequence marked along its length. The timeline, displayed across the bottom of the screen or on a separate monitor, is used to place key frames for all of the changes made to all of the objects in the scene. Every changeable aspect of each object will have its own track in the timeline. For example, a model dog might have separate tracks to control the motion of its body, head, eyes, ears, tongue, tail, legs, feet, and any of the other bodily functions that have been rigged for animation. The motion of every one of these elements can be addressed at any point by accessing its track in the timeline and adding, deleting or changing key frames. Key frames may also be used to control other aspects of a computer-animated scene, such as the camera and lights. A simple computer-animated sequence may ultimately have several dozen key-frame tracks while a complex scene with several characters may have hundreds of tracks, each of which can be accessed and altered at any time.

The animator begins by arranging the object in its first pose. Computer animators use an ordinary computer mouse to drag and position the joints of a digital model using handles that have been attached to the skeleton by the riggers. Some aspects of a character's motion can also be controlled by 'sliders' that animators use to dial in the performance they want. Sliders might be used to control the speed at which a character breathes, or the rate at which a dog wags its tail, for example. When the first position of the object is satisfactory, the animator sets the first key frame. The animator then moves the object to its second position. When happy with the second pose, the animator sets the second key frame.

The animator continues through the sequence, setting key frames whenever the object needs to change position significantly. If the object being animated is moving linearly, a key frame may be set perhaps once every 12 frames. With the start and end positions of a move identified, the computer interpolates the two poses and automatically 'in-betweens' – that is, calculates each of the incremental movements that need to take place in the intervening frames to produce smooth movement (fig. 6). Objects or characters with erratic movements that alter radically from one frame to the next may be key-framed for every frame of a sequence.

Animators typically deal with a single aspect of a performance at once. If animating a bird in flight, for example, the overall motion of the bird will be created first. If flying in a straight line this movement may be defined using just two key frames – one for the starting position of the body and one for its end position. Next the animator might create the more complex motion of the flapping wings, followed by the turning of the head, opening of the beak and swivelling of the eyes. Continuing in this manner, the animator gradually builds up the detail and complexity of a performance.

The fact that computer animators are able to repeatedly review and refine the movement of a character does not mean that creating a performance within the computer is any easier than when using traditional techniques. 'Many people think that computer animation is much simpler than stop-motion', remarks Todd Labonte, an animation supervisor at Tippett Studio, 'but it's still all about creating a performance. Animators still have the dilemma of deciding how, when and why they will create certain movements. The only thing that has changed is the tool used to translate those decisions.

'In some ways animating a convincing performance is harder with the computer', continues Labonte. 'For a start, using an external device like a mouse to move an on-screen character is hardly as intuitive as manipulating a stop-motion puppet with your hands. In fact, I often feel like I'm wearing boxing gloves while I'm animating!'

When animators receive a rigged character model, the first thing they determine is the way it walks. 'Walking is used as the basis for all character performances', says Labonte. 'This is where we really define the way a character moves. For example, a lion and a domestic tabby cat have pretty much the same basic physique. But the way we animate their walk will make that considerable difference between a large powerful-looking animal and a small harmless pet. Walk cycles show the way a character holds their body, what their weight and size is, and are a glimpse into how their brain works.'

During production several animators will often work with the same character simultaneously. To ensure that a performance is consistent from one shot to the next the animation supervisor will therefore create a character

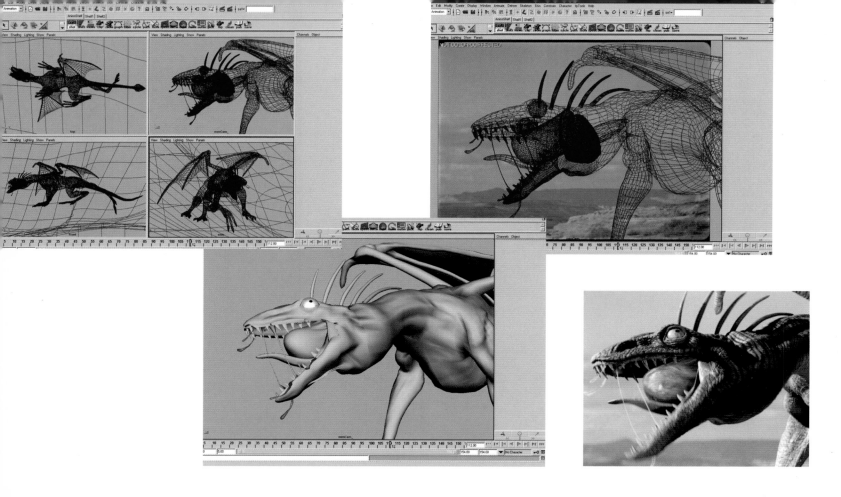

'bible', demonstrating how a character poses and moves in different situations. 'As animation supervisor I'm normally the first animator to get hold of a character', says Labonte. 'I then work with the movie's visual effects supervisor and director to lock down the way a character performs. This will include things like walks and runs, whether the character moves first from the shoulders or the hips, any small habits like the way they twitch their hands when standing still, and so on. I then produce a number of sequences and illustrations that I share with the animation team. I'm essentially an acting coach who has to make multiple animators deliver the same performance.'

Despite such guidance, animators do have their own distinctive style and so each shot will be assigned to someone considered most suited to produce the necessary motion. 'As supervisor I have to "cast" each shot', remarks Labonte. 'Sometimes I'll read a script and know instantly that a fast-moving piece of action should be handled by one animator, while a subtle piece of emotion should be given to another.'

Once a shot has been assigned, the supervisor and animator will discuss what is required. 'We will talk through the shot, look at the storyboard, discuss what the director has requested and throw any new ideas around', explains Labonte. 'The animator will then make a start by blocking out the basic motion of a character. Then we'll show that to the director for approval before starting on a refined performance. If the character is going to be composited into a live-action shot we will need to see how it will fit into the pre-filmed background plate. Often a director will ask for a particular action but then we'll find that it doesn't really work with the camera movement in the live-action plate. This is usually because some poor camera operator has had to guess how an as yet invisible character might look when moving through the frame. Then we'll have to design a performance that does what the director wants and also physically fits into the shot.'

In order to create a performance, animators will often act out their character's motions and videotape them for reference. They will also look at footage of real animals in action. 'Most animators have a mirror near their workstation so they can look at themselves performing', says Labonte. 'It's important that an animator can feel what their character is supposed to be doing and can identify where an action or emotion is coming from. I'm sure most animators are frustrated actors who have some kind of hang-up about putting themselves in front of the camera. If you look around the studio you'll see the animators at their desks repeatedly, almost subconsciously, acting out little movements and expressions. I've gone home with a sore neck many times!'

Ultimately a performance is revised numerous times as the result of suggestions made by many people involved in the production. 'We review shots each morning in dailies', explains Labonte. 'We'll loop a shot and watch it a hundred times so that everyone can study the work and make suggestions. I then have to filter those ideas and decide what changes to make before finals are sent for approval to the director.'

During the animation of a character, animators can view their work in a number of ways. These images from the production of *Evolution* (2001) show how a character was animated by Tippett Studio.

TOP LEFT: The basic computer-animation user interface. The character can be seen from four 'orthographic' views. The timeline for the scene runs across the bottom of the screen, and at the top a toolbar contains various animation tools.

TOP RIGHT: To check that their animation works within the live-action scene, the animator can superimpose the character over the live-action plate using the correct camera perspective.

ABOVE LEFT: The animator can give the character a simple shaded surface, concealing the wire-frame model and giving a clearer image of the performance.

ABOVE RIGHT: The final fully rendered shot as seen in the film.

PERFORMANCE CAPTURE

Since the earliest days of motion picture photography and animation, artists have sought ways to capture and reproduce naturalistic character motion. Eadweard Muybridge (<11) developed a system that enabled him to photograph and study the momentary poses of moving creatures; Max Fleischer designed the rotoscope (<174) so that animators could copy human motion for use in cartoons. Today, most computer animation is achieved using a mouse to manipulate digital models and set key frames within the digital environment. However, the idea of harnessing real movement is still attractive to film-makers, and a number of methods of channelling externally driven movement into the computer have been developed.

Initial plans for creating the dinosaurs in *Jurassic Park* (1993) involved a combination of full-scale robotic dinosaurs and traditional stop-motion puppets animated by Phil Tippett. Tippett's hand-animated dinosaurs were to be digitally composited into real landscapes by Industrial Light and Magic, who planned to give them added realism by applying digital motion blur (239>) to their movements.

Although at the outset of production digital technology was not considered capable of creating convincing dinosaurs, ILM's senior visual effects supervisor, Dennis Muren (<47), was convinced it would be possible to produce computer-generated dinosaurs of the quality required. Muren produced an early test that convinced Steven Spielberg of the potential of the computer. As a result, the task of creating 50 dinosaur shots was moved away from the traditional method of stop-motion and into the relatively unexplored territory of the computer.

Tippett was devastated that the computer had made its first serious incursion into the world of the stop-motion animator. Like many other artists, Tippett feared that his skills would soon become redundant. However, while ILM's computer wizardry was able to create convincing dinosaurs, the technology was not yet capable of producing reliably good performances. 'The first test I produced for Steven [Spielberg] was of a running tyrannosaur,' recalls Muren. 'Steven was bowled over by the first test and gave us the go-

ahead to produce all of the movie's dinosaurs in CG. But after our initial test we had real problems getting our CG dinosaurs to perform well. We started to worry that our test had been a fluke and we wouldn't be able to pull off a whole movie full of CG dinosaurs, so we spoke to Phil Tippett about ways to fuse traditional animation techniques with our new technology.

'We realized that there had to be a way to tap the experience and art of stop-motion animators and feed that into the computer,' says Tippett. 'By combining the two disciplines, we thought pretty amazing things ought to be possible.' In conjunction with ILM, Tippett and his staff built an interface between computer and traditional animator that they called the DID (dinosaur input device, later refined to direct input device).

'The DID was basically a traditional stop-motion armature,' states Tippett, 'but instead of being covered with foam latex and painted to look like a dinosaur, it remained just a skeleton. Each joint of the skeleton had a number of encoders that could measure the degree and direction of movement at that pivot point.' The DID device was linked to the computer, where a wire-frame model of the dinosaur had been built with corresponding joints. Using the DID, stop-motion artists animated a dinosaur's performance in the traditional way, then saw that movement translated to the digital model within the computer.

The process combined the best of both traditional and cutting-edge techniques. Animators were able to manipulate the armature to produce a nuanced performance, and unlike the old method of capturing movement on film, the new method allowed the animator to go back and refine any moves which they were unhappy with. After basic animation was approved, ILM added the digital muscle and skin to create lifelike animals. The DID device was used to create the terrifying tyrannosaurus attack on the Jurassic Park jeeps, and the sequence in which two children are stalked by velociraptors in the kitchen.

Following *Jurassic Park*, Tippett Studio animators used DID technology to help produce the stunning insect performances in *Starship Troopers* (1997). However, with the development of more sophisticated and intuitive software, today's animators now create subtle character performances using only their mouse to manipulate on-screen skeletons. Devices such as the DID are no longer necessary.

RIGHT: **Craig Hayes from Tippett Studio with the Dinosaur Input Device (DID) that he helped design and build for the production of the pioneering CG dinosaurs of** *Jurassic Park* **(1993).**

Although the motion of computer-generated creatures is generally created by animators, the complex and naturalistic motion of humans is normally captured directly from real life. In the 1980s, various medical establishments created methods of digitally recording and analysing the movement of patients who suffered from leg and spinal problems. This technology, known as motion capture, or 'mo-cap', has since been harnessed and developed for use in visual effects production.

'There are two main methods of capturing human movement for use in computer animation', explains Tom Tolles, CEO of House of Moves, a company that specializes in capturing movement data for use by visual effects facilities. 'Optical motion capture uses a number of cameras to "film" movement and translate it into computer data. Magnetic motion capture, on the other hand, uses a strong magnetic field to measure the movements of a person dressed in a bodysuit that is covered with magnetically active markers. Magnetic motion capture is generally more restrictive and complicated to use, but it does produce excellent data that can be utilized to create real-time performances. This means that a performer's actions can instantly affect the movement of a computer character in live-broadcast applications such as kids' TV, where animated characters need to interact with an audience.'

House of Moves uses the more popular optical method to capture movement. 'Our system works by using somewhere between 4 and 250 4-megapixel CCD [charge-coupled device] video cameras arranged around a performance area that is perhaps 8 m [26 ft] in diameter', states Tolles (see fig. 7 for basic set-up). 'The performer is dressed in a black suit to which we attach a number of small plastic balls. The balls are covered in a highly reflective material similar to Scotchlite, which was once used for front-projection purposes [<84]. Depending on the sophistication of motion detail needed, performers are dressed with between 20 and 60 markers at all the key joints. For basic movement, a hand can be represented by two markers, one at the wrist and one at the tip of the hand. Really complex movement can involve having a separate marker to capture the movement of each joint of each finger.' Optical motion capture can also be used to capture the subtle movements of a human face. Up to 300 markers can be attached to the skin and lips to capture the expressions of a performer.

FIGURE 7 **MOTION CAPTURE**

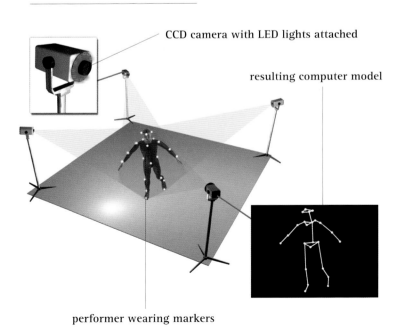

CCD camera with LED lights attached

resulting computer model

performer wearing markers

During the capture process, performers are filmed moving within the capture area. If their character needs to interact with any objects or surfaces these will be built in the studio – sets of stairs for them to walk up or fake cars for them to step out of, for example. Each CCD video camera emits infrared light, which hits the reflective body markers and is directed back into the camera it came from. The result from each camera is a black image containing a number of moving white dots – a 2-D representation of movement as seen from a single position. Seeing this cloud of dismembered floating points is a strange experience. Although nothing connects the markers, their movement fools the mind into making the logical connection between dots to form the impression of human movement – even the feeling that you can see limbs that do not exist.

To extract useful information, the computer to which this data is fed compares the centre of each white dot from several camera angles and triangulates the data to calculate its exact position in 3-D space. 'The computer needs to cross-reference continually between a number of camera angles', states Tolles. 'Looking at a performer from just one or two angles isn't enough, because each moving marker is continually being hidden, or "occluded", behind various parts of the body.'

Although the system is designed to calculate the position of each marker automatically, the resulting data normally has to be cleaned up manually. 'Motion-capture data has to be organized before it can be used', Tolles explains. 'The markers are continually moving about. Sometimes one can pass another, and then the computer can get confused and swap them. The result could be an arm movement getting mixed with a hip movement, which would result in a pretty weird-looking performance!'

'This system produces a huge amount of data', notes Tolles. 'Each CCD captures images at least 60 times a second, and with 50 markers on a body, that's 3,000 measurements per second per camera. However, it is because the system is so sensitive that it can capture recognizable performances. We do a lot of capture for the games industry, which hires famous sports stars to come and have their basketball or boxing movements captured for computer games characters. We've captured the distinctively recognizable moves of Bruce Willis for the action game *Apocalypse*, and of tennis player Andre Agassi for a Nike commercial. But we're best known for our work for the movies. An early mo-cap breakthrough was the work we produced for *Titanic* [1997], which allowed Digital Domain's CG characters to walk around on the decks of the model ship. More recently we've provided facial capture services for *Spider-Man* [2002] and *Spider-Man 2* [2004], and services and software for *The Polar Express* [2004] and *Monster House* [2006].'

Once motion data has been captured it needs to be applied to computer-generated characters in order to make them move. Each marker on the body of the live performer is mapped onto the body or skeleton of the digital character. In most cases the motion-capture data will need to be distorted somewhat – the markers used for motion capture are attached to the outside of the performer's body while the bones and joints that they drive in a digital character are a little way below the surface of the body. Similarly, any digital character that is a different shape or scale to the mo-cap performer will need to have its motion data mapped accordingly. For *The Polar Express* Sony Pictures Imageworks used data captured at House of Moves to drive the movement of the film's animated characters. Actor Tom Hanks played a number of characters in the film, including a seven-year-old boy. To create realistic movement, Hanks's motion-captured movements were scaled down to fit the smaller and differently proportioned body of the young boy. The props and scenery he interacted with during these scenes were also made larger to make his actions seem more like those of a young boy.

Mo-cap data is often only the starting point in the production of a performance. Once the natural movements of a character have been captured they can be altered using key-frame animation to produce a more dramatic or subtle performance. A character's motion is often captured in a series of discrete movements to build up a 'library' of moves. These small moves can later be edited together to produce a synthetic performance that is a combination of a number of natural movements. This technique is particularly

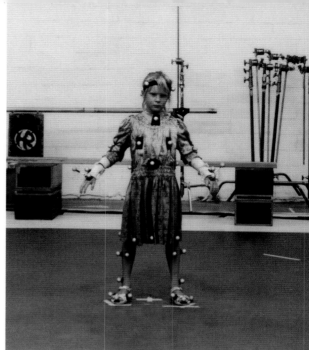

useful when creating large crowd scenes in which many characters need to move in reaction to various influences. In such cases the computer can judge what motion a character needs to make and assemble the appropriate pieces of motion-capture data to automatically create a performance (216>).

Motion capture has been used with great success in certain situations, but it does have its limitations. 'Mo-cap is really good at getting naturalistic human performances into the computer,' believes Tom Tolles, 'but some people tend to think that it is an easy way to achieve motion for all sorts of different animated characters. If the motion of a real animal is needed, such as that of a horse or a dog, we can bring those animals into the studio and record their movement just like that of humans. If it's a fantasy character being played by a human we can load performers with heavy weights so that they move in a slow, ponderous way – more like a giant or a monster. However, fantasy creatures are probably best created using key-frame animation techniques, which gives them a stylized performance. The monsters of Ray Harryhausen probably look so fantastic and appealing precisely because they have such a mysterious and undefinably inhuman way of moving.'

ABOVE LEFT: **A stunt performer covered with tracking markers slides down a tilted deck, providing motion-capture data for the creation of a computer-generated passenger in** *Titanic* **(1997).**

ABOVE: **Even the** *Titanic*'s **child passengers had their movements captured. This girl is wearing markers on her skirt: the swaying motion of the skirt will be transferred to the digital clothes of her animated double.**

LEFT: For this shot from *The Polar Express* (2004), Tom Hanks played all three characters. His movements were recorded in separate motion-captured performances applied to the different characters and later combined in a single shot.

JURASSIC PARK

Early plans for Steven Spielberg's (<39) adaptation of Michael Crichton's novel *Jurassic Park* involved a combination of full-scale animatronic dinosaurs and traditional stop-motion techniques. However, in the wake of its success with digital characters in *Terminator 2* (1991), Industrial Light and Magic was able to convince Spielberg that digital dinosaurs were a viable alternative to stop-motion.

To create their digital dinosaurs, the artists at ILM, under the guidance of effects guru Dennis Muren (<47), employed a number of groundbreaking techniques. The dinosaurs were first created as clay sculptures and then cyberscanned (<195) to produce digital models. These were then given a digital skeleton so that they could be animated using inverse kinematics (<201). ILM programmers created new 'Enveloper' software, which allowed the skin of the models to wrap round and move freely over internal muscles in order to create the look of a real animal.

ILM also created a program called 'Viewpaint', which allowed artists to paint the surface texture details of a dinosaur's skin directly onto the digital model. Such texture maps (<164) would previously have been painted as a flat design and then wrapped around the digital model, often causing stretching and distortion of the design. Viewpaint allowed skin designs to be painted in their correct place on the model itself, much like painting a physical model with paints. Several layers of texture map were applied to each dinosaur model, including bump maps to describe the texture of the skin and additional maps to describe skin colour and pattern, mud and dirt. For the sequence in which the T rex attacks jeeps in the rain, a special shader was written to create the effect of water running down the creature's back.

Computer animators created the dinosaur performances by referring to simple animatics – low-resolution test shots that were created and refined using traditional stop-motion puppets or basic computer models. The final dinosaurs were then animated using a combination of key-frame techniques (<205) and a 'dinosaur input device' (<207), which allowed stop-motion animators to transfer their traditionally animated performances directly into the computer.

Once dinosaurs had been animated and rendered (236>), they were composited (<100) into live-action background plates. The compositing process was vital to the credibility of the dinosaurs – even the most realistic digital characters will look fake if they do not convincingly integrate with their surrounding environment. As the T rex ran, small clouds of dust and dirt were added beneath its feet, shadows were cast on the ground and splashes of water were placed where it stepped in puddles. For shots in which dinosaurs emerged from behind objects each frame of footage of live action was rotoscoped by hand (<174). Individual leaves and blades of grass were painstakingly traced so that the digital creatures could be sandwiched into natural environments.

As production progressed, ILM became more confident in its ability to deliver photorealistic dinosaurs and the creatures were given a greater on-screen presence. A late addition to the schedule was a scene in which the actor Martin Ferrero is eaten by the T rex. According to the original plan the character would be seen disappearing out of frame when snatched from his seat on a toilet. The revised version showed the actor being picked up, tossed around and then eaten by the dinosaur in a single shot. During compositing, the real performer was swapped for a digital character just as the dinosaur's mouth closed over his body. Though a last-minute decision, the shot became a show-stopper.

During pre-production planning, digital dinosaurs had only been intended for use in long shots, with Stan Winston's animatronic puppets used for close-ups. However, as ILM's work became increasingly convincing, the CG creatures were brought closer to camera. For the last sequence featuring the T rex, the dinosaur's texture maps were repainted with extra detail and the creature brought right in front of the camera as it rampaged through the Jurassic Park visitor centre.

The public flocked to see *Jurassic Park*, smashing box office records to make it the highest-grossing film in history. The film later won Academy Awards for its visual effects and sound effects. Perhaps the film's greatest legacy was to prove that, finally, the computer could help special effects artists create almost anything the scriptwriter could conceive. Film-making was changed forever.

FACIAL ANIMATION

Expressive facial movement is the key to any convincing character performance and is among the hardest forms of animation to achieve successfully. Most computer-generated facial animation is currently produced using one of two different techniques. One method creates a physically based digital model that emulates the way muscles and flesh move on a real face. The other technique models the surface of the face as a series of fixed expressions. These are then arranged in a sequence to create a performance – the digital equivalent of replacement animation (<191).

Physically based animation requires the building of complex facial rigs that resemble the mechanics of the human face. Beneath layers of digital skin, tissue and ligaments lies a network of up to 200 muscles. Each muscle has a controller which allows it to be pushed and pulled by the animator. This movement translates through the layers of tissue to deform the high-resolution facial geometry of the face surface. The animation of each muscle usually affects the shape of the surrounding muscles so that if the mouth is moved, for example, the cheek will deform in response.

Individually animating each of the muscles used in such faces would be an arduous task and so interrelated muscles are normally clustered into a series of control groupings. Using these, animators can move discrete parts of the face to produce key facial movements such as 'right eye close', 'lip sneer', 'forehead wrinkle' and so on. These movements are key-frame animated to create changing facial expressions throughout a sequence. Techniques like these were used by Pixar to create facial animation for films such as *Monsters, Inc.* (2001) and *The Incredibles* (2004).

The animation of physically based face models can also be driven by motion-capture data derived from the performance of an actor. This technique was used to create the facial performances in *The Polar Express* (2004) and *King Kong* (2005). Commonly called 'performance capture' rather than 'motion capture', this method requires an actor to wear dozens, sometimes hundreds, of tiny facial markers. The movement of these markers during a performance is recorded like normal motion capture (<208) and then mapped onto the muscle groups in a digital facial rig in order to create an animated version of the original performance. Motion capture normally only provides perhaps 80 per cent of a performance, the remaining animation being created with normal key-framing techniques. In cases where the live performer's features do not directly translate to the geometry of the digital character's face, the motion-capture data will need to be distorted somewhat. For *King Kong*, for example, the motion around performer Andy Serkis's nose and mouth needed to be remapped to better fit the wide, protruding muzzle of the great ape.

The other popular method of producing facial animation relies on creating a series of pre-sculpted facial expressions. With this method the face model has no underlying flesh or muscle and so the geometry of its surface is directly sculpted using traditional digital modelling techniques. Sometimes each expression is first sculpted in clay and then scanned. Animators then select sculptures showing the expressions they want to use and place them at the key frames at which they are needed. The

ABOVE LEFT: **Tom Hanks undergoes performance capture for a scene from** *The Polar Express* **(2004). Dozens of tiny markers capture the movement of his face, while larger markers on his head, hands and shoulders are used to relay his overall body movement.**

ABOVE: **The finished scene on film.**

RIGHT: **Animators have traditionally used their own reflections in order to help them create convincing facial expressions for their characters, but to help his animators produce the right performance for Yoda, ILM animation director Rob Coleman created video reference shots of himself.** *Left:* **Here Coleman acts the part of Yoda for a shot in** *Revenge of the Sith* **(2005).** *Centre:* **The computer animator combines a number of blend shapes to give the CG Yoda a similar expression.** *Right:* **The shot as seen in the final film.**

computer then interpolates or 'blends' from one expression to the next over a designated number of frames to produce the required facial movement. This technique, known as 'blend-shape animation', was used to produce the facial performance of Gollum in *The Lord of the Rings* and Yoda in *Star Wars: Episodes II* and *III* (2002, 2005).

'The face of our CG Yoda began as a single digital sculpture in a neutral pose,' explains ILM animation director Rob Coleman, who oversaw character animation on all three modern *Star Wars* movies. 'From that starting point we digitally resculpted segments of Yoda's face to produce 40 separate facial elements, or "blend shapes". For example, two of our 40 blend shapes were a "right eyebrow up" shape and a "right eyebrow down" shape.'

Each of the 40 blend shapes was assigned a digital slider, creating an on-screen control panel similar to that of an audio mixing desk. Each blend shape in the animator's timeline could be faded up or down between 0 and 100 per cent. The higher the number, the more that shape influenced the overall facial pose. 'Using these sliders we were able to blend between our 40 differently sculpted shapes to produce Yoda's entire facial performance, including his speech,' says Coleman.

Creating a performance of nuanced emotions, expressions and speech from just 40 sculpted elements would seem like a tall order given that the human face uses hundreds of muscles to produce its range of movement. Yet ILM has found that it is not the number of shapes used but the way they can be selectively combined that creates a naturalistic performance, as Coleman explains: 'For earlier films we used to sculpt entire facial expressions. If we wanted an angry face we would have a bunch of models in which the whole face was pre-sculpted with different degrees of anger. There might be hundreds of fully sculpted faces altogether. During animation, one complete facial expression was blended into another. Performances created in this way worked well for non-human characters but they tended to be rather stylized and didn't really have the range and spontaneity that you find in a real face. We now have a much better understanding of how facial movement works, and by intelligently designing and then blending a relatively small number of facial elements, rather than overall facial sculpts, we could produce a very organic and expressive performance for Yoda. In actual fact, of the 40 blend shapes made for Yoda we used only 25 of them continually while the other 15 were used only occasionally.'

Although Yoda's facial expressions were created by a selective combination of blended facial elements rather than sculpted full facial poses, Coleman's team did rely on a number of pre-designed facial models. 'Our lead animator, Jamy Wheless, blended shapes to create eight master expressions,' says Coleman. 'Any time one of the fifteen animators working on Yoda wanted to create a particular emotion they could just press a button and up would pop the "meditative" face or the "angry" face. All the sliders would move to the correct blend positions to create these expressions. From there the animator could start blending shapes to create a performance, but it meant that everyone had a common starting point and could stay "on-model".'

Coleman describes how a Yoda facial performance was typically created: 'The first thing we do is block in the head action. This means simply key-framing the changing position of the head throughout the shot according to where he needs to look. We then listen to the recording of Yoda's dialogue and animate the jaw to indicate when he is or is not talking. This is simply jaw down, jaw up. The jaw controller is not one of our blend shapes, it's just a normally animatable part of the face.'

The next stage is to start layering in more specific mouth movement to produce the appearance of a voice performance. 'First we put in the mouth-closed phonemes – the Ms, Bs and Ps,' says Coleman. 'We then work on the mouth-open positions. At this stage we don't put in the individual phonemes, we start with the loudest sounds in the shot – where the mouth is at its widest. With those layered in we have an overall shape to the performance – we know when the mouth is open and closed. We then create the finer lip movements for the remaining phonemes – the Os, Es, Us and so on, in order to synchronize exactly with the pre-recorded dialogue. This is one of the tasks that uses the most blend shapes. For example an E will require three blend shapes to influence the form of the upper lips to a greater or lesser extent, then three more for the lower lips, plus we'll have the cheeks going up on either side and also a little crinkling at the corners of the eyes. With the basic words formed on Yoda's lips we would then add in any additional head moves that might be made in response to the dialogue. English speakers tend to emphasize certain words with a slight nod or tip back of the head.'

Finally the animators must give some thought to the performance of the upper portions of the face. 'Animating the mouth is just about getting the mechanics of talking right,' says Coleman. 'But the eyes are what really convey emotion. This is partly animating the face around the eyes – the way the brow furrows or the eyelids squint – but also about how the eyes themselves move.'

A character's eyes can be animated by using a controller that works like a handle protruding from the iris of each eye. The end of the handle can be moved around to sweep over the places that the character needs to look. The handles can also be attached to whatever the character is looking at so that their gaze remains fixed even as they walk around.

'Eyes are rarely still, even when we stare at a person's face during a conversation,' remarks Coleman. 'If the eyes don't move a character looks lifeless so we always have them scanning back and forth a little. In addition the pupils can widen or dilate to convey thought and emotion. We can also alter the convergence of the pupils, making the gaze of the eyes parallel when a character stares into the distance or cross slightly when staring at something very near.'

The hardest form of animation to create convincingly is undoubtedly that of the human face. We are all experts in what faces of all shapes, shades and emotions look like and are not easy to fool with any form of synthesized performance.

A startlingly realistic form of human facial animation was developed for use in *The Matrix Reloaded* (2003). To produce scenes in which the film's stars appeared to fight and perform in ways impossible for a real human,

a team led by George Borshukov was asked to find a way to create photorealistic computer-generated doubles that could be seen in close-up.

The technique they developed, called 'Universal Capture', was an image-based animation system. This meant that it used images of real moving faces to drive the synthetic motion of a computer-generated face. The CG face could then be attached to an animated body and be viewed from any angle under variable lighting conditions.

The system worked by surrounding performers with an array of five synchronized high-definition digital video cameras (fig. 8 (a)). Actors were then filmed as they performed the necessary expressions or dialogue. The result was a series of shots of the same action as seen from five different angles (b).

In the computer a high-resolution cyberscan (<195) of the performer's face (c) was then surrounded by five 'cameras', each of which was aligned to look at the digital head from exactly the same position as they had viewed the real head during filming (d). Each camera contained a record of the live-action footage that it had filmed from that same position during filming.

Each vertex on the surface of the cyberscanned face model was then 'projected' into each of the five surrounding cameras. Within each camera, each vertex from the surface of the 3-D cyberscan lined up with the 2-D coloured pixel that had been recorded at that exact spot on the face of the performer during filming (e). As the performer's face moved from one frame to the next, the changing position of every coloured pixel, and the vertex on the face of the cyberscan which it represented, was tracked. By triangulating the movement of each pixel from the position of each of the five cameras, an accurate reconstruction of the path of each pixel, and therefore vertex, through 3-D space was recorded. The motion of the vertices was then used to deform the surface of the cyberscanned head in order to create an animated performance that exactly copied that of the actor (f).

To complete the animation the 2-D video images filmed from each of the five camera angles were combined to produce an animated texture map that fitted the moving facial model perfectly. The result was highly controllable digital doubles that were indistinguishable from their real-world counterparts.

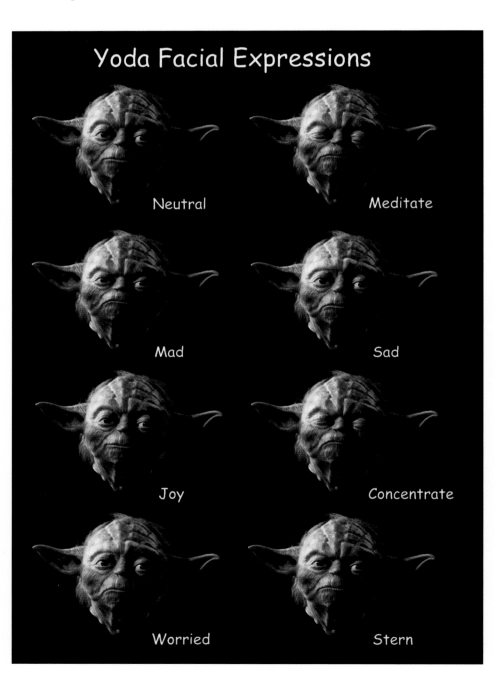

LEFT: **The eight master expressions of a Jedi Master, as used by ILM when animating their digital Yoda.**

BELOW: **Universal capture allowed dozens of photorealistic computer-generated clones of actor Hugo Weaving to appear in this scene from** *The Matrix Reloaded* **(2003).**

FIGURE 8 **UNIVERSAL CAPTURE**

c: cyberscan of performer's head

a: performer filmed by high-definition cameras

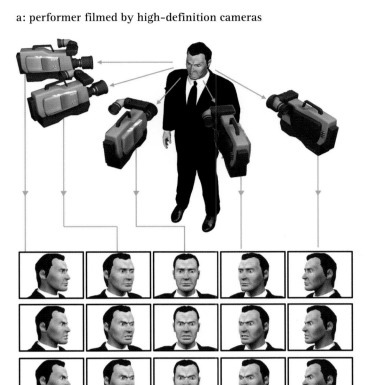

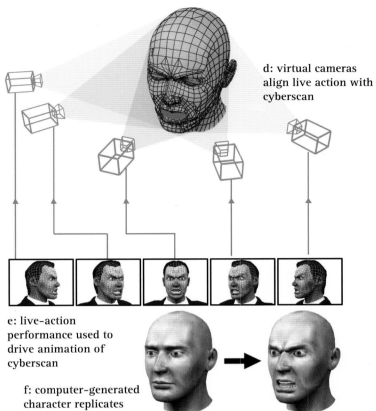

d: virtual cameras align live action with cyberscan

e: live-action performance used to drive animation of cyberscan

f: computer-generated character replicates actor's performance.

b: performance captured from five different angles

CROWDS

Film-makers have long realized that one of the most exciting movie spectacles can be the sight of hundreds or thousands of people involved in the on-screen drama. In 1915 D.W. Griffith employed 5,000 extras to populate the Babylon sequences of *Intolerance*, while an impressive 20,000 troops were recruited from the Soviet Red Army to re-enact Napoleonic battle scenes for the epic flop *Waterloo* (1970). But the record is held by Richard Attenborough's *Gandhi* (1982) which rallied over 250,000 extras for its funeral scenes.

But filling the screen with legions of people is time-consuming and very expensive. Because of this, film-makers have sought ways of making relatively few extras look like many more. Digital split-screen techniques now allow groups of extras to be filmed in several positions and then combined to look like a large crowd (<108). Even in the age of digital deception there are still some brilliantly simple methods of creating a crowd. For *Seabiscuit* (2003) and *Wimbledon* (2004), film-makers used hundreds of inflatable dolls wearing masks, clothes and wigs. Providing the camera was moving or the crowds were in the background of a shot, the conceit was undetectable.

However, some productions have called for tens and even hundreds of thousands of characters to perform in incredibly complex battle scenes. To produce these, film-makers have turned to the image-generating powers of the computer.

The largest movie battles ever created appeared in Peter Jackson's *Lord of the Rings* trilogy, with some sequences featuring over 200,000 battling orcs and elves. To produce these scenes Weta Digital created a unique crowd simulation software program called 'Massive'. 'Massive combined digital character animation techniques with a form of artificial intelligence that allowed us to control how thousands of characters looked and behaved', states visual effects supervisor Joe Letteri. 'We built a kind of artificial brain which was a system of rules governing how characters might behave or react in various situations. The brains were a network of 7,000 to 8,000 nodes, each node being the equivalent of a decision that had to be made, such as "Do I lift my sword or not?" or "Is this person so strong that I should run away?" Our characters could recognize who to attack, which weapons to use, and how to stand, run, or fall on different types of surface. Warriors even knew how to die in a manner suited to the way they were attacked and where they were standing'.

Once programmed, characters were let loose in environments that contained various obstacles and enemies. The computer then simulated a battle with each character behaving according to its own rules and drawing on a library of discrete motion-captured body moves to generate their actual performances (217>). 'Because we only told agents how to react in certain situations rather than exactly how to perform in every frame, the resulting battles were quite organic and could contain all sorts of surprises', says Letteri. 'In one shot a group of characters were so smart they actually decided they didn't want to fight and they turned around and ran away!'

Other notable computer-generated battles have appeared in *Troy* (2004) and *Kingdom of Heaven* (2005). In each case the fighting hordes were created by London's Moving Picture Company (MPC). 'For each of these films we had to produce dozens of battle shots in a very short time', states MPC technical director Carsten Kolve. 'Most shots needed to convey a specific part of a battle rather than just show a wide vista of thousands of combatants randomly fighting. Because we essentially needed to art-direct each shot, the artificial life solutions used for the *Lord of the Rings* battles weren't really appropriate for us. We couldn't spend the time programming all the variations and running simulations – we needed to determine exactly where and when events would occur. To solve this we created our own crowd simulation engine'.

MPC began by plotting every conceivable action that might be required on the battlefield, from troops waiting for battle to begin, to charging, hand-to-hand combat, throwing spears, climbing ladders, and so on.

Historical epics often call for a cast of thousands. Whereas once many hundreds of extras had to be hired and clothed, modern crowds are more often created by the computer, as in these shots from *Kingdom of Heaven* (2005, *above*) and *Troy* (2004, *below*), in which the majority of the soldiers are digital.

ABOVE RIGHT & FAR RIGHT: **For these shots from *Kingdom of Heaven*, the Moving Picture Company used a library of motion-capture moves to make thousands of computer-generated soldiers fight and die according to specific pre-programmed rules.**

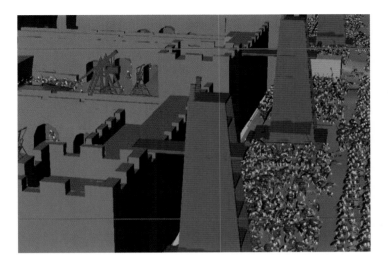

'Once we had a list of 500 or 600 actions we motion-captured stunt performers as they enacted them for us,' says Kolve. 'Where the action involved a prop, such as a swinging sword, we also captured the motion of the prop. In the end we had a library of many hundreds of discrete movements. We then grouped these movements together into motion libraries. A motion library is a set of movements that a character, which we call an "agent", can perform, like running to a halt, lifting and throwing a spear, and so on. The actions within a library are connected to each other with blends, allowing the movements to merge subtly from one to another over several frames. A motion library would typically contain only a small number of actions. Rather than enabling our agents to do absolutely anything in a shot, like the agents in *Lord of the Rings* – which is time-consuming and complex to control – we made our agents very good at performing specific tasks.'

In order to maintain the visual complexity of a crowd, MPC's artists created hundreds of different motion libraries that were distributed among the agents in a scene. Since shots are rarely longer than a few seconds, each agent's possible range of motion did not need to be very broad.

'For *Kingdom of Heaven*, Ridley Scott wanted very specific types of fighting to be happening at particular times in each area of a battle,' says Kolve. 'For example, at a certain point he would want the sword fighters to be battling with each other while archers shot their arrows at the people on castle battlements.' In order to arrange battles in the way the director wanted, customized fight sequences were first created by editing together the necessary sets of motion. 'We would simulate several hundred digital actors doing the right type of fighting,' says Kolve. 'We then copied or "instanced" that group of people and could rubber-stamp them across the landscape saying, "We'll have 500 here and 500 there," and so on. Each time we instanced a group the agents would automatically adapt to the new terrain. We would also rotate each new patch of people and offset their timing so they didn't look the same as their neighbours. Where groups overlapped we would go in and weed out any soldiers that merged or collided with one another, though at a distance it didn't really matter if one soldier's arm went through another's body – it wouldn't be seen.' MPC also created a library of characters performing exaggerated actions such as dying in a spectacular fashion. These were hand-placed wherever it was felt the action was a little sparse or lacking in interest.

As well as characters whose actions were determined by MPC's technical directors, each scene contained a number of characters whose movements were determined by the computer. 'We scattered a number of artificial intelligence characters in each shot,' explains Kolve. 'These characters could pick up on what the soldiers around them were doing and copy their general actions. This meant that their performance was a bit more random and always a little behind that of those around them.

They could run around with more freedom but were programmed not to bump into or walk through other characters. It just helped each shot look more natural.'

Artificially determined motion was also used when characters needed to react directly to the physical environment around them. 'We relied on motion capture whenever we could,' says Kolve, 'but there were times when we needed movement that was far more specific. For instance, if a character fell off a ladder we would use motion-captured movement for the fall, but when they hit the ground or landed on something like a piece of siege machinery, the characters would switch over to models that were programmed to react procedurally according to the laws of physics.' These characters were driven by software that gave them the physical properties of real humans, allowing them to react naturalistically to any forces applied to them. 'When we dropped a wounded character from a collapsing siege tower he would collide with the debris and crumple and deform just like a real human without us having to animate him in any way,' says Kolve.

Each battle contained a number of different armies and regiments, each with its own distinctive dress, style of armour and range of weapons. 'We had a series of controls that influenced the quantities of each type of costume, armour and weaponry there were in a shot,' explains Kolve. 'The director could just say "more wooden shields and fewer helmets" and we would adjust the look of the scene accordingly. On top of that the computer would add additional randomness to things like the patterns on shields, how people wore their clothes and so on. You would be very unlikely to see two identical characters.'

The combination of computer automation and manual intervention was also necessary when it came to killing performers that were struck by arrows. Making arrows shot by archers find and hit a target would have been a very complex task, as Kolve explains: 'Each archer would have to pick a target, predict its motion and the flight path of an arrow and then shoot in the hope of hitting. This might be what happened in real life but it is not very controllable in terms of computer simulation. The problem is further complicated by the fact that once a person is hit it might take the computer several frames to blend the "I've been hit by an arrow" motion clip into the performance, making their reaction appear too slow. So we would manually pick a number of people and tell them where and when their death would happen. During the simulation process a "marked" agent would tell the archer of his choice "Please kill me in 32 frames and, for your information, my right shoulder will be at exactly this position at that time." The archer then only had to make sure its arrow reached the right place at the right time while the suicidal agent made sure it blended into the right death motion.'

The resulting battles were made more realistic by the addition of minute puffs of dust that were spawned each time a character's foot hit the dusty ground.

CLOTH

Creating clothes for digital characters presents a number of challenges. Garments need to fit around characters and hang from their bodies naturalistically. The material needs to move freely and yet not intersect either with the body on which it is worn, or with itself as it folds and creases. It also has to react to external forces such as wind or objects with which it comes into contact.

The most widely used form of digital cloth is made from a polygonal mesh in which the segments that connect the vertices (<154) are programmed to act like tiny springs. The degree and direction in which these springs stretch and flex can be adjusted to produce materials ranging from the lightest silk to the thickest leather. The material is programmed to act according to the laws of gravity so that it will drape over any object that it is placed on. To do this it must also be capable of 'collision detection' – it needs to detect when it is touching another object so that it will lie on that surface, or be pushed by it, rather than pass through it. So that it can be creased and folded without intersecting with itself, cloth also needs to 'self-repel'. This is achieved by making the vertices of the cloth push away from each other like repelling magnetic poles.

The final look of cloth is achieved through a combination of texture maps and shaders (<164–7). A subtle bump or displacement map makes the weave look like anything from fine cotton to heavy canvas.

Using this material, clothes can be made in several ways. An item like a shirt can be sculpted as a single object much like any other piece of geometry, or the individual pieces of cloth can be cut out according to a pattern and 'stitched' together exactly as if a real shirt were being made by a tailor.

Once clothes are made they are draped over a character and left to fall naturally. If left alone the clothes will perform procedurally, moving and creasing as the character to which they are attached is animated. However, it is rare for digital clothes to move exactly as required without any additional input from artists.

'We spend lots of time creating a performance from digital clothing,' states Juan-Luis Sanchez, a digital clothing supervisor at ILM. 'When you watch a scene from a movie like *Revenge of the Sith* [2005] being filmed you notice how the actors are constantly being preened by wardrobe people. Their capes are straightened over their shoulders or pinned back with safety pins so that they look their best in every shot. We effectively do the same thing with our digital clothing. Once the clothes are on, we pin parts of them to the body so they won't move too far. We also specify areas where we want the cloth to be more flexible or stiff, such as seams and pockets. We can then adjust various parameters, making clothes react more or less to gravity. We can add a little wind to make them billow and then thicken the atmosphere so that they flow more slowly. This all allows us to sculpt the way clothing looks and moves in order to aid the drama. For *Attack of the Clones* [2002], George Lucas asked for Yoda's digital cape to move more "romantically". This meant choreographing its movement so that it acted slightly less realistically and more heroically. Instead of moving at the same time as Yoda we often made the cape move a beat or two later. We also made it glide and swirl to the floor after a fight rather than just dropping, for example.'

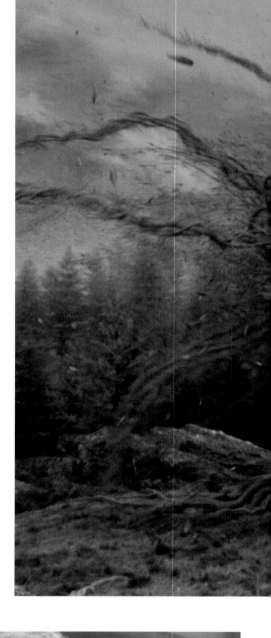

PROCEDURAL ANIMATION

Like digital model-making, a number of animation tasks can be achieved procedurally (<161). Such procedural tasks are normally used to produce complex forms of motion and interaction that would be too time-consuming or complicated to animate by hand. In such cases the necessary movement is determined by a series of mathematical formulas. These algorithms, often based on academic research, are written to synthesize the physical effects of natural forces such as velocity, gravity and the dynamic flow of fluids.

Procedural animation systems allow the animator to define the material properties and behaviour of the object to be animated. They then define the variable forces that are to be applied to that object. The computer then runs a simulation to calculate the resulting animation. Several simulations are typically needed, each time altering the various parameters until the required motion is achieved.

An example of a procedural animation might be the simulation of wind blowing through the branches of a computer-generated tree. Hand-animating thousands of branches and leaves would be highly impractical. However, by describing how flexible the branches are and the way in which the leaves move in a breeze, an artificial wind force could be applied to the tree to create a naturalistic animation. By varying the force of the wind or the flexibility of the tree, different types of motion could be achieved. A certain percentage of the leaves could even be told to blow away when the wind reaches a particular strength. Techniques like these were actually used by MPC to create the animated 'Whomping Willow' tree in *Harry Potter and the Prisoner of Azkaban* (2004).

There are many variations of procedural animation, some of which are described overleaf.

ABOVE: **The Moving Picture Company used procedural modelling and animation techniques to create small branches and several million leaves for the Whomping Willow in *Harry Potter and the Prisoner of Azkaban* (2004).**

LEFT: **To create digital cloth for Yoda's clothes, ILM used procedural tools that allowed materials to flow naturally according to the character's movements. *Left:* Animators could view the cloth's automatically generated movement and adjust it manually to refine its performance. *Right:* Yoda in his computer-generated clothes in *Revenge of the Sith* (2005). The procedurally generated cloth texture included subtle fluff and burrs.**

PARTICLE SYSTEMS

Procedural systems are particularly good at simulating the look and movement of moving materials such as dust, snow, smoke, water or even plagues of locusts. In such cases 'particle systems' are used to create and control large numbers of objects that would be impossible to handle using key-frame animation.

To use a particle system, a computer animator defines one or a number of 'emitters' – that is, points from which particles will emerge on screen. These emitters can be imagined as invisible fireworks from which thousands of sparks emerge when lit, although they can actually be of any size or shape and can themselves be animated to move.

The animator can define how fast particles are emitted, how many to have, how they are emitted, how far and fast they travel, how quickly they disperse, how they are affected by wind and gravity, whether they grow in size, and so on. After these parameters have been set the computer will produce a simulation, normally using a low number of particles, to show the animator what the flow looks like. The parameters can then be adjusted until the desired effect is achieved. During final rendering the particles can be rendered with shaders that make them look like dust, water, fire or any other material, or they can be replaced with objects such as pre-animated fish or insects, for example.

For the action-adventure movie *XXX* (2002) director Rob Cohen wanted a spectacular avalanche with a distinct personality to chase a skier down a mountainside. 'We needed to create a very controllable avalanche that we could direct according to Rob's very specific requirements,' recalls Digital Domain visual effects supervisor Joel Hynek.

After live-action plates were shot on locations around the world, Digital Domain's artists created accurate digital replicas of the mountainside topology down which the avalanche needed to flow. 'The first step in producing the avalanche was to design the way in which it would move – its overall speed and shape,' says Hynek. 'We did this by key-frame animating a spline (<158) that moved down the mountain, following the skier and conforming to any geographical features that might affect its progress. This moving line represented the leading edge of the avalanche. When the director was happy with that motion we had to create the snow itself.'

The bulk of the snow was produced by the animated spline, which was used as a particle emitter. The spline spewed out hundreds of thousands of particles that shot out in front of it as it travelled down the mountain. The particles moved at a slower rate than the spline itself so that a massive cloud of flowing particles built up behind the leading edge as it travelled forwards. Particle movement was programmed to be affected by the downward gravity of the slope and the pressure of the wind that built up in front of the avalanche and flowed over the top.

Rob Cohen wanted many tendrils of snow to leap out of the avalanche like arms grabbing for the escaping skier. 'We selected areas of the mountainside from which we wanted these fingerlike tendrils to emerge,' recalls Hynek. 'We then created the equivalent of a minefield, with lots of particle emitters lying dormant under the snow. When the leading edge of the avalanche went over these mines they exploded high-velocity plumes of particles that shot up out of the main body of snow. Some of these emitters birthed 3-D chunks of ice. The chunks themselves were also particle emitters so that a trail of snow streamed behind them as they flew through the air. When the projectile chunks of ice hit the ground in front of the avalanche another particle emitter would automatically generate a smaller impact plume.'

The clouds of snow particles were finally rendered using volumetric rendering techniques (236>) to produce dramatic clouds of billowing snow and ice that were composited into the live-action footage.

RIGID BODY DYNAMICS

Rigid body dynamics is an advanced form of particle animation that is used to simulate the motion of three-dimensional 'solid' objects as they collide and interact. This technique is usually used to create shots that show the destruction of buildings and machinery.

Using established laws of physics and mechanics in the form of highly complex algorithms, rigid body dynamic simulations calculate the way that objects of irregular shape, size and mass will move as they travel through 3-D space. For example, a triangular-shaped object that is heavier at one end than the other will fall with a unique tumbling, rotational action that would be hard to animate accurately by hand. Because computer-generated objects are not 'solid' and can pass through one another, the process also uses collision detection methods to recognize the time and place at which moving objects touch one another. It then calculates the forces at work as those bodies meet and sends them in other directions with the appropriate motion and velocity, as if they had actually been solid objects bouncing off one another. This technique is highly processor-intensive and so is normally only used to animate the most complex of shots.

Rigid body dynamics have been used for spectacular destruction scenes such as the explosive buckling of the USS *Arizona* in *Pearl Harbor* (2001) and the apocalyptic, twisting destruction of a road bridge in *War of the Worlds* (2005). The technique was also used to generate shots of the vast tower of Barad-dûr collapsing at the climax of *The Return of the King* (2003).

Most shots of Barad-dûr were achieved using a beautifully sculpted 8 m (26 ft) high model created by Weta Workshop. But trying to create a dramatic, controllable and repeatable performance from a collapsing miniature would have proved difficult. It was therefore decided to achieve the shot digitally. The first step was to create an extremely high-polygon digital model of the tower. If a digital model needs to divide into many pieces during its destruction then it must be constructed from a large number of polygons, allowing plenty of places for breaks to occur. The finished model of Barad-dûr, created by Weta Digital, comprised an incredible 250 million polygons.

In order for the tower to fall apart the points at which it would crack had to be defined. 'We used a 2-D particle system on the surface of the tower,' explains Jim Hourihan of Tweak Films, who wrote the simulation software for this sequence. 'We basically set a bunch of particles loose on the surface and they bounced around in all directions, drawing a line behind them wherever they went. The result was an elaborate and completely random jigsaw of lines where the surface of the tower would fracture. We then used a similar method to send particles into the actual body of the tower, dividing it up into 3-D chunks.'

Next the actual collapse of the tower had to be achieved. 'We did try doing it entirely according to the laws of physics,' states Hourihan. 'We essentially switched off the glue that was holding all the bits of tower together and let it fall according to our rigid body algorithms. But the result, however realistic, just didn't look spectacular enough. The thing about animating procedurally is that you need to build in lots of control. Naturalistic simulation is often not dramatic enough for the movies and directors always want to say exactly how things should look – whatever the math says. You therefore need to maintain control of as many variables as possible in order to influence the outcome of any simulation.'

To create a more spectacular collapse sequence, the tower had a large 'box' placed around it. This box worked like an invisible force field that held the tower together. By animating the box downwards so that the tower was gradually revealed, the building could be made to collapse from the top down. 'As the tower started to crumble, additional boxes were placed around the falling clusters of chunks,' explains Hourihan. 'As these larger chunks fell the boxes holding them together could also be animated to move around, allowing smaller sub-chunks out of their influence and letting them drop away independently.'

Using this technique, the crumbling of Barad-dûr was choreographed to look as spectacular as possible, with tens of thousands of chunks tumbling to the ground, realistically bouncing off one another on their way down.

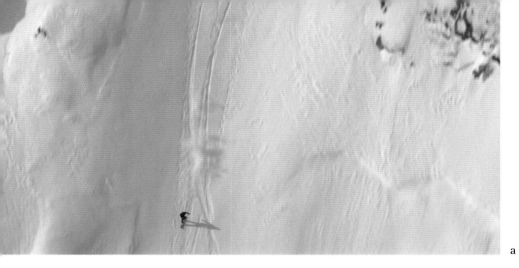

a

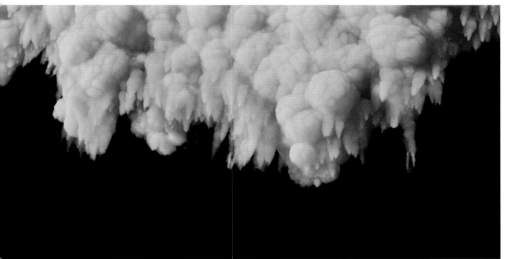

b

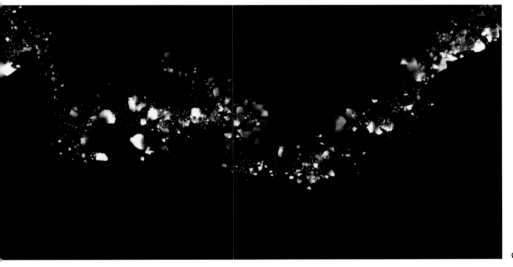

c

d

To create an awesome avalanche for *Stealth* (2005), Digital Domain added computer-generated snow to a live-action plate containing a real skier.

a: The skier was first filmed on location.

b: After a CG model of the mountain was built, an avalanche of small snow particles was created using particle animation and volume rendering.

c: Larger chunks of ice were also animated using similar techniques.

d: The elements were composited together to create an exhilarating and awesome scene.

THE LORD OF THE RINGS

After J.R.R. Tolkien's books were published in the 50s, filming *The Lord of the Rings* proved an unachievable goal for a number of notable film-makers. In 1978 the first half of the story was finally realized as a cartoon made by Ralph Bakshi – animation the only technique seemingly capable of portraying the saga's mythic characters and epic events. But it wouldn't be until the age of computer-generated imagery that Tolkien's dreams would finally be rendered with a brilliance to match their creator's imagination.

After several false starts Peter Jackson (<44) finally began shooting *The Fellowship of the Ring*, *The Two Towers* and *The Return of the King*, back to back, in 1998. Based in Wellington, New Zealand, Jackson's own facilities Weta Workshop (handling models, props and make-up) and Weta Digital (creating digital effects) worked for six years on the three films. In that time an astonishing array of techniques both old and new were adopted, adapted and combined to create some of the most awesome visual effects imagery ever seen.

Stunning New Zealand locations and full-scale sets were augmented by dozens of extraordinary miniatures, some so big that they were dubbed 'bigatures'. The regal city of Minas Tirith, for example, was 7.5 m (25 ft) high and 12.25 m (40 ft) wide with over 1,000 exquisitely detailed buildings. Once filmed the model was populated by digital characters and placed in a 3-D matte-painted mountain environment.

The trilogy's vast battle scenes were created using a custom-built artificial intelligence animation system called 'Massive'. In some shots up to 220,000 humans, orcs and elves fought according to a complex set of rules that told each how to move, react, fight and die.

A number of superb CG characters were created with absolute realism. These included the magnificent flame-spewing Balrog, the squidlike Watcher in the Water, herds of elephantine Mûmaks and the trilogy's signature achievement: Gollum. The new technique of subsurface scattering was used to render Gollum's photorealistic skin while actor Andy Serkis provided voice recordings and a motion-captured performance that was the basis of perhaps the first truly emotionally expressive CG character ever created for a film.

The films' central characters needed to vary in height from 1.25 m (4 ft) hobbits to 2 m (6 ft) wizards. To achieve this using normal-sized actors, a number of techniques were employed. For long shots, tall or small stand-ins wearing rubber masks made the main characters appear to be the right scale. Where large and small characters needed to interact, in-camera forced-perspective techniques were used – large characters like Gandalf being near the camera and small characters such as Frodo being further away. Deep-focus photography made the separated characters appear as if next to one another. Performers were also motion-control filmed in front of blue screens and adjusted for size during compositing. Many sets, props, plants and animals were also required in two sizes to make actors appear comparatively large or small.

Overseen by co-founder Richard Taylor, Weta Workshop produced thousands of elaborately detailed miniatures, costumes, weapons and props. The film's make-up requirements were also handled by the workshop, creating everything from full-body Uruk-hai warrior costumes to thousands of silicone hobbit feet.

Finally, the films were digitally graded, allowing the colour and tonal quality of every scene to reflect its place in the drama, from starkly threatening battle scenes to richly autumnal elven valleys.

After working tirelessly for eight years, Peter Jackson had created one of the most remarkable movie series ever produced. In terms of the range of techniques and quality of work, the movies were perhaps the most satisfying visual effects films for decades. The effort was rewarded handsomely at both the box office and the award ceremonies, with worldwide takings of $3 billion and a final count of 17 Academy Awards.

WATER

Water has traditionally been a problematic substance for special effects artists when trying to film miniature ships and floods. Perhaps not surprisingly it has continued to be one of the most demanding substances to replicate digitally.

The first successful digital water shots were of wide, unbroken surfaces such as the gently rolling seascapes in *Waterworld* (1995) and *Deep Blue Sea* (1999). The water for these films used a system pioneered by Areté Image Software that used oceanographic research to produce a model of how water surfaces move under varied conditions. By altering influences such as the speed and direction of the wind, an accurate animated model of the ocean surface could be produced procedurally. However, these early seas could not have breaking waves or interact with objects to produce foam or spray. The wake seen behind the ship in *Titanic* (1997), for example, was created by filming the water around a real ship and mapping that footage on top of digital water.

The movie widely recognized as the breakthrough for realistic digital water was *The Perfect Storm* (2000), for which ILM created dramatic shots of storm-tossed seas with naturalistic foam, spray and ships' wakes.

'Making CG water look real is always going to be tricky,' states Jim Hourihan, head of research & development at Tweak Films, where a number of spectacular flood shots were created for the environmental disaster movie *The Day After Tomorrow* (2004). 'Water just has so many natural facets that need to be spot on. And even though none of us has ever seen a giant tidal wave like the one in the movie, it's one of those things that people will feel looks fake unless everything is just right.'

Tweak Films was asked to create several shots showing vast quantities of water crashing through Manhattan. The first stage of the process was to produce an accurate simulation of how a massive body of water would flow through the city's streets. 'We used a physics-based fluid dynamics simulation in which the natural properties of water are defined as an algorithm,' explains Hourihan. 'This algorithm is a mathematical description of how water moves and reacts to various forces. As a result, we essentially have to tell the computer how large a volume of water we are dealing with and what environment that water is in. We then ask the computer to calculate exactly how that water would flow through the environment.'

One of the key shots in the flood sequence was an aerial view of the tidal wave swamping the New York public library. Tweak used an accurate digital model of the library and its environs that had been created for the production by Digital Domain. The model would eventually have highly detailed texture maps applied to its surfaces to create a photorealistic view of the city, but while working on the water the model contained only the basic geometry with which the water would interact. Once the computer had been given information about the real-life scale of the city environment and the volume of water required to flow through it, a simulation was run to calculate how the wave would look and behave.

The result of the initial simulation was not particularly exciting viewing. 'What we ended up with looked like a big blob of thick blue paint flowing past a bunch of grey boxes,' says Hourihan. 'It was quite hard to see how it would eventually look like a massive tidal wave because it didn't have any splashes or surface details that might indicate scale. It was just a blob. Nevertheless, it was a blob that was moving according to the laws of physics.'

Though accurate, the initial simulations didn't perform in the way that the film's director, Roland Emmerich, wanted. 'We had to do lots of simulations before the water behaved in the desired dramatic fashion,' says Hourihan. 'We influenced its performance by pumping more water into the simulation as it flowed along. We could make it swell or leap up by injecting more water at the places it was needed. We were effectively art-directing nature.'

When the director was satisfied with the character of the water, one problem still remained. 'We were pumping in so much water that it was totally engulfing the library. It was just flowing right up and over the roof,' says Hourihan. After trying more simulations Tweak eventually solved the problem by making the library building artificially high. Because the camera was looking down from above, it wasn't noticeable that the building had grown dramatically for the purposes of the simulation.

With the basic character and surface topology of the water simulated, the next task was to make it look less like paint and more like water. This was largely the job of shaders (<167) which would help to create the look of a large body of water during rendering (236>). However, a number of additional watery details had to be added. 'One of the things that makes rough water look real is the foam that floats on its surface,' explains Hourihan. 'We produced a number of two-dimensional animated texture maps to simulate what that foam looked like. They were basically procedurally produced black-and-white swirling patterns. We then scattered those maps all over the surface of the water.' During the initial water simulation the computer had also generated velocity vectors describing how the surface of the water moved in relation to the main body. 'We attached the maps to the main body of water so that they would be driven by its gross movement. We then used the velocity vectors to push the foam around on the surface so that it looked like it was floating over, rather than being fixed to, the main body. It was a bit like attaching the foam to the body of water with bits of elastic – the foam went

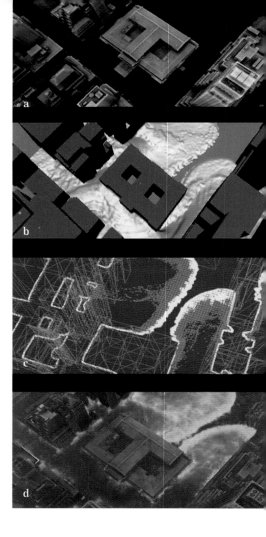

ABOVE: **To create incredible scenes of a flooded New York for** *The Day After Tomorrow* **(2004), Tweak Films used a high-resolution model of the city. Here (a) the New York Public Library model can be seen from above. Using procedural animation techniques, the flow of the flood waters is simulated as it engulfs buildings (b). Additional simulations create foam and spray on the top and leading edge of the water (c). The final composite is a chilling and dramatic demonstration of a city overpowered by the forces of nature (d).**

TOP RIGHT: **In this scene from** *The Day After Tomorrow*, **the steps and deep water through which people are struggling are an interior studio set. The background buildings were added later, along with a computer-generated tidal wave that smashes everything before it.**

RIGHT: *The Perfect Storm* **(2000) featured some of the first truly natural-looking CG water. Here, the gallant fishing boat** *Andrea Gail* **is dwarfed by ILM's spectacular digital tempest.**

where the water did but still had a fair amount of freedom to slip and slide'. Because the animated surface textures were attached to the body of water they would eventually be pulled down into that water as it churned. 'After a few frames the textures would get submerged or buckle and turn into a grey mush. So we had to continually recycle the maps, bringing fresh new ones onto the surface as the old ones disappeared'.

As the massive wave forced its way through the city it needed to produce spray wherever it struck objects and buildings. The computer was able to detect where the leading edge of the water hit or interacted with objects and at those points particle emitters sent spray into the air (<220). The amount and force of the spray was determined by the water velocity vectors calculated as part of the simulation. The movement of the spray was also influenced by surface wind

currents that were also calculated as part of the main water simulation.

Tweak's artists also manually placed emitters wherever they felt more white water was needed. 'The director particularly wanted a very dramatic surge of spray when the wave comes around the library from two directions and meets in the middle', remembers Hourihan. 'When we ran the simulation the two bodies of water met and there was just a bit of a ripple, but Roland Emmerich wanted a big dramatic moment. In the end we had to pump a lot of extra water under that area and then add a slightly delayed fountain of spray. It was completely unnatural but the timing and size of the splash certainly made for a dynamic moment'.

Considerable effort was put into making the spray look natural. 'If the particles were too small they looked granular and more like sand, and if they were too big they looked blobby. We eventually programmed the particles to expand until they reached the next-nearest particle – so some bits of spray were large and some were small', says Hourihan. But the key to getting the particles looking perfect was the way they created shadow: each tiny particle of spray needed to cast a shadow behind itself to make it stand out. Without this shadow the many particles in a plume of spray would look like one homogenous blob. As the airborne particles fell back down they intersected with the main body of water, remaining visible under the surface for a while to help produce a foamy, churning look.

The main body of water was rendered using subsurface scattering – a technique commonly used for skin (<204). 'The light would go down into the water and interact with things like the submerged foam texture maps and the sinking spray particles before coming back out of the water in a number of directions with a really naturalistic quality', says Hourihan.

The various water elements were composited with the photorealistic New York model that even included dozens of tiny vehicles being swept along in front of the wave. The result was some of the most awesomely apocalyptic images of natural phenomena yet created for the movies.

ABOVE: **Along with water, simulating realistic fur has been one of the greatest challenges for digital artists. This early CG monkey was created by ILM for** *Jumanji* **(1995).**

FUR AND FEATHERS

Along with water, the creation of lifelike hair and fur became a technical and creative holy grail from the earliest days of computer animation. The first sophisticated digital characters could only have smooth or solid outer surfaces, such as the metallic T-1000 character in *Terminator 2: Judgment Day* (1991), or the dinosaurs of *Jurassic Park* (1993). Creatures with a furry exterior, such as the computer-generated penguins in *Batman Returns* (1992), only looked effective in long shots – their appearance being the result of shaders (<167) that made light hitting them look as if it was bouncing off a furry surface.

With improvements in processor power and advances in modelling, animation and rendering, techniques progressed from producing the illusion of a hairy surface to the actual modelling of individual hairs themselves. An early landmark in computer-generated fur was *Jumanji* (1995), for which ILM created a digital menagerie with varying degrees of success. More recently, films such as *Harry Potter and the Prisoner of Azkaban* (2004) and *The Lion, the Witch and the Wardrobe* (2005) have proved that, though still a daunting challenge, the creation of convincing photorealistic hair, fur and even feathers is no longer an obstacle.

'Computer-generated fur has traditionally been one of the hardest things to create for two main reasons', explains Ben Morris, CG supervisor at London's Framestore CFC, where stunningly realistic digital squirrels were created for *Charlie and the Chocolate Factory* (2005). 'Fur has many natural qualities that make it complicated to replicate digitally', expounds Morris. 'The way it responds to light – reflecting, absorbing and shadowing itself, its colour, condition and distribution and the way it reacts dynamically to the movement of the creature – these are all aesthetic challenges that must be addressed to produce a

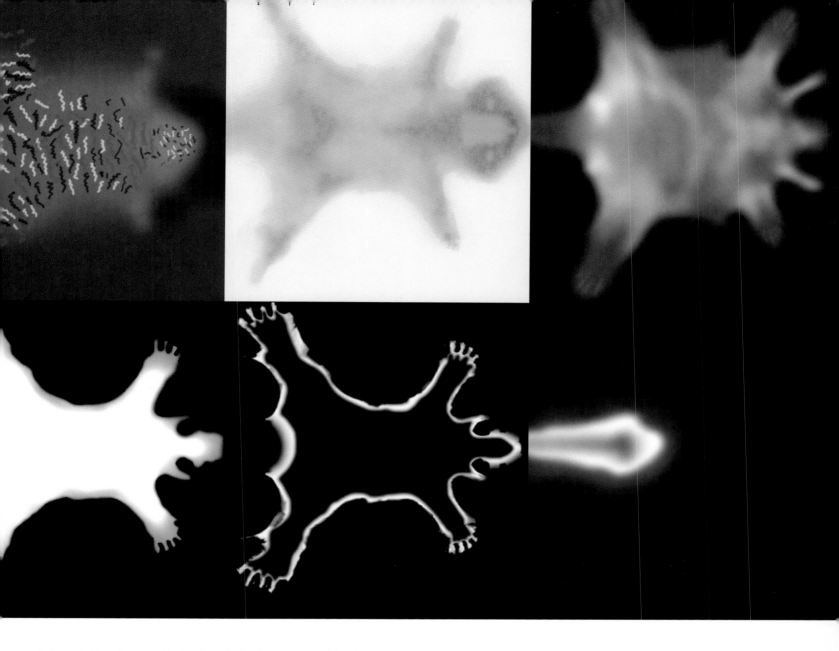

realistic result. The other complicating factor is the sheer amount of data involved. A single creature may have many millions of hairs, which traditionally created extremely large files and long render times.'

For *Charlie and the Chocolate Factory*, two dozen real squirrels were painstakingly trained for a scene in which they sort nuts before attacking one of Willy Wonka's young guests. Many tasks were too complex to achieve with live squirrels, however, so computer-generated rodents had to be used for over 60 shots. '*Charlie* was an immense challenge because our CG squirrels had to perform in parallel with real creatures – often very close to the camera and frequently cutting back and forth between live and CG squirrels,' states Morris. 'This meant our squirrels had to be absolutely indistinguishable from the genuine thing. From the start we knew that the success of our squirrels was going to depend on getting their fur to look right. We also had to find a way to do it efficiently. With almost 100 CG squirrels in some shots the amount of data would quickly become unmanageable without a highly optimized production pipeline.'

Morris and a team of 20 modellers, animators, technical directors and compositors spent eight months studying real squirrels and devising the systems and tools needed to create their CG doubles. Digital squirrel models were built using standard modelling techniques to create their skeleton, musculature and outer skin. 'Our squirrels were physically identical to the real thing except for some slight modifications to their paws,' says Morris. 'In nature a squirrel's hands are designed for holding nuts and climbing trees – but ours also had to be capable of roughing up small girls!'

With the basic body complete, attention turned to the all-important coat of fur. 'When you stare at squirrels all day you quickly realize that they look as different from one another as humans do,' says Morris. 'Many of these differences are due to their fur, which can have various patterns and colours, be fluffy or oily, flat or spiky, clumpy or very fine. These differences can be due to a squirrel's age, sex,

ABOVE: **To create the distinct appearance of genuine squirrel fur for** *Charlie and the Chocolate Factory* **(2005), texture and colour maps like these were applied.**

Top row:
(*left*) alterations to the angle of hairs
(*centre*) basic colour
(*right*) overall fur length

Bottom row:
(*left*) distribution of guard hairs
(*centre*) distribution of hair curl
(*right*) tail-fur length

condition or even mood. At first we thought we would just be making one generic squirrel but in the end we created 26 variations – each of which we named after musicians that they ressembled. David [Lee Roth] was a squirrel with a bit of an 80s hairdo, Iggy [Pop] was really scrawny with a bit of mange and Herbie [Hancock] was darker with heavier, clumpy fur.'

Morris and his team established that their squirrels would need seven different types of fur for the various areas of their body. Each squirrel had back fur, face fur, hand fur, belly fur, tail fur, underfur, and guard furs as well as whiskers and eyelashes. Each of these varied in length, thickness and colour and had to be distributed and intermingled in the correct way to look convincing.

To create its covering of fur the outer skin of the squirrel model was unwrapped to produce a flat template showing where the creature's legs, eyes, ears and other features were located. 'Painting on copies of the unwrapped skin we created a series of maps (<164) that would describe the various quantities and qualities of fur on different parts of the squirrels' bodies,' explains Morris. 'The maps were usually created in greyscale – the lighter the map the thicker or longer the fur in that area, for example. Separate maps defined the direction that the fur pointed, or places where it might be more clumpy. Other maps identified the seams around the animal's joints where extreme movements caused the hair to form a parting right down to the skin below. There was also a basic colour map that described what the squirrel's skin looked like at the base of the fur. In the end each squirrel had around 70 separate maps to control the look of the fur all over its body.' Additional maps also ran the length of each strand of hair. 'Squirrel hairs change colour several times between their base and tip,' says Morris. 'The most obvious example is the tail hairs. If you look at a squirrel's tail end-on you will see many concentric circles of colour changing from whites and creams to blacks, greys and browns.'

The fur itself was made up of thousands of simple geometric primitives – each piece being several vertices connected to form a curve. These hairs had no breadth or other physical characteristics. 'Our squirrel hairs didn't have a circular cross-section like real hairs do,' says Morris, 'They were actually completely flat. Whatever angle the camera viewed the hairs from, they always appear round because the shaders used during the rendering process instructed light to bounce off them in a way that made them appear cylindrical.'

Each squirrel was populated with approximately five million hairs, a quantity chosen through visual experimentation rather than by counting the actual number of hairs on a real squirrel. As a model covered in so much fur would be impractical to work with, most hairs were only ever generated

LEFT: Computer-generated squirrels used for close-up shots in *Charlie and the Chocolate Factory* (2005) were covered with as many as 5 million hairs. As the squirrels moved away from the camera, their coats were automatically 'pruned' until they comprised as few as 250,000 hairs.

BELOW: A contingent of computer-generated squirrels checks the quality of Willy Wonka's nuts. For some shots such as this, CG squirrels were used in the foreground, while background squirrels were animatronic puppets.

when the final squirrel images were rendered. Before then each squirrel was covered with approximately 2,000 'guide' hairs. 'Most fur movement was driven by the way the underlying skin to which it was attached travelled over the body as the squirrel moved around,' explains Morris. 'Even so, we had to continually groom the hair to make sure it looked at its best. Each of the two thousand guide hairs was programmed to influence the thousands of as yet invisible hairs around it. After each shot of a squirrel had been animated we would render a few final frames to check how the full fur coat looked and then rearrange any unsatisfactory areas by physically tweaking the nearest guide hairs. This hair-dressing took an immense amount of time and patience.'

Essential to the look of the final squirrel fur was the way it was lit. 'Any photographer will tell you that hair and fur is tricky to light,' says Morris. 'A common trick for making fur look good is to add a bit of backlighting to create a rim-lit feel which nicely shows off any detail and texture in the individual hairs.' Unfortunately the scene in which the squirrels were to appear took place in a large room with uniformly diffuse lighting. 'It was about the hardest environment in which to make the squirrels look good. Normally we replicate environmental conditions exactly, but in this case we often had to cheat the lighting of our models slightly to make them look their best.'

Another method used to create subtle lighting effects on the squirrels' fur was a pre-rendering process called 'ambient occlusion'. 'Getting accurate ray-traced [238>] shadows on the squirrels' fur during the final rendering process would have been an extraordinarily time-consuming process given the vast number of hairs contained in each image,' states Morris. 'Instead we rendered a pass for each shot in which the squirrels had no fur at all. During this render every point on the body of the animal sent out many rays in every direction in order to detect whether there were any other objects in the vicinity. Depending on how many of these rays hit another surface and how near that surface was, that area of the squirrel's body was given the appropriate amount of shadow darkening. The result was a scene in which the parts of the squirrel that were "occluded" – such as the self-shadowing areas inside the ears, mouth or armpits, for example – were grey or black while everywhere else was white. The ambient occlusion pass contained no detail other than these occlusion shadows. During the final render and compositing process this shadow information was applied to the squirrel's fur to produce very naturalistic, soft and subtle shadowing. It's a technique we use for all our animated characters and environments.'

With the appearance of the squirrel fur perfected it only remained to ensure that the production pipeline was as efficient as possible. 'The fact is that with enough time, technology and creative talent, any visual effect is now possible using computers,' remarks Morris. 'The real trick is making the process efficient.' One of the ways Framestore CFC made their squirrels faster to handle was to regulate the amount of fur on each squirrel according to its proximity to the camera. 'There's no point having five million time-consuming hairs on a squirrel when it's way off in the distance,' says Morris. 'For this reason we designed a system that regulated the number of hairs [level of detail, or LOD] on a squirrel depending on how near or far it was from the camera. A squirrel up close would have all five million hairs but as it ran away hairs would automatically disappear from its body. Meanwhile the remaining hairs would grow much thicker to fill in the gaps. At their furthest distance squirrels would have fewer than 100,000 hairs, but they were so thick that seen in detail they looked more like porcupines!' Another time-saving trick involved identifying which hairs were out of sight of the camera and then instructing the computer not to generate that fur data while rendering the image. 'If you could sneak a look at the other side of our squirrels while they are performing on screen you would see that the areas pointing away from the camera are completely bald!' reveals Morris.

Squirrel shots were finally rendered in up to 20 passes to provide compositors with the ability to alter their look almost infinitely as they placed them into scenes with actors and real squirrels.

PRE-VISUALIZATION

The complexity and expense of modern movie production means that directors now spend increasing amounts of time carefully planning their shots in advance of any filming.

Traditionally, storyboards have been a popular way of planning how a movie will look. Working closely with the director, artists produce drawings that illustrate the composition, action and camera movement of every shot in a sequence. Storyboard artwork can even be shot on video and then edited together with music and dialogue to create a more accurate sense of a scene's intended pace and movement. However, these moving storyboards, called 'animatics', are now being superseded by detailed sequences of 3-D animation that are created entirely within the computer. This process is called 'pre-visualization', or 'pre-viz'.

'Pre-viz is the ultimate planning tool for directors who are making complicated movies with a lot of action or effects,' states Colin Green, president of Pixel Liberation Front (PLF), which has created pre-viz sequences for movies such as *Minority Report* (2002), *The Matrix Reloaded* (2003), and *I, Robot* (2004). 'We start by creating correctly scaled digital models of everything that will be in a scene, such as props, scenery and vehicles,' explains Green. 'We also produce animated characters that resemble the actors in the movie. For *Superman Returns* [2006] we even had a Superman character with a fluttering cape. Once we have all our elements we then work with the director to produce animated sequences based on storyboards that have already been approved.'

Traditional storyboards are designed to capture the movement and action of a shot in one or two dynamic drawings but they are rarely truly representative of the way a scene will look once filmed. 'With pre-viz directors can see exactly what they are hoping to get in the final version of the movie,' states Green. 'For a start, the actors, props and camera will be moving, which makes a tremendous difference. Then there is the ability to constantly try new ideas; if the director doesn't like the way things look we can quickly try something else. We could move the actors in a different way, try another camera angle or lens, or perhaps a different camera move. Or we can see if the scene will work better if it is edited differently. Most pre-viz is done before shooting begins but we can also be on set during filming to quickly test new ideas before the real cameras and lighting equipment are set up for a new shot.'

Pre-viz tends to be used for the more action-oriented scenes in a movie and is used to solve technical problems, help plan complex stunts, and aid the design and conceptualization of visual effects.

'With a sequence like the freeway chase in *Matrix Reloaded* we were able to streamline the whole of the production process from a technical standpoint,' claims Green. 'For example, we could work out the best angle to shoot the action from and what lens to use for maximum impact. We could determine in advance how fast action vehicles needed to travel and how the stunts should be performed. We could also help work out what could be done as real stunts and what would have to be done as visual effects.'

One of the greatest advantages is in the planning of visual effects sequences. 'It's often hard to imagine what visual effects will look like when completed, but with pre-viz everyone involved can see how a shot is intended to work,' says Green. 'When live-action performances have been shot against green screen we can quickly composite them into our pre-viz shots to see if they work, right there on the set. We can also extract data from our pre-viz sequences for use during the actual production of visual effects. The most useful of this information is perhaps camera movement data. Once we have produced a virtual camera move for a pre-viz shot, that data can be exported and used to program motion-control cameras being used to film live action or models. It can also be applied to the virtual camera used to film any additional CG elements.'

Pre-viz has a trickle-down effect on all departments involved in a film. Because a pre-visualized sequence is an accurate blueprint of everything in a scene, art directors can determine exactly how large they need to build their scenery, cinematographers can plan how much lighting equipment may be needed, and producers can even work out how many extras they will need to hire to populate a scene.

A completed pre-viz sequence is normally given to a movie's editor so they can cut it into their working edit of a film. As filming progresses, pre-viz shots will gradually be replaced with live-action footage and completed visual effects shots until the finished sequence is achieved.

a

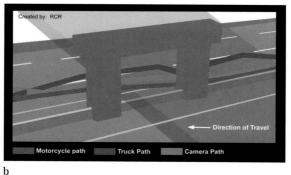

b

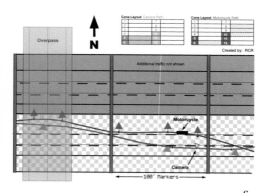

c

To plan complex action scenes, animated pre-viz graphics similar to these are created by Pixel Logic.

a: Original pre-viz animation using basic models to plot action and camera movement.
b: Layout of pre-viz animation as viewed from above and used to plan the movement of real vehicles and cameras during filming.
c: Exact plotting of all elements in a shot on a frame-by-frame basis, including additional detail such as compass directions to help plot direction of the sun.

DIGITAL LIGHTING

Just like shooting a movie in the real world, digital scenes must be properly lit before filming takes place. 'A model built in the computer exists within a totally dark environment', explains Craig Ring, visual effects supervisor at DreamWorks Animation, who has overseen lighting and effects in animated films including *Antz* (1998) and *Over the Hedge* (2006). 'During the animation process, a very flat type of light is used to view scenes in the computer. Without adding further specialized lights to the scene, it would be in total darkness when finally rendered. Every form of light and lighting effect you see in a CG scene is therefore designed and created by us.'

Much like cinematographers on real film sets, digital lighting designers have a full range of lighting tools at their disposal. The designer can choose from spotlights, which provide focused cones of light that cast shadows; radial lights, which cast light outwards in all directions like a real light bulb; ambient lights; non-directional diffuse lighting that illuminates a scene uniformly; and global lights, which cover the whole scene with parallel rays of light from a distant spot, much like the sun.

'As a visual aid the lights we use in our scenes are designed to look like real lights', explains Ring. 'We have little icons of fluorescent tube lights, and spotlights that even have movable barn doors on the front. It's just like having a miniature sound stage on the screen in front of you. These lights don't behave exactly like the real thing, but they are our nearest equivalent. When we want a light, we can pick up one of these icons and drag it to the place in the digital environment where we want to use it – just as a stage technician would pick up a light and place it where they want before plugging it in.' Digital lights themselves are invisible; only the light they produce can be seen, so they never have to be concealed behind props or scenery. Once a light has been positioned within the virtual environment, the lighting designer adjusts variables such as focus, fall-off, colour and so on.

The computer environment is very different from the real world in which light is automatically affected by how shiny a surface is or by how much dust is in the atmosphere. In particular, digital lights do not automatically produce any diffuse interreflectivity – the effect of light altering in quality as it bounces between objects – as Ring explains: 'In a real environment light hitting an object will automatically change colour and become more diffused when it is reflected off again. That reflected light will then hit other objects, where its colours and characteristics are changed even more. Digital lights don't automatically work like that, so we have to find ways to mimic nature.'

Until recently the only way to achieve such effects in a digital environment was to manually place lights that artificially reproduced a similar look. In the real world, for example, a white light pointing at a red brick wall results in a small amount of reflected soft red light illuminating other objects nearby. To fake this effect lighting designers will first place their white light pointing at the wall before placing a small red light within the wall to cast some 'reflected' light away from it. This can mean placing dozens of tiny lights in every scene in order to simulate the effect of natural light interactions.

It is now possible for physically accurate lighting interactions to be automatically calculated by the computer during rendering using a technique called 'global illumination' (237>). 'Global illumination mathematically calculates how light bounces around in a scene. We just have to place the main key lights and the bounced light is calculated and added by the computer. At DreamWorks we first used these techniques extensively for *Shrek 2* [2004] and it can look very naturalistic', says Ring. 'The problem is that the calculations can take a very long time during rendering, which is expensive.'

To save rendering time for shots using global illumination smaller objects in a scene can be 'switched off' so that they don't become part of the calculations. A shot of a room will have all the small objects used as set dressing switched off, so that only the large important objects like the furniture, walls and floor are included in the lighting calculations. 'The other thing we do is create proxy objects', comments Ring. 'If a character is standing on some grass by a tree we would want diffuse light to be reflected onto the

character from the green leaves of the tree above and the grass below. Calculating the way light bounces off thousands of leaves and blades of grass would be impractical so we can build a basic replacement tree that is just a green blob on a brown stick, and grass that is just a flat green surface. During rendering the light reflected off these and onto the character will be quick to calculate and we will have a character with natural-looking lighting on their skin. We then composite the shot of the character back into a shot of the trees and grass that has been rendered in the normal way.'

The ability of the computer to calculate realistic lighting effects means that digital lighting designers can spend less time trying to mimic nature and more time on the finer details of a shot. 'We can be much more like real-life cinematographers now that we don't have to spend so much time compensating for the inadequacies of the digital environment', says Ring. 'We can put more effort into using light to tell the story, to direct the viewer's eye, to make sure characters read well against the background.' Like cinematographers in the real world, digital lighting designers need to make the stars of the film look as good as possible. 'When lighting characters, there are certain small things that are important to get right', explains Ring. 'Real cinematographers are always careful to get a bright highlight in the actors' eyes – a little sparkle that helps to bring them to life. We do exactly the same thing, though luckily for us we can animate our lights to move along in front of a character and to light only the eyes, so the sparkle is always there.'

Being able to tell a light exactly which objects to illuminate is one of the great advantages of digital lighting. In the real world, cinematographers may spend hours arranging lights so that particular actors or areas of a set have just the right quality of illumination. In the digital world, a light can be told to light just one object and nothing else. Lights can even be given a negative value to take light away from objects that are overbright. 'The flexibility of digital lights is something that film and stage lighting people get really jealous of', exclaims Ring. 'Although we sometimes long to be able to place lights and automatically get all the lighting interactions that you do in the real world, the fact that we can animate the position of a light so that it follows a character around, or ask a light to illuminate the tip of a nose and nothing else, or drastically change the quality of the light at any time, is really very liberating.'

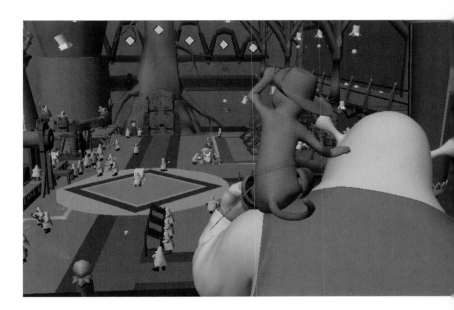

ABOVE: **In this scene from *Shrek 2* (2004), the main lights, displayed as yellow icons, are direct lights, such as spotlights and point lights. All bounced 'fill' lighting was created using global illumination, without which the number of lights needed for this scene would have been far greater.**

HIGH DYNAMIC RANGE IMAGES (HDRI)

Lighting entirely computer-generated scenes is a complex task, but lighting digital models that are to be placed within a real-world environment adds an additional level of complexity. Only when the lighting of digital models matches that of the filmed environment can the two elements be merged seamlessly.

Re-creating real-world lighting conditions in the computer is traditionally achieved by taking careful note of the intensity, position, and colour of the lights used during filming of the live-action plate. If a shot is filmed outdoors, the height and direction of the sun is also recorded. A highly reflective chrome sphere is often photographed in the environment, the reflection revealing the relative position of lights in the scene. A matte grey sphere may also be photographed to record the colour of the light. By studying these images the digital lighting artist will attempt to manually re-create the same lighting conditions within the computer.

For incredibly realistic results, the exact lighting of an environment can now be recorded photographically and used to directly generate the lighting used for a digital model. This technique is known as 'image-based lighting' and the photographs it uses are called high dynamic range images (HDRIs).

An HDRI is a high-quality panoramic photograph of the environment into which a computer-generated object is to be placed. Normal photographs are taken at an averaged exposure level to produce a balanced image. In these images most objects will be evenly exposed but areas of deep shadow will be completely black (underexposed) and contain no image information, while very bright areas will be white (overexposed) and will contain no image information. An HDRI image, however, is produced by photographing an environment several times, each time at a different exposure level. The result is a series of identical photographs that range from very overexposed to very underexposed. These images are then digitally combined to produce a single image containing a complete range of exposure detail, with information in both the brightest and darkest areas of the picture. This is an extremely accurate record of even the subtlest levels of light and colour within an environment.

Normal photographs only show a small section of an environment as seen from a single point of view. In order to accurately re-create the lighting in a scene, HDRI images must be able to show what the entire environment looks like. To create a complete image, HDRIs can be photographed with a 180° 'fish-eye' lens or by using a normal lens to photograph reflections from a 100 per cent reflective chrome ball. Either way, the result will be a number of photographs that collectively show a complete but distorted view of the environment. Using specialized software these images are unwarped and stitched together to create a single HDRI of the entire live-action environment. This image is called a 'light probe'.

The light probe image is then mapped onto the inside of a sphere that surrounds the digital model that needs to be lit (fig. 9). That sphere, with all of its information about the colour, position and intensity of light in a scene, then itself becomes one large light source that illuminates anything placed within it according to the HDRI information on its surface.

HDRI lighting is a complicated process but it produces reliably accurate lighting for any computer-generated object that needs to be placed into a live-action scene. It is particularly useful for highly reflective objects since they will reflect a realistic image of the surrounding scene, even though they were never actually present during filming.

FIGURE 9 **HIGH DYNAMIC RANGE IMAGES (HDRI)**

Once an HDRI has been obtained, the image is 'wrapped' around a scene and used to 'project' its environmental lighting information onto objects within that scene.

THE VIRTUAL CAMERA

FAR LEFT: **To create a High Dynamic Range Image (HDRI), a mirrored ball is photographed in the desired location. Several photographs will be taken at different exposures in order to capture the full range of light and shadow.**

LEFT: **The spherical photographs from the mirrored ball are unwrapped and used to produce an image which becomes the basis for the lighting of any CG objects placed in the environment.**

The 'virtual camera' is the device used to 'film' the world inside the computer. The digital domain does not, of course, actually exist as a physical location that can be photographed in any traditional sense. However, the virtual camera is used to describe the viewpoint that the computer will use during the final image-producing process of rendering (236>).

Live-action motion picture cameras are constrained by their physical size and weight as well as the manual methods used to adjust their aperture, focal length and focus. These constraints have created a series of visual storytelling conventions with which audiences are familiar and that they accept as the norm when they watch a movie.

The virtual camera suffers from none of the constraints of its real-world equivalent. The virtual camera does not actually exist as an object, so it has no size or weight – it can go anywhere, at any speed. Because it has no optical lenses and holds no film there is no need to worry about the amount of light in a scene or how that affects aperture, film speed, exposure or depth of field.

However, because audiences are so familiar with the look produced by the traditional movie camera, the virtual camera has had many of the characteristics of a real camera imposed upon it. 'The camera that we use to film our computer environments has been designed to replicate real cameras,' explains Damon O'Beirne, head of layout for *Over the Hedge* (2006) at DreamWorks Animation. 'We can give our camera any focal length lens and it will exactly replicate the look produced by that lens when used on a real camera. We can zoom, pan, tilt, dolly – all the moves that a normal camera can do. We can also do a lot of things that a normal camera can't do.'

Since the virtual camera has no constraints, it can be used to produce breathtaking rollercoaster rides through the artificial environment of the computer. 'That's fine in certain circumstances,' says O'Beirne, 'but we tend to use a more traditional style of cinematography that is more grounded in the real world. We

FIGURE 10 **THE VIRTUAL CAMERA**

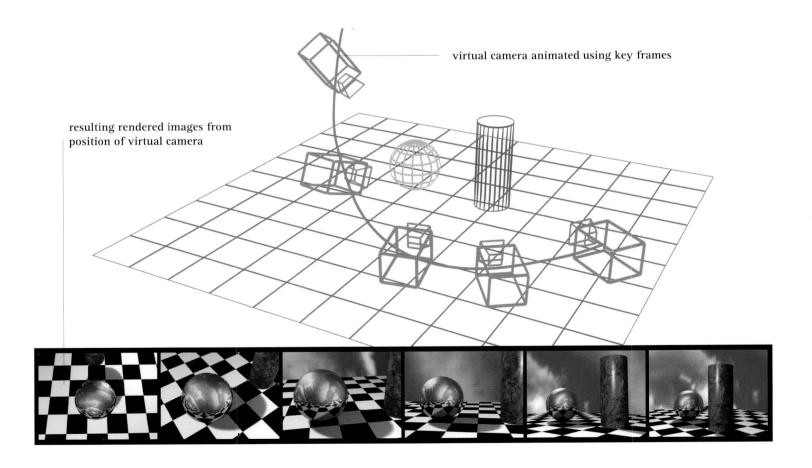

virtual camera animated using key frames

resulting rendered images from position of virtual camera

often watch movies shot on film and select a cinematic style that we will try to emulate. For *Over the Hedge* we used *Raising Arizona* [1987] as our main cinematic reference. It's important to impose a distinct style because instead of a single cinematographer as on a normal movie, we have half a dozen people creating the camera moves for a show. Each of these artists will have their own film-making influences – be it Steven Spielberg or John Woo – and they'll each end up making their own style of movie if there isn't a clear overall vision.'

To help replicate the look of real-world photography, O'Beirne likes to limit the toolset that his artists are able to use. 'In the real world cinematographers will have a limited range of lenses in their kit – a 35 mm, a 50 mm, and so on. But our virtual cameras can have any focal length lens we want. We can just dial in 33.062 mm and that's the lens we'll get. This can lead to an inconsistency of style so I'll put together a set of lens sizes that can be used in each film. If the artists are using a 24 mm lens and they want to go a little wider they can't just dial in another half-millimeter, they have to switch to the next lens down – say a 21 mm – just like a real cinematographer would.'

Virtual cinematographers also try to create camera moves that look as if they were produced by relying on any of the standard techniques used to move a camera on a real film set. These include the gentle glide of the steadicam shot, the sweeping arc of a crane shot, the uneven drift of the hand-held camera and the swift linear moves produced by a dolly track. It's not only the quality of the movement that is replicated in the digital world, as O'Beirne admits: 'We also sometimes build in small mistakes that you might expect to see in a live-action film. For example when a character walks and our camera pans to follow them, we might delay the start of the camera movement very slightly as if there were a real camera operator reacting momentarily after the movement of an actor. We might also put in a little camera shake when a camera moves, as if it's actually travelling along a dolly track.'

Layout artists don't always stick slavishly to the restrictions of real-world photography, however, and there are plenty of times that the virtual camera's abilities are used to positive advantage. 'In the real world cinematographers often struggle to get enough depth of field, especially when the light is fading,' says O'Beirne. 'We, on the other hand, can have a night-time scene with pin-sharp focus from the front to the back of a shot, if we wish. That's pretty handy.'

Virtual cameras are animated much like any other object within a computer-generated scene (fig. 10, <233). The digital artist begins by defining the size of the lens and the number of frames that the shot in question will last. The camera is then placed within the 3-D environment. When the artist is happy with the view from the camera's start position, he or she will set the first key frame. The artist then moves the camera to its second position and, if using a zoom lens, may adjust the focal length. In the real world the camera operator must concentrate on moving the camera to follow the important action within a scene. In the world of the computer, the camera can use 'target tracking' to keep the subject automatically in the centre of the frame, however extreme the movement of the camera is. The precision of target tracking tends to produce artificially perfect shots, but the method can be used as a starting point when animating a sequence.

The digital artist builds up the movement of the camera one key frame at a time, continually running the camera backwards and forwards, studying its motion and making refinements where necessary until a satisfactory shot has been achieved and the shot is ready to be rendered.

While the virtual camera and its cinematographer are capable of replicating any shot that can be captured with a traditional camera, some directors find it frustrating that they do not have a camera that they can physically handle during photography. This lack of interaction between camera and operator has driven some traditional film-makers to seek alternative ways to create their virtual camera moves. For *The Lord of the Rings: The Fellowship of the Ring* (2001) director Peter Jackson wanted to re-create the dramatic look and feel of a hand-held camera in a computer-generated scene involving a rampaging cave troll. The scene was first pre-visualized (<230) using motion-captured performances for the troll and the characters that he was attacking. In a motion-capture studio, Jackson was then able to view the animated fight scene using virtual reality goggles. A hand-held camera was created out of a wooden block on a pole. This was fitted with motion-capture markers so that as Jackson moved the camera around the set his motion was relayed to the computer and he was able to view what it was 'filming' through his goggles. In this way Jackson was able to follow the pre-planned fight, spinning around to see interesting action and leaping out of the way when the troll came in his direction. The resulting camera movements were edited and refined before being used to film the final CG environments and characters. The result was a thrilling action sequence that has the frenetic immediacy of combat-zone news coverage.

Another method of creating real-world camera moves was developed by Sony Pictures Imageworks for the shooting of its animated film *The Polar Express* (2004). When animated character performances had been edited to create final scenes they were 'filmed' using live camera moves created by cinematographer Rob Presley. Presley used a device that was built to resemble the mechanism used to control the movement of a real camera. By manually turning a set of wheels as he watched the animated action he could pan and tilt the virtual camera to shoot the film like a live-action movie.

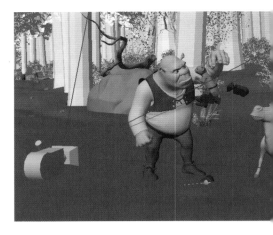

ABOVE: **In this scene from** *Shrek 2*, **the virtual camera is displayed as a yellow icon on the left. The digital cinematographer programs the camera to follow the pre-animated character movement. The grey lines emerging from the camera indicate the area of the scene that will be visible on screen.**

FAR RIGHT: **For this complex scene from** *Starship Troopers 2* **(2004) created by Tippett Studio, both the environment and the movement of the camera needed to be carefully tracked so that additional CG elements could be added.**

a: The live-action background plate of soldiers is filmed inside a studio.
b: The environment is modelled in the computer, matching the live-action set exactly. The scene is then replayed one frame at a time, adjusting the virtual camera so that it matches the movement of the real camera.
c: The CG environment with its matched camera move is used to produce animation effects, in this case hundreds of animated alien insects.
d: The CG creatures are tested against the live-action environment. Their exploding bodies appear to interact with the match-moved concrete barricades.
e: The animated aliens and explosions are rendered.
f: The rendered elements are composited with the live action to produce the final shot.

MATCH MOVING

Designing camera movements for completely computer-generated scenes gives digital artists all the freedom that real-world camera operators have to move a camera and produce the best compositions. However, many digital effects are eventually composited into footage of real-world environments that have already been filmed with a moving camera: animated dinosaurs are seen crashing through real forests, digital ships land their simulated armies on actual beaches, and computer-generated vehicles race along genuine roads. In such cases the movements of the virtual camera used to film the computer-generated elements must precisely match those of the camera used to film the live-action environment. The resulting images, created at different times and using differing technologies, will have identical camera movements, allowing them to be layered together seamlessly during compositing.

To replicate the movement of the real-world camera in the computer, a process known as '3-D camera match moving' is used. During photography of the live-action plate, special effects supervisors take accurate measurements of the position of each significant object in a scene, including specially placed markers. The starting position of the camera is also measured and details of its lens type are noted. These measurements are sometimes recorded using the highly accurate laser measuring equipment that is used by cartographers and architects. The information collected on location is used to construct a basic yet precise 3-D model of the real location within the computer. This digital reconstruction of the real environment is essential because any CG objects that will eventually need to appear to interact with the real world, for instance digital vehicles, must be animated to move over an accurate representation of the real ground plane and avoid, or possibly interact with, any of the scene's real objects.

To create a camera match-move, the footage of the live-action background plate is viewed on a monitor. The digital model of the environment is then superimposed over the background plate, and the virtual camera is manoeuvred until its view of the model is perfectly aligned with the viewpoint of the camera used to film the live action. When the first frame of the live-action plate and the digital environment are perfectly aligned, the operator moves through the shot a few frames at a time, altering the position of the virtual camera so that its perspective remains identical to that of the live-action camera. By working through the whole shot in this way, the virtual camera is programmed to produce a perfect copy of the location camera's movements.

Another method of match moving does not involve creating a model of the real environment but instead relies on identifying and tagging a series of fixed points within the live-action plate. These points might be anything that is small yet detailed or of high enough contrast to be identified in each subsequent frame, such as the corner of buildings or possibly specially placed tracking markers. With a number of points identified, sophisticated match-moving software will advance through the sequence, frame by frame, detecting the changing position and relationship of each identified marker point and extrapolating accurate camera motion data. Once the live-action camera motion data has been gathered it can be applied to the virtual camera used to 'film' the necessary computer-generated elements. The data can also be exported to motion-control cameras for the shooting of additional live-action footage or visual effects elements such as miniatures. As a result of using the same camera movement to film every element in a shot, the layers will sit perfectly on top of one another in the final composite.

Another important form of tracking involves recording not simply the movement of the camera used to film a scene, but also the movement of the actual objects within a scene. With the motion of real objects tracked they can be modified digitally. An example might be to track the movement of a real pick-up truck filmed as it drives through a shot so that a computer-generated farm dog can later be placed riding in the back. To track the motion of a real object a digital model is first made with the same basic shape and scale. This 'proxy' object is then displayed on a monitor with the live-action footage displayed behind it. The digital artist then adjusts the position of the proxy model, in our example the pick-up truck, until its perspective perfectly matches that of the real truck and the two are aligned, one on top of the other. The shot is then advanced one frame at a time and the position of the model truck is changed incrementally so that it keeps pace with the real-world version. The result in our example will be a model pick-up truck that drives in exactly the same way as the real vehicle did during filming. Our computer-generated farm dog can then be animated standing on the back of the digital truck. The shot can then be rendered without the digital truck and the resulting shot of the dog gliding along on thin air can be composited together with the live-action vehicle footage, the two matching perfectly. Interesting examples of this technique have been the replacement of the actor Ralph Fiennes's nose with a digital nose in *Harry Potter and the Goblet of Fire* (2005) and adding a digital blade to a bladeless sword handle wielded by Tom Cruise when filming fight scenes for *The Last Samurai* (2003).

It is difficult to overestimate the importance of match moving to modern special effects production. The ability to synchronize the performance of virtual and real-world cameras and to layer moving digital objects onto real ones is the key to the invisible integration of live action and digital effects. Film-makers are becoming increasingly reliant on the computer to provide not only the expected animated monsters and spaceships, but also set details such as period buildings, trees and replica historical vehicles.

a

b

c

d

e

f

RENDERING

The last process in the production of computer-generated imagery is 'rendering'. Rendering is a highly complex mathematical operation that conjures a completed, high-quality, 2-D image from the mass of instructional data that is generated during the digital production process. It is one of the most important, and probably least understood, parts of the visual effects pipeline.

When a shot has been finished by an artist, it is launched into a render. During this process, the computer studies every piece of information that it has been given about a scene. As it processes this data, the final image is constructed one pixel at a time. Examining a tiny part of the scene, the computer calculates the geometry of the object that the virtual camera is looking at; what animation, texture maps and shaders have been assigned to that object; and the quality and quantity of lights that surround it. Some objects within a scene will only be generated during the rendering process. For example, a character covered in fur will have only a few guide hairs (<228) placed on it during modelling. The renderer will use the information provided by these guide hairs to calculate the position of the thousands of surrounding hairs. These will then be generated as pieces of geometry that will be included in the calculation of a final 2-D image. When every influence has been considered and calculated, the computer produces a number that represents a colour. The colour is assigned to one pixel, which is then placed in a grid. The computer then begins to calculate the colour for the next pixel along. After the process has been repeated several million times, the result is a single computer-generated image which might be recorded directly onto film or composited with other elements to produce a final image.

Rendering is the most time-consuming and processor-intensive task in the production of digital images. Most large special effects facilities have powerful render 'farms' with hundreds, sometimes thousands, of processors dedicated to rendering. At ILM the server room houses over 3,500 AMD processors that work all day to create the company's groundbreaking images. At night the processors in the artists' desktop workstations also become part of the system, resulting in one of the world's most powerful computing networks with over 5,000 processors.

Rendering is often the deciding factor in the quality of the visual effects that appear in a film. Using modern modelling and animation software, digital artists have the potential to create almost any conceivable image. However, it is the time that such images may take to render that often affects how much can be achieved on the budget of a feature film. The amount of information contained in a scene directly affects the time that it takes to render, and much effort is put into finding ways to make shots more efficient to render. One frame of complex computer animation might typically take four hours to render, though some can take many more. With 120 frames in a five-second sequence, such a shot would take one processor 480 hours – 20 days – to render. Using many processors, however, the shot could be completed overnight. Although the power of processors increases yearly, the growing complexity of the scenes that they are expected to handle means that render times are not much faster now than they were a decade ago.

The final version of a shot is usually rendered in several different layers or 'passes'. Each of these will render a different aspect of the scene, such as the specular, diffuse, or ambient lighting (<166), ambient occlusion (<228), Z-depth information (<103), and mattes. The result will be a number of elements that can be composited together to produce the final image at a later stage. By breaking a shot into its constituent parts, far greater versatility is possible during compositing.

Many types of rendering software are available on the market and visual effects facilities tend to employ several types, depending upon the specific requirements of their work. By far the most popular is Pixar's RenderMan. RenderMan was one of the first effective pieces of rendering software and was developed at Lucasfilm in the mid-80s by Dr Edwin Catmull, now the executive vice-president of Pixar. It was this software that allowed breakthroughs in computer-generated imagery for films such as *The Abyss* (1989) and *Jurassic Park* (1993) and which continues to be used for much of the most spectacular feature film work.

RENDERING LIGHT

An important part of the rendering process is calculating the way that any lights placed in a scene will affect the final image. The way that light is absorbed, reflected or refracted within a CG scene can have considerable impact on the appearance and ultimate realism of a shot.

At a basic level, lighting calculations are achieved by combining information about the quality and angle of lights pointing into a scene with information about objects in the scene as defined by their geometric attributes and the texture maps and shaders that are assigned to them.

Until relatively recently the realism of lighting in a scene was largely a result of the way that the virtual lights were set up by the lighting designer. This was because the computer had no efficient, physically accurate way of calculating the properties of light in a digital scene, meaning designers had to 'fake' the way that light works in the real world (<231). A great deal of academic

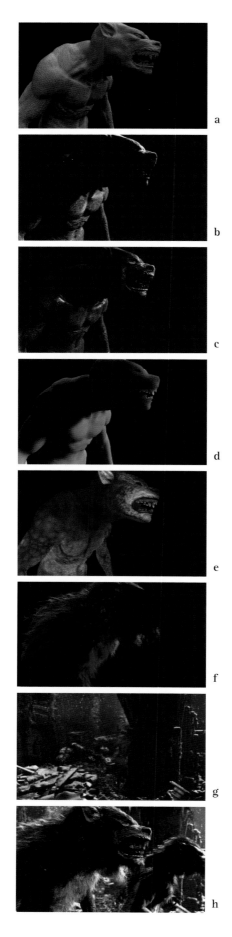

a

b

c

d

e

f

g

h

LEFT: Many elements are typically rendered for each CG object in a shot. Here are some of those rendered by Luma Pictures to produce a shot of a werewolf for *Underworld: Evolution* (2006).

a: ambient light pass
b: diffuse light pass
c: specular light pass
d: subsurface-scattering pass
e: colour pass
f: fur pass
g: original live action
h: final composite

research has gone into finding ways of accurately re-creating the physical behaviour of real light within computer-generated environments. The aim of such techniques is to produce natural-looking lighting by simulating the way that all light sources and object surfaces within an environment interact with one another. This is achieved by accounting for all possible combinations of diffuse and specular reflections and transmissions. Such techniques are grouped under the umbrella term 'global illumination'.

Using global illumination methods a CG environment can, in theory, be illuminated using only a few lights to represent the sources of direct illumination that would naturally occur in that scene. The light from these direct sources then bounces around in the environment to create the diffuse (soft) interreflected illumination that most objects in the real world are lit by. An outdoor scene should therefore only need to be lit by the sky, while an indoor scene should only need lights placed in the windows and at any internal sources of illumination – such as ceiling lamps. By rendering such environments using global illumination algorithms, the light from each source bounces around the scene in accordance with the laws of physics (or at least models of those laws) to produce very realistic lighting. In reality this natural-looking light is rarely sufficient for the purposes of film-making and, just like cinematographers filming outside on a sunny day, the lighting designer will usually place additional artificial lights in order to achieve the dramatic look they require.

Global illumination is a very general term for a number of techniques that aim to create natural-looking lighting by applying the physics of light to the rendering process. Different visual effects companies and rendering packages use a combination of these approaches in order to achieve what they consider to be global illumination.

RAY TRACING

One method of producing realistic-looking images that include accurate reflections is to use a rendering method called 'ray tracing'. To determine the colour of a pixel, a ray is traced from the virtual camera to the spot in the scene that is being studied (fig. 11, 238>). According to the quality of the surface that the ray hits, as described by an object's geometry and the texture maps and shaders that have been assigned to it, the ray will either be absorbed, reflected, or, in the case of translucent materials, refracted.

Any light that is reflected will continue its journey bouncing through the scene until it is either absorbed, exits the scene, or reaches a light source. When the ray has finished its journey, the colour of the single pixel that it represents is adjusted according to how the light has been affected during the ray's journey. This process has to be repeated for each of the millions of pixels in a frame of computer animation and is view-dependent, meaning that the lighting calculations need to be recomputed as soon as the camera moves. Ray tracing is actually the reverse of what happens in

ABOVE: **Global illumination techniques now make the creation of natural-looking CG environments possible, as this New York street scene from *King Kong* (2005) illustrates. While the foreground buildings, road, traffic and pedestrians were filmed outside, most of the buildings and distant detail are computer-generated.**

BELOW: **The machine room at The Motion Picture Company is an atmosphere-controlled environment where hundreds of processors work to create spectacular visual effects. The massive banks of servers, processors and hard disk arrays make this feel more like the control room of NASA than a place where movies are made.**

FIGURE 11 **RAY TRACING**

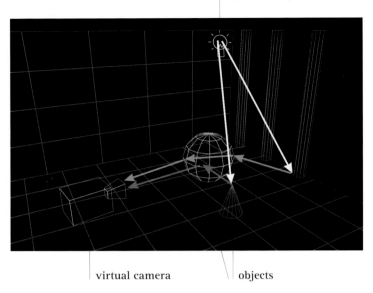

light source

virtual camera   objects

rendered ray-traced image from position of virtual camera

surface. When a tile first looks into a scene everything will be dark except for any sources of direct illumination (lights). The tile will therefore shade itself according to the information coming only from those lights. However, once every tile in a scene has made its initial response to the direct light that they can see, the whole scene will immediately look very different. Now there will be two types of available illumination in the scene: the original direct light sources and the thousands of lit tiles which are themselves now indirect light sources. The lighting calculation is therefore repeated, each tile taking into account the colour and intensity of both the direct illumination (the lights) and indirect illumination (the other tiles) in the scene. This is a recursive process and after each repeated calculation, or pass, the lighting in a scene will become more subtle and realistic. After a number of passes (perhaps several dozen) the changes become increasingly fine and so the process is stopped.

Unlike ray tracing, radiosity calculations are independent of viewer position, so providing that none of the lights or objects within an environment moves, only one, very demanding, calculation is necessary per scene. Once a radiosity calculation is complete the resulting lighting effects are 'baked' into the surfaces in a scene. Wherever that environment is used in a film the same radiosity calculations can be used to light the surfaces during rendering.

Calculating radiosity is an extremely intensive process and is impractical for use in every situation. It is often used for the production of digital matte paintings and environment models (260>).

FIGURE 12 **RADIOSITY**

After dividing a scene into coloured tiles, several cycles of radiosity are rendered, each creating a more refined and realistic image.

basic render using direct illumination

tiles applied to surfaces

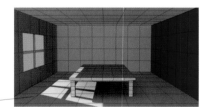

first-pass radiosity render

second-pass radiosity render

the real world where photons are emitted by a light source and travel through a scene until they reach our eye.

Ray tracing is particularly useful for calculating reflections and shiny surfaces. The technique does not, however, calculate the diffuse interreflection of light between various surfaces and it produces very sharp shadows that tend to look unrealistic in natural environments.

RADIOSITY
Radiosity was one of the first algorithms developed to compute both direct and indirect illumination.

Radiosity works by dividing the surfaces in a scene into thousands of tiny patches or tiles (fig. 12). Each of these tiles, which start life unilluminated and therefore black, looks out into the scene and gathers information about any light source that it can see. It then calculates a colour and brightness for its

FIGURE 13 **CAUSTICS**

Vital to the realism of scenes containing water and glass, caustic rendering simulates the way that light is refracted and focused by transparent materials.

PHOTON MAPPING

Photon mapping offers another method of calculating the diffuse interreflection of light between surfaces in a computer-generated environment. Using this technique millions of photons (particles of light energy) are fired in random directions from all the lights in a scene. Each photon has a known amount of energy and moves through the scene until it hits an object. The geometry and shaders of that object determine how much of the photon's energy is absorbed, refracted or reflected. They will also determine the angle in which any reflected energy is redirected. The photons continue bouncing from surface to surface within the scene until all their energy is absorbed.

As the photons bounce around in a scene a record of their behaviour is stored as a 'photon map'. This map details the points at which photons hit a surface, their incoming angle and their energy upon arrival.

Photon mapping is a preprocess that is calculated before the main rendering of an image. Once a map has been calculated in a 'first pass' it is stored and then referenced during a later 'second pass' rendering of each frame. The second pass rendering calculates the direct lighting in a scene using standard ray tracing (<237). The indirect light is also calculated using ray tracing but when a ray hits the surface of an object it references the photon map to discover the intensity of light at that point.

As well as producing very natural interreflected diffuse lighting in a scene, photon mapping is very good at calculating a particular lighting phenomenon called 'caustics' (fig. 13). Caustics are formed by light that is reflected or transmitted by a number of specular surfaces before hitting a diffuse surface. Examples of caustics with which we are all familiar are the shimmering patterns of light on the bottom of a swimming pool and the way that light can be focused through a magnifying glass.

Other important lighting effects include subsurface scattering, used to simulate the realistic appearance of translucent skin (<204), and volume rendering, which uses methods similar to ray tracing to calculate the appearance of the large numbers of particles used to form smoke, fire or clouds.

OTHER RENDERING TASKS

In addition to lighting effects, many of the most subtle yet important visual qualities of a scene are generated during the rendering process. These qualities can make the difference between mediocre-looking graphics and successful photorealistic images.

Motion Blur

All fast-moving real-life objects filmed with a movie camera feature motion blur, a streaky effect that results from the subject's movement during exposure. Since computer models do not actually move while they are being photographed (or rather rendered), fast-moving objects can have natural-looking motion blur added to them during the rendering process. The computer, knowing an object's position in previous key frames and in-between frames, is able to calculate how much blur should emanate from an object according to the speed at which it is travelling.

Anti-Aliasing

Anti-aliasing helps to make the 'rough edges' of computer-generated objects look more smooth and natural. A digital image is made up of many thousands of discrete square pixels, each of which can only represent a single colour. In some situations, the picture definition created by these tiny pixels is not good enough to make the edges of an object look naturally smooth, resulting in jagged edges. During rendering, the computer can study the edges of objects and set the characteristics of pixels on boundary edges to be a mixture of the background and foreground qualities, resulting in much smoother edges (fig. 14).

When a shot has been rendered, its frames are assembled in the correct order and the sequence is either viewed on a monitor or transferred to videotape. Once the work has been approved by the film's effects supervisor and director, it is combined with other elements during compositing or recorded onto celluloid film, or to a digital storage device, ready to be edited into the final version of the movie.

FIGURE 14 **ANTI-ALIASING**

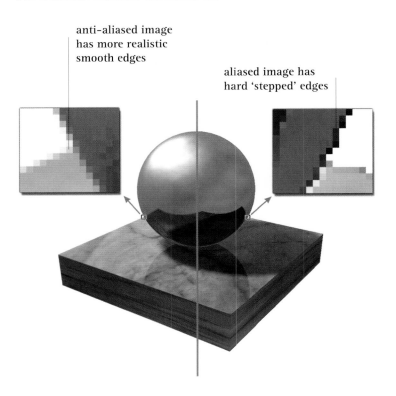

anti-aliased image has more realistic smooth edges

aliased image has hard 'stepped' edges

STAR WARS: EPISODE I *THE PHANTOM MENACE*

Star Wars (1977) and its two sequels, *The Empire Strikes Back* (1980) and *Return of the Jedi* (1983), were among the most innovative and important special effects films ever made. Fans who knew these movies were intended as the middle chapters of a planned nine-part saga waited patiently for more sequels. But for 15 years George Lucas (<39) insisted that effects technology was not yet capable of creating the new worlds he had in mind.

When ILM created dazzling computer-generated dinosaurs for *Jurassic Park* (1993), Lucas realized that technology had finally caught up with his imagination, and he began work on the very first chapter of the story: *Stars Wars: Episode I The Phantom Menace* (1999). In terms of scale and ambition, this was to be the greatest visual effects film yet made. Of the 2,000 shots in the film, some 1,900 would be digitally generated or enhanced (a major effects film might normally contain 200 effects shots).

Where previous *Star Wars* films had always been heavily populated by a mixture of lovable and loathsome creatures – usually produced using make-up, animatronics or stop-motion – many of the stars of *The Phantom Menace* were entirely digital, walking, talking and interacting with all the freedom of human actors. The most complex digital character was the clumsy alien Jar Jar Binks. With a face capable of over 400 expressions, Jar Jar was the most emotive and expressive digital character yet created for a movie. Other notable digital characters included the hovering, trunk-nosed junk dealer, Watto, and the toad-like Gungan leader, Boss Nass. Sophisticated cloth-simulation software was developed to create the convincing costumes worn by these and other digital stars. Despite the film's awesome digital menagerie, many characters were still realized using more traditional techniques. These included Yoda, who, two decades after his screen debut, was still simply a hand puppet operated by ex-Muppet performer Frank Oz.

More than any film before, *The Phantom Menace* explored the potential of the 'digital backlot' (262>), filming actors and minimal sets against a blue screen and adding digital or miniature scenery during post-production. Locations such as the planet-city of Coruscant were created almost entirely within the computer and then composited with the live action. Other locations, such as the ornate city of Theed, were traditional models filmed with motion-control cameras and combined with digital extensions. Some methods used to bring locations to life were charmingly old-fashioned, however. The magnificent waterfalls that surround Theed were created by filming dry table salt as it was poured over black velvet – a traditional effects trick.

Star Wars films have always relied on miniatures and models and *The Phantom Menace* was no exception. The film was one of ILM's biggest miniature assignments ever, with hundreds of spacecraft and locations being constructed under the watchful eyes of model supervisor Steve Gawley and chief model-maker Lorne Peterson (<153). While many flying spaceships were digitally animated, those that needed to be destroyed were still blown up using miniature pyrotechnics and filmed at high speed with motion-control cameras.

Some of the film's most interesting effects were invisible. During editing, Lucas was able to radically alter images and even create entirely new ones with remarkable freedom. Many original scenes were digitally manipulated, allowing shots to be assembled from several different takes, choosing each actor's best performance. Some dialogue was rewritten after filming, so actors' mouths were filmed speaking new lines and composited over original footage. Entirely new scenes were created by selecting and manipulating images of performers taken from various scenes and combining them with new backgrounds.

With *The Phantom Menace* and its even more spectacular sequels, *Attack of the Clones* (2002) and *Revenge of the Sith* (2005), George Lucas achieved what he had always dreamt of – total creative freedom without any of the physical and optical constraints that have hampered film-makers for over a century. These were perhaps a glimpse of the way that all films will be made in cinema's second century.

5

MATTE PAINTINGS

INTRODUCTION

When scripts call for distant planets or primeval vistas, often the only way to realize such visions on film is with an eye-deceiving painting. Matte painting – the art of combining painted artwork with live-action footage – is perhaps the most fascinating and magical of all visual effects illusions. If the matte painter is successful, an audience will see what appears to be a real location, never aware that they are viewing an artificial scene that exists only as several layers of paint on a sheet of glass.

While they are commonly used to create impossible and outrageous locations, matte paintings are equally effective at re-creating the most ordinary of settings that might otherwise be unsuitable for filming due to traffic problems, unhelpful local laws or even inclement weather conditions.

Matte painting offers the film-maker unparalleled creative possibilities, free from the laws of physics and nature. Any location that can be imagined can be conjured with breathtaking realism. Like the best examples of *trompe l'œil*, a good matte painting, created from only a few licks of paint on a flat surface, can trick the eye into perceiving landscapes that appear to stretch to infinity.

Today, with the help of the computer, new barriers of illusion are being broken. Matte paintings are now produced digitally and can combine computer-generated models and animation, traditional two-dimensional artwork and live-action film. Thanks to the extraordinary skills of the matte artist, it is now truer than ever before to say that modern movie audiences simply cannot believe their eyes.

GLASS SHOTS

The use of painted elements to improve a film scene is generally thought to have originated with the pioneer film-maker Norman O. Dawn (1884–1975; see panel). As a young man, Dawn worked at the Thorpe Engraving Company in Los Angeles, where, among other things, he took photographs of properties that were for sale. In 1905, Dawn's boss showed the young photographer how to improve the desirability of a site by obscuring or amending unsightly aspects with a few well-placed dabs of paint on a sheet of glass positioned in front of the camera. Slender cypress trees were used to hide telegraph poles and fake fountains concealed piles of rubbish.

Although stills photographers had used this method to enhance their shots for many years, Dawn is believed to be the first to have applied the technique to moving pictures when he made *California Missions* (1907). The film documented the historic mission buildings built by the Spanish along California's coast, many of which had fallen into a state of disrepair. By placing a sheet of glass in front

FIGURE 1 **GLASS SHOTS**

Glass shot used during the filming of *Cleopatra* (1963).

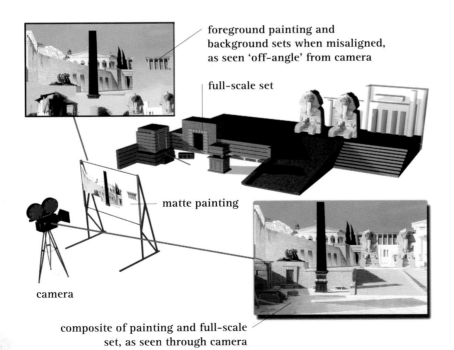

foreground painting and background sets when misaligned, as seen 'off-angle' from camera

full-scale set

matte painting

camera

composite of painting and full-scale set, as seen through camera

TOP: A glass-shot set-up used by Norman O. Dawn during the filming of *For the Term of His Natural Life* (1927) in Tasmania. The element painted on the glass is a replacement roof for the building in the far distance.

ABOVE: A glass shot made by Norman O. Dawn. Except for the small balcony area in which the actors are visible, the image was entirely created using scenery painted on a sheet of glass placed in front of the camera.

PRECEDING PAGES: An imam calls the faithful to prayer over the rooftops of medieval Jerusalem in *Robin Hood Prince of Thieves* (1991). In fact, the holy man is matte painter Michael Pangrazio, appearing in a scene painted almost entirely by himself.

PROFILE **NORMAN O. DAWN**

Born in a tent in a Bolivian railroad camp, Norman O. Dawn (1884–1975) was the son of a pioneering American railway engineer and keen photographer. Dawn learned how to produce glass shots during his work as a stills photographer in 1905 (<244). The following year, he travelled to France, where he took courses in classical art and even met Georges Méliès (<14) and the Lumière Brothers (<12). After spending the huge sum of $500 on a French-made movie camera, Dawn returned to the United States in 1907 to look for work in Hollywood's fledgling film industry.

Dawn produced the film *California Missions* (1907) using what are thought to be the first glass shots in any moving picture and then spent four years making documentary travelogues throughout the world, often embellishing shots with his own glass-painted artwork. He returned to Hollywood in 1911 and became a freelance special effects artist, specializing in combining live-action footage with paintings. He also created effects such as miniature explosions, fires, avalanches and earthquakes, and even experimented with crude rear-

projection methods (<82). His work for the film *Oriental Love* (1917) was key in bringing Hollywood's attention to the creative and financial potential of special effects.

Between 1916 and 1923, Dawn directed a number of effects-filled feature films for Universal, including *Sinbad the Sailor* (1917). In 1923 he became special effects producer for MGM, immediately embarking on a 1,300 km (800 mile) dog-sledge journey into the Alaskan wilderness to film scenes for *Masters of Women* (1923).

In 1926 Dawn travelled to Australia, where he constructed an entire studio and film-processing laboratory before shooting *For the Term of His Natural Life* (1927). Excited by news of the arrival of the 'talkies', Dawn returned to the US in 1927 to purchase sound equipment, which he used for the production of Australia's first-ever sound feature, *Showgirl's Luck* (1931).

Dawn moved back to the States in 1934, settling down to direct a series of movies that would reflect his own adventurous and pioneering spirit, including *Trail of the Yukon* (1937) and *Orphans of the North* (1940).

of the camera on which columns, roofs and bell towers were painted to align with the real buildings that were visible through the glass, Dawn was able to restore the crumbling cloisters to their former glory. Dawn used his glass-shot method extensively in the many travelogue films that he made around the world. In 1908, for example, he photographed South American Indian women bathing in a pool behind his hotel. Setting up his camera to peer through a hotel window, Dawn painted a Mayan temple on the pane of glass to change the background of the scene.

Although hailed by many as the inventor of the glass shot (often referred to as the 'Dawn process'), Dawn himself was uncomfortable taking all the credit, saying in later life, 'I should dispel any notion that I invented this technique – I merely built onto it and took advantage of conditions to advance an art in the making...'.

The use of glass shots in film-making was initially a laborious process. As with hanging foreground miniatures (<117), the camera was positioned to film the scene in question, its tripod fixed in place, and sandbags arranged around its legs to prevent any movement during the lengthy preparation process (fig. 1). A sheet of glass, held in a secured wooden frame, was positioned about 3 m (10 ft) in front of the camera. It was vital that the combination of camera lens, film stock and lighting produce sufficient depth of field (<115) to keep both nearby painting and background landscape in perfect focus.

To create the painting itself, the matte artist looked through the camera viewfinder and directed an assistant, who marked the glass to show the points at which real scenery and painted areas were to merge. The artist then sketched the scene on the glass with a wax pencil, frequently checking the marriage of drawing and background elements through the camera viewfinder. The required image was then painted directly onto the glass, usually in oil paint, using tones and colours that blended perfectly with the scenery in the background. While painting the image, the artist had to judge how light and shadow would look at the time of day that the scene was to be filmed, in order to ensure that the painting would blend with the live-action

component of the shot. For this reason, glass shots were often prepared on the day before filming, so that the artist could see exactly how shadows looked at the required time of day. However, an experienced artist could paint a scene in the morning with shadows that would accurately match those of the real scenery later in the same day. Once the sun had moved to a position where shadows on both painting and background scenery matched, the director had perhaps an hour to capture the scene before the quality of light in the two halves became too dissimilar.

It was vital that there was no movement of glass or camera during filming. If either moved fractionally, the background scenery and foreground painting would appear to shift, destroying the illusion that the two elements were one. During bad weather, filming could only proceed between gusts of wind, which might wobble both camera and painting. Some camera movement was possible during filming if the camera was mounted on a nodal-head tripod (<118), which allowed basic pans and tilts to be achieved without painting or background becoming separated.

Even after the development of more sophisticated methods of combining live-action images with paintings, the basic glass shot remained popular for many years. During World War II, the process was used during the production of newsreel films in armaments factories. To avoid having to remove all sensitive equipment, plans, or signs from a factory floor, a sheet of glass was placed in front of the camera, and any visual information considered useful to the enemy painted out or disguised. However, the process was most typically used in the feature film industry to save money on set construction by adding roofs or extra storeys to the lower portions of studio sets. The results can be seen in films such as *Cleopatra* (1963), where partially built full-size sets were built at the cost of hundreds of thousands of dollars while the impressive tops of buildings were painted and added for just a few thousand more (<244).

The inconvenience of preparing and painting a shot on location while a whole film crew waited for the results led Norman O. Dawn himself to look for an alternative technique.

ORIGINAL NEGATIVE MATTE PAINTING

For his 1911 film *Story of the Andes*, Norman O. Dawn pioneered an alternative method of combining live-action and painted elements known as 'original negative matte painting'. This involved exposing only the live-action area of the frame while on location and leaving a portion of the image unexposed for the painted elements to be added later. Such split-screen or in-camera double exposures had already been used by pioneers such as Georges Méliès and Edwin S. Porter (<14,17) around the turn of the century to combine two or more live-action elements. However, Dawn was the first to adapt the process for the combination of live action and matte paintings on the original negative. Although he first tried the idea in 1911, it wasn't until Dawn acquired the new Bell and Howell type 2709 camera (<19) in 1914 that he was able to perfect the technique.

As with the basic glass shot, a large sheet of glass was placed in front of the camera on location (fig. 2). Rather than paint replacement scenery directly onto the glass, the appropriate areas of the glass were painted an opaque black to produce a matte (a), which would prevent areas of the negative film in the camera from being exposed during filming. Mattes could also be made of carefully trimmed black cardboard, which was slotted into a specially designed 'matte box' on the front of the lens.

The edges of the matte were carefully designed to follow natural borders within the scene, the straight roofs and walls of buildings being particularly suitable junctions to integrate real life with the artificial. Sometimes several glass mattes were separately placed at several distances from the camera to produce varying qualities of matte line in different parts of the image. For example, mattes that followed the edges of straight objects, such as buildings, might be placed some distance in front of the camera to produce in-focus, 'hard' matte lines where the live action was to be butted up to the edges of the painted scene. Mattes that followed the edges of more irregular objects, such as bushes or grass, might be placed much nearer to the camera, resulting in an out-of-focus, 'soft' matte line where the edges of the painted material would later 'mix' with the live action.

Once the mattes were satisfactorily arranged, the scene was filmed using a pin-registered 'matte camera', which held the film absolutely steady during shooting. Unsteady film would produce an image that weaved around, resulting in an unconvincing final union between the painting and the scene. While filming the scene, an additional 15–30 m (50–100 ft) of test footage was first exposed for use during later stages of the process. After filming, the footage was removed from the camera and stored undeveloped in a refrigerator. Original negative matte painting is sometimes referred to as 'latent image matte painting', because the original negative with its 'latent' image was stored undeveloped until ready for combination with a painting (b).

At the art studio, another pin-registered matte camera was fixed to a solid base and aimed at a sheet of glass (or art board) mounted on a solidly fixed easel. This camera had a light behind its lens, so it was capable of operating as both camera and projector.

A few frames of the test footage were then removed from the undeveloped roll of original film and processed. The resulting piece of film would show an area of live action that was filmed on location and a blank area where no image had yet been added. A frame of this developed film was placed in the camera and projected onto the easel (c). Using the projected image for reference, perspective lines and elements such as walls or foliage that needed to extend from the live-action area into the matte painting area were carefully drawn onto the glass in a process called 'delineation'. When the sketch was complete, the area of the glass on which the already filmed live action was visible was painted black, producing a counter-matte.

The matte artist then began to paint the appropriate landscape or buildings in the remaining clear area of glass. As painting progressed, the

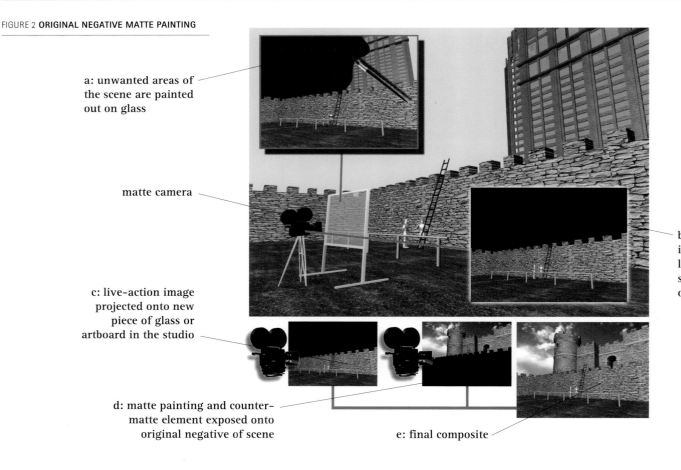

FIGURE 2 **ORIGINAL NEGATIVE MATTE PAINTING**

a: unwanted areas of the scene are painted out on glass

matte camera

c: live-action image projected onto new piece of glass or artboard in the studio

b: undeveloped image of live-action scene held on film

d: matte painting and counter-matte element exposed onto original negative of scene

e: final composite

This original negative matte painting was created by matte-painting specialists Matte World (now Matte World Digital) for *Robin Hood Prince of Thieves* (1991). Michael Pangrazio first created a matte painting of medieval Jerusalem (*above left*), leaving space for the live-action element to be added. The live-action parts of the image were filmed on a studio stage (*above*). Pangrazio, dressed as a holy man, performed in front of a small section of painted-sky backing and behind a small piece of railing that looked as if it was part of the minaret. The rest of the frame remained black. Cooking fires and smoke were pre-filmed at high speed and then rear-projected into the black areas of the frame for photographing onto the same piece of film. The sun was also a backlit exposure, producing a brighter glow than a painted sun could. The partially exposed film was rewound and exposed to the painting to produce an extremely high-quality composite image (*left*) on a single original negative.

artist would periodically check how well the painting and live action matched by looking through the camera viewfinder at the combination of the filmed and developed image held in the gate of the camera, and the image on the easel. When the matte painting was complete, the remaining undeveloped test footage was loaded into the camera and exposed to the painting (d). The black areas on the glass (the counter-matte) would not affect the already exposed areas on the negative; the painted artwork, which had been appropriately lit with studio lamps, would be printed into the corresponding unexposed areas of the negative. The result was a test composite of live action and painting (e).

This test was done at a number of different exposure levels to produce what is known as a 'wedge' – a series of differently exposed composites. The

wedge was studied to determine what the best exposure level for the final composite would be. When an exposure that produced the best match of colour and contrast had been found, the whole roll of original undeveloped production footage was loaded into the camera and exposed to the painting. When developed, the result should have been a perfectly balanced combination of live-action footage and matte painting, all on the original first-exposure negative.

The great advantages of the original negative system over the glass-shot method were that it allowed the artist sufficient time to complete the matte painting to perfection without the pressure of performing a miracle on set while the whole crew was waiting; the live action could be filmed quickly during production and the painted elements did not have to be

ABOVE: **For this shot from** *Earthquake* **(1974), Albert Whitlock exposed smoke and fire elements onto film holding an undeveloped image of his Los Angeles matte painting.**

added for many weeks, allowing last-minute creative decisions to be made about the style and content of the painted elements; furthermore, the artist could match the lighting of the painting to that of the live-action plate exactly, whatever time of day it was filmed. Perhaps the greatest advantage of all was that since both live action and artwork were captured on the original negative, the quality of the combined image was excellent.

There were some disadvantages to capturing both live action and matte painting on the original negative, however. The smallest mistake when exposing a matte painting onto an original live-action negative might ruin original footage that could cost hundreds of thousands of dollars to re-film. Matte cameramen also had to make repeated sample exposures using the test footage before they were able to achieve the final composite, and there was always the danger that the supply of this footage would run out before a satisfactory match of painting and live action was found.

The undisputed master of the original negative technique was the matte artist Albert Whitlock (see panel). Once Whitlock had combined the live action with a matte painting, he often exposed additional elements onto the undeveloped image. For *Earthquake* (1974), Whitlock produced a number of paintings of Los Angeles after it had been shaken to destruction. Once painting and live action had been combined, Whitlock developed a small piece of the exposed composite. In a studio that was draped entirely in black velvet, he placed a developed frame of the film into a camera and studied it through the viewfinder. Whitlock then directed assistants to parts of a stage that corresponded with positions at which he wanted to place additional elements. Once these places were marked, Whitlock set up small fires and plumes of smoke and exposed them directly onto the original undeveloped negative footage. He also positioned black mattes in the studio that corresponded to the shape and position of buildings on the original negative. The plumes of smoke disappeared from camera view behind these black shapes so it appeared to drift between the painted buildings on the final image.

Until the arrival of digital matte painting techniques (260>), the original negative matte painting technique was used regularly. However, for many artists the advantage of the high-quality, first-generation image produced by the method did not outweigh the risk of spoiling the original negative. A number of safer methods were therefore devised.

RIGHT: Matte paintings were vital to the rich imagery of *Gone with the Wind*. Even Tara, the grand house at the centre of the drama, was largely the product of the artist's brush. The bottom half of the image contains live action, while the top half, added to the original negative, is a painting by Jack Cosgrove.

PROFILE **ALBERT WHITLOCK**

Albert Whitlock (1915–2000) began his movie career at the age of 14 as an errand boy at London's Gaumont British Studio. Eventually graduating from errands to painting signs and scenery, Whitlock was employed by the young Alfred Hitchcock (<27) to paint a newsstand sign for *The Lady Vanishes* (1938). His work as a scenic artist led Whitlock to matte painting, and he was taught by the pioneering British matte painter W. Percy Day (1878–1965), whose own work appeared in films such as *The Thief of Bagdad* (1940) and *Black Narcissus* (1947).

In 1954 Whitlock moved to the United States, working first at Disney before becoming head of the matte department at Universal in 1963. A gentleman who always wore a suit and tie even when painting, Whitlock was admired for his highly naturalistic matte paintings. He was particularly skilled at creating dramatic lighting effects and moody atmosphere. He was also known for his extremely fast working pace. For *Earthquake* (1974), he created and filmed 22 paintings for 40 shots in under 12 weeks. He painted the impressive mountaintop city in *The Man Who Would Be King* (1975) in just six hours.

Most of Whitlock's paintings were achieved using the original negative technique (<246) and he frequently used complex multiple exposures to add additional details such as smoke and fire – a risky practice that can destroy the entire image if one mistake is made.

Whitlock's skill at bringing a painting to life was so highly prized that many directors came to rely on him. Robert Wise wouldn't agree to direct *The Hindenburg* (1975) until he knew the artist was available to produce the 85 matte shots called for by the script. Whitlock is best known for his work with Alfred Hitchcock, a director who had great faith in the ability of matte paintings to tell stories. Whitlock created scenes for all of Hitchcock's movies after 1961, including *The Birds* (1963, <68), *Marnie* (1964) and *Frenzy* (1972). He won Oscars for his work on *Earthquake* and *The Hindenburg*.

BI-PACK CONTACT MATTE PRINTING

From the mid-20s, the bi-pack contact matte printing technique was used to combine already developed live-action images with matte paintings. Once film that needed a painting added to it had been filmed and developed to produce a positive image (fig. 3(a)), a single frame was placed in a matte camera and projected onto a large sheet of glass. The artist then created the matte painting on the glass so that it corresponded to the projected image, painting over areas that needed to be altered and leaving clear the areas that were to remain unchanged (b). When the glass matte painting was complete, a piece of evenly illuminated white card was placed behind it. The white light reflected from the card was clearly visible through the unpainted areas of the glass. The front of the painting was left unlit. The rest of the already developed live-action film was then loaded into the camera and bi-packed (sandwiched; <58) with fresh, unexposed film.

The painting was then filmed. During exposure, the light from the white card shining through the unpainted areas of the glass hit the live-action plate footage and copied these areas of live action onto the new piece of film. No light came from the unlit, painted areas of the glass, so these areas of the new film remained unexposed (c). The film in the camera was then rewound and the pre-filmed live-action film (the plate) was removed. The white card behind the painting was then replaced with black card or velvet and the front of the matte painting was evenly illuminated. The undeveloped

negative film in the camera was then re-exposed, so that the painting appeared in the previously unexposed areas. The black card behind the painting prevented any additional exposure in those areas of the film that had already received the image from the live-action plate (d).

The bi-pack matte process allowed great freedom of choice over the placing of the matte lines in an image. Since the painting was added to a live-action plate that had been filmed without any matted-out areas, the method could be used to add matte paintings to any piece of footage, whether or not it was originally planned as a matte shot. Another advantage came from the fact that the live-action plate could be divided into three colour separations (<61). The unexposed camera negative could therefore be variably exposed to each of these separations to produce a highly controlled colour balance between live action and painting.

The biggest disadvantage to the method was that the live-action portion of the composite image (e) was in fact a second-generation image and therefore of an inferior quality to the area holding a first-generation image of the painting with which it was combined (the same is also true when using rear- and front-projection methods; 251>). The difference between the first-generation footage of the painting and the second-generation footage of the live action often becomes apparent when matte shots created using this technique are viewed on television. Since television has a lower resolution than film, it is a medium less capable of conveying subtleties of colour and contrast, and the live-action portion of a matte shot can therefore sometimes appear to stand out from the painting around it.

FIGURE 3 **BI-PACK CONTACT MATTE PRINTING**

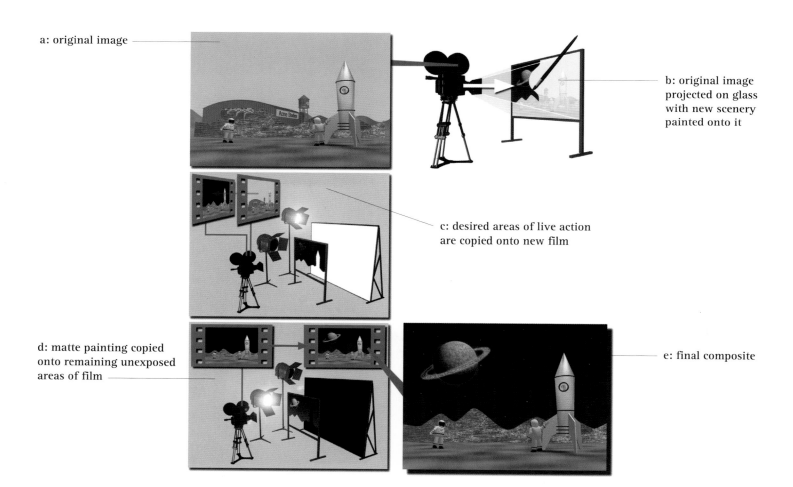

a: original image

b: original image projected on glass with new scenery painted onto it

c: desired areas of live action are copied onto new film

d: matte painting copied onto remaining unexposed areas of film

e: final composite

REAR PROJECTION, FRONT PROJECTION AND OPTICAL PRINTING

REAR PROJECTION

Rear projection (<82) was probably the simplest and most popular method of combining moving images and paintings. Once filmed and developed, the live-action footage was threaded into a projector and projected onto a sheet of glass from behind (but back-to-front so that it appeared the right way round when viewed from the front (fig. 4)). Working on the other side of the glass, the matte artist delineated, sketched and then painted the required image in the appropriate areas. When the painting was complete, a frosted glass screen was attached to the back of the unpainted areas of the glass.

The frosted glass allowed the rear-projected live action to be focused on the surface of the glass. Without it, the glass would allow the projected image to pass through unseen. A camera looking at the front of the painting then filmed the combination of painting and rear-projected live action. It was difficult to achieve a balanced combination of painting and rear-projected image with one exposure, however, so the live-action and painted elements of each shot were often filmed separately. First, the painting was filmed by illuminating it appropriately and replacing the frosted glass used for rear projection with black velvet. The rear-projected image was then added in a second exposure, in which the lighting on the painting was switched off to ensure that the film was exposed to only the live action.

Rear projection was particularly useful for matte paintings that needed many small areas of live action added to them. By using several projectors, live-action elements could be projected onto a number of different 'windows' in the painting.

Depending on the number of elements required, the projectors could be moved to new positions and more live action projected into other areas of the painting for filming in any number of additional exposures. This technique was used by Industrial Light and Magic during the making of *Return of the Jedi* (1983) to project 12 live-action shots of the furry Ewoks as they danced around bonfires in their painted treetop village.

FRONT PROJECTION

A less frequently used method of combining live action and matte paintings was front projection (<84). Front-projected matte shots were created in a similar way to rear-projected ones, the main difference, as the name would suggest, being that the live-action element was projected into the image from the front rather than from behind. The windows for live action in a matte painting were backed with Scotchlite, which reflects light directly back to its source. Just like the front-projection systems once used to combine actors with live action, camera and projector were mounted at 90° to one another in front of the matte painting. The projector threw the image of the live-action plate onto a half-silvered (two-way) mirror that

FIGURE 4 **REAR–PROJECTION MATTE PAINTING**

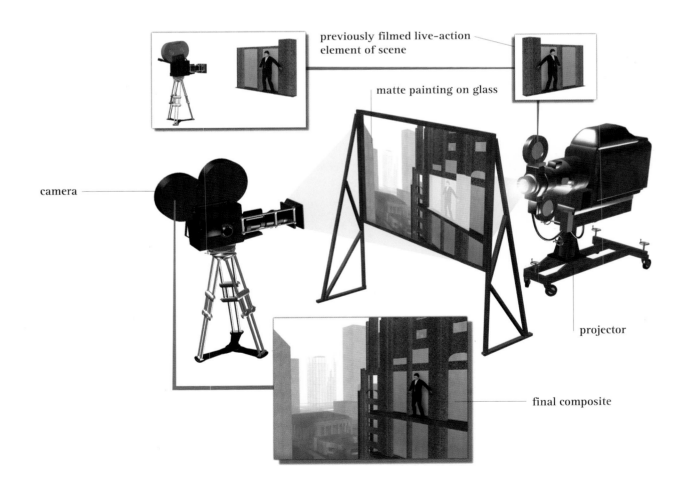

previously filmed live-action element of scene

matte painting on glass

camera

projector

final composite

was placed at an angle of 45° to both camera and projector (fig. 5). The projected live-action footage passed through the mirror and hit the painting, where most of its light was absorbed. The footage that hit the Scotchlite areas was reflected directly back to the mirror, through which it passed into the camera. The camera therefore filmed both live action and matte painting.

Front projection was a more complicated process than rear projection, but the reflected live-action images were generally brighter and sharper than those achieved with rear projection. Most of the scenes that included matte painting elements in *The Empire Strikes Back* (1980) were achieved using front projection.

OPTICAL PRINTING

Probably the least common method of combining matte paintings with live action involved producing mattes and counter-mattes of each of the elements that were to be combined. These were then assembled in an optical printer (<70), much as in any other form of optical compositing (<76). This method allowed maximum control over the image characteristics (such as focus, colour and size) of each of the elements being combined, but a little less control over subtleties like the way that the matte lines between painting and live action could be varied. Matte paintings often had blue-screen travelling matte elements (<68), such as characters or spaceships, printed on top of them using the optical printer.

RIGHT: To position Sylvester Stallone precariously on a vast cliff-face for *Cliffhanger* (1993), Boss Films rear-projected footage of the actor climbing on a small area of rock into a large matte painting. The live action was first projected onto glass and the matte line marked up *(top left)*. Leaving a gap for the live action, the cliff face was painted *(top right)*. Model mountain sections were built around the painting *(centre left)* so that the camera could move past them during filming to create realistic changes in perspective *(centre right)*. In the final composite, the join between live action and painting is undetectable *(bottom right)*.

FIGURE 5 **FRONT-PROJECTION MATTE PAINTING**

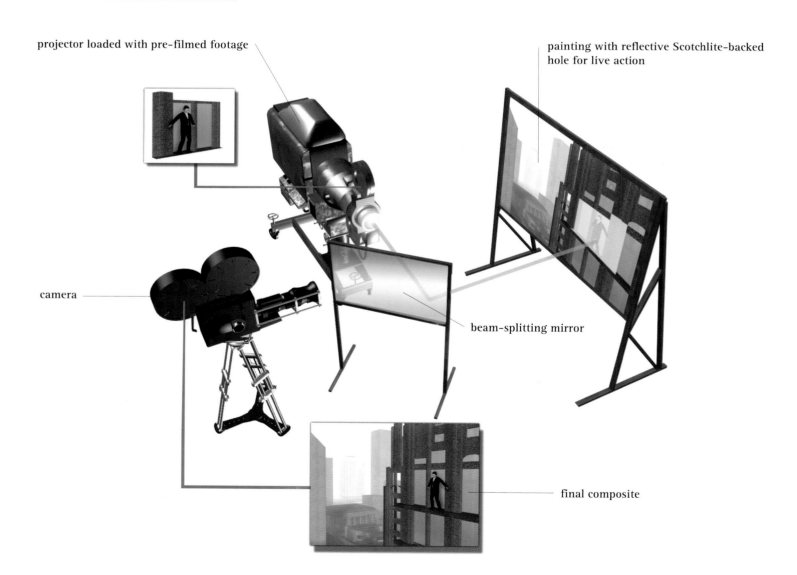

projector loaded with pre-filmed footage

painting with reflective Scotchlite-backed hole for live action

camera

beam-splitting mirror

final composite

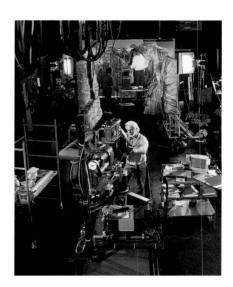

THE ART OF MATTE PAINTING

The first stage in producing an image that will fool an audience into accepting a painting as real is careful planning. Whether created using old-fashioned techniques or within the computer, matte shots are not simply high-quality paintings; they are illusions cleverly designed to deceive the eye.

'Matte shots tend to be held on screen for longer than the average special effects shot', explains Craig Barron, who was once a matte cameraman at ILM and is now a co-founder of matte painting specialists, Matte World Digital. 'Matte shots are normally used for establishing shots that are quite contemplative. They tell a story or establish a scene and people look at these images for a relatively long time. That means that the quality really has to be there, otherwise people will notice that something is wrong. The whole idea of an establishing shot is that it confirms the location or period of a scene in the mind of the audience. If this first image is not convincing, the realism of the whole scene will be destroyed, no matter how good the other elements.

'Good matte paintings are as much about design and planning as anything else', continues Barron, who is also co-author of the book *The Invisible Art*, the definitive study of matte painting. 'Long before anything is filmed, a matte shot will be carefully planned by us and the film's production designer. This usually entails producing a number of small test paintings in which we figure out composition, colour schemes, lighting effects and how live action will integrate with painting.'

The key to planning a successful matte shot is devising a composition that will quickly impart an authentic sense of location. 'There are a number of basic rules about how to compose a matte shot', says Chris Evans, a senior artist at Matte World Digital. 'These help us to create images that tell a story effectively and efficiently and allow us to disguise the fact that what an audience is looking at is not reality, but an artificially created environment.'

The artist begins by deciding which parts of an image should be live action and which should be painted. The human eye tends to scan images in a uniform way – most of us read an image from left to right. Some people believe that our eyes also move up towards the top of an image in a triangular motion during this left-to-right scan. 'This is what I call the "pyramid of believability"', says Evans. 'If a viewer's eye scans these three broad areas of an image and reads them as real, then he or she will probably accept the whole image as genuine. These are the parts of an image that we tend to reserve for the live-action portion of a shot. We also consider the fact that the eye is always drawn to the lightest areas of an image. The live action therefore tends to be situated in the brightest regions of a composition, while the painted areas tend to be darker and more shadowy.'

Once an image has been planned, the matte artist begins to produce the painting. Most matte shots are now 'painted' directly in the computer, although some people still like to create traditional paintings that are later photographed and manipulated digitally. Their methods remain a fascinating insight into the way that matte paintings were produced for over half a century.

There is some difference of opinion about whether oil paints or acrylics are the better material for matte painting. Oil paints dry slowly, which allows the artist to push them around and alter them for some time after they have been applied. The rich colours of oil paints do not alter when they dry, which is useful when a painting has to match live-action footage. Acrylics, on the other hand, dry in a matter of minutes and can be painted over almost immediately. However, acrylics do tend to dry a slightly different colour. Some artists like to combine the two mediums, developing and perfecting a design in acrylic and then laying oil paints over the top to create the final image.

Matte paintings can sometimes be a combination of original artwork and other materials. 'The purpose of a matte painting is to tell a story without the deception being discovered', says Harrison Ellenshaw, who oversaw the matte paintings for *Star Wars* (1977) and *The Empire Strikes Back* (1980) before becoming the head of Disney's matte painting department, where he supervised paintings for films such as *Dick Tracy* (1990). 'The method you use to create that image is really not important. If you are trying to create an image of something that already exists, then you might as well make use of that object or location by photographing it and adding the photo to your painting. I used this method for matte paintings of the Jawa sandcrawler in *Star Wars* and Boba Fett's spaceship in *The Empire Strikes Back*. We had models of these machines, so I lit them appropriately and photographed them from the correct angle. I then stuck the photographs onto glass, painted on top of them and added the correct environment around them.'

ABOVE: **Matte artist Michelle Moen works on an atmospheric painting of Gotham City for** *Batman Returns* **(1992).**

LEFT: **Matthew Yuricich works on a matte painting for** *Star Trek: The Motion Picture* **(1979). The close-up shows the level of detail required to produce photorealistic images.**

The traditional matte artist must create the illusion of a spatial environment that may be many miles in width and depth, merely by applying a few thin layers of paint to a flat surface that is perhaps 1.2 m (4 ft) wide and 1 m (3 ft) high. 'When a director of photography films a real landscape, they don't have to worry too much about the atmosphere and sense of distance in their image, because the sun does all of that for them,' explains Chris Evans. 'However, a matte artist has to make decisions about every single visual aspect of an image. What is the quality of the atmosphere? How does the sun penetrate that atmosphere? How does the quality of light affect the relationship between every object between the camera and the horizon? Composition and planning are very important, but in the end the success of a painting comes down to lighting. Natural light is very consistent; it reacts in certain ways according to the weather and the location, and it has a consistent transition of tonality and colour over distance. We are all used to those relationships; we see them every day without being aware of it. The physics of light and optics and atmosphere are locked into everyone's brains and we have to get those relationships right in our paintings. If something is not quite perfect in a painting, an audience will know it immediately. They will rarely think, "That's a bad matte shot," but they will sense that there's something not quite right about what they are seeing. That can pull them out of the narrative very quickly.'

As well as accurately reproducing the qualities of light, the matte artist must also be able to reproduce a realistic sense of scale and perspective. Matte painter Chesley Bonestell, who created paintings for classic films such as *Citizen Kane* (1941) and *Destination Moon* (1950), believed that it was his training as an architect that enabled him to produce such convincing images. In an examination he was once asked to produce a painting of a mirror that was tipped at an angle of 10° from a wall, and its reflection of a chair that was tipped at 10° from the mirror. Only those with an unerring eye for such visual relationships are likely to produce convincing matte paintings.

The effectiveness of a traditional matte painting also stems from the way in which paint is applied to its surface. For paintings to combine seamlessly with photographed images, a style of painting is required that is photorealistic when filmed. From around 2 m (6 ft) away, most good matte paintings do look like photographs. Closer inspection usually reveals an impressionistic style of painting in which the artist has 'stabbed' rough areas of colour with surprisingly little intricate detail. 'Creating traditional matte paintings is actually a case of painting something that mimics the way our eyes perceive a scene', explains Harrison Ellenshaw. 'If we look into the distance, we don't actually see very much detail at all. A window on a far-off building looks just like a small grey smudge, a tree looks like a dull green blob, perhaps with a bit of brown in it. What makes these distant objects look like windows or trees is the fact that our brains see them in context and tell us what they are – our brains fill in the fine details that our eyes don't actually perceive. If you were to create a matte painting in which every little detail was visible, you might think that it would look incredibly realistic. In fact, it would look like the most fake image that you have ever seen. Matte paintings are therefore impressionistic in style. They are made up of lots of little blobs and lines of colour that look pretty nondescript up close, but when you step back they look very natural.'

Matte painter Matthew Yuricich, whose paintings have appeared in films such as *Ben-Hur* (1959), *Star Trek: The Motion Picture* (1979) and *Dances with Wolves* (1990), tells the story of a film director who came to see his painting of a pirate ship for a particular production. The director was insistent that Yuricich paint every one of the ship's many cannons in extreme detail. The painter tried to show the director that a single stroke of black paint would suffice for each gun, but the director ordered him to paint each barrel in minute detail. On seeing the finished shot, the director thanked the artist for taking the effort to include the detail he had asked for. Yuricich had, of course, used only a single streak of black paint for each gun – the director's imagination had supplied the rest of the detail.

'When creating a matte painting, I use all sorts of painting techniques', notes Chris Evans. 'If you look at a real building or a mountain, there are layers of history and weathering and decay. All those nuances of surface texture need to be suggested in a painting. I often lay on colours in broad strokes and then push them around and stipple them with a rag or a piece of newspaper. However, an important aspect of matte painting is destroying any sense of there being a painted surface', he cautions. 'Modern artists like Jackson Pollock and impressionists like Claude Monet draw attention to the surface of the canvas through their painting techniques. We have to make sure that there is absolutely no sense of surface on matte paintings – they need to be more like windows opening out onto a view. No part of the painting should catch the light in a way that indicates a surface. Some matte painters have even been known to sand down each layer of paint so that it is totally smooth before applying the next layer, as if making a lacquer box.'

No matter how well crafted, a traditional matte painting can only ever be a still image – a moment in time that has been captured like a photograph. Even on a windless day, a real scene is never static – grass and trees always sway, clouds drift, heat waves distort the distant view and small insects or dust float past almost unnoticed. Matte paintings can look

PROFILE **PETER ELLENSHAW**

London-born Peter Ellenshaw (1913–2003) learned the art of matte painting from his stepfather, W. Percy Day (1878–1965). Ellenshaw's early work with Day appeared in many of the classic films made at London's Denham Studios by producer Alexander Korda, including *Things to Come* (1936) and *The Thief of Bagdad* (1940).

After serving in the Air Force during World War II, Ellenshaw returned to painting, providing images for films such as *Stairway to Heaven* (1946) and *The Red Shoes* (1948). In 1948 Walt Disney began producing live-action feature films in Britain and Ellenshaw was one of the artists chosen to create matte paintings for classics such as *Treasure Island* (1950) and *The Story of Robin Hood* (1952). Disney was so impressed with Ellenshaw's work that he asked the artist to move to Hollywood to work for the Disney Studio permanently.

In 1953 Ellenshaw became head of the Disney matte department in Burbank, providing paintings for films such as *20,000 Leagues Under the Sea* (1954) and even creating early concept paintings of Disneyland. He also became increasingly involved in the planning and production of visual effects in general. *For Darby O'Gill and the Little People* (1959), Ellenshaw planned the use of huge sets and deep-focus photography to create shots of 'little people' interacting with full-size characters without using any additional optical processes (<118). Between 1950 and 1979 Ellenshaw worked on 34 Disney films, winning an Academy Award for whimsical depictions of Victorian London in *Mary Poppins* (1964).

After working as production designer and supervisor of miniature effects for *The Black Hole* (1979), Ellenshaw retired from the film business but has continued to enjoy great success as a landscape artist. His son, Harrison, is also a successful matte painter and visual effects supervisor (<254).

LEFT: **Artist Caroleen Green adds the finishing touches to a matte painting by Chris Evans from** *Indiana Jones and the Temple of Doom* **(1984). Footage of the hero emerging from a tunnel was rear-projected into a hole in the cliff on the left of the painting and a real river was added at the bottom of the ravine. The composite was filmed with a moving camera to give the impression it was shot from a helicopter.**

artificial without these almost imperceptible movements. 'There are many ways to bring a little life to an otherwise still painting when it is being filmed,' explains Harrison Ellenshaw. 'Perhaps the most popular and versatile method is to scrape small areas of paint off the glass of a matte painting. During filming, any moving object or light source can be placed behind the painting. Where the changing light pattern is seen through the glass, the scene will appear to have some movement. A small change in light can make painted grass look as if it is swaying or water look as if it is flowing.' For *Scaramouche* (1952), this method was used to give life to the painted theatre audience during the final fight sequence. The same trick was used by Ellenshaw to make the stars sparkle above Tracy Town in *Dick Tracy* (1990).

A traditional matte painting can also be brought to life by adding some camera movement during photography. 'Traditional matte paintings are 2-D images, so camera movement will produce no perspective change and will quickly spoil the illusion of depth,' explains Craig Barron. 'However, a shot with no camera movement can also tip off the audience that an image is a special effect, especially in modern films that otherwise have a lot of camera action in them.' When filming a matte painting that has rear-projected live action (<82), it is possible to add subtle camera pans and tilts and to track in and out of the image (since there will be no change in perspective, a tracking shot will look like a zoom).

However, because these rear-projection matte paintings were filmed in a number of passes (painted and projected elements being photographed separately in order to obtain the correct exposure), any camera moves had to be created using a motion-control system (<146) that allowed the moves to be repeated precisely. 'One way of adding movement to a shot was to combine matte paintings with models,' says Barron. 'With a model in front of the painting, a small camera move would produce a much better sense of there being a change in perspective. A good example is the complex combination of rear-projected live action, matte paintings and models that we used for the last shot of *Batman Returns* [1992].' The shot in question shows Bruce Wayne's Rolls-Royce driving into the distance along a snowy Gotham City street. As snow falls, the camera moves upwards, past a maze of gantries and pipework, to reveal the Gotham City skyline. In the final moments of the shot, the bat signal throws its beacon into the night sky. 'This shot was achieved using a single piece of negative in the camera, the final image being gradually built up by exposing over 50 different passes on the motion-control matte camera,' explains Barron. 'We filmed a live-action plate of the car driving down the street on large-format VistaVision film (<55). That film was rear-projected into a matte painting of the street and surrounding buildings, which was itself built into a miniature Gotham City set. The matte camera filmed the rear-projected car and its model surroundings and then craned up past the model, which included various small lights as well as additional projected elements such as plumes of steam. Finally, the camera came to rest on the Gotham City skyline, which was composed of several layers of model buildings in the foreground with 2-D painted buildings in the background. The bat signal was projected onto clouds that were made of fibrefill, a cotton wool-like material that is used to stuff pillows, and attached to a moving backing so that they appeared to drift. The signal was actually done in two exposures – one for the round bat symbol itself and one for the funnel-shaped beam of light – because we found it impossible

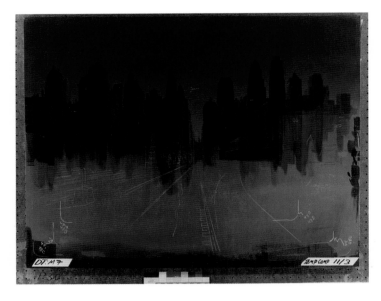

to get a balanced exposure when doing both parts at once. Finally, the shot had several layers of falling snow added to it. We filmed the snow – actually potato flakes and shredded plastic – in several exposures so that it appeared to fall at different speeds and varying distances from the camera.'

Perhaps the greatest challenge for traditional matte painters was concealing the matte line – the junction of painting and live action. 'Matte lines were the constant, recurring difficulty in any traditional matte shot,' states Barron. 'We had to make the matte line invisible so we always had to figure out an effective way to disguise it.' If a matte painting was part of a miniature model set, as in the final shot of *Batman Returns*, the edges of the live-action plate could be concealed by parts of the miniature set. In most matte paintings, however, the live-action and painted areas would adjoin directly. 'Hiding a matte line began with designing a shot that made use of "natural" matte lines,' explains Barron. 'We always looked for divisions of colour or texture in the live-action plate that could be used as the point where live action turned into painting. Shots of cities or perhaps rocky environments were relatively simple because there would be lots of distinct lines, such as the edges of walls or boulders that could serve as boundaries.

The hardest matte lines to achieve were where the live-action plate had to end in a consistent area of colour, like the sand in a desert or a blue sky. When that happened, we had to match the colour of the photographed painting with the colour of the live action exactly.'

In situations where blending the matte line was likely to be problematic, matte artists began by conducting a number of tests. 'We'd start by testing what colour paints would match the live action when photographed,' explains Barron. 'The difficulty was that paints actually change colour when they are photographed, partly because of the way film reacts to different colours and partly because of the qualities of the artificial light that we would use to illuminate our paintings.

'Once we knew what colours would match, the painting was created using the right range of colours around the matte line. Throughout this process, we would do a number of photographic tests to make sure that the painting and live action still matched reasonably. When the painting was finished, we would do a "wedge" – 128 different exposures of the painting combined with the live action. Then we would go through every one of those different iterations to decide which particular match was the nearest.

Sometimes the artist would go back and make a few changes to the painting just to get the match absolutely perfect. Before we did the final exposure of a front- or rear-projected matte painting, we often used a scalpel blade to scrape small flakes of paint away from the glass all around the edges of the live-action areas of the painting – this would help the painting to merge with the live action in a more gradual way, without any hard lines.'

Despite the matte artist's best efforts, there were some matte lines that refused to be blended to perfection. 'One of the hardest paintings we did while I was at ILM was the famous final shot of *Raiders of the Lost Ark* [1981]', comments Barron. 'The shot was of a man pushing a trolley along a concrete floor in a warehouse. Only a small part of the floor was live action and everything else was painted by matte artist Mike Pangrazio. Because the floor was grey – which is made up of every colour in the spectrum – it took us endless tests to get a good enough colour match, and even then we were never able to make it completely perfect.' Despite Barron's reservations, the shot is perhaps one of the most successful matte paintings ever used and remains convincing even though it is on screen for over 30 seconds. Even the best traditional matte paintings can normally only be shown for three to five seconds before an audience begins to spot their flaws.

Once the matte artist's work is completed, the final success of a matte shot may depend on the decisions made by the film's director and editor. 'How and where a matte painting is used in a film is crucial to its success,' says Harrison Ellenshaw. 'A matte painting needs to be on screen just long enough for the audience to read what it says, but not so long that they will start to scrutinize it and notice problems. The difference between a matte shot being a success or a failure can literally be a few frames.' Chris Evans agrees, believing that directors can fall in love with a good matte painting and spoil it by showing it off. 'Any longer than a few seconds and an audience will begin to notice the conceit – even the best matte paintings will be spotted if they are on screen for too long. Even I can miss half of the traditional matte paintings in a film if they are used well. A director who keeps a matte painting on screen for too long is like a magician who can't resist repeating his best tricks. When you keep showing them the trick, the audience soon works out how it is done.'

LEFT: **Comic-strip caper *Dick Tracy* (1990) relied on matte paintings to bring its colourful cityscapes to life.** *Top left:* This matte painting in its early stages shows how the artist has sketched delineation lines to help plan the shot and create the right perspective. *Bottom left:* To create a shot of a car arriving at a dockside warehouse, a painting was created leaving spaces for live-action car footage and live-action shimmering river water. *Top right:* To create twinkling stars, tiny holes were scraped in the sky areas of the painting. During filming, a sheet of clear acetate with random ink markings was moved between the painting and a light source to vary the amount of light reaching each star. *Bottom right:* The final image. Note that live-action smoke has also been added to a warehouse chimney.

BELOW: **The famous closing shot from *Raiders of the Lost Ark* (1981). The warehouse is a matte painting by Michael Pangrazio, and the live-action plate of an old man pushing a trolley occupies only a small area of the central aisle.**

DIGITAL MATTE PAINTING

Like all other aspects of visual effects production, matte painting has been revolutionized by the arrival of the computer.

In the early days of digital image manipulation, matte artists took advantage of the computer to alter and composite traditionally produced artwork. 'For a while we continued creating traditional matte paintings in oils and acrylics,' comments Chris Evans of Matte World Digital. 'When a painting was complete, we would photograph it and scan it into the computer. Once [it was] digitized we could do all sorts of things that just weren't possible with the old optical techniques.'

One of the earliest examples of the computer encroaching on the territory of the matte painter was during the production of *Young Sherlock Holmes* (1985).

'For *Young Sherlock* I did a number of traditional paintings and we scanned them into the computer and combined them digitally,' explains Evans. 'For a sequence in which a computer-animated knight leapt out from a stained-glass church window, I painted the window in watercolours and then created the surrounding church environment as a separate oil painting. These elements were scanned into the computer and then joined together. Where we had once spent all our time trying to blend matte lines – the edges where various elements join together – the computer actually allowed us to select colours from either painting and seamlessly blend the two elements across the matte line. It was a very exciting time because it was just beginning to dawn on us how much computers were going to allow us to do in the future.'

The key to creating convincing matte paintings within the computer has been the development of sophisticated computer paint software that allows images to be 'painted' directly within the computer. The software most commonly used for this purpose is Adobe Photoshop. Developed in the late 80s by ILM effects supervisor John Knoll and his brother Thomas, Photoshop was designed to manipulate digitized images for use in the print and publishing trade. However, the software's powerful ability to manipulate and even create original digital images has made it a favourite in the visual effects industry for creating texture maps (<164) and digital matte paintings.

For some artists, putting down the brush and palette and learning to use a graphics pen has been a difficult process, but others have found it liberating. 'I learned to paint in oils,' says Evans. 'When I first started working at ILM, I had to get used to working with acrylics, which is what they used for their matte paintings. Learning to paint within the computer was really just the same process. We still have to create the same balance of tone and colour and light and shade – the only things that have

RIGHT: Sets for *The Truman Show* (1998) were only constructed as high as the first storey. Matte World Digital then match-moved wire-frame models of the desired set extensions to the original footage (*above*). After rendering, the digital models were composited into the live-action plate to produce a natural-looking small-town environment (*below*).

BELOW: Matte painter Chris Evans (*right*) discusses his stained-glass matte painting for *Young Sherlock Holmes* (1985) with Dennis Muren (*centre*) and John Lasseter (*left*). Once completed, several paintings were scanned into the computer and digitally manipulated and combined.

changed are the tools and materials. Probably the biggest difference between traditional painting and digital painting is the brush that you use. When using paints, you choose a brush that is the right size and shape for what you want to achieve. You can dip that brush into two or three paints, collecting a little more of one particular colour on one part of the brush. Then when you're painting you can jam that brush into the surface and twist it around to achieve hundreds of variations of colour and texture, all from that single loading of paint. Painting with a graphics pen is more like airbrushing – you can only use one colour at a time and the tool doesn't actually make contact with the surface of the artwork; it's more like spraying paint from a distance.'

Despite the artists' lack of physical interaction with their work, digital matte painting has many compensations. 'There are lots of amazing things that you can do with a digital brush that you can't do with a real one,' says Evans. 'Probably the most useful thing is the ability to paint with textures rather than just colours. If you're creating a painting of some rocks, instead of painting every detail of every rock, software like Photoshop allows you to sample an area of real stone from the live-action plate or a reference photograph and then "paint" with that texture. After spending years meticulously painting every subtle detail, it's amazing just to be able to say "I'll have some of this grass over here, and some of this brickwork over there," and then see it just appearing on the screen.'

'A large part of digital matte painting is manipulating photographic elements that have been collected on location,' explains Evans' colleague Craig Barron. 'There isn't much point spending time painting something new if you can use a photograph of a real object. Digital matte paintings are often a collage of photographic elements woven together with digitally painted original elements. That may make creating a digital matte painting sound easy, but it's no easier than producing a convincing image by gluing together lots of disparate photos that have been cut out of different magazines.'

Once a live-action plate has been scanned into the computer, the matte artist can begin painting directly on top of the image. 'We used to spend a lot of time matting off the image while filming the original plate,' says Barron. 'But now the whole shot can be filmed without any masking, and once it's on our computer monitors, we can decide at which points the digital matte painting is going to start. If the live action is the wrong size or in the wrong part of the frame, we can simply reposition the image on the monitor and create a new environment around the edges. The other major difference about the way live action is filmed for digital matte painting is that we don't need to worry too much about where the matte line is eventually going to be. We used to place actors and props very carefully so that no moving object would pass over the point where the painting began – otherwise an actor's head might disappear behind the painting. Today, moving objects can be digitally rotoscoped [<102], effectively cutting out an object from its real background so that painted areas can be brought right down behind characters and objects in a scene.'

With the live-action image displayed on the computer monitor, the matte artist begins to produce a digital matte painting in much the same way as a traditional matte painting. First, the artist looks for perspective lines in the live action and extends them out into the area that is to be artificially created. The artist then 'sketches' the composition of major elements on the screen before starting to paint. As well as having a digital palette with which to mix any colour of paint, the artist can also clone colours and textures directly from the live-action plate itself.

The artist then begins to build up the painting. 'A digital matte painting can be created in layers,' explains Evans. 'With traditional painting, you physically layered coats of paint on top of one another to create an effect. If you painted something undesirable on top of a good bit of work, you had pretty much lost the work beneath it. In the digital realm, we can paint one layer, then tell the computer we want to paint on top of that in a separate layer. This way every object or area in a scene can be stored as a different piece of art, like sheets of painted glass stacked on top of one another. If we decide we want to change any aspect of an image at any

stage of the process, we can simply access the layer in question and change it without affecting anything else. For example, if the image does not appear to have enough atmospheric depth to it, we could go back to some of the more distant layers and tone down some of the colours or cast a haze over the image. A digital matte painting might be made up of 50 or more layers. We can render each of these layers separately [<236] and give them to the compositor as individual elements, allowing them tremendous scope for refining the image when it is combined with the live action in the final composite.'

Like traditional matte paintings, digital matte paintings can be used to create 2-D extensions to live-action establishing shots filmed with a locked-off, unmoving camera, but the potential of the computer is now being harnessed to produce far more dynamic images. Traditionally, a production might build only those sections of sets which actors are to interact with – in the case of buildings, usually only the first storey. These would then be extended using matte paintings or miniatures. However, the limitations of these techniques meant that the camera normally had to remain in a fixed position for the duration of a shot. Moving it could result in a change of perspective, causing 3-D set and 2-D painting to become misaligned. Today, however, computer technology allows real environments to be supplemented with 3-D digital set extensions, allowing the camera to move around freely within a scene.

'The key to digital set extensions is camera match moving [<235], which gives us an accurate record of the movements of the live-action camera,' explains Barron. 'The ability to recover a camera move from a live-action plate means that instead of being limited to expanding a locked-off shot with a 2-D matte painting, we can create 3-D digital set extensions and then "film" them in the computer with identical camera moves. When rendered, these computer-generated elements can be composited into the footage of the partially built live-action environments. With a dimensional model instead of a flat painting, the camera can change perspective and the artificial additions to a scene will alter accordingly. We refer to the building of artificial environments in this way as the "digital backlot".'

A fine early example of a digital backlot created by Matte World Digital is the town of Seahaven, location for *The Truman Show* (1998). The production designer planned the downtown area of Seahaven using a CAD (computer-aided design) program. The resulting plans were used by construction crews to build full-size sets up to the first storey. Matte World Digital then used the same plans to create 3-D digital models of the top half of the buildings.

'Once we had the live-action location footage, we tracked the camera movements and applied those movements to the virtual camera that was used to film the digital models within the computer,' says Barron. 'We then combined these models with the bottom halves of the location sets. The result was shots in which the camera moved around real buildings with computer-generated extensions.'

With the digital models attached to their live-action foundations, Matte World Digital artists Evans and Brett Northcutt created texture maps to make the digital models match the real buildings. 'To make the top half of the buildings look like the bottom, we used photographs that Craig Barron had taken of the location sets,' explains Northcutt. 'We sampled areas of wood and entire items like windows and used them to make digital matte paintings, which were then applied to each side of the wire-frame digital models.'

To help the digital models match the real sets, Evans and Northcutt painted lighting effects such as highlights and shadows directly onto the digital matte paintings. 'Normally when you build digital models you have to light them digitally,' explains Northcutt. 'In this case, the lighting in the live-action scenes remained constant, so we actually painted the lighting effects directly onto our texture maps. The texture maps were therefore self-illuminating – that is, they needed no additional lighting to produce their look. However, we did add a few small lights around the periphery of the digital models, just to change the quality of their edges slightly and help them blend perfectly with the real sets.'

A common method of creating digital matte paintings is to first create a 2-D digital painting – much like a traditional matte painting – and then turn that 2-D image into a 3-D environment using a process called 'camera mapping'. Camera mapping works by projecting a 2-D painting into a computer-generated scene from the point of view of the virtual camera from which the scene is viewed. While looking at that painting, digital artists create a number of basic 3-D objects that correspond in shape, size and position to objects that appear in the painted image. If the painting were of a city, for example, a series of box meshes would be made and placed exactly where each of the buildings in the image appears. The 2-D image of each building would therefore be projected onto the side of an actual 3-D object. If the camera through which the scene is being viewed then moves, while the camera projecting the 2-D painting stays in the same place, the audience will be able to move past objects that move with a realistic sense of parallax, or perspective. Scenes created in this way are not truly 3-D; if the camera through which we view the scene moves too far from the position of the camera that projects the 2-D painting it will become clear that the objects in the scene have no real depth to them. For this reason the process of camera mapping is often referred to as '2½-D'. If truly dynamic shots are required, with the camera moving through the environment, more usual methods of CG model construction, texturing and lighting will be used.

With traditional matte painting shots, artists and technicians strove to disguise the matte line – the point at which two-dimensional painting and live-action footage met. But modern matte shots rarely have a single definable point at which reality stops and artifice begins. Digital matte shots are now often much more than the clever combination of two 'flat' elements and can be a complex interweaving of live-action footage, painted and photographic textures, 3-D digital models, animated characters, computer-generated particle and environment effects such as rain, water and trees, and interactive lighting effects, all filmed with a roving camera. 'Increasingly we find ourselves creating

ABOVE: **To create a shot of 1870s San Francisco for** *The Last Samurai* **(2004), Matte World Digital first filmed Tom Cruise and Billy Connolly using partial sets and a large green screen on the studio backlot (***top left***). San Francisco was then modelled using reference photographs from the period (***top right***) and rendered using global illumination to create naturalistic lighting. Animated cable cars and horse-drawn carriages were also combined with live-action extras to populate the streets. The distant sky, water and harbour were digitally painted (***above***).**

ABOVE: The 'digital backlot' is now vital to the creation of period settings on a grand scale. The Moving Picture Company used a combination of digital models and matte paintings to create historic vistas for *Troy* (2004, *top*) and *Kingdom of Heaven* (2005, *above*).

LEFT: To create a pan-down from an idealized New York skyline to the entrance of Grand Central station for *Down with Love* (2003), Matte World Digital filmed the station entrance set surrounded by green-screen material. They later match-moved that camera pan-down with a 3-D matte painting of famous New York buildings to create a seamless composite.

entire environments instead of just a snapshot of a scene as viewed from one angle,' states Craig Barron. 'An example of this was an establishing shot of 1870s San Francisco that we created for *The Last Samurai* [2004]. Visual effects supervisor Jeff Okun shot a live-action plate of Tom Cruise and Billy Connolly on the backlot street at the Warner Brothers Studios. As the actors walked out of an alleyway, the period set ended and they walked toward a large green screen while the camera craned upwards to see what would eventually become a view looking down a San Francisco street towards the Bay. We created all the rest of the shot with a 3-D environment. Referring to photographs from the period our digital matte artist Chris Stoski created 3-D buildings with painted textures that were lit using global illumination rendering techniques [<237]. We also added animated CG cable cars, horses and carriages, and additional extras who were our employees filmed in period costume.'

While matte painting was once a very distinct stand-alone visual effects technique, the place where matte painting stops and other forms of computer-generated effect take over is now as blurred as the very best of matte lines. 'What we do now is not really matte painting in the traditional sense,' admits Barron. 'We strive to create believable scenes and environments using whatever techniques help to sustain the illusion. We still call the work we produce "matte painting" because it's a term and a concept that people understand, though a better description might be "environment creation".'

However, Barron cautions against the tendency to believe that the rendering power of the computer can replace the skill of the trained artist. 'Many people think the computer can fix anything and that anything can be achieved digitally,' he says. 'To a degree that is true, but it's really the people working on the computers that make the shot. In our experience it still takes an accomplished artist, skilled in traditional and digital methods of image creation, to know if and why a shot is working and how to make it better. The artist knows how light, colour and composition work to sell a shot. Whatever new technology there might be around the corner always requires an artist who can make good aesthetic choices to make it work; that part will never change.'

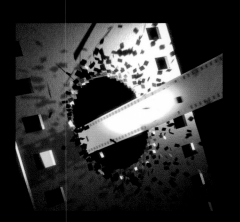

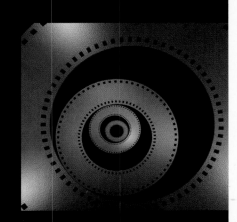

MAKE-UP

INTRODUCTION

Before the advent of the movies, theatre performers used make-up to strengthen their appearance when seen from a distance, making themselves more attractive, dramatic or loathsome as required. Their features had to be visible to the whole audience, even to theatre-goers in the most distant, low-priced seats.

Actors appearing in films quickly found that they needed a different kind of make-up. Appearing in close-up on the larger-than-life silver screen, there was little chance of their features being missed. A more subtle, tonal make-up was therefore required.

Appearing on film also presented actors with a new set of problems. Early black-and-white film was not capable of capturing every skin tone. Many actors, such as romantic idols Ramón Novarro and Rudolph Valentino, ringed their eyes with a wide rim of dark make-up so that the whites of their eyes would not blend in with the surrounding skin which became very pale when photographed.

The sensational subject matter that quickly became the staple of the movies often called for more than simple tonal make-up – monsters and madmen were the order of the day. Actors such as Lon Chaney (see panel) began to specialize in fantastic three-dimensional makeovers, using a range of primitive materials to transform the actual shape of the face. Mortician's wax or putty was smeared on and built up in thick layers, then sculpted to

PRECEDING PAGES: The sleek malevolence of one of cinema's greatest monsters would never have been possible without the extraordinary art and craft of the special effects make-up artist. This is the Queen Alien from *Alien Vs. Predator* (2004).

LEFT: The first great make-up artist, Lon Chaney, as he appeared in *The Phantom of the Opera* (1925).

BELOW LEFT: Wearing his Mr Hyde make-up for *Dr. Jekyll and Mr. Hyde* (1931), actor Frederick March enjoys afternoon tea with director Rouben Mamoulian and co-star Miriam Hopkins.

create false noses, scars and other horrific appendages. Perhaps the most unpleasant of these early materials was collodion, a syrupy liquid plastic normally used in the production of photographic plates. It was highly flammable and often irritating to the skin. Collodion, combined with cotton, was built up layer by layer to give Boris Karloff his freakishly high forehead in *Frankenstein* (1931; 272>).

The mechanical and optical principles of cinematography provided film actors with opportunities not available to stage actors. The frame-by-frame nature of film meant that radical changes could be made to a performer's appearance between takes. This technique was used in *The Wolf Man* (1941) to show Lon Chaney Jr (1906–73) changing from gentleman to werewolf. To effect the transformation, Chaney was positioned against a set of curtains that were starched to prevent any movement. The camera was also heavily weighted to hold it in place. When the actor had assumed a suitable stance, tiny nails were hammered into his costume to pin him to the wall and a few frames of film were shot. Make-up maestro Jack Pierce (271>) then applied make-up to begin Chaney's transformation from man to wolf. When the first stage of the make-up was ready, a few more frames were filmed and the process repeated. It took 21 make-up changes and 22 hours to film the scene. The transformation still looks remarkably eerie today, due in part to Pierce's remarkable make-up and, perhaps to some degree, because Chaney was quite exhausted by the time the final Wolf Man frames were filmed.

The optical characteristics of film were cleverly utilized during the filming of *Dr. Jekyll and Mr. Hyde* (1931). Actor Frederick March, who played the dual roles of Jekyll and Hyde, had two types of make-up applied to his face. His Mr Hyde character was created using green make-up while the Dr Jekyll make-up was applied in red. During filming, a green filter was placed over the camera lens, causing the red Dr Jekyll make-up to appear dark on the final black-and-white film while the green Mr Hyde make-up remained almost invisible. Replacing the green filter with a red one made the red make-up vanish and the green make-up appear – morphing the pleasant Dr Jekyll into the horrible Hyde before the audience's eyes.

A significant breakthrough in make-up came in the late 30s with the development of foam latex technology, used to make false noses, chins and other parts that could be stuck directly onto the actors' faces and bodies. The first major film to use foam latex appliances on a large scale was *The Wizard of Oz* (1939). The make-up artist Jack Dawn, among others, created the magical make-up for the film's much-loved characters. The pre-prepared foam latex pieces could be glued to the actors' faces at the start of each day, removing the need to build up fresh make-up each morning and guaranteeing consistent results. Foam latex appliances and costumes form the basis of many make-up effects to this day.

PROFILE **LON CHANEY**

The son of deaf-mute parents, Lon Chaney (originally Alonso Chaney; 1883–1930) learned to communicate through mime and facial expression at an early age. As an aspiring actor, Chaney toured in musical comedies for several years before arriving in Hollywood in 1912. Over the next five years, Chaney directed a number of films for Universal and appeared as a bit player in around 75 films, gradually gaining a reputation as an actor who could create almost any character through the use of make-up.

Chaney's big break came with *The Miracle Man* (1919), in which he played a con man who pretends to be contorted by paralysis. The film was the biggest hit of the year and established Chaney as a star. For his subsequent roles, Chaney created increasingly complicated and physically painful make-up designs. In *The Penalty* (1920), the actor tied his legs behind him and walked and jumped on wooden pegs strapped to his knees.

Chaney is best remembered for his monstrous but sympathetic characters in two epic films, *The Hunchback of Notre Dame* (1923) and *The Phantom of the Opera*

(1925). To create Quasimodo in *Notre Dame*, Chaney wore an 18 kg (40 lb) rubber hump that was strapped to a leather harness weighing a further 13.5 kg (30 lb). The actor filled his mouth with wax and covered one eye with putty. For the Phantom, Chaney gave himself painfully stretched features by inserting wires beneath his lower eyelids and inside his mouth and nostrils.

Chaney was secretive about his techniques, working on his own make-up behind locked doors until he was ready to appear before the camera. As a result, many of his methods remain a mystery. Chaney enjoyed hiding behind his make-up, and despite being one of Hollywood's greatest stars, was rarely recognized in public. A popular saying in the 20s was: 'Don't step on that spider – it might be Lon Chaney.'

Chaney died of bronchial cancer in 1930, just after the release of his first sound film, *The Unholy Three* (1930), directed by Tod Browning, for whom he had produced much of his best work. His life story was told in the film *The Man of a Thousand Faces* (1957), starring James Cagney.

LEFT: *The Wizard of Oz* (1939) became one of the most loved movies of all time. Characters such as Scarecrow and Tin Man were among the first to be made using foam latex, still the basis of many special effects make-up creations.

RIGHT: False teeth, contact lenses and foam-latex facial appliances contributed to the make-up effects of *The Exorcist* (1973), some of the scariest ever created. It was one of many graphic horror films made in the 70s and 80s.

The changing style and subject matter of the movies has been the cause of many revolutions and evolutions in the work of the make-up artist. The 1950s saw a rash of lurid science fiction films that required a range of aliens and atomically mutated creatures. This was the age of the rubber suit and a generation of stunt performers were dressed in latex to flail about in front of the cameras. The most fashionable couturier of the day was Paul Blaisdell, whose monstrosities added colour to films such as *It! The Terror from Beyond Space* (1958) and *Invasion of the Saucer Men* (1957).

From the 60s, mainstream movies became increasingly explicit, and film-makers dared show their audiences gruesome details of murders and mutations. Make-up artists became as adept at re-creating the appearance of the insides of the body as its exterior details. *The Exorcist* (1973) brought new levels of horror to the screen and inspired a generation of make-up effects artists specializing in fantasy and horror creations. Artists such as Bob Keen (*Hellraiser*, 1987; *Nightbreed*, 1990) and Tom Savini (*Friday the 13th*, 1980; *Day of the Dead*, 1985) populated our screens with increasingly realistic, if outrageously fantastic, characters.

Whether a film requires an actor to age by a decade or decompose before our eyes, to be subtly altered with a new nose or transformed into an astonishing character from our worst nightmares, special effects make-up artists the world over now use the same basic materials and methods.

PROFILE **JACK PIERCE**

The son of a Greek goatherd, Jack Pierce (born Janus Piccoulas, 1889–1968) emigrated to the US as a teenager. After early stints as a stage actor, stuntman, projectionist and cameraman, he settled for the greasepaint-and-powder life of a make-up artist. He became arguably the most celebrated and influential of Hollywood's make-up men.

One of Pierce's earliest monster make-ups was for the Fox production *The Monkey Talks* (1927), in which he used chamois leather, putty and spirit gum to build the features of a monkey onto the face of the actor Jacques Lerner. Pierce then moved to the make-up department at Universal where, over the course of the next 15 years, he created some of Hollywood's most memorable monsters.

Universal launched its celebrated cycle of horror films with *Dracula* (1931). The Count, played by Bela Lugosi, needed little physical alteration, but Pierce created a special green make-up that, when photographed with black-and-white film, gave the Prince of Darkness his eerie porcelain glower.

Later the same year Universal firmly established its

horror cycle, and Pierce his place in make-up history, with the production of *Frankenstein* (1931). Pierce's designs, applied to actor Boris Karloff, gave us the towering creature now recognized as the definitive image of Frankenstein's monster.

Pierce followed *Frankenstein* with *The Mummy* (1932), wrapping Karloff in bandages and thereby creating the prototype for the legions of movie mummies that have stumbled through horror films and comedies ever since. Pierce's other creations included the stars of *Bride of Frankenstein* (1935), *The Wolf Man* (1941) and *Phantom of the Opera* (1943).

Pierce became head of Universal's make-up department in 1936, where he stayed until the mid-40s when new management, keen to use modern materials and faster methods, clashed with the notoriously bad-tempered Pierce and his methodical use of traditional techniques. Pierce left Universal to become a freelance make-up artist, working on various television series throughout the 50s, but never again having the chance to startle and amaze the world with his glorious big-screen monsters.

FRANKENSTEIN

Following the enormous success of *Dracula* (1931), Universal began production of a series of horror films, starting with an adaptation of a recent stage version of Mary Shelley's classic tale of Gothic science fiction, *Frankenstein*. It would later film *The Mummy* (1932), *The Wolf Man* (1941) and *Phantom of the Opera* (1943), among others, stretching the skills and resources of the studio make-up department to the full.

The task of bringing *Frankenstein* to the screen was assigned to the English director and Hollywood newcomer James Whale (<25). Whale chose to cast a virtually unknown English actor, Boris Karloff (born William Henry Pratt, 1887–1969), as the monster – having spotted him lunching quietly in the studio canteen. The 44-year-old Karloff was offered the part of the monster only after it had been turned down by Bela Lugosi, who thought being almost entirely concealed behind make-up, as the role demanded, would do nothing for his career as a serious actor. Fortunately Karloff had no such misgivings, and ironically his subtle and sympathetic portrayal of the monster made him one of the best-known and best-loved stars of the 30s.

Turning the slight, mild-mannered Karloff into Frankenstein's monster was a make-up artist's dream come true. James Whale, an accomplished artist, produced detailed sketches of how he imagined Karloff as the monster. Universal's resident make-up genius, Jack Pierce (<271), took Whale's sketches and threw himself into the project, reading the original novel as well as books on human anatomy, medicine and surgery. With his new-found knowledge, and in close consultation with the director, Pierce designed a monster that he believed would be the most likely outcome of the processes described by Shelley, given that the book itself does not provide a definitive description of the monster's physical appearance.

Pierce began with the monster's head. 'I discovered that there are six ways that a surgeon can cut the skull,' he later explained. 'I figured that Dr Frankenstein, who was not a practising surgeon, would take the easiest. That is, he would cut the top of the skull straight across like the lid of a pot, hinge it, pop the brain in and clamp it tight.' The result of Pierce's reasoning was the tall square head with clamps and scars that is perhaps the most recognizable aspect of Karloff's monster.

Pierce built up the monster's head on top of Karloff's own features using many layers of cheesecloth soaked in collodion, a liquid made from cellulose dissolved in ether and alcohol which was once painted onto cuts like a form of liquid band-aid. It took six hours to apply the finished make-up and another one and a half to remove it. During these lengthy sessions Karloff, a heavy smoker, couldn't even relax with a cigarette as collodion was explosively flammable. Facial make-up also included a pair of heavy wax eyelids which, when attached to Karloff's own features, caused them to droop halfway over his eyes. Small wires were used to pull the corners of the actor's mouth out and downwards. Grey-green greasepaint helped to give the monster's face its deathly pallor when photographed. His other famous features – the conductive bolts in his neck – were so securely glued to Karloff's skin that he was left with small scars for years to come.

Karloff's height was increased to 2.3 m (7½ ft) with heavy platform boots and his legs were strapped to steel struts that prevented him from bending his knees, producing the awkward shuffling walk for which the creature became well known. Having read that the blood in decomposing bodies flows to the extremities, Pierce added a final grim touch by blackening the monster's fingertip. Sensing the visual power of Pierce's creation, Universal shrouded the production of the film in mystery, keeping the appearance of the monster a heavily guarded secret.

Frankenstein was a sensation on its release. The primitive methods of early sound mean that the film has lost a great deal of its power to shock, and in places it can seem as stiff and slow as the monster himself. However, film-goers of the day were genuinely involved by the sheer strangeness of the whole production, scared by Karloff's appearance and touched by his performance as the tormented, vulnerable monster.

The stark image of Pierce's monster is now so deeply embedded in our consciousness, and has been so frequently imitated, that it is difficult to imagine that Pierce was the first person to conceive such a design.

The film made a star of Karloff, secured the reputation of Pierce as one of Hollywood's foremost make-up artists and made Universal a box office fortune. Success led to the inevitable sequels, with Karloff sharing the screen with some sophisticated effects work for *Bride of Frankenstein* (1935) and returning again for *Son of Frankenstein* (1939) before handing the role on to other actors including Lon Chaney Jr and even the man who first refused the role – Bela Lugosi.

PROSTHETICS

Prosthetics – the art of creating three-dimensional make-up – depends on producing artificial appliances that can be accurately, and invisibly, attached to the performer. To create appliances that can transform the regular features of John Hurt into the hideously disfigured subject of *The Elephant Man* (1980), or Tim Roth into an ape warrior for *Planet of the Apes* (2001), the make-up artist must first acquire an accurate template of the face, or other body part, on which he or she will be working. These templates are created by taking a 'life cast' directly from the body of the performer.

LIFE CASTS

'Life casts are the first part of the process of creating prosthetic make-up', explains Tom Woodruff, who, with partner Alec Gillis, runs the Los Angeles-based special effects make-up company Amalgamated Dynamics Incorporated (ADI), which has created stunning make-up effects for films including *Alien*[3] (1992), *The Santa Clause* (1994) and *Alien Vs. Predator* (2004).

'Whatever we need to create – be it a simple blemish or a major facial mask – must be designed so that it perfectly fits the face or body of the actor beneath. To do that, we need a completely accurate representation of that performer'.

'The most common type of life cast is probably a face cast', says Woodruff. 'This is used to create things like masks, scars, false noses, bags under the eyes, double chins and so on'. To create a face cast, the performer is first fitted with a skullcap to prevent their hair from becoming entangled in the casting material. The back of the head is then covered with strips of plaster-covered bandage. The bandages are applied as far as a straight line running over the top of the head from ear to ear. The plaster back-piece takes around ten minutes to set, after which work can begin on the face.

'The face is the important part', comments Woodruff. 'We have to capture the exact shape of a performer's face with a neutral expression. In this way, the finished prosthetic appliance can be effectively glued to the actor's face and will easily conform to whatever expression they create when performing. For the front of the face, we use dental alginate – the waxy material that dentists use to take a cast of your teeth if you're having any major dental work done'. Dental alginate is a seaweed-based powder that, when mixed with

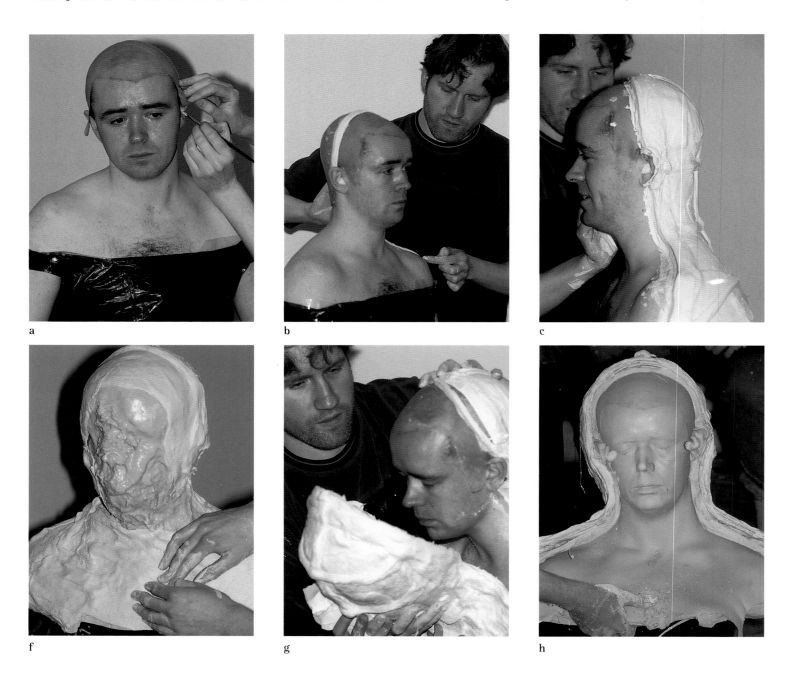

a

b

c

f

g

h

water, creates a paste that sets hard in less than 10 minutes. 'We carefully spoon it onto the performer's face, making sure that it gets into all the wrinkles and corners,' explains Woodruff. 'Too much will pull the lips and cheeks downwards, resulting in a misshapen cast. This is the point where people always expect to have straws stuck in their nose so that they can breathe. Actually, we don't do that because nostrils are never perfectly round, so straws don't fit them very well. Straws also tend to distort the nose shape and produce a bad cast. Instead, we leave the nostrils uncovered and carefully paint the alginate around them, which leaves the nasal cavities open.'

Once the layer of alginate has set and the performer's features are captured, the whole cast is reinforced with strips of plaster bandage that are wrapped over both the front and back of the head (still leaving the nasal holes unblocked). When this layer has set, after about 20 minutes, the cast is carefully cut in half from ear to ear across the top of the head, so that it separates into a plaster-and-bandage back-piece and an alginate-and-plaster front-piece.

Sitting completely still for half an hour, unable to talk, see or even hear properly, can be an intimidating experience, and the procedure affects

different people in different ways. 'Some people are fine having their cast done,' says Woodruff. 'Others are very nervous. These people cannot communicate with us – other than by moving their hands to let us know that they are still conscious under the plaster – so we just have to keep talking to them, reassuring them that everything is OK. Some people find the whole experience quite pleasant – it's dark and warm, and some describe it as kind of a womblike experience. Some people fall asleep, some pass out and some totally freak out and rip the plaster from their faces. We once did a cast of a Navy diver who was used to being in deep water and mud. However, when we got the alginate on his face, he just panicked and pulled it all off! You can never tell how it will affect someone, so you have to monitor each person constantly.'

Casts of body parts, or even the entire body, are produced in much the same way as facial casts. The performer stands upright and is often strapped to a frame to ensure that the same stance is maintained throughout the process. 'We normally cast bodies in neutral positions, with arms and legs open, so that the final shape allows access to all areas of the body,' says Woodruff. 'However, for *Demolition Man* [1993] we had to produce models

d

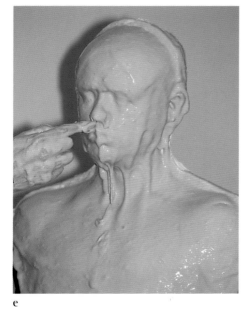

e

i

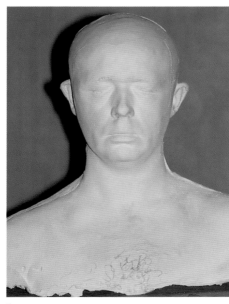

j

LEFT: **With a protective plastic cape around their body, the subject first has a bald cap glued over their head to cover the hair (a). Make-up artist Brendan Lonergan uses plaster bandages to build a ridge across the top of the head (b). The back of the head and shoulders are completely covered in plaster bandages (c). Powdered alginate is mixed with water and poured over the face (d). Keeping the nostrils clear, the mixture is gently worked into all areas of the subject's face to ensure an accurate cast (e). When the alginate has set, the front of the head is bandaged to the plaster back piece (f). After carefully cutting through the plaster across the seam, the life cast is gently removed in two halves (g). The two halves of the mould are bound together with another layer of plaster bandages (h). The empty mould is then filled with liquid casting plaster (i). When the plaster has set, the mould is carefully removed to reveal a perfect copy of the subject (j). This plaster life cast is normally used to create another exact copy of the face on which prosthetic appliances will be sculpted in clay.**

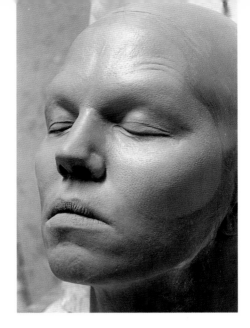

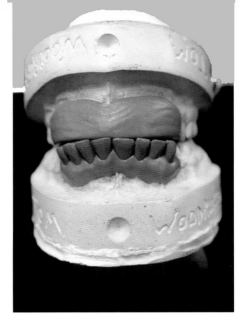

FAR LEFT: **Prosthetic facial appliances are created by sculpting the additions in clay over a life cast. Here subtle changes have been made to the cheeks, brows and forehead of the actor. Even the quality of the performer's skin has been carefully re-created.**

LEFT: **Here a new set of teeth has been sculpted on top of the cast taken from a performer's actual teeth. The new teeth will be cast in dental acrylic and will fit over the performer's teeth perfectly.**

RIGHT: **The functional exterior of fibreglass moulds gives little clue as to the delicately detailed foam-latex appliances that can emerge from within.**

of Wesley Snipes, Sylvester Stallone and about twenty other characters frozen in agonized positions. We didn't actually use the stars' bodies; we used body doubles and later grafted the stars' facial casts onto them. The body doubles had to be taped to metal poles in very uncomfortable positions in order to create their life casts.'

When the cast of a face or body feature has been produced, the result is a fragile two-part shell that is a perfect 'negative' of the performer. This shell is fitted back together and filled with a very fine gypsum plaster mix. When the plaster has set, the mould is opened and the result is a plaster bust – a 'positive' copy of the performer that replicates their form in every way. 'The live performer who we cover in plaster is the original positive, then we make a cast of that person and end up with a negative mould; says Woodruff. 'We fill this mould with plaster and end up with another positive – a perfect copy of the performer made in plaster. The rest of the process of producing prosthetic make-up operates on exactly the same principles – we continue making positive and negative copies of our original life cast together with the changes we make to it.'

SCULPTING

Having obtained a positive copy of a face or body part, the make-up artist can begin to design the prosthetic appliances. 'If we are producing a false nose for example, we take some clay and sculpt it directly on top of the nose on the plaster-cast head; explains Woodruff. 'What we are doing is producing a new face for the performer – it's their old face plus the new changes sculpted in clay over the top.' Any changes made in clay will ultimately become prosthetic appliances made in rubber.

The process of sculpting appliances is a fine art that combines the aesthetics of creating naturalistic body parts with the practical challenge of producing make-up pieces that can be easily reproduced and effectively fitted onto the performer. 'You want to get the best-looking appliance you can; says Woodruff, 'which means creating new shapes that complement the face below. At the same time, you have to think about practical aspects, such as where the finished appliance will blend into the real face, the way it will bend and perform, and how it will be moulded and cast.'

Designing the way that an appliance blends into the face of the performer is vitally important. 'The giveaway is the blend line; explains Woodruff. 'This is the edge of the rubber appliance where it tapers into the actor's skin. The trick is to make that line as delicate and subtle as possible.'

Part of the art of concealing the blend line is finding a good place for the line to run. 'If it's possible, good places are the natural creases of the performer's face, such as the crow's feet at the corners of the eyes, or under the eyebags if it's an older person. These wrinkles will be dark because they are in shadow, so it's easier to hide the join there. If it's a face without a lot of wrinkles, we just have to design the blend line so that it conforms to the natural contours. We always spend a lot of time making sure that there's a really smooth, delicate transition between clay and plaster life cast.'

Most prosthetics are designed to increase the size of a performer's features, and are simply applied over the top of the natural face and body. Sometimes, however, a sculpture is used to create features such as scars, which must appear to cut into the performer's skin. 'Obviously, we cannot actually take anything away from a performer's face; says Woodruff. 'To create an indentation, such as a scar or a bullet wound, we have to build up the area around the scar realistically, subtly thickening the flesh so we can then gouge out a scar that goes down until it reaches the performer's real flesh.'

The sculpted clay additions must match the performer's physical features exactly. 'If we are creating prosthetics to fit a face, we replicate the condition of that performer's skin on the sculpture. Using intricate tools, we individually create pockmarks and pores that look just like the ones on the performer's real skin. If we are creating an appliance to make the performer look older or fatter, we redesign the skin patterns on the model to account for these changes.'

When the clay additions that have been sculpted over the plaster life cast are complete, a mould of the new design is produced in much the same way that the original life cast of the performer was made.

A simple head mould can be made in two halves. If the sculpture is a complicated shape, however, such as the entire body of a creature that has been sculpted over the life cast of a performer's body, it may be necessary to create the mould in several pieces. This makes it easier to apply the finished prosthetic or creature costume to the performer and to remove it when shooting is finished.

The mould is created a section at a time by painting wax sealant over the life cast and its sculpted clay additions. Several layers of fibreglass resin called a 'gel coat' are then applied, taking care that the resin fills every detail of the sculpture. Chopped glass fibre is then sprinkled onto the resin and another layer of resin is painted on top of that. After several layers of sandwiched glass fibre and resin have been applied, a thick layer of tissue is arranged on the surface to prevent the sharp glass fibre shards from causing any harm. When the mould has dried the life cast is removed and the result is a fibreglass shell that is a perfect negative of the plaster life cast and its sculpted clay additions. The life cast then has the sculpted clay scraped off so that it returns to a perfect unadulterated replica of the performer.

Next, the life cast is placed back inside the newly created fibreglass mould. Between the cast and the mould there are now gaps – the space that was occupied by the sculpted clay additions. These gaps are filled with liquid foam latex, which when set results in an appliance that on the inside fits the features of the performer perfectly, and on the outside transforms the performer into the person or creature that was sculpted in clay.

MATERIALS

Foam latex, from which most prosthetics and creature skins are made, is a rubbery, spongelike material that is lightweight and easy to paint and glue. Every item requires a different type of foam latex, depending on its size and shape and the way in which it will be used. Producing the foam is both an art and a science.

At Jim Henson's Creature Shop, the foam lab is run by Marie Fraser, who spends her days carefully measuring, mixing and cooking noxious substances. 'First, we decide what the character needs to look like and how it will perform,' explains Fraser. 'This determines the type of foam latex that we will create. A large creature whose skin does not move very much, such as a dinosaur, would probably have a skin of sturdy, dense foam latex. A creature such as a puppy, with wrinkly, flexible skin, would be made out of a foam latex that is thinner and much softer.'

The first stage in the production of foam latex involves mixing together the basic ingredients in the correct proportions. The most important constituent is liquid latex, a milky white fluid that comes from the Malaysian rubber tree. Various chemicals, including preservatives and fungicides, are added to the liquid before use. The mix is carefully measured out and a foaming agent added to it. Foaming agents are a type of soap that causes the latex to produce bubbles. Different grades of soap produce different qualities of bubble, and the soaps are carefully weighed and combined before being used to produce the desired foam. Next a curing agent is added, to turn the mixture into a solid sponge when it is finally baked. The result is a syrupy, somewhat smelly substance. At this stage a dye may be added so that the foam will be the correct base colour for the creature in question. Once combined, the ingredients are placed in a food mixer. The machines used at Henson's range from ordinary household kitchen appliances that can mix a couple of pints or litres at a time, to a battery of industrial-sized machines that can work on much larger quantities. 'We can control the softness of the final foam latex by the amount that we whip it up at this stage,' explains Fraser. 'If we only whip it for a short while, the bubbles will be small and this will produce a heavier, more solid foam. If we really whip the mixture until it is light and fluffy, the resulting foam will look more like a bath sponge.' As

the foam begins to reach the desired consistency, a gelling agent is added to the mix. This will cause the foam to set in its risen state when it is in the mould.

Small, simple-shaped moulds have the foam mixture carefully spooned into them. Larger or more complicated moulds have the foam injected into them using a giant syringe that forces the foam into every cavity. Small air holes are drilled into the mould to allow air to escape the gushing foam. If the item being cast will be put under stress during filming, the mould may first be lined with pieces of nylon or Lycra, which help to reinforce the finished foam piece.

In the case of entire creature suits to be worn by the performer, a Lycra or spandex suit is stretched over the mould's inner core before the foam latex is introduced. The result is a stretchy bodysuit with a sculpted foam latex outer skin.

Once filled, the mould is left for around 15 minutes so the gelling agent can set the foam. The entire mould is then placed in an oven and cured at 80–100°C for an hour or two. When the oven is opened, the unpleasant smell of sulphur – released from the foam during the curing process – wafts out. The mould is then opened and the foam rubber piece allowed to cool before being removed and thoroughly washed to remove its sulphurous stench.

The resulting foam latex item is a perfect positive copy of the mould in which it was cast. Every minute wrinkle and skin pore of the original sculpture appears on the surface of the latex. When the small flanges of latex that result from the seams of the mould have been trimmed from the cast, it is ready to be painted with acrylic paint that has been mixed with Pros-Aide (a type of flexible glue that helps the paint to adhere to the latex).

While foam latex has been the mainstay of special effects make-up since the late 30s, a number of alternatives are becoming increasingly popular. 'Foam latex is great for a lot of things,' explains Tom Woodruff. 'It is fine for creatures that have tough, leathery skin – an elephant, for example. However, if you look at some creatures, humans included, you realize that their skin is actually translucent. You can actually see the roots of the hairs below the surface. Even when it is painted really beautifully, foam latex can never have this quality – it will look like a painted, solid surface.'

To produce more subtle flesh effects, silicone is becoming increasingly popular. 'Silicone is

RIGHT: **Once removed from the moulds, foam-latex skins and appliances are thoroughly soaked and washed to remove their unpleasant odour.**

FAR RIGHT, ABOVE: **A one-piece foam-latex hedgehog skin ready to have its internal head and body mechanisms fitted.**

FAR RIGHT, BELOW: **ADI created this silicone bust of actor Christopher Lloyd for a scene in** *My Favorite Martian* **(1999). Silicone is often favoured for its translucence, making it visually similar to human skin.**

BELOW: **Using giant syringes, technicians pump gallons of liquid foam latex into fibreglass moulds at Jim Henson's Creature Shop.**

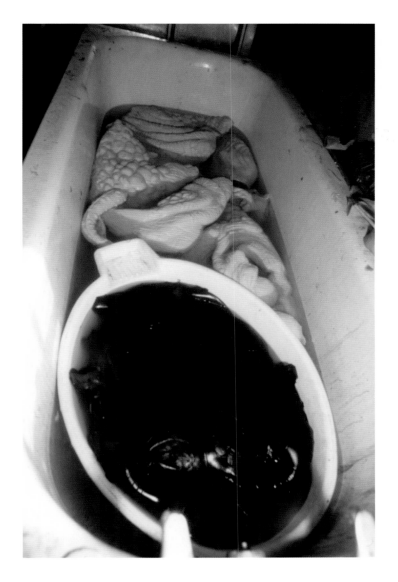

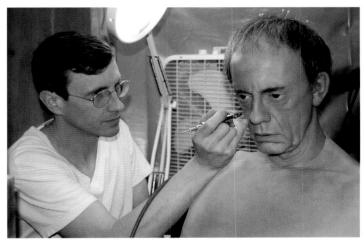

translucent like real flesh, and it jiggles like flesh. It is a far more convincing material for many purposes', claims Woodruff, who first used silicone for the animatronic human bodies that he created for *Death Becomes Her* (1992). 'It is especially good for animatronic faces, because it transfers the mechanical movements under the flesh into convincing and supple movements on the surface'.

Silicone comes in the form of a greasy cream, rather like soft petroleum jelly. Unlike foam latex, silicone is not baked in order to solidify it. Instead, a chemical catalyst that hardens the silicone is mixed into the liquid before it is injected into the mould. Other ingredients can also be added, including softeners to produce a silicone that is less rubbery, and dyes to create the appropriate colour. Dying silicone is important because the material continually exudes a sort of oily sweat, which makes painting its surface difficult. 'We have to seal silicone to cut down its oiliness, and then we paint over it in many thin layers of translucent oil-based paint to slowly build up the colour that we want', explains Woodruff. 'Building up the colour in this way gives a finer effect and is much more like the way our own skin colour is built up layer by layer'.

Although silicone looks good, it does have disadvantages. 'Silicone is very heavy', says Woodruff, 'so it's fairly impractical for use on a whole creature, especially one with a human operator inside. Instead, we might use a mixture of foam latex and silicone on a character, only using the silicone for the particularly expressive areas like the face. Also, because it's so oily, it

is very hard to stick silicone to the skin when it is used for prosthetic appliances. The edges are especially tricky to get right when applying silicone prosthetics. Foam latex can be squashed and crushed into shape at the edges, but silicone won't change its shape at all'.

Woodruff and his partner Alec Gillis are always searching for new materials that can be used for their make-up creations. 'Many industries are continually inventing new types of plastics, polymers and resins for their own purposes, and we need to keep our ears to the ground because they could be making the perfect materials for us', says Gillis.

Woodruff and Gillis accidentally found a new material while working on *The Santa Clause* (1994). 'We were trying to figure out what we should use to make a fat belly for Tim Allen', explains Gillis. 'This was for a really important scene in the movie, because it was the one time that we would see that Allen actually had a fat body and wasn't just wearing clothes with some stuffing underneath. We were thinking about using silicone – which is fleshy like fat but not quite as wobbly – when a salesman turned up with a block of this amazing blubbery material that was the accidental result of a failed experiment into a new type of glue. We experimented with it, and discovered how to work with it, which involved melting it at 200°C [400°F] and designing moulds that wouldn't squirt the pressure-injected boiling liquid onto anyone, and we made a totally convincing wobbly fat belly for Tim Allen. He was really pleased with the result, because he overheard someone at a screening say that he had eaten lots of potatoes to get fat for the film!'

AGEING

Artificial ageing is perhaps one of the most common movie make-up effects. Many actors are required to age subtly by a matter of a few years, or perhaps a decade, during the course of a film. Some films have even required young actors to be transformed into characters two or three times their own age.

The undisputed master of old-age make-up effects for film and television is Dick Smith (1922–). Smith began his career in 1945 when, fresh out of Yale University, he became the first staff make-up artist at the newly formed NBC television station. The quality of the early television images was poor, and make-up artists were able to use relatively crude make-up effects. As the quality of television images improved, however, artists such as Smith found themselves having to develop increasingly sophisticated make-up techniques that would stand up to closer scrutiny.

In his 14 years at NBC, Smith became an expert in the art of quick-change make-up. At that time, many television dramas were performed live, and as a performer left the set, Smith might have mere seconds to age them before their next appearance. Smith's quick-change masterpiece was *Victoria Regina* (1957), an hour-and-a-half live drama starring Claire Bloom as Queen Victoria.

During the broadcast, the actress had to age from a young princess to an elderly queen. As the actress moved between sets during the three-minute commercial breaks, Smith and his assistants applied foam latex neck, jowl and nose appliances to her face. With successive breaks more appliances were added on top of the existing make-up, including foam latex eyebags, eyelids and a sagging lower lip and chin. The lines and wrinkles of old age were printed onto the queen's brow using a specially designed rubber stamp. Her final aged appearance was too much to achieve in only a few minutes, however. Instead, a one-piece rubber mask was created and worn by another actress, who mouthed the lines of the 80-year-old queen as Bloom recited them from behind the camera.

In the 60s, Smith – by now recognized as one of the leading make-up artists – began to work in feature film production, where image quality demanded far greater subtlety, and budgets allowed longer design and preparation time.

Smith's first widely recognized feature film success came when he added nine decades to the youthful face of actor Dustin Hoffman for *Little Big Man* (1970). Until this time, old-age make-up was generally achieved using a one-piece sculpted mask that had all the sags and wrinkles built into it. One of Smith's innovations was a make-up design that consisted of a number of small, overlapping foam latex appliances built up on the face. These were produced by sculpting the entire old-age face using Plasteline (a material rather like Plasticine) on a life cast of the actor that had first been given a thin coating of rubber.

Smith spent six weeks sculpting Hoffman's old-age face. Referring to photographs of elderly people, Smith realized that, contrary to common belief, people actually become less wrinkled in extreme old age. After a certain point, the skin becomes so thin that the lines and wrinkles that have gathered over the years actually melt away into expansive areas of soft skin. When the sculpture was satisfactory,

RIGHT: Using overlapping facial appliances for the first time, Dick Smith aged the 33-year-old Dustin Hoffman by 90 years for *Little Big Man* (1970).

FAR RIGHT: Dick Smith won an Oscar for the old-age make-up that he used to transform F. Murray Abraham into the composer Antonio Salieri for *Amadeus* (1984).

BELOW LEFT: Dick Smith carefully applies old-age stipple to wrinkle Marlon Brando's skin for *The Godfather* (1972).

BELOW: Brando, then aged 47, as he appeared in the finished film.

Smith divided the face into the different sections that he would use as final prosthetic pieces – eyelids, cheeks, nose and upper lip, lower lip and chin, and the front half of the neck. These sections were individually cut from the surface of the sculpture with a scalpel and then peeled away. The sculpted pieces were then used to produce moulds for the prosthetic appliances.

The resulting foam latex appliances were pre-painted to save time when applied to the actor. Even so, the 33-year-old Dustin Hoffman was subjected to over five hours in Smith's make-up chair each time he was transformed into the film's 121-year-old survivor of Custer's last stand.

Smith paid particular attention to the bald skullcap that went over Hoffman's own hair. Traditionally, these caps were made of an elasticated plastic material that stretched over the actor's head. The caps were smooth and featureless and, once fitted, had to have additional make-up applied to give them texture. However, shortly before Smith worked on *Little Big Man*, the British make-up artist Stuart Freeborn had perfected a method of making a foam latex cap that had every anatomical detail sculpted onto it. The cap, developed to age the actor Keir Dullea for *2001: A Space Odyssey* (1968), was made in two pieces – front and back – with gently overlapping edges. Smith improved on Freeborn's innovation by punching individual hairs into the edges of the cap to create a realistic fringe around the ears and neck.

One of Smith's other innovations was the development of more realistic eyelids. Traditionally, fake eyelids were sculpted and fitted slightly in front of an actor's own eyelids like a fixed shield. When a performer blinked, their own eyelids would move down behind the fake appliances. For Hoffman's make-up, Smith created a complicated mould and developed a specially thin and flexible type of foam latex. The resulting appliances were placed over Hoffman's own eyelids and glued to his skin at the top and bottom edges – just under the eyebrows and above the eyelashes. These artificial eyelids actually blinked whenever Hoffman blinked. Ironically, despite Smith's efforts, Hoffman's ancient character does not blink in any of his close-ups.

Smith also created foam latex appliances for the back of Hoffman's hands. These caused some problems because Hoffman's character smoked, and the ash from his cigarette occasionally melted their rubber surface. Once the array of prosthetic appliances was attached to Hoffman's face and hands, Smith applied make-up on top, accentuating wrinkles where necessary and adding liver spots, one of the sure signs of old age.

The following year, Smith was asked to age Marlon Brando by around 20 years for *The Godfather* (1972). For this altogether more subtle make-up, Smith was prevented from using prosthetic appliances because the star did not relish the time and trouble that such techniques involved. Instead, he devised a simpler make-up that did not entail making life casts or quite so many hours spent in the make-up chair.

The 47-year-old Brando's hair was already grey, but Smith actually dyed much of the actor's hair black. Brando's remaining grey hair, and some that was dyed white, was then combed back through the black hair to look more like hair that was in the process of ageing. Brando's eyebrows were also greyed. Since Brando did not want the shape of his face changed by prosthetics, Smith used a 'dental plumper' – a thick wire that runs around the lower teeth to give the appearance of pronounced gums. Attached to the sides of this wire were pieces of moulded dental plastic, which pushed out the lower cheeks to give the appearance of jowls. The actor's teeth were also painted a shade of brown to represent nicotine stains.

To give Brando's skin the appearance of old age, Smith applied several layers of old-age stipple – a mixture that includes liquid latex, gelatin and talcum powder that is dabbed onto the skin with a sponge. Immediately after application, the actor's skin is stretched and the latex dried with a hairdryer. When the latex has set, the skin is released but is prevented from returning to its original shape by its coat of latex, causing it to wrinkle like old skin.

One of Smith's most successful old-age make-ups was the addition of 30 years to the face of actor Max von Sydow as Father Merrin in *The Exorcist* (1973). Von Sydow was not required to age during the course of the film, but was chosen by the director William Friedkin for his ability to play the role despite the fact that he was some 30 years younger than his character. Smith's make-up scheme involved the use of prosthetic appliances on the cheeks, upper lip and chin, and a wrinkled wattle for his neck. These were supplemented by coats of old-age stipple on the forehead, neck, hands and around the eyes. An unusual requirement of Smith's make-up for von Sydow was that it be heat-resistant. Some scenes were to be filmed in the deserts of Iraq, and Smith knew from experience that the latex stipple could melt in warm conditions. As a result, Smith used a particularly stubborn stipple formula that he had accidentally discovered while working in television many years before. Later scenes were filmed in a bedroom set that was built within a giant refrigerator so that the actor's breath would be visible. Different make-up formulations were developed to prevent the stipple from becoming too brittle in the cold.

Smith's make-up on Max von Sydow was so convincing that many people have seen *The Exorcist* without realizing that the old priest is played by a young actor with heavy and elaborate make-up.

In 1985 Smith won an Oscar for his remarkable old-age make-up work for *Amadeus* (1984). Smith's old-age make-up for F. Murray Abraham, who played the composer Antonio Salieri, was particularly challenging since the narrative of the film continually moves back and forth using flashbacks. Both young and old Salieri characters are seen in quick succession, which could have made the use of make-up all the more obvious to the audience. Smith's job was made even more demanding because Abraham has pockmarked skin, and his old-age prosthetics had to be sculpted to represent the same skin in later life.

Since entering semi-retirement Smith continues to design make-up and work as a make-up consultant on films including *Death Becomes Her* (1992) and *House on Haunted Hill* (1999).

ANIMATRONICS

The term 'animatronic' was first coined in the early 60s when Walt Disney attempted to bring three-dimensional mechanical figures to life for his revolutionary theme park, Disneyland. Among the Magic Kingdom's attractions when it opened in July 1955 were a cruise through jungle waters populated by simplistic mechanical beasts, and a mechanical barber-shop quartet whose members moved and sang by virtue of a series of metal spindles or cams.

As part of the ongoing improvements to his park, Disney planned a restaurant called the Enchanted Tiki Room, where mechanical birds would perform and sing to diners at the end of their meal. With help from the studio's electrical and sound departments, Disneyland's engineers created a system that employed the magnetic audio recording used for the birdsong to send electrical signals to the motors that controlled the mechanical creatures. The Enchanted Tiki Room opened in 1963, and the success of its 200 performing birds led Disney to build a more elaborate exhibit called the Hall of Presidents, using the same electromechanical system to make a moving, talking re-creation of Abraham Lincoln. Since the system combined sound, animation and electronics, Disney christened the method 'audio-animatronics'.

Although the practice of bringing life to mechanical creations was not given a name until the 60s, film-makers had relied on such techniques since the earliest days of film. Edwin S. Porter's (<17) *The Eagle's Nest* (1907) featured a crude model of a giant eagle. The bird, which had hinged wings, was suspended on piano wire and filmed 'flying' in front of a moving scenic background with a snatched baby clutched in its talons. In a climactic clifftop scene, the eagle lurched and juddered in battle with future director D.W. Griffith, then an aspiring young actor.

In 1911 Georges Méliès (<14) created the 7.5 m (25 ft) bust of a giant ice monster for *The Conquest of the Pole* (1912). The creature had rolling eyes and a gaping mouth, and its unwieldy 6 m (20 ft) arms were raised and lowered by two men pulling on cables from an overhead gantry.

A landmark mechanical monster was created at Germany's technologically advanced UFA studios (<21), where a huge model of the legendary dragon Fafner was constructed for Fritz Lang's *Die Niebelungen* (1924). The 18 m (60 ft) dragon had an articulated skeleton, which allowed its body and limbs to flex naturalistically. It also had a flexible outer skin of scales made of vulcanized rubber, and could even drink water, breathe fire and bleed when stabbed. Seventeen technicians laboured to create the dragon's performance – four were concealed within the creature itself, while others worked below in a trench containing rails on which the whole contraption moved back and forth.

Early animatronic creatures were necessarily large, because the mechanical systems used to produce their movement relied on bulky, low-tech cables, levers, gears and hinges. Subtle expression was not an option – creatures were brought to life through the large-scale movements of major limbs, with perhaps the occasional roll of an eye and gape of the mouth to suggest higher consciousness. These mechanical monsters, simplistic by today's standards, nevertheless proved popular characters in adventure and fantasy films of all varieties. The star of *King Kong* (1933) was a stop-motion (<181) animated gorilla just 46 cm (18 in) high, but for scenes in which the creature was seen in extreme close-up, a 4.6 m (15 ft) 'life-sized' bust of the great ape was constructed. This was built using a wood and metal frame interwoven with cloth to create what looked like a wickerwork ape. This frame was clothed in 30 tailored bearskins. The beast's plaster eyes were 30 cm (12 in) in diameter, he had a 60 cm (2 ft) nose and 120 cm (4 ft) eyebrows, and his wooden incisor teeth were 25 cm (10 in) long. Three men squeezed inside Kong's head to operate the cables, levers and compressed-air mechanisms that controlled the eyes, eyebrows, nose, mouth and lips. Kong's facial performance, particularly in his scenes with Fay Wray, is surprisingly expressive. Other full-size props included an articulated hand that could close around Fay Wray, and a huge foot and lower leg used to trample extras.

The alternative to building entirely mechanical creatures was to build them around existing life forms – usually human performers. Dressing people in creature costumes had, of course, been done in the theatre for hundreds of years. The technique was first used on film by Georges Méliès, who created a troupe of stylish lunar nymphs with papier mâché heads for *A Trip to the Moon* (1902). The technique flourished with the rash of science fiction movies that were made in the 50s – the skimpy budgets of many could not stretch to anything more sophisticated than a man in a rubber suit. Perhaps the most popular rubber-suit creation of the era was the star of *Creature from the Black Lagoon* (1954). The film's monster, the Gill Man, was played by several performers, including the swimmer Ricou Browning, who swam underwater in a heavy rubber suit while holding his breath for several minutes. The Gill Man was so popular that he appeared in two sequels. In Japan, Toho Studios used 'suitmation' methods to create the enduring star of *Gojira* (1954) and its many sequels (300>).

The birth of the sophisticated modern rubber suit, which allows a performer to control the overall body and limb movements while an

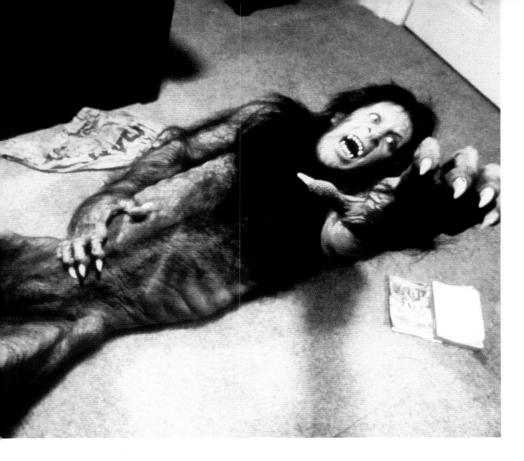

external puppeteer operates subtle facial expressions, can be traced to the work of the British make-up artist Stuart Freeborn. Freeborn designed and built the prehistoric apes that appear in the opening sequence of *2001: A Space Odyssey* (1968). Unhappy with the level of facial expression that he was able to achieve with a performer wearing layers of prosthetic appliances or a cover-all rubber mask, Freeborn devised an ape make-up with facial movement that could be controlled by the wearer. To make the rubber lips of an ape curl, Freeborn fitted a plate to the underside of the performer's chin. The plate was attached to cables that operated a lip-control mechanism attached to the ape's mouth. When the performer opened their mouth, the plate would move and the ape would snarl. For occasions when a snarl was needed while the mouth remained closed, Freeborn devised a toggle that fitted into the mouth of the performer. By using their tongue to pull the toggle, the performer could curl the lips of the face mask.

Freeborn built the Chewbacca costume for *Star Wars* (1977) using a similar internally controlled face mask and was subsequently asked to produce creatures for the film's sequel, *The Empire Strikes Back* (1980). Among the menagerie of the follow-up was the Jedi Master Yoda, an ancient green wizard who was actually a sophisticated glove puppet, operated and voiced by Muppet performer Frank Oz (1944–).

Executive producer George Lucas (<39) was worried about relying on an artificial performance for one of the film's most pivotal characters, and asked fellow fantasy film-maker Jim Henson (284>) for help and advice. Freeborn received a great deal of valuable guidance from Jim Henson's Creature Shop, which was at the time developing revolutionary creature performance techniques for *The Dark Crystal* (1982, 284>).

Freeborn's Yoda and Henson's creations for *The Dark Crystal* were the first steps in an animatronic revolution that used increasingly sophisticated technology to create subtle and naturalistic creature performances. Other influential animatronic work was seen in *The Howling* (1981) and *An American Werewolf in London* (1981), both of which combined make-up and mechanics to turn humans into werewolves. In the mid-90s, the art of animatronics was fused with computer-control technology to produce the frighteningly convincing dinosaurs that roamed *Jurassic Park* (1993) and farm animals so lifelike that they could be intercut with the real thing for *Babe* (1995).

Today, animatronic work fits into two broad categories. The simpler method is the person-in-a-suit approach. Such creatures usually have their major limbs operated by a performer encased within a sculpted rubber suit, but have a mechanical head and other moving appendages operated by remote control. The alternative is an entirely mechanical creature – hosting an interior packed with motors, gears and wires – that is operated by external puppeteers. Whichever method is used, the goal of such creations is to produce convincing, lifelike characters whose existence will not be questioned by the audience.

TOP: **Ricou Browning is helped into his rubber costume for *Creature from the Black Lagoon* (1954), perhaps the most famous monster suit of all time.**

ABOVE: **With a little help from Muppet performer Frank Oz, the wizened Jedi Master Yoda was able to give a convincing performance alongside luminaries such as Alec Guinness in *The Empire Strikes Back* (1980).**

ABOVE LEFT: **Rick Baker won an Academy Award for the incredible transformation scenes in *An American Werewolf in London* (1981). Oscars for special effects make-up were historically awarded only occasionally, but after 1981 the category became a permanent one.**

FAR LEFT, ABOVE: **Though a stop-motion animated puppet was used for most shots of the giant star of *King Kong* (1933), close-ups were achieved using a 4.5 m (15 ft) mechanical bust and a full-size articulated hand and forearm.**

FAR LEFT, BELOW: **A dragon named Fafner was one of the earliest mechanical film stars. Seventeen technicians worked to create his performance in *Die Niebelungen* (1924).**

THE DARK CRYSTAL

From the beginning of his career in the mid-50s, Jim Henson (1936–90) strove to create increasingly sophisticated puppets that would produce ever more subtle and convincing performances. Most of Henson's work centred on The Muppets, the gang of zany animal-inspired puppets that appeared in their own television show (1976–81) and even feature films, beginning with *The Muppet Movie* (1979).

But the Muppets, for all their lovable antics, could never be anything more than colourful glove puppets. Henson longed to use the talented artists, technicians and performers with whom he worked to create a new form of storytelling.

Henson dreamt of creating a magical world, populated entirely by extraordinary creatures, but didn't actually have a screenplay, or even a particular story in mind – more of a sense of time and place from which he would ultimately extract a tale. Henson asked the British fantasy illustrator Brian Froud to begin designing a new world and its inhabitants. Froud produced thousands of intricately detailed sketches, and even small sculptures, of the imaginary inhabitants of a fantastical planet. It was these characters and locations that eventually inspired the story Henson called *The Dark Crystal* (1982).

Henson's idea was a bold one. He wanted to create a film in which no humans appeared – only imaginary characters created from foam latex and cloth. In 1979 Henson set up a workshop in London to begin designing and building the creatures that would populate the world of *The Dark Crystal*. It was the first time that such complex puppet characters had been created for a film. Many of the techniques commonly in use today were first developed here, bringing life to characters such as the evil vulture-beaked Skeksis, the wise and melancholy Mystics and the film's most humanlike characters, the Gelflings.

Large creatures such as the Skeksis were designed to fit around human performers. The body of each Skeksis was built onto a lightweight metal harness which was cantilevered from the performer's hips. As a result, the character would appear to 'float' above the performer below in a peculiarly nonhuman form of movement. The performer hidden beneath each Skeksis's swath of robes would provide the creature's gross body movements, while up to four additional puppeteers manipulated rods and cables to control the movement of other bodily features.

Performers also crouched inside the 30 kg (70 lb) shells of the crablike Garthim foot soldiers. These costumes were so heavy that between takes the shells were hung on racks while the performers, still strapped to their underside, relaxed below. Perhaps the most extraordinary performer-based characters were the Land-Striders, batlike creatures perched atop a set of spindly 4.5 m (15 ft) legs. Carbon-fibre stilts were attached to the arms and legs of a performer who strode forwards in a crouched fashion. Rubber tendons were attached between the creature's pelvis and the top of each stilt, and covered with a fleshlike fabric that stretched realistically with each stride.

By modern standards, the creature control mechanisms were basic. The wooden keys of an organlike contraption could be played to create the movement of a character's hand. Breathing movements were achieved by inflating and deflating balloons inside characters' cheeks. Radio control was at first used sparingly to operate the eye movements of some characters, but during production more sophisticated methods were developed. The two lead Gelfling characters were given all of their most subtle facial movements via radio control – a considerable breakthrough then, but now common practice.

The Dark Crystal was not a box office success, perhaps because its fantastic special effects were not matched by an equally compelling story. However, the film had proved that convincing, naturalistic performances could be coaxed from a collection of foam-rubber contraptions. The Henson organization today remains a pioneer in the field of animatronics.

CHARACTER DESIGN

Building an artificial creature – even a down-to-earth domestic animal – always begins with a period of intensive design work. The design of a character not only determines its physical appearance, but also has considerable influence on the way in which it will be built, performed and filmed.

'All character design starts with the script,' comments Mark 'Crash' McCreery, the character designer who shaped the inhabitants of the *Jurassic Park* movies (1993, 1997, 2001), the beastly star of *The Relic* (1997), the bionic stars of *Hulk* (2003), and the ghouls of *Pirates of the Caribbean* (2003) and *Van Helsing* (2004), among many others. 'Some scripts have elaborate descriptions of a character that tell us exactly what it should look like, but sometimes all we have to go on is what we are told about the way it moves or behaves. Occasionally you'll get a director like Tim Burton or James Cameron, who already has a very strong idea about what something should look like and may already have made some sketches of their own. Then it's a case of reinterpreting their ideas to produce a practical character. For *Edward Scissorhands* [1990], Tim Burton had already drawn some lovely concepts – they really conveyed the fragile nature of the Edward character. However, his designs didn't really relate to reality. I had to find a way of turning the drawings into practical designs that could be manufactured and fitted to a performer, while keeping to the original spirit of Tim's vision.

'When designing a character, there are a number of things to consider other than just the look of a character,' explains McCreery. 'I need to know what the budget constraints are – is this going to be a fully animatronic creature, or a guy in a suit? If it is a guy in a suit, anything I create will have to be fitted around the human anatomy, which can be very limiting. It also helps to know what kind of schedule we're dealing with. It's no good designing the most fantastic and elaborate character if we only have one month to build it or there will only be a few days to film it. All these mundane but very important practical aspects have to be considered before I can begin to get creative.'

The design process may involve weeks of research and many dozens of development sketches. 'I look at a lot of books, watch wildlife documentaries, sometimes visit the zoo – whatever it takes to be inspired before I start drawing,' comments McCreery. 'Sometimes it can take a lot of scrappy little sketches before something starts to look right. Other times you can think about it for a while before getting it right in just one or two drawings.'

However well conceived, McCreery's initial designs are unlikely to end up on the screen. 'Once I have a design, it goes out to the director or the producer or the studio. Very often these people have no preconceived idea of what the character should look like, but as soon as they see a design, they start to tell you what they definitely don't want and how it should change. I often get quite attached to a character that I have developed over a period of time, and it's frustrating having to change all the things that you think are neat about it. At the end of the day, though, this is a business and we have to do what the client wants, not what satisfies us personally.'

According to McCreery, the design of a creature can involve much more than its physical appearance. 'If there's time, I try to do what I call "attitude" drawings. Most design work involves simply planning the physique of a character – its dimensions and form – but by drawing the creature in action, in its own environment, we can really impart a sense of what or who this character is – how it thinks and moves.' The way a creature will eventually move is an important part of the design

equation for McCreery. 'Sometimes you see creatures in a film whose movements just don't seem to match the way they look. That's because they haven't really been designed with their performance in mind. It's very important to know what animatronic or puppetry method will be used, because that will affect the way creatures move and how they should be designed.'

McCreery spent over a year producing concepts for the cast of *Jurassic Park* (1993). McCreery's designs not only dictated the appearance of the beasts, but also influenced their eventual behaviour. 'I spent a couple of weeks on a sketch of the T rex coming out of some trees,' remembers McCreery. 'The current thinking was that dinosaurs had evolved into modern-day birds, so I gave the T rex very birdlike talons and eagle-like eyes. It was kind of pouncing out of the jungle rather than lumbering in the way that dinosaurs had traditionally been depicted. The ultimate design changed somewhat, but that drawing really affected the way the dinosaurs were approached in the whole film – as warm-blooded, fast-moving animals, not slow, old reptiles.'

When the design of a character has been approved on paper, a small clay sculpture called a maquette is produced. 'Even though you have been working on a paper design for weeks, you never really know how it's going to look until you get this little sculpted clay model. Then you can see if there's something a bit funny about the legs or the neck, and maybe it doesn't work as well from some angles as it does from others,' says McCreery. 'Maquettes are also a really useful way of checking a design with the mechanical guys. They will be able to tell if a limb is going to be too small to get a hydraulic mechanism into it, or if some other aspect isn't going to work for them.'

As well as helping to decide the final shape of a character, maquettes are used to plan its colour and texture. 'When we have nailed the shape of the character, we'll spend time on the fine details. In the case of a dinosaur, this might involve working on the exact pattern of its scales,' says McCreery. 'We also think about colour design, which is the icing on the cake. The colouring of a creature can make a big difference to its success on screen, but you really can't tell how well a colour scheme will work until you see it on the model.'

Many character designers are starting to switch from the traditional artists' materials of pen, paper and modelling clay to more modern alternatives. Many now draw and paint characters using 2-D design software while others sculpt their character maquettes directly into the computer using 3-D sculpting software such as Z-Brush (<196).

LEFT: **Creature designer Mark 'Crash' McCreery works on character designs at Stan Winston Studio.**

BELOW FAR LEFT: **Ray Harryhausen's evocative sketch of the Kraken from** *Clash of the Titans* **(1981) is a fine example of a character design that illustrates attitude as well as physical appearance.**

BELOW LEFT: **Crash McCreery's colour design for the T rex in** *Jurassic Park* **(1993).**

BELOW: **Although Crash McCreery's original concept for the T rex was not used for the final design, the creature's pose and attitude ultimately informed the approach to every animal that appeared in** *Jurassic Park*.

PROFILE **STAN WINSTON**

After studying painting and sculpture at the University of Virginia, Stan Winston (1946–) headed for Hollywood in 1968 with hopes of becoming an actor. While waiting for stardom, Winston was selected for an apprenticeship in make-up at the Walt Disney Studios, where he discovered that make-up was his true calling.

Winston won an Emmy for his creations for the telefilm *Gargoyles* (1972). He next aged the actress Cicely Tyson to 110 years for the TV movie *The Autobiography of Miss Jane Pittman* (1974), and collected another Emmy alongside fellow newcomer Rick Baker (292>).

Winston contributed to several low-budget horror films before creating the make-up that transformed Rod Steiger into W.C. Fields for *W.C. Fields and Me* (1976), and the fantasy characters of *The Wiz* (1978), for which he began to experiment with mechanically articulated faces.

Following a recommendation from make-up guru Dick Smith, Winston was awarded the job of creating facial prosthetics and full-scale robotics for James Cameron's modestly budgeted *The Terminator* (1984). The scale of the work led to the establishment of Stan Winston Studio, now one of Hollywood's leading facilities. The studio has created animatronic creatures for films such as *Aliens* (1986), *Predator* (1987), the *Jurassic Park* films (1993, 1997, 2001), two *Terminator* sequels (1991, 2003) and the robotic teddy bear in *A.I.: Artificial Intelligence* (2001). The studio has also created more traditional but no less spectacular make-up effects for films including *Edward Scissorhands* (1990), *Batman Returns* (1992) and *Interview with the Vampire* (1994). The studio's digital visual effects division created environments and character animation for *Sky Captain and the World of Tomorrow* (2004).

Winston has directed two films, *Pumpkinhead* (1989) and *The Adventures of a Gnome Named Gnorm* (1991). He has won Oscars for his work for *Aliens*, *Jurassic Park*, and *Terminator 2*. With James Cameron and former ILM chief Scott Ross, Winston was a co-founder of leading Hollywood visual effects company Digital Domain.

ANIMATRONIC SCULPTING

Once an animatronic character's appearance has been approved, the design must be translated into a full-sized operational creature. 'We begin by converting the maquette of a character into a full-sized sculpture,' explains Alec Gillis of Amalgamated Dynamics Incorporated. 'Depending on the shape and size of a character, this may be done in one of several ways. If the creature is going to be completely mechanical, we build a metal frame that roughly complies with the anatomy of the character. This is like a skeleton on top of which we will build the clay sculpture. The frame is usually modular, so that we can later carve up the finished sculpture and remove the various limbs to be moulded and cast as individual pieces.

'For some large characters, like the Brain Bug we made for *Starship Troopers* [1997], we take a copy of a maquette and cut it into slices. These cross-section profiles are then enlarged and reproduced in wood or foam before being reassembled to create an accurately shaped, full-size framework over which we can sculpt in clay. In the case of a character that is eventually going to have a performer inside it, we start with a life cast of the performer and then sculpt clay directly over the top of that.'

A sculpture is created using various types of clay, depending on the subject matter and the material in which the character will later be produced. 'If the creature is going to be made from silicone, we have to use a special clay that has no sulphur in it – sulphur residue in a mould will react badly with silicone,' explains Gillis. 'If we are doing a really big sculpture, we might use a water-based clay that we can keep damp and soft by wrapping it in wet towels. We have to be especially careful that parts of a sculpture where the clay is particularly thin don't dry out and crack. We normally create the gross shape of the character using wet clay – which is easy to push into shape – then we'll let it dry a little so we can sculpt the finer details into a harder surface. If a sculpture is going to be worked on for a very long time, we might use an oil-based clay that doesn't dry out at all.'

Sculpting is perhaps the most crucial stage of bringing an animatronic character to life. 'Every little detail, each skin blemish or hairline wrinkle that is created during the sculpt will be transferred to the final piece,' continues Gillis. 'A good sculpture can make so much difference. This is where a character is really created.'

As with the creation of prosthetic appliances, making animatronic creatures from foam latex or silicone is a matter of producing a series of negative and positive copies of a sculpted clay shape. When the clay sculpture of a character has been completed and finessed in every minute detail, it is used to make a negative fibreglass mould – a shell that has every detail of the clay sculpture recorded on its inner surface. If this shell were filled with liquid foam latex, the result would be a solid foam copy of

RIGHT: **Some large characters are not ever sculpted in clay. Instead, costumes are built up, or 'fabricated', using pieces of shaped foam to represent flesh and muscle. When a fabricated suit is complete, a skin, coat of fur, or costume is placed over the top. Here a fabricated Minotaur suit is being assembled at KNB EFX for *The Chronicles of Narnia: The Lion, the Witch and the Wardrobe* (2005).**

FAR RIGHT ABOVE: **An artist at ADI works on the sculpt for a scale model of the Alien Queen for *Alien Vs. Predator* (2004).**

FAR RIGHT BELOW: **Some larger sculptures may be worked on by numerous artists. This *Alien* sculpture being created at ADI has various aspects of its detail created by different sculptors.**

the clay sculpture. Animatronic creatures are not made from solid foam, however. They need to be filled with electronics, mechanical devices and sometimes performers, so the negative mould of the sculpture must be used to produce a hollow skin.

If the character will be a rubber suit brought to life by a human performer, a positive life cast of the performer is placed inside the negative fibreglass mould. The gap between the negative mould of the sculpture and the positive life cast is then filled with foam latex to produce a skin that is perhaps an inch or two thick. 'We often shave the life cast of the performer down a little bit,' explains Gillis. 'By making the life cast slightly smaller – especially around the joints where costumes tend to wrinkle a bit – we ensure that the resulting rubber suit will be a really tight fit on the performer's body.'

If a character is to have an entirely mechanical interior, a thin skin of clay is built up inside the negative fibreglass mould of the original sculpture of the creature. This layer of clay will later be replaced with the character's rubber skin. Various features may be sculpted into this layer of clay to determine the way that the final skin will respond when moved by various animatronic mechanisms. Parts of the anatomy that might later need subtle mechanical manipulation, such as a face, are given a very thin layer of clay, which will ultimately result in a delicate rubber skin. Areas of a character's body that need less subtle movement may be given a much heavier clay lining to produce a thicker, less agile skin.

When the inside of the mould has been lined with clay, another fibreglass mould is made from it. The result is an inner core that fits inside the original mould of the sculpture. This core will later be used as part of the internal structure of the finished character. When the clay layer has been stripped from inside the original mould, and the new core is placed within it, there will be a gap between the two moulds where the layer of clay once was. By filling that gap with foam latex or silicone, a rubber skin is formed.

The result of the sculpting and moulding process is a floppy rubber skin that looks as if some poor creature has had its insides sucked out by a giant mosquito. It is this skin that must be filled with a skeleton, motors and cables to produce a lifelike performing creature.

INNER MECHANISMS

Planning the internal mechanism of an animatronic creature begins during the design stage – electronics and mechanical mechanisms evolving in tandem with a character's outer appearance. However, most of the physical work on a character's inner mechanisms only begins after the creature has been sculpted in clay to produce a foam latex skin.

'Almost as a by-product of the moulding process that produces the skin, we create a fibreglass inner core, which is exactly the size and shape of the underside of the skin,' comments Jamie Courtier, creative director at Jim Henson's Creature Shop. This inner core – a lightweight fibreglass shell – is, in effect, the 'body' of the character. It will have the finished foam latex skin fitted around it, and the internal metal framework of the character will fit within it. The core is often cut into sections so that the various limbs and joints can move independently. For particularly flexible parts of a character's body, such as the neck, the fibreglass shell of the core may be too rigid to provide the necessary underlying body movement, and may be replaced with a specially created articulated body piece.

Though the fibreglass core presents a perfect ready-made body over which the foam latex skin can be fitted, its rigidity does have limitations. 'When the fibreglass core is moved mechanically, the skin can move over the top of it quite realistically,' says Courtier. 'However, the pieces of core itself do not actually change shape. In real life, the body under the skin would change

shape as the character moves – tendons would stretch, flesh and muscle would bulge and contract. These days, if a character has to move and behave just like a real animal, we create an inner body that actually replicates those natural movements.'

To achieve this, the internal metal framework of the character is built to resemble the skeleton of the creature in question. The fibreglass core is then assembled around this skeletal framework. Where muscles need to be seen working beneath the surface of the skin, the fibreglass is replaced with sculpted soft foam muscles.

These are encased in an elasticated material such as spandex, which is secured to the skeleton of the creature. A layer of fabric is laid over the foam muscle structure to prevent friction, thus allowing the muscle to move freely below the foam latex outer skin, which is wrapped over the whole framework and generally glued in place at a few key points. Henson's used such anatomically precise techniques to create incredibly realistic animals for both *Babe* (1995) and *101 Dalmatians* (1996).

With the body under construction, attention turns to the actual mechanisms that will be used to make the character move. With large limbs, movement is generally only required in one or two directions around each joint. Such movement can be achieved by attaching hand-controlled metal rods directly to the limbs. These rods normally protrude from the body, and end with a control handle that might be a simple one-handed grip or a complex mechanism resembling a set of bicycle handlebars. By pulling, pushing and twisting these handles, a puppeteer is able to give a creature its overall body movement.

'We now find that controlling characters with rods is a much more viable option than it was a few years ago,' comments Jamie Courtier. 'We used to spend a lot of time concealing control rods from camera view, which inevitably meant that one part of a creature – usually its rear end – would have to be off-camera. However, it's now relatively fast and inexpensive to digitally remove items like control rods and even puppeteers from a shot after filming. Rod puppetry has two advantages. Firstly, a rod-puppeteered creature is generally easier and cheaper to build than a character that is operated by other, more complicated means. Secondly, having a direct attachment to the creature via a rigid rod means that the puppeteer can create a more fluid, interactive performance, because the puppeteer's own movements are transferred directly to the character.'

For large-scale animatronic creatures, hydraulics may be used to control movement with amazing grace and precision. The 12 m (40 ft) T rex built by Stan Winston Studio for *Jurassic Park* (1993) was mounted on a sophisticated hydraulic motion platform of the type used for flight simulators. To create the dinosaur's movement, the rig could move the huge and potentially dangerous automaton at great speed, bringing it safely to rest within inches of cast and crew.

While hydraulics and rods are suitable for creating big movements, small actions such as facial expressions require more finesse. As many as 30

individual movements may be needed to give an animatronic head the appearance of naturalistic life. These include the eyebrows, cheek muscles, lips, nose and eyes. The movement itself is supplied by a relatively simple interior mechanism that can push, pull or swivel the fibreglass core below the creature's foam latex skin, or, for more subtle movement, can be attached directly to the underside of the skin itself. 'Half the game with getting the movement of a face right is the way in which you actually attach the mechanisms to the costume,' explains Nick Dudman, special effects make-up supervisor on films including *The Mummy* (1999), *Star Wars*: Episode I *The Phantom Menace* (1999) and all of the *Harry Potter* movies. 'The mechanisms need to be fixed to the foam latex skin so that it will absorb the underlying mechanical qualities of the movement, blurring them to produce an organic feeling at the surface level of the skin.'

Such movement can be supplied either via cable or radio control. 'Cables are usually used when there is no problem with having a large number of unsightly wires coming out of the underside of a creature,' comments Dudman. 'However, if the character needs to be a stand-alone creation, without any wires coming out of it, then its internal mechanisms may have to be operated by radio control.'

Cable-controlled movement works on the same principle as bicycle brakes. A thin cable is threaded inside a slightly thicker tube and lightly lubricated to prevent friction. One end of the cable is manipulated by a puppeteer, who pulls or releases the cable using a handgrip or lever. The other end of the cable is arranged so that it pulls a tab or operates a lever that directly affects the movement of the puppet whenever the puppeteer pulls the handgrip. The cables used for this work – which range from wires as thin as fishing line to heavy-duty cables capable of pulling several tons – are kept as short as possible. 'The further a cable has to reach between creature and puppeteer, the more effort is needed to pull it and the harder it is to achieve a subtle performance,' explains Dudman. 'Cable control is really only suitable for characters that can be kept a relatively short distance from the puppeteer.'

Radio-controlled animatronics operate in much the same way as with cables, the difference being that a small electric motor within the creature itself is used to push and pull the skin. This motor is controlled by radio waves from a hand-held unit. 'We use the servomotors that are normally used to operate radio-controlled model aircraft,' explains Dudman. 'Instead of having a small spinning drive shaft, these motors operate an axle that twists backwards and forwards. We attach this axle to a rod or cable that in turn moves the latex skin. The only real difference between radio and cable control is that with radio control, there is no physical link between the puppeteer and the character.' Servomotors work under proportionate control, which means that the further and faster the puppeteer moves the joystick of the device, the further and faster the servomotor moves its axle, making puppeteering with servos an intuitive process. Servos are chosen for their size and power. A small motor, perhaps the size of a box of matches, may fit more easily into the confines of an animatronic head, but it can only produce small, relatively weak movements. Larger motors can produce greater movement but are much harder to conceal – especially when as many as 30 of them are required in the case of an animatronic head. 'We often find that there just isn't enough room to put all the servos we need into a head, especially if it's part of a costume that has to have room for the performer's head as well,' comments Nick Dudman. 'In such cases, we have to secrete the motors in other places around the body and route their movement through the costume using internal cables.'

Dudman created sophisticated animatronic heads for the law-enforcement characters known as Mangalores in *The Fifth Element* (1997). 'The Mangalores were performers dressed in rubber suits,' notes Dudman. 'The suits themselves were relatively simple, then they were topped off with a silicone animatronic head that went over the performer's own head. The mask was fixed to the bodysuit with poppers that kept the skin taut. Normally with heads, there may be two places where the performer below is actually visible – around the mouth and also the eyes. In this case, the eyes

FAR LEFT BELOW: **The hydraulically operated T rex built by Stan Winston Studio for** *Jurassic Park* **(1993) was mounted on a computer-controlled motion platform similar to those used for flight simulators.** *Above:* **The mechanical understructure of the T rex, revealing the complex collection of joints, motors, cables and hoses required to produce lifelike movement.** *Below:* **The T rex on the stage at Universal Studios. The creature was so huge that it remained in one place while sets were rebuilt around it. The mechanical monster was only filmed from the waist up; shots of it walking were created digitally.**

LEFT: **A mechanical bird built by Jim Henson's Creature Shop for** *The Flintstones* **(1994). The character's performance was puppeteered using a simple rod and cable-grip mechanism protruding from the back of its body.**

BELOW: **The complex animatronic workings of an alien character built by ADI for** *My Favorite Martian* **(1999).**

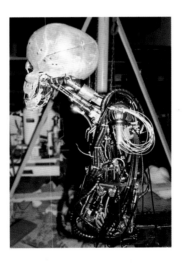

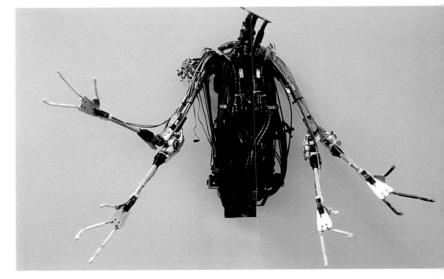

of the performer were fitted with contact lenses and we made little silicone eyebags – like slugs – that were glued under the performer's eyes to blend them with the mask. I wanted to see right into the mouth of the Mangalores, so the mask was built with a rubber throat that had several rows of teeth. The rubber throat actually rolled down inside the throat of the performer, who also wore a rubber tongue. If the Mangalores opened their mouths, you could see right down into their gullets, which really gave the impression of living, three-dimensional creatures. However, because the masks were so close to the faces of the performers, there was no room to hide the servomotors that controlled the facial movement, so we built a special backpack that hung the sixteen facial servos and their batteries down the spine of each performer. The radio-controlled movement of the motors was then transferred via cables that went up through the costume and into the head.'

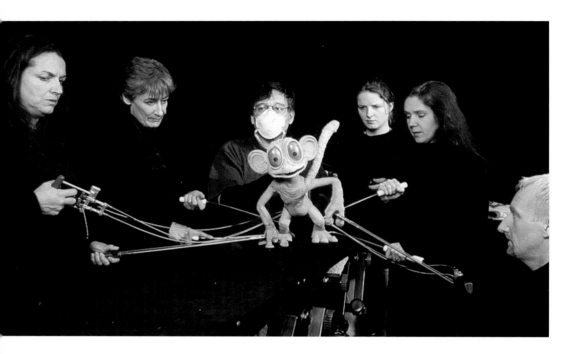

PROFILE **RICK BAKER**

Rick Baker's (1950–) fascination with make-up emerged when, as a child, he would give himself hideous wounds and dress up as monsters. It was then that Baker also developed his passion for re-creating the great apes – a skill for which he has become most celebrated.

Baker began his career building stop-motion puppets, but got his first make-up break on the no-budget monster movie *Octaman* (1971), for which he created an octopus-like rubber suit. Baker's next assignment, *Schlock* (1971), brought his first opportunity to construct an ape-like creature. The low-budget movie was the debut for the writer/director John Landis – who also wore the missing-link apeman suit created by Baker.

Baker's next opportunity to create an ape was for *The Thing with Two Heads* (1972) – the 'Thing' being a two-headed gorilla. Baker thought he would have the chance to create the ultimate gorilla suit for the remake of *King Kong* (1976), but disagreements with the producers led to an unhappy experience and work of

which Baker is not particularly proud. He next produced some of the cantina scene aliens for *Star Wars* (1977) before creating the landmark transformation make-up in *An American Werewolf in London* (1981).

Greystoke: The Legend of Tarzan, Lord of the Apes (1984) brought Baker his first chance to make truly sophisticated simians. Baker built 30 amazingly convincing apes with cable-controlled faces. Incredibly, he achieved even finer results for *Gorillas in the Mist* (1988). His great apes were so convincing that they were seamlessly intercut with footage of real mountain gorillas. He later created the ultimate in great apes – the huge gorilla star of *Mighty Joe Young* (1998).

Baker has won Oscars for his work on *An American Werewolf in London*, *Harry and the Hendersons* (1987), *Ed Wood* (1994), *The Nutty Professor* (1996), *Men in Black* (1997) and *How the Grinch Stole Christmas* (2000), but was denied even a nomination for his superbly expressive make-up for *Planet of the Apes* (2001).

EYES

The eyes, it is said, are the windows to the soul. Lon Chaney was one of the first to recognize the importance of a character's eyes. To play a blind man for *The Road to Mandalay* (1926), Chaney peeled the translucent white skin from inside an eggshell, cut it into circles and pressed it over his eyeballs. This gave his eyes the cloudy look of cataracts, but like many of Chaney's efforts, caused the actor considerable pain.

Contact lenses are the safer and generally more comfortable method now used to change the appearance of an actor's eyes. For many years, make-up artists used 'scleral lenses'. These were produced by taking a mould from the performer's eyeball – a difficult and unpleasant task – which was then used to create a tightly fitting, rigid plastic lens that covered the whole of the front of the eye. These lenses were uncomfortable to wear and had to be removed regularly to allow oxygen to reach the surface of the eye. Today, 'corneal lenses' – which cover only the iris and corneal area of the eye – are the more comfortable alternative. These are the same type as the soft lenses that are used for normal sight correction, and once applied, can be worn all day. Corneal contact lenses can now be made with any colour or pattern desired.

Once a design has been created, artwork is sent to a specialist optometrist who transfers the pattern onto lenses ready for use. Contact lenses are a relatively cheap and simple way to create a striking eye design, such as the eerie mirrored eyes of Yul Brynner in *Westworld* (1973), or the threatening, brightly coloured eyes of Darth Maul in *Star Wars*: Episode I *The Phantom Menace* (1999). They can also be used to enhance old-age make-up. During extreme old age, the eyes often develop a feature called arcus senilis – a fatty deposit around the edge of the iris that makes the eye look grey and soft.

Lenses with pale blue-grey rims can be used to mimic this condition in young, healthy eyes, and were effectively used for the old-age make-up created by Dick Smith for *Little Big Man* (1970) and *Amadeus* (1984).

For animatronic creatures, entirely artificial eyes must be created. 'Eyes are one of the most important focal points that bring any character to life,' says Jamie Courtier of Jim Henson's Creature Shop. 'It really is worth spending a disproportionate amount of time and money on getting a creature's eyes to look good. Dull, lifeless eyes can immediately give a creation away as artificial.'

As with contact lenses, artificial eyes start life as conceptual artwork. 'For models of real animals, we design an eye that is identical to the genuine thing,' explains Courtier. 'For fantasy-type creatures, however, we design original eyes that are in keeping with the character. For the Bark Troll from *NeverEnding Story III* [1994], for example, we designed an iris that was based on the cross-section of a tree trunk.' There are other aspects to the eye that help an audience to judge a character's personality.

'A key part of eye design is deciding the size of the pupil,' says Courtier. 'If a character has large pupils, it will tend to look cute and friendly. Smaller pupils create a more beady-eyed, evil look.' Eyeballs are made from spheres of plastic resin, ranging from tiny bead-sized globes for mice and birds, to football-sized ones for dragons and dinosaurs. The spheres, which are normally ivory-coloured to mimic the whites of the eyes, have one curvature ground off, leaving a flat surface onto which the painted eye artwork is laid. This flat-sided sphere is then placed in a mould which is filled with clear resin. When set, this gives the whole eyeball a thin transparent skin, and fills out its flattened side to a normal curve. The clear dome of set resin over the eye artwork also acts like a magnifying glass, making the flat design look three-dimensional, especially after the eye has been polished.

Resin eyeballs can be startlingly realistic, but they cannot physically react in the way that a real eye does. In bright conditions, a real iris contracts to limit the amount of light that enters the eye; while in the dark, the iris expands. This phenomenon was cleverly replicated in *Jurassic Park* (1993), for which Stan Winston Studio built a tyrannosaurus with motorized diaphragms that dilated its pupils. In one of the film's most chilling moments, the huge creature peers into a jeep containing two children. When a torch is shone into its eye, the beast's iris dilates dramatically, giving a true sense of an animal on the prowl.

Henson's found an ingeniously simple way to control the size of eye pupils for the piglet star of *Babe* (1995). A small rubber ball was fixed to the end of a rod and placed inside a hollow eyeball filled with silicone oil. When pressure was applied to the rod, the rubber ball squashed against the inside surface of the eyeball, resulting in a large iris. When the pressure was released, the rubber ball moved away from the inside of the eye and the iris appeared smaller.

Once completed, eyeballs are mounted in a radio- or cable-controlled mechanism that enables them to be rotated in any direction. Remote-controlled hard-shell eyelids made from plastic or metal are mounted just in front of the eyes and pivoted so that they roll over the eyeball when a blink is required. When the eye mechanism is placed in the skull of the creature under construction, the character's skin is glued to these eyelids so that the flesh around the eyes moves as the eyelids open and close.

FAR LEFT: **Cheeky sidekick Blawp from *Lost in Space* (1999) was brought to life by six puppeteers using rod and cable controls. The cables and rods, once carefully concealed behind or beneath a character, are now easy to remove digitally.**

LEFT: **Bruce Willis is surrounded by Nick Dudman's Mangalores – performers wearing foam-latex costumes and animatronic heads – in *The Fifth Element* (1997).**

BELOW: **Famed for his wandering eye, Ragetti (Mackenzie Crook) was one of the most popular characters from the *Pirates of the Caribbean* movies. His fake eye was a scleral lens painted to look like wood by specialist contact-lens artist Cristine Ceret of Professional VisionCare Associates.**

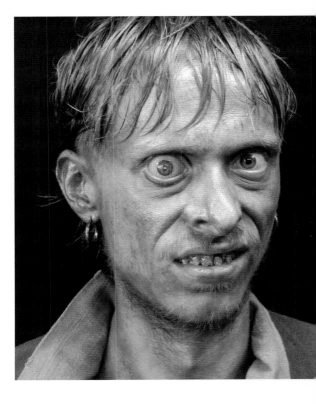

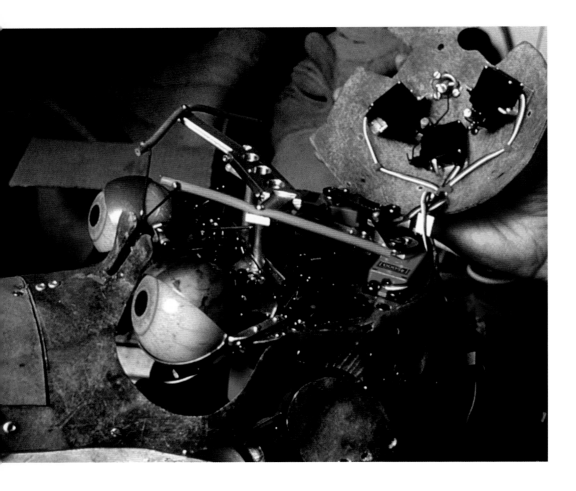

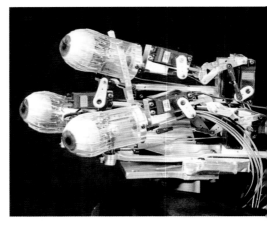

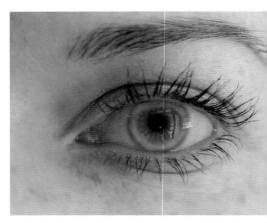

The hard-shell blink mechanism used in most animatronic creatures is effective when seen from a distance, but in close-up there is something rather artificial about the technique. 'As we've progressed into producing ever more realistic creatures, the eyelid has been one of those things that we have had to finesse,' says Jamie Courtier. For the film *Buddy* (1997), Henson's aimed to create the most realistic-looking animatronic gorilla ever made for a film. 'Animatronic gorillas had got pretty good over the years,' explains Courtier, 'but something that had never been addressed properly was the eyeball and the eyelid. If you watch a person sleep, you will notice the eyeballs moving around beneath their closed eyelids. This is because eyeballs are not perfectly smooth-sided spheres; they actually have quite a pronounced bulge on the surface over the cornea. It is this corneal bulge that you can see moving under a sleeper's eyelid, and which also moves the skin of an eyelid as it slides over the eyeball during a blink. Such a bulge could never occur with a traditional animatronic blink, because the eyelid is a hard shell mounted just above the surface of the eyeball.'

For *Buddy*, Henson's designed a new type of artificial eyeball that had a realistic corneal bulge. Although the bulge itself is barely noticeable, the quality of reflection produced by the shape of the new eyeball brought an additional spark of life to the character. While normal animatronic blink mechanisms swing a solid, semicircular lid over the surface of the eyeball without touching it, Henson's designed a new type of flexible eyelid that actually touched the eyeball and changed shape as it was dragged over the corneal bulge.

Finally, Buddy's eyes featured an electronic detail that made the life of the puppeteer a little easier. 'When we look at something while our body is moving around, our eyes automatically adjust so that they continue looking at the same object even though the position of our head may have changed radically,' notes Courtier. 'To replicate this trait during a performance, a puppeteer must physically alter the position of the eyes so that they still look in the same direction, however much the head moves. To solve this, Buddy's eye mechanism included a gyroscopic feature that actually sensed the movement of the head and applied a counter-movement to the eyes. Once the eyes were locked into looking at something, Buddy could move freely while his eyes continued to look at the right spot.

'As with a lot of the improvements that we make in animatronics, no one in the audience will actually notice such changes,' remarks Courtier, 'but we keep making lots of little breakthroughs that all together help us to create more convincing characters.'

TOP: **This unusual eye mechanism was built by ADI for a triple-eyed alien from** *My Favorite Martian* **(1999).**

ABOVE: **A corneal contact lens has been painted to resemble the medical condition arcus senilis, making the youthful wearer appear much older. Lenses such as these are frequently used as part of an old-age make-up design.**

ABOVE LEFT: **The complex inner workings of an animatronic creature's eye mechanism. In this case, the character has traditional brass hard-shell eyelids to which the foam-latex skin will later be glued.**

FUR

Once the body of a creature has been designed, sculpted and cast, some thought must be given to the finished look of its exterior. Leathery creatures, such as lizards and dinosaurs, are sculpted with every exterior scale and wrinkle already in place. The rubber skin therefore only needs to be painted before looking complete.

Creatures that are covered with fur or feathers, on the other hand, are sculpted bald and must have an appropriate exterior attached to their smooth rubber skin. 'There are various ways to give a creature a coat of fur,' explains Tom Woodruff of ADI. 'One way is to buy ready-made fake fur that can be cut up and fitted to the creature in question. This fur is normally either entirely synthetic, or is sometimes made from yak hair, which is humanely shaved from the belly of yaks and dyed various colours. We generally find that this off-the-shelf fur is not quite near enough in colour and texture to what we need, and so our specialist manufacturer will actually make fur according to our specifications. Using samples that are sent to us, we blend different grades and colours to create the type that we want. We then ask the manufacturer to produce a fur that has 10 per cent of one variety of fur, 40 per cent of another and so on.'

An alternative to using ready-made fur is to create it from scratch. 'For really good hair, we find that we normally have to make our own,' explains Woodruff. One way to do this is to hand-tie every single hair into a piece of elasticated material such as spandex. The finished fur, which can take weeks or even months to produce, is then cut into the appropriate shapes and attached to the body of the creature, or stretched over the limbs and body parts like a tightly fitting sock.

Instead of producing a hand-tied body sock, hairs can be hand-punched directly into the foam latex or silicone skin of the creature, a painstaking and laborious process. Using a tool made from an ordinary sewing needle with the top of the eye cut off to create a prong, the artist selects a single hair and punches it into the skin. The hair does not need to be glued because the natural grip of the rubber skin holds it in place. Blending and mixing grades and colours of hair is an art in itself, as is punching the hair into the skin so that it stands at the correct angle. This is perhaps the most effective, if labour-intensive, method of creating realistic fur – the coat shifts and bristles naturally as the rubber beneath creases and bulges during a performance. The method is particularly effective when used with silicone, because the translucent material leaves the roots of the hair just visible below the skin.

BELOW: **For an even coating of short hairs, a character can be flocked. Here (*below left*) the head of Aslan from *The Chronicles of Narnia: The Lion, the Witch and the Wardrobe* (2005) is being flocked in the workshop of KNB EFX. The object that looks like a flashlight is the flocking machine, from which electrostatically charged hair is emitted. In this case, the fur was a mixture of different shades of human hair. The final result (*below*) shows how the flocked hairs have been carefully brushed to create natural-looking patterns. Coarser whiskers have been hand-punched into the skin and the mane is made from custom-produced fabric-backed artificial fur.**

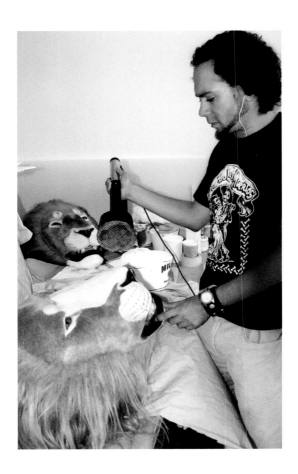

BELOW: **To create convincing long fur, a character's hairs may be individually punched into its skin in a process that can take many weeks. Here, Buddy the gorilla is given a coat of fur at Jim Henson's Creature Shop.**

To produce a covering of very fine short hairs, hand-punching would be impractical. In this case, the body of the creature can be 'flocked' – finely chopped fur is sprayed directly onto the body of a creature that has been covered in glue. During the spraying process, the body is given a negative electrostatic charge, while the chopped hairs are given a positive electrostatic charge. These opposing charges cause the hairs to stand upright in the glue. Before the glue dries, an electrostatic wand can be waved over the standing hairs to encourage them to point in various directions and resemble the way that real fur grows on animals.

Despite the incredible range of fake furs that are available, it is sometimes impossible to re-create nature realistically. 'On principle, I, like most people, will always use fake fur if possible,' says special effects make-up designer Nick Dudman. 'Unfortunately, it occasionally proves impossible to create a fake version of an unusual variety of fur, and the real thing will have to be used. We always use legitimate suppliers who only supply fur from recognized sources, and we certainly never use anything that comes from any sort of threatened species.'

To prepare real animal fur, a strong, water-soluble glue is combed through the pelt. When the glue has set, the leather backing is scraped from the fur using a razor blade. The back of the fur is then painted with liquid latex, which replaces the leather and holds the roots of the fur in the correct position. When the latex has set, the water-soluble glue is washed away to leave a perfect coat on a flexible, hygienic rubber backing.

Using real fur and hair is becoming increasingly unacceptable by most people's standards, and new ways of creating substitutes are constantly being sought. When faced with finding realistic-looking dog fur for *101 Dalmatians* (1996), Jim Henson's Creature Shop developed a method of treating sheep's wool to produce the type needed. Many other types of fur are used to create alternatives to the real thing.

No matter how good the hair on a creature may appear, however, the success of an artificial hairdo can ultimately depend on the way in which it is filmed. Flattering lighting and some well-chosen filters can make all the difference.

PERFORMANCE SYSTEMS

When one imagines the work of a puppeteer, visions of a sole performer hunched over a dangling marionette or crouched under a table with their hands buried inside a glove puppet come to mind. However, the sophisticated animatronic creatures now built for feature films need to have more than a few simplistic body movements in their repertoire. To be adequately expressive, a character's face alone may have as many as 30 separate control functions.

Bringing such creations to life can require some high-tech solutions. Although Jim Henson's Creature Shop is known for the craftsmanship of its animatronic creations, the organization is most proud of its commitment to character performance. 'Our company sprang from Jim Henson's desire to create amazing characters,' comments Jamie Courtier. 'The technology behind a character was not important to Jim; it was the final performance that counted. Some of his greatest characters – Kermit, Miss Piggy – were, after all, only simple glove puppets. However, as our feature film work has developed, the devices that we use to bring life to our characters have become more and more complicated.

'Imagine a radio-controlled face with 30 motors in it,' continues Courtier. 'It would be impossible for a single person to operate so many channels of movement effectively. We might need four or five puppeteers, each operating half a dozen of a character's expressions. Simply coaxing a smile from a character could require a considerable team effort. To reduce the number of performers, we came up with our Performance Control System.' The system works on the premise that any character's facial performance is made up of a limited repertoire of expressions – sadness, smiling, confusion and so on. The manner and degree to which these emotions are expressed is what differentiates the personality of each character. If a puppet with a sophisticated animatronic face were brought to life by a team of puppeteers, each member would need to work in perfect harmony. A simple smile might involve one performer creating a grin, another the flaring of the nostrils and yet another a slight widening of the eyes. By linking an animatronic creature to a computer, however, a puppeteer is able to program the key expressions of a character into the computer's memory. The computer then knows that when a character smiles, each of the motors controlling the face should move in a particular way. 'The system allows puppeteers to work with pre-set expressions – you simply ask for a smile and get one,' explains Courtier.

'The puppeteer can create an amazing performance simply by asking the computer for a little more sadness or a little more anger. The computer will automatically mix and match those expressions to create something that is unique, but within the pre-set parameters for that character.' To operate the system, the puppeteer uses both hands to manipulate a set of controls. The right hand slips into a

ABOVE: To produce synchronized lip movements for the *Teenage Mutant Ninja Turtles* (1990), Jim Henson's Creature Shop used infrared light to measure the movements of a puppeteer's mouth, reproducing similar movement in the puppet. There are now a number of so-called 'waldo' systems available to record a performer's movements and translate them to a puppet.

ABOVE RIGHT: The most common way to create the performance of an animatronic character is by radio control. Standing behind the camera, puppeteers manipulate various aspects of each character using hand-held control consoles. Here a set of radio-control eye mechanisms is being tested.

ABOVE LEFT: The Henson Performance Control System allows puppeteers to choreograph the action of their characters by remote control. The performer places their hands in a pair of sensor gloves and uses their fingers to manipulate the character; a video camera and monitor are used to view the puppet's actions when it is some distance away.

LEFT: Digital technology now allows controlling cables, rods, or even entire puppeteers to be erased from the finished shot. For scenes featuring a see-through C-3PO in *The Phantom Menace* (1999), a puppeteer and puppet were linked by rods so that the robot copied the human's movements exactly. The human was later digitally removed from the shot.

mechanical glove that measures every twist, turn and clench of the puppeteer's hand. These movements directly affect the puppet – by twisting his or her hand, the puppeteer can turn the puppet's head; opening and closing the hand will cause the character's mouth to open and close. The left hand grips a joystick that can swivel in all directions. Each finger rests on a control dial, while the thumb slots into a cup that acts as an independent miniature joystick. It is this set of controls that is normally used to navigate between the pre-set expressions. 'The whole system is totally flexible,' says Courtier. 'If a puppeteer wants to control a frown with the forefinger, we can set it up that way. If the puppeteer would rather use the thumb, then we will change things accordingly.' To create the farmyard characters for *Babe* (1995), Henson's refined the system to include speech controls. The company had already used a system of puppeteering lip movements for *Teenage Mutant Ninja Turtles* (1990), in which performers wore a facial device that used infrared to measure their mouth position 100 times a second and transfer those moves to the turtles' lips. The system worked but the results were crude. 'For *Babe*, we needed to create refined lip movements that synchronized with pre-recorded character dialogue,' says Courtier, 'so we created the Henson Performance Recording System.'

The computer system uses the pre-recorded dialogue from a scene and analyses the phonemes in each word to form the lip movements of the character. The facial performance is displayed as a graphic wave on a computer monitor, and the puppeteer can use a graphics pen to alter it manually in order to refine the performance. 'The beauty of this system is that it is only the speech that is pre-recorded,' states Courtier. 'The puppeteer will perform the creature as usual and the computer will only take control during the time that the character has to perform a line – it's a perfect combination of new technology and old-fashioned puppeteering.'

New technology has made many of the great creature performances of recent years possible. While Henson's used computers to help create the movement of the tiny star of *Babe*, Stan Winston has used digital technology to control work of a very different scale. 'Although many of the dinosaurs of *Jurassic Park* [1993] were computer-generated, we could never have got our live-action dinosaurs to look so good without computers,' states Winston. 'Our 12 m [40 ft] T rex was mounted on an enormous motion platform and we controlled its movements via a computer.' Winston's team built a 1:4 scale 'waldo' – a model of the animal with encoders at each of its joints. When this puppet was moved by hand, the encoders measured the movement of its joints and sent the signals to a computer. The computer then scaled up the moves and relayed them to the hydraulic joints of the full-scale dinosaur. The waldo could transfer real-time puppeteering directly to the dinosaur, or could be used to program each of the 57 joints (also known as 'channels of movement') individually to create a performance that could easily be repeated. 'Our other great innovation with the T rex was the elimination of what we call "wagga-wagga",' explains Winston. 'When a big but flexible device like the T rex comes to a halt after a fast move, the whole thing wobbles – an instant giveaway that the creature is fake. We used the computer to detect all potential wobbles and apply a counteractive movement to another part of the character. This effectively cancelled out the wobble. It worked beautifully.'

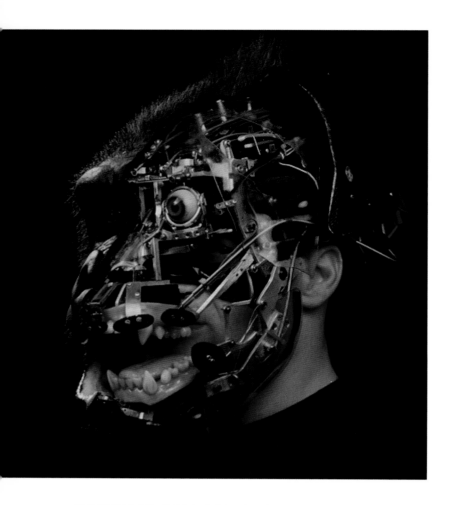

COSTUME PERFORMERS

No matter how fine the design and engineering of an animatronic character, without a good puppeteer on the outside – or an able performer on the inside – the creation will remain nothing more than a lifeless collection of metal, rubber and fur.

One of the world's most experienced costume performers is Peter Elliot, whose speciality is re-creating the lifelike movements and expressions of apes for films including *Greystoke: The Legend of Tarzan, Lord of the Apes* (1984), *Congo* (1995), *Buddy* (1997) and *Instinct* (1999). 'I approach an ape performance as a form of method acting,' explains Elliot. 'The only way to behave like an ape is to "become" an ape – to understand how an ape thinks, why they do the things that they do.'

After working as a professional acrobat and diver, Elliot trained as an actor before landing the part of an ape in *Greystoke*. Although production of the film was postponed, Elliot was asked to spend two years researching ape behaviour. In that time he became an accepted member of a family of chimpanzees, and learned to communicate and interact freely with them. 'One of the greatest personality traits of an ape is that it lives in the now, whereas we humans are continually living in the past or the future,' he comments. 'If an ape has a problem, it comes to a conclusion there and then. Apes also have a very short attention span. It's a survival mechanism. If you sit and think about anything for too long in the jungle, something will leap on your back and eat you.'

To demonstrate the way an ape thinks, Elliot sits on the floor with a collection of household items. Within seconds, he transforms himself into a chimpanzee, speaking its thoughts aloud as it plays with the items – smelling them, tasting them, throwing away those it does not like or trust. To add to the performance, Elliot uses the five basic chimp sounds: hoots, grunts,

barks, growls and screams. His resemblance to a chimp is uncanny. 'Many people think that one ape is just like another, but chimps are vastly different to gorillas, which move and react in their own unique way,' emphasizes Elliot. 'Gorillas have a particular social structure that makes their reactions very different. They also move in a very different way because they are so massive and so strong. Playing a gorilla largely comes down to getting the breathing right. They have this amazing presence, a heavy but graceful way of moving, and that stems from the way they breathe.'

As Elliot talks, his facial expression begins to resemble that of a gorilla, with a down-turned mouth and heavy brow. A deep growling comes from within his chest and his nostrils flare with each breath. 'When you get the breathing right, everything else falls into place – the sense of weight and natural rhythms of movement seem to follow.'

Acting like an ape in normal circumstances is one thing, but translating that into a convincing practical performance when sealed inside a heavy rubber suit is something else altogether. 'I might spend quite a while getting the movement and presence of an ape correct during rehearsal,' says Elliot, 'but when the costume is finished and I start to wear it, it can be very demoralizing. When you put on a 7 kg [15 lb] gorilla head that protrudes 15 cm [6 in], the size of the head multiplies your own head movement. As a result, I have to pare back my internal performance to produce an accurate external performance.'

Working inside a suit offers other impediments. 'A real gorilla may weigh 180 kg [400 lb]. It would be impossible to perform inside a costume that actually weighed that much, so the weight has to be suggested by the way I move, and that comes down to the breathing. However, 90 per cent of a gorilla's expressions are done with the mouth shut, so I will be trapped in an artificial head, with no fresh air, breathing my own carbon dioxide. You need to do this slow, heavy breathing to get the performance right, but you're actually near to suffocation. The heavy breathing and growling also tends to upset the sound recordist. If the scene has dialogue, they will want as much silence as possible so they can get a clean recording of the actors' voices. However, I need to growl and grunt to perform properly – not to mention the noise that comes from the 30 or so motors that will be operating the face mask.'

Working inside a suit can be an exhausting and uncomfortable experience. 'It can be so hot in a suit that I will sweat off 3 kg [7 lb] a day. Then there is the itching. If you have an itch or blisters – which often result from wearing the costume – you can't scratch because it's under a layer of rubber and fur. I've developed a form of self-hypnosis so that things like that don't drive me mad.'

A large part of a gorilla performance comes from the facial expressions of the creature, operated not by Elliot but by a puppeteer working with radio control. 'I work very closely with the puppeteer during rehearsals,' explains Elliot. 'I will act all the facial expressions as I move and they will learn how those expressions match my actions. It has to become a symbiotic relationship. It's no good if they create a facial expression after I've done a movement – it should be simultaneous. When performing, I try to give subtle indicators of the movement I'm about to make, and those guide the puppeteer.' The external puppeteer also has a role to play in guiding Elliot's own performance. 'The only way I can see when I'm in a suit is through a tiny gap in the nostrils, so when I'm walking on all fours, all I can see is the floor below me. The puppeteer normally uses a microphone linked to my earpiece to guide me around the set.'

Elliot's understanding of apes also enables him to guide those who make the costumes. 'I can make suggestions that will help the engineers and artists produce a better costume. For *Instinct* [1999], I asked the Stan Winston Studio to construct a new form of arm extension [a gorilla's arms are disproportionately long, and costumes include crutch-like arm extensions]. For the first time ever, I had wrists that flexed just like a real gorilla's. Before then, it was the one thing that was never quite right. I think that we can really do gorillas justice now.'

PROFILE KEN RALSTON

Growing up in Los Angeles, Ken Ralston (1953–) developed an early passion for film-making and spent much of his childhood creating 8 mm home movies full of models, animation and other effects.

As a result of his early experiments, Ralston found work at Cascade Pictures, one of Hollywood's leading visual effects houses, in the 70s. There he built sets, sculpted models, animated puppets and created numerous optical effects for hundreds of television commercials.

In 1976 Ralston was invited to join a group of young effects artists to create the effects for *Star Wars* (1977). Having started at ILM as a special effects camera assistant, Ralston graduated to camera operator for *The Empire Strikes Back* (1980) before helping to design and animate the Go-Motion dragon for *Dragonslayer* (1981). The following year he earned his first credit as special effects supervisor for *Star Trek II: The Wrath of Khan* (1982), sharing credit with Jim Veilleux. Ralston won his first Oscar for co-supervising the landmark effects in *Return of the Jedi* (1983), for which his achievements included the amazingly complex space battle sequences. As supervisor at ILM, Ralston was responsible for the creation of astounding effects for a string of landmark films. Perhaps his most memorable work has been produced in collaboration with Robert Zemeckis (<43), for whom he has supervised effects such as the flying time-travelling cars of the *Back to the Future* trilogy (1985, 1989, 1990), the interaction of humans and cartoons in *Who Framed Roger Rabbit* (1988), characters with holes through their bodies in *Death Becomes Her* (1992), the removal of an actor's legs in *Forrest Gump* (1994), an incredible trip through the universe in *Contact* (1997) and the groundbreaking motion-captured performances of *The Polar Express* (2004).

Ralston left ILM in 1995 to become senior visual effects supervisor at Sony Pictures Imageworks, where he continues to oversee the creation of innovative visual effects. He has won Academy Awards for his work in *Return of the Jedi*, *Cocoon* (1985), *Who Framed Roger Rabbit*, *Death Becomes Her* and *Forrest Gump*.

ABOVE: Ape impersonator Peter Elliot dressed in his gorilla costume for *Buddy* (1997).

FAR LEFT: This cutaway head of the gorilla from *Buddy* shows the intricate array of servomotors and control mechanisms fitted into the space between the mask and the performer's head.

LEFT: Among the many discomforts endured by costume performers are leg extensions, designed to make characters taller than average humans. Here experienced costume performer Brian Steele tests the leg extensions for a werewolf character created by Patrick Tatopoulos for *Underworld: Evolution* (2006).

GODZILLA

In early 1954, the Japanese producer Tomoyuki Tanaka (1910–97) found himself desperately looking for a 'blockbuster' film subject after the collapse of a major production that he had been planning. At the time, science fiction was the rage in Hollywood, and films such as *Monster from the Ocean Floor* (1954), and *Them!* (1954) featured plots that capitalized on the popular fears of nuclear radiation. Tanaka reasoned that while Americans had a fear of radiation, only the Japanese had direct experience of the horrors of nuclear war, and so a film based on this subject could prove popular. The result of Tanaka's thoughts was one of the most famous monster films of all time, *Gojira* (1954), known in the West as *Godzilla*.

Gojira was made by Japan's Toho Studios – a production company as famous for the films of the celebrated Japanese director Akira Kurosawa as it is for its long-running series of *kaiju eiga* (literally meaning 'monster movies'). The plot of the film centres on a 120 m (400 ft) amphibious creature that is awakened by an A-bomb explosion. The beast wreaks havoc on various Japanese cities – conventional weapons being unable to stop him. Eventually, Japanese scientists invent a device that removes all the oxygen from the sea, thus suffocating the creature. The monster was called 'Gojira' after an overweight studio technician whose nickname was a combination of the words 'gorilla' and '*kujira*' – the Japanese for 'whale'.

The head of Toho's special effects department was Eiji Tsuburaya (1901–70), who had produced the effects for Japanese propaganda films during the war and had learnt how to re-create convincing battle scenes using models and miniatures. His simulated attack on Pearl Harbor was so convincing that American occupying forces who later saw the footage thought they were watching film of the actual battle. Tsuburaya supervised the construction of the beautifully intricate model cities that Gojira would trample. Tsuburaya's 1:25 scale model buildings were complete with miniature interiors and delicate small-scale brickwork so that they would collapse convincingly. Miniature vehicles were cast in iron so that they would look appropriately heavy when kicked or crushed by giant feet.

Gojira himself underwent several design phases, starting life as a mutated octopus-related creature before evolving into a giant dinosaur-lizard. The monster was created by dressing performers in suits made of foam latex reinforced with bamboo and urethane. The suits were painted dark grey, not green as is often assumed. Gojira's mouth could be operated by the performer, while his tail was manipulated by wires from the outside. Toho called their suit method 'suit-mation'.

The monster's scenes were filmed at high speed to make him and the buildings he destroyed look far larger than life. Because high-speed photography required extremely bright lights, the performers that played Gojira (Katsumi Tezuka and Haruo Nakajima – who would play the role until 1972) would become unbearably hot inside their unventilated suit – losing half a pint of sweat during some scenes, and frequently fainting.

In addition to the full Gojira suit, a bottom-half suit worn with suspenders was used for foot and leg shots, and a hand puppet of the beast's face was used for expressive close-ups.

Gojira, and the more than 30 sequels that it spawned, are often mocked in the West as the ultimate in badly made monster movies. This misinformed view is the result of the badly doctored versions that are usually shown outside Japan. Original dialogue is frequently dubbed into foreign languages, changing the meaning and plot of the original. Dubbing has also led to criticism of the acting. In fact, some of Japan's greatest actors have starred in Gojira films. Additional inferior footage is sometimes added to the Western versions, and the original musical soundtrack, often by the highly respected classical composer Akira Ifukube, is replaced by a different score altogether.

Although some of the later Gojira films suffered from inferior production values, the early films of the series are vibrant and well made, and should be viewed in their original versions to be fully appreciated.

DIGITAL MAKE-UP

While computers can now produce spectacular creatures that perform in ways that animatronic creations simply never could, the silicon chip has also started to encroach on some of the more traditional areas of special effects make-up – it is now being used to apply what would once have been prosthetic appliances to the features of living performers.

An early glimpse of things to come was seen in *Death Becomes Her* (1992). Directed by Robert Zemeckis (<43), the film tells the story of what happens to two women (Goldie Hawn and Meryl Streep) when they consume an elixir that promises immortality. As a result of their mutual jealousies, the women subject one another to the kind of physical abuse that would kill ordinary mortals, but in their case results in all sorts of hilariously macabre afflictions. '*Death Becomes Her* was quite a test for us at ILM', recalls the film's visual effects supervisor Ken Ralston, now senior visual effects supervisor of Sony Pictures Imageworks (<299). 'A lot of shots were achieved using physical make-up and animatronic effects, but some of what we had to do was so off-the-wall that it was just impossible to do the old way'.

One of the film's most memorable sequences sees Meryl Streep twisting her neck so severely that her head faces in the wrong direction – the result of a spectacular fall down a flight of stairs. 'The twisted neck thing was originally tried as a practical effect', explains Ralston. 'The idea involved fitting a backwards-facing Meryl Streep mask on a twisted neck prosthetic attached to the performer's body. It looked quite good but it just didn't quite work, so we realized it would have to be done digitally'.

It was decided that the effect would be achieved through using a combination of traditional prosthetics and digital compositing. Meryl Streep would be filmed in the studio set wearing a prosthetic twisted neck and a blue Lycra bag over her head. The blue head bag would then be digitally removed from the shot and the resulting hole filled with the appropriate background area, taken from a separate shot of the empty set. A separately filmed shot of Streep's head would then be composited on top of the twisted neck so that it faced the wrong way. Unfortunately, Streep developed an allergic reaction to the prosthetic make-up, so the neck itself was also produced as a computer-generated element.

'We were a little bit nervous about making a computer-generated neck', recalls Ralston. 'This was still the very early days of CG and we had previously only done fantasy-type figures like the metallic man in *Terminator 2* [1991]. This project meant putting a CG body part on a living person, which involved making a CG model that really looked like it was made of human skin – something we all see every day and which anyone can spot when it looks fake'. The prosthetic neckpiece to which Streep was allergic was cyberscanned (<195) to produce a digital copy that was used as the basis for a neck modelled entirely within the computer. Streep's backwards-facing head was filmed by seating the actress on a swivel chair that was moved to match the movement of her body in the live-action footage.

The digital twisted neck and the backwards-facing head elements were then digitally composited onto the footage of the actress's headless body. The result was the disconcerting combination of front-facing body and back-facing head linked by a horribly twisted computer-generated neck.

Today, digital make-up techniques can be far more subtle and are increasingly being used where traditional make-up was once employed. The key to the computer's ability to create convincing make-up effects is the ability to replicate the movement of performers, enabling digital additions to be applied to them. This is done using match-moving techniques (<235). Typically, a performer will have their face scanned to produce a 3-D digital model. When the actor's live-action performance has been filmed, the digital model of their head is layered on top of the footage and painstakingly repositioned by hand one frame at a time until it copies precisely the motion of the filmed head. Any necessary make-up changes can then be created using the digital head and later composited back onto footage of the real head. Methods such as these were used by Lola VFX, who re-sculpted the faces of Ian McKellen and Patrick Stewart to make them look 10 years younger for a flashback scene in *X-Men: The Last Stand* (2006). Lola specialize in digital cosmetic enhancement (DCE), the computerized equivalent of plastic surgery, which gives stars blemish-free skin, breast enhancements and even longer legs.

Although computer-generated make-up and creature effects have become increasingly sophisticated and convincing in recent years, Nick Dudman does not believe that the days of the traditional make-up artist are numbered. 'Digital methods will never be as fast or economical as practical make-up. Computers have the potential to do some amazing make-up effects, but one person with a few bits of rubber can do in a few hours what it will take a team of highly paid computer experts weeks or months to achieve. I'm sure that will never change significantly'.

Ultimately, Dudman believes that practical make-up will remain a popular option because of the life that a flesh-and-bone actor can bring to a character. 'I think that our work will continue to be used as long as audiences want to see actors and not cyber-performers', says Dudman. 'People definitely enjoy seeing computer-generated performers, and CG films like *Toy Story* [1995] are very entertaining. At the end of the day, however, I think most viewers want to see real actors. Even if a film character is a hideous beast, that character can be given so much more life, and so many more emotions, if there is a good actor beneath the make-up'.

MF57/10 Background plate

a

b

c

d

e

Stan Winston is in broad agreement with Dudman about the way that computers will affect his art in the future. 'I was absolutely thrilled when I first saw the computer-generated dinosaurs in *Jurassic Park*,' comments Winston. 'Many people panicked and started predicting the end of traditional make-up and practical creature effects, but CG will never replace live effects, never. From a film-maker's point of view, you can almost guarantee that if an effect can be done live, it will be done live. It normally looks better, it's cheaper to produce and it allows you to achieve a performance on set with actors and technicians interacting with it. However, CG allows us to do things that we just can't do practically, and often now it's a case of mixing CG with practical effects on a shot-by-shot basis. Take *The Lost World* [1997]. In that film, there are shots of animatronic dinosaurs, and the audience might work out that it's a mechanical creature, but then you suddenly get a shot where the dinosaur leaps into the air and the audience will think "Oh, that can't be real, it must be done another way." Then we go back and forth, between different methods, depending on what the needs of the shot are. Ultimately, if the story is well told, we can have a mix of practical effects and computer effects and people won't have the time, or the inclination, to sit and think about how any of it is done – they will just enjoy the story.'

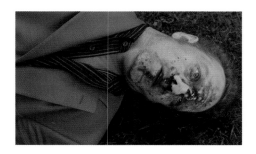

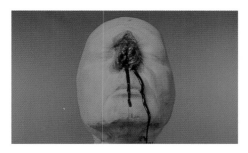

For Winston, digital effects are just another way of allowing film-makers to realize their visions more fully. 'Even now people argue about which is better – practical effects or computer effects? For me, it has nothing to do with technology; it's all about creating convincing characters for film. Whatever the method used, the end result is the important thing. There is a place for totally CG movies, but they won't replace movies with live actors. People often ask if we will ever reach the stage where we can do completely convincing computer-generated actors. Of course we will; it's only a matter of time. But does that mean that we will be able to replace Al Pacino? I don't think so. Any live performer brings something to the mix that no animator ever will. And where animatronics is concerned, it thrills people to know that what they are looking at is real, that something is a genuine, full-blown, mechanical creation that can be touched. People want us to do more, to keep pushing the limits of live effects. As long as an audience wants to see this kind of thing, it will be done.

'*Toy Story* is a wonderful CG movie, the *Star Wars* movies have some great CG characters, and in the future there will be even more realistic CG movies that people will flock to see,' says Winston. 'However, these are just different ways of telling a story. As audiences, we like things to be presented to us in different ways. We still go to the theatre, we still like traditional cel animation, we still like to see Muppet movies where the characters are really nothing more than crude sock puppets. These are all different ways of telling stories, of presenting characters – none is more valid than any other. CG won't replace other things, it will exist alongside them, and one will complement the other.'

LEFT: **Early digital make-up effects were created for *Death Becomes Her* (1992). ILM filmed Meryl Streep with a blue hood over her head and a twisted prosthetic neck (a). The blue head was erased from the picture (b). Streep's head was filmed surrounded by blue (c). Streep's head was extracted from the plate (d). The actress's back-to-front head was added back onto her body. As a final touch, even the reflection in the nearby mirror was adjusted to reflect the new, twisted reality (e).**

ABOVE RIGHT: **Digital effects are increasingly used to create more naturalistic, if hideous, make-up effects. For this shot of a gruesome nose injury in *A History of Violence* (2005), effects company Mr X filmed a prosthetic disfigured nose and digitally applied it to a performer's face. Since the nose is smaller than the performer's real nose, this would have been impossible to achieve with prosthetics.**

RIGHT: **The elegant amphibian Abe Sapien from *Hellboy* (2004) was created by make-up studio Spectral Motion. Actor Doug Jones was dressed in prosthetic appliances and a mask. The slim design of the mask meant there was little room for animatronic mechanisms and so eye blinks were added digitally during post-production.**

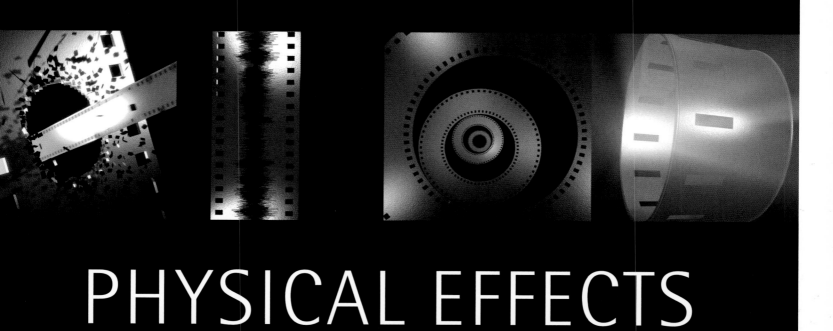

PHYSICAL EFFECTS

7

INTRODUCTION

The term 'special effects' has been adopted by both the media and the general public to describe any method that is used to produce filmed images that somehow deceive the eye. However, as this book demonstrates, a wide variety of different yet interrelated disciplines can be used to create such deceptions, including animation, miniatures, matte paintings, make-up and pyrotechnics. Designating these diverse techniques with the single all-encompassing term 'special effects' is not very satisfactory and past attempts to distinguish between different types of effects in the credits of a film have created some confusion. Terms such as special effects, special photographic effects, mechanical effects, optical effects and visual effects, among others, have been used to refer to different categories of technique from one film to another.

Today, there is broad agreement about how different techniques should be defined. The credits of a modern film are likely to group effects into several distinct categories. 'Visual effects' describes any process that takes place separate from, and usually after, the shooting of the main live action of a film. This includes computer animation and digital compositing. 'Special effects make-up' (sometimes 'special make-up effects') describes any form of three-dimensional make-up process, including prosthetics and animatronics. The catch-all title 'special effects' is generally reserved to describe any form of effect that is performed 'live' in front of the camera during principal photography, such as explosions, bullet hits, collapsing buildings, rain, wind and so on. What the credits of most films now refer to as 'special effects' may also sometimes be called 'mechanical effects', or, as in this book, 'physical effects'.

In the early years of the burgeoning film industry, many effects that have since been achieved more safely and conveniently using sophisticated optical or digital techniques could only be achieved by staging them as live events. Many of the early slapstick comedies featured relatively sophisticated physical effects. The madcap antics of Mack Sennett's Keystone Kops (<18) entailed incredibly complex preparations so that telephone poles collapsed, trams collided, cars drove through houses and people flew through the air on cue. Simple 60-second sequences took teams of 'gag men' days to prepare. For effect more than safety, these 'Sennett stunts' were often performed in slow motion and filmed with an under-cranked camera to make the final sequence appear madly frenetic when the film was projected at the normal speed.

Perhaps the most consummate early physical effects artist was the silent comedian Buster Keaton (1895–1966). The young Keaton had planned to become a civil engineer, but when he began working in films his

engineering skills were employed solving technical problems and devising complicated mechanical stunts. Keaton always worked in collaboration with his technical director Fred Gabourie (1881–1951), who helped him to design, build and operate the gags for all of his films. Gabourie later became head of the prop department at MGM.

One of Keaton's best mechanical effects was the hurricane sequence in *Steamboat Bill, Jr.* (1928), in which entire houses collapse on cue or are blown into the air. In the most spectacular stunt in the sequence, the entire front of a house falls forwards and Keaton only manages to avoid being crushed by standing where an open window falls over him. Meticulous planning and engineering by Gabourie ensured that the wooden house frontage cleared Keaton's head by just a few inches.

Despite changes in technology and safety regulations, the physical effects work of Keaton and the Keystone Kops remains typical of what physical effects must achieve today. Modern physical effects supervisors may find themselves planning anything from violent storms to enormous explosions, from sinking ships to crashing cars. Physical effects is therefore one of the most diverse and consistently challenging areas of special effects work.

PRECEDING PAGES: **James Bond (Timothy Dalton) narrowly escapes a huge explosion in *Licence to Kill* (1989).**

ABOVE: **In *Steamboat Bill Jr.* (1928), Buster Keaton avoided injury by standing exactly where the open window fell. The potentially deadly house missed the actor by just inches, thanks to the skills of Fred Gabourie, Keaton's special effects engineer.**

ABOVE RIGHT: **Rain stands shower the crew of the *Enterprise* as they perform in a studio tank for a scene in *Star Trek IV: The Voyage Home* (1986).**

LEFT: **The outrageous gags performed by Mack Sennett's Keystone Kops involved highly complex physical effects engineering.**

ATMOSPHERIC EFFECTS

Though not particularly glamorous or exciting, a large proportion of physical effects work involves providing what are known as 'atmospheric effects' – meaning wind, rain, snow, fog and smoke. Such effects are required to some degree in almost every film whatever the subject or budget.

RAIN
Rain can make location filming impossibly uncomfortable and often causes long delays. When it is actually needed on screen, the real thing can rarely be relied upon to arrive at the right moment, and it is almost impossible to film effectively when it does. The best policy, therefore, is to hope for dry weather and create the perfect rain when it is called for.

FIGURE 1 **STUDIO RAIN**

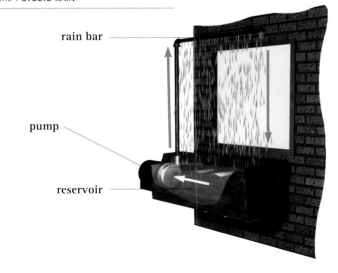

rain bar

pump

reservoir

Rain, of course, is nothing more than water that falls from the sky. Making fake rain simply involves getting water up above a scene so that it can fall back down again in a controlled manner. When filming in a studio, rain is produced either by pumping water into an overhead system of pipes that are filled with holes, or by employing rain stands – tall pipes topped with a nozzle to spray water in the desired direction. Different types of nozzle can create anything from a fine mist to heavy droplets. The amount of water sprayed during each take of a rain scene can be surprisingly large, and a waterproof wall may be built around the edge of a set so that the water can be drained away or pumped back into the system. If a studio set needs to have rain falling outside its windows, a rain bar may be fitted just above each window to sprinkle a curtain of water outside. This falling rain is collected in a small trough underneath the window, where it is pumped back up to the rain bar and recycled (fig. 1).

Creating rain on location can be more complicated. Water is easy to find in towns and cities. With a permit from the necessary authorities, fresh water can be drawn directly from the mains supply using the hydrants intended for use by the fire services. However, films are often shot in exotic or inaccessible locations where a supply of fresh water is not readily available. In such places, large tanker trucks that hold thousands of gallons of water may be used to pump water to rain stands. If rain is needed for a prolonged period, a small fleet of tankers may be kept busy providing a constant supply of fresh water. If performers do not have to be soaked by the water, it may be collected from local rivers – providing the water has been tested for safety. Sterilizing chemicals are almost always added to the water used for rain, and in cold conditions it is heated to keep performers comfortable.

Location rain often has to fall over far larger areas than studio rain. To cover a wide area, heavy-duty valves of the type used as fire sprinklers on oil tankers can be adapted and hung from an overhead crane. These can spray water over a distance of several hundred feet, though large pumps may be needed to provide the necessary pressure. The noise of these pumps and the deluge that results normally means that any dialogue recorded during a scene will need to be replaced (348>).

Since creating consistent artificial rain over a large area is practically impossible, downpours are often only staged immediately in front of the camera in the foreground of a shot. However, background surfaces that are

FIGURE 2 **STUDIO TANK WAVE MACHINE**

FIGURE 3 **TIP TANKS**

Floats plunge up and down. Waves are created according to the speed of floats.

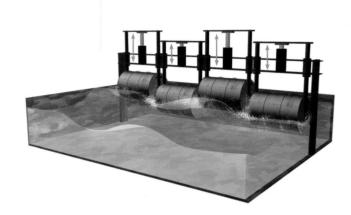

tip tank

adjustable chute

studio tank

pump

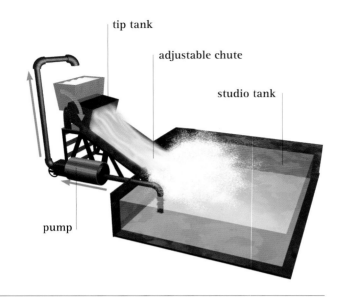

hard or smooth, such as roads, rivers and lakes, will plainly reveal that the rain is not falling on them. By framing a shot so that areas of smooth ground are not visible, the impression of deep rain can be created by producing patches only where it will be noticed most – such as just in front of the camera and on the roofs of distant cars and houses. Soft ground surfaces such as grass do not reveal whether rain is falling on them or not, so as long as there is a blanket of rain across the screen, an effective rainstorm can be created without having to spray rain onto every square inch of ground.

Finally, effective rain only results from the appropriate photography. To be seen properly, rain must be lit from behind or from the side at an angle. This way, light refracts through the water rather than reflecting off it. Even a downfall of biblical proportions can be rendered almost invisible on film if it is lit from the front. Some technicians add milk or paint to the water to help make it more visible, but without suitable lighting, even this will not make rain obvious.

Film-makers have always enjoyed re-creating destruction wrought by the might of water. For *The Ten Commandments* (1923), director Cecil B. DeMille used thousands of gallons of water to film the parting of the Red Sea.

On four occasions, DeMille released massive waves of stored water, and the resulting floods washed from Paramount Studios to downtown Hollywood, resulting in arrests each time. For the flood scenes in *Noah's Ark* (1929), director Michael Curtiz released 15,000 gallons of water onto crowds of extras from tanks positioned immediately above the set. The extras were smashed to the ground, resulting in serious injuries.

For scenes that actually take place in water, rough sea conditions are re-created in the safety of the studio tank. A system of mechanical paddles or floats that plunge in and out of the water can produce quite large waves (fig. 2). Massive walls of water are created using tip tanks – large metal containers filled with hundreds or thousands of gallons of water (fig. 3). When a wave is required, the tank is either tipped over or a valve at its base is opened. The released water gushes down an adjustable chute with an upturned lip at its bottom. As the water leaves the chute, it sprays into the air and atomizes. This atomized water looks like a dense wall of water as it travels across the screen, but if properly controlled it can engulf a performer without any danger. Large pumps are used to quickly refill the tip tanks between takes.

ABOVE: **Enormous fans were used to create violent winds for the storm sequences in** *Black Narcissus* **(1947). Similar fans are still used today, while jet engines can create extreme blasts of wind and air cannon can use compressed air to produce very strong, short bursts of air.**

FAR LEFT: **The creation of a storm for** *The Mosquito Coast* **(1986). Rain stands provide a deluge, while outboard motorboat engines churn the water and huge fans whip up storm-force winds.**

LEFT: **Tip tanks dump thousands of gallons of water onto the deck of HMS** *Surprise* **during the filming of** *Master and Commander: The Far Side of the World* **(2003). When the water leaves the end of the chute, it turns into relatively harmless spray.**

WIND

To create wind for films, fans that vary in power – from hairdryers to jet engines – are used. The most commonly used wind machines employ a converted automobile or aircraft engine to drive a set of propellers that are from 1m (3 ft) to 2m (6 ft) in diameter. The blades are mounted within a protective wire cage and the whole unit is mounted on a turntable. These fans can create enough wind to move large trees at a distance of several hundred feet. For *Twister* (1996), the jet engine from a Boeing 707 was used to create the film's tornado-blasted scenes.

An alternative method is to employ a device called a 'wind mover', which operates on the Venturi principle. A metal funnel pointing in the direction of the desired breeze has compressed air pumped into it. As the air rushes from the front of the tube, it creates a vacuum behind it that sucks in and then propels even greater quantities of air in the same direction.

Because wind itself cannot be seen, lightweight and harmless materials such as dust and leaves are usually thrown into its path to indicate its speed and strength. It is possible to create the impression of powerful wind by using smaller-sized fans to ruffle the hair of actors in the foreground, while objects such as distant trees are agitated using ropes pulled by hidden technicians.

Perhaps the most famous wind effect in film history is the twister from *The Wizard of Oz* (1939). This effect did not actually involve any wind at all, though it was a major mechanical achievement. Special effects supervisor Arnold Gillespie (<141) built a 9m (30 ft) funnel of muslin that was motorized to spin at high speed. The funnel was suspended from a gantry in the roof of a stage, while the base of the contraption was connected to a winding track that followed a different path to the top of the tornado. The base of the funnel sat in a pan that blew fuller's earth (a very fine powdered clay) into the air around it. As the spinning funnel moved across the studio, the differing paths of its top and bottom gave it the realistic twisting look of a tornado.

SMOKE

It is said that there is no smoke without fire. But starting a fire whenever smoke is needed for a scene would be impractical, unpredictable and potentially dangerous. Instead, a number of methods are used to create the effect of smoke without having to set fire to anything.

To quickly create a large volume of billowing smoke, smoke 'bombs' can be used. These are simply canisters that can produce huge quantities of smoke when activated. The smoke is the same type used by aeronautical display teams. It comes in a range of colours and can be purchased in canisters that last for varying periods of time. This smoke is produced chemically and is quite noxious, making it unsuitable for indoor use or around performers.

The most commonly used method of creating smoke is to use a specially built machine that can make the exact quality and quantity of smoke required. These machines all take advantage of the fact that oil produces smoke when it is heated. A typical smoke machine consists of a heating element – similar to that found in an electric kettle – that is used to heat oil. The vapour from the boiling oil is sprayed from a nozzle whereupon it condenses to create plumes of white smoke. The machines used to create this type of smoke range from small hand-held devices to enormous vehicle-based machines that are capable of smoking up large areas of a landscape. In windless conditions, this smoke will hang in the air long enough for most scenes to be filmed. Wafting the smoke with a paddle as it sprays from the machine will cause it to form a consistent misty haze. This type of smoke is commonly used to create an atmosphere in outdoor scenes such as woodlands, where sunshine streaming through the branches of trees will form dramatic shafts of light in the smoke.

Over the years, various types of oil have been used for the creation of smoke, some of which have been outlawed due to their detrimental effect on the health of film workers. The substances now commonly used are a type of mineral oil which has no serious effects on health, and an oil alternative called ethyl glycol. An alternative method, which does not involve heating the oil, uses a liquid called 'cracked oil'. This substance has pressurized air passed through it until it slowly begins to emit a very fine white mist. Unlike the heated oil method that creates smoke at the touch of a button, this technique takes some time to produce a large volume of smoke. The method is most commonly used when shooting miniatures in a sealed studio (<116). The smoke machine can be connected to a device that measures the density of the atmosphere, and will regulate the output of smoke to ensure a consistent density. This is particularly important if a model is being filmed with a motion-control camera over a period of many hours. The consistent density of cracked oil smoke makes it particularly suitable for emulating underwater conditions. The underwater model sequences for movies such as *The Hunt for Red October* (1990) and *Star Wars*: Episode I *The Phantom Menace* (1999) were filmed in a studio full of fine smoke, a technique known as 'dry for wet'.

An effect sometimes seen in horror films, music videos and stage shows is the distinctive ground-hugging mist created by dry ice. Dry ice is crystallized carbon dioxide, created by reducing the pressure and temperature of carbon dioxide gas to produce a 'snow' that is pressed into blocks of solid ice. When dry ice is warmed, it 'melts' from a solid to a gas, creating clouds of foglike smoke. This fog is heavier than air, so it falls to the ground to form a dense white carpet that will roll down walls and creep across floors.

To create a fog, pieces of dry ice are dropped into warm water, either in a simple bucket or a specially made dry ice machine. The warmer the water, the more fog will be produced. The impressive dense clouds created by dropping dry ice into boiling water will dissipate quite quickly, while the less impressive quantities created by cooler water will hang in the air longer. The pressure of the fog created using this method is usually enough to pump it some distance through pipes to the point where it is to emerge. Because dry-ice fog is heavy, it will collect on the floor, building in depth according to the quantity produced. To create a layer of a specific depth, a wall the correct height can be built around the stage. When the fog reaches the top of this wall it will overflow and escape to other areas of a room.

When solid, dry ice remains at a constant temperature of –79°C. Handling the ice without protection can cause severe skin burns. Despite this, however, dry ice wrapped in insulation material and placed in actors' mouths to vaporize breath has in the past been used to give the impression of a very cold atmosphere when filming in a warm environment.

COBWEBS

No spooky house or jungle cave would be complete without a thick veil of cobwebs across every corridor and doorway. The device used to make an artificial spider's web is a type of hand-held fan that has a small pot of cobweb cement fitted to the shaft that spins the fan blades. As the fan spins, a small hole in the cement pot emits a thin stream of liquid cobweb that is blown out to land and set on nearby props. The method is similar to the one used to spin cotton candy in fairgrounds. The threads produced by a cobweb spinner are relatively short and weak, so large curtains of cobweb are prepared with a network of supporting monofilament fishing line before being sprayed with web. A handful of fine dust is then thrown over the web for the finishing touch. The cement traditionally used for cobwebs was a type of rubber that was noxious when sprayed, would disintegrate after a few days, and would ignite if in contact with a naked flame. Modern cobweb cement is made from liquid latex that solidifies as soon as it is sprayed. Thicker cobwebs can be made by drizzling a thin stream of melted synthetic polymer into a bath of cold water where it instantly sets. The resulting tangle of rubber strings can then be stretched across sets to form the main body of giant webs. These are then dressed with finer cobweb and dust. This technique was used to produce the webs made by the giant spider Shelob in *The Lord of the Rings: The Return of the King* (2003).

ELECTRICAL EFFECTS

Lightning and electrical effects have charged the air of many horror films. Lightning and the bright dancing tendrils of electrical charge are now animated and added to a scene after filming, but in the past many electrical effects were filmed live. Probably the most famous electrical effects are those created by the Universal Studios electrician Kenneth Strickfaden (1896–1984) for *Frankenstein* (1931, <272). Known in Hollywood as 'Mr Electric', Strickfaden created a range of fabulous-looking electrical contraptions for Frankenstein's laboratory – giving them exotic names such as 'bariton generator' and 'nucleus analyzer'. These devices encouraged massive electrical discharges to leap from one antenna to another, filling the air with electricity. Thousands of volts surged through equipment just feet from the main players. As Boris Karloff lay half-naked on the operating table, technicians above him touched together white-hot carbons to create showers of sparks that fell down on him. Strickfaden's scientific devices turned up in many films over the years, including *The Wizard of Oz* (1939), *The Face of Fu Manchu* (1965) and the TV series *The Munsters* (1964–6). Late in his life he was hired as a consultant by the director Mel Brooks, who restored devices created for the original *Frankenstein* and plugged them back in for use in his Gothic parody *Young Frankenstein* (1974).

SNOW AND ICE

Snow is perhaps the hardest of all the natural elements to reproduce artificially on film. However, fake snow is infinitely preferable to the real thing. Although genuine snowy locations allow immense creative freedom in terms of camera movement and shot expanse, natural snow may look less than pristine after a film crew has arrived, set up equipment, built sets and conducted rehearsals. Once disturbed, real snow can be extremely hard to rearrange, allowing shots to be repeated just once or twice before a fresh location has to be used. Natural falling snow is also highly unpredictable. It arrives when it is not wanted and refuses to fall when it is required. The majority of movie snow is therefore faked.

Historically, the most commonly used snow substitute was salt. Salt looks good on film, has the frosted appearance of snow, can be arranged into crests and drifts and can be watered down to produce a convincing slush. However, salt can kill plant life, contaminate watercourses and, when used in large quantities, pollute land for years. A popular recipe for Hollywood snow in the 1930s was a mixture of gypsum, salt and bleached cornflakes. It took 46 tons of this mixture to cover a street in snow for *Elmer, the Great* (1933). Incredibly, another early popular snow substitute was asbestos dust. Before it was recognized as a potentially deadly health hazard, truckloads of the powdered material were delivered to studios and spread across every surface. It was even arranged on actors' hair and clothing, and shovelled into wind machines to create picturesque but toxic blizzards.

Much of David Lean's epic *Doctor Zhivago* (1965) was filmed not in frozen Russia but in the sweltering heat of a Spanish summer. For the scene in which the Red Army charges across a frozen lake, a Spanish field was levelled and covered with sheets of iron on top of which thousands of tons of marble dust were spread. This was then steamrollered flat so that the charging horses would slip and slide as if on a real frozen lake. To complete the illusion, 'lakeside' trees were frosted with a spray of whitewash and a rowing boat was positioned as if trapped in the ice.

Today, creating snow for the movies is big business, involving considerable investment and research into methods and materials. One of the world's leading snow men is Darcy Crownshaw, who can supply snow for every occasion. 'We actually have more types of snow than the Eskimos have words for!' says Crownshaw, whose company, Snow Business, has branches in 17 countries. 'We have over 100 types of snow, each of which is used to create a different look or to perform in a different way. Our snow is made from all sorts of materials, including plastics, foams and even potato starch, but much of the snow that we supply is made from paper'.

Paper has been used to make snow for some time, but the snow that Crownshaw pioneered is fundamentally different from its forerunners. 'Most

ABOVE: **When activated, a cobweb spinner emits a string of silky material from the container at the centre of its rotating fan.**

ABOVE FAR LEFT: **Smoke from heated oil is fed into a fan to create a dense fog bank during the filming of *The Lost Continent* (1968).**

ABOVE LEFT: **A dry-ice machine billows a heavy freezing fog into woodlands, where it will hug the ground to eerie effect.**

RIGHT: **The Red Army charges across a frozen lake – actually a Spanish plain covered with fake snow in *Dr Zhivago* (1965).**

paper snows were small flakes that had been cut or punched out of larger sheets. This gave them straight edges that made them fall rather unrealistically and blow away as soon as there was any wind,' he explains. 'However, we make our paper snow differently. Instead of being cut, our paper is ripped so that it has very fluffy edges. When ripped paper snow falls, it meanders and tumbles like real snow. When it's on the ground, it clumps together like real snow. When the wind is really strong, it doesn't blow away, but forms drifts just as real snow does.'

Paper snow is just one product in Crownshaw's arsenal and he usually employs a variety of fake snows, according to the needs of a scene. 'We might use six or seven different types of snow in any one scene,' explains Crownshaw. 'In fact, if you look at real snow on the ground, you will see lots of different textures and sizes, so although we use different materials for speed, economy or performance, the more types we use in one shot, the better it seems to look.'

The majority of snow work does not involve the simulation of actual snowfalls but rather the dressing of sets and locations with a layer of already settled snow. To cover wide areas of distant landscape quickly, large volumes of water-based 'wet foam', similar to that used by firefighters, can be pumped from a large-diameter hose. For one shot in Kenneth Branagh's *Hamlet* (1997), Snow Business covered 35 hectares (86 acres) in snow, much of it foam. Although this method is fast and cheap, foam degrades quickly and will only last for a few hours before breaking down, so it is best when used for single shots.

For areas in the middle distance, large-sized paper snow can be used; the size of the flakes helps to give some texture to the covered area. In the foreground, much finer grades of paper snow are used. Rather than smothering delicate features such as grass and twigs, finer paper snows cling to them and give definition, much as real snow would. Altering the water content of paper snow controls its characteristics. The snow is held in large hoppers from which it is blown along pipes up to 500 m (1,640 ft) in length. As the snow is sprayed from the pipe, the paper is mixed with the desired quantity of water using adjustable nozzles. A dry, fluffy snow can be kicked up as people run through it; wetter snow forms distinct tracks when vehicles drive through it and, when sprayed, will stick to vertical walls and even

TOP LEFT: A light covering of snow and ice can make a location look as wintry as a full-scale snow scene. Here a Scottish village has been given a touch of frost for *The Winter Guest* (1997).

ABOVE LEFT: Clouds of C-90 are sprayed onto trees to create a convincing snow scene.

LEFT: Members of the Snow Business team give the forecourt of London's St Pancras station a coat of damp paper snow for a wintry scene in *Bridget Jones's Diary* (2001).

RIGHT: Using a range of materials, Snow Business iced up this interior library set for *The Day After Tomorrow* (2004).

ABOVE RIGHT: To create instant permafrost on fixtures and fittings, various waxes were sprayed over objects such as this reading lamp. Shredded polymer mixed into the wax made the ice glisten realistically.

ceilings. Wet paper snow can even be scooped up and formed into snowballs for throwing. The paper used to create outdoor snow is unbleached and chemical-free to lessen its impact on the environment.

Rather than covering everything with snow, Crownshaw often creates a convincing winter scene by coating an area with fake frost. 'If deep snow is not absolutely necessary to the plot, an equally effective impression can be given using a product called C-90. It's actually a pure cellulose powder that is used by the food industry, so it's completely environmentally friendly,' he states. 'To apply C-90, we first spray water onto the areas we want to coat. Then we blow thick clouds of the white dust into the air, and it sticks to anything that is wet. This material only gives a thin coating but creates a really convincing heavy frost that is every bit as effective as a thick blanket of snow. As soon as filming is finished, we spray the area with water again and the C-90 is washed away.'

Other set-dressing materials include types of clear silicone rubber that can be melted and spread over areas to form glistening ice, and liquid paraffin wax that sets when tipped into bodies of water to form a floating sheet of ice. Crownshaw uses a range of high-tech equipment to melt and spray different types of wax to create the appearance of frozen snow and ice. The wax can be semi-clear like ice or solid white like snow. The addition to the wax of shredded polymers and other materials will make it sparkle like real frozen snow. Much of this technology was used to create the chillingly realistic frozen interior scenes for *The Day After Tomorrow* (2004).

To create falling snow, a number of different methods can be used. Inside studios, hoppers or pipes can be set up in the roof to release paper or plastic snow. Paper snow is generally used to produce blizzard conditions while foams and plastics produce more gentle effects. The snow used inside studios must be grade-1 fireproof to meet safety regulations and dust-free to protect the lungs of performers and technicians. The most commonly used falling indoor snows are a plastic snow that is made from grinding up blocks of polyethylene to produce realistic flakes of fluffy snow, and a form of dry foam. 'Dry foam is produced from a liquid but unlike the large amounts of "wet foam" used to cover the ground in exterior shots, it isn't mixed with water to produce the foam; the machines just use the foam liquid and froth it up to produce very dry, fluffy flakes,' explains Crownshaw.

'Dry foam snow floats nicely in the air, drifting slowly to produce gentle-looking snowfall. As soon as the snow hits an object each flake melts away just like real snow so it can't be used to produce ground cover. Dry snow works really well when characters are seen coming indoors from a snowstorm because the flakes stuck to their hair and clothes gradually melt realistically. It's also hypo-allergenic so there are no problems having it land on people.'

On location, small hand-held machines can be used to spray foam into the air; when handled correctly, they can provide quite a convincing snowstorm. A quick and easy way of creating a blizzard is to use snow candles – hand-held incendiary devices that emit plumes of white paper ash into the air for several minutes. Several candles waved randomly in the air will cover a large area with remarkably realistic snow. 'Although paper ash doesn't melt realistically in the way that dry foam does, snow candles generally produce a better quality of falling snow,' says Crownshaw. 'However, from a vanity point of view, it can be quite pleasing when you create a really convincing blizzard and a paper snowflake lands on someone and doesn't melt. That way some observant viewers will realize that it's not a real storm, but a really good imitation.'

Another increasingly popular snow is called polymer snow. Polymer snow is a petrochemical product supplied as a very fine powder. When added to water the powder expands to over 40 times its original volume. The resulting snow makes an excellent ground dressing. It is slippery and free-flowing and so is ideal for creating avalanches.

When asked if digital techniques have diminished the need for artificial snow, Crownshaw reveals that modern methods have actually had the reverse effect. 'Producers used to delete really big snow scenes from their scripts because they knew what it could involve. Today, snow isn't a problem. The CGI guys can do a great job of painting vast distant landscapes white, and we can concentrate on doing better-quality work that performers can interact with in the smaller foreground areas. We now do more snow than ever before, so we actually like the CGI people.'

BREAKAWAY EFFECTS

In the movies, no bar brawl would be complete without beer bottles being smashed over heads, and few action-adventure films can resist sending at least one person, vehicle or object flying through a plate-glass window.

For stunts where injury seems avoidable – such as vehicles smashing through windows – real glass is likely to be used. Stunt performers will also sometimes jump through panes of real glass. In such cases, a sheet of tempered glass is normally fitted with a glass breaker – a small spring-loaded arm tipped with a sharp metal point. Glass breakers fitted to the bottom of a window are triggered momentarily before a stunt performer is about to jump through it. If the timing is correct, the window will shatter just as the performer hits it, giving the impression that it is the performer's body that is doing the breaking. If the glass breaker fails to work, the stunt performer is more likely to bounce dramatically off the glass than plunge through it.

When the risk of serious injury is too great to use real glass, a safer alternative is employed. Fake glass, as well as other objects that are to be safely broken or smashed during filming, are called 'breakaway effects'.

The earliest breakaway effects were achieved using a variety of simple materials. Objects such as plates and vases were handmade from bread or pie dough, which was baked hard and then painted. Such items were solid enough to withstand rough handling and would break when required. A popular alternative to dough was ordinary casting plaster. This material, mixed with sand or sawdust to make it brittle, is still sometimes used for items such as vases and pots.

Breakaway glass was first made by dissolving white sugar in a small quantity of boiling water. When cooled, this solution would crystallize into a glasslike material that would shatter without any sharp edges. Bottles were produced by pouring the sugar solution into plaster moulds, and slabs of glass were made by pouring it onto a flat surface. Sugar glass was never a perfect alternative to real glass, however. Objects made from the material were only semi-transparent and were full of rough crystals and flow lines. The addition of a little cream of tartar helped to make sugar glass look slightly more realistic, but real glass objects normally had to be used in establishing shots, and the sugar glass substituted at the last moment for shots of the actual breakage. A better-looking fake glass was made from stearic acid (an extract of animal and vegetable fats). Although stearic acid produced a much more convincing glass substitute, it was subject to 'cold flow' – once cast, an object would gradually 'melt', slowly sagging like a wax object under heat. For this reason, stearic acid breakaway objects had to be made shortly before use.

Today, breakaway glass is made from a pre-prepared plastic resin that can be purchased in thick slabs. This resin is melted down in a saucepan over a stove to produce a clear liquid. Dyes can be added to this liquid to produce glass of any colour. Glass made with undyed liquid resin tends to be slightly yellow, so uncoloured clear glass is usually made with a tiny amount of green dye to give it the greenish tint that glass normally has. Once in liquid form, this resin is poured into plaster moulds to create objects of almost any shape and size. Provided they are handled carefully, the glasses and bottles that result from this process are strong enough to be filled with liquids and will shatter quite

a

b

c

d

FAR LEFT: **Using standard moulding techniques, breakaway glass and ceramic objects can be produced in almost any shape and colour.**

LEFT: **To make breakaway glass, pieces of solid resin are first melted over a stove (a). The liquid resin is then poured into moulds (b). As the resin sets, its surface is warmed to prevent bubbles and ripples (c). The set resin is carefully removed from its mould, ready for use (d). This piece is one quarter of a lighthouse lens made for the film *The Lighthouse* (2000).**

ABOVE: **A stuntman playing James Bond plunges through a breakaway window during a thrilling chase in *GoldenEye* (1995).**

realistically when smashed. Sheets of glass up to 2 m (6 ft) square can be produced by pouring the liquid resin onto a smooth metal or marble tabletop on which lengths of angle-iron have been laid to produce a mould of the correct size. The tabletop is often heated slightly to avoid the flow lines that can occur when the resin sets too quickly.

Once the resin is poured, its surface may be warmed with a hot-air gun to prevent small bubbles and other inconsistencies from setting into the surface of the glass. Once cooled, resin glass can be set into any window frame, just like the real thing.

Some movie scenes require glass that has already been shattered. Many sets need to be strewn with broken glass after an action sequence, for example, and in scenes where a stunt performer has performed the dangerous act of diving through a window, the real star has to be seen landing on the ground in a shower of glass splinters. To make ready-shattered glass, a special silicone-based plastic is cast into sheets and then broken into thousands of tiny pieces that look exactly like the bright, sharp fragments that result when real glass is shattered with great force. These fragments can be safely thrown at actors without fear of injury.

Breakaway china objects such as plates and vases are made from paraffin wax, which is opaque and, being less brittle than breakaway glass, breaks into larger chunks in the same way that real china would. Just like glass resin, paraffin wax is melted and poured into moulds to make the required object. However, wax is harder to colour than glass resin, so any colouring is normally painted onto the surface of the finished object. When under the hot lights of a film set, warm paraffin wax objects will break into relatively large pieces, so they are often refrigerated prior to use to make them more brittle and easily shattered.

GUNS AND BULLETS

Since Edwin S. Porter's (<17) historic film *The Great Train Robbery* (1903), guns have played a vital role in the movies. 'Most people think the guns that they see in the movies are special prop guns. In fact, whenever you see someone firing a gun in a film, the chances are that it's probably the real thing,' explains Dale Clarke, an armourer at Bapty & Co, one of the world's longest-established suppliers of movie weaponry.

Bapty & Co supplies film-makers with guns that range from 17th-century matchlock rifles to the very latest laser-guided assault weapons and even enormous artillery pieces. In the company's London warehouse, tens of thousands of weapons hang in neat rows, carefully cared for between appearances in films as diverse as *The Bridge on the River Kwai* (1957), *Alien* (1979), *The Killing Fields* (1984), *Batman* (1989) and the *Star Wars*, *Indiana Jones* and James Bond films.

The work of an armourer may begin in the early stages of pre-production. 'Guns are a complicated affair, so film-makers rarely leave it to the last minute before they think about weapons for their characters,' explains Clarke. 'Our job begins by reading the script and then discussing its requirements with the art department and prop buyer. We first decide what type of gun will suit a particular character. This involves a show-and-tell session in which we demonstrate what we consider to be the most suitable weapons and their various attributes.'

Once the type of gun has been chosen, the armourer considers how the weapon will be used during filming and what versions are required. 'We actually supply a number of specifications of gun,' explains Clarke. 'These are mixed and matched according to the requirements of each scene in a film. Firstly, we have the practical guns. These are 100 per cent real guns that are used to fire blank ammunition during filming.

'Then there are non-practical guns. Again these are real guns, but they have been deactivated so they cannot actually fire anything. Then we have replica guns that are made in metal or plastic to look like the real thing. These are quite detailed and can function mechanically, but obviously they can't fire, so they are fine for use by background characters when some degree of realism is needed.

'Then there are dummy guns that are simply a shell and do not work mechanically. These are

ABOVE: This unique boat-mounted, belt-fed sniper rifle was customized by gunsmiths at Bapty & Co for the opening scenes of *The World Is Not Enough* (1999).

LEFT: Bapty & Co created this unique disassembling AK47 Kalashnikov sniper rifle – the only one of its kind in the world – for the *The World Is Not Enough*.

RIGHT: James Bond (Pierce Brosnan) creates havoc in the opening sequence of *Die Another Day* (2002). Bapty added a flash enhancer to the Ingram Mac-10 sub-machine gun so that it would produce spectacular muzzle flashes when fired.

used for basic background action or as "holster fillers". Finally, we have rubber guns. These are moulded in rubber to look like the real thing, and can safely be used when there is any running or stunt work involved. Deciding exactly what guns are needed early in the production schedule is particularly important if we will be taking the weapons abroad. In most cases we're not exporting film props, we're exporting weapons of war – foreign officials tend to want to know why you want to fly a dozen Kalashnikovs into their country on a commercial flight! It can take a while for us to arrange all the necessary government permits.'

Before they can be used, real guns are modified to make them capable of firing blank cartridges and incapable of firing real bullets. 'Some guns, such as revolvers and bolt-action rifles, can fire a blank cartridge just as well as a live one,' explains Clarke. 'However, many weapons actually use the firing of a bullet as part of their operating system. For example, a Kalashnikov uses the gas pressure created by firing a bullet to help load the next cartridge. In order to fire blanks, which don't create much gas, we must restrict the inner size of the barrel in order to keep the gas pressure high. With guns that eject their cartridges after they have been fired, major modifications may have to be made to the ejection port so that the spent blank cartridges, which are often longer than spent live cartridges, can be expelled safely.'

The scientific refinement of modern military guns can actually render them unsuitable for film work. 'Most of the people who use military guns want to keep the location of a firing rifle a secret, for rather obvious reasons,' explains Clarke. 'To achieve this, all military self-loading rifles are built with an extremely efficient flash eliminator – a cleverly designed device that sits on the barrel of a gun and minimizes the flash of light it produces when a bullet is fired. This, of course, is the exact opposite of what film-makers want – an action film needs its guns to have great bursts of flashing light when they are fired. We therefore remove the flash eliminators on our guns and replace them with our specially designed flash accentuators.'

The alternative to having real guns with flash accentuators is to use specially built 'gas guns' that produce a huge flash of burning gas when the trigger is pulled. 'Gas guns are of limited use because they need to be plumbed into a source of gas,' explains Clarke. 'Most of the time it is not practical to have a performer who is required to run around with a gun connected up to gas pipes, so we stick with the real thing.' Occasionally, extremely bright strobe lights are used to simulate the bright flashes of a firing machine gun. For *Indiana Jones and the Last Crusade* (1989), strobe-light machine guns were fitted to a real Messerschmitt aircraft for scenes in which the hero and his father are attacked from the air.

The technicians at Bapty commonly perform major conversions to turn 'off-the-shelf' weapons into something that better suits the needs of film-makers. 'The design team of the James Bond film *The World Is Not Enough* [1999] fell in love with the look of a certain type of sniper rifle,' recalls Clarke. 'However, sniper rifles are designed to discharge a single bullet very accurately, and Bond films normally require something a lot more spectacular. As a result, we took a standard machine gun and created what was probably the world's first belt-fed sniper rifle that was also totally reliable when mounted on a fast-moving boat.'

In addition to the extensive alterations that the Bapty gunsmiths make to the internal mechanisms of their weapons, the external appearance of a gun can also receive considerable attention. Many science fiction or fantasy films require fully functioning guns that look very different from commercially available contemporary weapons. 'We've witnessed the evolution of so-called "special" weapons over the past 25 years,' explains Clarke. 'We began by changing the appearance of real guns so that they

looked like laser blasters for *Star Wars* [1977]. The film had a pretty low budget, so we made fairly simple modifications to existing weapons. Luke Skywalker's blaster was just a Sterling sub-machine gun with a few bits of angle aluminium strapped to the barrel and a piece of artillery sight on the top. If you study parts of the original film closely, you will actually see the so-called laser weapons discharging spent 9 mm cartridges – the laser beams were put in afterwards and help to distract you from noticing that it is really a down-to-earth machine gun being fired. After *Star Wars*, we made the blaster for *Aliens* [1986]. This was a Thompson sub-machine gun strapped over a pump-action shotgun. These two weapons were then mounted inside a fairly crude aluminium outer case to make it look like some special sci-fi gun.

'Today, we create weapons like those seen in *Judge Dredd* [1995]. Those were a range of weapons including Berettas, Remington pump-action shotguns and Kalashnikovs that were mounted in sophisticated fibreglass outer shells designed by the film's art department. The outer shells had lights and digital read-outs and included built-in mechanisms for reloading the weapons within. Being able to reload a weapon easily is vital, because we need to fill up the magazines, cock the weapon and get it back to a performer before the crew is ready for the next take.'

Occasionally, a film requires a completely unique gun that cannot be converted from existing weapons. For *Mission: Impossible* (1996), Bapty & Co was asked to create a gun that could be made from the various parts of a portable radio. The gun did not have to be seen firing, so it was a simple case of designing a clever and convincing-looking weapon. Once made, however, the production decided that the weapon should also be practical, so a fully working gun capable of discharging two rounds of ammunition was retro-engineered to the same design. 'It was an extremely challenging engineering job,' comments Clarke.

Once the technical aspects of gun design and modification have been tackled, the armourer starts to work with the people who will actually use the weapons. 'The first thing we do is teach people how to be safe with the weaponry,' says Clarke. 'Even though we are not dealing with guns that fire real bullets, very serious injury can occur from the misuse of a blank-firing weapon. The first thing to remember is that blanks can be just as loud as real guns, so anyone using a gun – and all of the surrounding crew – should wear ear defenders or earplugs whenever there is any gunfire.'

TOP: **Ripley (Sigourney Weaver) brandishes a customized weapon that combines a Thompson sub-machine gun with a pump-action shotgun encased in a fibreglass housing in *Aliens* (1986).**

ABOVE: **The blasters used in *Star Wars* (1977) were modified Sterling sub-machine guns that fired blank 9 mm cartridges.**

LEFT: **Hundreds of real weapons ranging from pistols to artillery guns await use in the warehouse of Bapty & Co.**

Although no bullets come out of a blank-firing weapon, the discharge from a blank can cause serious injury. 'When a blank shell is fired, it propels a cloud of super-heated gases hot enough to set fire to nearby materials'. To demonstrate this point, Clarke fires a single round from a revolver into a polystyrene tailor's dummy from a distance of around 1 m (3 ft). A deep hole filled with many black flecks is melted into the polystyrene. 'The black bits are grains of unburned gunpowder,' points out Clarke. 'If you were fired at with a blank, these bits of powder could embed themselves in your skin and scar you permanently, just like a tattoo. As well as the powder, there is sometimes a small piece of cardboard wadding used to pack the gunpowder in the shell that effectively becomes a cardboard bullet that can penetrate flesh at close range.'

There is also the danger of brass shards. Blanks are made of brass – like normal shells – and because there is no bullet to hold in the powder, the end of the shell is crimped shut. When fired, this crimp is blasted open and small pieces of hot brass will travel some distance from the weapon, which could result in injuries. 'Blank guns should never be fired at anyone. They are always pointed to one side of a target person, and the camera angle hides the fact that the aim is off.'

Once a performer is aware of the danger posed by the weapon, the armourer teaches him or her how to use the device. 'We feel that the better a performer knows the weapon, the better they will look and feel when using it,' explains Clarke. 'If you watch Bruce Willis in *Die Hard* [1988], you'll notice how well he uses a weapon. That's because he fully understands how guns work and is able to load them, strip them down and clear any stoppages himself. He doesn't need to think about how he uses his gun and, as a result, gives a convincing performance and is able to do little bits of interesting action – like reloading his weapon – without thinking about it. We try to ensure that all performers whose characters are meant to be experienced with guns reach that standard. Another reason for intensive training is to calm a performer's nerves. Many people are understandably nervous about using a gun, and nerves can easily lead to accidents.'

As well as training the performer to use a weapon, an armourer has a good knowledge of how any character is likely to use a gun. 'Throughout the ages, the way people have handled weapons has changed,' notes Clarke. 'The way an 18th-century person held and used a pistol was quite different to the way we do now. It's part of our job to know these details and pass them on to the performer.'

During filming, armourers work with the director, fight coordinator and special effects supervisor to plan each shot. 'We have to help the director achieve the shot they are thinking of, but at the same time we can sometimes tell them that what they are planning is dangerous. Very often we will come up with more exciting alternatives that a director didn't know were possible. We then rehearse performers, and get them used to the rhythm of the shot – they walk it through saying, "Bang, bang, bang!" whenever they are going to fire their gun. This is very important because in the turmoil of an action sequence, it's easy for a performer to get confused and shoot at the wrong time and place. This rehearsal is also useful for the special effects crew, who use it to practise when they are going to operate their bullet-hit effects [320>], which is a totally different part of the equation.'

ABOVE LEFT: **This unique pistol from** *Mission: Impossible* **(1996) was designed to be assembled from the parts of a portable radio.**

ABOVE: **The Peacemaker gun from** *Judge Dredd* **(1995) used a custom-made fibreglass outer shell to conceal a blank-firing Kalashnikov.**

BELOW: **A gun using compressed air to fire capsules containing fake blood, silver paint or zirconium can be used to create a range of bullet-hit effects.**

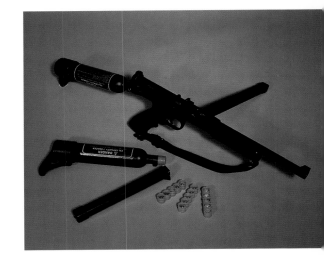

Finally, when the scene is fully rehearsed, the armourer loads all weapons and hands them to the performers. 'Once we have stepped away, it is over to the performers and, if we've done our job, there won't be any problems,' states Clarke. 'We still need to keep an eye on all the weapons, though, to make sure there are no stoppages or other mechanical problems. When the director shouts "cut", nobody relaxes. This is potentially the most dangerous time because people lower their guard. We go in and take the weapons from the performers and make them safe. Only when we give the all-clear can the crew relax.'

BULLET HITS
When a gun has been fired, the audience naturally expects to see its effect – a person or object struck by a bullet. When film was a young medium, the only way to achieve this effect was to fire real bullets. A hired sharpshooter or a fixed-position rifle would actually fire bullets into the scenery surrounding an actor. Providing the target was relatively soft, the performer would not be harmed by flying debris or a ricocheting bullet. In the classic gangster movie *G Men* (1935), actor Edward G. Robinson appears in several shots in which his surroundings are strafed by real bullets: his look of fear probably had nothing to do with his skill as an actor.

In the late 30s, the Screen Actors Guild put a halt to this traumatic and dangerous practice. Bullet hits were then achieved as a split-screen effect, the performer on one side of the screen being filmed in one take, and the bullet hits on the other side of the screen in another. A safer alternative was to fire small chalk pellets from a slingshot to create a puff of white dust where they hit an object. These pellets would not harm an actor, but they didn't create the dramatic burst of destruction that a real bullet would.

One early method of producing the explosive effect of a real bullet hitting scenery involved carving a small crater in the target object and plumbing it with a pipe connected to a source of compressed air (fig. 4). The pipe was fed through the back of the object, while the crater on its front was filled with an appropriate material such as loose plaster or sawdust. A burst of compressed air would blow this material out of the

hole on cue. A sequence valve could be used to create the staggered blowing of holes to simulate machine-gun fire. This method is still occasionally used.

Today, the effect of a bullet hit can be produced either pyrotechnically or non-pyrotechnically. Non-pyrotechnic methods involve firing small capsules from a specially designed airgun. The capsules, which are made of a thin gelatin, can be filled with various substances, and when fired at a solid object, burst to release their contents. If firing at a wall, these capsules are filled with powder of the appropriate colour to produce a puff of dust for each bullet hit. If strafing the side of a car, capsules can be filled with a thick silver paint that splatters to produce what looks like metallic holes in the paintwork. To produce the effect of sparks when a bullet ricochets off metal, capsules are filled with a metallic element called zirconium, which produces sparks when it hits a hard surface.

Pyrotechnic bullet hits use a small explosive device called a 'squib'. A squib resembles an ordinary domestic fuse with a wire protruding from one end. The wire is connected to a source of electrical power, and when the power is switched on, the squib will explode. 'Squibs come in all sorts of shapes and sizes,' explains the special effects supervisor Chris Corbould, who, having worked on more than 10 James Bond films, has probably simulated as many gun hits as anyone in the business. 'Squibs are basically an off-the-shelf item that we use for any number of purposes, not just for bullet hits. Some squibs just produce a smokeless blast, some create smoke and a flash, and some create a shower of sparks like a bullet hitting metal. We use different types of squib for different types of job. They're quite useful little devices.'

Pyrotechnic bullet hits have to be set up long before any weapon is fired (fig. 5). Each required bullet hole is carefully dug into a surface, primed with a squib and then camouflaged. For example, a target such as a plaster wall is pre-prepared by having a cone-shaped hole dug out and the squib placed at the bottom. The thin electrical wire of the squib is threaded through a small hole at the base of the crater and out the back of the wall, where it is connected to a power source.

The back of the wall immediately behind the squib may have a type of

FIGURE 4 **COMPRESSED–AIR BULLET HIT**

hole in the wall

debris blown from hole   compressed air

FIGURE 5 **PYROTECHNIC BULLET HIT**

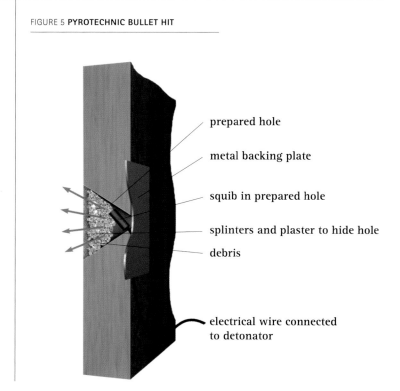

prepared hole

metal backing plate

squib in prepared hole

splinters and plaster to hide hole

debris

electrical wire connected to detonator

putty or a metal plate fitted over it to ensure that the blast of the squib is directed forwards. The cavity is then filled with plaster (sometimes mixed with materials such as sawdust to make it brittle) and painted. When an electric current is applied to the squib, the pre-prepared hole is blasted out. Objects made of wood will have a bullet hole gouged out, and after the squib has been positioned, the wood splinters will be lightly glued back into position. In fact, the types of holes created by movie bullets are rarely true to life. A real bullet hitting an object such as a plaster wall would make a relatively small hole on impact and would only create a large crater on the reverse of the wall where it exits.

Part of the art of using squibs is in hiding their presence before they are detonated. 'Fixing squibs into scenery in a studio is relatively easy,' explains Corbould. 'It's just a case of drilling a hole through the plywood or plasterboard walls, and then threading the squib through from behind. It's also usually pretty easy outdoors because it's just a case of burying the wires in the ground – for The Mummy [1999], we just buried the wires in the desert sand. It's a lot more difficult if you're working on location in some historical building. People obviously don't want you making holes through their walls, so you have to find ways of attaching squibs and hiding wires without drilling into anything. Sometimes it's a case of fabricating fake walls or door frames that can be destroyed. Hiding the wires from squibs can be fairly easy if a scene is only being filmed with one camera. If we know where the camera is, we can tape wires behind objects like the legs of furniture and then run them under carpets. However, these days action scenes are often filmed with multiple cameras and even moving hand-held cameras. Not knowing what parts of a location are going to be seen by the camera can make hiding wires very difficult and involve a lot of work.'

The cables that come from a squib are wired into a device that allows each one to be detonated on cue. Sophisticated firing mechanisms called 'clinker boxes' can be programmed to detonate each squib at exactly the right moment in a sequence. Once the firing sequence is triggered, each detonation will be accurate to within hundredths of a second. 'Although we use some hi-tech ways to trigger the detonation of bullet hits, we often prefer the old-fashioned nailboard method,' explains Corbould. A nailboard is simply a board on which a number of metal 'nails' are fixed in a row. Each nail is connected to a terminal into which a single squib is wired. A special effects technician holds an isolated metal rod that is connected to a source of low-voltage power. As each nail is touched with the live part of the hand-held rod, an electrical current travels to the squib and detonates it. Rapid machine-gun fire can be simulated by dragging the rod over the nails at the desired speed. 'We find nailboards useful because a competent technician can perfectly match the firing of bullet hits to whatever live action is going on in a scene. The firing can be slowed down or speeded up depending on the movements of characters, ensuring that no one is near a bullet when it goes off,' says Corbould.

Keeping track of bullet hits can be a logistical headache if a scene requires a large number of hits. 'One of the biggest shots we have done in terms of the sheer quantity of hits going off was for the Russian archive sequence in GoldenEye [1995],' notes Corbould. 'We initially prepared the shot with just a few hundred bullet hits, but the director, Martin Campbell, filmed the shot once and then decided he wanted a lot more bullets. Every qualified pyrotechnician we could find was brought in, and we wired and prepared 1,800 squibs overnight – a shot like that would normally take at least a couple of days to set up. Every single wire in the spaghetti-like mass was numbered so we knew exactly which bullet would go off and when. During filming, a number of technicians each had their own area to watch and detonate. The 1,800 squibs all went off in about ten seconds – it was pretty impressive. Keeping track of every bullet hit was vital because, even though most of what was being destroyed in the scene was books and paper, a piece of flying card could be quite painful. When you will be working with actors for nine months on a project, it's important to retain their confidence in you.'

FIGURE 6 **PYROTECHNIC BODY HIT**

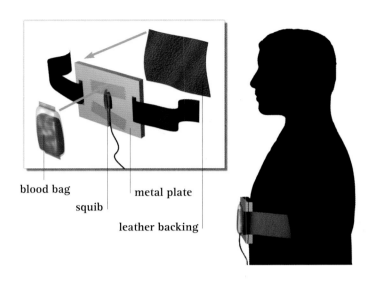

blood bag | squib | metal plate | leather backing

When bullets are required to hit a performer, there are pyrotechnic and non-pyrotechnic options. Non-pyrotechnic methods include firing blood-filled gelatin capsules that burst when they hit the performer. Alternatively, a small piece of blood-soaked cotton wool can be fired at the actor using a blowpipe. Another option is to prepare a realistic bullet wound and conceal it with a piece of foam rubber made to look like normal skin. A thread attached to this fake skin can then be pulled, causing the skin to fly off and reveal the wound.

The pyrotechnic method of simulating body hits again involves the use of squibs (fig. 6). A metal plate backed with a layer of leather is strapped to the body of the performer under his or her clothes. A low-powered squib is taped against an indentation or channel in the metal plate. The wire from the squib normally runs down the trouser leg and out to the detonating device, although performers who are to be shot on the run may wear a self-contained battery-operated squib that they can detonate themselves during the action. If the gunshot wound needs to include blood, a small bag of fake blood is placed next to the squib to produce a trickle, or directly over the squib to create a dramatic spurt. For an even bloodier effect, pieces of meat can be added to the blood mixture.

For a scene in which a criminal accidentally shoots his own foot in Straw Dogs (1971), effects supervisor John Richardson filled a leather boot with fake blood, steak and squibs. When detonated, blood and flesh burst through the shoe leather. 'For family films like the Bond movies, we rarely use any blood when characters are shot,' explains Corbould. 'It's usually enough to see the burst of dust and fabric caused when a squib goes off under some clothing. Often we don't use body hits at all. If a run of machine-gun bullets hits a wall behind a character, the audience will assume the person has been hit as well, and they can fall to the floor without any visible wounds. This is especially true if the person being hit is a stunt performer, because they always like to jump in the air and make a bit of a performance when hit!'

Although the squibs used for body hits are low-powered, they can still be dangerous. 'When anybody is near a squib, you have to be careful,' emphasizes Corbould. 'The devices are detonated electrically, so you have to make sure you don't give anyone a shock. Actors have to be trained to move without letting their hands pass in front of the squib, as it could burn a hand. Even the shredded clothing that flies out when a squib is detonated can be dangerous.'

PYROTECHNICS

Pyrotechnics – the art and science of creating fire and explosions – can produce some of the most visually stunning special effects. Although explosions for the movies are designed to look spectacularly devastating without presenting any danger to those involved, the potential threat to life and limb is still very real. Explosions are created using powerful and dangerous materials, and must only be attempted by professionals with years of training and experience, and for whom safety comes above any other consideration.

The laws governing the use of explosives and explosive materials vary in different countries and states. Those wishing to buy and work with such materials must demonstrate that they have expert knowledge of the safe storage, preparation and use of explosives before they will be awarded a licence to do so. Such explosives licences are normally divided into a range of different grades, and as pyrotechnicians gain more knowledge and experience of their craft, they become eligible for licences that bestow greater responsibility upon them.

At the heart of many pyrotechnic effects is a highly inflammable material called 'black powder'. Composed of a number of basic ingredients, including charcoal and potassium nitrate, black powder comes in various grades, from a fine dust to small chunks like pieces of gravel. Although a few grams or ounces of this powder will do little more than burn furiously when lit with a match, the same quantity is capable of reacting violently when used under certain conditions. 'The key to using black powder for explosions is the way in which you prepare the powder for the job', explains John Richardson, who has supervised special effects for films such as *The Omen* (1976), *Superman* (1978), *Aliens* (1986) – for which he won an Academy Award – *Starship Troopers* (1997) and every James Bond film since *Moonraker* (1979). 'A small quantity of black powder in a heap will do little more than go off with a flash if you ignite it', continues Richardson. 'However, if you take the same amount of powder and try to restrict its combustion by packing it into a container, the powder will be unable to burn slowly, and the only way it can release its energy is to explode with great force. Like most aspects of pyrotechnics, it's not what you use, it's how you use it.'

To create explosions, black powder is packaged in plastic or cardboard containers to create 'bombs'. An electrically controlled detonator, similar to the squibs used to make bullet hits (<320), is planted in the powder before the container is sealed and wrapped with tape. The tighter the powder is packaged, and the thicker the wrapping of tape, the more violent the resulting explosion. When detonated, black-powder

ABOVE: **The basis of most pyrotechnic explosions, black powder comes in a number of grades which produce different effects. Fine and medium grades (*top*) are very fast burning and are used for most types of explosion. Coarser grades (*bottom*) might be used to fire cannon or guns, when the powder needs to continue burning while a projectile is forced along the length of a barrel.**

LEFT: **When detonated, a black-powder bomb throws smoke and debris into the air.**

ABOVE RIGHT: **Black-powder bombs mixed with gasoline can blow oil drums high into the air.**

BELOW RIGHT: **Pyrotechnics and bullet hits are detonated electrically using a firing box or 'clunker box'. Each explosive charge is wired to a separate terminal and can be either programmed to go off sequentially or operated manually by a technician.**

bombs create a powerful blast with a bright flash and a quantity of white smoke. Various materials can be mixed with the black powder to create a more interesting flash – copper filings make the flash green; zinc makes it blue; strontium nitrate, red; and iron filings produce a shower of sparks.

However, this blast is rarely visual enough to fulfil the needs of film-makers. 'Black-powder bombs are normally just the basis for creating much more visually impressive explosions', explains Richardson. 'We use the blast to lift various materials into the air using mortars'. Mortars are variously shaped heavy-gauge steel tubes or pans that are used to hold black-powder bombs and the material that the bombs will be blasting into the air. A simple round tube will blast its contents straight up into the air in a relatively thin column. A wide, shallow mortar with sloping sides will create a lower blast that spreads material out over a wide distance.

'Mortars are normally buried in the ground or placed out of sight wherever an explosion has to occur', says Richardson. 'A black-powder bomb is placed in the base of the mortar, and over that goes the material that we want to throw into the air. Only very soft materials are used, such as peat, cement powder or chunks of foam – basically, anything that won't do serious damage if it hits someone at great speed. We have to be extremely careful that no small stones find their way into the mortar. A piece of gravel turns into a bullet when blasted from a mortar and could potentially kill someone'.

As well as flying debris, movie explosions often require huge clouds of billowing fire. 'We create fireballs using a variety of liquid fuels', explains Richardson. 'The most commonly used fuel is ordinary gasoline, which creates a brilliant orange ball of fire. Sometimes we use diesel, which produces a redder flame that is tinged with oily black smoke at the edges. We often use naphthalene, which creates explosions that look a bit like a cross between petrol and diesel, or isopropanol [pure alcohol], which is useful for indoor explosions because it has a relatively cool flame that is safer when performers are involved'. Naphthalene and isopropanol are useful because both fuels have very little 'residue'. When used in an explosion, petrol or diesel continues to burn after the initial ignition, and any fuel that does not burn in the air rains to the ground or sticks to scenery, where it burns until depleted. Naphthalene and isopropanol, on the other hand, both burn immediately and are depleted in one very fast explosion, creating potentially safer balls of fire.

To create fireball effects, plastic bags full of the chosen liquid are placed on top of a black-powder bomb in a mortar [fig. 7, 324>]. 'We usually use two bombs when creating a fireball explosion', explains Richardson. 'The force of the bomb that vaporizes the fuel can actually be enough to extinguish any fire, with the result that gallons of vaporized fuel just float off into the sky. A second bomb placed on the edge of a mortar will ensure that the vaporized fuel is ignited properly as it rises into the air'. The alternative method of creating fireball explosions is to use a gas mortar – a metal funnel that releases and ignites a cloud of compressed propane gas.

In addition to fireballs, a number of other distinct types of explosion are frequently used in the movies. 'One of the most popular effects is for great plumes of sparks to rocket out of an explosion', notes Richardson. 'These can be created using an off-the-shelf pyrotechnic item called a "directional spark charge". These charges come in various sizes to simulate anything from a sparking electricity socket to a 90 m [300 ft] high fountain of sparks'.

Each movie explosion is a carefully controlled balance of various charges and materials. 'We actually choreograph explosions to get something that has the right combination of different shapes, colours and types of fire and debris', says Richardson. 'On *A Bridge Too Far* [1977], there was an explosion when a character accidentally turned a flamethrower on an ammunition dump. That explosion involved 56 detonations in a period of just 5 seconds, each one carefully designed and timed to complement the others'.

Explosions are almost always filmed at high frame rates in order to make them last longer on the screen (<133), and, as a result, the choreography of pyrotechnics can involve time delays that are calculated in tenths or even hundredths of seconds. 'What looks like a gap of one second between different parts of an explosion on film can actually be a difference of a quarter or an eighth of a second during filming', Richardson explains. 'We therefore have to

have a pretty good sense of exactly how each detonation will interact with the others.' Whenever more than one charge is to be detonated, care has to be taken with the wires. 'An explosion can go wrong because the first bang either burns or cuts the wires to the other charges,' continues Richardson. As a result, all wires are carefully arranged and often channelled inside protective metal tubing.

Directors often like to show people being thrown through the air as a result of impressive explosions. If filled with soft materials, mortar explosions should not present too much danger to stunt performers a reasonable distance from the blast. Performers can be made to look as if they are closer to an explosion if a scene is filmed with a long lens, which has the effect of reducing the apparent distance between objects (<52). The dramatic force of an explosion can be suggested by using a pneumatic springboard called a 'kicker plate' to throw stunt performers a considerable distance into the air. Kicker plates are basically hinged metal plates that, when activated, spring open with great force. As an explosion is detonated, stunt performers jump onto kicker plates, depressing a trigger which causes them to be fired dramatically into the air. The violent force of a kicker plate is more likely to cause injury than the explosion itself and stunt performers must take great care to bend their knees correctly when they are flung into the air.

Explosions using black powder are designed to look visually impressive but, though potentially extremely dangerous, are not usually powerful enough to do serious damage to property. 'We can rig impressive-looking explosions inside real buildings, and after the fireball has died down, the place is perfectly intact

FIGURE 7 **FIRE BOMB**

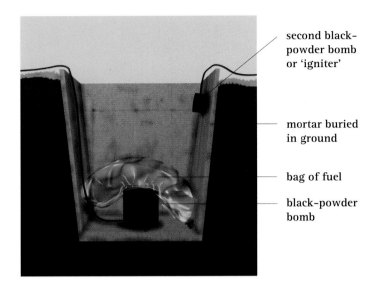

second black-powder bomb or 'igniter'

mortar buried in ground

bag of fuel

black-powder bomb

and unharmed,' says Richardson. 'Sometimes, however, we are required to physically destroy buildings or sets. Such explosions are made up of two distinct parts. There is the "cosmetic", colourful-looking bit that is achieved using black powder and gasoline devices, and then there is a totally separate process designed to inflict the actual damage to the property.'

Destroying real buildings can require far more explosive force than is safe in most film-making situations. 'We always search for a way of using the minimum amount of explosive,' Richardson explains. 'We first weaken any structure so that it is barely standing and it wouldn't take much more than a high wind to make it come to pieces. Then we place explosives in strategic positions, such as the last remaining support posts. Once these points are blown, the building will collapse, and it will appear as if it was the work of the cosmetic explosion that we set off at the same time.' The best material for cutting objects such as support posts is a high explosive cord known variously as det cord, Cordtex or Primacord. 'Cordtex is a sharp, violent explosive that is rather like a plastic clothesline that can be wrapped or taped around any object. By putting a piece around a tree trunk, you could blow a tree in half. It's a very useful material, and we use a lot of it.'

As well as creating explosions on land, effects supervisors are also asked to create them in the water. 'We often have to produce explosions in rivers or in the sea, especially for James Bond movies where boat chases are almost one of the staple ingredients,' states Richardson, who has executed impressive water explosions in films such as *Moonraker* (1979) and *Deep Blue Sea* (1999). 'We need a great deal of force to get water up in the air, but black powder-based explosions are rarely strong enough. Instead, we usually use industrial high explosives. These need to be very securely anchored to the river or seabed, with no chance of their being moved by tides or current. The explosive itself has a float attached to it so that it will remain at the correct depth under the surface of the water.'

The depth at which the charge goes off is vital and has to be correct to within a few inches. If it is too deep, it will not lift the water high enough; if it is too shallow, it will lift an unimpressive quantity of water a very long way. 'Due to the difference the depth of water makes to an explosion, we have to be very knowledgeable about local tidal patterns and be able to judge the depth of waves – a wave going over a charge can add another couple of feet to the depth of the water.'

Unlike land-based explosions whose position can be clearly marked, underwater explosives are not easily visible to either stunt performers or

BELOW LEFT: Gas mortars are used to create short, intense bursts of flame by releasing and igniting compressed propane. The funnel is positioned wherever the explosion needs to come from – typically behind a door or window.

BOTTOM LEFT: Stunt performer Ray Parks is propelled into the air by a pneumatic kicker plate during the filming of *Star Wars*: Episode I *The Phantom Menace* (1999).

RIGHT: In a complex set-piece such as this from *Tomorrow Never Dies* (1997), dozens of charges will be detonated with split-second accuracy. Massive explosions must be carefully choreographed both to impress and to protect cast, crew and equipment.

BELOW: Special effects supervisor Chris Corbould safely created huge water explosions in the heart of London for *The World Is Not Enough* (1999).

pyrotechnicians. 'With any form of explosive, it is absolutely imperative that the area of the explosion is always in full view of the person who will be detonating the charge. If a scene involves a number of explosions, there may be a team of people in different positions to keep an eye on each charge,' explains Richardson. 'It is also important that performers know exactly where an explosion will occur, so that they can avoid them. With water, this can be difficult because the explosive is hidden below the surface. We normally arrange small cork floats that bob on the surface immediately above the explosive, and anyone driving a boat keeps a lookout for them. However, when driving a speedboat at 50 mph, spotting and avoiding a tiny float can be quite tricky. The technician overseeing each charge has to decide if a boat is at a safe distance before detonating an explosion – a few feet can make the difference between a safe stunt and blowing the boat up.'

An important consideration when detonating explosives in water is the power of the resulting shock waves. 'Shock waves travel through water with a far greater force than through air,' explains Richardson. 'If a person is in the water near an explosion, they can suffer physical harm. The shock wave could result in internal injuries to organs like the kidneys, and if somebody's head is under the water, the shock wave could rupture their eardrums. I have been standing in water when dynamite has been detonated some considerable distance away, and the shock wave felt like a very strong slap against my legs.' Shock waves are not only harmful for humans. 'Underwater explosions can kill all the aquatic life in the immediate area,' says Richardson. 'We therefore tend to detonate a few small explosions before the bigger explosion to frighten the fish away.'

During the filming of the high-speed boat chase for the opening sequence of *The World Is Not Enough* (1999), special effects supervisor Chris Corbould used ultrasonic equipment to scare the fish of the River Thames away from the enormous explosions that he had devised. 'The equipment was the type used by power stations to discourage fish from swimming up their water outlet pipes,' he explains.

This sequence was a particularly complicated operation. 'We were filming on the River Thames near famous landmarks like the Houses of Parliament as well as the actual headquarters of the British secret service, MI5, and many waterfront residential properties. Some of our explosions involved sending up to five tons of water into the air, so we had to be extremely careful that we did not cause any alarm or damage. In the event, our explosions merely set off a few car alarms.' As well as ensuring that the film's pyrotechnics did not interfere with the city and citizens of London, Corbould had to consider the effect that filming in a major city could have on his own plans. 'Explosions are almost always detonated electrically,' explains Corbould, 'and because of this, mobile telephones and radios are strictly banned on the set – it is possible that such equipment could induce an electric current in a wire and cause an accidental explosion. However, in a city like London, there is no way to control the signals that are flying around. So, instead of using electrical detonators, we wired our

high explosives with a system that detonated them by shock. The cable we used was lined with explosive, and when we detonated that cable from the land, it sent an instantaneous shock to the high explosives tethered in the water.'

High explosives are sometimes just too dangerous to be used when filming water sequences. This is particularly true if actors need to be anywhere near an explosion, or if the explosion is taking place within the confines of a shallow studio tank. 'Within a tank, we would normally use an air mortar to create a water explosion,' says John Richardson. 'This involves using an underwater reservoir of compressed air and an underwater valve. When the valve is opened, the compressed air blasts up through the water with such force that it pushes water up into the air. This method tends to atomize water into very fine spray, so it is good for creating explosions around models. We used air mortars to create all of the explosions around the stealth boat in *Tomorrow Never Dies* [1997].'

Perhaps the most popular form of transport to be given the explosive treatment is the ordinary motor car. Whether the car is to be the victim of a terrorist bomb or the casualty of an action-packed chase, directors simply cannot resist blowing them up. As with most movie pyrotechnics, the destruction of a car is usually achieved through a combination of techniques, each designed to add to the visual appeal of the shot. Cars to be destroyed are first weakened so that the minimum amount of explosive can be employed to blow them apart. The fuel tank, fuel lines and often the engine itself are removed. Doors and panels that are to fly off are disassembled before being put back into place and held with temporary fixtures. The doors on the opposite sides of a vehicle will be removed from their hinges, placed back into position and held by a cable that stretches across the interior of the car to hold the doors together. Similarly, the hood over an engine compartment might be removed and put back in place with only a length of cable connecting it to the vehicle. During the explosion, this cable acts as a tether that determines how far the hood is flung by the blast.

FIGURE 8 **THE CANNON CAR**

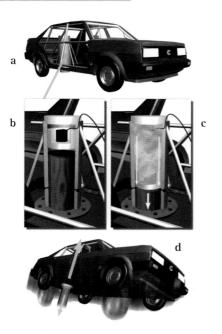

a: **vehicle with cannon welded into chassis**
b: **black-powder bomb and telephone pole**
c: **exploding bomb fires pole**
d: **vehicle is fired into air**

LEFT: Dramatic explosions must often be achieved in close proximity to performers. Here, Pierce Brosnan and Izabella Scorupco dive for cover as a large fireball ignites safely just a few yards behind them in *GoldenEye* (1995).

RIGHT: To tip this large truck onto its side for a scene in *Raiders of the Lost Ark* (1981), a pyrotechnic cannon was fitted to the underside of the vehicle in order to fire a wooden pole at the ground below.

BELOW: John Richardson gave added drama to this fireball explosion in *Blue Thunder* (1983) by adding directional spark charges to create plumes of sparks.

The explosion itself will commonly be created by as many as a dozen separate charges, set off within a fraction of a second of each other. To emulate the way in which a real car might explode, black-powder charges might be detonated sequentially, starting in the fuel tank and working along the inside of the car to the engine. Additional charges may be placed within the car to blow the doors and windows out. The trunk and hood may be blown out by placing a mortar underneath both of them. A tiny amount of black powder will be placed in the mortar tube and a plunger – simply a wooden disc – placed over it. On detonation, the wooden plunger rockets out of the mortar and blasts out any part of the vehicle in its path. An additional black powder and gasoline fireball detonated at the same time will look as if it is actually doing the work of ripping these parts away from the body of the car.

To turn them over during a chase or an explosion, vehicles are fitted with an explosive cannon that, when detonated, forces them into the air (fig. 8). The vehicle to be flipped is fitted with a roll cage to protect the stunt driver, and a huge mortar approximately 1 m (3 ft) in length is welded into the frame of the car, its open end protruding from one side of the undercarriage of the vehicle (a). The mortar is charged with a black-powder bomb that contains just a few grams or ounces of explosive. A section of telephone pole is pushed into the cannon from below the car and held in position by several nails that slot through the wall of the mortar and into the wood (b). The vehicle is driven by a stunt driver who uses a button fitted to the steering wheel to detonate the cannon at the right moment. When the bomb detonates (c), the pressure from the exploding black powder shoots the wooden pole out at great velocity, firing the vehicle into the air (d). With careful planning just 170 g (6 oz) of black powder can force a car off the ground and into a 360° flip before it lands back on its wheels. Instead of using black-powder bombs, many effects supervisors now prefer to employ non-pyrotechnic cannon, which use compressed air or nitrogen to force a projectile from the bottom of the vehicle. Cannon are not used solely to turn cars over. A cannon placed horizontally in the rear of a vehicle can be used to fire it through the air and is useful when cars need to jump long distances or smash into objects at great speed.

The key to creating safe pyrotechnic effects is thorough planning and testing. 'Even though we may have done a particular type of explosion dozens of times in the past, we still spend a lot of time testing equipment and materials before we start work on each new show', stresses Chris Corbould. 'The watchword is consistency – we need to know exactly how every explosion we are going to create during filming will work. During the test stage, we take detailed notes on what types and quantities of explosive we are using; we video each explosion with distance markers so that we know what its reach will be; and we measure the temperature of the flames at various distances. These tests enable us to say with certainty what the safety parameters of each explosion are, and how close performers and crew can get. There is no room for improvisation with explosives; we must always know exactly what we are dealing with.'

Before each shot is attempted, effects supervisors write a risk assessment document that is circulated to every member of the cast and crew. 'We write down what materials will be used, what the crew can expect to see and hear, we make suggestions about safety precautions and list anything that the emergency services may need to know.' Due to the dangerous nature of pyrotechnics, supervisors always have the final say on the nature of an effect. 'We get asked to do all sorts of potentially dangerous things, and most can be achieved safely when carefully planned', says Corbould. 'We will never do anything that we consider to be a genuine risk. If we are asked to do something and we say no, then that is final. If directors or producers insist, we can walk off the set and have nothing more to do with it. No film is worth risking personal safety.'

FIRE

Although setting fire to objects sounds simple, fires for films need to be totally safe, predictable and controllable. What's more, although objects may need to appear to burn fiercely, they must often remain unharmed so that they can continue to be used over the many days that it may take to film a scene.

Special effects technicians are often asked to set fire to buildings without causing them any harm. To make a building look as if it is burning without actually setting light to anything, self-contained boxes are constructed behind each window on the inside of the building. These cubicles are then filled with smoke which billows from the windows. The smoke is brightly backlit with flares or powerful lights. to create the impression that a fierce fire is raging behind the windows, although the interior remains untouched.

To produce real flames either indoors or out, a number of carefully controlled techniques are employed. For both small and big flames, flame bars – metal tubes with holes or slits at regular intervals – are used. Propane gas, or, if outdoors, diesel, is pumped into the bars and squirted through the holes, whereupon it is ignited by a pilot light.

Flame bars come in various shapes and sizes to produce different qualities of flame. They are positioned at a safe distance behind objects that need to appear to be on fire, and immediately in front of the camera to create foreground fire. As well as using flame bars, pyrotechnicians may smear a highly inflammable gel onto objects that need to be seen burning. This burns for a limited period, so only enough to last the duration of the shot will be applied to fireproofed objects before each take. Film sets that are to be set on fire during the making of a film are largely built with fireproof materials, and only the parts that need to burn are covered with gel and set alight.

Spectacular fire effects were created by the special effects supervisor Neil Corbould for the opening battle sequences of *Gladiator* (2000). 'We had to unleash all kinds of fire effects in a large area of woodland near London to re-create a battle between Romans and German tribesmen. This presented a number of challenges, not least how to avoid burning down a whole forest full of actors and film crew', explains Corbould, who won an Oscar for his work on the film.

Corbould's team spent six weeks building various fire precautions in the forest before filming could begin. 'The forest itself was scheduled to be cut down by the local forestry commission so we could do anything we needed to achieve our effects. First we widened a surrounding road to a width of 80 feet [24 m] to create a fire break. Then we dug three 40,000-gallon reservoirs for the 30-man fire crew to draw water from.'

With safety precautions installed, Corbould's team rigged the forest to produce the fire effects required by director Ridley Scott. 'We buried thousands of feet of 2 in [5 cm] diameter steel pipe throughout the forest. Some of this was under the ground to create lines of fire for the performers to run past and some was buried in trees so that they would appear to burst into flames and burn when hit by flame bombs fired by catapults. The pipes were connected to three 20,000-gallon liquid propane tankers that were positioned 250 m [812 ft] away. Before we started the fires the fire crews would hose down surrounding trees and forest floor with water so that they wouldn't catch light in the intense heat. Then we would light pilot lights and, on the call of "action", open valves that pumped propane into the forest to create an instant inferno. The fires would burn for up to five minutes, then we'd turn off the valves, the fire would die right down, and the fire crews would go in and extinguish any remaining flames.'

Neil Corbould's *Gladiator* fire effects allowed raging fires to be turned on and off in a controlled and repeatable manner over a period of several days. However, one of the most famous fires in the history of the movies was a one-off affair that could not be repeated. The burning of Atlanta for *Gone with the Wind* (1939) was filmed on 10 December 1938 at the RKO-Pathé studio in Culver City, California. The fuel for the fire was the Skull Island set from *King Kong* (1933), which itself had been adapted from exterior sets originally built for Cecil B. DeMille's *King of Kings* (1927). This set was dressed to resemble 19th-century Atlanta and plumbed with a network of pipes through which a thousand gallons of fuel per minute were pumped to produce an enormous conflagration that many citizens of Hollywood turned up to watch. The 60 m (200 ft) flames burned with such ferocity that the site was demolished in just six minutes. The resulting footage was used both in *Gone with the Wind* and later for the burning of the mansion in Hitchcock's *Rebecca* (1940).

ABOVE LEFT: **A variety of different flame bars can be used to burn propane gas and other fuels to create controllable fires.**

LEFT: **Cliff Richardson created this dramatic scene for *Battle of Britain* (1969) without actually damaging any of the buildings that appear to be on fire.**

RIGHT: **Neil Corbould used thousands of gallons of liquid propane to create the spectacular forest-fire effects for the opening battle scenes of *Gladiator* (2000).**

PROFILE **CLIFF RICHARDSON**

The pioneering British effects supervisor Cliff Richardson (1905–85) began work in London's film industry as a prop boy in 1921. Richardson's fascination with the technical aspects of film-making, especially his interest in guns and gunpowder, quickly gained him a reputation as the person to tackle any unusual request.

Richardson worked his way through the ranks at a number of Britain's leading film studios, including British International Pictures, where the young Alfred Hitchcock made his early films; Ealing Studios, home of the famous Ealing comedies; and Denham Studios, where classics such as *The Thief of Bagdad* (1940) were produced. His first job as supervisor was on *The Big Blockade* (1940).

As someone who earned the title of supervisor at a time when many war movies were being made, Richardson became best known for planning scenes of mass destruction in films such as *Ships with Wings* (1942) and *San Demetrio London* (1943). However it was later, bigger-budget movies that allowed him greater destructive freedom; he created the impressive steam train derailment in *Lawrence of Arabia* (1962) and the explosion of a real aircraft hangar for *Battle of Britain*

(1969), as well as the many pyrotechnic stunts for *The Dirty Dozen* (1967). However, Richardson equally excelled at the smaller challenges. For the swamp scene in *The African Queen* (1951) real leeches refused to perform as required, so Richardson made rubber leeches with internal blood sacs that bled when Humphrey Bogart pulled them from his skin. For the same film Richardson created a swarm of mosquitoes by filming through a fish tank filled with floating tea leaves.

Richardson invented many devices that became widely used in the film industry. These included an oil-vapour smoke machine, a gas-powered machine gun, a nozzle for spraying foam snow, and the 'Dante' – a contraption used to create enormous blankets of fire. Richardson used the Dante in what he considered one of his most successful scenes, the burning of a huge warehouse for *Battle of Britain*.

Before his retirement Cliff Richardson often worked in partnership with his son John Richardson (1940–), who has himself become a world-class special effects supervisor, working on many James Bond films and all of the Harry Potter movies. Father and son are shown here using an early snow machine.

SPECIAL PROJECTS

Whenever a script calls for anything beyond the ordinary, the physical effects supervisor gets the job of providing the action. For this reason, physical effects supervisors need a thorough understanding of an incredibly wide range of subjects. 'When you get a script, you go through it and identify all the scenes that might require some sort of effects input,' says George Gibbs, whose ingenious effects for *Indiana Jones and the Temple of Doom* (1984) and *Who Framed Roger Rabbit* (1988) have won him Academy Awards. 'Sometimes it's a simple case of making a note to use breakaway glass bottles in scenes where there may be the possibility of a breakage. Other times the effect is something massive that will require months of planning – those are the type of projects that I tend to specialize in. My job is to think about the requirements of a shot and apply my knowledge of subjects as diverse as electrical and mechanical engineering, pneumatics, hydraulics, explosives, carpentry, plumbing, metalwork and chemistry. Of course, no supervisor can be expert in all these things, but we should know enough to have a good idea of how an effect might be achieved. Then it's up to us to do the research, and find the people who are the real experts.'

One of Gibbs's biggest assignments was to build a 75 m (250 ft) rope bridge for *Indiana Jones and the Temple of Doom*. 'Of course, an Indiana Jones film is full of effects challenges,' notes Gibbs, 'but most films have one really big or difficult job that takes up a disproportionate amount of time and energy. On *Temple of Doom*, it was the rope bridge.'

To build the rope bridge, which was far longer than any that exists in real life, Gibbs enlisted the help of a British engineering company that was constructing a dam near the Sri Lankan location chosen for the sequence. 'To get the bridge in place, we first had to dynamite 60 cm [2 ft] of solid rock from a cliff top on one side of the gorge, to make it the height we needed. We then drilled 1.5 m [5 ft]

RIGHT: George Gibbs supervised the major engineering project that was necessary to build and then destroy the huge rope bridge in *Indiana Jones and the Temple of Doom* (1984).

BELOW: Supervisor John Richardson performs a stunt worthy of James Bond himself as he attempts to dislodge a boat stranded on rocks during the filming of *Moonraker* (1979).

down into the rock so that we could secure the steel I-beams that the bridge would be suspended from. The bridge itself was made from flexible 2.5 cm [1 in] crane cable – this had been calculated to be the correct specification by several world-class engineering companies. We strung four cables across the gorge – two for the handles and two for the bottom part of the bridge. The bottom two cables had wooden slats fixed between them to make the walkway. We then had to wrap real rope around the steel cables to make them look like rope, and connect rope banisters between the top and bottom cables.'

After ensuring that he had built the safest, strongest bridge possible, Gibbs had to find a way to destroy it. 'In the film, Indiana Jones cuts through the bridge with a knife. In reality, the steel cable had a combined breaking strain of hundreds of tons,' says Gibbs. 'The only way to break it was to use explosives. After lots of experiments and research, we had some explosive cutting devices made for us by a French company that produces the explosive bolts used for escape hatches in spacecraft. They were about the size of a polystyrene teacup and had a groove into which the bridge cable slotted. When detonated, the cutters blasted a kind of chisel right through the cable.'

In the film, the bridge breaks and falls with a full complement of passengers. 'We built dummies that had a compressed air mechanism inside them to make their arms and legs flail around during the fall. These dummies were very basic and were made at the last minute, but they really made the million dollars spent on the sequence worthwhile.'

Sometimes special effects supervisors come across problems to which no one knows the answer, and which only experimentation can solve. 'For *A Fish Called Wanda* [1988], I was asked to crush an actor into wet cement with a steamroller,' remarks Gibbs. 'The set-up was relatively simple. We dug a 1 m [3 ft] wide, 75 cm [30 in] deep trench in the runway at London's Heathrow Airport. This allowed a wide steamroller to drive over a stunt performer in the trench. To establish the fact that it was a genuinely heavy machine that was going to go over our stuntman, the steamroller first drove over some wheelbarrows that we made from zinc – a very soft metal that we often use because it crushes easily. Obviously, we couldn't fill the trench with real cement because the stunt performer had to be submersed in the stuff. Also, the scene would take several days to film and we didn't want the cement to set. We discovered that porridge mixed with a little black paint looks just like cement and was quite safe to use, so we made hundreds of gallons of porridge in cement mixers.

'However, the problem was that the porridge went mouldy very quickly. We tried all sorts of preservatives without success, but eventually we discovered that the best thing to keep the porridge fresh was to mix it with Camp coffee [a brand of liquid coffee concentrate]. No one in the world could have told us that we needed to use coffee, it's just one example of the strange problems that we can often only solve through experimentation and imagination.'

Physical effects are often potentially dangerous to anyone involved. 'Effects can often present an actual risk to those working and performing around them. Of course, everything we do is designed with safety as the number-one priority, but some stunts are just inherently risky.' Gibbs considers one of his most potentially dangerous assignments to be the giant ship propeller that he built for *Indiana Jones and the Last Crusade* (1989). In the film, Indiana Jones fights an opponent while his speedboat is dragged into a rapidly rotating ship propeller. 'We built a giant propeller with a huge hydraulic engine to turn it at great speed,' remembers Gibbs. 'Harrison Ford had to perform on the speedboat as it was being physically chopped up by the propeller. When you've got a star like Harrison Ford actually doing his own stunts and a 3.5 ton propeller revolving just 3 m [10 ft] away, your calculations have to be spot on. If we had miscalculated how quickly we could stop the propeller or the way the boat broke up, then Harrison could have been minced. The danger was very real.'

Physical effects can also present danger to those who design and operate them. In his years as an effects supervisor on the James Bond films, John Richardson has gained a reputation as someone who becomes more than usually involved with his effects. 'Our work with physical effects often crosses boundaries with the work of the stunt team,' claims Richardson. 'Much of our work is designed and planned in tandem with the stunt guys because they are often the ones who will end up performing with the effects on screen. However, sometimes our own work can be physically strenuous. As well as the risks involved when working with dangerous chemicals and high explosives on a day-to-day basis, there are all kinds of perilous situations involved with rigging effects at great heights, underwater or even hanging out of aeroplanes.'

One of Richardson's most dangerous tasks came during the filming of *Moonraker* (1979). 'We wanted a shot of a speedboat going over the 90 m [300 ft] Iguazu waterfalls in Brazil,' recalls Richardson, 'so we put the boat in the river about half a mile upstream from the falls. However, because the water was quite shallow, five of us had to get into the water and manhandle the boat around rocks until we got it in the right position. We then released it and it floated towards the edge of the falls. Then, right at the very edge of the drop, it got impaled on a rock and we couldn't move it. After much discussion, and in a moment of madness, I offered to hang from the underside of a helicopter and try to push it off, so we flew up to the boat with me clinging to the end of a rope. After dropping me in the water and then in the trees, the pilot eventually got me onto a rock and I tried pushing the boat but it wouldn't budge. So I decided to grab the boat and signal the helicopter to move away. The idea was that the helicopter would drag the boat free and I would be the human link. As I held on to the boat and the helicopter moved away, I could feel my arms getting longer, but by this time, I was determined to shift the boat. Then I heard this ping, ping, ping noise. It was the stitching of my harness breaking. I realized then that I should probably let go, and we flew back to land with me hanging on to the skid of the helicopter looking just like James Bond. Later that night it rained somewhere upstream and the extra water flushed the boat over the falls when we weren't there to film it.'

Animals, particularly horses, have always played an important part in the movies, often resulting in accusations of cruelty. The most controversial technique used for equine stunts was called the 'running W', a method that involved wiring a horse's front legs with a W-shaped arrangement of cables that ran up to the underside of the horse's belly and from there to a stake secured to the ground. When a running horse reached the end of the cable, its front legs would be pulled from underneath, causing it to turn head over heels. If done properly, the trick was said to cause the horse no pain, but there is no doubt that many horses have been injured by this and other stunts over the years.

'Today stunts like the running W are outlawed,' comments Nick Allder, whose physical effects have appeared in films such as *Alien* (1979), *Léon* (1994) and *Hellboy* (2004). 'We now try to find ways that allow animals to appear in films without any form of cruelty. For *Braveheart* [1995], Mel Gibson wanted to see horses doing somersaults and all kinds of stunts that we can no longer expect real animals to perform. To provide such shots we built a pneumatic sling that would fire an artificial horse and a stunt performer 6 m [20 ft] along a track in one and a half seconds before launching them into a jump or a fall. We used the device for shots where horses run into wooden stakes during a battle and for a shot where Mel Gibson appears to jump his horse from a castle into a lake. The results were

FAR LEFT: **John Fulton engineered the simple but effective illusion of an unseen person walking through the snow for** *The Invisible Man* **(1933).**

LEFT: **For** *Who Framed Roger Rabbit* **(1988), George Gibbs created hundreds of 'gags' in which objects reacted to characters that would be added during post-production. For this shot, a coat was made to bulge as if it contained a wriggling rabbit.**

so convincing that we decided to video the process because we thought we might receive complaints, and sure enough the animal rights people were on to us as soon as the movie was released.'

Physical effects supervisors are often asked to suggest the presence of an invisible character or force on screen. For *The Invisible Man* (1933), John Fulton (<69) used clever mechanical gags and wire work to make doors open, chairs move and items float around as if the unseen hero of the film was actually interacting with them.

In one scene, the presence of the invisible man is indicated by the appearance of his footprints in fresh snow. To achieve the effect, Fulton created a wooden floor with foot-shaped holes in it. These holes were stopped up from below and artificial snow laid over the top. During filming, the foot-shaped holes were opened sequentially, causing the layer of snow to collapse downwards as if being compressed by invisible feet.

The use of wires and other hidden mechanical methods to move objects during filming was resurrected by George Gibbs during the making of *Who Framed Roger Rabbit* (1988; <176). Although the stars of the film were largely animated cartoons, many of the props and environments with which they interacted were real. 'We devised dozens of mechanical methods of creating the impression that the animated characters were actually present during filming,' explains Gibbs. One of the most complicated sequences in the film involved a bar-tending octopus whose eight arms each performed a different task. 'The octopus, which was animated and added into the scene later, used its cartoon tentacles to move real items – it took a glass from a shelf, made a martini, poured a beer, wiped down the counter, lit a cigarette and took money from a customer. Each of the real items was carefully puppeteered using rods or wires concealed below or above the stage. We also built robotic arms controlled by tiny motors that could move objects like real cigars up to the mouths of cartoon characters. Such rigs were eventually hidden behind the cartoon characters, which were later added over the top. Other props included a computer-programmed piano whose keys worked

automatically so that Donald Duck and Daffy Duck looked as if they were playing a real piano.'

While Gibbs created the physical effects for the scenes shot in England, those filmed in the United States were supervised by Michael Lantieri (335>). 'Although we didn't know it at the time, *Roger Rabbit* was actually a practice run,' states Lantieri, whose responsibilities included staging the film's opening sequence in which cartoon character movie stars are seen working in a real film studio. 'What we didn't realize back then was that making objects and environments respond to characters not present during filming would one day turn out to be a very significant aspect of physical effects work. In 1988 the age of digital visual effects was still a distant dream, but when it did eventually arrive, this was just the kind of work that we would need to produce time and time again.'

After *Roger Rabbit*, Lantieri worked on several films that were among the first to explore the computer's potential to manipulate images of props and environments. 'When we made *Back to the Future Part II* [1989], we had characters flying around on hoverboards, which were like skateboards that hovered instead of using wheels,' recalls Lantieri. 'To get the boards and the people to fly, we hung them in a very traditional way using thin piano wires that were almost invisible on screen. We went to great lengths to build sets that had a lot of vertical lines in them so that the vertical wires would blend into the background and be less noticeable. On the few occasions that the wires were very visible, ILM used old-fashioned rotoscoping techniques to hand-trace the wires and remove them optically [<67].

'However, just two years later when we did *Hook* [1991], digital technology had advanced to the point where cables could easily be removed from a shot using a computer. For the flying scenes in that film, we hung Robin Williams from cables that were ten times stronger and very much thicker than those used in *Back to the Future*. Today, wires are so easy to remove from a shot that we actually paint them to make sure the computer guys can see them clearly!'

BELOW LEFT: George Gibbs built this fully operational 28 ton reconstruction of a World War I tank for *Indiana Jones and the Last Crusade* (1989). A huge transport aircraft was required to deliver the massive vehicle from England to the location in Spain.

RIGHT: Many physical effects are easier and safer to execute now that computer technology can be used to erase the evidence from a shot. For this sequence in *Back to the Future 2* (1989), the wires that suspended the performers were digitally removed.

PROFILE **MICHAEL LANTIERI**

Michael Lantieri was born and raised in Burbank, the heart of Hollywood film production, so it was hardly surprising that he wanted to become involved in film production from an early age.

After leaving school Lantieri started work at ABC television for a year before finding employment in the special effects department of Universal Studios, where he created effects for television series such as *The Six Million Dollar Man* (1973–8). Lantieri spent eight years at Universal, learning all the basic special effects crafts until he was offered the opportunity to supervise the effects for *Flashdance* (1983). After several similarly modest effects films, Lantieri began to create major-league physical effects for films such as *Poltergeist II* (1986) and *Star Trek IV: The Voyage Home* (1986).

After supervising the ingenious mechanical effects for the American shoot of *Who Framed Roger Rabbit* (1988), Lantieri provided increasingly sophisticated effects for a string of films directed or produced by Steven Spielberg, including the two *Back to the Future* sequels (1989 and 1990), *Hook* (1991) and *Jurassic Park* (1993), for which he received an Academy Award.

Lantieri has gained a reputation for creating large-scale physical effects that seamlessly integrate with computer-generated animation to give the perfect illusion of fantastic characters interacting realistically with live-action environments. In films such as *The Flintstones* (1994), *Congo* (1995), *Casper* (1995), *The Indian in the Cupboard* (1995), *Jurassic Park: The Lost World* (1997), *Wild Wild West* (1999), *Hulk* (2003) and *Lemony Snicket's A Series of Unfortunate Events* (2004), Lantieri has continually pushed the limits of physically achievable effects, leaving only the most impossible feats to the computer. Lantieri made his debut as a director with the feature film *Komodo* (1999).

PROFILE **THE CORBOULDS**

In the past two decades one family has come to dominate the field of spectacular physical effects production. Though based in and around London, the Corbould brothers, Chris, Neil, Paul and Ian, now work all over the world on some of Hollywood's biggest movies.

The brothers' interest in special effects was sparked by their uncle, leading British effects supervisor Colin Chilvers. Chilvers has overseen effects for films from *Superman* (1978) to *K-19: The Widowmaker* (2002) and gave some of his young relatives their first start in the industry with summer jobs while still at school.

The most prominent names in the family are the two brothers Chris (*above*) and Neil (*below*), each of whom runs his own successful business based at Pinewood Studios.

Chris (1958–) is the oldest brother and has become best known for his work on the James Bond films. Starting as a technician on *The Spy Who Loved Me* (1977) and working his way up to supervisor on *GoldenEye* (1995), Chris has a particular talent for complex engineering challenges and sequences that involve specialized vehicles. He oversaw the tank chase for *GoldenEye*, the helicopter attack in *The World Is Not Enough* (1999) and the ice chase in *Die Another Day* (2002). Other projects have included the *Tomb Raider* movies (2002, 2003) and *Batman Begins* (2005), often working in association with leading stunt co-coordinator Simon Crane.

Neil Corbould (1962–) has supervised many equally spectacular sequences, frequently creating large-scale battle scenes and their bloody consequences. He oversaw the battles for *King Arthur* (2004) and *Kingdom of Heaven* (2005), and the harrowing opening scenes of *Saving Private Ryan* (1998), for which he fitted amputees with false limbs that were blown off on screen. He won an Oscar for his work on *Gladiator* (2000). His other work includes *The Day After Tomorrow* (2004) and *Superman Returns* (2006). Neil also works with his sister Gail, a project manager, as well as his parents Cliff and Jean.

Ian and Paul work as freelance technicians and supervisors, often in conjunction with their brothers. Ian specializes in prosthetic work, having worked on *Saving Private Ryan*, *Gladiator* and *Kingdom of Heaven*. Paul specializes in atmospherics and pyrotechnics in films including *Entrapment* (1999) and *King Arthur*.

Just two years after *Hook*, Lantieri provided the physical effects for *Jurassic Park* (1993), perhaps the most influential digital effects film ever made. 'Jurassic Park was really the first film in which major physical effects had to be designed to complement digital characters that would be added much later in the production process,' says Lantieri. 'In a way, it was very similar to what we had done for *Roger Rabbit* – we had to create the impression that invisible characters were interacting with a real environment. Probably the most complex sequence in which we had to fake the presence of a dinosaur was the scene in which the T rex chases a jeep. The dinosaur had to emerge from some trees, smash through a fallen log and ram a moving vehicle. To accomplish this scene, we rigged full-sized trees so that they would fall out of the way as if an invisible dinosaur were pushing through them. A full-sized tree trunk that lay across the road was rigged to blow apart and be knocked to one side as if a dinosaur had smashed through it. The jeep was rigged so that its windshield was smashed off by the flying log, and then jumped into the air as hydraulic rams imploded the side of the vehicle as if it had been hit and damaged by the dinosaur.'

Planning such effects is a time-consuming and highly detailed process for Lantieri. 'We really have to know a lot about the digital character that we are supposed to be representing on the set,' he explains. 'I sit with the people who are going to create the computer-generated creature for days on end, discussing its characteristics. We need to know how fast a character can move when running at full speed, how far apart its tail and head might be at full stretch, how heavy it should appear to be – all the details of a character's physique that will allow us to create live effects that digital animators can match their characters to.'

LEFT: **Michael Lantieri orchestrated the mayhem caused by an invisible T rex for this shot in *Jurassic Park: The Lost World* (1997). The dinosaur was animated and added during post-production.**

Lantieri himself makes considerable use of computers during the creation of his physical effects. 'We use CAD [computer-aided design] programs to design our effects rigs and all kinds of specialized software to work out the complex engineering problems that we encounter. We also design whole sequences by creating computer-generated pre-viz animations [<230]. These allow us to determine exactly how and when all of our effects will work and to try out various alternatives. We also use computers to control our equipment during filming. We can program events to happen so that an effect occurs when a camera or actor is in exactly the right position.'

Although many of the physical effects that Lantieri creates live can now be produced in the computer, he believes that physical effects will continue to be used for a long time to come. 'Physical effects are generally much cheaper than digital effects. However, the cost of digital effects is coming down all the time, so eventually that will be less of a consideration,' reasons Lantieri. 'I think physical effects will still continue to be used for several reasons. Firstly, they enable actors to feel as if they are interacting with a character; pretending that you are appearing with some imaginary creature is actually very hard. This is especially true when extras – who are not necessarily skilled actors – are asked to react to something that isn't actually there. When we tossed real cars through the air and sent them smashing into each other for *Hulk* [2003], the extras didn't need to pretend that they were seeing something spectacular. Secondly, most directors like to get as much accomplished during the shoot as possible. This means that they can have maximum control over what happens on the set, and they end up with an image that they can use when editing rather than having to wait a long time while computer effects are added. This is why we go to incredible lengths to create even the most difficult shots live, and we leave only the impossible things for the computer guys to achieve. Finally, unless it's a completely computer-generated film, there always has to be a point at which live effects meet computer-generated effects – wherever that line is drawn is where our physical effects will occur. The more CGI characters that appear in the movies, the more there will be for us to do.'

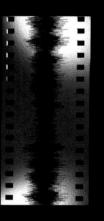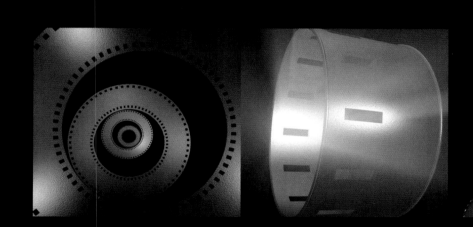

SOUND

INTRODUCTION

For three decades after their invention, moving pictures contained no pre-recorded sound. However, the movies were rarely silent. Early films were often accompanied by live commentary – an orator would explain the story, speak characters' lines and create crude synchronized sound effects using a range of props. Sometimes a special sound effects machine was used, producing a range of noises such as car horns and horses' hoofs at the touch of a button. An audience's emotional response to a film was frequently guided by live music – in provincial theatres solo musicians would improvise musical accompaniment on the piano, violin or clarinet, while in grand metropolitan venues full orchestras played specially composed scores.

Many critics now consider that the silence of the silver screen resulted in many masterpieces; early cinema was visual storytelling in its purest form. But for many film-makers of the time, the goal was always to create films with pre-recorded synchronous sound. By the mid-20s a number of systems that effectively linked sound and image were being perfected. The first sound feature film to be released was Warner Brothers' *Don Juan* (1926). While it had no recorded dialogue, the film was accompanied by a soundtrack of synchronous music and sound effects played on a phonographic record. *Don Juan* was not the success that the studio had hoped for, but its next sound production, *The Jazz Singer* (1927) – which included synchronous singing and dialogue – became an overnight sensation. By 1930 all the major studios had converted to sound production, replacing Warners' clumsy sound-on-disc system with a more effective sound-on-film system, storing soundtrack alongside images on the film itself.

Film sound is now almost as important a part of the film-going experience as the images themselves. While crackly, dull sound once marred many screenings, modern theatres have invested in state-of-the-art digital sound reproduction systems that can project a sound to any part of the screen or auditorium, creating a convincing three-dimensional soundscape that places the audience 'within' the action. This chapter deals with the intricacies of creating a modern film soundtrack.

SOUND RECORDING

The first practical step in the creation of a modern movie soundtrack is the recording of all the dialogue spoken by performers during filming. This is the job of the sound recording mixer, who is responsible for placing microphones as near to the actors as possible. This may mean using a boom (a long pole to which a microphone is attached) or, in the case of action scenes or long shots, fitting performers with radio microphones that are hidden discreetly about the body and which transmit sound in the form of radio waves.

Dialogue is the most important sound in any scene, and the mixer will attempt to record it with as little other extraneous noise as possible. After recording, the mixer may also collect various noises that are specific to the location. These additional sounds, which may be used when creating the final soundtrack, include a location's 'ambience' – the almost imperceptible quality of sound that is unique to every place as a result of its geography, vegetation, construction materials, weather conditions and so on. Ambience is normally recorded as near to the time of filming as possible, since it may change subtly throughout the day.

For many years, a large machine called a Nagra was used during filming to record analogue sound on reel-to-reel quarter-inch tape. Nagras have now been replaced by digital recording systems such as DAT (digital audio tape) and, increasingly, portable hard disk recorders. Modern recording devices are capable of simultaneously recording the sound from a number of different microphones on separate audio tracks. This means that dialogue spoken by each performer can be treated separately during the editing process.

Sound mixers often complain that they are treated as the least important part of the filming process. This is perhaps because dialogue is one of the most easily replaced elements of any scene and is therefore often re-created during post-production in a process called ADR (automated dialogue replacement, 348>). Because the cost of filming is so great, most producers would rather have inferior original sound, or even no sound at all, than delay the filming process just to make the sound people happy.

After filming, the sound recorded on location is synchronized with the images so that the two can be edited simultaneously. Synchronization is made possible by using the clapperboard, or 'slate', that appears at the beginning or end of each take as a point of reference. The frame of film in which the iconic black-and-white-striped board snaps shut is aligned with the clearly audible bang at the beginning of the soundtrack. Today, electronic clapperboards are commonly used. These are linked to both camera and sound equipment and generate an electronic time code that allows the easy and accurate synchronization of image and sound, especially when both are digitized for use with the digital non-linear editing systems now employed to edit most films (342>).

SOUND EFFECTS

While spoken dialogue is recorded on location, almost every other sound in a film's soundtrack will be recorded separately. Noises such as footsteps, wind, birdsong, rustling clothes, slamming doors and car engines are all recorded individually and mixed together at a later stage. Ultimately, all film soundtracks comprise two distinct parts: a track that contains nothing but dialogue, and 'M & E' tracks that contain nothing but music and effects. Keeping these elements separate means that when versions of a film are produced for foreign release, the original dialogue can be replaced by speech in the appropriate language while the sound effects and music remain unaltered.

Sound effects are prepared in three distinct ways. Ordinary sounds that exist in the everyday world can be recorded especially for the production or can be found in existing sound recording libraries. Traditionally, each of the Hollywood studios maintained a large sound library containing every imaginable sound effect on tape. The most commonly found effects were reused in countless films – and can easily be recognized in movies made, sometimes decades apart, by the same studio. Among the most famous is the recording of a thunderclap originally made for Universal's *Frankenstein* (1931). This recording, known as 'Castle Thunder', is the stylized Hollywood thunderclap that we all recognize from the movies but have never heard in real life. The effect has been used in countless films throughout the decades including *Citizen Kane* (1941), *Bambi* (1942), *Cleopatra* (1963), and *Back to the Future* (1985), among many others. Another frequently used sound effect is a scream originally recorded for *Distant Drums* (1951). The recording has become known

PRECEDING PAGES: Foley artist Gary Hecker smashes a watermelon with a baseball bat to create the sound of exploding bugs for *Starship Troopers* (1997).

ABOVE: Cinemagoers line up outside the Warners' Theatre in Hollywood, eager to see *The Jazz Singer* (1927) and experience their first 'talkie'.

LEFT: When manually operated during screenings, devices such as the Allfex Machine (c. 1910) supplied a range of exciting sound effects to accompany otherwise silent films.

as the 'Wilhelm scream' after it was used to dramatize the shooting of a character called Private Wilhelm in *The Charge at Feather River* (1953). The rasping shriek, believed by Ben Burtt (350>) to be the voice of the musician and character actor Sheb Wooley, has been used hundreds of times. Burtt himself has used it as a signature sound effect in his work for all of the *Star Wars* and *Indiana Jones* films. It can also be heard prominently in *Poltergeist* (1982), *Toy Story* (1995), *Planet of the Apes* (2001), *Pirates of the Caribbean* (2003), *The Lord of the Rings: The Two Towers* (2002), *Madagascar* (2005), and dozens more.

Today the average recording studio has an extensive library of sound effects that is stored on thousands of compact discs and in digitized libraries on a computer system. Unusual sounds that are needed in order to convey a particular mood or situation, or sounds for films that contain locations, characters or machines that do not exist in real life, may be specially created by mixing and modifying one or more existing sounds to create entirely new ones. This process is called sound effects mixing (342>).

Simple, non-specialized sounds that relate directly to the movements of characters or objects on screen are created in a process called 'Foleying' (345>). Foley artists typically re-create the sounds of characters' footsteps, breathing, clothes rustling, doors opening and closing and so on, which are then added to the final edited film.

SOUND EFFECTS MIXING

The sound effects mixer is responsible for combining and manipulating recordings to create new sounds. Sound effects and dialogue were traditionally edited on magnetic tape. Edits were achieved by cutting the tape and splicing it back together with adhesive tape, in the same way that film was traditionally edited. Mixes were achieved by simultaneously running a number of tapes on separate machines and re-recording the resulting combination of sounds on a separate tape.

Today, sound editing and mixing is achieved digitally. All sounds are played into the memory of a computer, where they can be endlessly altered and mixed. A soundtrack can be built up by laying sounds into an almost limitless number of tracks (fig. 1), which can be individually accessed and altered at any point during the editing process. While sound effects editors once went to enormous lengths to create new sounds by mixing, layering, distorting, speeding up or slowing down their tape recordings, individual sounds can be digitally sampled and played on a keyboard, each key producing a variation of the original sound.

The basic sound effects for a suit of armour might be sampled and, as the image of a sword-fighting knight is viewed, the sound effects mixer can play the appropriate sound effects, move by move, like music on the keyboard. Any sounds that do not perform in the required way can be displayed on a monitor as a wave form – a visual representation of the characteristics of the sound wave. This wave can then be altered by directly manipulating its frequency range and amplitudes to affect the noise produced.

Curiously, when the sound of a specific object or event is required for a film, a recording of that actual sound usually proves neither convincing or dramatic. As a result the sounds of often very different objects or actions are recorded to create a better representation of the desired sound. One of the most commonly used sounds in any action film, the gunshot, is a good example of this. When real gunfire is recorded, the sound is normally rather disappointing, often sounding rather thin and high-pitched, and rarely as loud or as dangerous as most audiences would expect. The gunfire used for soundtracks is normally manufactured from as many as a dozen different noises, which might include a thunderclap, a dog barking, a door slamming and possibly even the sound of real guns. Each of these constituent sounds will be slowed down, speeded up, changed in pitch or given a little reverberation before being mixed together to produce a violent boom worthy of James Bond's Walther PPK or Dirty Harry's Magnum. Simpler examples include the rustling of loose audio tape to mimic the sound of walking through grass or crinkling a potato chip packet to create the sound of a crackling fire.

Often, many of the sounds that need to be created are for everyday objects or locations whose natural sounds the director feels are not dramatic or emotive enough. For *Body of Evidence* (1993), Sandy Genler, a sound effects mixer at Sony Pictures Studios, was asked to make a room sound 'sexy'. 'This is typical of the kind of strange request that we often get from directors,' explains Genler. 'How do you make a room – which in itself doesn't make a distinct noise – sound sexy? In this case, there was a fan rotating

RIGHT: **For a sequence such as this truck chase from *Raiders of the Lost Ark* (1981), every sound would be separately created, recorded and mixed after filming. In this case, truck noises, a horse galloping, punching sounds and numerous other effects would be layered together.**

FIGURE 1 **DIGITAL EDITING SOFTWARE**

Modern soundtracks are edited digitally. Once recorded sounds have been digitized, the editor can use software to manipulate and mix them in almost limitless ways.

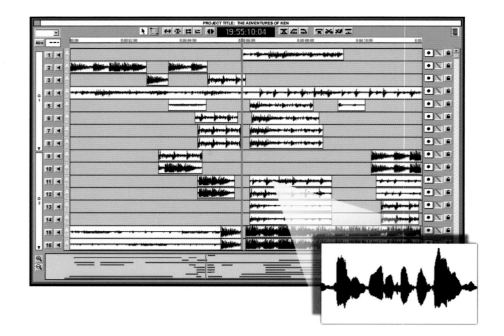

on the ceiling, so we mixed the sound of the fan with the husky breathing of a woman. The breathing was barely audible, but it worked on a subliminal level to give the room the sultry feeling that the director had requested.'

Using unusual sounds to exaggerate the noise made by everyday objects is known as 'sweetening', and is commonly employed to add a touch of melodrama to a scene. For the exhilarating desert truck chase in *Raiders of the Lost Ark* (1981), the roar of a lion was used each time the vehicle changed gear, making the sequence more sensational as a result.

With the rise in popularity of films that are set in extraordinary locations, or that feature fantastic events or characters, there has been an increased need for unusual sound effects. No longer simply technicians who are commissioned to create a few unusual noises towards the end of a film's production, sound effects mixers are increasingly being asked to create entire 'soundscapes' that are as much a part of a film's fabric as the set design, costumes and visual effects. The artists who work to create this all-encompassing sound illusion are known as 'sound designers'.

Ben Burtt (350>) was one of the first artists to use the term 'sound designer' to describe his work. 'Sound design is a term that has only been around for a couple of decades, and has never been fully accepted by some people in the industry,' notes Burtt. 'Traditionally, the sound on a film has been broken down into a number of distinct processes that were performed by different people who often never even communicated with one another – they simply did their job and passed their material on to the next person in the chain. However, I, along with an increasing number of other people, believe that sound is as important in the telling of a story as the images. Sound design is not simply about creating a few clever sound effects; it's about how music, dialogue, sound effects and images interact with one another, often very subtly, in the telling of a story.'

Burtt was first given the chance to put his theories to the test when he was hired to create the sound effects for *Star Wars* (1977). 'Like the visual effects for *Star Wars*, George Lucas wanted the sound effects for his film to be unlike anything that audiences had experienced before. He didn't want to use sounds that had been pulled from some sound effects library. He wanted an exciting and dynamic range of new sounds, and this gave me the opportunity to create unique effects for spaceships, creatures, weapons and alien environments.'

Burtt approaches the creation of sound effects in two ways. 'When I read a script, the type of sound needed for an effect might instantly come to mind. Sometimes I have a very clear idea of how that sound can be created, but other times I have to experiment with all kinds of things before I can get the sound I'm thinking of. My other method is to put together tapes of assorted sounds that are interesting to me – I've been collecting sounds for over 25 years, so I have thousands and thousands of them. Then, when I'm looking for a new sound but I'm not sure what is needed, I listen to my tapes until I hear something that hits a chord, I may then develop that sound further through mixing and editing. Suitable sounds can come from the most unexpected places. I once went to a missile testing range to record the sound of rockets to use for spaceships, but it was the throbbing noise of the malfunctioning air-conditioning unit in my motel room that ended up being the basis for many of the spaceship sounds in the *Star Wars* movies!'

Burtt's experience with *Star Wars* and its sequels offered unparalleled opportunities. '*Star Wars* was so unique – everything in that film could have sounded almost any way we wanted it to. There was no right or wrong, but I did have some basic rules to help create the sounds I used. The story is essentially about good and evil, so I designed sounds that reflected that. Imperial ships and weapons tended to be shrieking and howling, frightening and ominous. Rebel spaceships, locations and weapons, on the other hand, sounded less threatening, less sleek and more organic.'

For the shrieking roar of the Imperial TIE fighters, Burtt mixed a number of original sounds. 'For the basic roar, I used a very old recording of an elephant trumpeting. I slowed that sound right down and lengthened it. To that I added the sound of a car going past on a wet highway – the sort of swish made by tyres on a waterlogged surface. Then I added a kind of rasping roar from a military rocket. In fact, I originally created this sound for the laser beam that comes from the Death Star, but it was so popular that it ended up being used extensively for the TIE fighters.'

Perhaps Burtt's most famous sound is the crackling electrical hum of the glowing laser swords used by the Jedi Knights. 'The light sabres were the very first sounds that I made for the film,' says Burtt. 'After seeing some early concept paintings, I immediately knew the noise that I wanted to create. At the time I had a part-time job as a projectionist. One of the projectors I used was very old and its motor made a wonderful electrical humming noise. This noise alone did not sound threatening enough for a weapon, and I knew it needed something else. A few weeks later, I was using my tape recorder at home and I had a microphone cable on which the shielding was faulty. As I carried the microphone past my television, it picked up a humming noise from the picture tube. When I combined this with the projector noise, I had the sound of the light sabres. I actually produced two different versions of this sound: one for Darth Vader's sword, which was pitched in a minor key to sound threatening, and one for Ben Kenobi's sword, which was more of a C-major chord. Together, the two noises clashed and created a disharmony that was symbolic of the struggle between good and evil.'

Since the light sabre sound effects were supposed to emanate from swords as they moved through the air during fight sequences, Burtt further manipulated the recording to create 'whooshing' sounds. 'Whenever an object moves towards you and then away from you, the pitch of its sound

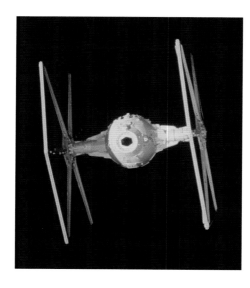

ABOVE: **The sounds of an elephant, a car driving past on a wet road and a military rocket engine were all combined to create the rasping noise of the TIE fighters in the *Star Wars* movies.**

BELOW: **A typical modern sound-mixing suite. Digitized sounds are mixed in a computer and can even be played like music on an electronic keyboard. Close at hand is a library of CDs containing a range of pre-recorded sound effects.**

changes', explains Burtt. 'This happens when police vehicles pass you by – you hear a strange change in the tone of the sirens as they pass. This is called the "Doppler effect". To re-create this phenomenon, I set up a loudspeaker and played back the basic light sabre noises. I used another tape recorder to re-record this noise through a microphone that I held in my hand and waved back and forth past the loudspeaker at different speeds. The result was these amazing whooshing sounds, just as if the swords were being moved through the air. I used the same process to make all the spaceships sound as if they were moving past the camera.'

Burtt spent much of his time on *Star Wars* creating the language of alien characters. 'Developing voices is always the most time-consuming task,' claims Burtt. 'Voices are always judged very critically, and audiences are pretty adept at recognizing and reading languages. It is important that an alien language does not sound as if it is derived from any that exists on Earth, but at the same time, it needs to possess the same emotional range as real language so that an audience can tell what is being expressed. I have used real languages as a basis, though – for the Ewoks in *Return of the Jedi* [1983], and the Huttese language, first used in *Star Wars* and expanded for *Jedi*, was based on an Inca language called Catua.'

Burtt also uses animal sounds as the basis for many alien voices. 'Chewbacca's voice is basically the noise of various bears with a few bits of walrus, lion and dog added in for extra texture,' he explains. 'I went out and recorded the sound of animals at various zoos and parks and then divided up the recordings into individual sounds that were like the phonemes of human speech. I then catalogued these bits according to the way I thought they sounded, so that I had angry sounds, cute sounds, a bunch that sounded like information, others that sounded questioning and so on. When I had this library, I then constructed sentences by editing sounds together according to what Chewbacca was supposed to be saying in each scene. I also had to make sure that these sounds synchronized with the way his lips had moved during filming, which made things quite difficult. I used the same method for the chirps and whistles of the robot R2-D2, though that was much easier as R2 doesn't have a mouth!'

Fifteen years after last creating sounds for the *Star Wars* universe, Burtt began working on the design of sounds for *Star Wars*: Episode I *The Phantom Menace* (1999). 'I was very conscious of creating exciting new sounds but ones that also remained consistent with the style of the original films,' claims Burtt. 'One of the major changes has been the type of equipment available. Many of the sounds for the original films were created using physical tricks that had essentially been used for decades – like manually dragging tape through a tape player to affect the sound it made. However, we now work with computers that can do almost anything. The Doppler effect that I created for the lightsabers by swinging a microphone past a speaker can now be created by a standard piece of software at the touch of a button. I wouldn't say that we can produce better sound effects now, but we can certainly work much faster and we have far more control.'

FOLEYING

When pre-recorded sound effects have been selected from a library, and specialized original sound effects have been created, the remaining sounds that are required for a film are created in a process known as 'Foleying'.

The process is named after Jack Foley (346>), a sound editor employed for over 30 years at Universal Studios. Working on a film called *Smuggler's Island* (1951), Foley found himself editing pre-recorded sounds of splashing water to match the actions of an actor paddling a small boat in the ocean. Cutting a sound to match each movement was a laborious process, so Foley decided to get a bucket of water and 'act' the scene while watching the film. The resulting recording of splashing water synchronized perfectly with the picture, and the whole process took a fraction of the time that it would have taken to edit pre-recorded splashes manually. Sound effects artists had in fact been doing this kind of thing for years, but throughout his career Jack Foley probably did more than anyone to refine the technique and make it popular.

Today, the Foley process is responsible for creating a large proportion of the sounds that we hear in any film. If the dialogue and music were

RIGHT: **Footsteps are one of the most commonly required sound effects. Here the sound of someone walking on sand is being recorded for** *The Beach* **(2000). A selection of other walking surfaces can be seen in the background.**

PROFILE **JACK FOLEY**

Jack Donovan Foley (1891–1967) grew up in Coney Island, NY, where his classmates included the future actors James Cagney and Bert Lahr. Although his face would never be as famous as those of his friends, Foley's name would eventually appear, indirectly, in the credits of almost every modern feature film.

In 1914 Foley relocated to Los Angeles where he worked as a stuntman in silent movies. He then moved to the foot of California's Sierra Mountains, working in a hardware store before promoting the spectacular local scenery as a location for Westerns. Foley was soon something of a jack of all trades for Universal, making props, writing screenplays and directing inserts – close-up shots of small details that aren't filmed during normal shooting.

Foley was working as a props assistant on the film *Show Boat* (1929) when the coming of sound meant the production was hastily turned into a talkie and Foley found himself assisting with the sound. With the studios clamouring to employ anyone that knew anything about sound, Foley found himself in demand as a 'sound man'.

For *Show Boat* Foley had helped create sound effects that were recorded at the same time as the music.

For later movies he created separate sound effects that were then edited together and added to the finished film. However, this was a time-consuming process and so he later perfected the art of viewing finished movies a reel at a time and creating and recording 'live' sound effects to match the picture.

Foley was a master at producing convincing sounds from almost anything that came to hand, but it was his footsteps for which he was best known. To create the sound of a group of people walking he would use his own feet plus two walking sticks to make the sound of additional footsteps. During his career he estimated that he walked 5,000 miles on the spot, carefully mimicking the differing footstep styles of stars including James Cagney, Rock Hudson, Tony Curtis and Marlon Brando – even female stars such as Jean Simmons.

In his 40-year career at Universal, Jack Foley enhanced hundreds of films from *Dracula* (1931) to *Spartacus* (1960). Though other studios used similar techniques, Foley was so admired that it was his name that became most associated with the technique of performing sound effects.

removed from the soundtrack of any typical movie, the noises we would hear might include the footsteps of people walking on various surfaces, clothes rustling, light switches being turned on and off, objects being picked up and set down – all the creaks and bumps that occur when people and objects move. These sounds may seem natural when heard in a film, but they are almost always entirely artificial creations, and are the last to be recorded and added to a soundtrack.

The Foley process begins when the sound editor and a Foley artist carefully study each scene of a film and make a list of every possible sound that is likely to occur as a result of the action that they see. With a complete list of required sounds, the Foley artist decides exactly how each noise is to be created. Most recording studios have a room piled with a range of props that Foley artists can hit, squeeze, rub, twist, shake and rip to create the sounds they need. These props will have been accumulated over the years and are valued for the sounds they can produce. 'The objects that we use to make sounds often bear no relationship whatsoever to the objects whose sound we are trying to re-create,' admits Gary Hecker, senior Foley artist at Sony Pictures Studios. 'This is because when you record the sound of the actual object that you are trying to represent, the recording process can alter the quality of that sound somewhat. So, paradoxically, the sound made by a completely different object is often more real-sounding than the sound of the real thing.'

Most Foley artists have favourite props that they use time and again. 'One of my best props is a creaky old chair,' states Hecker. 'By treating this chair in different ways, I can make the sound of creaking floorboards, a ship at sea, doors opening and closing, people walking up stairs – all kinds of noises – even the sound of a creaky old chair!'

When all the necessary props have been selected and tested, the Foley artist begins work on a Foley stage, where the sounds for each sequence are created and recorded. 'The first sounds that we record for each scene are the footsteps,' explains Hecker. 'This means getting two surface sounds correct. One is the type of shoe that an actor in a scene is wearing, the other is the type of ground or floor on which he or she is walking. We have hundreds of pairs of shoes in my size. Each one produces a different sound when used.

We also have a large variety of walking surfaces – small square areas of sand, gravel, wooden flooring, carpet, concrete and so on. Sometimes we have to create mud or other special surfaces to walk on. For *The Empire Strikes Back* [1980], we wanted a squishy sound for the scene when Han Solo and Princess Leia walk on the floor of a cave that is actually the inside of a giant monster's mouth. For that we got large pieces of steak and cracked eggs onto them to produce a really gooey noise when they were stepped on.'

While watching the action – which is repeatedly displayed or 'looped' on a large screen – the Foley artist must mimic the movement of each performer, reproducing the exact pace of walk, run or shuffle. If the scene involves dancing, the Foley artist may even have to learn the dance routine in order to re-create the rhythm of the footsteps. 'Creating footsteps really is a form of performance in its own right, because you have to become the actor that you are watching on the screen,' comments Hecker. 'There is quite a knack to walking in a way that will make you sound like a particular performer. In the case of Arnold Schwarzenegger in *Terminator 3* [2003], I wore very heavy shoes that gave the appropriate beefy sound. Even so, he has a very particular stride that is quite hard to replicate when you can't actually walk up and down – we have to do all our walking "on the spot" standing on small areas of surface that are near to the fixed microphone.'

When the footsteps of each character in a scene have been recorded, the next sounds to be re-created are the subtle, often almost imperceptible, rustling noises made by their clothes. The 'moves' track is recorded as Foley artists sitting near to a microphone hold, move, flap and rub the appropriate types of material while watching the scene in question.

Next any additional sound effects are created. 'You would be amazed by the hundreds of tiny little sounds that there are in each scene,' says Hecker. 'Every time actors move there is the squeak of their shoe leather, the jangle of the keys in their pocket, the creak of their chair as they stand up or the clink of a coffee mug as it is placed on a table. We go through each scene and create every one of those sounds – and it's a real art. Depending on how you handle it, the same prop could be used to make sounds with many different qualities. If we are breaking some glass, I can

ABOVE: **The Foley stage at London's Shepperton Studios, where a Foley artist is at work creating sounds to match the images on the screen. A range of props is at hand on the far wall, including a selection of doors, locks and latches.**

produce a crack, a break, a smash or a shatter – it all depends what I do to the glass and how near we place the microphone.' Foley artists also produce many subtle sounds that will seem as if they have come directly from the performers on-screen – breathing, sighing, coughing, sniffing, chewing, and even kissing. 'I've spent plenty of time kissing the back of my own hand over the years!' laughs Hecker.

While Foleying has traditionally only been used to create the mundane sounds in a scene, advances in technology have meant that the process is now being used to produce increasingly complex sound effects. 'Once, the only way to create some sound effects was for a sound designer painstakingly to mix and layer various pre-recorded sounds,' states Hecker. 'However, with the use of modern sound-processing equipment, a lot of complex sounds are now being created live during the Foley. A good example is the sound of an explosion. This would once have been created by layering many different pre-recorded sounds, including real explosions. However, recently we have created a lot of explosion sounds right here on the Foley stage. To create a big bang, I might use a large hollow vinyl-shelled suitcase. This would be laid on its side and covered in dirt and gravel, and then I would hit it really hard with a baseball bat. This nice, hollow noise would be recorded through a special six-thousand-dollar microphone that can record noises as loud as 150 decibels. Then the sound would be slowed down and processed through a harmonizer which will pitch the sound down, making it deep and full of bass. The result sounds like the most enormous explosion that you've ever heard in your life.'

Hecker is increasingly being asked to adapt the Foley process for the creation of vocal performances for screen creatures. 'Creature sounds have traditionally been made by mixing lots of sounds, including those of real animals,' states Hecker. 'This is an incredibly laborious process in which you are largely dependent on the quality of the available animal noises to create any form of performance or emotion. If the sounds are not really well mixed, the result can end up sounding just like something that has been derived from real animals. For films such as *Godzilla* [1998], *Mighty Joe Young* [1998] and *Hollow Man* [2000], I actually made the noise of the animal characters by coming up with a vocal performance that, when processed through various software and hardware, became the voice of each character. The great advantage of doing this is that the director of a film can direct me as a performer and tell me that the character needs to sound a little sadder or crosser or happier. It takes me a matter of seconds to make a "sad" noise, whereas a sound designer might spend hours on remixing to get the same result. Sometimes additional noises – in the case of *Godzilla*, the odd animal growl or the sound of screeching metal – are later layered on top of my performance to get the final effect, but the emotive performance comes from my voice. I also produced many of the horse vocals for *Seabiscuit* [2003] – snorts, whinnies and breathing. But the hoof beats and running sounds were mostly produced using that most famous of all sound props – coconut shells.'

AUTOMATED DIALOGUE REPLACEMENT

During the editing of a film, images are cut together using the original production recording as a soundtrack. As a result of conditions during filming, however, much of the dialogue in these recordings is often obscured by the sound of buzzing studio lights, background chatter, overhead aeroplanes and the hum of production generators. This disrupted dialogue therefore has to be replaced before a film can be completed. 'The original recording of dialogue as spoken by actors on set is often completely unintelligible', remarks Max Hoskins of ReelSound, a sound studio based at London's Pinewood Studios. 'This is often simply due to unsympathetic conditions during filming. The common perception among production crews is that sound recording is not very important because sound can always be fixed at a later stage. While it is true that we can do almost anything with sound, it's often the case that if producers and directors spoke to us for five minutes before filming began, it could later save us weeks of time and save them an awful lot of money.

'Once the picture element of a film has been edited, we go through and listen to the dialogue of each actor', Hoskins explains. 'Ideally, we need the words of each character to be heard perfectly clearly, with no extraneous background noise. Sometimes a small background noise will drown out a single word spoken by an actor and that word will have to be replaced; other times, there is so much noise in the background or it has been so poorly recorded that the whole scene has to be re-recorded.'

The process of deciding which words are to be replaced and noting where they occur in a scene is called 'spotting'. Once a film has been 'spotted', the actors are called back for automated dialogue replacement sessions (ADR). 'ADR often takes place when actors are already working on their next project, and they may have to take time off to fly across the world and re-record dialogue that they originally spoke many months before', says Hoskins. 'Performers appearing in the same scene can rarely be reassembled at the same time, so actors usually have to speak their lines to no one. As a result, re-recorded dialogue is generally considered inferior, in performance terms, to original production sound. For this reason, we try to replace as little dialogue as possible, but some films – especially action films – may have as much as 70 per cent of their dialogue re-recorded and replaced.' Some directors, however, enjoy the freedom and flexibility that this process allows them, and some films, such as *Once Upon a Time in America* (1984), have had every single piece of original dialogue replaced.

During an ADR session, performers are shown a scene repeatedly while listening to the original sound on headphones, so that they can learn to say their lines in exact synchronization with the image. Before videotape made things simpler, scenes were repeated by editing film into a loop that went round and round in a projector. For this reason, ADR is still sometimes called 'looping'. 'When a performer is learning to repeat his or her lines parrot-fashion, it is the last chance for a director to make alterations to the performance', explains Hoskins. 'Sometimes directors ask the actors to alter the emphasis or intonation of the dialogue slightly. Sometimes they even ask the actors to say a completely new word or line, and they have to find a way to synchronize it with the sentence that is being spoken on the screen. We also find alternatives to swear words so that we can produce a toned-down version of the film for use on television or on board aircraft.'

If part of a script has been rewritten since filming, it is likely that the new words will not fit the movement of the mouths already filmed. In such cases, the new dialogue must be recorded so that it fits the movements of the back of an actor's head in the reverse-angle shots that are used in most dialogue scenes.

When actors are ready to repeat dialogue so that it perfectly matches the lip movements on screen, they watch the image once more and perform while their voice is recorded. 'The synchronization of performers' words with the image of their lips has to be exact', notes Hoskins, 'though these days we can edit words digitally, stretching or shrinking them fractionally to ensure

FIGURE 2 **MOVIE THEATRE SOUND SYSTEM**

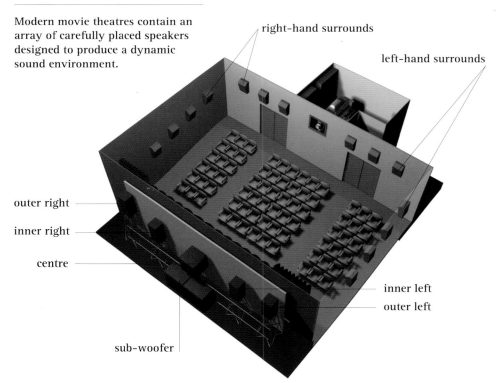

Modern movie theatres contain an array of carefully placed speakers designed to produce a dynamic sound environment.

right-hand surrounds

left-hand surrounds

outer right

inner right

centre

inner left

outer left

sub-woofer

ABOVE RIGHT: **The re-recording stage at Pinewood Studios. The room is designed to replicate conditions in a movie theatre so that the re-recording mixer can create the best balance of music, dialogue and sound effects.**

RIGHT: **The final stage of sound production. An operator at Pinewood Studios converts the final soundtrack mix into an optical or digital signal so that it can be printed onto the film and added to release prints or mastered onto a CD.**

that every word fits absolutely perfectly. When the film is finished, no one in an audience should ever be aware that much of what they hear is actually recorded long after the images were filmed.'

RE-RECORDING

When each sound effect and piece of dialogue has been recorded and edited, every element is brought together and assembled to create a completed soundtrack in a process called the 're-recording mix'.

'The re-recording mix is where we produce the final soundtrack for a film, and it is generally the last creative process in the production of a feature film,' explains Graham Hartstone, head of post-production at London's Pinewood Studios. Each of the individual edited sounds – some lasting only a second or two – is held on what adds up to dozens, or sometimes even hundreds, of separate tracks. These have to be gradually combined and reduced down to the six or eight tracks that will be added to the final version of the film.

As the many tracks of sound are combined, they are manipulated and balanced to sound the way that the director wants them to be heard by the audience. One of the important tasks at this stage is dividing each sound between the various loudspeakers used in film theatres (fig. 2). 'Most film theatres now have a minimum of six channels of sound,' explains Hartstone. 'Behind each movie screen there are typically four loudspeakers: a centre speaker, a left-hand speaker and a right-hand speaker, which give the impression that sounds are coming from the correct place on the screen, and a subwoofer speaker, which emits low-frequency, non-directional sounds – the type that make your chair vibrate when a spaceship goes past or a gun goes off. Then in the auditorium

FIGURE 3 **SOUNDTRACK FORMATS**

A modern film print holds soundtrack information in a number of formats, which theatres select according to their sound reproduction system.

a: SDDS (Sony Dynamic Digital Sound) optical soundtrack.
b: Dolby SR optical digital soundtrack.
c: Variable width analogue optical soundtrack.
d: DTS (Digital Theatre Sound). In this system the film print does not contain the soundtrack itself. Signals on the film control the playing of a separate CD.

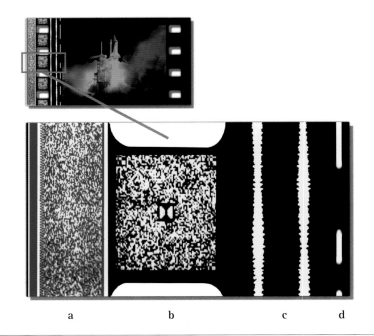

a   b   c   d

itself there are speakers down the walls – these are the left-hand and right-hand surround channels that give the impression that the environment in the film actually extends out beyond the screen. As well as these standard arrangements, some other sound systems use additional speakers. The Sony system uses five speakers behind a screen – a subwoofer and then outer and inner left- and right-hand speakers – so that it can locate sound even more accurately on the screen. The latest Dolby system uses a third surround channel to send sound to speakers on the back wall of the auditorium.'

During the mixing process, the supervising sound editor and the director will decide which of these speakers each sound should come from. As a sound is being copied onto the new mix, a joystick can be used to determine where that sound should come from, and it is then recorded onto the appropriate tracks. A sound that needs to come from the far right of the screen might therefore be divided equally between the right-hand speaker behind the screen and the right-hand surround channel. The source of each sound can also be moved throughout the duration of a shot so that, for example, an aircraft can sound as if it is coming from behind the audience before actually appearing on the screen.

PROFILE **BEN BURTT**

Ben Burtt (1948–) became fascinated by sound when, bed-ridden for weeks at the age of six, his father brought home a tape recorder as a form of entertainment. The machine sparked a passion that would become a career.

After gaining a degree in physics, Burtt's short film *Yankee Squadron* (1970) won first prize at the National Student Film Festival, winning him a scholarship to the USC film school, where he specialized in sound.

After leaving USC, Burtt found work as a sound recordist and editor on low-budget films before being asked to create the sound effects for a new science fiction film called *Star Wars* (1977). *Star Wars* gave Burtt the unique opportunity to design sound for entire worlds and their inhabitants. His work for the film changed the way we think about film sound and won him an Academy Award.

Burtt has since become closely associated with the films of George Lucas and Steven Spielberg, designing the sound for all subsequent *Star Wars* films, the

Indiana Jones trilogy, *Willow* (1988) and *E.T. the Extra-Terrestrial* (1982), among others.

The soundscapes designed by Burtt are so inventive and rich that they not only provide a backdrop to the action of a film, but are also an integral part of a film's fabric, adding humour, drama, spectacle and pace in their own right. As a result, Burtt's work has inspired a new generation of sound professionals.

As well as working in the field of sound effects, Burtt has directed episodes of the *Young Indiana Jones* TV series (1992–6) and several IMAX movies including *Special Effects: Anything Can Happen* (1996), a documentary about the history of special effects.

After finishing work editing *Star Wars*: Episode III *Revenge of the Sith* (2005), Burtt announced that he had signed a deal to work at Pixar Animation Studios. He has won Oscars for his work on *Star Wars*, *Raiders of the Lost Ark* (1981), *E.T.*, and *Indiana Jones and the Last Crusade* (1989).

350 SPECIAL EFFECTS THE HISTORY AND TECHNIQUE

PROFILE **GARY RYDSTROM**

Gary Rydstrom (1959–) was raised in Chicago and had set his sights on a career in the movies by the age of 12. Rydstrom's childhood obsession with the movies was sparked by watching old silent movies on TV, something of an irony given that he would become one of the world's top sound designers.

In 1977 Rydstrom enrolled at USC's highly respected School of Cinema and soon found that his talents lay in post-production, in particular sound. In 1983, following a number of jobs that included working as Francis Ford Coppola's projectionist, a professor at USC recommended Rydstrom for a job at Sprocket Systems, George Lucas's famed sound studio (later renamed Skywalker Sound).

Rydstrom started learning the business of sound production under mentor Ben Burtt (<350), cutting his teeth as an engineer on films such as *Indiana Jones and the Temple of Doom* (1984). Rydstrom quickly moved on to designing sound for small projects including *Luxo Jr.* (1986), John Lasseter's ground-breaking computer-animated short for which he created the highly personable metallic language of an animated lamp.

As sound designer Rydstrom has created some of the most striking and memorable soundtracks for dozens of modern movies. Among his most memorable work have been the hauntingly primeval voices of the dinosaurs in *Jurassic Park* (1993) and the chillingly subjective orchestra of gunfire in the opening scenes of *Saving Private Ryan* (1998).

Rydstrom has become most associated with the work of Pixar Animation Studios, having created playful and energetic soundscapes for films including *Toy Story* (1995), *Monsters, Inc.* (2001) and *Finding Nemo* (2003). In 2003 he left Skywalker Sound to embark on a new career as an animation director at Pixar.

To date Rydstrom has won seven Oscars for his work on *Terminator 2: Judgment Day* (Best Sound, and Best Sound Effects, 1991), *Jurassic Park* (Best Sound, and Best Sound Effects, 1993), *Titanic* (Best Sound, 1997), and *Saving Private Ryan* (Best Sound, and Best Sound Effects, 1998).

The re-recording process takes place in several stages. The hundreds of individual tracks of sound are first reduced to a number of more manageable tracks called pre-mixes. Each pre-mix contains the mix for a particular category of sound. Before the proliferation of digital technology in the late 80s, all sound was stored and played on reels of magnetic tape. Each reel contained several tracks of sound, so pre-mixing meant running dozens of reels of sound simultaneously and re-recording the hundreds of sounds that they output onto a single reel of tape. Today, the various audio tracks are stored as digital information on hard disks, tapes or CDs, and re-recording is a case of selectively combining various digital files.

'The first thing we do is make the dialogue pre-mix,' explains Hartstone. 'Each character's dialogue may be split up on several tracks, because some of it will be original production sound that was recorded on location, and some will be sourced from ADR sessions [<348]. These separate pieces are combined to create one complete track. At the same time as assembling these bits of dialogue, we may make various acoustic alterations to the quality of the sound, so that dialogue spoken in an ADR studio will sound as if it were recorded in the same location as the original dialogue. Next we do pre-mixes for the sound effects. These fall into several categories. We do a mix of what we call "spot effects". These are individual sounds that relate directly to actions on the screen – sounds like doors closing, cars starting, guns firing and so on. Again, these sounds will be held on a large number of tracks, so we re-record them and mix them onto one new track. During this mix, we will also compare the sounds to the dialogue pre-mix that we have already done, adjusting their volume levels so that none of the noises will drown out important dialogue.'

The next stage is to do an atmosphere pre-mix in which sounds such as distant traffic, wind, birdsong and so on are mixed together. 'Generally speaking, we use the director's choice of lens as our cue for how to treat atmospheric effects,' states Hartstone. 'For a big, wide-angled establishing shot, we would probably use the surround speakers to give the audience the impression of actually being in that environment, but for an intimate shot between two characters, we probably wouldn't want the audience to be too aware of the general world around them, so the atmospheric sound may only go to the speakers behind the screen. Our next pre-mix is footsteps and movements. If people are just moving about within the confines of the screen, then their body movements and footsteps will be kept on the centre channels. However, if they move off screen, or run onto it, we may pan the sound accordingly. The final pre-mix is for the film's musical score. This is usually the last element to arrive, and we do the music pre-mix while taking care that it does not swamp the dialogue, or that the music is not spoilt by intrusive sound effects. Music is a very individual thing, and while it is often easy for us to create a satisfactory balance of dialogue and sound effects without the director present, the director is the only one who knows how he or she wants the music to play against the other sounds.

'When we have done our pre-mixes, everyone important who is involved with a film and its soundtrack will assemble for the final mix,' continues Hartstone. 'This can often be a tense time, because it is literally the last chance to make any creative alterations to a film. When we have done the final mix, the result is three "stems". These are the dialogue stem, the music stem and the effects stem. It is important to keep dialogue separate from music and effects because foreign versions of a film will replace the English-language dialogue with their own language.'

When the soundtrack for a theatrical release version of a film is completed, it is optically printed onto a 35 mm negative, the sounds being represented either by a variable-width black area at the side of the picture, or by a matrix of black and clear dots that contains the information for digital sound reproduction. There are a number of sound reproduction systems in use today, so each copy of a film may have as many as four separate soundtracks printed onto it so that its sound can be reproduced in any movie theatre (fig. 3). When the negative of the soundtrack has been created, it is sent to a laboratory, where it is married with the negative of the fully edited picture. Hundreds of copies of the film are then made and distributed to cinemas.

9

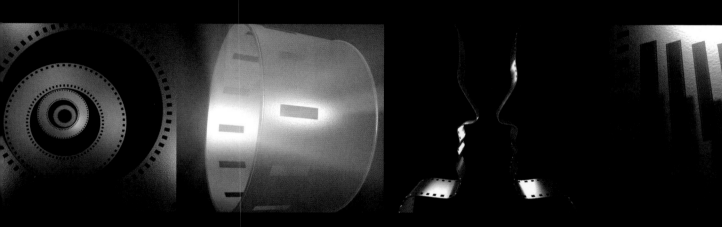

CONCLUSION

The most influential of all 50s presentation experiments was 3-D, a technique that makes the normally flat images of a cinema screen appear to reach out towards the audience. Though there had been a number of earlier experiments, 3-D cinema only became widely popular with the release of the independently produced *Bwana Devil* in 1952. In fact, the 3-D effects in *Bwana Devil* were actually quite poor – spears waved towards the camera hardly threatened to poke the audience's eyes out, and the occasional encounters with skinny ex-circus lions were barely as thrilling as the 'lion in your lap' promised by the film's zealous marketing campaign. Despite this, and some appalling reviews, *Bwana Devil* was a box office hit. Thinking it had found a way to revive its ailing fortunes, Hollywood plunged into the production of 'stereoscopic' films. The trade began to think and talk in terms of 'depthies' and 'flatties' in much the way that 'silents' and 'talkies' had been distinguished on the arrival of sound. But all too often, 3-D was used as a substitute for other production values and some truly terrible films were produced, including *Robot Monster* (1953), a popular candidate for worst movie ever made. There were some more worthy attempts to use the method creatively, however, as in Hitchcock's *Dial M for Murder* (1954) – perhaps the subtlest expression of the technique. But 18 months after the release of *Bwana Devil*, and with the public already bored of the process, the production of stereoscopic movies dried up. The studios transferred their hopes to other technical innovations such as the widescreen process CinemaScope (<55).

Perhaps the greatest limitation of the 50s 3-D films was the varying quality of their stereoscopic effects. Images rarely 'leapt' from the screen as promised by the publicity and viewers had to wear uncomfortable red and

Over the last 100 years, the art and technology of special effects has been tirelessly improved until, as the cinema enters its second century, few creative barriers remain to be broken. With the extraordinary advancements that have been made in computer-generated imagery, it is now possible to produce artificially any image that the human mind can conceive. Most future developments in special effects production are likely only to be refinements of current technology – allowing imagery to be created more efficiently and cheaply.

Future technological developments are likely, therefore, to concentrate less on the type of images that we create, and more on the way we consume them. Now, as in the past, we pay to sit in rows and watch an oblong image displayed on a flat screen. But an array of alternative methods of consuming filmed images are now being developed.

The cinema stands on the threshold of one of the most revolutionary eras since its invention. Some of the technology now being explored, with its emphasis on increased interaction between image and viewer, looks set to revolutionize the way we perceive visual entertainment for generations to come.

3-D

Since the invention of moving pictures, there have been many experiments in film presentation technology. Few ideas got any further than the drawing board since, during the first half of the century, cinema was the dominant entertainment medium of the world – and Hollywood saw no reason to tinker with a formula that worked. However, the idea of finding new ways to present films was taken more seriously in the 50s, when television began to steal huge audiences from the cinema. Desperate to halt the decline in movie-going, the Hollywood studios showed themselves willing to try anything that might distinguish cinema from television and tempt audiences away from their living rooms. Some ideas – such as widening the shape of a cinema screen – were both practical and popular, and remain in use to this day. Other ideas were more hare-brained, often seeing the light in only a few movies before fading into obscurity.

PRECEDING PAGES: **Leaping off the screen and 'into' the theatre,** *Terminator 2: 3-D – Battle Across Time* **wows visitors to the Universal Studios theme park. Could this be how all movies will look in the future?**

FAR LEFT: **A 50s audience wearing anaglyphic glasses enjoys the thrills of a 3-D movie.**

LEFT: *Bwana Devil* **(1952) was the first big 3-D hit, though its promises of 'A lion in your lap!' and a 'A lover in your arms!' were perhaps a little optimistic.**

ABOVE: **After the surprise success of** *Bwana Devil* **(1952), Hollywood plunged into the production of 3-D movies.** *House of Wax* **(1953) was the first 3-D production by a major studio.**

ABOVE RIGHT: **Gillman from** *Creature from the Black Lagoon* **(1954) was one of the most popular 50s monsters to lunge at the audience in stereoscopic glory.**

green spectacles that resulted in a murky-looking image and, in many cases, gave them a headache. Today, however, new technology allows 3-D films to be produced far more effectively than ever before. Anyone viewing a modern stereoscopic production will see images that appear to extend (and recede) from the screen so realistically that many people cannot resist the urge to reach out and 'touch' them. However, despite their sophistication, the new 3-D techniques still work on the same basic principles that were utilized in the 50s and before.

At the heart of all 3-D processes is the principle of binocular vision. The Greek mathematician Euclid (circa 325–265 BC), who was the first to note the phenomenon over 2,000 years ago, demonstrated that because our eyes are about $2\frac{1}{2}$ inches apart, each one sees a slightly different perspective of the same scene. By merging these two differing perspectives, our brains create the perception of depth. The phenomenon is easily demonstrated by holding one finger up at arm's length. Looking at it alternately with one eye and then the other, the finger will appear to shift in position because it is being viewed from two slightly different angles. Only by looking at the finger with both eyes at once will a real sense of three-dimensional depth be achieved. In order to replicate the way that our eyes work, all 3-D film techniques require a scene to be photographed in stereo – using two cameras to film the scene from slightly different angles. Each of these perspectives must then be presented to just one of our two eyes in order to simulate the impression of binocular vision and three-dimensional depth.

Historically, there have been three basic ways of ensuring that each of our eyes receives just one of the two perspectives necessary to create the 3-D experience. One, the anaglyphic process, uses coloured lenses either to transmit or block images of a certain colour. The polarized process, on the other hand, uses the principles of polarized light to separate each image, while the frame sequential process mechanically blocks the view from each eye intermittently. Today's 3-D systems apply new technology to maximize the potential of these processes.

The anaglyphic process was first used for the projection of 3-D images in 1856 when J.C. d'Almeida gave a demonstration at the Académie des Sciences in Paris. Using a magic lantern, he alternately projected two images that had been photographed by two cameras whose lenses were the same distance apart as two eyes. The two images, one coloured red and one coloured green, were viewed by an audience wearing glasses which themselves held one red and one green lens. Each lens effectively obscured the image that was shown in its own colour and highlighted the image shown in the opposite colour. The result was that each eye received only the correct image, producing the illusion of a three-dimensional picture (fig. 1, 356>). The anaglyphic system, with its familiar red and green glasses, is the most widely known way of creating and viewing 3-D films, and it was the method widely used during the 50s. The images themselves can be projected from a single film that either has both the left and right, red and green images superimposed on each frame, or has the red and green images printed on alternate frames. Alternatively, two separate films can be shown simultaneously using two projectors.

FIGURE 1 **THE ANAGLYPHIC PROCESS**

The anaglyphic process works by using a
red lens to block green (or blue, or cyan)
light from one eye and a green lens to
block red light from the other eye.

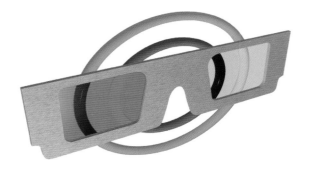

FIGURE 2 **THE POLARIZED LIGHT PROCESS**

Polarizing filters placed over each of the
projectors showing a 3-D film make the
light travel either horizontally or vertically.
Polarizing glasses ensure that only one
image reaches each eye.

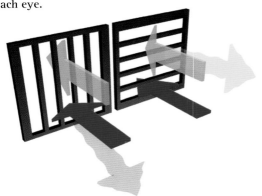

The anaglyphic system can achieve good 3-D images but it certainly has its drawbacks. Audiences tend to tire of peering through the coloured spectacles for the duration of a whole film. The reliance on coloured pictures and spectacles also means that the anaglyphic system cannot be successfully used in full colour.

The polarized light process was discovered in the 1890s and applied experimentally to moving pictures as early as 1896. In the late 30s the innovations of Dr Edwin H. Land (1909–91), inventor of the Polaroid camera, made the use of polarized light a truly practical method of producing 3-D images.

Polarizing filters work rather like a grid that is made up of microscopic angled slots and bars. Only light that travels at exactly the right angle will pass between the bars, while that travelling at any other angle will hit them and bounce off. The polarization of light cannot be recorded on film during photography, so polarizing filters are placed over lenses during projection. Using two separate projectors, one image of a scene is projected through a polarizing filter with horizontally angled slots, and the other image through a filter with vertically angled slots. A viewer wearing glasses with one vertically slotted lens and one horizontally slotted lens will therefore see a separate image with each eye (fig. 2). Polarizing filters in themselves are neutrally coloured, and since colour is not used as a way to separate left and right images, the polarizing method can be successfully used to show 3-D films in natural-looking hues.

The Teleview process that was installed in New York's Selwyn Theatre in 1922 was the first to use the frame sequential method of creating 3-D images by using a mechanical means of presenting separate images to each eye. Each viewer looked through a device that contained left and right shutters, which were mechanically opened and closed in synchronization with left and right images that were alternately thrown from a single projector. Looking through a cumbersome contraption attached to the seat in front of them, viewers would be shown one image through the right eyepiece and then one through the left, in rapid succession, to create the impression of depth.

Stephen Hines, one of a number of people who specialize in the increasingly popular field of modern stereography, says that while the basic methods of viewing 3-D films haven't changed, modern equipment does allow far more control over the actual production of spectacular three-dimensional images. 'Today there are several ways of capturing images for a 3-D film,' explains Hines. 'Some systems use a single camera with a special double lens that records two slightly different views next to each other on the same piece of film. But the best way is to use two separate cameras on a platform that allows the cameras to be moved independently to produce different effects. Once you have those images on two separate reels of film, you can print them and filter them in any way you want depending on how they are going to be shown.'

Hines has invented a camera system that gives film-makers total control over the way their 3-D images will look. 'There are several factors that affect the characteristics of a 3-D image,' he explains. 'Our eyes are about two and a half inches apart. Reproducing this gap, known as interocular distance, will produce images that match our normal perception of images. However, if the distance between the two camera lenses is increased or decreased, it has startling visual implications.' By moving the two lenses farther apart, the final 3-D image looks very small. This phenomenon, called perceptual miniaturization, can often be seen in the popular View-Master 3-D binocular toys. 'View-Master-type pictures are often photographed by using two standard 35 mm still cameras that have been bolted side by side,' says Hines. 'Frequently, the result is that the lenses used to take the pictures are twice as far apart as the eyes that we use to view them. As a result, everything looks like it is somehow miniaturized. The reverse happens if the lenses are too close.'

The other major factor that affects 3-D images is the convergence distance of the two lenses. 'Imagine a line that comes from the centre of each of the two lenses being used for 3-D filming. If the lenses are angled very slightly inwards, these lines will eventually intersect. This is known as the convergence point,' explains Hines. 'When a 3-D film is projected, any object that was beyond the convergence point during filming will appear to be behind the plane of the theatre screen, objects that are at the convergence point will appear to be on the screen, and objects that are in front of the point will appear to be sticking out towards the audience.'

The rig that Hines has built, called the 'StereoCam', is a platform that can hold two standard 35 mm or 65 mm motion picture cameras or high-definition video cameras. One camera is mounted vertically aiming downwards, while the other is horizontal. Both cameras point at a 45° beam-splitting mirror, which makes it possible for each to film exactly the same scene (fig. 3). However, during operation, the horizontal camera can be moved so that it records a slightly different image to the vertical camera. Moving the horizontal camera can affect both the interocular distance between the two lenses, and their point of convergence, in order to make objects in different parts of a scene appear to leap off the screen. Small video cameras attached to the rig transmit images to a special viewing device which enables the director and camera operator to see a 3-D video image of the scene being filmed.

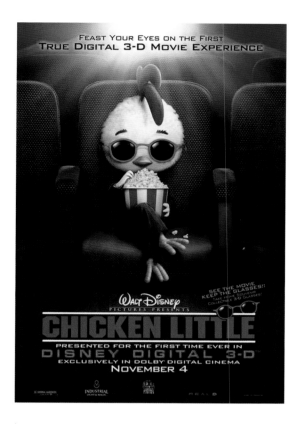

FEAST YOUR EYES ON THE FIRST
TRUE DIGITAL 3-D MOVIE EXPERIENCE

SEE THE MOVIE!!
KEEP THE GLASSES!!
TAKE HOME EXCLUSIVE
COLLECTIBLE 3-D GLASSES!

WALT DISNEY
PICTURES PRESENTS

CHICKEN LITTLE

PRESENTED FOR THE FIRST TIME EVER IN
DISNEY DIGITAL 3-D
EXCLUSIVELY IN DOLBY DIGITAL CINEMA
NOVEMBER 4

INDUSTRIAL
LIGHT & MAGIC

REAL D

are put on each of the two projectors and audiences wear polarized glasses, which present each eye with the correct picture and which have no adverse effect on the quality of the images being projected.' Another system, similar in principle to the Teleview system of the 20s, uses liquid crystal glasses that react to a beam of infrared light from the projector that causes them to flicker at around 50 hertz (times per second) and give each eye alternate views of the synchronized pictures on the screen. This system is used by IMAX (358>), which projects its large-format 3-D films at twice the regular speed so that each eye can see a different image in turn.

Using up-to-date filming and projection techniques, modern 3-D is hugely superior to the gimmicky process that once produced murky images of varying quality. Creating the convincing illusion that objects and environments on the screen do actually exist in three dimensions, modern 3-D is now a powerful entertainment medium with considerable potential.

In the 50s a downturn in audience numbers led the Hollywood studios to seek presentation technologies, including 3-D, that might encourage people back into theatres. 2005 saw a 6 per cent fall in US box office returns and was the third year in a row to see a decline in cinema-going. It is perhaps no coincidence, therefore, that the studios have shown a marked resurgence of interest in 3-D as a method of presenting mainstream movies.

In 2005 Disney released its animated CG movie *Chicken Little* in 3-D. Because, like all CG movies, *Chicken Little* was created and animated using 3-D models and environments, the final version could be released as a normal 2-D movie and re-rendered from the point of view of two virtual cameras (<233) for release in stereographic 3-D. The 3-D version was rendered by ILM and presented in theatres equipped with digital projectors (359>) using glasses, screens and software technology developed by a company called Real D.

3-D works well in theatres equipped with digital projectors because they are capable of displaying far more than the 24 frames per second shown by normal projectors. The system developed by Real D and used for *Chicken Little* displays 144 fps. These frames are divided between left and right views so that when polarized glasses are worn each eye receives 72 fps. A special silvered screen also helps to ensure high-quality viewing.

Chicken Little was a notable success in 3-D, earning considerably more per 3-D screen than it did in 2-D venues. Importantly, audiences and critics commented that watching the film felt quite natural, and was unlike the 'gimmicky' experience normally associated with traditional 3-D

Once the two separate films have been developed, they can be treated according to the method by which they are to be presented. 'Some films are still shown using the red–blue/green anaglyphic process,' explains Hines. 'I've managed to find an optimum balance of coloured filters so that the effect of muddy colours and fringing is minimal. But there is always some fringing when using the anaglyph technique – objects that are in front of the convergence point will have red fringing to their right and objects beyond it will have their fringe to the left. Polarization remains the most practical and satisfactory method of separating the images,' says Hines. 'Polarizing filters

ABOVE: Disney's *Chicken Little* (2005) was the first computer-animated movie to be widely distributed in a 3-D format. Computer-animated films are ideal for release in 3-D because a second, stereographic version of the film is easily rendered using an additional virtual camera.

FIGURE 3 **THE HINESLAB STEREOCAM**

A beam-splitting mirror allows a vertically mounted camera and a horizontally mounted camera to film from almost identical perspectives. The horizontal camera can be moved to change the quality of the 3-D image achieved.

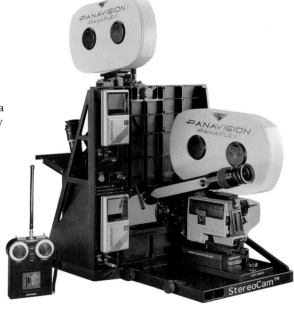

presentations. Such reaction augurs well for those who hope stereographic film can break away from its widely held perception as a gimmick to become a viable alternative method of consuming films.

When *Chicken Little* was released in November 2005, just 84 screens in the US were equipped to show the film in 3-D. It was planned that 500 screens would be available for the release of Disney's second stereographic CG film *Meet the Robinsons* (2006). Disney has announced that all of its future CG animated films will be released in a 3-D version, and other studios look set to follow.

Other film-makers are showing interest in 3-D as a method of making mainstream films. James Cameron has announced that he will make all of his future movies in 3-D, saying that he believes 3-D could change movies in the way that sound and colour did when first introduced. He has already directed the stereographic special-venue film *Terminator 2 3-D* (1996) as well as producing the documentaries *Ghosts of the Abyss* (2003) and *Aliens of the Deep* (2005) in IMAX 3-D. He has developed a new system of filming in high-definition 3-D which will be used to shoot his feature film *Avatar* (2008).

There is now even a way to create films for presentation in 3-D without having to film stereographically during initial production. A Californian company called In-Three has developed a complex and closely guarded system that can take normal 2-D images and convert them into 3-D. In this process the left-eye image remains the same while the right-eye image is altered to create the impression of 3-D. The technique is intensive and requires trained operators to selectively apply a series of differing digital processes to each shot in order to add depth information that is not present in the original frame, a process they call 'Dimensionalization'. In-Three has persuaded a number of Hollywood studios to convert classic films for re-release in 3-D. The system has been endorsed by directors including Peter Jackson (<44), Robert Rodriguez, Robert Zemeckis (<43) and George Lucas (<39), who is planning to convert all of his *Star Wars* films into 3-D for future re-release.

It remains to be seen whether such high-profile enthusiasm for 3-D will this time be reflected at the box office.

SPECIAL-VENUE FILMS

In addition to 3-D, there are a number of other systems that use unusual techniques to achieve a spectacular result. So-called 'special-venue films', in which the film itself is the star, are found in theme parks, major museums and science parks, or as stand-alone sites in city centres. Special-venue films normally use an unusual film format to produce a particularly high-quality image, while in theme parks the images are often accompanied by motion, smoke, lighting effects and even performers who interact with the on-screen action.

A system called 'Showscan' invented by the effects pioneer Douglas Trumbull uses 65 mm film that runs vertically through the camera and projector at 60 fps to produce images that are brighter and sharper than with any other system. Looking at a Showscan film really does feel like looking through a window into the real world. Showscan is normally combined with motion platforms that are programmed to move in response to the images seen on screen in order to immerse the audience in the action.

The most commonly used special-venue system is IMAX, which runs 65 mm film horizontally through the camera at 24 fps (the 65 mm equivalent of VistaVision, <55). IMAX films are projected onto enormous screens up to eight storeys high that completely fill the viewer's field of vision.

IMAX films have traditionally tended to be documentaries set in impressive landscapes such as the Rocky Mountains or the Arctic. IMAX cameras have even been used by NASA to film breathtaking views of the Earth from space.

Though IMAX has been available since the 60s, it has only recently become widely popular, resulting in an explosion of production using the format. This includes, for the first time, fictional films such as the dramatic 40-minute feature *T-Rex – Back to the Cretaceous* (1998) – a spectacular 3-D movie featuring computer-generated dinosaurs. IMAX is also starting to show digitally remastered giant-screen versions of selected Hollywood

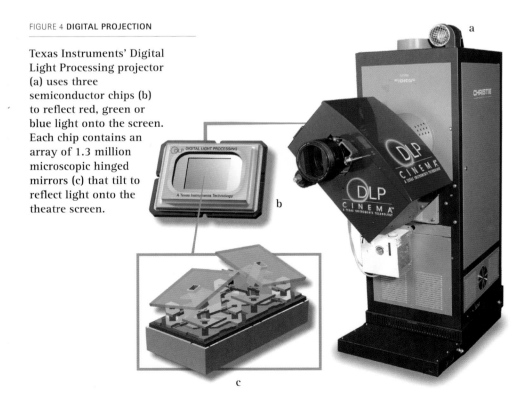

FIGURE 4 **DIGITAL PROJECTION**

Texas Instruments' Digital Light Processing projector (a) uses three semiconductor chips (b) to reflect red, green or blue light onto the screen. Each chip contains an array of 1.3 million microscopic hinged mirrors (c) that tilt to reflect light onto the theatre screen.

ABOVE RIGHT: **Computer-generated characters leap from the screen in this promotional still from** *Terminator 2: 3-D – Battle Across Time.*

BELOW RIGHT: **The enormous size of an IMAX screen fills the viewer's field of vision, making it the most spectacular way of viewing filmed images.**

blockbusters at around the same time as their general release. These have included the *Star Wars* prequels, *Poseidon* (2006) and the *Harry Potter* films. The company's 3-D technology has also been applied to films such as *The Polar Express* (2004), which took a considerable portion of its initial box office returns from stereoscopic screenings in IMAX theatres.

There are now over 250 IMAX screens worldwide and many more are planned for major cities. While they can only ever represent a small percentage of the tickets sold to see a mainstream film, Hollywood is starting to see IMAX as an important additional source of income for selected 'event' movies.

DIGITAL DEVELOPMENTS AND VIRTUAL REALMS

While the reproduction of sound has evolved significantly in the digital age, the projection of images that are recorded and stored on 35 mm film has remained essentially unchanged for decades.

However, digital projectors are now able to project film-quality images onto large screens using millions of microscopic mirrors (fig. 4). Digital projection is attractive to studios and film distributors because it will reduce the huge costs currently involved in manufacturing, transporting and ultimately destroying thousands of prints of each new film. Using digital projection, cinemas will receive films on disks, download them via the internet, or have them relayed by satellite. It is hoped such methods will help cut the risk of piracy from stolen film prints and make it easier and quicker for a theatre to adjust the number of screens that are showing a film according to its popularity. Film prints become progressively dusty and degraded with each showing; digital projection, however, means that a film will look as good for its hundredth screening as it does at its first.

The first digitally projected public screenings of a major movie were of *Star Wars*: Episode I *The Phantom Menace* (1999), for which four US theatres were equipped with the new projectors. Later the same year *Toy Story 2* (1999) became the first feature film to be entirely created, mastered and exhibited digitally, with digital theatres projecting copies of the movie that had come directly from the computers at Pixar Animation Studios.

The entirely digital production and distribution of movies is set to increase as more movies are both filmed and finished digitally. At the time of publication over 1,000 screens worldwide were equipped for digital projection but this number is expected to rise rapidly. The future, for major theatre chains at least, will undoubtedly be the exhibition of movies without film.

The continued use of a large screen to communally view the newest films is by no means a certainty. Falling box office revenues are in part due to many people's increasing preference for consuming movies and other entertainment at a time and place most convenient to them. DVD and home cinema systems have contributed to falling theatre attendance by making movie-watching at home a more enjoyable experience. In an attempt to find new business models in response to the digital revolution, Hollywood studios are even contemplating a service that will send, for a premium fee, latest releases directly into homes while they are still on theatrical release.

Even viewing movies on a screen could become a thing of the past. A technology that dispenses with any form of screen by projecting images directly onto the retina of the eye is already available. The system, called Virtual Retinal Display (VRD), was originally developed for military, medical and industrial applications – but its potential for entertainment purposes is being explored. The system requires the user to wear a headset which rapidly scans high-resolution images through the pupil and directly onto the retina. To the viewer, these images seem just like ordinary vision – exactly as if they are being seen directly through the eyes and without the black boundaries that we see around the edge of a cinema screen. By linking such a headset to a powerful computer, the viewer's head and eye movements can be tracked so that as the head is turned, they are able to 'look around' within the virtual environment. In the future it is conceivable that, rather than being rendered out as a 2-D final product, computer-generated movies may be released – perhaps via the internet – in an unrendered 3-D state. A viewer wearing a VRD headset could then act as their own virtual camera – as they move their head to see another area of the action, the movement will be measured and used to render, in real time, their own individual view of the pre-orchestrated action. Furthermore, because the system is binocular, it can send a slightly different view of a scene to each eye – making it ideal for viewing films in 3-D.

In the future, new technologies such as VRD will undoubtedly see widespread use in gaming applications – giving participants a highly interactive relationship with the game they are playing. However, the impact of such 'virtual reality' technology on cinema-going is more open to speculation. 'In the future, there will undoubtedly be many more ways to receive visual entertainment,' the cinematic visionary Douglas Trumbull believes. 'The scope for our increased interaction with such entertainment is huge – individuals will be able to choose what they see and even make decisions about how on-screen characters behave. But how that will affect the cinema is hard to tell. I believe that some new form of entertainment that uses computer-generated characters and environments will evolve. This will probably be a highly interactive mixture of the computer game and the cinema as we know it. People may go to the future equivalent of the multiplex to participate in this type of entertainment or, more likely, plug in through the internet. Ultimately such entertainment may even plug directly into our brain, supplying images and sound and even stimulating certain nerves to control our feelings and emotions. However, despite the increased opportunity for direct interaction with our entertainment, we shouldn't forget the power of the traditional cinema. People do actually enjoy sitting with hundreds of other people in a theatre – where they can laugh and scream in response to a piece of filmed entertainment over which they have no control. Whatever additional new forms of entertainment we create, they will probably exist alongside the old method. There are many entertainment marvels ahead, but the cinema as we know it will be hard to beat, and I believe it will still be around for some time to come.'

It may be decades before the techniques now being developed for the display and consumption of moving images settle into established new forms of mass entertainment. However, the incredible advances of the last two decades mean that the actual images that these technologies will display are not likely to change vastly; given enough time and money, any image imaginable can now be conjured with the computer. ILM's senior

visual effects supervisor Dennis Muren believes that anything film-makers want to see is possible. 'We can now create pretty much anything anyone asks of us,' Muren states. 'That's not to say that things aren't a challenge any more, but I rarely lie awake at night worrying whether or not we can pull something off. For me the big challenge in digital effects is now about getting things done faster. I want to see results more quickly and I want individual artists to be able to have much more control over their own shots rather than being just part of a pipeline.'

For some, however, there remains one goal: the creation of 'virtual performers' – digital actors indistinguishable from the real thing. Such characters would be the wholly owned property of entertainment companies and would never have to be paid salaries or royalties, nor would they need an expensive entourage of assistants, drivers and make-up artists. Such performers would become cross-media stars, appearing in both films and computer games.

Amazingly lifelike digital characters currently appear in many films, but these are often nonhuman characters such as aliens and dinosaurs whose unfamiliarity helps to disguise their artificial origins. Computer-generated humans tend to be used only very briefly, or in long shot, so that detailed scrutiny is impossible. They certainly aren't yet capable of giving a completely naturalistic performance. There is no doubt that a totally convincing computer-generated human can and will be created, but in the near future, perfect virtual actors will be so time-consuming and expensive to produce that, other than the publicity gained by the film that features the first virtual cast, the advantages of creating artificial performers are debatable. As Muren says: 'I just don't see the point of virtual performers. If you want great performances, then hire great actors – there are plenty out there. Visual effects are all about creating what doesn't already exist.'

The most frequently cited attraction of so-called 'synthespians' is the possibility of making new films with the stars of the past. Humphrey Bogart and Marilyn Monroe are two personalities commonly tipped for a comeback. The creation of convincing-looking Bogart and Monroe replicas is already a possibility, but aside from an appropriately hard-boiled face or accurately rendered curves, whether any animator could re-create their glamour, or indefinable on-screen presence, remains debatable. Nevertheless, some enterprising companies have already negotiated for the rights to resurrect certain deceased icons in future movie productions.

Hollywood has always sought to provide ever more spectacular images in order to keep audiences coming back for more. But the advent of digital effects has started to challenge the old rules. In 1993, cinema-goers lined up around the block to see the computer-generated wonders of *Jurassic Park*. Just a few years later such images were almost commonplace and certainly didn't warrant lining up to see. In the future, film-makers will find it increasingly difficult to impress audiences with outstanding images and will instead have to work even harder to create entertainment in which audiences are genuinely swept up by the drama and intrigued by well-observed characters.

A century ago, Georges Méliès was the first film-maker to discover that sheer spectacle was not enough to keep audiences coming back, and when he failed to offer anything more than tricks, his films began to lose their popular appeal. Visual effects artists will continue to perfect the creation of whatever wonders are asked of them. But in a new century, where films can be made without film, and where dramas may not need actors, the challenge for film-makers will be to find new ways of using moving pictures to awe, inspire and entertain us.

RIGHT: **Lifelike CG characters are already possible, but will the silicone chip replace the need for real actors in the future? Many believe the computer is best used only for the creation of fantasy characters, such as the giant green star of *Hulk* (2003).**

APPENDIX
SPECIAL EFFECTS LANDMARKS

This section details some of the most significant special effects films ever made. In compiling this list, I have considered hundreds of key effects films from the first one hundred years of the cinema; however, it is beyond the scope of this book to cover completely such a wide range. While this list is necessarily restricted, it aims to cover the most important and interesting effects movies to have been released over the decades, though readers will no doubt have their own favourites. Selection is based on the standard and importance of a film's effects at the time of production, and is not intended as a guide to the overall quality of the movies themselves, since, sadly, the two do not always equate.

Special effects credits are included for each film, an endeavour not without complications. Early films tended to give screen credits to departmental heads only and not necessarily to those responsible for creating the work. Nevertheless, every attempt has been made to correctly identify those involved in the production of effects in each case. The creation of modern effects films can involve so many people (many hundreds of digital artists in the case of a major film) that only departmental heads or supervisors have been listed. Running times are for original theatrical release.

THE ABYSS (1989)
DIRECTOR: James Cameron. VISUAL EFFECTS SUPERVISOR: John Bruno. VISUAL EFFECTS SUPERVISORS: Walt Conti (Walt Conti Productions), Robert Skotak (4Ward Productions), Dennis Muren (ILM), Gene Warren Jnr (Fantasy II Film Effects), Hoyt Yeatman (Dream Quest Images). SPECIAL EFFECTS CO-ORDINATORS: Joe Unsinn, Joe Viskocil. ALIEN CREATURE EFFECTS: Steve Johnson (Steve Johnson's XFX). 145 mins (special edition: 172 mins). Twentieth Century Fox.

The crew of a deep-sea oil rig become involved in a rescue mission to a sunken nuclear submarine where they encounter a strange life form.

A milestone in the evolution of computer-generated effects, *The Abyss* contained ILM's first major computer-generated organic 'character' – a snakelike entity formed of sea water called the Pseudopod. With the surrounding environments reflected and refracted in its surface, the character genuinely looks as if it is made of water. At one point, its tip even mimics the faces of the leading characters. Though digitally created, the Pseudopod was still optically composited. Traditional effects included the combination of live action and models – such as a split-screen shot in which a model mini-submarine being dropped into the water was combined with a life-size ship deck with actors on it. Filming of underwater sequences took place in the largest freshwater tank ever built for film use – inside a decommissioned nuclear power station. **Academy Award for Best Visual Effects.**

ALIENS (1986)
DIRECTOR: James Cameron. VISUAL EFFECTS SUPERVISORS: Robert Skotak, Dennis Skotak. POST-PRODUCTION VISUAL EFFECTS SUPERVISOR: Brian Johnson. SPECIAL EFFECTS SUPERVISOR: John Richardson. MINIATURES TECHNICAL SUPERVISOR: Pat McClung. ALIEN EFFECTS: Stan Winston. 137 mins (director's cut: 154 mins). Twentieth Century Fox.

After 57 years in hibernation, Officer Ripley (Sigourney Weaver) – the sole survivor of *Alien* – returns to the home planet of the monstrous life form that caused so many problems in the original film. With a crew of Combat Patrol Marines, she attempts to destroy the alien threat.

Aliens features some of the finest multi-element in-camera visual effects ever produced. For many shots, beam splitters were used to combine models, live action, matte paintings and other elements. An early shot of the Gateway space station was an in-camera composite produced using a photographic blow-up of a painting of the earth, a glass painting of sections of the space station, a model of sections of the space station, a sun element and a model spacecraft flying on wires. Beam splitters were also used to introduce smoke and fire elements to small models to help with the perception of scale. Other model shots were combined with live action using front and rear projection. Shots of the alien nest were created by combining a partially built full-scale set with a hanging miniature. A variety of aliens ranging from full-sized people-in-a-suit versions to miniature puppets were built. Perhaps the most ingenious alien creation was a small 'facehugger' which ran along a wire that controlled the scuttling movement of its legs. Major physical effects achievements included a 'powerlifter' – a servo-controlled walking forklift. **Academy Awards for Best Visual Effects and Sound Effects Editing.**

AN AMERICAN WEREWOLF IN LONDON (1981)
DIRECTOR: John Landis. SPECIAL MAKE-UP EFFECTS: Rick Baker. SPECIAL MAKE-UP EFFECTS ASSISTANT: Steve Johnson. SPECIAL EFFECTS: Martin Gutteridge, Garth Inns. 97 mins. Polygram.

Bitten by an English werewolf, an American tourist creates havoc in the streets of London.

American Werewolf achieved some of the most remarkable human-into-wolf transformations ever seen on screen. The basis for this was the 'change-o-head' technique conceived by Rick Baker for this film, but which, due to delays, was first used for the transformations created by Rob Bottin for *The Howling* (1981) – on which Baker was a consultant. The technique involved using life masks of actors and manipulating and distorting them from behind with rods or inflatable bladders to look as if major changes were happening under the skin. For *Werewolf*, Baker used the technique for the whole body so that the character's face, legs, feet, arms, hands and back are all seen stretching and rippling as if the bones below are reorganizing themselves. Fur growing on the body of the wolf was achieved by pulling hair into the latex skin and running the film backwards. Other make-up included a fully changed wolf puppet and the lacerated faces of werewolf victims. **Academy Award for Best Make-up.**

THE BIRDS (1963)
DIRECTOR: Alfred Hitchcock. PROCESS CINEMATOGRAPHY: Ub Iwerks. OPTICAL CINEMATOGRAPHY: Roswell A. Hoffman. MATTE ARTIST: Albert J. Whitlock. ADDITIONAL VISUAL EFFECTS: L.B. Abbot, Linwood C. Dunn, Robert R. Hoag. ANIMATION: David Fleischer. MECHANICAL EFFECTS SUPERVISOR: Lawrence W. Hampton. MECHANICAL EFFECTS TECHNICIAN: Marcel Delgado. 120 mins. Universal.

The residents of a quiet Californian town are unaccountably besieged by flocks of angry birds.

Hitchcock's greatest effects achievement, *The Birds* used sodium vapour, blue screen and hand-drawn travelling mattes to combine real birds filmed flying in a studio with location scenes. Shots in which thousands of birds gathered were created by optically combining up to thirty separate elements. For the final attack sequence, Tippi Hedren spent a week having real birds thrown at her and tied to her clothes with string. Mechanical birds that flapped and pecked were also used on location. Locations filmed in the Californian town of Bodega Bay were expanded with superbly atmospheric matte paintings by Albert Whitlock.

BLADE RUNNER (1982)
DIRECTOR: Ridley Scott. SPECIAL PHOTOGRAPHIC EFFECTS: Entertainment Effects Group. SPECIAL PHOTOGRAPHIC EFFECTS SUPERVISORS: Douglas Trumbull, Richard Yuricich, David Dryer. SPECIAL PHOTOGRAPHIC EFFECTS DIRECTOR OF PHOTOGRAPHY: Dave Stewart. OPTICAL PHOTOGRAPHY SUPERVISOR: Robert Hall. MATTE ARTISTS: Matthew Yuricich, Rocco Gioffre, Michelle Moen. ANIMATION & GRAPHICS: John Wash. CHIEF MODELMAKER: Mark Stetson. MECHANICAL EFFECTS SUPERVISOR: Terry Frazee. VISUAL DISPLAYS: Dream Quest Inc. VISUAL FUTURIST: Syd Mead. 114 mins (director's cut: 117 mins). Warner Bros.

In the Los Angeles of 2019, an ex-cop (Harrison Ford) is hired to track down and eliminate a group of dangerously intelligent 'replicants'.

Most of *Blade Runner*'s sumptuous effects are used to portray the LA of the future. Large forced-perspective models of the city were filmed in thick smoke to create long shots of the heavily polluted environment. Many shots were extended with brilliant matte paintings. A shot looking up at a passing airship through the glass roof of the Bradbury building was created by sticking a photo cut-out of the roof onto glass. This photo, and the camera used to film it, were moved past a stationary model blimp that had advertising images projected onto its silk sides. The 'Spinner' aircraft were created in a range of sizes from eighteen-inch models to full-size mock-ups. Rear projection was used to create the passing backgrounds for shots inside the Spinner cockpit, while front projection provided the backgrounds in the Tyrell Corporation Headquarters.

CITIZEN KANE (1941)
DIRECTOR: Orson Welles. SPECIAL EFFECTS: Vernon L. Walker. OPTICAL EFFECTS: Linwood Dunn. MATTE ARTIST: Mario Larrinaga. EFFECTS CAMERA: Russell Cully. SOUND EFFECTS: Harry Essmanti. SPECIAL MAKE-UP EFFECTS: Maurice Seiderman. 119 mins. RKO Radio Pictures.

After the death of newspaper tycoon Charles Foster Kane (Orson Welles), a journalist interviews the man's acquaintances in an attempt to discover the meaning of his last word: 'Rosebud . . .'

Hundreds of subtle effects shots made the modestly budgeted *Citizen Kane* look like a lavish epic. Matte paintings enlarged the interiors of Kane's mansion 'Xanadu' and the exterior of the Kane newspaper offices. Clever optical printing multiplied the crowds at a political rally and combined live action and models to exaggerate the size of an opera house. Hanging miniatures were used to add ceilings to sets, and stop-motion animation created the movement of vehicles on the Xanadu building site. Convincing make-up effects made Welles look both younger and considerably older than his real age (<74).

CLOSE ENCOUNTERS OF THE THIRD KIND (1977)
DIRECTOR: Steven Spielberg. SPECIAL PHOTOGRAPHIC EFFECTS: Douglas Trumbull. DIRECTOR OF EFFECTS PHOTOGRAPHY: Richard Yuricich. MECHANICAL EFFECTS: Roy Arbogast, George Polkinghorne. MATTE ARTISTS: Matthew Yuricich, Rocco Gioffre. CHIEF MODELMAKER: Greg Jein. MOTHERSHIP CINEMATOGRAPHER: Dennis Muren. EXTRATERRESTRIAL REALIZATION: Carlo Rambaldi, Isidoro Raponi. 135 mins (1980 special edition: 132 mins; 1998 collector's edition: 137 mins). Columbia Pictures.

Though kept secret by the government, mankind's first contact with alien life cannot be hidden from a number of ordinary people who find themselves mysteriously drawn to the chosen landing site.

Spielberg's first major visual effects film used a combination of traditional techniques and cutting-edge technology to create some awe-inspiring effects sequences. Shots of the Indiana landscape were produced using forced-perspective models with miniature houses as small as one inch in height. These models were photographed and used as front-projection backgrounds for full-scale sets used during live-action scenes. Front projection was also used to create the shimmering light patterns on the belly of the alien mothership. The mothership itself was a 2 m (6 ft) model with thousands of tiny lights created using individual internal bulbs, fibre optics and neon-filled aluminium tubes drilled with minute holes. Using a pioneering motion-control system, spacecraft models were filmed in a smoke-filled environment to give them a magical glowing effect and, in the case of the mothership, vast scale. Physical effects included turning a car and a camera upside down simultaneously to create a shot in which the contents of the car float upwards as a spaceship moves overhead.

DARBY O'GILL AND THE LITTLE PEOPLE (1959)
DIRECTOR: Robert Stevenson. SPECIAL EFFECTS: Peter Ellenshaw. OPTICAL PROCESSES: Eustace Lycett. ANIMATION EFFECTS: Joshua Meador. 90 mins. Walt Disney Productions.

An Irish caretaker (Albert Sharpe) falls down a well and into the kingdom of the leprechauns.

One of the best effects films of its day, *Darby O'Gill* used a range of techniques, including deep-focus photography and sodium-vapour travelling mattes, to create shots of full-sized people interacting with leprechauns. Normal-sized sets were combined with oversized replicas using split-screen techniques. Leprechauns interacted with huge models of human limbs while actors playing humans sometimes appeared with small puppets. There are excellent animation effects such as the addition of an animated mouth to a real horse, and some beautiful matte paintings create the rural Irish locations.

DESTINATION MOON (1950)
DIRECTOR: Irving Pichel. VISUAL EFFECTS TECHNICAL SUPERVISOR: John S. Abbott. MECHANICAL EFFECTS SUPERVISOR: Lee Zavitz. EFFECTS PHOTOGRAPHY: Lionel Lindon. MATTE PAINTINGS AND BACKDROPS: Chesley Bonestell. ANIMATOR: Fred Madison. MAKE-UP: Webster Phillips. 91 mins. United Artists.

After governmental budget cuts, an inventor persuades private investors to pay for his rocket so that the USA can reach the moon before the Russians.

The first great science fiction movie of the 50s, *Destination Moon* was designed to be as scientifically accurate as possible. The surface of the moon was built on a sound stage where forced-perspective landscaping combined with small people dressed as astronauts helped to give a huge sense of scale. Two thousand car headlamps were used to create the stars in the sky. A full-size 150-foot-high rocket set was built in the Mojave Desert, but a model was substituted for the take-off scenes. Stop-motion was used for the landing of the ship and scenes in which astronauts walk along its hull. Full-scale spacewalk scenes were created by hanging actors from wires and manipulating them like puppets. Rubber membranes fitted to actors' faces and operated by hidden levers stretched their skin to produce the effects of G forces when taking off. Academy Award for Best Special Effects.

EARTHQUAKE (1974)
DIRECTOR: Mark Robson. SPECIAL EFFECTS CINEMATOGRAPHER: Clifford Stine. SPECIAL

PHOTOGRAPHIC EFFECTS/MATTE PAINTINGS: Albert J. Whitlock. MINIATURES SUPERVISOR: Glen E. Robinson. MECHANICAL EFFECTS: Frank Brendell, Jack McMasters, Lou Ami. 122 mins. Universal.

When Los Angeles is rocked by a huge earthquake, its citizens are affected in different ways.

Much of *Earthquake*'s full-scale destruction was real – pre-weakened full-scale sets were built on enormous shaker platforms, and six-ton blocks of concrete were dropped just feet from leading actors. Perfect miniature re-creations of landmark buildings were designed to shake apart, and the footage of miniature destruction carefully combined with that of real locations. The Hollywood dam was re-created as a 17 m (56 ft) long miniature – though the problems of miniaturizing water marred some shots of its actual destruction. Over 40 exquisite matte paintings expanded the damage done to the city. **Academy Award for Special Achievements in Visual Effects and a Scientific and Technical Academy Award for the invention of a camera–shaking device.**

THE EXORCIST (1973)
DIRECTOR: William Friedkin. SPECIAL MAKE-UP EFFECTS: Dick Smith. OPTICAL EFFECTS: Marv Ystrom. SPECIAL EFFECTS SUPERVISOR: Marcel Vercoutere. SPECIAL SOUND EFFECTS: Ron Nagle, Doc Siegel, Gonzalo Cavira, Bob Fine. 122 mins. Warner Bros.

A young girl (Linda Blair) becomes possessed by a demon.

For one of the most notorious horror films ever made, Dick Smith turned actress Linda Blair into a child possessed by the demon Pazuzu. In one shot, the words 'help me' appear on the child's stomach. This was achieved by painting the phrase in a chemical that made the skin on a foam rubber stomach swell. The fake stomach was then filmed as heat guns evaporated the chemical, returning the skin to normal. When the resulting film was projected backwards, the words seemed to appear in the flesh. To make the child spew green vomit, hidden pipes were run along the cheeks and into the mouth of stunt double Eileen Dietz. A nozzle in the mouth then sprayed pea soup on cue. The film marked the first use of 'bladder effects' – for a shot in which the girl's neck puffs up, a balloon was concealed under disguised false skin and inflated with air. Smith's subtlest achievement was to transform the 44-year-old actor Max von Sydow into a 70-year-old. So that performers' breath would be visible in some scenes, the child's bedroom was built within a giant refrigerator. **Academy Award for Best Sound.**

FANTASTIC VOYAGE (1966)
DIRECTOR: Richard Fleischer. VISUAL EFFECTS: L.B. Abbott. OPTICAL CINEMATOGRAPHY: Art Cruickshank. MATTE ARTIST: Emil Kosa. MINIATURE SUPERVISOR: Howard Lydecker. MINIATURISTS: Marcel Delgado, Roy Arbogast. WIRE FLOATING/FLYING EFFECTS: Peter Foy. 100 mins. Twentieth Century Fox.

An assassination attempt is made on an important scientist who is defecting to the West. A team of doctors and a submarine are shrunk to microscopic size and injected into the scientist's bloodstream in the hope of repairing the damage to his brain.

Fantastic Voyage re-created the inside of the human body as a series of huge, accurately detailed sets. The brain set was 30 m (100 ft) long and 11 m (35 ft) wide while the heart set was 130 feet long and 30 feet high complete with working valves and muscles. A full-sized submarine 13 m (42 ft) in length and weighing 4 tons was built for use in these scenes. Transparent arteries were made to look as if they had blood cells moving within them by using a colour wheel that projected violet and pink discs onto their walls. Shots of actual cells moving through the bloodstream were created by filming blobs of heated Vaseline and mineral oil,

which floated in water. Scenes in which the explorers swim through the body were created by suspending performers on wires and filming at three times normal speed. **Academy Award for Best Visual Effects.**

FORBIDDEN PLANET (1956)
DIRECTOR: Fred McLeod Wilcox. SPECIAL EFFECTS SUPERVISOR: A. Arnold Gillespie. MATTE ARTISTS: Warren Newcombe, Howard Fisher, Henri Hillinick. MINIATURES SUPERVISOR: Maximillian Fabian. ANIMATION SUPERVISOR: Joshua Meador. ANIMATORS: Joe Alves, Dwight Carlisle, Ronn Cobb. OPTICAL PHOTOGRAPHY: Irving C. Reis. 98 mins. MGM.

A team of astronauts lands on the planet of Altair IV to search for survivors from a previous mission. Only two people and their robot are found, but a strange creature begins to attack the newly arrived visitors. A science fiction update of Shakespeare's *The Tempest*.

One of the best effects films of the 50s, *Forbidden Planet* still looks good when seen today. The *United Planets Cruiser* spaceship was a combination of models flown on wires and filmed at high speed; a full-scale studio mock-up of the bottom half of the craft was also built – the top section was matted in for long shots. Simple but effective techniques included the use of split screens to make a leaping tiger vanish when shot by the Captain (Leslie Nielsen), and a hand-drawn animated Monster of the Id. Impressive sets included the surface of the planet Altair IV and the spacecraft cockpit – its flashing lights and control panels required 43 km (27 miles) of electrical wiring. For many people the film's most memorable character is Robby the Robot – a bulbous two-legged droid with a transparent domed head and concertina arms. Robby's flashing lights, spinning antennae and other moving parts required 762 m (2,500 ft) of electrical wiring which emerged from one heel and ran to a nearby control panel. Robby was so popular (and expensive) that MGM reused him in *The Invisible Boy* (1957) the following year.

FORREST GUMP (1994)
DIRECTOR: Robert Zemeckis. SPECIAL VISUAL EFFECTS: Industrial Light and Magic. VISUAL EFFECTS SUPERVISOR: Ken Ralston. OPTICAL SUPERVISOR: Bruce Vecchitto. CG SUPERVISORS: George Murphy, Stephen Rosenbaum. SPECIAL EFFECTS SUPERVISOR: Allen Hall. SOUND DESIGN: Randy Thom. 142 mins. Paramount.

A slow-witted man (Tom Hanks) drifts through life and experiences a number of extraordinary historic situations along the way.

Robert Zemeckis has always made use of visual effects for storytelling purposes rather than simply for show, and *Gump* is typical of the way in which he employs effects to enhance realism rather than create the unbelievable. The opening sequence of a feather drifting through the sky was created by digitally blending together dozens of blue-screen shots of a real feather. Scenes set in Vietnam involved digital matte painting, and actor Gary Sinise had his legs digitally removed for his portrayal of a Vietnam veteran. Other highlights included the digital manipulation of stock footage to show Hanks interacting with historical figures such as Richard Nixon, John F. Kennedy and John Lennon. Crowd replication was used to create huge numbers of people in a stadium and a political rally. **Academy Award for Best Visual Effects.**

JASON AND THE ARGONAUTS (1963)
DIRECTOR: Don Chaffey. SPECIAL VISUAL EFFECTS: Ray Harryhausen. 104 mins. Columbia.

The fabled Jason (Todd Armstrong) travels on board his ship, the *Argo*, in search of the Golden Fleece, encountering a host of mythical gods and beasts along the way.

Considered by many (including the animator himself) to be Harryhausen's best work, *Jason* contains some of the most memorable stop-motion sequences ever committed to film. Highlights include Talos, an enormous bronze statue who comes to life when the treasure he guards is threatened. With his startlingly impassive face, the character creaks and grinds as he moves – a deliberate attempt to indicate the rusting of joints rather than the bad animation claimed by some critics. Other characters include a seven-headed Hydra and a pair of hideously devilish half-bird, half-human harpies. The film is most remembered for the amazing sequence in which three men fight seven sword-wielding skeletons. The extraordinary interaction between actors and puppets makes this perhaps the most complex and thrilling stop-motion scene ever achieved.

JURASSIC PARK (1993)
DIRECTOR: Steven Spielberg. SPECIAL VISUAL EFFECTS: Industrial Light and Magic. FULL-MOTION DINOSAURS: Dennis Muren. LIVE-ACTION DINOSAURS: Stan Winston. DINOSAUR SUPERVISOR: Phil Tippett. SPECIAL DINOSAUR EFFECTS: Michael Lantieri. SOUND DESIGN: Gary Rydstrom. 126 mins. Universal.

Using fossilized DNA, scientists genetically re-create living dinosaurs for display in an island theme park. Based on the novel by Michael Crichton.

Jurassic Park was the film that finally convinced the world that the computer was the effects tool of the future. ILM's computer-generated dinosaurs had a life never before captured in an artificially created performance. Highlights include a tyrannosaurus rex attack at night, in which a digital dinosaur snatches a real actor from a toilet – the actor being replaced by a digital performer at the last moment – and a stampeding herd of Gallimimus. Computer animation was complemented with animatronic creations that ranged from a 12 m (40 ft) T rex to a tiny hatchling, as well as a number of close-up feet, arms and heads which intercut seamlessly with the CG work. Dinosaurs were made all the more convincing by brilliant sound design which created their growls and roars by mixing a number of real animal calls. As well as creating the interaction of digital dinosaurs with real environments, physical effects included a number of impressive set pieces, such as an artificial tree with breakaway branches to enable a full-sized jeep to be dropped through it. **Academy Awards for Best Visual Effects, Sound and Sound Effects Editing.** (<210)

KING KONG (1933)
DIRECTOR: Merian C. Cooper, Ernest B. Schoedsack. SPECIAL EFFECTS SUPERVISOR: Willis O'Brien. ANIMATION PUPPETS: Marcel Delgado. SPECIAL EFFECTS TECHNICIANS: E.B. Gibson, Orville Goldner, Fred Reefe, Carroll Shepphird. ARTISTS: Mario Larrinaga, Bryon L. Crabbe. OPTICAL EFFECTS: Linwood Dunn, William Ulm. REAR PROJECTION: Sydney Saunders. DUNNING PROCESS SUPERVISORS: Carroll H. Dunning, C. Dodge Dunning. WILLIAMS PROCESS SUPERVISION: Frank Williams. 103 mins. RKO Radio Pictures.

A film producer discovers an island populated by dinosaurs and a gigantic ape. The ape is captured and taken to New York in chains where it escapes and causes havoc.

The greatest effects film of its day, and one of the best ever, *Kong* used every technique available at the time. A full-size bust, arm and leg were built for close-ups, but most shots of Kong were created using an 46 cm (18 in) stop-motion puppet. Stop-motion animation was also used for the Skull Island dinosaurs, various shots of human characters, and the attacking aircraft and elevated train sequences. Traditional 2-D animation created a flock of seagulls on the approach to Skull Island. Composite shots were created using Williams process and Dunning process travelling mattes, double-exposure split screens and both miniature and full-sized rear projection. Glass shots were used to portray many locations including the establishing shots of Skull Island and the New York skyline. The front of

the Skull Island wall was a full-size set but the reverse of the wall was created by combining a miniature wall and foreground with footage of extras on the roof of a studio building. (<184)

KING KONG (2005)
DIRECTOR: Peter Jackson. WETA WORKSHOP SUPERVISOR: Richard Taylor. WETA WORKSHOP CONCEPT ARTIST: Miles Teves. VISUAL EFFECTS SUPERVISORS: Scott E. Anderson and Joe Letteri, George Murphy, Ben Snow, Marc Varisco. VISUAL EFFECTS DIRECTOR OF PHOTOGRAPY: Alex Funke. SOUND RE-RECORDING MIXER: Christopher Boyes. 187 mins. Universal.

Closely following the story of the original, Peter Jackson's labour of love is an outstanding visual effects triumph. New York was re-created digitally using global illumination to render sumptuous views of the city in intricate period detail. The ship *Venture* was produced using a combination of full-size craft and a finely detailed scale model floating on beautifully animated digital water. Skull Island was created almost entirely using painstakingly crafted miniature environments that were seamlessly combined with live action filmed on partially dressed full-size sets. The island is populated by many fabulous and often vile beasts, all rendered with incredible realism and integrated with the live action with great skill. The highlight of the show is the all-digital Kong which, apart from its size and range of expressions, appears indistinguishable from a live ape. Kong's stirring performance was based on motion-captured acting from actor Andy Serkis, who previously provided the performance of Gollum in the *Lord of the Rings* films. Kong's fur also puts in a great performance, looking totally realistic, even in extreme close-up, when flowing in the wind, brushing against objects or when matted and coated in mud. *King Kong* was a critically lauded epic that, while not a flop, mysteriously failed to do epic business. **Academy Awards for Achievement in Visual Effects, Sound Mixing and Sound Effects.**

THE LAST STARFIGHTER (1984)
DIRECTOR: Nick Castle. DIGITAL SCENE SIMULATION: John Whitney Jnr, Gary Demos (Digital Productions). SPECIAL EFFECTS SUPERVISOR: Kevin Pike. SPECIAL EFFECTS: James Dale Camomile, Michael Lantieri, Darrell D. Pritchett, Joseph C. Sasgen. 101 mins. Universal/Lorimar.

When he achieves a high score on his favourite video game, a teenage boy (Lance Guest) discovers that the game is actually a recruitment device used by a race of aliens.

An important landmark in the development of computer-generated images (or 'Digital Scene Simulation', as it was then commonly called), *The Last Starfighter* created all of its spaceship shots digitally. The new technology was still lacking many of the subtleties that make today's animation so convincing – most surfaces look too 'perfect' and there is no motion blur in shots of fast-moving spaceships. However, this film made the potential of the technique obvious. The building and animation of computer models took two-and-a-half years using a $15 million Cray Supercomputer – one of the most powerful computers in the world at that time. Gary Demos and John Whitney Jnr received a Scientific and Technical Academy Award for 'the practical simulation of motion picture photography by means of computer-generated images'.

THE LORD OF THE RINGS:
THE FELLOWSHIP OF THE RING (2001)

THE LORD OF THE RINGS:
THE TWO TOWERS (2002)

THE LORD OF THE RINGS:
THE RETURN OF THE KING (2003)

DIRECTOR: Peter Jackson. VISUAL EFFECTS SUPERVISORS: Jim Rygiel, Joe Letteri (*Towers* & *Return*), WETA Digital. ANIMATION SUPERVISOR: Randall William Cook. SUPERVISOR OF SPECIAL EFFECTS MAKEUP, CREATURES, ARMOUR & MINIATURES: Richard Taylor, Weta Workshop. VISUAL EFFECTS DIRECTOR OF PHOTOGRAPHY MINIATURE UNIT: Alex Funke. VISUAL EFFECTS CONSULTANT: Mark Stetson. VISUAL EFFECTS ART DIRECTOR: Paul Lasaine. PHYSICAL EFFECTS SUPERVISOR: Steve Ingram. ADDITIONAL VISUAL EFFECTS: Animal Logic, Digital Domain, Hatch Productions, Hybrid Enterprises, Oktober, Rhythm and Hues, Rising Sun Pictures, Sandbox Pictures, Sony Pictures Imageworks, Tweak Films. 178 mins (*The Fellowship of the Ring*); 179 mins (*The Two Towers*); 201 mins (*The Return of the King*). New Line Cinema.

The epic journey of a hobbit and his friends on a quest to destroy a powerful ring and prevent it from falling into the hands of evil.

Peter Jackson's towering trilogy has become one of the most financially successful movie franchises ever. Superb attention to detail combined with both cutting-edge and traditional technologies also produced among the most satisfying and substantial effects films for years. In a trilogy overflowing with masterful visual effects, highlights included Gollum, a truly expressive CG character produced using subsurface scattering for lifelike skin; vast computer-generated battles on a scale never before seen; stunning locations created through the use of traditional models and digital matte paintings; the convincing interaction of differently scaled human and humanlike characters using both sophisticated and cleverly simplistic methods; and a range of convincingly ghoulish characters produced with superb prosthetics. Each film won an Academy Award for Best Visual Effects and there were additional awards for Make-up and Sound Effects Editing. (<222)

THE LOST WORLD (1925)
DIRECTOR: Harry Hoyt. RESEARCH AND TECHNICAL DIRECTION (STOP-MOTION ANIMATION): Willis O'Brien. CHIEF TECHNICIAN: Fred W. Jackman. TECHNICAL STAFF: Marcel Delgado (ANIMATION PUPPETS), Homer Scott, F. Devereaux Jennings, Vernon L. Walker. ART TECHNICIAN: Ralph Hammeras. 108 mins. First National Pictures.

After claiming to have discovered the existence of dinosaurs, Professor Challenger (Wallace Beery) persuades a national newspaper to finance a scientific expedition to a remote jungle plateau. Based on the novel by Sir Arthur Conan Doyle.

The first great creature movie, *The Lost World* is a silent masterpiece that still makes remarkable viewing. Puppet dinosaurs animated by Willis O'Brien were built by Marcel Delgado using wood and wire skeletons covered with foam rubber – a great improvement over the clay puppets which until then had been the norm. Animation highlights include a stampede of some 15 dinosaurs on the run from an erupting volcano and morning-after shots in which herds of dinosaurs browse on vegetation and the carcass of a dead creature. The dinosaurs were not the film's only animated elements; an apatosaur in a swamp was surrounded by pliable gelatin which was remoulded between shots to look like mud. Animation and live action were effectively combined with clever split screens. The brontosaur which rampages around London had both its tail and head built full-size. The film was originally around 108 minutes in length (depending on the speed of projection) but was later re-edited to half this length. Much of the original footage has been lost over the years but a campaign to find and restore the lost scenes is gradually returning the film to its full glory.

THE MATRIX (1999)
THE MATRIX RELOADED (2003)
THE MATRIX REVOLUTIONS (2003)

DIRECTORS: Larry & Andy Wachowski. VISUAL EFFECTS SUPERVISOR: John Gaeta and Dan Glass, John DesJardin. PROSTHETICS: Bob McCarron. ANIMATRONICS: Paul Katte, Nick Nicolaou (Make-up Effects Group). SPECIAL EFFECTS SUPERVISORS: Brian Cox, Steve Courtley, Clay Pinney. CG SUPERVISOR (ESC): George Borshukov. MODELS AND MINIATURES SUPERVISOR: Fon Davis. VISUAL EFFECTS: Amalgamated Pixels, Animal Logic, BUF, Bullet Time, CIS Hollywood, ESC, Giant Killer Robots, Hatch Productions, Manex Visual Effects, Mass. Illusions, Pacific Title, Sony Pictures Imageworks, Spectrum Studios, Tippett Studio, Tweak Films. 136 mins (*The Matrix*); 138 mins (*The Matrix Reloaded*); 129 mins (*The Matrix Revolutions*). Warner Bros.

A computer programmer (Keanu Reeves) is recruited to help fight a form of artificial intelligence which, having defeated mankind in a global war, now keeps most of humanity plugged into an artificial reality.

Among the most visually innovative movies of the decade, the *Matrix* trilogy used groundbreaking digital techniques to produce some stunning action sequences. The films are best remembered for their 'bullet time' shots in which performers supported on wires were photographed with hundreds of still cameras to create a single shot that moved around an extreme slow-motion performance. Considerable advancements were also made in aspects of 'virtual cinematography' – the creation of photorealistic environments, models and characters through the use of image-based techniques. Photographs of real buildings were used to produce computer-generated buildings using projection mapping techniques and actors filmed with high-definition video from multiple angles were used to produce unnervingly realistic digital doubles – most particularly for a sequence in *Reloaded* in which hundreds of versions of the same character take part in a brawl. Physical effects included impressive gunfight sequences and spectacular highway chases, though, like everything else in the films, they were heavily reliant on digital manipulation. *The Matrix* won Academy Awards for Best Visual Effects, Sound and Sound Effects Editing.

METROPOLIS (1926)
DIRECTOR: Fritz Lang. SPECIAL EFFECTS: Eugen Schüfftan. 120 mins. UFA.

In the year 2000 the suppressed working classes of a great city live and work below ground. When the workers become agitated, they are calmed by a saintly girl called Maria. But a mad scientist, Rotwang, creates a robot version of Maria who incites the peasants to revolt.

The first great science fiction film, *Metropolis* used a range of effects to conjure its vision of a great city of the future. The city itself was a miniature brought to life by animated cars and aircraft. Matte paintings were used for aerial views of the city and for shots such as that of the sports stadium. Other tricks included multiple-exposure shots to indicate the hero's confused state of mind and early rear projection to create images on television screens. (<124)

MIGHTY JOE YOUNG (1949)
DIRECTOR: Ernest B. Schoedsack. VISUAL EFFECTS DESIGNER AND DIRECTOR: Willis O'Brien. STOP-MOTION ANIMATOR: Ray Harryhausen. SECOND STOP-MOTION ANIMATOR: Peter Peterson. STOP-MOTION TECHNICIANS: Marcel Delgado, George Lufgren, Harry Cunningham. MATTE ARTISTS: Fitch Fulton, Louis Litchtenfield, Jack Shaw. VISUAL EFFECTS CINEMATOGRAPHERS: Harold Stine, Bert Willis. OPTICAL CINEMATOGRAPHY: Linwood Dunn. MECHANICAL EFFECTS: Jack Lannon. 94 mins. ARKO (Argosy Pictures Corporation/RKO Radio Pictures).

A giant gorilla, 'Joe Young', is taken from his home in Africa to become a theatrical attraction in America. However, the unhappy ape escapes and causes panic on the streets.

Mighty Joe Young contains some of the subtlest stop-motion characterization ever created. Though Willis O'Brien supervised the effects for the film, most of the animation was achieved by his young apprentice, Ray Harryhausen. Harryhausen brought an incredible sense of personality to the giant ape, Joe. This is particularly apparent in scenes where the despondent ape aimlessly plays with the dirt on the floor of his cage and stares, with watery eyes, longingly from his window. The film's action sequences are thrilling. Highlights include a scene in which live-action cowboys on horseback attempt to lasso Joe. The real lassoes blend seamlessly with their animated replacements. At times the cowboys and their horses are also animated. Perhaps the most thrilling part of the film is its emotional ending in which Joe rescues a baby from a burning orphanage – a perfect synthesis of stop-motion, models, mattes and rear projection. O'Brien won a long overdue Oscar for his work on the film.

1941 (1979)
DIRECTOR: Steven Spielberg. VISUAL EFFECTS SUPERVISOR: Larry Robinson. VISUAL EFFECTS CINEMATOGRAPHER: William A. Fraker. OPTICAL EFFECTS: Frank Van der Veer. OPTICAL CONSULTANT: L.B. Abbott. MATTE ARTIST: Matthew Yuricich. MECHANICAL EFFECTS SUPERVISOR: A.D. Flowers. MINIATURES SUPERVISOR: Greg Jein. MINIATURE LIGHTING DESIGNER: Robin Leyden. 118 mins. Universal/Columbia.

After the Japanese attack on Pearl Harbor, the sighting of a submarine convinces the citizens of Los Angeles that they are also under attack.

1941 contains some of the most exquisite model work ever filmed. Beautiful miniature re-creations of 1940s Los Angeles included a forced-perspective Hollywood Boulevard and an oceanside amusement park complete with working 3.5 m (12 ft) Ferris wheel. The flight of model aircraft was achieved through a combination of radio control (Grand Canyon sequence) and an improved version of the Lydecker technique which allowed complex aerial manoeuvres to be achieved over the Hollywood Boulevard set. Major physical effects included pushing a full-sized house off a cliff. A Scientific and Technical Achievement Award was given by the Academy in recognition of the system used to fly model aircraft.

RAIDERS OF THE LOST ARK (1981)
DIRECTOR: Steven Spielberg. SPECIAL VISUAL EFFECTS: Industrial Light and Magic. VISUAL EFFECTS SUPERVISOR: Richard Edlund. MECHANICAL EFFECTS SUPERVISOR: Kit West. OPTICAL EFFECTS: Bruce Nicholson. MATTE PAINTING SUPERVISOR: Alan Maley. MATTE ARTIST: Mike Pangrazio. SUPERVISING ANIMATORS: Samuel Comstock, Dietrich Friesen. CLOUD EFFECTS: Gary Platek. SPECIAL MAKE-UP EFFECTS: Christopher Walas. 115 mins. Lucasfilm/Paramount.

Indiana Jones (Harrison Ford), dashing professor of archaeology, is dispatched by the US government with a mission to capture the lost Ark of the Covenant before the Nazis do.

Though created in the style of the Saturday morning serials of the 40s and 50s, *Raiders*' effects are anything but crude. Matte paintings include the docks around a 30s Clipper plane, a Himalayan village and the closing shot of a vast warehouse – one of the lengthiest matte shots ever. Models include a Nazi U-boat and a German jeep which, with its passengers, is stop-motion animated to appear as if falling from a matte-painted cliff. The sequence in which the Ark of the Covenant is opened is a torrent of special effects animation ending with some unusual cloud tank shots. The same sequence includes a gruesome melting head – achieved by building up layers of coloured wax on a skull before melting it with heat guns while filming at a slow frame rate. Impressive physical effects include a giant boulder that chases the hero through a tunnel, and a full-scale replica of a Nazi flying-wing aircraft which is blown up spectacularly. The film was followed by two sequels, each crammed with equally stunning effects. **Academy Awards for Best Visual Effects and Sound.**

STAR WARS:
EPISODE I **THE PHANTOM MENACE** (1999)
STAR WARS:
EPISODE II **ATTACK OF THE CLONES** (2002)
STAR WARS:
EPISODE III **REVENGE OF THE SITH** (2005)

DIRECTOR: George Lucas. SPECIAL VISUAL EFFECTS: Industrial Light and Magic. VISUAL EFFECTS SUPERVISORS: John Knoll (Ep I, II, III), Dennis Muren (Ep I), Scott Squires (Ep I), Roger Guyett (Ep III). ANIMATION DIRECTOR: Rob Coleman. CREATURE EFFECTS SUPERVISOR: Nick Dudman (Ep I). MODEL SUPERVISOR: Steve Gawley (Ep I), Brian Gernand (Ep II & III). SPECIAL EFFECTS SUPERVISOR: Peter Hutchinson (Ep I), Frank W. Tarantino (Ep I), David Young (Ep II & III). SOUND DESIGN: Ben Burtt. 133 mins (*The Phantom Menace*); 142 mins (*Attack of the Clones*); 140 mins (*Revenge of the Sith*). Lucasfilm/Twentieth Century Fox.

A peaceful and democratic galaxy is justly overseen by the noble Jedi Knights. However, a trade federation has started a conflict that will lead to the downfall of democracy and the rise of a new, evil Empire.

At the time of its release, *The Phantom Menace* was the most sophisticated digital effects film in the history of the cinema. The highlights of the film were its computer-generated characters such as Watto, Sebulba, Boss Nass and, above all, Jar Jar Binks – totally convincing computer-generated performers that interacted with live-action actors at a level never achieved before. The film used the 'digital backlot' technique more than any previous film – shooting actors with minimal sets and props and creating the rest of the environment in post-production. Digital technology also allowed the director to combine action filmed at different times and locations, giving him the freedom to create any shot he required. Though many models and environments were digitally created, the film was still one of the biggest physical model assignments ever – some 500 models of ships, cities and robots were built and filmed. Despite the prevalence of characters created in the computer, many were still brought to life using traditional prosthetic effects and puppeteering techniques. *Attack of the Clones* and *Revenge of the Sith* built on the achievements of *Phantom*, relying increasingly on sophisticated computer-generated environments and finessing character animation techniques. *Clones* and *Sith* were filmed entirely on high-definition video. (<240)

STAR WARS: EPISODE IV **A NEW HOPE** (1977)
DIRECTOR: George Lucas. SPECIAL VISUAL EFFECTS: Industrial Light and Magic. SPECIAL PHOTOGRAPHIC EFFECTS SUPERVISOR: John Dykstra. SPECIAL EFFECTS CAMERAMEN: Richard Edlund, Dennis Muren. SPECIAL PRODUCTION AND MECHANICAL EFFECTS SUPERVISOR: John Stears. MAKE-UP SUPERVISOR: Stuart Freeborn. COMPOSITE OPTICAL PHOTOGRAPHY: Robert Blalack. MATTE ARTIST: Harrison Ellenshaw. MINIATURE PYROTECHNICS: Joe Viskocil, Greg Auer. STOP-MOTION ANIMATION: Jon Berg, Phil Tippett. SOUND DESIGN: Ben Burtt. 136 mins. Lucasfilm/Twentieth Century Fox.

An idealistic young farm boy becomes involved in the rescue of a princess and the struggle between a band of rebels and the evil galactic Empire.

Probably the most important effects film ever made and responsible for kick-starting the special effects revolution of the 80s and 90s, *Star Wars* used every category of effect with stunning results. Computerized motion control was developed to film the many blue-screen model spaceship shots with realistic motion blur. The interior and exterior of the Death Star was largely portrayed using seamless matte paintings. Effects animation created laser beams, blaster bolts and the famous light sabres. Stop-motion animation produced an unusual game of chess. Early computer animation was used for battle graphic sequences. Special effects make-up created a range of aliens and Han Solo's shaggy sidekick Chewbacca. Superb sound design was as responsible for the creation of new worlds as were the visual effects. A 1997 special edition contained new scenes and digital effects. **Academy Awards for Best Visual Effects and Sound Effects.** (<150)

STAR WARS:

EPISODE V **THE EMPIRE STRIKES BACK** (1980)
DIRECTOR: Irvin Kershner. SPECIAL VISUAL EFFECTS: Industrial Light and Magic. SPECIAL VISUAL EFFECTS SUPERVISORS: Richard Edlund, Brian Johnson. MECHANICAL EFFECTS SUPERVISION: Nick Allder. SPECIAL CREATURE DESIGN: Stuart Freeborn. EFFECTS DIRECTOR OF PHOTOGRAPHY: Dennis Muren. STOP-MOTION ANIMATION: Jon Berg, Phil Tippett. ANIMATION AND ROTOSCOPE SUPERVISOR: Peter Kuran. MATTE PAINTING SUPERVISOR: Harrison Ellenshaw. MATTE ARTISTS: Ralph McQuarrie, Mike Pangrazio. MINIATURE PYROTECHNICS: Joe Viskocil, Dave Pier, Thaine Morris. SOUND DESIGN: Ben Burtt. 124 mins. Lucasfilm/Twentieth Century Fox.

After the temporary victory of the Rebel Alliance in *Star Wars*, the Imperial forces track down and destroy the rebels' hidden base.

Incredibly, the second film in the *Star Wars* series managed to top the effects achievements of its predecessor. The first half-hour contains one of the greatest optical effects sequences ever achieved – a battle in the snow that includes superb stop-motion animation of Imperial AT-AT walkers and snow creatures animated using an early form of Go-Motion. The battle is also notable for excellent travelling matte work that placed white snowspeeder craft against snow backgrounds without noticeable matte lines. A major new character, Yoda, was perhaps the most convincing screen puppet yet created. Beautiful matte paintings created Cloud City on Bespin. The action highlight of the film is a chase through an asteroid field – the most complex optical compositing achieved to that date. A 1997 special edition contained new scenes and digital effects. **Academy Awards for Best Visual Effects and Sound.**

STAR WARS:

EPISODE VI **RETURN OF THE JEDI** (1983)
DIRECTOR: Richard Marquand. SPECIAL VISUAL EFFECTS: Industrial Light and Magic. VISUAL EFFECTS SUPERVISORS: Richard Edlund, Dennis Muren, Ken Ralston. MECHANICAL EFFECTS SUPERVISOR: Kit West. MAKE-UP AND CREATURE DESIGN: Stuart Freeborn, Phil Tippett. STOP-MOTION ANIMATOR: Tom St. Amand. MATTE PAINTING SUPERVISOR: Mike Pangrazio. MATTE ARTISTS: Chris Evans, Frank Ordaz. OPTICAL PHOTOGRAPHY SUPERVISOR: Bruce Nicholson. SOUND DESIGN: Ben Burtt. 131 mins. Lucasfilm/Twentieth Century Fox.

The Empire is building a huge new space station which the Rebels must destroy before it becomes fully operational.

A special effects tour de force which contains some of the greatest effects work of the *Star Wars* series. The film begins with a major creature sequence, the star of which is Jabba the Hutt – the largest and most complex animatronic

character built to that date. Other characters in the film include rod puppets, rubber suits, stop-motion puppets and dozens of furry Ewoks – teddy bear-like creatures performed by dwarfs wearing costumes. Highlights of the film include a stunning speeder-bike chase through a forest, stop-motion animated scout walkers that strut around during a forest battle, and space battles that rank among the most sophisticated examples of optical compositing ever achieved – some shots containing as many as 300 separate elements. Over 150 model spacecraft and locations were created for the film. A 1997 special edition contained new scenes and digital effects. **Academy Award for Best Visual Effects.**

TERMINATOR 2: JUDGMENT DAY (1991)
DIRECTOR: James Cameron. VISUAL EFFECTS SUPERVISORS: Dennis Muren & Robert Skotak. SPECIAL MAKE-UP AND TERMINATOR EFFECTS: Stan Winston. COMPUTER GRAPHICS: Industrial Light and Magic. OPTICAL PHOTOGRAPHY SUPERVISOR: Bruce Vecchitto. SPECIAL VISUAL EFFECTS: Fantasy II Film Effects. SUPERVISOR: Gene Warren Jnr. SPECIAL VISUAL EFFECTS: 4ward Productions. SUPERVISOR: Robert Skotak. TERMINATOR POV/GRAPHIC DISPLAYS: Video Image. 137 mins. Carolco/Tri-Star.

A robot from the future (Arnold Schwarzenegger) arrives on Earth on a mission to protect a young boy who is destined to save humanity from destruction. However, a shape-shifting robot (Robert Patrick) comes with more sinister intentions.

ILM created *T2*'s amazing liquid metal T-1000 character using breakthroughs in 3-D morphing technology and software that could map 2-D images onto the surface of 3-D animated objects – used for shots such as the T-1000 rising out of a chequerboard floor. Digital work was complemented by perfectly executed traditional effects work – miniatures were used for the opening war sequences and the climactic crashing truck scene. A model Schwarzenegger was Go-Motion animated on top of a model truck with rear-projected background scenery. A model of Los Angeles blown apart by air cannon was combined with a CG nuclear shockwave. The body of a character disintegrating in the blast was a papier mâché model filled with shredded paper and blasted by air cannon. Make-up effects included a walking endoskeleton puppet, a life-cast bust of Schwarzenegger which when hit by bullets revealed the robot beneath, and various T-1000 reincarnations including a 'splash head' that sprung into two halves when shot at point-blank range – digital effects were used to create a shot of the head resealing itself. This was the first film to have all of its digital effects digitally composited – though other effects were still composited optically. **Academy Awards for Best Visual Effects, Make-up, Sound and Sound Effects Editing.**

THE THIEF OF BAGDAD (1940)
DIRECTORS: Ludwig Berger, Michael Powell, Tim Whelan. TRAVELLING MATTES: Tom Howard, Stanley Sayer. MATTE ARTISTS: W. Percy Day, Wally Veevers. MINIATURES: Johnny Mills. MECHANICAL EFFECTS: Lawrence W. Butler. SPECIAL SOUND EFFECTS: Jack Whitney. 106 mins. United Artists.

After an evil grand vizier (Conrad Veidt) deposes a good caliph (Miles Malleson), a young boy (Sabu) – the eponymous thief – helps to restore the throne to its rightful owner.

Thief was the first film to use Technicolor blue-screen travelling mattes for scenes such as a mechanical horse riding through the sky, the appearance of a giant djinni and shots of a flying carpet. Other effects included glass shots, matte paintings, and forced-perspective sets for the re-creation of the exotic city of Bagdad (filmed in a London suburb), model ships and giant mechanical props such as

an oversized djinni's foot and a spider. **Academy Award for Best Special Effects.**

THINGS TO COME (1936)
DIRECTOR: William Cameron Menzies. SPECIAL EFFECTS DIRECTOR: Ned Mann. SPECIAL EFFECTS ASSISTANTS: Lawrence W. Butler, Wally Veevers. SPECIAL EFFECTS PHOTOGRAPHY: Edward Cohen ASC, Harry Zech. MINIATURE DESIGNS: Ross Jacklin. MATTE PAINTINGS: W. Percy Day. ASSISTANT MATTE ARTIST: Peter Ellenshaw. 92 mins. London Films.

After a catastrophic world war, the citizens of Earth form a futuristic new society. Based on the book *The Shape of Things to Come* by H.G. Wells.

Though the production of *Things to Come* did not involve the development of any new techniques, the sheer number and quality of effects ensure its status as a landmark film. Superb matte paintings established the city Everytown, its destruction and eventual rebuilding. Thirty years of war were depicted by a series of scenes in which futuristic model tanks rumble across battlefields and aircraft swarm overhead. Live-action footage of real cities was carefully combined with scenes of miniature destruction using split-screen work. Optical printing effects superimposed text to show the passing of the years as well as legions of soldiers on the march. The film is best remembered for its scenes of a utopian technological future. Society reconstructs itself in an exciting montage of excellent effects work in which models, matte paintings and live action are combined using split screens, optical printing and rear projection. The vast city of the future was created by combining full-scale sets and models (complete with working lifts and monorails) with foreground miniatures and the Shuftan process.

TITANIC (1997)
DIRECTOR: James Cameron. SPECIAL VISUAL EFFECTS: Digital Domain. VISUAL EFFECTS SUPERVISOR: Rob Legato. DIGITAL EFFECTS SUPERVISOR: Mark Lasoff. 2-D DIGITAL EFFECTS SUPERVISOR: Michael Kanfer. ADDITIONAL VISUAL EFFECTS: Banned from the Ranch, Cinesite, CIS Hollywood, Digiscope, 4ward Productions, Hammerhead Productions Inc, Industrial Light and Magic, Light Matters Inc, Matte World Digital, Pacific Title Digital, Perceptual Motion Pictures, Pop Film. SPECIAL EFFECTS SUPERVISOR: Thomas L. Fisher. SPECIAL MAKE-UP EFFECTS: Greg Cannom. SOUND DESIGN: Christopher Boyes. 194 mins. Paramount/Twentieth Century Fox.

The romance between two young people of differing social backgrounds is played out against the doomed maiden voyage of the *Titanic*.

An effects film on an epic scale, *Titanic* combined cutting-edge effects technology and old-fashioned tricks to create some stunning sequences. Long shots of the ship were created by filming a 13.5 m (44 ft) 'miniature' with motion control and combining it with CG water, smoke, passengers and other elements. Larger-scale sections of the ship were built and sunk in a specially created tank and a full-scale ship was constructed in Mexico. Some interiors, such as the first-class lounge and the engine room, were exquisite miniatures with actors composited into them. Beautifully executed morph sequences acted as transitions between the present day and the past and even as a link to footage of the genuine *Titanic* wreck. Motion-captured performances allowed digital actors to perform many stunts, and digital face replacements put the faces of leading actors onto the bodies of stunt performers. Major physical effects included flooding full-scale sets with thousands of gallons of water. The soundtrack contained more sound elements than any other film in history. **Academy Awards for Best Visual Effects, Sound and Sound Effects Editing.**

TOY STORY (1995)
DIRECTOR: John Lasseter. ART DIRECTOR: Ralph Eggleston. SUPERVISING ANIMATOR: Pete Docter. DIRECTING ANIMATORS: Rich Quade, Ash Brannon. 80 mins. Disney/Pixar.

A young boy's collection of toys comes to life when nobody is looking. However, the harmony of the group is threatened with the arrival of a new high-tech spaceman, Buzz Lightyear.

The world's first computer-generated feature film, *Toy Story* thrilled children and adults alike with its mix of action and comedy. Director John Lasseter proved that computer-generated performances could be as good as anything in an ordinary animated film. Lasseter received a special Oscar for the production of this landmark film. (<198)

TRON (1982)
DIRECTOR: Steven Lisberger. VISUAL EFFECTS SUPERVISORS: Harrison Ellenshaw, Richard W. Taylor. COMPUTER ANIMATION: Digital Effects Inc, Triple-I, MAGI, Robert Abel & Associates. 96 mins. Walt Disney Productions.

A computer games designer (Jeff Bridges) finds himself inside the world of his computer where he is forced to fight for his life in an all too real video game competition.

Tron was an early showcase for computer animation, using the technology to create the action and environments within a computer. The film's non-computer-generated scenes were also a major effects task, requiring actors to be filmed in black and white so that glowing neon costumes and backgrounds could be added optically. (<162)

20,000 LEAGUES UNDER THE SEA (1954)
DIRECTOR: Richard Fleischer. VISUAL EFFECTS CINEMATOGRAPHER: Ralph Hammeras. PROCESS CINEMATOGRAPHER: Ub Iwerks. OPTICAL CINEMATOGRAPHY: Art Cruickshank, Eustace Lycett. ART DIRECTOR: Harper Goff. ANIMATION EFFECTS: Joshua Meador, John Hench. MATTE ARTIST: Peter Ellenshaw. MECHANICAL EFFECTS SUPERVISOR: Robert A. Mattey. MINIATURE CONSULTANTS: Howard and Theodore Lydecker. GIANT SQUID MODELLER: Chris Mueller. GIANT SQUID TECHNICIAN: Marcel Delgado. 127 mins. Walt Disney Productions.

An armed frigate sets out to discover the truth behind a strange beast that has been terrorizing sailors. The ship is attacked by the 'beast', and its survivors rescued by Captain Nemo (James Mason) in his futuristic submarine. Based on the novel by Jules Verne.

The effects highlight of *20,000 Leagues Under the Sea* is a sequence in which the submarine *Nautilus* is attacked by a giant squid. Weighing 2 tons and with eight 12 m (40 ft) tentacles, the mechanical beast was operated by a combination of electronics, hydraulics, pneumatics and old-fashioned puppeteering – each tentacle was controlled by some twelve hand-operated wires. The *Nautilus* was built as a 61 m (200ft) mock-up that actually floated in the sea, and as half a dozen miniatures ranging from 46 cm (18 in) to 7 m (22 ft) in length. Due to the difficulty of filming miniatures with early Cinemascope lenses, some models were built in artificially compressed proportions. These 'squeezed' models were filmed with normal camera lenses and then unsqueezed to the correct proportions when the resultant images were projected with an anamorphic lens. Glass shots by Peter Ellenshaw include a crater around the surfaced submarine and the landscape of Vulcania island. **Academy Awards for Best Special Effects and Art Direction.**

2001: A SPACE ODYSSEY (1968)
DIRECTOR: Stanley Kubrick. SPECIAL EFFECTS SUPERVISORS: Wally Gentleman, Tom Howard, Con Pederson, Douglas Trumbull, Wally Veevers. ADDITIONAL SPECIAL EFFECTS SUPERVISORS: Les Bowie, Charles Staffell. MATTE ARTISTS: Roy Naisbitt, John Rose. ADDITIONAL MATTE CINEMATOGRAPHY: Richard Yuricich. MAKE-UP: Stuart Freeborn. 161 mins. MGM.

After the discovery of a mysterious black obelisk on the surface of the moon, mankind is forced to search for answers about his place in the universe. Based on the short story *The Sentinel* by Arthur C. Clarke.

A towering special effects achievement, *2001: A Space Odyssey* used a range of innovative techniques to portray space flight as accurately as possible. The film made the first major use of front projection for the opening 'Dawn of Man' scenes, a shot in which Earth is seen from a window during a phone call, and for projecting live action into the windows of model spacecraft. Huge model spaceships, up to 16 m (54 ft) in length, were filmed using an early type of motion control. Optically produced travelling mattes were avoided by using multiple-pass exposures on the original negative, and hand-drawn mattes. The famous 'Stargate' sequence was created using the innovative slit scan animation technique. Convincing scenes of weightlessness were created with ingenious wire work. Physical effects achievements included a massive 12 m (38 ft) vertical barrel that rotated at 5 km (3 miles) per hour. This set represented the centrifuge of the Jupiter Mission spacecraft and was used to create shots of crew members walking around the walls of their ship. **Academy Award for Best Special Effects.** (<88)

THE WAR OF THE WORLDS (1953)
DIRECTOR: Byron Haskin. VISUAL EFFECTS SUPERVISOR: Gordon Jennings. VISUAL EFFECTS CINEMATOGRAPHER: W. Wallace Kelley. MATTE CINEMATOGRAPHY: Irmin Roberts. OPTICAL CINEMATOGRAPHY: Paul K. Lerpae. PROCESS CINEMATOGRAPHY: Farciot Edouart. MATTE ARTISTS: Ian Domela, Chesley Bonestell. MINIATURE SUPERVISOR: Ivyl Burks. MECHANICAL EFFECTS SUPERVISOR: Walter Hoffman. MARTIAN MAKE-UP: Charles Gemora. 85 mins. Paramount.

The Earth is invaded by a race of Martians against whom even the most powerful weapons are useless. Adapted from the novel by H.G. Wells.

Hugely expensive to make, and a smash hit at the box office, *The War of the Worlds* is the film that the effects producer George Pal is perhaps best remembered for. Three Martian ships, each 107 cm (42 in) in diameter, were built from copper and translucent plastic – allowing them to glow ominously from internal lights. The ships glided through the sky suspended on wires that were connected to an overhead gantry. The Martian craft's famous death-rays were created by burning welding wire with a blowtorch to create a stream of sparks. This was filmed against black and superimposed onto shots of the models. People and objects vaporized by the Martians were made to glow and disappear with effects animation. Large areas of Los Angeles and various Californian landscapes were built and destroyed in miniature. A Martian, complete with flapping gills and pulsating veins, was created from papier mâché, wire and sheet rubber – though it is most remembered for its spindly three-fingered hand. **Academy Award for Best Special Effects.**

WHO FRAMED ROGER RABBIT (1988)
DIRECTOR: Robert Zemeckis. SPECIAL VISUAL EFFECTS: Industrial Light and Magic. VISUAL EFFECTS SUPERVISOR: Ken Ralston. MECHANICAL EFFECTS SUPERVISORS: George Gibbs (UK), Michael Lantieri (US). DIRECTOR OF ANIMATION: Richard Williams. OPTICAL PHOTOGRAPHY SUPERVISOR: Edward Jones. VISUAL EFFECTS CAMERA OPERATOR: Scott Farrar. 103 mins. Warner Bros./Touchstone/Amblin.

In a world where cartoon characters interact with humans, a private detective (Bob Hoskins) is on a murder case in which the chief suspect is animated film star Roger Rabbit.

Roger Rabbit combined human performers with new and classic cartoon characters ('Toons') in the most spectacular film of its type ever made. During filming, physical props were manipulated on wires as if being used by invisible characters – bicycles rode on their own and pianos were played with invisible fingers. Cartoon characters were then hand-drawn and animated to match these physical effects before being optically composited into the live action. Animated characters genuinely look as if they are within the real environments; in the Ink and Paint Club scenes, where actors and Toons mingle, the Toons move in and out of pools of light in a smoky atmosphere with the same subtle changes of tone and colour as the human characters. **Academy Awards for Best Visual Effects and Sound Effects Editing.** (<176)

WILLOW (1988)
DIRECTOR: Ron Howard. SPECIAL VISUAL EFFECTS: Industrial Light and Magic. VISUAL EFFECTS SUPERVISORS: Dennis Muren, Phil Tippett, Michael McAlister. SPECIAL EFFECTS SUPERVISOR: John Richardson. STOP-MOTION ANIMATOR: Tom St. Amand. MAKE-UP SPECIAL EFFECTS: Nick Dudman. OPTICAL SUPERVISORS: John Ellis, Bruce Nicholson, Kenneth Smith. MATTE PAINTING SUPERVISOR: Chris Evans. MATTE ARTISTS: Caroleen Green, Paul Swendsen. CG SUPERVISORS: Douglas Scott, George Joblove. MORPHING SOFTWARE: Doug Smythe. 125 mins. Lucasfilm/MGM.

In a land of magic, a midget (Warwick Davis) tries to protect a baby boy from an evil queen who, according to prophecy, he will one day destroy.

Important as the first film to use 2-D digital morphing (for a sequence in which a number of creatures change into one another), *Willow* is an effects treat made in the final glory days of optical effects work. A pair of tiny pixies were created through a combination of travelling mattes and oversized props. Stop-motion brought to life a two-headed dragon, an enchanted brazier and the wings of a fairy queen. Effects animation created lightning and sparks. Animated smoke effects seen during the destruction of the evil queen were created using a complex form of slit scan. Special creature effects included dogs dressed as hellhounds and an animatronic possum. Includes some beautiful matte paintings.

YOUNG SHERLOCK HOLMES (1985)
DIRECTOR: Barry Levinson. SPECIAL VISUAL EFFECTS: Industrial Light and Magic. VISUAL EFFECTS SUPERVISOR: Dennis Muren. MOTION SUPERVISOR: David Allen. EFFECTS CAMERAMEN: Scott Farrar, Michael Owens. GO-MOTION ANIMATION: Harry Walton. OPTICAL SUPERVISOR: John Ellis. MATTE PAINTING SUPERVISOR: Chris Evans. PHOTOGRAPHY SUPERVISOR: Craig Barron. COMPUTER ANIMATOR: John Lasseter. 109 mins. Paramount.

Sherlock Holmes and Watson meet while at school and have their first adventure when they investigate a number of mysterious deaths.

Young Sherlock contained some beautiful matte paintings of Victorian London and some excellent animated sequences of small cakes that come to life as part of a drug-induced hallucination. The movie is most important for having the first computer-generated character to appear in a feature film – a stained-glass knight who leaps from a church window.

APPENDIX
ACADEMY AWARDS

Listed below are the recipients of awards given by the Academy of Motion Picture Arts and Sciences, better known as Academy Awards or Oscars. From 1937 until 1964 Oscars were awarded jointly for both special photographic effects and sound effects, after which the categories received dedicated awards. In each case awards are given to the individuals who supervised or contributed most to the effects in each film. Sadly only the film titles can be listed here. For more information about Academy Awards see page 46. Full details of Oscar winners and the recipients of Technical, Scientific and Engineering awards can be found on the Academy's own website: www.oscars.org

Winners are listed in bold, the name of the award in italic.

1929
Engineering Effects
Wings

1937
Achievement in Special Effects
Spawn of the North

1939
Achievement in Special Effects
Gone with the Wind
Only Angels Have Wings
The Private Lives of Elizabeth and Essex
The Rains Came
Topper Takes a Trip
Union Pacific
The Wizard of Oz

1940
Achievement in Special Effects
The Blue Bird
Boom Town
The Boys from Syracuse
Dr. Cyclops
Foreign Correspondent
The Invisible Man Returns
The Long Voyage Home
One Million B.C.
Rebecca
The Sea Hawk
Swiss Family Robinson
The Thief of Bagdad
Typhoon
Women in War

1941
Achievement in Special Effects
Aloma of the South Seas
Flight Command
I Wanted Wings
The Invisible Woman
The Sea Wolf
That Hamilton Woman
Topper Returns
A Yank in the R.A.F.
Dive Bomber

1942
Achievement in Special Effects
The Black Swan
Desperate Journey
Flying Tigers
Invisible Agent
Jungle Book
Mrs. Miniver
The Navy Comes Through
One of Our Aircraft Is Missing
The Pride of the Yankees
Reap the Wild Wind

1943
Achievement in Special Effects
Air Force
Bombardier
Crash Dive
The North Star
So Proudly We Hail!
Stand by for Action

1944
Achievement in Special Effects
The Adventures of Mark Twain
Days of Glory
Secret Command
Since You Went Away
The Story of Dr. Wassell
Thirty Seconds Over Tokyo
Wilson

1945
Achievement in Special Effects
Captain Eddie
Spellbound
They Were Expendable
A Thousand and One Nights
Wonder Man

1946
Achievement in Special Effects
Blithe Spirit
A Stolen Life

1947
Achievement in Special Effects
Green Dolphin Street
Unconquered

1948
Achievement in Special Effects
Deep Waters
Portrait of Jennie

1949
Achievement in Special Effects
Mighty Joe Young
Tulsa

1950
Achievement in Special Effects
Destination Moon
Samson and Delilah

1951
Achievement in Special Effects
When Worlds Collide

1952
Achievement in Special Effects
Plymouth Adventure

1953
Achievement in Special Effects
The War of the Worlds

1954
Achievement in Special Effects
Hell and High Water
Them!
20,000 Leagues Under the Sea

1955
Achievement in Special Effects
The Bridges at Toko-Ri
The Dam Busters
The Rains of Ranchipur

1956
Achievement in Special Effects
Forbidden Planet
The Ten Commandments

1957
Achievement in Special Effects
The Enemy Below
The Spirit of St. Louis

1958
Achievement in Special Effects
Tom Thumb
Torpedo Run

1959
Achievement in Special Effects
Ben-Hur
Journey to the Center of the Earth

1960
Achievement in Special Effects
The Last Voyage
The Time Machine

1961
Achievement in Special Effects
The Absent-Minded Professor
The Guns of Navarone

1962
Achievement in Special Effects
The Longest Day
Mutiny on the Bounty

1963
Achievement in Special Effects
The Birds
Cleopatra

1964
Achievement in Special Visual Effects
Mary Poppins
7 Faces of Dr. Lao

1965
Achievement in Special Visual Effects
The Greatest Story Ever Told
Thunderball

1966
Achievement in Special Visual Effects
Fantastic Voyage
Hawaii

1967
Achievement in Special Visual Effects
Doctor Dolittle
Tobruk

1968
Achievement in Special Visual Effects
Ice Station Zebra
2001: A Space Odyssey

1969
Achievement in Special Visual Effects
Krakatoa, East of Java
Marooned

1970
Achievement in Special Visual Effects
Patton
Tora! Tora! Tora!

1971
Achievement in Special Visual Effects
Bedknobs and Broomsticks
When Dinosaurs Ruled the Earth

1972
Special Achievement in Visual Effects
The Poseidon Adventure

1973
No award

1974
Special Achievement in Visual Effects
Earthquake

1975
Special Achievement in Visual Effects
The Hindenburg

1976
Special Achievement in Visual Effects
King Kong
Logan's Run

1977
Achievement in Visual Effects
Close Encounters of the Third Kind
Star Wars

1978
Special Achievement in Visual Effects
Superman

1979
Achievement in Visual Effects
Alien
The Black Hole
Moonraker
1941
Star Trek: The Motion Picture

1980
Special Achievement in Visual Effects
The Empire Strikes Back

1981
Achievement in Visual Effects
Dragonslayer
Raiders of the Lost Ark

1982
Achievement in Visual Effects
Blade Runner
E.T. the Extra-Terrestrial
Poltergeist

1983
Special Achievement in Visual Effects
Return of the Jedi

1984
Achievement in Visual Effects
Ghostbusters
Indiana Jones and the Temple of Doom
2010

1985
Achievement in Visual Effects
Cocoon
Return to Oz
Young Sherlock Holmes

1986
Achievement in Visual Effects
Aliens
Little Shop of Horrors
Poltergeist II: The Other Side

1987
Achievement in Visual Effects
Innerspace
Predator

1988
Achievement in Visual Effects
Die Hard
Who Framed Roger Rabbit
Willow

1989
Achievement in Visual Effects
The Abyss
The Adventures of Baron Munchausen
Back to the Future Part II

1990
Special Achievement in Visual Effects
Total Recall

1991
Achievement in Visual Effects
Backdraft
Hook
Terminator 2: Judgment Day

1992
Achievement in Visual Effects
Alien 3
Batman Returns
Death Becomes Her

1993
Achievement in Visual Effects
Cliffhanger
Jurassic Park
The Nightmare Before Christmas

1994
Achievement in Visual Effects
Forrest Gump
The Mask
True Lies

1995
Achievement in Visual Effects
Apollo 13
Babe

1996
Achievement in Visual Effects
Dragonheart
Independence Day
Twister

1997
Achievement in Visual Effects
The Lost World
Starship Troopers
Titanic

1998
Achievement in Visual Effects
Armageddon
Mighty Joe Young
What Dreams May Come

1999
Achievement in Visual Effects
The Matrix
Star Wars: Episode I The Phantom Menace
Stuart Little

2000
Achievement in Visual Effects
Gladiator
The Hollow Man
The Perfect Storm

2001
Achievement in Visual Effects
Artificial Intelligence: AI
The Lord of the Rings: The Fellowship of the Ring
Pearl Harbor

2002
Achievement in Visual Effects
The Lord of the Rings: The Two Towers
Spider-Man
Star Wars: Episode II Attack of the Clones

2003
Achievement in Visual Effects
The Lord of the Rings: The Return of the King
Master and Commander: The Far Side of the World
Pirates of the Caribbean: The Curse of the Black Pearl

2004
Achievement in Visual Effects
Harry Potter and the Prisoner of Azkaban
I, Robot
Spider-Man 2

2005
Achievement in Visual Effects
Chronicles of Narnia: The Lion, the Witch and the Wardrobe
King Kong
War of the Worlds

GLOSSARY

ADDITIVE PROCESS
A method of creating colour pictures by combining two or three images, each of which contains one of the three primary colours (red, green and blue). Red, green and blue light will produce white light when mixed equally and can be combined in different quantities to produce any colour in the spectrum.

ALGORITHM
A set of instructions written in a computer language which instructs the computer to perform a specific task.

ALIASING
A phenomenon present in digital images when the number or size of pixels used to describe an image are insufficient to create enough subtlety or detail, with the result that edges of objects can appear jagged. Anti-aliasing algorithms used during rendering help to identify and reduce the effect of aliasing.

ALPHA CHANNEL
When a computer-generated object or scene is rendered the result is a 2-D image in which each pixel is represented by four values. Three of these values describe the amounts of red, green and blue that combine to produce the pixel's final colour. The fourth value represents how transparent the pixel is. This is known as the 'alpha channel'. When one computer-generated image is combined with another during compositing, the alpha channel is therefore used to define how objects will look when layered on top of one another. In the case of animated scenes, the alpha channel is a form of built-in travelling matte.

AMBIENT LIGHT
A constant level of light that falls on CG objects no matter what lighting effects are in the scene.

AMBIENT OCCLUSION
Each point on the surface of a computer-generated object fires beams out in all directions in order to discover if any other objects in the scene will prevent light from reaching that point of the surface. Ambient occlusion is calculated as a separate pass during rendering and the result is a model whose surface has a certain amount of shadow 'built in'.

ANALOGUE
Used to describe any method of recording or transmitting sounds, images or data by creating and storing modulations such as size, width or density that are directly analogous to the subject in question.

ANAMORPHIC LENS
A lens that horizontally squeezes images during filming so that a disproportionately wide picture can be recorded on the almost square frame of standard 35 mm film. During projection, a second anamorphic lens is used to unsqueeze the image to its normal proportions.

ANIMATIC see PRE-VISUALIZATION

ANIMATION
The process of creating the illusion of movement in either models, puppets, pictures, artwork or computer-generated objects by causing them to move incrementally from one image to the next. When the resultant images are viewed at the normal speed of 24 frames per second (for normal 35 mm film), the subject appears to move independently.

ANIMATION CAMERA
Camera capable of photographing a single frame at a time, which points down at a flat table where artwork is arranged. Also called animation stand, rostrum camera or down-shooter.

ANIMATRONIC
Any remotely controlled system that uses pneumatics, hydraulics, cables, rods, or motors to produce lifelike performances from puppets or models.

ANISOTROPIC SHADING
A method of shading CG objects that have many small grooves in their surface. Used for materials such as straight hair and brushed metals. A good example of this type of shading is the reflected highlights seen on the surface of a CD.

APERTURE
An opening through which light passes on its way to or from the film. In a camera, the aperture regulates how much light passes through the lens and is controlled by an adjustable hole called a 'diaphragm' or 'iris'. The amount of light is measured in 'f-stops' or 't-stops'. In a projector, the aperture is a changeable mask that determines the aspect ratio of the image being projected.

ARMATURE
The underlying framework or skeleton of a model or puppet. Armatures are extremely tough and carefully engineered to withstand the rigours of filming.

ASPECT RATIO
The relative width and height of an image when viewed on a cinema screen or television. Aspect ratios are measured in terms of width against height. A standard frame of 35 mm film has an aspect ratio of 1.33:1, which is known as 'Academy ratio' and is the same as with a traditional television screen. 35 mm cinema images are typically projected in one of two standard ratios: 1.85:1 ratio is usually produced by masking off the top and bottom of a normal 1.33:1 image during printing or projection. 2.35:1 is a much wider image that is the result of using anamorphic lenses to 'squeeze' a wide image onto a standard-sized piece of film and then decompressing it during projection. 70 mm films are normally projected with an aspect ratio of 2.2:1.

ATMOSPHERIC EFFECTS
Physically produced effects that alter the quality of atmosphere in a studio or on location. These include smoke, rain and snow.

AUTOMATED DIALOGUE REPLACEMENT (ADR)
The replacement of dialogue originally spoken and recorded during filming with new dialogue recorded at a later date. Also called dubbing or looping.

BALD CAP
A rubber cap stretched over a performer's head to create the illusion of baldness, or ensure that a wig fits snugly.

BALL-AND-SOCKET JOINTS
Small joints used in the construction of the armatures used for animation puppets. A ball on the end of one limb is fitted into a precisely fitting socket on the adjoining limb. The joint is loose enough to allow the easy manipulation of a puppet but tight enough to ensure that the puppet keeps its shape when posed.

BEAM SPLITTER
An optical device such as a prism or two-way, half-silvered mirror that divides and redirects the light that hits it. A single image projected into a beam splitter will be equally divided and exit as two identical images of the same scene. The device can work in reverse so that two separate images entering the beam splitter exit as a single beam of light. Used extensively in the creation of optical visual effects.

BEAUTY PASS see PASS

BI-PACK
Some optical effects shots required two separate films to be run through a camera simultaneously. Each reel of film was usually held in a separate magazine, but the two strips were sandwiched together or 'bi-packed' when they ran through the gate where they were exposed to light.

BITMAP
A file that describes a 2-D digital image. The information in a bitmap includes the number of horizontal and vertical pixels that make up an image, the number of bits per pixel, and the colour of each pixel.

BLACK POWDER
A fast-burning material that comes in grades ranging from a fine powder to small chunks and is the basis of most pyrotechnic explosions and fireworks.

BLUE SCREEN
A screen of a carefully balanced blue colour which is placed behind performers or objects during filming to allow the optical or digital creation of travelling mattes. Today's digital matting processes can produce a matte from a surface painted blue, green or any other consistent colour.

BLUE-SCREEN PROCESS
An optical process by which subjects filmed in front of a blue screen were combined with a separately filmed background. There were two basic systems, the blue-screen colour separation process and the superior blue-screen colour difference process. Now replaced by digital alternatives.

BLUE OR GREEN SPILL
Any blue or green light that is reflected onto the subject, and hence into the camera, during the filming of blue- or green-screen footage. If not corrected, these areas may become transparent during compositing.

BOOLEAN OPERATION
A method of creating a 3-D digital model by performing an addition, subtraction, union or intersection between two or more 3-D objects.

BREAKAWAY EFFECTS
Props designed to break easily and safely during the filming of action sequences. These include chairs made from lightweight balsa wood, which can be smashed over heads, and windows for stuntmen to jump through.

BUMP MAP see TEXTURE MAPPING

CABLE CONTROL
The remote-controlled operation of puppets or models via cables that are pushed and pulled either by hand or by small motors.

CAD (COMPUTER-AIDED DESIGN)
Specialized engineering or design software used in the planning and construction of models, props, sets, lighting set-ups and complex special effects equipment.

CAMERA MAPPING
A digital texturing technique by which a 2-D image is projected into a scene from the position of the virtual camera being used to view the scene. If simple 3-D objects are placed within the scene so that they line up with the 2-D image, the impression of fully textured 3-D objects will be created. Used to produce 3-D (or '2½-D') moves on 2-D digital matte paintings.

CANNON CAR
A specially modified vehicle which uses a pyrotechnic or pneumatic cannon to fire a projectile from its base in order either to propel it forwards or turn it over.

CARTESIAN COORDINATES
Named after the French mathematician and philosopher René Descartes (1596–1650), the coordinates that locate any point in space relative to at least two perpendicular axes. A point in 2-D space is defined by its X and Y coordinates, while a point in 3-D space also has a Z or depth coordinate.

CATHODE-RAY TUBE (CRT)
The component in a traditional television or computer monitor that enables an image to be displayed on its screen. Streams of electrons emitted by a cathode inside a vacuum bombard a phosphorous screen causing it to glow. Electromagnets are used to deflect the electrons so that they hit the correct part of the screen in order to form an image.

CCD (CHARGE-COUPLED DEVICE)
An electronic chip used in video cameras and film scanners to convert images into digital or analogue signals. Small light-sensitive cels (photosites) on the surface of the chip convert the light that hits them into an electrical charge proportional to the quality of the light. This electrical charge is either recorded as an analogue signal, or is converted and stored as a digital signal in the form of a series of binary digits.

CEL ANIMATION
The traditional method of creating hand-drawn 2-D 'cartoon' animation. Each changing frame of movement is drawn and painted on a clear cel (made from cellulose acetate). This cel is placed on top of a painted background before being photographed. Twenty-four cels are needed per second of action and there are some 130,000 in a typical animated feature.

CGI
Computer-generated imagery (or computer graphic images). Any 2-D or 3-D images created entirely within a computer. Often abbreviated as 'CGI' or 'CG'.

CINEMATOGRAPHER
The cinematographer designs the overall look of a film by choosing the type of camera, film, lenses, lighting, filters, and other equipment used during filming. He or she will work closely with the visual effects supervisor to ensure that effects shots conform to the overall style. Also called director of photography (DOP or DP) or lighting cameraman.

CLOUD TANK
A glass tank filled with saline solutions of various densities and used to film billowing cloud and smoke formations.

COLOUR SEPARATIONS
By copying a colour image onto black-and-white film through red, green and blue filters, it can be broken down into three black-and-white positive records of the red, green and blue content of the scene. These black-and-white records (called colour separation masters) can be successively printed back onto normal colour film stock through the same colour filters to produce another colour image. Colour separations were used in the creation of optical travelling mattes, to control colour balance during optical compositing, and are used as a method of archiving important films in a black-and-white format so that their colour detail will not fade over time.

COMPOSITE
Any image that is made up from a combination of two or more elements filmed at different times or places. Compositing, the process of combining these various images, can be done in camera, in an optical printer, or now almost exclusively using a computer. Also known as a composit.

CONTACT PRINTING
The copying of images from one exposed and developed piece of film onto raw stock by sandwiching the two together and shining light through them.

CYBERSCAN
A method of transcribing a real object into a digital model by accurately measuring its features with a laser.

DAILIES
The previous day's filming that has been developed and printed overnight. At the beginning of each working day, director and key crew members assemble to watch the 'dailies' or 'rushes'. Productions shot digitally have no need for dailies as footage can be reviewed as soon as it has been shot.

DENTAL ALGINATE
A quick-setting plaster made from seaweed extracts used to make life casts of faces and body parts for make-up purposes.

DEPTH OF FIELD
The distance in front of the camera over which objects appear to be acceptably in focus. When objects both near and far from the camera are in sharp focus, a shot is said to have a 'deep' depth of field. When objects near the camera are in focus but those just a few feet behind them are out of focus, a shot is said to have a 'short' (or 'narrow' or 'shallow') depth of field. Depth of field is affected by the focal length and aperture of the lens on the camera, the amount of light in a scene, the shutter speed of the camera, and the speed rating of film being used.

DEPTH PERCEPTION
The illusion of distance in shots of models or miniatures. Depth perception is artificially created by filling the set with a fine smoke, stretching large sheets of fine cloth or bridal veil between planes, or painting distant objects in dull colours.

DEVELOPING
The laboratory process during which chemicals are used to make visible the latent image on an exposed piece of film. Also called processing.

DIFFERENCE MATTE
A digital method of creating a matte by comparing two almost identical images. Changes detected in the second image, such as the movement of an object, can be used to create a matte to remove the object from the scene.

DIFFUSE INTERREFLECTION
A CG rendering process whereby light bounces from one object and then strikes other objects in the surrounding area, thus illuminating them with the reflected light. Light is reflected from non-shiny, diffuse surfaces such as the ground, walls or objects, to illuminate areas that are not necessarily in direct view of a light source. If the diffuse surface is coloured, its reflected light is also coloured, resulting in similar colouration of surrounding objects. Diffuse interreflection is an important component of global illumination (see below).

DIFFUSE REFLECTION
Light hitting a textured CG surface that is reflected at a number of differing angles. It is the complement to specular reflection (see below). An example of the difference between specular and diffuse reflection can be seen in surfaces painted with either matt or glossy paints. Surfaces painted with matt paint have a higher amount of diffuse reflection, making them look evenly lit, while those in gloss have a higher amount of specular reflection, making them look shinier.

DIGITAL
Used to describe methods of recording, storing and transmitting images, sounds and data through the conversion of analogue information into binary numbers (combinations of ones and zeros). Digital information can be copied and transmitted repeatedly with no loss of detail, making it ideal for visual effects production where images need to be copied and combined many times.

DIGITAL BACKLOT
3-D computer models used to replace or extend real film sets, reducing the time and money spent in physically constructing major sets. An extension of the art of matte painting.

DIGITAL CINEMA
The creation and distribution of movies by entirely digital means. Productions are filmed using high-definition video, edited and finished digitally and then displayed in theatres using a digital projector.

DIGITAL INTERMEDIATE
The digital post-production of a movie during which all processes once achieved optically are handled by a computer. Movies shot on film have their negatives scanned at a high resolution to create digital data that can be edited, colour-corrected and integrated with visual effects. The finished movie can be digitally projected, recorded back onto film for distribution to theatres, or mastered to DVD for home video release.

DIGITAL MATTE PAINTING
The extension, manipulation and improvement of filmed images using 2-D digital paint methods to create objects, buildings and locations that do not exist. Increasingly involves the creation and integration of 3-D objects and environments as well as animation and other effects.

DIGITAL PAINT
The digital equivalent of paint and brushes. Digital paint may be used to touch up individual frames of film, create texture maps for digital models, or paint entire scenes for digital matte paintings. As well as painting with colours, artists can paint with 'textures' that have been sampled from real photographs or paintings. The most widely used digital paint software is Adobe Photoshop.

DIGITIZE
To convert the characteristics of any object, sound, image or analogue recording into digital information so that it can be used or manipulated by a computer.

DISPLACEMENT ANIMATION
A method of animation in which parts of a model are physically moved between the photography of each frame. This differs from replacement animation in which the model is substituted with a new one in a different pose.

DISPLACEMENT MAP *see* **TEXTURE MAPPING**

DISSOLVE
Scene-changing technique in which one image slowly fades out as the new image fades in. Dissolves are normally used as a narrative device to indicate the passing of time between scenes.

DOLLY
The moving platform on which camera and camera crew are pushed around to create a moving camera or 'dolly' shot. The platform is usually mounted on tracks that are laid on the ground to ensure smooth movement.

DOUBLE EXPOSURE
Two overlaid images on a piece of film caused by running the film through a camera twice. The technique can be used to create in-camera dissolves or the appearance of transparent ghosts.

DUBBING
The process of laying down new dialogue and sound effects onto filmed images. The term is also commonly used to describe the copying of sound and images from one videotape to another.

DUNNING–POMEROY PROCESS
The first method to use the principles of coloured light to create travelling mattes on black-and-white film. The technique bi-packed an orange-dyed positive of the required background image on top of raw stock inside the camera. In the studio, an actor lit with orange light performed in front of a blue screen. The image of the actor passed through the orange-dyed background image film in the camera to be recorded on the new film, while the blue light had the effect of printing the orange background image into the areas around the actor.

DYNAMATION
The name given by Ray Harryhausen and producer Charles Schneer to their split-screen method of combining stop-motion animation with rear-projected live action in *The 7th Voyage of Sinbad* (1958). For later Harryhausen films the same basic technique was variously renamed as 'Superdynamation' and 'Dynarama', while non-Harryhausen animated films hailed similar effects as 'Regiscope', 'Fantamation' and 'Fantascope', among others.

DYNAMICS
Methods that create movement in computer-generated objects by applying a set of predefined rules (an algorithm). An example is the movement of digital fur on a CG creature's body. This could be key-frame animated by manually moving 'guide hairs' which affect the movement of all surrounding hairs, or by programming the hair to react 'dynamically' in response to the animated movement of the body to which it is attached and the movement of neighbouring hairs. Most fur movement is created with a combination of manual and dynamic methods. Also commonly used to produce the movement of fluids and particulate masses such as dust clouds.

EDGE DETECTION
Traditionally, complex objects that moved in a 3-D fashion in animated feature films had to be painstakingly drawn, frame by frame, by artists skilled at portraying changing perspective. Today, complex objects are first created as 3-D computer models and then animated to produce the desired movement. Edge detection software then analyses the image in each frame and produces a series of 2-D black-and-white outline cels as if drawn by hand. These are then coloured and integrated into the traditionally animated elements.

EFFECTS ANIMATION
In 2-D animated feature films, the animation of any form of complex moving object or substance other than the characters. Includes moving water, falling leaves, fire, smoke, clouds and shadows. In live-action feature films, effects animation is drawn, painted and composited optically and now digitally, to create lightning, the muzzle flash on guns, sparks and smoke.

ELEMENTS
Images assembled during compositing in order to create a finished shot. A typical visual effects shot may contain digitally created elements such as animated characters or matte paintings, as well as filmed elements such as live action or miniatures. Many elements are created solely to help the major components of a scene merge together more realistically. For example, a movie containing CG dinosaurs might need mud, dust and water splashes added when each foot touches the ground, showers of bark and leaves when the creatures smash through forests, and puffs of vapour that will be added to mouths when the weather is supposed to be cold. A separate unit will often film these separate elements to create a library for use during compositing.

EMULSION
The layer of photochemically sensitive gelatin mixture that coats a strip of clear flexible material to create photographic film. Colour film has three layers of emulsion, each being sensitive to one of the three primary colours.

ESTABLISHING SHOT
The first image in a sequence which is used to establish a location, time and mood before cutting to close-ups of the main action. Matte paintings are commonly used to create establishing shots of fictitious locations.

EXPOSURE
The act of directing light onto a piece of undeveloped film in order to record an image. When film receives too much light it is said to be 'overexposed'. When too little light makes an image too dark it is 'underexposed'.

EXTRUSION
A digital modelling method by which a 2-D template of an object's cross-section is first drawn before being extended to the desired depth to produce a 3-D model. An extruded circle creates a cylinder, for example.

FADE
A technique by which an image gradually changes from a normally exposed picture into a solid colour – normally black – as a scene transition. A fade-out is where the picture turns black, while a fade-in is where the picture emerges from black.

FILM FORMAT
The type of film used for a project, either in terms of the physical width of the film as measured in millimetres (e.g. 35 mm or 70 mm), or by trade name (e.g. IMAX or VistaVision).

FILM RECORDER
A device used to record digital images from a computer onto the analogue medium of film. CRT film recorders use a camera to film the images from a high-quality computer monitor, while the now more common laser recorders shine a beam of coloured light directly onto a piece of film.

FILM SCANNER
A device that converts the analogue information held on film into digital information for manipulation within a computer. Light is shone through a frame of exposed and developed film and onto a CCD chip, converting the image into electrical signals which are recorded as digital information.

FILM SPEED
The 'speed' of photographic film refers to the sensitivity of its emulsion to light. 'Fast' film needs little light to record a correctly exposed image while 'slow' films need much more. Film speed is measured in terms of an exposure index, which is stated by film manufacturers and measured by a number of international standards.

FILTER
Any material such as glass or gauze that affects the quality of light passed through it. Filters can be attached to camera lenses, over lights, or within optical printers. In the digital world, filters are algorithms that are applied to digital images in order to affect the characteristics of groups of pixels, for instance by making them blurred or warped.

FLUID DYNAMICS
The study of how particulate matter and fluids flow under different circumstances. Such characteristics can be reduced to a number of mathematical rules, or algorithms, that may be used to create realistic computer-generated water and smoke.

FOLEY
The recording of synchronized sound effects to match silent images. Most noises heard in a film are created during a Foley session rather than being recorded during original filming. The process is sometimes called 'Foley walking' or 'footsteps' since a large part of the job involves reproducing the sound of walking. Named after Jack Foley (1891–1967; <345).

FORCED PERSPECTIVE
A false illusion of depth or size created during the

construction of models or sets by artificially shortening the distance over which objects would naturally appear to change in size. This means that exceptionally large-looking sets can be built in much smaller spaces and for less money than would otherwise be the case. Sets with dramatic forced perspective are sometimes peopled with tall people in the foreground and small people in the distance, as in the case of the engine room set of the *Enterprise* in *Star Trek: The Motion Picture* (1979).

FRAME RATE
The number of frames of film that are exposed per second during filming. Normal 35 mm motion picture photography is filmed and projected at 24 frames per second (fps).

FRONT PROJECTION
An optical method of simultaneously filming performers in a studio and pre-filmed background images which were projected onto a highly reflective backdrop from the front. The projector and camera were positioned at 90° to one another, yet were able to share the same optical path due to the positioning of a beam-splitting mirror at an angle of 45° between them. The method was also used to combine live action and matte paintings.

F-STOP
The amount of light that travels through the lens of a camera is controlled by opening and closing a diaphragm or iris. Each successive opening of a diaphragm lets in twice as much light as the last and is called an f-stop or just 'stop'. F-stop numbers range from f1, which allows all the light entering a lens to reach the film, to f32, where almost all the light entering the lens is blocked from the film. T-stops, sometimes confused with f-stops, are an electronic calculation of the actual amount of light that reaches the film plane.

GATE
The place behind the lens of a camera or projector where a frame of film stops momentarily to be exposed to light or, in the case of the projector, to be projected onto a screen.

GENERATION
Each time a filmed image is copied it is one generation on from the original negative. Since image quality is lost with each subsequent generation, film-makers try to ensure that images seen in the cinema are of a generation as close to the original negative as possible. Digital processes have removed the problems of generational loss since each subsequent copy of a digitized image (or sound) retains all the original information.

GEOMETRY
The geometric 'wire mesh' that forms the underlying structure of most computer-generated objects.

GLASS SHOT
A method of integrating painted image with live action by painting the desired additions to a scene onto a sheet of glass positioned in front of the camera. The camera films a combination of the image on the glass and the background scenery seen through the glass.

GLOBAL ILLUMINATION
A rendering method used to produce photorealistic CG images. Global illumination algorithms simulate the way that light energy is exchanged between all objects in a scene by taking into account both direct illumination (the light which has taken a path directly from a light source) and indirect illumination (the light that has undergone reflection from other surrounding surfaces).

GO-MOTION
A sophisticated variation of stop-motion animation in which the puppet is pre-programmed to perform each incremental move while the shutter of the camera is open. The result is an animated character that moves with lifelike motion blur.

GRAIN
The emulsion on photographic film is made of tiny grains of silver halide suspended in gelatin. The larger the size of these grains, the more sensitive the film is to light, but the more 'grainy' the image appears when projected. Grain can clump together in the emulsion of a film, becoming quite visible on a cinema screen. Grain becomes more noticeable the further away each generation is from the original negative.

GRAIN MANAGEMENT
Shots created by digitally compositing numerous images from different sources will need to have the grain (see above) in each element carefully managed. This may mean trying to suppress the appearance of grain in some filmed elements, or adding grain to digitally created elements which inherently contain no grain. The aim is to create multi-layered composite shots in which the final appearance of the grain matches that of the ordinary shots in the rest of the movie.

GRAPHICS TABLET
A sensitive desktop device which can be used by computer operators to draw using a special pen. Anything drawn on the tablet will simultaneously appear on the computer monitor. The graphics pen can also be used like a paintbrush – the amount of digital paint applied varies with the pressure applied by the pen. A graphics tablet can also be used like a mouse to give instructions to a computer.

HDRI (HIGH DYNAMIC RANGE IMAGES)
Photographs that capture a full range of exposure detail in both the lightest and darkest areas of the image. Created by combining over-, under- and correctly exposed images of a scene, often photographed in a highly reflective sphere. These are used as a light source when lighting CG objects that are to be composited into real-world environments.

HIERARCHY
A chain of interdependent elements in any jointed digital model – typically a limb of a computer-generated character's body. The position of an object in a hierarchical chain affects the way that it reacts when the objects to which it is linked are moved during animation, and how those other objects react when it is moved.

HIGH-CONTRAST FILM
A variety of black-and-white film that only records extreme contrasts of tone – converting most tones and colours into either black or white. Used in the production of optical mattes and titles.

HIGH-CONTRAST MATTES
A method of producing optical mattes that relied on the subject being separated from its background by extreme differences of contrast. Typically, a model spacecraft might be filmed by a motion-control camera in two passes. In the first pass, the model was lit perfectly (the 'beauty pass') but no light was allowed to fall on the backdrop, which remained dark. In the second pass, no light was allowed to fall on the model but the backdrop was lit brightly – making it a stark white. The model became a black silhouette against the white backdrop and, when filmed with high-contrast black-and-white film, was used to produce male and female mattes.

HIGH-DEFINITION VIDEO
High-definition (HD) video generally refers to any video system of higher resolution than standard-definition (SD) formats such as the NTSC and PAL systems normally used for broadcast and home video. The increased quality of images produced by HD video results from the additional number of horizontal lines used to record an image (e.g. 1080 as opposed to the 525 or 625 used by NTSC or PAL) and the methods used to process, compress and store image information.

HIGH-SPEED PHOTOGRAPHY
Filming at higher than normal frame rates will result in 'slow motion' images when the film is projected at the normal rate of 24 frames per second. High-speed photography is often used to create a sense of scale when filming miniature effects such as models, smoke or water. While most miniature photography is achieved at two to four times normal speed, some shots involve filming several thousand frames per second using highly engineered cameras made by the Photosonics corporation.

IMAGE-BASED LIGHTING
The use of photographs of real-world locations to generate the lighting used to illuminate CG scenes and objects. See HDRI.

IMAGE-BASED MODELLING
The creation of 3-D CG models by cross-referencing 2-D images of an object that has been photographed from several different angles.

IMAX
A large-format film process which uses 65 mm film horizontally, resulting in a frame that is three times larger than that in normal 65 mm photography and ten times the size of the frame in standard 35 mm photography. As a result, the image quality is superb and can be projected onto an enormous screen.

IN-BETWEENER
During the drawing of traditional 2-D animation, a lead animator draws only the key poses of a character in each scene – perhaps two or three key frames for every second of action. In-betweeners draw the stages of action between these frames.

IN-CAMERA EFFECT
Any visual effect that is achieved during filming without having to manipulate the film after processing. In-camera effects can include fast and slow motion, fades, dissolves, split-screen effects, glass shots and hanging miniatures. Though they can give superior results because they are achieved on the original negative, such effects are generally avoided since they risk damaging the original negative image. Now largely redundant due to digital processes.

INTERLACING see PROGRESSIVE SCAN

INTROVISION
An intricate variation of front projection which effectively enabled the 2-D projected background image to be split into various planes. Performers could be made to appear as if they were actually acting within the environment of the projected image.

INVERSE KINEMATICS
A method of digital character animation by which only the end joints or limbs in a hierarchical skeleton are moved to the desired position. The way that the rest of the body moves in response is calculated automatically by the computer according to pre-set rules.

KEY FRAME
In traditional 2-D animation, the most important images are drawn by lead animators to indicate the major changes in character movement. (Less experienced animators complete the in-between frames.) In computer animation key frames are still used, with the animator setting the position of any object every few frames, and the computer calculating the transitions in between (interpolating). Key-framing is the most common method of controlling all aspects of a computer-generated scene and is used to control lights, cameras and other aspects of the virtual environment.

KEYING
The digital process of selectively laying one image on top of another involves producing a matte or

'key' that is derived from some quality of the image to be overlaid. A 'key' can be 'pulled' from a number of attributes in an image including its luminance (luma-keying), and its chrominance (chroma-keying).

KICKER PLATE
A pneumatically operated springboard used to fling stunt performers or objects into the air when filming action sequences.

LATENT IMAGE
The invisible image that lies dormant on a piece of film after it has been exposed to light and before it has been developed. Some optical visual effects processes involved keeping an exposed but undeveloped piece of film in the camera, or in storage, before re-exposing it to other elements, for instance a matte painting, at a later stage. Such methods are called 'latent image' or 'held take' processes.

LATEX RUBBER
A liquid produced from the sap of the rubber tree. When combined with fungicides and other chemicals, it is used to create various densities of solid rubber including the foam rubber for prosthetic make-up and animatronics.

LATHING
A digital modelling method by which a basic 2-D shape is rotated about an axis to create a 3-D object with the same profile. A circle lathed around a nearby axis would create a torus (doughnut shape), for example.

LIFE CAST
A mould bearing the exact features of a performer, used for the creation of prosthetic make-up and costumes to ensure a perfect fit. The process usually involves covering the performer's body and face in quick-drying plaster to produce a negative mould from which a positive cast can be taken. Instead of the traditional method of producing a life cast, which can be unnerving for the subject, a cyberscan (see above) can now be used to create an accurate replica of a performer's features in a computerized milling process.

LOCKED-OFF CAMERA
A camera which has been rigidly secured to ensure that it will not move or shake during filming.

LOFTING
A digital modelling technique in which a number of differing 2-D shapes are arranged along a path (a spline) and then linked together to create an object with a changing profile.

LYDECKER TECHNIQUE
A method of suspending and flying models from tensioned wires. Perfected by brothers Howard and Theodore Lydecker in the 1930s (<145).

MAGAZINE
The detachable light-proof compartment which holds the film for a movie camera. Magazines generally have two chambers, one containing a reel of unexposed film, the other a take-up chamber which receives the film after it has been exposed in the camera.

MAPPING
The fitting of 2-D textures and images to the surface of a 3-D object in order to create natural-looking CG models.

MASSIVE
Artificial intelligence software used to control the complex movement of thousands of CG objects. Originally written by Stephen Regelous to create the battle scenes for *The Fellowship of the Ring* (2001) but now available commercially.

MATCH MOVING
When computer-generated elements need to be placed into a live-action scene that has been filmed with a moving camera, the CG elements must be

'filmed' with an identical camera move so that they can be merged realistically with the live action during compositing. Match moving is the process of matching the movements of the computer's virtual camera to those of the live-action camera. Also known as 3-D camera tracking.

MATTE
Any form of mask that prevents light from reaching and exposing areas of film. The area of film left unexposed is usually filled with an image from another source at a later stage. Mattes always exist in two complementary parts: one matte allows exposure on one part of the film and prevents it in another, while a counter-matte covers the already exposed area and allows the rest of the frame to receive a different image. A matte and its counter-matte are often referred to as a male and female matte. Today, mattes are produced digitally using a number of processes.

MATTE BOX
A slotted frame that is attached to the front of a camera in which metal or cardboard mattes can be inserted to prevent the film's exposure to parts of an image.

MATTE LINE
The place in a composite image where two separately created elements meet. When the combination of elements is not entirely successful, a discernible black line may be visible between them. With optical printing, matte lines were virtually impossible to avoid completely but the precision of digital compositing techniques means that matte lines are generally a thing of the past.

MATTE PAINTING
A painting, usually of a location, which is combined with live-action footage, animation or models to produce a realistic composite image. Paintings were traditionally done on large sheets of glass and combined with other images through a variety of optical processes, such as rear or front projection. Matte paintings are now usually painted directly within a computer before being digitally combined with live-action and animated elements.

MESH
The vertices, segments and polygons which collectively create the structure, or geometry, of a digital model.

MINIATURE
Any object or location that is reproduced at a smaller scale for filming purposes.

MODEL
Any object or location that has been reproduced for filming purposes. Models are not necessarily smaller than the real thing – they may be the same size or, when actors need to look small by comparison, larger than the real object. Though models are usually perfect re-creations of the exterior of an object, they are often dummies that lack interior details such as motors or mechanisms.

MORPHING
The process by which one image appears to transform seamlessly into another. Digital morphing can merge one 2-D image into another, or change one 3-D model into another. Morph sequences often involve a series of objects that will be transformed into one another over a set period of time. Each object in the sequence is called a 'morph target' or 'blend target'. Often used in action sequences to transition between a real or computer-generated stunt performer and the star of the film in time for a close-up.

MORTAR
A pipe, funnel or dish used to control the characteristics of pyrotechnic explosions.

MOTION BLUR
The blurring that occurs if an object moves when the shutter is open during photography. Though it

is actually a technical shortcoming, motion blur helps moving images to look more natural to the human eye by preventing the strobing that would occur if objects moved from frame to frame without blur.

MOTION CAPTURE
Methods of capturing the natural movement of bodies or faces so that it can be used for the animation of computer-generated characters. Often called 'mo-cap'.

MOTION CONTROL
A method of recording or programming the movements of a film camera so that a shot can be achieved exactly as required, and repeated whenever necessary. Particularly useful for filming a number of different elements in separate takes or 'passes' so that they can be effectively combined at a later date.

MULTIPLANE EFFECTS
Naturalistic changes in focus and perspective in 2-D animation achieved by arranging artwork in a number of layers or 'planes' in front of the camera. Such effects were first successfully used after the construction of Disney's multiplane camera in 1937, and are now achieved by arranging layers of artwork in a computer.

NEGATIVE
When an image has been photographed and the film from the camera developed, the result is normally a negative image – in the case of black-and-white photography the dark and light areas are reversed, while in colour photography dark and light are reversed and the colours are 'complementary' to the original. When copied or 'printed' onto print film, the negative image is reversed into a normal positive image.

NODAL HEAD
A special tripod head that tilts or pans a camera around the nodal point of a lens so that the view of a scene changes but the perspective from which it is seen does not.

NODE
A point at which any decision is made during the creation of procedural computer-generated animation. For example, when a procedurally animated character reaches a chasm they could decide either to jump, fall, or turn around. This decisional 'node' is written into the character's set of operating rules and the final choice will be made by referencing all available information and options.

NOISE
A random signal generated by the computer that can be used for a number of digital imaging purposes. Noise added to a texture map will add a more mottled appearance and a naturalistic appearance of randomness. Noise added to any form of animation, such as the movement of a virtual camera or the motion of a character, can also help to modify the smooth performance sometimes produced by automation.

NURBS (NON-UNIFORM RATIONAL B-SPLINE)
A digital modelling technique which generates model surfaces as a number of separate square patches, each of which is influenced by a set of continuous curves (or splines).

OPACITY MAP *see* TEXTURE MAPPING

OPTICAL EFFECTS
Visual effects that were created with an optical printer. Strictly speaking, only effects actually created using an optical printer were 'opticals', but the phrase is widely used to distinguish any process that involves using the properties of light, film and lenses (such as front and rear projection) from physical effects that are achieved on the set, or digital effects that are produced in the computer.

OPTICAL PRINTER
A device used to create optical visual effects by manipulating photographic images while copying (printing) them from one film onto another. At its simplest, the optical printer was simply a projector and a camera facing one another; the projector shone its image through a lens and onto the new film held in the camera. Effects achieved using an optical printer included the compositing of travelling matte photography, split-screen effects, dissolves, fades and wipes. Optical printers have now been entirely replaced by digital alternatives.

OPTICAL SOUND
A system of reproducing film sound which involves converting electrical sound signals into an analogue pattern that is printed as a continuous strip alongside the images on a piece of film. This signal is read optically and converted back into sound during projection.

ORIGINAL NEGATIVE MATTE PAINTING
A method of combining paintings and live action by exposing both onto the same original negative film without any additional processes. Also known as 'latent image matte painting'.

OVERCRANKING
Running a film through a camera faster than the normal speed of 24 frames per second. When the developed film is projected at the normal speed, the action appears in slow motion. Running a camera slower than the normal speed to create speeded-up images is called 'undercranking'.

PARTICLE SYSTEM
A digital method of generating and animating the random movement of large numbers of particles for the creation of swarms, clouds, tornados, fireworks, water and so on. Particle systems control various parameters such as the number of particles in a shot, where they come from, how they move in relation to one another, their velocity and drop-off. Changing any one aspect will change the entire pattern of movement. The particle flow in a shot is determined using basic particles before they are replaced with the objects required for the scene – which may in themselves be animated, such as swimming fish.

PASS
During the photography of models or miniatures, an image is often filmed in several 'passes'. Each one captures a specific aspect of the image, usually on a separate piece of film. In the case of a model spaceship, separate passes might be used to film the model's internal lighting, the glow from its engines, a smoky atmosphere, and a silhouette for the production of a travelling matte. In a 'beauty pass' the model in question is lit to look its best. The different passes are combined optically or digitally. The result is a shot in which all elements are balanced to produce an image difficult or impossible to achieve in a single take. When a shot involves a moving camera, motion control is essential for ensuring that the camera movement is identical for each pass. Different passes are also produced when rendering computer-generated models and animation.

PHOTOSHOP
Leading 2-D image creation and editing software used by most companies to create digital matte paintings and texture maps for CG models.

PHYSICAL EFFECTS
Any effects that are physically achieved on set during filming. Includes the use of pyrotechnics, atmospherics and large-scale mechanical props. Also known as 'mechanical effects' and 'special effects'.

PILOT PIN REGISTRATION
Most visual effects processes require every image in a sequence to be positioned in exactly the same place on each subsequent frame of film. This allows elements held on separate films to be precisely

combined, ensuring production of a successful composite image. To ensure perfect 'pin registration', cameras and projectors used in visual effects use special pilot pins which fit snugly into the perforations in a piece of film, holding it absolutely steady in the aperture during photography or projection.

PIXELS
An abbreviation of 'picture elements'. Pixels are the tiny squares of colour which make up a digital image. Each image comprises many thousands of pixels – the more used to describe a picture, the higher its resolution. For film images the appearance of each pixel is the result of a combination of four channels of information. Three channels specify the amounts of red, green and blue that combine to produce the pixel's colour. The fourth channel, known as the alpha channel, contains information about the transparency of the pixel and is used during compositing.

PLATE
Any still or moving image used as a background for front or rear projection, optical travelling matte processes, or in a digital composite shot. To ensure that backgrounds will be suitable for use later in production, plate photography is often overseen by visual effects supervisors who travel to locations with the film's main crew. Lighting and camera movement in a plate are carefully planned so that effects elements can be effectively matched to them. The word 'plate' originates from the early days of still photography when negatives were made of plates of glass with photographic emulsion on their surface.

POLYGON
A simple two-dimensional geometric shape. Polygons are the building blocks of 3-D digital models.

PRE-VISUALIZATION
The planning of complex action sequences by first animating them using 3-D software. 'Pre-viz' allows visual effects supervisors to design shots, physical effects supervisors to plan what equipment they will need, stunt coordinators to calculate distances and speeds, cinematographers to plan lighting and camera angles, and editors and directors to pre-cut a scene to achieve the best result.

PRIMACORD
A high-explosive 'rope' that can be wrapped or taped around objects in order to destroy them on detonation. Also known as det cord.

PRIMITIVES
Basic 3-D geometric objects that are often used as a basis for the construction of more complicated digital models within the computer. Primitives such as spheres, cubes and pyramids may be squashed, squeezed, distorted or intersected to create other more interesting forms.

PROCEDURAL MODELLING/PROCEDURAL ANIMATION
Time-saving digital modelling and animation techniques by which the form or movement of objects is calculated by the computer according to pre-programmed mathematical formulas (algorithms).

PROCESS CAMERA/PROCESS PROJECTOR
A camera or projector which uses pin registration to ensure that each frame of film is held absolutely steady during the photography or projection of visual effects elements.

PROCESS SHOT
Usually describes composite shots achieved using rear projection. The term is sometimes also used to describe a shot achieved using optical travelling matte processes.

PRODUCTION/PRE-PRODUCTION/POST-PRODUCTION
The process of creating a film is divided into three distinct phases. Pre-production refers to the parts of the film-making process that occur before principal photography begins. This includes scriptwriting, the design and construction of props and sets, casting of actors, financing and scheduling. Production is the actual phase of shooting a film in a studio or on location, and is usually the shortest part of the film-making process. Post-production refers to the processes that occur after shooting. This includes editing, the creation of visual effects, dubbing and sound effects, and recording the musical score. The actual timing of these phases may overlap somewhat – editing usually begins during the production phase, for example.

PROGRESSIVE SCAN
A video recording method in which the picture information for each frame is recorded, stored and displayed one line after another (progressively) to produce a whole image. Traditional video systems instead use a system by which alternate lines of picture information are recorded separately and later interlaced to form a complete picture during display. Progressive scan technology is analogous to the way whole frames are photographed by traditional film cameras. Video shot in this way can therefore be transferred directly to film on a frame-by-frame basis.

PROPRIETARY SOFTWARE
Most computer-generated imagery is created using standard 'off the shelf' software. Larger visual effects studios often write their own software to achieve unusual or difficult effects. This 'proprietary' technology is often widely promoted but carefully guarded, being one asset that sets a studio apart from its rivals.

PROSTHETICS
False limbs, noses or other appendages which are seamlessly affixed to the face or body of a performer.

PYROTECHNICS
The creation of explosions and bullet hits by using real explosives and other highly flammable materials. Non-pyrotechnic alternatives are available – using compressed air to blow debris into the air, for example.

RADIOSITY
A method of creating realistic lighting for 3-D digital images by calculating the diffuse interreflection of light between every surface in a scene. Radiosity produces convincing digital images but is extremely time-consuming and machine-intensive.

RAW STOCK
Unexposed and undeveloped film.

RAY TRACING
A method of calculating physically accurate lighting in 3-D digital scenes by tracing the path of light beams emanating from the camera as they bounce around an environment before reaching sources of light.

REAR PROJECTION
A method of combining live-action foregrounds with pre-filmed background scenery. Actors perform in front of a translucent screen which has still or moving images projected onto it from behind. A camera films the composite image. Animation, models and matte paintings can also be combined with background footage in this way. Also called rear-screen projection, back projection or process photography.

REGISTRATION PINS
Metal pins that precisely fit into the sprocket holes in a piece of film in order to position each frame exactly and hold it absolutely steady during exposure in a camera or projector.

RELEASE PRINT
The final version of a film, produced in large quantities for distribution to cinemas.

RENDERING
The final process in the production of computer-generated images. During rendering, every instructional aspect of a 3-D scene (lighting, camera, geometry, texture maps, shaders, animation, etc.) is studied by rendering software in order to calculate the final 2-D image.

REPLACEMENT ANIMATION
A method of stop-motion model animation in which puppets to be animated have all or part of their body replaced between photography of each frame, rather than being moved and repositioned by hand, as in displacement animation.

RE-RECORDING
The process of copying and mixing various pre-recorded sound effects and dialogue to create the final soundtrack for a film.

RESOLUTION
The quality of a digital image expressed in terms of pixels or pixels per unit area.

REVERSE BLUE SCREEN
An unusual method of creating blue-screen travelling mattes used in the early 80s. Rather than using a blue background screen to create a matte of a foreground object, the object was painted with a special translucent ultraviolet paint. The model was first filmed with normal lighting in front of a black screen. Using separate film, another identical pass was then filmed. This time the model was lit with ultraviolet light which turned the model blue, resulting in an image of a blue model against a black background. This film was used to create the travelling mattes. The reverse blue-screen process was first used for shots of a model fighter aircraft in *Firefox* (1982).

RIGID BODY DYNAMICS
A method of procedurally animating supposedly solid CG objects so that they collide and interact automatically, according to the laws of physics. Typically used to show objects crashing or disintegrating.

ROTOSCOPE
A combined camera and projector that is mounted on a rostrum and points down at a table. Images from a film can be projected downwards and traced onto paper or cels, which can then be used to create artwork for lightning, ghosts, or other hand-animated effects. The artwork is then rephotographed and optically combined with the original footage. The digital version of rotoscoping is mainly used for dividing each frame of a sequence into areas that will become either background or foreground when additional elements are composited into the scene.

SCALE
The comparative size of a model compared to the real object on which it is based. A 1 m model of a 4 m car has a scale of 1:4. Solid objects can be effectively re-created at smaller scales, while certain natural elements such as fire and water are difficult to miniaturize convincingly.

SCOTCHLITE
Trade name for a highly reflective material manufactured by the 3M company. With 250,000 tiny glass beads on each square inch of its surface, Scotchlite is 'retroreflective' – the majority of light hitting it is reflected directly back to its source. Generally used for reflective road signs and safety clothing, Scotchlite was also used in the effects industry for front-projection processes.

SEGMENT
A basic piece of geometry that links vertices during the construction of a digital model.

SHADER
An algorithm used by computers during rendering to calculate the way that light interacts with the surface of a digital model. Shaders determine the final look of computer-generated objects and scenes. Also called surface shaders.

SHAPE INTERPOLATION
A method of creating movement by instructing the computer to interpolate, or 'morph', between a number of fixed shapes. It is commonly used to create facial performances by interpolating between a number of pre-made facial expression models. Also called shape blending or blend-shape animation.

SHOWSCAN
A high-quality film format that moves 65 mm film vertically through the camera and projector at a speed of 60 frames per second. Showscan is also the name of a corporation that uses the process to create theme-park film attractions.

SHUFTAN PROCESS
A traditional method of using mirrors to combine full-scale live action and miniatures in camera.

SHUTTER
The device inside a camera that intermittently allows light to enter and expose the film within. Shutters are normally rotating discs with openings that let light reach the film while it is held motionless in the gate for exposure, and block light while the film is being advanced to the next frame. The shutter on a film projector prevents light from reaching the screen while each frame is being pulled into place.

SIMULATION
Methods of computer animation or modelling that draw on predetermined rules (algorithms) to generate the models' appearance or behaviour. Usually used to produce shots that would be too complicated or time-consuming to animate or model manually.

SLIT SCAN
A type of optical animation that produced images of streaking light. The effect was achieved by exposing a single frame of film, over a long period, to artwork seen through a slit in a screen. The camera, artwork and even the slit could be in motion during photography.

SLOW MOTION
Slowing the apparent speed of filmed objects by running film through the camera faster than the 24 frames per second normally used for filming and then projecting the resulting images at the normal speed. A scene filmed at 48 frames per second and projected at 24 will move at half its original speed. Some visual effects shots may be filmed at speeds as high as 500 frames per second, making a one-second event stretch to over 20 seconds on screen. Slow motion can now be created digitally by interpolating frames to produce artificial in-between frames that extend the sequence. Also called overcranking.

SODIUM VAPOUR PROCESS
A travelling matte process that used two films mounted in a single camera simultaneously to produce both the foreground element of a shot and its complementary travelling matte during original filming. The matte was created by placing the foreground element (e.g. an actor) in front of a yellow backdrop lit by sodium vapour lamps. A beam-splitting prism inside the camera sent the light from the yellow backdrop to one film to produce the matte, and all other light to the second film to record the image of the foreground element.

SPECULAR REFLECTION
The brightest areas of highlight on the surface of a computer-generated object. Created by light from external sources being reflected directly toward the camera.

SPLINE
A path created within the computer by joining two or more vertices. Although straight lines can be used to connect the vertices, more commonly the connecting lines can be influenced to produce a series of smoother curves. A spline could control the movement of a virtual camera by manually defining various key camera positions in a sequence and allowing the computer to calculate the path that links them. Spline-based modelling defines the surface of a digital model by using a relatively small number of control points, which are linked to produce a shape that influences the contours on the surface of the model.

SPLIT SCREEN
Any optical or digital process that allows an image to contain two or more elements that were photographed at separate times. Typically used to allow the same actor to appear twice in the same frame. To achieve the effect photographically, one side of the screen is matted off during exposure before the film is rewound. The matte is reversed, the film re-exposed. Some split-screen effects try to hide the fact that the image is produced by more than one exposure, others use the technique for dramatic effect – for instance, to show two people in different locations speaking on the telephone. Split screens need not be stationary – the line dividing the two exposures can be moved from frame to frame.

SPROCKET HOLES
Small perforations along the edges of a film strip that are engaged by the teeth of sprocket wheels to move film through a camera or projector.

SQUIB
A small pyrotechnic device used to simulate bullet hits. Squibs come in various sizes and are detonated electrically – either directly through a wire or occasionally by radio control.

STOP-MOTION
A method of animating models by physically altering their position in between the photography of each frame. When the resulting images are projected at the normal speed, there is the illusion of autonomous movement. Also called stop-action.

SUBDIVISION SURFACES
A method of selectively subdividing the polygons that form the mesh of a digital model in order to create more refined surface detail. Pioneered by Pixar in their short animated film *Geri's Game* (1997).

SUBSURFACE SCATTERING
A method of rendering realistic translucent materials by calculating the way that light penetrates their surface and is absorbed and diffused before exiting at different angles. Developed in the late 90s by Pat Hanrahan, Henrik Wann Jensen and Stephen Marschner.

SUBTRACTIVE PROCESS
A method of creating colour photographic images by combining three images, each of which contains just one of the three primary 'complementary' colours of cyan, magenta and yellow. Individually, these colours work to filter out the other colours in the spectrum that make up white light; when the separations are projected together they therefore produce a resulting image that is the desired colour. This method is used in all modern colour film processes.

SUPERIMPOSITION
The layering of two or more filmed images so that they are transparently visible at the same time. Also called double or multiple exposure.

SUPERVISOR
The senior effects technician responsible for overseeing the production of effects for a film.

Most major films have two types of effects supervisor: the special effects supervisor works on the physical and mechanical effects in a film, while the visual effects supervisor oversees the production of visual effects such as matte painting, animation, travelling mattes and miniature photography. Supervisors begin working on a film during pre-production, when they study the script and plan how each effect can be best achieved using the allocated budget. This is followed by a period of research and development during which techniques are tried, materials tested, and specialized equipment or software created. During production, supervisors oversee the safe and efficient filming of scenes in which physical effects are used, or the shooting of plates to which visual effects will be added during post-production. The special effects supervisor's job normally ends when shooting finishes, while the bulk of the visual effects supervisor's work takes place during post-production when the live action has been filmed and is ready for any changes. A film normally has an overall visual effects supervisor who is hired by the production to plan and budget each effects shot. They then contract visual effects studios, or vendors, to create the work. Each effects studio will have its own visual effects supervisor to oversee its own work.

SURFACE NORMAL
The surfaces of CG models are normally made up of thousands of triangular polygons. The flat surface of each polygon usually faces a slightly different direction in order to describe the contours of the model. The direction in which each polygon faces is its 'surface normal'. This information is used when calculating the way that light bounces off the model during rendering.

TAKE
Each time the camera is started and then stopped to film a shot. Several takes of each shot are normally filmed and the best is selected and used during editing. After the first take, each subsequent version of a shot is called a retake.

TANK
A large area of water in a film studio that is used for the filming of scenes involving boats and water. Tanks normally have a large painted backdrop and contain underwater tracks and pulleys for the manoeuvring and sinking of boats, plus equipment for creating waves.

TECHNICAL DIRECTOR
Though different visual effects facilities tend to give their staff different titles, technical directors, or TDs, usually have a highly specialized role in the production of computer-animated sequences. Ordinary animators or modellers create the basics of each shot before handing it over to TDs, who will deal with any out-of-the-ordinary requirements such as interactive water effects, the behaviour of hair, or any unusual lighting conditions. TDs will often need to write new software applications in order to achieve the desired effect.

TECHNICOLOR
An American company formed in 1915 by Herbert T. Kalmus, Daniel F. Comstock and W. Burton Wescott, who invented a number of pioneering colour film processes. Their first system was a 'two-strip' additive process (see above) that used a beam splitter in the camera to send two copies of an image to two separate strips of negative film, each filtered through a red or green filter. The two resulting black-and-white prints were then projected back through a red or green filter to produce a colour image. A later two-strip process used the subtractive process (see above) to combine cyan and magenta to create a colour image. In 1932 the company introduced the three-strip Technicolor process for which it is best known. This system used a special camera that held three films to record the red, blue and green colour

components of a scene. All three colour records were then used to print their complementary colour onto a single positive film for projection. The colour produced using this system was bold and lush, as seen in *Gone with the Wind* (1939), for example. The system became outmoded after 1952 when Kodak introduced its single-strip Eastman Color film, which could be used in ordinary cameras. Technicolor still exists as a company that processes and develops movie film, duplicates consumer video and DVD and operates major digital intermediate facilities (see above). It also owns the visual effects facility The Moving Picture Company (MPC).

TEXTURE MAPPING
A method of adding colour or surface detail to digital models. To create texture maps, photographs or artwork of surfaces and patterns can be scanned into the computer, or created using digital paint software. Texture maps are then applied to the model using mapping coordinates to ensure that they fit correctly. As well as adding 2-D detail to a model, certain texture maps can change the appearance of a model's shape. Bump maps are greyscale maps that can make a flat surface look bumpy by the way that light is reflected from it. Alternatively, displacement maps can be applied to a model's surface to physically alter its shape during rendering. Opacity maps can be applied to a 'solid' model to make areas of its surface appear see-through.

THREE-DIMENSIONAL/3-D
Most images that we see have the two-dimensional aspects of height and width. Stereoscopic photography (using two cameras) can create images that, when combined, appear to have the third dimension of depth. Traditional cartoon animation is 2-D, since characters and backgrounds are flat pieces of artwork that can only be viewed and filmed from one angle. Model animation is 3-D because the camera and the models are able to move in all dimensions during animation. However, unless filmed stereographically, the resulting filmed images are two-dimensional. Computer-generated animation is often called 3-D animation because the models and environments are constructed in three-dimensional space within the computer, allowing the computer's virtual camera to roam around and 'film' them from any angle. Like normal motion picture photography, the usual result is, however, a 2-D image of a 3-D scene. Some computer-generated films have been rendered in both normal 2-D and stereographic 3-D versions, including *The Polar Express* (2004) and *Chicken Little* (2005).

THREE-STRIP PROCESS see TECHNICOLOR

TIME-LAPSE PHOTOGRAPHY
A method of filming slow-moving events to produce a sequence in which they appear to occur far more quickly. Once a camera is set up it can be programmed to photograph one frame every second, every hour or even every week. Usually used to create speeded-up images of naturally slow processes such as the growth of plants or the movement of clouds.

TIME-SLICE PHOTOGRAPHY
An effect produced by editing together images of the same subject that have been photographed simultaneously from different perspectives. The effect is of a motion picture camera moving through a moment that has been 'frozen in time'. Also called bullet time.

TIP TANK
A large tank of water that can be tipped or emptied to create waves during the filming of floods and storms. Also called tipper tank or dump tank.

TRACKING SHOT
A shot in which the camera moves in a linear fashion either towards, away from, or past the

subject. The camera is normally mounted on a crane, track or wheels to allow smooth movement. Also called dolly shot, trucking shot or travelling shot.

TRAVELLING MATTE
Travelling mattes are used to combine two separately filmed elements when the foreground element (e.g. a person) changes shape or position from frame to frame – necessitating a new matte for each frame. Many methods of producing travelling mattes have been used – most rely on the foreground object being filmed in front of a coloured background. Traditional techniques such as the sodium vapour process and the blue-screen colour difference process created mattes optically. Today, all travelling matte shots are created digitally. *See* mattes

TWO-STRIP PROCESS see TECHNICOLOR

UNIVERSAL CAPTURE
A form of motion capture that uses the facial performance of a live actor as recorded by multiple video cameras to drive the performance of a computer-generated character with identical facial features. Pioneered for use in *The Matrix Reloaded* (2003).

UV MAPPING
The process of producing a 2-D image or 'map' that represents the surface of a 3-D model. U and V refer to the horizontal and vertical coordinates of the image. Once they have had colour and texture applied in 2-D, UV maps are reapplied to a 3-D model to produce its final appearance.

VERTEX
A single point in two- or three-dimensional digital space. By linking three or more vertices, basic shapes called polygons can be created and used to construct complex digital models.

VIRTUAL CAMERA
The hypothetical camera used to film animation and environments created within the computer. The virtual camera is not a physical camera but rather the 'device' used to determine the viewpoint that the computer will use when deriving information about the digital world during the process of rendering. Virtual cameras have been designed to replicate the abilities of real cameras and can be programmed to use different types of lenses and animated to move like real cameras.

VIRTUAL REALITY
Images of computer-generated environments and characters that are displayed to a single viewer using a form of headset or projected directly onto the retina of the eye (Virtual Retinal Display) to give the viewer the impression that he or she is immersed within a scene. VR systems react to the movements and actions of the viewer, allowing him or her to directly influence events. Used for military, medical and gaming purposes, they have the potential to develop into new forms of interactive entertainment.

VIRTUAL SETS/VIRTUAL STUDIO
Photorealistic computer-generated environments that replace the need for large film sets or location filming. Actors perform within an empty studio using minimal sets and props. During filming, cameras that move freely around actors relay their exact movements to a computer, determining how the virtual camera reacts. Filmed live action and computer-generated backgrounds are then composited to produce the final sequences.

VISTAVISION
35 mm film that is run horizontally through the camera (rather than vertically, as is normally the case) to create a negative that is eight perforations wide – twice the size of a normal 35 mm image. First developed in the 50s, VistaVision produces images that are sharper and less grainy than those in normal 35 mm photography, making them ideal

for optical visual effects processes that require the repeated copying and therefore degradation of an image.

VOLUME RENDERING
The rendering of large numbers of often semi-transparent computer-generated particles used to simulate snow, rain, dust, clouds, etc. The computer studies the 3-D volume of particles at various depths from the camera in order to calculate a final 2-D image of the combined effect.

WEDGE
A strip of identical images, each of which has been photographed at different exposure levels. It is used to find the best exposure or balance.

WILLIAMS PROCESS
Early travelling matte process that filmed foreground images against a black or white backdrop and used high-contrast film to produce a matte.

WIPE
The replacement of one image with another through some form of decorative transition rather than by a straight cut, dissolve or fade. The second image normally replaces the first by appearing to 'wipe' across the screen.

WIRE-FRAME MODEL
The most basic visual form of a computer-generated model before it has had any textures applied to it. Also called a mesh.

WIRE REMOVAL
The removal of wires or rigs used to hang or support characters or objects during filming, as well as other unwanted elements, from a scene. A painstaking task when attempted optically, it is now achieved digitally with relative ease. Also called rig removal.

Z-DEPTH
During the rendering of computer-generated objects, a Z-depth pass (also called an 'ID pass' or simply 'depth pass') renders information about the distance of parts of an object from the camera in a visual form. Typically, distance from camera (or from the top to the bottom of an object) is denoted using greyscale (parts of an object that are nearest to the camera are white and furthest are black, with shades of grey in between) or hue (bands of colour that travel through the spectrum). This 2-D representation of an object's 3-D characteristics is used during compositing in order to relight an object, change focus on it, or allow the realistic addition of depth cues such as mist or fog.

ZOOM
The process of altering a shot during photography so that the camera appears to get closer to or further from its subject. In fact, a camera does not actually move during a zoom in or out, it is only the focal length of the zoom lens that is altered.

ZOPTICS
A variation of front projection in which the zoom lens on a camera was linked with the zoom lens on a projector. By simultaneously increasing the size of the projected image and the field of view of the camera, the projected image would appear to remain the same size when rephotographed while any foreground object would appear to shrink. Invented by Zoran Perisic and first used in *Superman* (1978) to make Superman fly towards or away from the camera without actor Christopher Reeve having to physically move.

BIBLIOGRAPHY

Abbott, L.B., ASC. *Special Effects, Wire, Tape and Rubber Band Style*. California: The ASC Press, 1984.

Bacon, Matt. *No Strings Attached: The Inside Story of Jim Henson's Creature Shop*. London: Virgin Publishing, 1997.

Bizony, Piers. *2001: Filming the Future*. London: Aurum Press, 1994.

Bouzereau, Laurent, and Jody Duncan. *Star Wars: The Making of Episode I The Phantom Menace*. London: Ebury Press, 1999.

Brosnan, John. *Movie Magic*. London: Macdonald and Jane's, 1974.

Brownlow, Kevin. *The Parade's Gone By . . .* London: Columbus Books, 1989.

Burum, Stephen H. (ed.). *American Cinematographer Manual* (ninth edition). California: The ASC Press, 2004.

Clark, Frank P. *Special Effects in Motion Pictures*. New York: Society of Motion Picture and Television Engineers, Inc., 1966.

Coe, Brian. *The History of Movie Photography*. Westfield, NJ: New York Zoetrope, 1981.

Dunn, Linwood G., ASC, and George E. Turner (ed.). *The ASC Treasury of Visual Effects*. California: The ASC Press, 1983.

Fielding, Raymond. *The Technique of Special Effects Cinematography* (fourth edition). London: Focal Press, 1985.

Finch, Christopher. *Special Effects: Creating Movie Magic*. New York: Abbeville Press, 1984.

Fry, Ron, and Pamela Fourzon. *The Saga of Special Effects*. Englewood Cliffs, NJ: Prentice Hall, Inc., 1977.

Goldner, Orville, and George E. Turner. *The Making of King Kong*. New York: A.S. Barnes & Co., Inc., 1975.

Harryhausen, Ray, and Tony Dalton. *Ray Harryhausen: An Animated Life*. London: Aurum Press, 2003.

Hutchison, David. *Film Magic: The Art and Science of Special Effects*. London: Simon and Schuster, 1986.

Hutchison, David (ed.). *Fantastic 3-D*. New York: Starlog Press, 1982.

Imes, Jack Jr. *Special Visual Effects*. New York: Van Nostrand Reinhold Company, Inc., 1984.

Johnson, John. *Cheap Tricks and Class Acts*. Jefferson, NC: McFarland & Company, Inc., 1996.

Katz, Ephraim. *The Macmillan International Film Encyclopedia*. London: Macmillan, 1994.

LoBrutto, Vincent. *Sound-on-Film: Interviews with Creators of Film Sound*. Westport, CT: Praeger, 1994.

Mitchell, Mitch. *Visual Effects for Film and Television*. Oxford: Focal Press, 2004.

Monaco, James. *How to Read a Film* (revised edition). Oxford: Oxford University Press, 1981.

Noake, Roger. *Animation: A Guide to Animated Film Techniques*. London: MacDonald and Co, 1988.

Pinteau, Pascal. *Special Effects: An Oral History*. New York: Harry N. Abrams, 2004.

Salisbury, Mark, and Alan Hedgecock. *Behind the Mask: The Secrets of Hollywood's Monster Makers*. London: Titan Books, 1994.

Salt, Barry. *Film Style & Technology: History & Analysis* (second edition). London: Starword, 1992.

Shay, Don, and Jody Duncan. *The Making of Jurassic Park*. London: Boxtree, 1993.

Sklar, Robert. *Film: An International History of the Medium*. London: Thames & Hudson, 1993.

Smith, Thomas G. *Industrial Light and Magic: The Art of Special Effects*. New York: Ballantine, 1986.

Taylor, Al, and Sue Roy. *Making a Monster*. New York: Crown Publishers, Inc., 1980.

Thompson, David. *Georges Méliès: Father of Film Fantasy*. London: Collins, 1992.

Timpone, Anthony. *Men, Makeup, and Monsters*. New York: St Martin's Press, 1996.

Vaz, Mark Cotta, and Craig Barron. *The Invisible Art: The Legends of Movie Matte Painting*. London: Thames & Hudson, 2002.

Vaz, Mark Cotta, and Patricia Rose Duignan. *Industrial Light and Magic: Into the Digital Realm*. New York: Ballantine, 1996.

Wilkie, Bernard. *Creating Special Effects for TV and Films*. London: Focal Press, 1977.

Wilson, Steven S. *Puppets and People*. San Diego, CA: A.S. Barnes & Company, Inc., 1980.

MAGAZINES

American Cinematographer (monthly). P.O. Box 2230, Hollywood, CA 90078, USA. www.cinematographer.com

Cinefex (quarterly). PO Box 20027, Riverside, CA 92516, USA. www.cinefex.com

USEFUL WEBSITES

www.visualeffectssociety.com

www.vfxpro.com

www.vfxhq.com

www.fxguide.com

www.vttbots.com

www.awn.com

INDEX

Principal entries are in **bold**; illustrations are in *italics*

PICTURE CREDITS

ADI = Amalgamated Dynamics Inc; AVE = Artem Visual Effects; BFI = British Film Institute; FCFC = Framestore CFC; JFC = Joel Finler Collection; JHCS = Jim Henson's Creature Shop; KNB = Kurtzman, Nicotero, Berger/KNB EFX Inc; Kobal = The Kobal Collection; MWD = Matte World Digital; MPC = Moving Picture Company; PVA = Professional VisionCare Associates; REF = Richard Edlund Films Inc; RGA = The Ronald Grant Archive; RR = Richard Rickitt; SWS = Stan Winston Studio

l = left; r = right; t = top; b = bottom; c = centre

2 Universal/Wing Nut Films (courtesy Kobal)
4–5 l to r: RR; courtesy Universal Studios; RR; Paramount (courtesy Kobal); Danjaq/United Artists (courtesy John Richardson); Paramount (courtesy Kobal)
6 BFI
7 Columbia (courtesy Kobal)
8 Méliès (courtesy Kobal)
10 RR
11t RR; 11b Science Museum/Science & Society Picture Library
12 RR
13t RR; 13b Science Museum/Science & Society Picture Library
14 RR
15l RR; 15r Kobal
16 RR
17l Kobal; 17r RR
18t RGA; 18b RR
19l RR; 19r United Artists (courtesy Kobal)
20t 20th Century Fox (courtesy Kobal); 20b BFI
21 First National (courtesy Kobal)
22 RR
23 RR
24l RR; 24r 20th Century Fox (courtesy Kobal)
25 RR
26t Paramount (courtesy Kobal); 26b JFC
27t RGA; 27b RR
28 RR
28–9c 20th Century Fox (courtesy Kobal)
29t Paramount (courtesy Kobal)
30l 20th Century Fox (courtesy Kobal)
31 20th Century Fox (courtesy Kobal)
32 Danjaq/United Artists (courtesy Kobal)
33t Kobal; 33b MGM (courtesy Kobal)
34 RR
35 tl Universal (courtesy Kobal); 35 tr Columbia (courtesy Kobal); 35b Universal (courtesy Kobal)
36 Ladd Company/Warner Bros (courtesy Kobal)
37 Universal (courtesy Kobal)
38 Lucasfilm/Paramount (courtesy Kobal)
39 BFI
40t Carolco (courtesy Kobal); 40b Amblin/Universal (courtesy Kobal)
41 RR
42t 20th Century Fox (courtesy Kobal); 42b Marvel/Sony Pictures (courtesy Kobal)
43t Kobal; 43b Dreamworks/Universal (courtesy Kobal)
44t Dreamworks (courtesy Kobal); 44b Kobal
45 Lucasfilm/20th Century Fox (courtesy Kobal)
46 Paramount (courtesy Kobal)

47 courtesy ILM; 47b © Academy of Motion Pictures Arts and Sciences
48 RR
50 courtesy Panavision Europe
53 Universal (courtesy Kobal)
58 RR
59 Universal (courtesy Kobal)
62 Paramount (courtesy Kobal)
63 Disney Enterprises (courtesy Kobal)
65 Paramount (courtesy Kobal)
66 Warner Bros/DC Comics (courtesy Kobal)
68 Universal (courtesy JFC)
69t RR; 69b courtesy REF
71 RKO (courtesy BFI)
72t RR; 72b RR
73 MGM (courtesy Kobal)
75 RKO (courtesy Kobal)
77l courtesy JFC; 77r RR
78 courtesy REF
79t courtesy REF; 70b Lucasfilm Ltd/20th Century Fox (courtesy Kobal)
80–1 Canal+/DA (courtesy Joe Viskocil)
83tl courtesy of Amicus/BFI; 83tr Paramount (courtesy Kobal); 83bl & 83br courtesy Pinewood Studios
85 Warner Bros/Marvel Comics (courtesy Kobal)
87t Warner Bros (courtesy Kobal); 87b Danjaq/United Artists (courtesy RGA)
89 MGM (courtesy Kobal)
90–91 courtesy Quantel
94 RR
95 RR
96b courtesy Sony Broadcast
97 courtesy of Lucasfilm Ltd
98t Warner Bros (courtesy Technicolor); 98b courtesy Autodesk
99 courtesy Silicone /Efilm
100t courtesy REF 100b/101b Paramount (courtesy FCFC)
101t Paramount (courtesy Kobal)
102 20th Century Fox/Paramount (courtesy Asylum)
103 courtesy New Deal Studios
104–5 New Line Cinema (courtesy Magic Camera Company)
106 (courtesy FCFC)
107 (courtesy FCFC)
108 Imagine/Touchstone (courtesy MWD)
109 Paramount (courtesy BFI)
111 Warner Bros (courtesy Kobal)
112 Warner Bros (courtesy REF)
114 Universal (courtesy REF)
115 Disney Enterprises (courtesy RGA)
116 Universal (courtesy Kobal)
117 courtesy Kevin Brownlow
118 Danjaq/United Artists (courtesy John Richardson)
119 courtesy Snow Business
120tl & 120bm courtesy New Deal Studios; 120bl courtesy REF
121 20th Century Fox (courtesy Kobal)
122/123 courtesy New Deal Studios
125 UFA (courtesy Kobal)
126 Universal (courtesy BFI)
127 Universal (courtesy Weta Workshop)
128 Universal (courtesy Weta Workshop)
129t 20th Century Fox (courtesy 4ward Productions); 129b (courtesy 4ward Productions)

130t & 130bl courtesy Joe Viskocil; 130br 20th Century Fox (courtesy Kobal)
131t courtesy 4ward Productions; 131b Carolco (courtesy Joe Viskocil)
132 courtesy Joe Viskocil
133 Lucasfilm Ltd/20th Century Fox (courtesy Kobal)
134t RR; 135b courtesy Effects Associates
135l courtesy Effects Associates; 135r 20th Century Fox (courtesy Kobal)
136–7 20th Century Fox/Paramount (courtesy Weta Workshop)
138 20th Century Fox/Paramount (courtesy Asylum)
140t courtesy BFI; 140b 20th Century Fox (courtesy Kobal)
141t RR; 141b Lucasfilm Ltd/20th Century Fox (courtesy Kobal)
142 courtesy 4Ward Productions
142tl courtesy BFI; 142bl courtesy Joe Viskocil
144t & 144c courtesy New Deal Studios; 144b courtesy Aero Telemetry Corporation photo by Bridger Neilson
145t Michael Bailey, vttbots.com;145b Amblin/Universal (courtesy BFI)
146l Paramount (courtesy Kobal); 146r MGM (courtesy Kobal)
147 RR
148 courtesy Sony Pictures Imageworks
149t courtesy Mark Roberts Motion Control; 149b RR
151 Lucasfilm/20th Century Fox (courtesy Kobal)
151 courtesy New Deal Studios
152t courtesy ILM; 152b Warner Bros (courtesy Kobal)
154 courtesy Evans and Sutherland
155 Lucasfilm/20th Century Fox (courtesy Kobal)
159 courtesy Magic Camera Company
160 courtesy Gentle Giant Studios
161 courtesy Digital Domain
163 Disney Enterprises (courtesy Kobal)
165b courtesy Headus
168 RKO (courtesy Kobal)
170 RR
171 Disney Enterprises (courtesy BFI)
171 Kobal
172 courtesy Jon Brooks
174 Paramount (courtesy Kobal)
175t RR; 175b Lucasfilm Ltd/20th Century Fox (courtesy Kobal)
177 Disney Enterprises (courtesy Kobal)
178 MGM (courtesy Kobal)
179 courtesy DreamWorks
180 Tohokushinsha Film Corp/Ntv/Tokuma Shoten (courtesy Kobal)
181 The Arthur Melbourne-Cooper Film Archive/photo repro Tjitte de Vries
182 RR
183 First National (courtesy Kobal)
184–7 RKO (courtesy Kobal)
188 BFI
189t Warner Bros (courtesy Kobal); 189b courtesy Ray Harryhausen
190 Columbia (courtesy Kobal)
191t RR; 191b Touchstone/Burton/Di Nov (courtesy Kobal)
192t DreamWorks/Aardman (courtesy Kobal); 192b Columbia (courtesy Kobal)
193t Warner Bros (courtesy MPC); 193c courtesy ILM
194t courtesy Tippett Studio; 194b RR
195 RR
196 Screen Gems, Inc./Lakeshore Entertainment (courtesy Luma Pictures)

197t Screen Gems, Inc./Lakeshore Entertainment (courtesy Luma Pictures); 197b courtesy Pixar

199 Disney Enterprises (courtesy Kobal)

200 courtesy Tippett Studio

201–3 Sony Pictures (courtesy Tippett Studio)

204t New Line Cinema (courtesy Kobal); 204 courtesy Henrik Wann Jensen

206 DreamWorks (courtesy Tippett Studio)

207 courtesy Tippett Studio

209t courtesy House of Moves; 209b Castle Rock/Shangri-La Entertainment (courtesy Kobal)

211 Amblin/Universal (courtesy Kobal)

212 Castle Rock/Shangri-La Entertainment (courtesy Kobal)

213–14 Lucasfilm Ltd/20th Century Fox (courtesy ILM). *Star Wars*: Episode III – *Revenge of the Sith* © 2005 Lucasfilm Ltd. & ™. All rights reserved. Used under authorization. Unauthorized duplication is a violation of applicable law.

215 THE MATRIX RELOADED © WV Films III LLC. Licensed by Warner Bros. Entertainment Inc. All rights reserved. Courtesy Kobal.

216t 20th Century Fox (courtesy Kobal); 216b Warner Bros (courtesy Kobal)

217 20th Century Fox (courtesy MPC)

218 Lucasfilm Ltd/20th Century Fox (courtesy ILM). *Star Wars*: Episode III – *Revenge of the Sith* © 2005 Lucasfilm Ltd. & ™. All rights reserved. Used under authorization. Unauthorized duplication is a violation of applicable law.

219 HARRY POTTER AND THE PRISONER OF AZKABAN © P of A Productions Limited. Licensed by Warner Bros. Entertainment Inc. All rights reserved.

221 Columbia/Revolution Studios (courtesy Digital Domain)

223 New Line Cinema (courtesy Kobal)

224 20th Century Fox (courtesy Tweak Films)

225t 20th Century Fox (courtesy Kobal); 225b THE PERFECT STORM © Warner Bros., a division of Time Warner Entertainment Company, L.P. All rights reserved. Courtesy Kobal.

226 Tri-Star (courtesy Kobal)

227 Graphic representation by RR

228–9 CHARLIE AND THE CHOCOLATE FACTORY © Theobald Film Productions LLP. Licensed by Warner Bros. Entertainment Inc. All rights reserved. Courtesy Kobal.

230 Graphic representation by RR

231 courtesy DreamWorks

232 RR

234 courtesy DreamWorks

235 Sony Pictures (courtesy Tippett Studio)

236 Screen Gems, Inc./Lakeshore Entertainment (courtesy Luma Pictures)

237t New Line (courtesy Kobal); 237b RR

241 Lucasfilm Ltd/20th Century Fox (courtesy Kobal).

242 Morgan Creek/Warner Bros (courtesy MWD)

244–5 RR

247 Morgan Creek/Warner Bros (courtesy MWD)

248 Universal (courtesy Kobal)

249 Selznick/MGM (courtesy Kobal); 249b RR

253 courtesy REF

254 courtesy BFI

255 courtesy REF

256 Lucasfilm Ltd/Paramount (courtesy Kobal)

257 courtesy Harrison Ellenshaw

258 Touchstone Pictures (courtesy Harrison Ellenshaw)

259 Lucasfilm Ltd/Paramount (courtesy Kobal)

260 Paramount (courtesy ILM)

261 Paramount (courtesy MWD)

263 Warner Bros (courtesy MWD)

264 20th Century Fox (courtesy MWD)

265t Warner Bros (courtesy MPC); 265b 20th Century Fox (courtesy MPC)

266 20th Century Fox (courtesy Kobal)

268t Universal (courtesy Kobal); 268b RR

269 RR

270 MGM (courtesy Kobal)

271t Warner Bros (courtesy Kobal); 271b Universal (courtesy Kobal)

273 Universal (courtesy Kobal)

274–5 RR

276 courtesy ADI

277–9 courtesy JHCS

279br courtesy ADI

280 Paramount (courtesy Kobal)

281l Cinema Center (courtesy Kobal); 281r The Saul Zaentz Company (courtesy Kobal)

282t RKO (courtesy RGA); 282b; Courtesy RGA

283l Polygram/Universal (courtesy Kobal); 283tr Universal (courtesy Kobal); 283bl Lucasfilm Ltd/20th Century Fox (courtesy Kobal)

285 Hensons/Universal (courtesy Kobal)

286tr courtesy SWS; 286bl Columbia (courtesy Ray Harryhausen); 286br Amblin/Universal (courtesy SWS)

287 Amblin/Universal (courtesy SWS)

288 courtesy SWS

289l courtesy KNB; 289tr& 289br courtesy ADI

290tr courtesy JHCS; 290cl & 290bl Amblin/Universal (courtesy SWS)

291 courtesy ADI

292tl courtesy JHCS; 292tr Columbia/Tri-Star (courtesy Kobal); 292bl courtesy Cinovation

293 courtesy PVA

294l courtesy JHCS; 294tr courtesy ADI; 294br courtesy PVA

295 courtesy KNB

296tl & 296cr courtesy JHCS; 296br Lucasfilm Ltd/20th Century Fox (courtesy ILM). *Star Wars*: Episode I – *The Phantom Menace* © 1999 Lucasfilm Ltd. & ™. All rights reserved. Used under authorization. Unauthorized duplication is a violation of applicable law.

297l Golden Harvest/Clearwater Holdings (courtesy Kobal); 297r courtesy JHCS

298 courtesy JHCS

299t courtesy Sony Pictures Imageworks; 299bl courtesy Patrick Tatopoulos Studios; 299br courtesy JHCS

301 Toho (courtesy Kobal)

302 Universal (courtesy BFI)

303t Bender/Spink (courtesy Mr X); 303b Sony Pictures (courtesy Spectral Motion)

304 Danjaq/United Artists (courtesy Kobal)

306 RR

307 courtesy BFI

308bl courtesy RGA; 308br courtesy Kobal

309 RR

310l courtesy BFI; 310r courtesy AVE

311 MGM (courtesy Kobal)

312–13 courtesy Snow Business

314 RR

315 Danjaq/United Artists (courtesy Kobal)

316 Danjaq/United Artists (courtesy Kobal)

317t MGM/Eon (courtesy Kobal); 317b RR

318t 20th Century Fox (courtesy Kobal); 318b RR

319r RR; 319b courtesy AVE

322–3 courtesy AVE

324tl courtesy AVE; 324bl Lucasfilm Ltd/20th Century Fox (courtesy ILM). *Star Wars*: Episode I – *The Phantom Menace* © 1999 Lucasfilm Ltd. & ™. All rights reserved.

325 Danjaq/United Artists (courtesy Eon)

326 Danjaq/United Artists (courtesy Eon)

327t Lucasfilm Ltd/Paramount (courtesy BFI); 327b courtesy John Richardson

328t courtesy AVE; 328b MGM (courtesy Kobal)

329t courtesy John Richardson; 329b DreamWorks/Universal (courtesy Kobal)

330 courtesy John Richardson

331 Lucasfilm Ltd/Paramount (courtesy Kobal)

332 Universal (courtesy Kobal)

333 Disney Enterprises (courtesy Kobal)

334 Lucasfilm Ltd/Paramount (courtesy Kobal)

335t Amblin/Universal (courtesy Kobal); 325 courtesy Michael Lantieri

336 Amblin/Universal (courtesy Kobal)

337t courtesy Chris Corbould; 328b courtesy Neil Corbould

338 courtesy Gary Hecker

340 RR

341 courtesy Kobal

343 Lucasfilm Ltd/Paramount (courtesy BFI)

344t Lucasfilm Ltd/20th Century Fox (courtesy Kobal); 344b RR

345–7 RR

348t RR; 348b courtesy Pinewood Studios

350–1 courtesy ILM

352 courtesy Universal Studios

354t RR; 354b Gulu Picture Co. (courtesy Kobal)

355l RR; 355r Universal (courtesy Kobal)

357t Disney Enterprises (courtesy RGA); 357b courtesy HinesLab

358 courtesy Texas Instruments

359t courtesy Universal Studios; 359b courtesy Imax

361 Universal/Marvel Entertainment (courtesy Kobal)

AUTHOR'S ACKNOWLEDGEMENTS

Firstly I would like to thank my parents, Martin and Barbara; I hope this book serves as some compensation for the explosions, fires, crashes, floods and enormous electricity bills that I inflicted upon them during my youthful film-making experiments.

I would like to thank everyone at Aurum Press, who made working on this book such a pleasure. In particular Karen Ings, who dealt calmly and efficiently with whatever muddles and surprises I threw at her and was at all times a great support. Many thanks to Ashley Western, who did a superb job wrangling the huge amount of text and images into a beautiful book that I am proud to have on my shelf. A big thanks to my agent, Ben Mason, who helped set everything up and made sure it all ran smoothly.

Many thanks to Richard Taylor at Weta Workshop for his enthusiastic support of the project and for supplying a generous review of the results. Very special gratitude goes to Ray Harryhausen for supplying the foreword. One of the most gracious and generous people I have ever met, Ray's continuing delight in the magic of special effects is both infectious and inspiring. I will treasure the times we have spent chatting about the movies.

I am indebted to my old friend Simon Winstanley who created the graphic illustrations with the combination of creative flair and technical brilliance that he brings to all of his work. May the Fourth be with you.

A big thank-you to the studios and effects professionals who have helped along the way and are listed below. Dozens of individuals have generously volunteered to explain their craft, review the resulting text and supply images. Without you, this book would have been impossible.

Finally, and above all, I thank my fabulous wife Varsha, who has supported and encouraged me in all my endeavours over the past ten years. This book is dedicated to you and to our number-one son, Charlie, who, I have no doubt, is already planning his own explosions, fires, crashes and floods . . .

THE AUTHOR AND PUBLISHER WISH TO THANK THE FOLLOWING PEOPLE AND COMPANIES FOR THEIR HELP IN CREATING THIS BOOK.

Dennis Skotak, Robert Skotak (4ward Productions), Tom Woodruff Jr, Alec Gillis (ADI), Rob Hertz (Aerotelemetry), Lucy Cooper, Mike Kelt, Bob Thorne (Artem), Nathan McGuinness (Asylum), Helen Arnold, Mitch Mitchell, Kevin Wheatley (Cinesite), Joanna Capitano, Joel Hynek (Digital Domain), Melissa Taylor (Double Negative), Amanda Cramer, Wendy Elwell, Fumi Kitahara, Harold Kraut, Arnauld Lamorlette, Oliver Mouroux, Damon O'Beirne, Craig Ring, Eric Tabellion (DreamWorks Animation), Leslie Huntley, Gene Warren (Fantasy II Film Effects), Wolfgang Lempp (Filmlight), Ben Morris, Martin Parker, Sean Varney (Framestore CFC), Steve Chapman, Brian Sunderlin (Gentle Giant Studios), Phil Dench (Headus), Howard Berger (KNB), Richard Edlund, Jeanette Kremer (Richard Edlund Films), Sophie Trainor, Martin Hobbs, Carsten Kolve, Anders Langlands, Andy Middleton, Max Wood, Melody Woodford (The Moving Picture Company), Tom Tolles (House of Moves), Ben Burtt, Rob Coleman, Megan Corbett, Steve Gawley, John Knoll, Dennis Muren, Lorne Peterson, Juan Luis Sanchez, Suzy Starke (ILM/Lucasfilm), Matthew Gratzner, Ian Hunter, Emily Bowen (New Deal Studios), Ryan Kingslein (Pixel Logic), Joel Freisch, Eric Jeffery, Todd Labonte, Lori Petrini, Tom Schelesny,

Phil Tippett (Tippett Studio), Craig Barron, Krystyna Demkowicz, Chris Evans, Brett Nortcutt (Matte World Digital), Vince Cirelli (Luma Pictures), Rama Dunayevich (The Orphanage), Mandy Abbott, Roger Thornton (Quantel), Mike Elizalde (Spectral Motion), Lisa Pistachio (SGI), Mark Chiolis (Thomson Grass Valley), Seth Rosenthal, Jim Hourihan (Tweak Films), David Singer (Mr X), Sean Cushing, Colin Green (Pixel Liberation Front), Darcy Crownshaw (Snow Business), Sandy Genler, Gary Hecker, Ken Ralston (Sony Pictures), Crash McCreery, Stan Winston (Stan Winston Studio), Bob Hoffman (Technicolor), John Baster, Daniel Birch, Tania Rodger, Richard Taylor, Jenny Williams (Weta Workshop/Digital). Nick Alder, Michael Bailey, Steve Begg, George Borshukov, Jon Brooks, Kevin Brownlow, Mike Boudry, Cristine Ceret, Jamie Courtier, Dale Clarke, Chris Corbould, Neil Corbould, Gary Coulter, Phil Donovan, Nick Dudman, Harrison Ellenshaw, Peter Elliot, Roy Field, Marie Fraser, George Gibbs, Dr Rolf Giesen, Martin Gutteridge, Helen Hamilton, Graham V. Hartstone, Stephen Hines, Darin Hollings, Henrik Wann Jensen, Michael Lantieri, Brendan Lonergan, John Richardson, Mark Roberts, Nigel Stone, Douglas Trumbull, Joe Viskocil, Sean Ward.